MW01069814

COOKING SCHOOL

Mastering Classic and Modern French Cuisine

ALAIN DUCASSE

Benoît Witz, Sébastien Serveau, Romain Corbière, Hisayuki Takeuchi

New York · Paris · London · Milan

écoledecuisine
ALAIN

TABLE OF CONTENTS

EASY 5

INTERMEDIATE 136

DIFFICULT 402

APPENDIX

The chef's toolbox 502
Information about basic ingredients 510
Basic recipes and techniques 544
Index by level of difficulty 572
Alphabetical index of recipes 574
Index by types of dishes 577
Index by ingredient 580
Index by cooking utensils 583
Index by cooking time 587

EASY

4 SPREADS
AND DIPS
AÏOLI
EGGPLANT
CAVIAR

ANCHOÏADE
TAPENADE

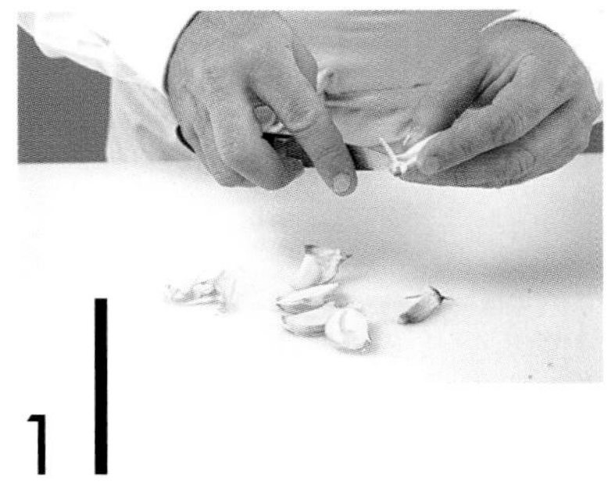

1

2

3

AÏOLI

Makes about 300 g – 10.5 ounces (1 1/4 cups) spread

Preparation time 10 minutes

3 cloves garlic
1 egg yolk
1 teaspoon freshly squeezed lemon juice
Salt
Freshly ground pepper
100–120 ml – 1/3 cup plus 1 tablespoon plus 1 teaspoon–1/2 cup olive oil

1 Halve and peel the garlic cloves. Remove the green cores and squeeze through a garlic press into a mortar.

2 Add the egg yolk. Mix with a pestle. Add the juice to the mortar. Season with salt and pepper.

3 Add all the oil in a thin stream while stirring vigorously with the pestle to make an emulsion. Stir until all the oil is absorbed.
Cover with plastic wrap (cling film). Store at room temperature (never in the refrigerator) before serving.

TIPS FROM OUR CHEFS

SWEET GARLIC

Make aïoli in summer with young garlic, sometimes labeled green garlic. Its sweeter flavor means you can add more.

POTATO

French home cooks often use potato to tone down the flavor of the garlic. If you want to do the same, boil a potato (60 g – 2.12 ounces) in its skin and crush it while it is still hot, then add it to the mixture in the mortar and pound with the pestle to combine.

ANCHOÏADE

1 Mix the water with the vinegar and set aside. Halve and peel the garlic cloves. Remove the green cores. Combine the garlic, anchovies, and olives in a blender. Add a little of the vinegar mixture. Blend.

2 When the ingredients have been reduced to a puree, gradually add the olive oil while blending. When the mixture has thickened a little, dilute with a little more of the vinegar mixture.

3 Add about one third of the grapeseed oil and blend. Scrape down the sides of the blender jar with a spatula (scraper). Add the rest of the grapeseed oil while blending. Transfer to a bowl, cover with plastic wrap (cling film), and refrigerate. Serve cold.

Makes 750 ml – 3 cups spread

Preparation time 10 minutes
Rest time 2 hours

120 ml – 1/2 cup water
80 ml – 1/3 cup distilled white vinegar
2 cloves garlic
250g – 8.8 oz anchovy fillets in oil, drained
30 g – 1.06 ounces pitted black olives (or 36 small olives)
200 ml – 3/4 cup plus 1 tablespoon olive oil
180 ml – 3/4 cup grapeseed oil

TIPS FROM OUR CHEFS

FOR THE TASTE BUDS

It is better to use anchovies in oil rather than salted anchovies, which have a very strong flavor. Taste the anchoïade once you have finished making it. If it's too strong, add more olive oil to tone down the flavor.

STORAGE

This anchoïade will keep for about two weeks in a tightly closed jar in the refrigerator.

EGGPLANT CAVIAR

1

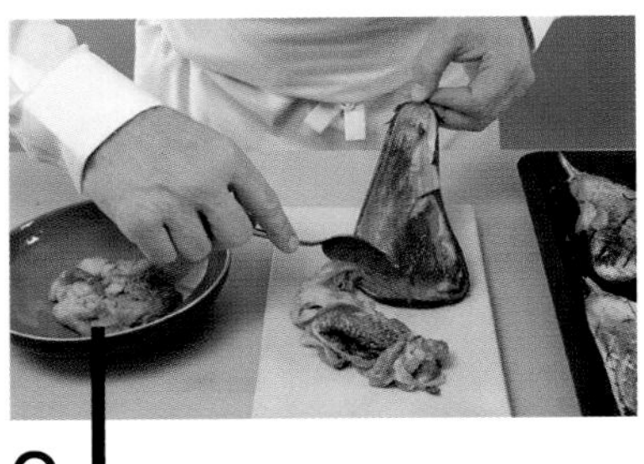

2

Makes about 800 ml – 3 1/3 cups spread

Preparation time 20 minutes
Cooking time 45 minutes
Resting time 2 hours

EQUIPMENT

Mortar and pestle
Blender

1 kilogram – 2 pounds 4 ounces (about 2 small) eggplants (aubergines)
3 cloves garlic
Leaves of 1 sprig thyme
About 1/2 cup olive oil, divided
Salt
Freshly ground pepper
Juice of 1/2 lemon
2 scallions (spring onions)

1 Preheat the oven to 200°C – 400°F (gas mark 6). Halve the eggplants.
Score the cut surfaces of the eggplant to a depth of 5–10 mm – 1/4–3/8 inch. Cut the garlic cloves in half without peeling.
Put the eggplants cut-sides up in a broiler pan. Sprinkle the garlic and thyme over them. Add 4 tablespoons – 1/4 cup of olive oil and season with salt and pepper.

2 Bake for 45 minutes. Check if done by pressing lightly on the thickest part with your fingertip; the flesh should be tender.
Scoop out the flesh from the eggplants with a tablespoon. Peel the garlic and place it in the blender with the eggplant.

3 Add the remaining 1/4 cup olive oil and the lemon juice and blend for 2 minutes. Adjust the seasoning with salt and pepper and blend again. Transfer to a container.
Cut the tops from the scallions, leaving 5 cm – 2 inches of green. Peel off the outer layer of skin. Slice the scallions (opposite). Mix with the eggplant caviar.
Cover with plastic wrap (cling film). Store in the refrigerator and serve cold.

TIPS FROM OUR CHEFS

THE EGGPLANTS
If the eggplants have an excessive amount of seeds, press the caviar through a strainer (sieve) to remove some of them.

VARIATIONS
You can customize this caviar by adding goat milk curds, bell pepper confit, dried tomatoes, tuna belly, or sliced black olives.

1

2

Makes about 300 g – 10.5 ounces (1 1/4 cups) spread

Preparation time 20 minutes
Resting time 15 minutes

A WORD FROM OUR SOMMELIER

Pair with rosé Champagne.

TAPENADE

1 clove garlic
400 g – 14 ounces (4 cups) pitted black olives
5 anchovy fillets in oil, drained
50 g – 1.76 ounces (1/3 cup) capers
2 sprigs basil
30 ml – 2 tablespoons sherry vinegar
60–80 ml – 1/4 cup–1/4 cup plus 1 tablespoon and 1 1/2 teaspoons olive oil

1 Halve and peel the garlic clove. Remove the green core. Combine the garlic, olives, anchovies, and capers in a blender.
Wash the basil and gently pat dry. Pluck the leaves off into the blender, then pour in the vinegar and oil.

2 Blend in short bursts. Scrape down the sides of the blender jar with a spatula (scraper) and mix.
Transfer to a container and cover with plastic wrap (cling film).
Store in the refrigerator and serve cold.

Suggested accompaniment

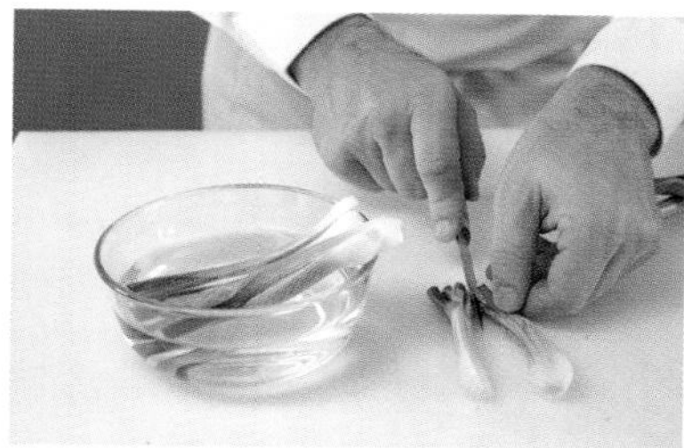

Trim the tops of five or six scallions (spring onions), or use small onions with leaves. Cut off the roots and remove the outer skin. Then cut the scallions in half lengthwise.

Trim off the large outer leaves and roots from radishes. Scrape off the small leaves sticking to the top. Immerse the radishes in cold water.

Cut a flute loaf (similar to a baguette) into thin diagonal slices. Arrange them on a baking sheet. Drizzle the bread with a little olive oil. Place the baking sheet as near as possible to the broiler (grill) or burner and toast the bread for 2 minutes.

FOIE GRAS BUTTER

Preparation time 5 minutes
Cooking time 30 minutes

Veins of 1 deveined foie gras (page 531)
Butter equivalent in weight to the veins, softened
Fine salt
Freshly ground white pepper
1 dash cognac
Fleur de sel
Coarsely ground pepper
1 ficelle loaf (thin baguette), sliced and toasted

1 Push the veins through a strainer (sieve). Use a silicone spatula (scraper) to collect the foie gras and transfer it to a plate.

2 Cut the softened butter into small cubes and add it to the foie gras. Season with a little fine salt and white pepper, then add the cognac. Mix gently with the spatula.

3 Spread out a sheet of plastic wrap (cling film) on the work surface and place the foie gras mixture in the middle. Roll into a cylinder inside the plastic wrap and refrigerate for 30 minutes to harden.

4 Slice. Sprinkle with fleur de sel and coarsely ground pepper and serve with toasted ficelle slices.

TIPS FROM OUR CHEFS

THE PERFECT THICKENER
Foie gras is expensive, so you can make use of the parts surrounding the veins of the raw liver you have deveined (page 531) to make foie gras butter.
Foie gras butter can also be used to thicken a jus or gravy.

1

2

3

4

NIÇOISE SALAD

Serves 4

Preparation time 25 minutes
Cooking time 3 minutes

Salad

6 quail eggs
2 tomatoes
1 bell pepper
3 stalks celery
Juice of 1/2 lemon
2 poivrade artichokes
1/2 cucumber
1/2 fennel bulb
3 scallions (spring onions)
1 (120-g – 4.23-ounce) can tuna
1 ficelle loaf (thin baguette)
200 g – 7 ounces mesclun
8 anchovy fillets in oil, drained
1 sprig basil

Vinaigrette

3 tablespoons sherry vinegar
1 tablespoon balsamic vinegar
Salt
Freshly ground pepper
55 ml – 1/2 cup plus 1 tablespoon extra-virgin olive oil

1 Immerse the eggs in cold water in a saucepan. Bring to a boil and cook for 3 minutes. Drain, then plunge into cold water.

2 Remove the stems from the tomatoes and cut an X in the bottom of each. Immerse the tomatoes for 10 seconds in boiling water, then in ice water (page 521). When cold, take out of the water, cut into quarters, remove the cores and seeds, and cut each piece in half.

3 Slice off the top and bottom of the bell pepper. Stand the pepper upright and cut the flesh away around the core. Cut along the ribs to separate into four lobes. Peel each piece with a peeler (page 513). Cut into batons.

4 Peel the celery stalks with a vegetable peeler. Cut into even lengths, then into batons, and finally into very small dice. Reserve some of the most tender celery leaves.

5 Add 1 tablespoon lemon juice to a small bowl full of water. Remove the hard outer leaves from the artichokes and pare all around the artichoke hearts (page 516). Peel the stems and trim the tops of the leaves to one third of their length. Immerse the artichokes in the water and lemon juice.

6 Peel the cucumber half. Cut in half lengthwise, removing the seeds. Cut into batons, and then dice.

7 Peel the quail eggs. To avoid damaging them, roll them gently over the work surface to break their shells, then remove. Rinse to remove any traces of shell.

8 Cut the fennel bulb half in two. Using the finest setting on the mandoline slicer (page 515), cut it into fine slices over a large bowl of cold water.
Cut a 10-cm – 4-inch length of the scallions into thin slices, starting at the bulb. Drain and break up the tuna. Halve the quail eggs. Drain the artichokes. Slice them on the mandoline slicer. Drizzle with the remaining lemon juice.
Slice the bread and toast under the broiler (grill).

9 For the vinaigrette, combine the vinegars and add salt and pepper. Add the oil and mix to an emulsion.

10 Drain the fennel. Wash and dry the mesclun, then use it to make a bed on the plates.
Distribute all the ingredients on top of the mesclun, inserting the pieces of toast and basil leaves among the greens. Drizzle generously with vinaigrette.

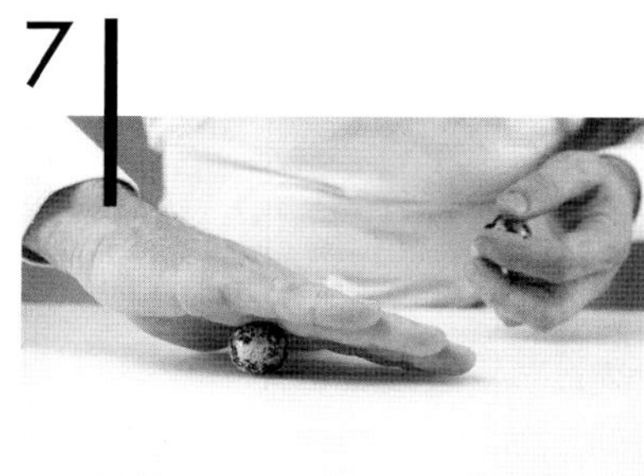

CELERIAC AND APPLE RÉMOULADE

Serves 4

Preparation time 20 minutes

EQUIPMENT

Mandoline slicer
Mold

1 small celeriac
400 g – 14 ounces (about 3 small) Ida Red or Braeburn red apples
1 individual container plain (natural) yogurt
Juice of 1 lemon
Salt
Freshly ground pepper
1 Granny Smith green apple
1 square (or circular) mold,
10-cm – 4-inch square (or diameter)

1 Trim the base of the celeriac flat. Peel vertically, following the round shape of the celeriac. Cut into quarters and slice with the mandoline (page 504).
Wash and dry the red apples. Set aside a few batons for garnish, then slice with the mandoline (page 513).

2 Put the yogurt into a bowl, add the lemon juice, and season with salt and pepper. Mix well. The sauce should be smooth but not runny.
Pour the sauce over the celeriac mixture, then incorporate gently.

3 For each serving, fill the mold with the rémoulade, pressing lightly to make it even. Unmold by lifting the ring carefully.

4 Cut very fine slices of green apple (page 513). Fold each one over without breaking. Hold a folded slice between your thumb and index finger, then place another one next to it, overlapping. Continue until you make a flower. Repeat with remaining green apple slices. Garnish the salad with the green apple flowers and the red apple batons.

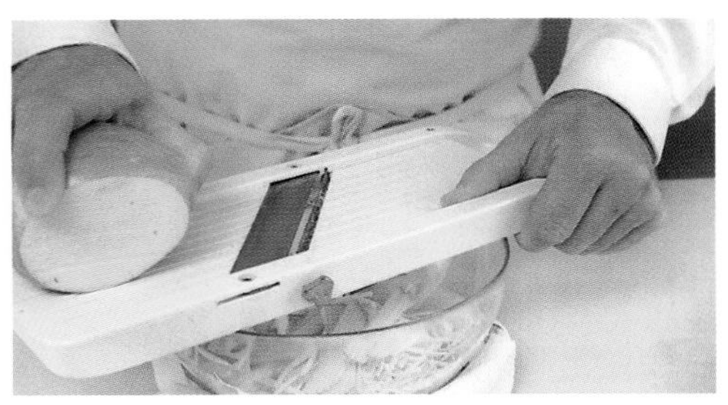

TIPS FROM OUR CHEFS

A LITTLE VARIATION

If you are able to adjust the shredding blades on your mandoline slicer, choose a medium size for the celeriac and a finer one for the apple.

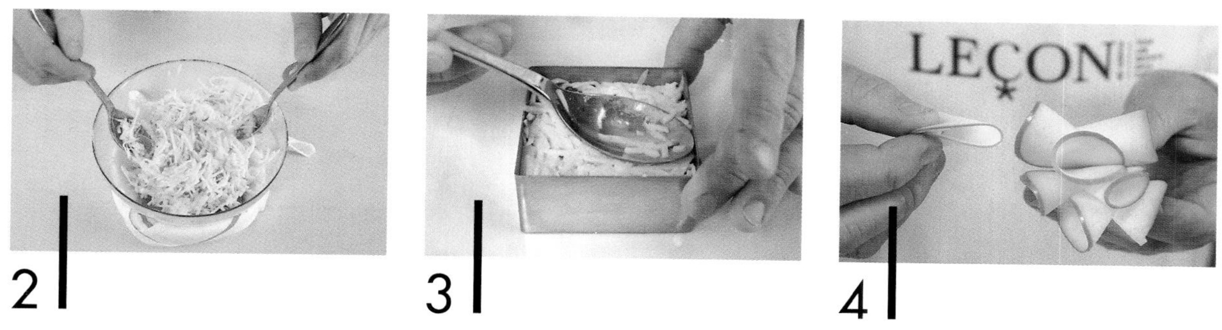
2
3
LEÇON
4

APPLE, ARTICHOKE, AND BEET CARPACCIO

Serves 4

Preparation time 25 minutes

EQUIPMENT

Mandoline slicer

2 large artichokes
1 lemon, halved
1 beet (beetroot)
20 green almonds
4 Pink Lady (or Starking) apples
Olive oil
200 g – 7 ounces (aged) Parmesan cheese
1 scallion (spring onion) or small fresh white onion
Freshly ground pepper
Fleur de sel

TIPS FROM OUR CHEFS

FINISHING

If you can, adjust the blades on your mandoline slicer to vary the thickness of the slices: medium size for soft fruit, such as apples, and fine for firm vegetables, such as the beet.

1 Use a very sharp knife to cut off the stems (stalks) at the bottom of the artichokes. Remove the outermost leaves from the base.
Pare the artichokes around the bottom, leaving only the tender part (page 516).
Rub each artichoke bottom with the cut side of one lemon half. Keep this half so that you can repeat this operation with the artichoke slices (step 4). Squeeze the other half of the lemon into a bowl filled with cold water. Immerse the artichokes in it.

2 Use a vegetable peeler to peel the beet. Immerse in a bowl filled with cold water.

3 Cut the green almonds in half. Take the kernel halves out of their shells and peel (page 510).

4 Drain the artichokes. Slice finely with the mandoline slicer (page 504), stopping when the core (with the choke) appears. Rub the slices with lemon.
Drain the beet and slice very finely (almost translucent) with the mandoline slicer.
Wash and dry the apples. Core (page 512) and slice very finely with the mandoline slicer (page 513).

5 Pour a generous amount of olive oil on four small plates and spread evenly.
Place one apple slice on a plate. Add one beet slice and one artichoke slice, overlapping. Continue around the plate to make a rosette. Slide the last slice under the first. Do the same for the other plates.

6 Wash the scallion and chop (both white and green parts) with a chef's knife.
Sprinkle the scallion over the carpaccio. Drizzle with olive oil and add a sprinkling of freshly ground pepper and fleur de sel. Decorate with green almond pieces. Serve immediately.

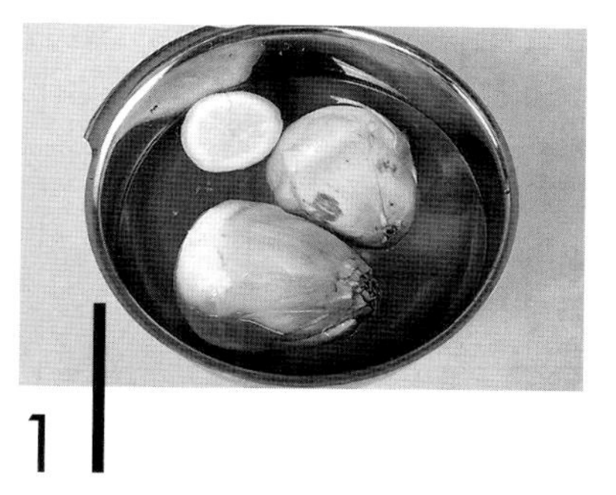
1

2

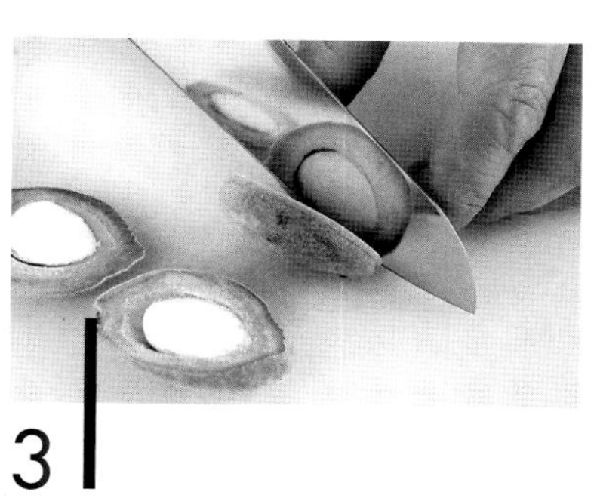
3

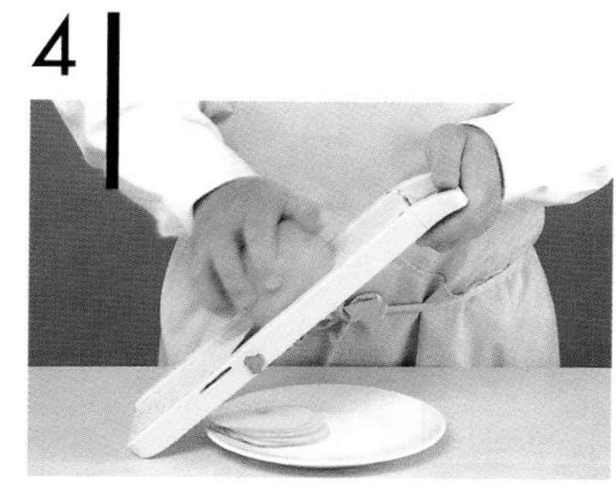
4

5

COLD COUSCOUS SALAD WITH CRUNCHY VEGETABLES

Serves 4

Preparation time 30 minutes
Resting time at least 3 hours

200 g – 7 ounces (1 cup plus 2 tablespoons) fine-grain couscous
Salt
100 ml – 1/3 cup plus 1 tablespoon plus 1 teaspoon olive oil
125 ml – 1/2 cup cold water
3 tomatoes
1 small Marketmore cucumber
Juice of 3 lemons
1/2 bunch mint
1/2 bunch parsley
Tabasco sauce
1 yellow bell pepper
3 scallions (spring onions) or 1 small fresh white onion

TIPS FROM OUR CHEFS

REAL TABBOULEH
Authentic Lebanese tabbouleh—the inspiration for this dish—is more green than white, because it mainly contains parsley, mint, and sometimes fresh cilantro (coriander). Bulgur wheat is used instead of couscous and plays only a secondary role.

1 Put the couscous into a bowl and add 3 pinches of salt and 50 ml – 3 tablespoons plus 1 1/2 teaspoons olive oil. Rub the couscous between your outspread palms for 3 minutes to coat the grains with the oil (page 552). Add the water and let stand for 5 minutes without stirring.
Wash all of the vegetables. Shred two tomatoes and the cucumber. Set aside. Fluff the couscous with a fork to separate the grains. Add the lemon juice and let stand for 5 minutes without stirring.

2 Wash and dry the mint and parsley. Pluck the leaves, arrange them in small bunches, and mince (page 524). Fluff the couscous again.

3 Add the shredded vegetables, parsley, and mint to the couscous. Add the remaining olive oil.
Season with a dash of Tabasco, stir, and adjust the seasoning with salt. Cover with plastic wrap (cling film) and let rest for 3 hours in the refrigerator.

4 Remove the stem (stalk) from the third tomato and cut into 12 wedges. Peel by passing the blade of your knife between the skin and flesh (page 521). Remove the seeds, then dice.

5 Slice off the top and bottom of the bell pepper. Stand the bell pepper upright on a cutting board and cut the flesh around the core. Cut at the ribs to leave four lobes. Remove the core, seeds, and white ribs. Peel each piece with a vegetable peeler (page 513). Cut the pieces into strips, then into a 2-mm – 1/16-inch dice (brunoise).

6 Add the scallions and the diced tomatoes and bell pepper to the salad. Mix well and serve.

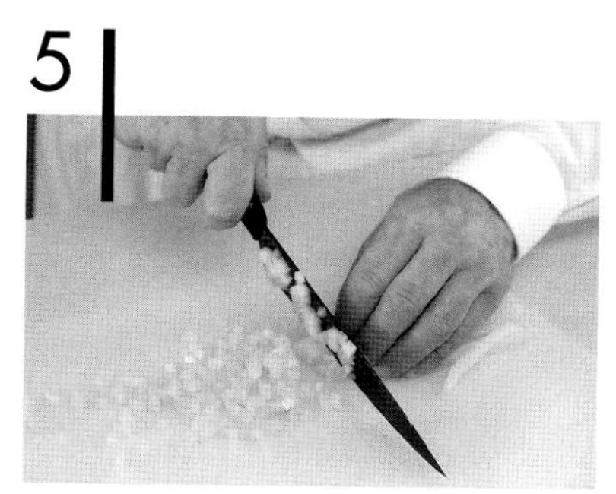

TIPS FROM OUR CHEFS

ONE OR THE OTHER
The Marketmore cucumber has bumpy skin and has firmer and less watery flesh than the smoother and longer common cucumber. If you can't find this variety, use half of a smooth cucumber.

CHICKEN AND GRANNY SMITH APPLE SALAD WITH TANGY CREAM

Serves 4

Preparation time 20 minutes

200 g – 7 ounces Emmental or Comté cheese
2 stalks celery
1 chicken breast, cooked
1 small fresh white onion
4 Granny Smith apples
A few chives, minced
Olive oil
Freshly ground pepper
Fleur de sel
2 tablespoons crème fraîche
Juice of 1 1/2 lemons
Salt

1 Use a chef's knife to cut the rind off the cheese. Cut into 5-mm – 1/4-inch slices. Cut the slices into batons, and then into a 5-mm – 1/4-inch dice.

2 Wash the celery and remove any leaves. Peel the stalks with a vegetable peeler, being careful to remove all the strings. Cut into 8-cm – 3 1/8-inch lengths, and then into batons with a thickness of 3–4 mm – 1/4 inch. Slice the chicken breast, then cut into matchsticks the same size as the celery batons.

3 Peel and slice the onion (page 525).
Wash and dry the apples. Core (page 512) and slice into matchsticks (page 512).

4 Mix the cheese, celery, chicken, and apple together in a bowl. Sprinkle with the chives and drizzle with olive oil. Season with pepper and fleur de sel.
Whisk the crème fraîche with the lemon juice for extra tang (it should be smooth but not runny), season the mixture with salt and pepper, and serve it alongside the salad.

TIPS FROM OUR CHEFS

DILUTE

If your crème fraîche is very thick, rather than adding more lemon juice and rendering it overly sour, dilute it with a little whipping cream.

1
2
3

LYONNAISE SALAD

Serves 4

Preparation time 30 minutes
Cooking time 1 hour 5 minutes

EQUIPMENT

Immersion (stick) blender

Salad

8 slices smoked side (streaky) bacon
1 clove garlic
1/2 ficelle loaf (thin baguette)
Olive oil
1 frisée heart
12 fresh quail eggs
2 tablespoons distilled white vinegar

Dressing

1 (120-g – 4.23-ounce) onion
1 clove garlic
Fine salt
1 egg
30 ml – 2 tbsp sherry vinegar
70 ml – 1/4 cup plus 2 1/4 teaspoons olive oil
Freshly ground pepper

1 Preheat the oven to 170°C – 325°F (gas mark 3). Lay the bacon on the work surface and trim off the rind. Transfer to a baking sheet (tray), cover with parchment (baking) paper and another baking sheet, and place an ovenproof weight on top. Cook in the oven for 35 minutes.

2 Peel the garlic clove. Cut the bread on the diagonal into thin slices and rub with the garlic. Transfer to a rack. Drizzle with olive oil. Select the best frisée leaves. Tear the leaves into small pieces. Wash and dry.

3 Use a serrated knife to make an incision close to the top of each quail egg. Use a paring knife to take the tops off the eggs and empty each one into a small bowl. Prepare a bowl with water and ice cubes. Oil a dish. Heat a saucepan of water. When the water in the saucepan boils, add the vinegar. Stir with a spoon to create a whirlpool at the center. Drop one egg into the whirlpool. Cook for 30 seconds.

4 Use a skimmer or slotted spoon to take the egg out of the pan and drop it into the ice water. Repeat, one at a time, with remaining eggs. Let the eggs cool for 3 minutes. Drain each egg in your hand and use a teaspoon to gently trim off any strings of egg white. Place the prepared eggs on the oiled dish.

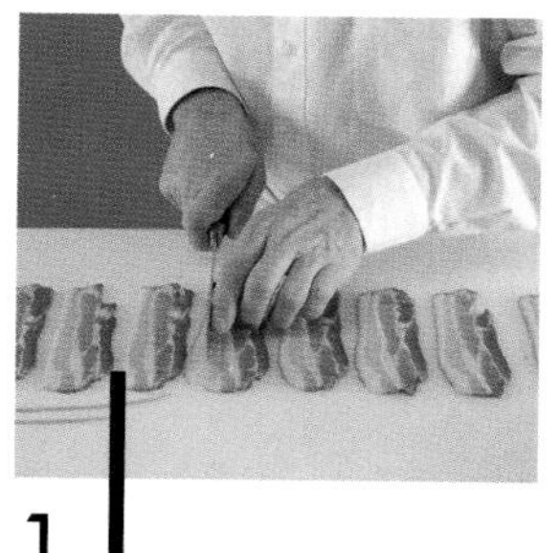

1

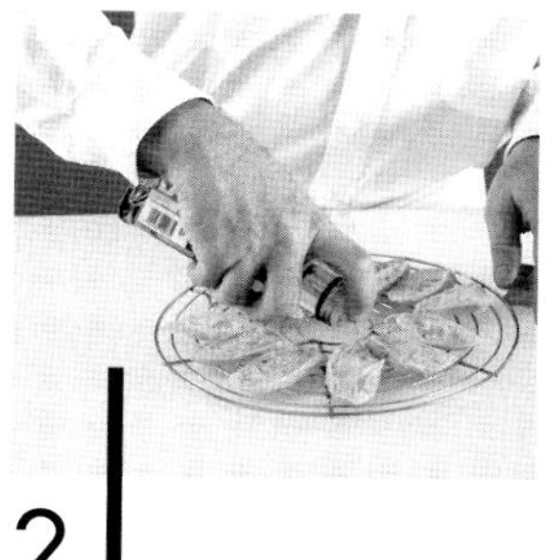

2

3

4

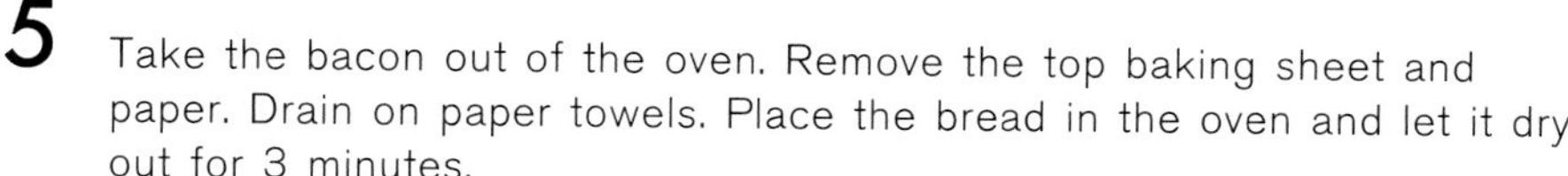

5 Take the bacon out of the oven. Remove the top baking sheet and paper. Drain on paper towels. Place the bread in the oven and let it dry out for 3 minutes.

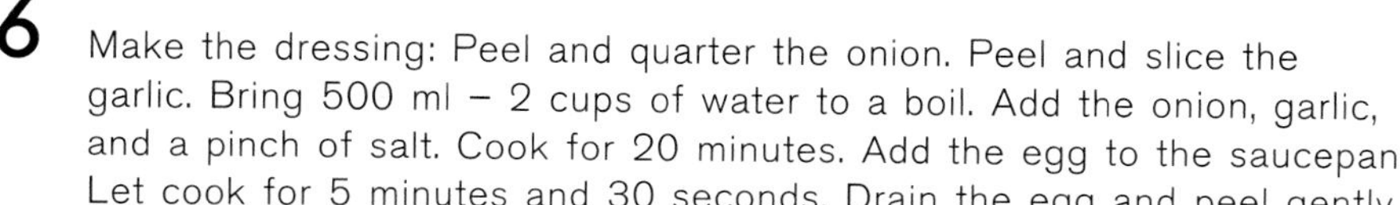

6 Make the dressing: Peel and quarter the onion. Peel and slice the garlic. Bring 500 ml – 2 cups of water to a boil. Add the onion, garlic, and a pinch of salt. Cook for 20 minutes. Add the egg to the saucepan. Let cook for 5 minutes and 30 seconds. Drain the egg and peel gently.

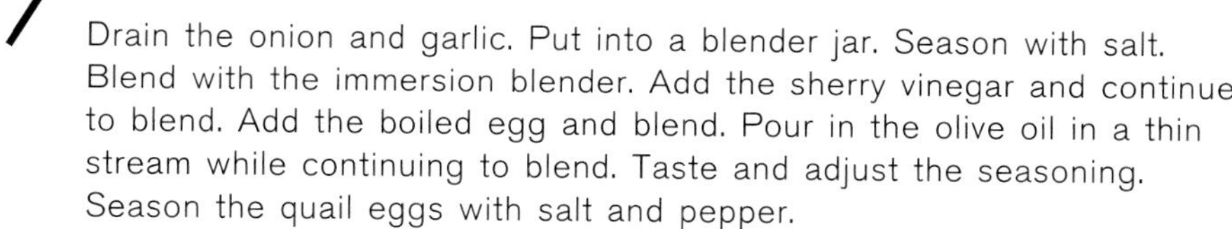

7 Drain the onion and garlic. Put into a blender jar. Season with salt. Blend with the immersion blender. Add the sherry vinegar and continue to blend. Add the boiled egg and blend. Pour in the olive oil in a thin stream while continuing to blend. Taste and adjust the seasoning. Season the quail eggs with salt and pepper.

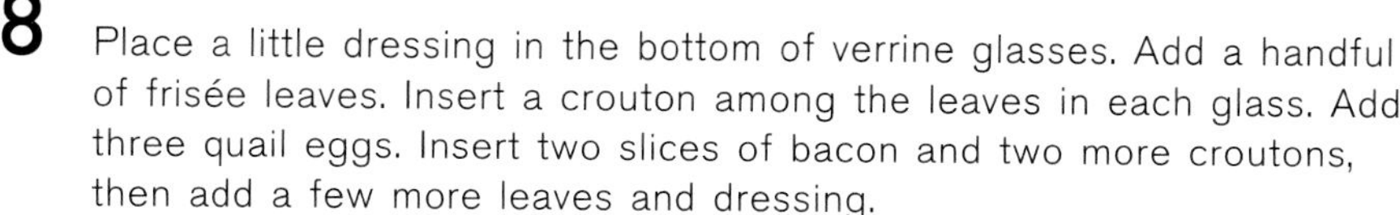

8 Place a little dressing in the bottom of verrine glasses. Add a handful of frisée leaves. Insert a crouton among the leaves in each glass. Add three quail eggs. Insert two slices of bacon and two more croutons, then add a few more leaves and dressing.

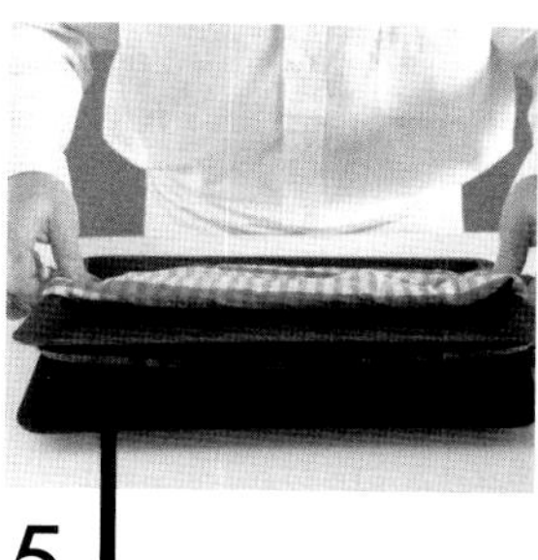

5

6

7

TIPS FROM OUR CHEFS

FRESHNESS IS A MUST

Keep in mind that if an egg (whether quail or chicken) is not fresh enough, its white will not set well around the yolk when poaching and will spread out in strings in the water.

GENTLY DOES IT

Gently make a cut into the shell with a serrated knife without going any farther. Then cut off the top of the egg. If you crack the shell as you would for a chicken egg, you will pierce the membrane and probably break the yolk.

STORAGE

This garlic dressing can keep for a few days in the refrigerator.

WARM RATTE AND VITELLOTE POTATO SALAD

Serves 4

Preparation time 10 minutes
Cooking time 15–20 minutes

Potatoes

400 g – 14 ounces Ratte potatoes of the same size (or other heirloom fingerling potato)
400 g – 14 ounces Vitelotte potatoes of the same size (or other deep blue–purple potato)
12 g – 0.42 ounces (2 1/2 teaspoons) kosher (coarse) salt
1 clove garlic
2 sprigs thyme
2 bay leaves

Vinaigrette

1 white onion
2 tablespoons sherry vinegar
1 tablespoon Meaux mustard
1/4 cup olive oil
Leaves of 1 bunch flat-leaf parsley and other fine herbs of your choice
1/2 teaspoon fine salt
Freshly ground pepper

1 Clean the potatoes, using a brush to remove any soil. Bring 1 liter – 4 cups water to a boil in a saucepan. Add the kosher salt, whole unpeeled garlic clove, thyme, and bay leaves and cook the potatoes until easily pierced with the tip of a paring knife, 15–20 minutes. Drain the potatoes, discarding the garlic and bay leaves, and let cool a little. Peel while still hot.

2 Cut the potatoes into about 4-mm – 1/8-inch-thick round slices (page 518). Place in a bowl, being careful not to break them.

3 Make the vinaigrette: Mince the onion (page 525). Put into a bowl with the vinegar, mustard, and oil. Stir well. Finely chop the herbs. Add the herbs, salt, and pepper to the vinaigrette and whisk to combine.
Pour the vinaigrette over the potatoes. Mix gently. Serve immediately. This salad is best when eaten warm.

TIPS FROM OUR CHEFS

PEELING
Peeling the potatoes is easier when they are hot. Let them cool just enough that you can handle them without burning yourself.

STOP STICKING
Before slicing the potatoes, very lightly oil the knife blade so that it doesn't stick. The cuts will be clean.

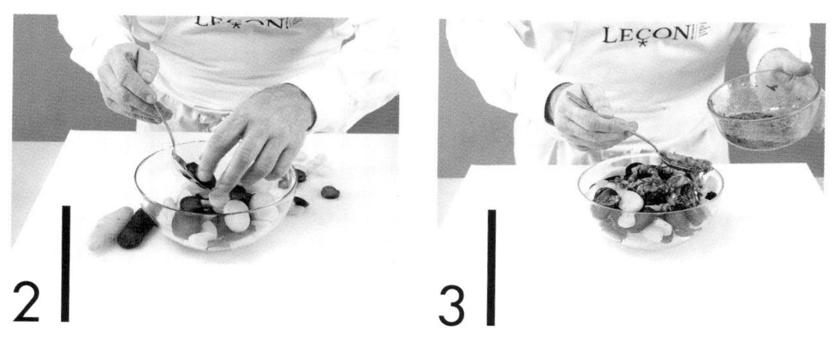

2

3

CHILLED TOMATO SOUP

Serves 4

Preparation time 40 minutes
Cooking time 30 minutes
Resting time 12 hours + 15–20 minutes

EQUIPMENT

Blender

Soup

400 g – 14.11 ounces ripe tomatoes
1 fresh onion
2 tablespoons tomato paste
2 tablespoons olive oil, plus more for drizzling
1 dash Tabasco sauce
2 sprigs cilantro (coriander)
Fine salt
40 g – 1.41 ounces bread
1 cucumber
1 clove garlic
12 tomato bonbons (page 562)

Tomato syrup

2 tomatoes on the vine
Olive oil
Fine salt
Pinch of sugar
Freshly ground pepper
1 tablespoon tomato paste
1 g – 0.04 ounces sheet (leaf) gelatin (1/2 sheet)

TIPS FROM OUR CHEFS

RELEASE WATER

Tomatoes and cucumbers contain a lot of water. Sprinkling salt over them helps them to release part of this so water it doesn't collect at the bottom of the finished dish in an unsightly manner.

NO SPACE IN THE FREEZER?

In this case, place the dishes containing the syrup in the refrigerator, but allow a little more time for the gelatin to set. Whether the syrup sets in the freezer or the refrigerator, it should not be allowed to harden.

1

Make the soup: Wash and dry the tomatoes. Cut into slices, then into pieces. Peel the onion, cut into pieces, and add to the tomatoes in a bowl.
Add the tomato paste, 2 tablespoons of oil, the Tabasco, a few cilantro leaves, and two large pinches of fine salt.
Cut the bread into medium slices, then into large cubes, and add to the bowl.

2

Peel, then slice off the top and bottom of the cucumber. Cut in half lengthwise, then cut in half again. Scrape the seeds out with a small spoon into a bowl.
Add the cucumber juice and seeds to the bowl containing the tomatoes and bread, and set aside the cucumber in the refrigerator.

3

Peel and halve the garlic, then mince. Also add to the bowl. Cover the bowl with plastic wrap (cling film) and let marinate for 12 hours in the refrigerator.
After 12 hours, cut the cucumber into thin batons, and then into a 5-mm – 1/4-inch dice. Place in a strainer (sieve), sprinkle with salt, toss gently, and let stand to release liquid.

4

Make the tomato bonbons.
Set aside the tomato skins (page 562). Make the tomato syrup: Cut the 2 vine tomatoes in half. Heat a little oil in a saucepan. Place the tomato halves in the oil, skin upward. Add the tomato skins set aside from the bonbons, plus a pinch of salt and a pinch of sugar.
Add a sprinkling of freshly ground pepper and the tomato paste. Cover and let cook for 30 minutes over low heat.

5

Soak the gelatin for 5 minutes in cold water (page 596). Strain the contents of the saucepan through a strainer (sieve) into a bowl, pressing with the back of a spoon. Drain the gelatin with your hands. Add to the hot tomato syrup. Mix well. Place the bowl with syrup inside a container filled with ice cubes and let cool, stirring from time to time.

Divide the syrup among four small serving dishes. Allow to set in the freezer for 15–20 minutes.

6

Transfer the soup ingredients from the bowl to a blender and blend. Transfer to another bowl. Taste and adjust the seasoning. Drizzle with a little olive oil.

7

Pluck the leaves from 1 sprig of the cilantro and mince the leaves with a knife. Add to the cucumber.

Make a layer of cucumber over the lightly set tomato syrup in the dishes. Gently pour the soup over the top. Garnish each serving with a cilantro leaf.

Trim off the excess plastic wrap from the tomato bonbons. Arrange the bonbons around the dishes of soup and serve.

LEEK AND POTATO SOUP

Serves 6

Preparation time 15 minutes
Cooking time 30 minutes

EQUIPMENT

Blender

600 g – 1 pound 5 ounces Agria potatoes
2 leeks (white part only)
20 g – 0.71 ounces (1 1/2 tablespoons) butter
1/2 teaspoon fine salt, plus more for seasoning
750 ml – 3 cups chicken broth or stock
200 ml – 3/4 cup plus 1 tablespoon whole milk
Freshly ground pepper
150 ml – 2/3 cup whipping cream
A few sprigs of chervil

1 Wash, brush, and peel the potatoes. Cut in half lengthwise. Cut each half into slices (page 518).

2 Wash the leeks. Cut in half lengthwise. Slice each half finely.

3 Use a wide and deep skillet or frying pan to sauté the leeks in the butter. Add the 1/2 teaspoon of salt. Once the leeks are soft, add the chicken broth and the milk.

4 Add the potato slices and additional salt and pepper. Bring to a boil and let cook for 25 minutes. When cooked, stir in the cream.
Transfer to a blender (or use an immersion/stick blender) and blend until very smooth.

5 Strain the soup through a fine strainer (sieve).
Reheat just before serving.
Serve in bowls and garnish with snipped chervil just before serving.

3

4

5

TIPS FROM OUR CHEFS

AS VICHYSSOISE

This creamy soup is also delicious served cold, as vichyssoise, in verrine glasses. To make vichyssoise, add the cream only after straining the soup. Or for a tangier cold version, try it with crème fraîche.

CREAM OF SQUASH SOUP

Serves 4

Preparation time 25 minutes
Cooking time 10 minutes

EQUIPMENT

Pressure cooker
Immersion (stick) blender

1 kg – 1 (100-g – 3.5-ounce) onion
175 g – 6.17 ounces potatoes
1 (150-g – 5.3-ounce) carrot
1/2 vanilla bean (pod)
1.2 kg – 2lb 10 oz butternut squash
2 chicken bouillon (stock) cubes
3 tablespoons olive oil, divided
1 teaspoon salt, plus more for seasoning
50 g – 1.76 ounces stale bread
100 g – 3.53 ounces thin lardons or chopped bacon
250 ml – 1 cup light (single) cream
Freshly ground pepper

TIPS FROM OUR CHEFS

DON'T FORGET
Wash the potatoes and carrot after peeling.

GO GENTLY WITH THE SALT
Use salt in moderation because bouillon cubes already contain salt.

STRAINING?
You don't absolutely have to strain the soup, but doing so will give it a very smooth texture. If you skip this step, you may end up with a grainier soup.

1

Peel and chop the onion (page 525). Peel the potatoes. Peel the carrot and slice off the top and bottom. Cut the potatoes and carrot in half lengthwise. Cut the carrot into pieces about 3 mm – 1/8 inch in thickness. Split the vanilla bean in half without separating the two pieces completely.

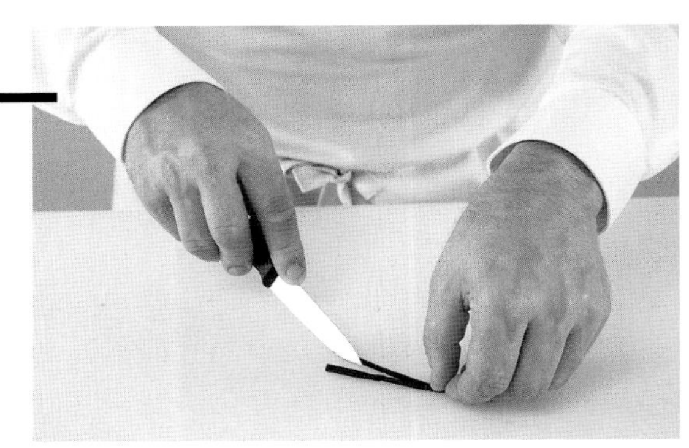

2

Halve the squash. Remove and discard the seeds. Stand each half upright and cut off the skin. Cut each half into slices about 1 cm – 3/8 inch-thick. Set aside 100 g – 3.53 ounces for the garnish. Cut the rest into batons, and then dice.

3

Dissolve the bouillon cubes in 600 ml – 2 1/2 cups boiling water. Put 2 tablespoons of the olive oil into a pressure cooker. Add the onion and sauté for 1 minute over medium heat. Add the carrot and lightly cook for 1 minute.
Add the squash, split vanilla bean, and 1 level teaspoon of salt. Sauté the squash for 4–5 minutes, stirring from time to time.

4

Brush the sides of the pot with a wet pastry brush.
Add the stock and increase the heat. Add the potatoes. Place the lid on the pressure cooker and lock.
Bring the pressure cooker to high pressure. Lower the heat as much as possible while maintaining high pressure and cook for 10 minutes.

5

In the meantime, prepare the garnish: Cut up the squash set aside into batons, and then into about 5-mm – 1/4-inch cubes. Cut the bread vertically into slices, then into batons, and then into about 5-mm – 1/4-inch cubes.

6

Thinly slice the lardons. Heat the remaining 1 tablespoon of olive oil in a deep skillet or frying pan. Brown the lardons for 1 minute. Add the bread, stirring until golden.
Add the diced squash and sauté. Season lightly with salt. Cook for 4 minutes.
While this is for the garnish and not an integral part of the dish, it unquestionably enhances the dish, both visually and in flavor.

7

When the soup is cooked, turn off the heat and timer. When it is safe to remove the lid, open the pressure cooker and remove the vanilla bean.
Blend the soup with the immersion blender. Add the cream while blending, then taste and adjust the seasoning with salt and pepper.
Strain the soup through a fine strainer (sieve).

8

Pour into plates, small bowls, or small glasses. Serve with the garnish.

SOUPE AU PISTOU (PROVENÇAL VEGETABLE SOUP WITH PISTOU)

Serves 4

Preparation time 25 minutes
Cooking time 1 hour 15 minutes
Resting time 12 hours

A WORD FROM OUR SOMMELIER

Pair with a Provençal rosé (e.g., Bandol).

TIPS FROM OUR CHEFS

LIKE A PRO

If you have a mortar, pound the garlic (after removing the cores), pine nuts, grated Parmesan, basil, and salt to a smooth paste. Slowly add olive oil in a thin stream, continuing to mix until smooth (page 504).

Soup

- **125 g** – 4.41 ounces (2/3 cup) small dried navy (haricot) beans
- **2** medium zucchini (courgettes)
- **250 g** – 9 ounces green beans
- **500 g** – 1 pound 2 ounces potatoes
- **3** tomatoes
- **1** large white onion
- **2** tablespoons olive oil
- **1** tablespoon kosher (coarse) salt

Pistou (pesto)

- **2** cloves garlic
- **30 g** – 1.06 ounces Parmesan cheese
- **30 g** – 1.06 ounces (2 tablespoons) pine nuts
- **1** teaspoon salt
- **6** tablespoons olive oil
- **6** sprigs basil

1 Put the navy beans into a bowl. Cover with plenty of cold water and soak for 12 hours. When the time comes to make the soup, wash all the vegetables. Slice off the ends of the zucchini. Cut in half. Cut the pieces into batons, and then dice (page 522).

2 Trim off the ends of the green beans. Cut into 2-cm – 3/4-inch lengths. Peel the potatoes. Cut into 4-mm – 1/8-inch-thick slices. Cut the slices into batons, and then dice.

3 Cut each of the tomatoes into 8 wedges. Peel them by passing the knife blade between the skin and the flesh (page 521). Remove and discard the cores and seeds. Cut the tomato pieces into batons, and then dice.

4 Peel the onion. Halve and chop (page 525). Place 2 tablespoons of oil in a stewpot. Add the onion. Mix and let sauté for 1 minute.

5 Drain the navy beans. Add them to the pot with the tomatoes and pour in 1.25 liters – 5 1/4 cups of water. Bring to a boil. Cover the pot and simmer for 1 hour. Add the potatoes. Cover and cook for 15 minutes. Add the zucchini and the green beans. Season with the kosher salt. Mix and let simmer for 15 minutes. Don't cover the pot; this will cause the green beans to discolor.

6 Make the pistou: Cut the garlic cloves in half, then peel and remove the green cores. Grate the Parmesan—you should have about 1/3 cup.
Place the garlic in a food chopper (for use with an immersion/stick blender) together with the pine nuts and the salt. Add 3 tablespoons of olive oil and the grated Parmesan. Blend.

7 Remove the stems (stalks) from the basil and chop the leaves coarsely. Add the basil leaves to the food chopper together with the remaining 3 tablespoons of olive oil. Blend again. Transfer to a bowl. Serve the soup in bowls. Place a little pistou in the center of the soup, or serve separately.

Makes 12 fritters

Preparation time 20 minutes
Cooking time 4 minutes per batch
Resting time 40 minutes

Batter

1 large egg
150 g – 5.29 ounces
(1 1/4 cups) flour
Salt
Olive oil

12 zucchini flowers
Salt
Freshly ground pepper

Oil for deep-frying

TIPS FROM OUR CHEFS

A WELL-NEEDED REST
The batter needs to rest for 30 minutes at room temperature so that the flour can absorb the liquid. This Nice-style batter can also be used to coat zucchini sticks, eggplant (aubergine) slices, and acacia flowers before frying.

FRESHNESS IS A MUST
The zucchini flowers must be very fresh. Make this dish the same day you buy the flowers.

SERVING
Serve these hot and crispy fritters as an appetizer, or as an accompaniment to fish or stuffed vegetables.

ZUCCHINI FLOWER FRITTERS

1 Make the batter: Break the egg into a small container. Place the flour in a bowl. Add a pinch of salt and mix. Add the egg. Add a little olive oil. Mix gently. Add a little water and mix. Continue to add water while whisking the mixture until you have a smooth batter.
Strain the batter through a strainer (sieve) to remove any lumps, pressing down with a spatula (scraper). Let stand for 30 minutes.

1

2 Cut the zucchini flowers off of the zucchini, if attached, and reserve zucchini for another use.
Remove and discard the bottoms of the flowers and the pistils (page 522).

2

3 Gently open out the flowers without tearing. Spread them out on paper towels.
Mix the batter well. Use a brush to apply the batter to the flowers. Turn them over and do the same on the other side.
Arrange the coated flowers in a single layer on a baking sheet (tray). Let rest for 10 minutes.

4 During this time, heat the oil in a deep fryer (deep-fat fryer) with the basket inside to 160°C – 320°F.
Gently lay four zucchini flowers inside the basket. Fry for 2 minutes in the oil. Turn over. Fry for another 2 minutes.

5

5 Take the basket out of the fryer. Remove the flowers and drain on paper towels.
Cook the rest of the flowers the same way. Season with salt and pepper. Serve immediately.

RATATOUILLE

Serves 6

Preparation + Cooking time
1 hour 30 minutes

2 onions
2 eggplants (aubergines)
2 yellow bell peppers
1 green bell pepper
2 red bell peppers
4 medium zucchini (courgettes)
3 cloves garlic
6 (130-g – 4.59-ounce) vine tomatoes
Leaves of 1 bunch basil
150 ml – 1/2 cup plus 1 tablespoon olive oil, divided
Salt
Freshly ground pepper

TIPS FROM OUR CHEFS

KEEPING THE BEST QUALITIES
Cooking the ingredients separately allows them to stay crisp, keep their color, and retain their vitamins (the cooking time is shorter), and it makes it easy for the water they contain to evaporate.

RINSING
It's essential to rinse the pan after cooking the tomatoes, because their acidity could cause the zucchini to change color.

SERVING
Serve this ratatouille as an accompaniment to meat or fish, or serve it as a one-course meal with scrambled eggs. Serve hot or cold.

1

Peel the onions. Halve and chop (page 525). Slice off the top and bottom of the eggplants. Use a vegetable peeler to remove alternating bands of skin. Cut the eggplants in half widthwise, then quarter each half lengthwise. Cut each piece into 1.5-cm- – 1/2-inch-wide batons, then dice.

2

Cut off the top and bottom of the bell peppers. Stand them upright. Cut off the flesh around the core. Cut each pepper into four lobes at each of the ribs. Peel each piece with a vegetable peeler (page 513). Cut the pieces into batons, and then dice.

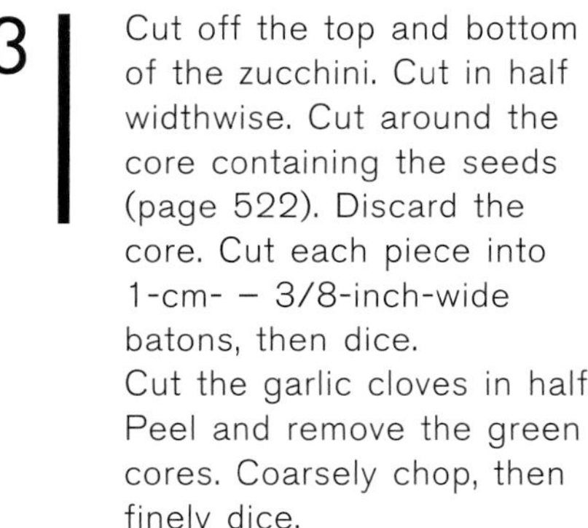

3

Cut off the top and bottom of the zucchini. Cut in half widthwise. Cut around the core containing the seeds (page 522). Discard the core. Cut each piece into 1-cm- – 3/8-inch-wide batons, then dice.
Cut the garlic cloves in half. Peel and remove the green cores. Coarsely chop, then finely dice.

4

Remove the stems (stalks) from the tomatoes and discard. Cut an X in the base of each tomato. Immerse for 10 seconds in boiling water, then in ice water (page 521).
Once the tomatoes have cooled, remove them from the water. Peel.

5

Halve them horizontally and scoop out the seeds with a small spoon. Quarter each tomato half in one direction, then in the other direction. Rinse the basil and dry gently.

6

Put 1 tablespoon of oil into a deep skillet or frying pan. Add the onions. Season with salt and mix. Add 4 or 5 basil leaves. Brown for 3 minutes over medium heat. Add the bell peppers. Season with salt and pepper. Add a few more basil leaves. Mix gently and cook for 5 minutes. Transfer to a bowl.

7

Heat 1/4 cup plus 1 tablespoon of olive oil in the same pan. Add the eggplants and season with salt and pepper. Add 10 basil leaves. Cover the pan and cook for 10 minutes, stirring from time to time. Transfer the contents of the pan to a colander and let drain.

Heat 1 tablespoon of olive oil in the same pan. Add the garlic and sauté to soften for 1 minute. Add the tomatoes and season with salt and pepper. Add 6 or 7 basil leaves. Mix and let cook, uncovered, for 8 minutes. Add to the onion mixture.

8

Rinse and dry the pan. Heat 2 tablespoons of olive oil. Add the zucchini and season with salt and pepper. Add 4 or 5 basil leaves.

Cook for 5 minutes, shaking the pan from time to time. Add to the onion–tomato mixture. Add the eggplant. Mix gently. Transfer the ratatouille to a serving dish and decorate with a few basil leaves.

DUCHESS POTATOES

Makes 40 puffs

Preparation time 30 minutes
Cooking time 10–15 minutes

EQUIPMENT

Pastry (piping) bag
Fluted pastry tip (nozzle)

500 g – 1 lb 2 oz (2 1/3 cups) mashed potatoes (see p. 555)
3 eggs
50 g – 1.76 ounces (3 1/2 tablespoons) butter, softened
1/2 teaspoon fine salt

1 Break and separate the eggs. In a bowl combine the egg white and egg yolks.
Incorporate the butter into the hot mashed potatoes.
Add the salt.
Add the egg mixture. Mix quickly until smooth.

2 Fit the pastry bag with the tip and fill with the mixture.
Preheat the oven to 200°C – 400°F (gas mark 6).

3 Pipe small, even mounds, with a little space between them on all sides, onto a buttered or nonstick baking sheet (tray).
Cook in the preheated oven until golden and firm to the touch, 10–15 minutes.

TIPS FROM OUR CHEFS

BUTTER FIRST
The butter has to be incorporated first to stop the potatoes from becoming pasty. Flavoring the mash with herbs or spices is a nice touch.

1

2

POTATO CROQUETTES

Makes 40 croquettes

Preparation time 35 minutes
Cooking time 6–7 minutes
Resting time 1 hour

EQUIPMENT

Pastry (piping) bag
Size 10 plain pastry tip (nozzle)

Duchess potato base (page 46)

Crumb coating

80 g – 2.82 ounces (2/3 cup) unbleached all-purpose flour
2 eggs, beaten
100g – 3.53 oz (1 cup) dried bread crumbs

Oil for deep–frying

TIPS FROM OUR CHEFS

PLANNING
If the piped mixture is too hard to cut when you take it out of the freezer, let it thaw a little, but don't allow it to get soft again. The croquettes need to be firm when they are dredged in the breadcrumbs or they will lose their shape.

1 Make the Duchess Potato base (page 46). Fit the pastry bag with the tip and fill with the mixture (page 507). Dust a baking sheet (tray) with some of the flour. Pipe lines of the potato mixture the length of the sheet. Pipe parallel lines with space in between.

2 Dust with sifted flour. Place in the freezer for at least 1 hour. Take the croquettes out of the freezer. Cut into 5-cm – 2-inch lengths on a cutting board. Roll in flour.

3 Dip in the beaten eggs. Heat the oil in the deep (deep-fat) fryer to 180°C – 355°F.
Dredge the croquettes in the breadcrumbs to coat well. Immerse in the oil. Fry until golden, 6–7 minutes.

1

3

DAUPHINE POTATOES

1 Make the Duchess Potato base (page 46).
Make the choux paste (page 545): Heat the milk and butter in a saucepan over medium heat. Add grated nutmeg (to taste) and salt. Heat the oil in the deep fryer (deep-fat fryer) to 180°C – 350°F. Bring the milk mixture to a boil. Add all of the flour. Stir immediately with a whisk.

2 As soon as the mixture thickens, reduce the heat. Stir constantly with a silicone spatula (scraper) to dry out the mixture. When the mixture comes away easily from the bottom of the pan, add the eggs, one at a time. Continue to stir with the spatula. Add the choux paste to the potato base. Mix well.

3 Make quenelles: Use two tablespoons. Fill one with the preparation and shape into a well-rounded oval. Use the second spoon to detach the quenelle from the first and gently let drop into the frying oil. Be careful, because the oil may splash. Fry the dauphine potatoes until browned, 6–7 minutes, shaking the frying basket from time to time to stop them from sticking.

Makes 40 fritters

Preparation time 40 minutes
Cooking time 6–7 minutes

Duchess potato base (page 46)

Choux paste

125 ml – 1/2 cup whole milk
60 g – 2.12 ounces (4 tablespoons) butter
Freshly grated nutmeg
1 pinch salt
70 g – 2.47 ounces (1/2 cup plus 1 tablespoon) flour, sifted
2 large eggs

Oil for deep–frying

1

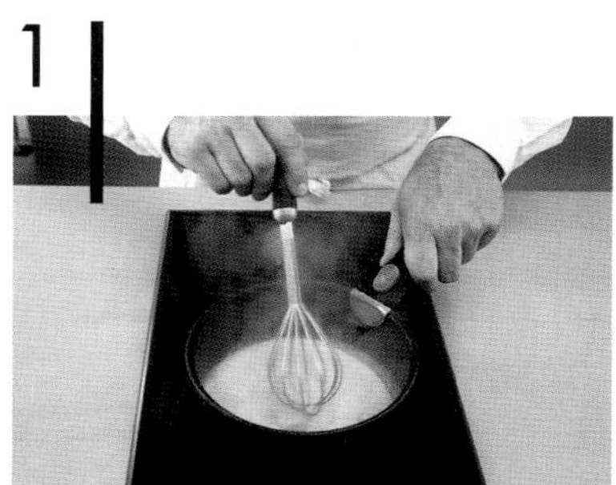

3

TIPS FROM OUR CHEFS

EQUAL MEASURES
Keep in mind that for the potato base and choux paste to mix thoroughly, they should both be hot—more or less at the same temperature—and be equivalent in weight.

GRATIN DAUPHINOIS

Serves 4

Preparation time 25 minutes
Cooking time 1 hour

1 kg – 2 pounds 4 ounces Mona Lisa (or other smooth white) potatoes
2 cloves garlic
20 g – 0.71 ounces (1 1/2 tablespoons) butter, softened
300 ml – 1 1/4 cups whole milk
300 ml – 1 1/4 cups whipping cream
1/2 teaspoon fine salt
A little freshly grated nutmeg
Freshly ground white pepper
20 g – 0.71 ounce (3 tablespoons) dried breadcrumbs

1 Wash, brush, and peel the potatoes. Preheat the oven to 200°C – 400°F (gas mark 6). Use a mandoline slicer or knife to cut the potatoes into 4-mm- — 1/8-inch-thick slices (page 519). Peel the garlic. Use a wide chef's knife to crush one of the cloves by pressing on the blade with your fingers (page 523). Rub the bottom and sides of a gratin dish with the other clove.

2 Coat all over the inside of the dish with the butter by pressing on it with the back of a spoon.

3 Combine the milk and cream in a saucepan. Heat over medium heat until the mixture boils. Add the potatoes. Add the salt and the nutmeg. Add the crushed garlic clove. Sprinkle generously with freshly ground pepper (six turns of the peppermill). Stir well. Cook for 5 minutes. The potatoes will release their starch as they boil, thickening the milk-cream mixture.

4 Use a slotted spoon to remove the potato slices. Arrange in the dish, spreading out evenly.

5 Pour the liquid into the dish. Bake in the preheated oven for 45 minutes.

6 Take the dish out of the oven. Check that the potatoes are cooked through by piercing a slice or two with the tip of a knife. Sprinkle breadcrumbs evenly over the top. Return to the oven until deep golden, an additional 5–10 minutes.

TIPS FROM OUR CHEFS

IN PROPER ORDER
Rub the baking dish with the garlic before you butter it. The butter should be left to soften in advance to make it easier to spread.

BOILING
The potatoes have to boil very quickly in the milk-cream mixture so that they release their starch without soaking up too much liquid.

THE RIGHT SHADE OF GOLD
If the breadcrumbs are toasting too quickly in the oven, cover with aluminum foil (shiny side facing outward). Leave the oven drip pan inside the oven while baking to collect any excess liquid.

BOULANGÈRE POTATOES

Serves 4

Preparation time 25 minutes
Cooking time 1 hour 30 minutes
Resting time 40 minutes

Gratin

1kg – 2 lb 4 oz medium potatoes
50g – 1.76 oz (3 1/2 tbsp) butter
1/2 tsp fine salt
2 leeks (only white part)

Bouquet garni

2 leek leaves
1 bay leaf
3 sprigs thyme
1 bunch parsley, only stems (stalks)

600 ml – 2 1/2 cups chicken broth or stock, hot

TIPS FROM OUR CHEFS

A LONG TRADITION
The word boulangère ("baker") comes from the old tradition of taking a dish of potatoes and meat to the local bakery. It was cooked slowly in the oven after the bread had been baked and the fire was put out. Likewise, the Alsatian dish baeckeoffe actually means "baker's oven."

1 Preheat the oven to 180°C – 350°F (gas mark 4). Wash the leeks. Cut off the tops. Set aside. Cut the roots off the leeks. Cut the leeks into approximately 3-mm – 1/8-inch slices. Make the bouquet garni: Cut two leek leaves into lengths of 7–8 cm – 2 3/4–3 1/4 inches. Lay the bay leaf, thyme, and parsley stems on top. Wrap the leaves around the herbs. Tie the bundle closed with kitchen twine (page 544). Bring the chicken broth to a boil. Add the bouquet garni. Let infuse for 20 minutes.

2 Wash, brush, and peel the potatoes. Soak in water. Drain. Use a mandoline slicer to cut the potatoes into slices approximately 3-mm – 1/8-inch thick (page 519).

3 Grease the dish with some of the softened butter using the back of a spoon. Make a layer of potato slices over the bottom of the dish. Then line the sides of the dish, overlapping the slices.

4 Add the leek slices, placing them side by side. Make a second layer of overlapped potato slices. Alternate rows of leeks and potatoes.

5 The final layer should be a rosette of potatoes covering the entire dish. Season with salt. Cut the rest of the butter into cubes and distribute over the dish. Pour the hot chicken broth over the potatoes. Bake in the oven for 1 hour 30 minutes. When cooked, collect the liquid with a spoon. Drizzle it over the dish to prevent the potatoes from drying out.

TIPS FROM OUR CHEFS

MOISTEN WELL

Measure out the amount of chicken broth according to the size of your dish; the dish should be filled to the rim with liquid so that the potatoes remain tender and don't dry out.

A CLASSIC

According to Provençal tradition, you can cook a leg or shoulder of lamb, with the fat removed, on a bed of potatoes. There is no need for butter, because the potatoes will soak up the meat juices.

POTATO PIE

Serves 4

Preparation time 25 minutes
Cooking time 1 hour 10 minutes

900 g – 2 pounds Charlotte (or other long, waxy) potatoes
Fine salt
1 (100-g – 3.53-ounce) white onion, peeled
12 long and thin strips of salted side (streaky) bacon, rind removed
80 g – 2.82 ounces (3/4 cup) shredded Emmental cheese
Leaves of 1 sprig thyme
60 ml – 1/4 cup dry white wine
300 ml – 1 1/4 cups chicken broth or stock
Freshly ground pepper

1 Preheat the oven to 230°C – 450°F (gas mark 8). Wash, brush, and peel the potatoes. Use a mandoline to cut the potatoes into slices 2–3 mm – 1/8 inch thick (page 518). Season lightly with salt. Cut the root of the onion. Chop finely (page 525).

2 Line a gratin dish with the bacon strips, letting them stick out over the edge of the dish. Cover the sides of the dish with slices of bacon cut in half so that there is just a single layer of bacon everywhere in the dish.

3 Make a layer of slightly overlapped potato slices in the bottom of the dish. Make a layer of about one third of the chopped onion, followed by one of about one third of the shredded cheese. Sprinkle a little thyme over the top. Make a second layer of potatoes, followed by one of onion, then one of cheese. Sprinkle a little more thyme over the top.

4 Cover them with a final layer of potatoes. Sprinkle the rest of the onions over it. Do the same with the remaining cheese. Finish with a little more thyme. Pour in the white wine. Fold the ends of the bacon over the top. Heat the chicken broth. Pour the hot broth over the potatoes. Season lightly with salt.

5 Cut out a sheet of parchment (baking) paper the same shape as the dish. Cover the dish. Cover with aluminum foil (shiny side facing outward). Bake in the preheated oven for 15 minutes. Reduce the temperature to 200°C – 400°F (gas mark 6) and bake for an additional 15 minutes. Take the dish out of the oven. Remove the foil and parchment paper. Check that the potatoes are cooked through using a knife tip, which should pierce the potatoes easily. Press on the pie with the flat part of a skimmer so that the potatoes are submerged in the cooking liquid.

6 Reduce the oven temperature to 180°C – 350°F (gas mark 4). Return the dish to the oven without covering for another 40 minutes. After this time, the top should have turned a deep golden color. Take the dish out of the oven. Pour off any remaining liquid. Season with pepper. Serve the pie directly from the baking dish, or let it cool and unmold it before slicing.

TIPS FROM OUR CHEFS

A MEAL IN ONE

This pie, inspired by a traditional recipe from the Auvergne region, can be served as a single-course meal, accompanied with a green salad and a well-ripened cheese. It can be made ahead of time and very gently reheated in the oven.

VARIATIONS

The Emmental can be replaced with any kind of cheese, such as mozzarella or fresh tomme cheese. To recall the flavors of this dish's native land, try a salers or Cantal cheese.

FOR A SOFT TEXTURE

To prevent the pie from drying out, the wine and broth should be poured over the top and during initial cooking it should steam. This is why it is covered with parchment paper and aluminum foil (or sometimes cooked in a steam oven). This process can also be accomplished using an earthenware dish with a tight-fitting lid.

MEDITERRANEAN TIAN OF ZUCCHINI, TOMATOES, AND MOZZARELLA

Serves 4

Preparation time 30 minutes
Cooking time 30 minutes

EQUIPMENT

Immersion (stick) blender and food chopper attachment

3 long zucchini (courgettes)
2 small onions (or 1 large)
4 tomatoes
2 **125-g** – 4.41-ounce mozzarella balls
1 clove garlic
2 sprigs cilantro (coriander)
1 tablespoon plus 1 1/2 teaspoons olive oil, plus more for drizzling
Salt
Freshly ground white pepper
1 tablespoon tomato paste

1 Wash and dry the zucchini. Use a paring knife to carve out curved slices.

2 Peel and quarter the onions. Set aside the cores. Detach the outer layers and cut into petals. Chop up the scraps (trimmings). Wash, dry, and halve the tomatoes. Cut off the stems (stalks) and cut each half into two or three wedges, depending on their size. Peel by passing the blade of a paring knife between the skin and flesh (page 521). Remove the core and seeds. Set aside for the sauce.

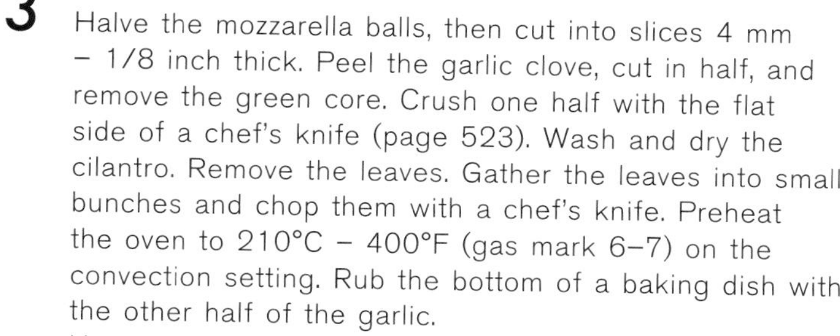

3 Halve the mozzarella balls, then cut into slices 4 mm – 1/8 inch thick. Peel the garlic clove, cut in half, and remove the green core. Crush one half with the flat side of a chef's knife (page 523). Wash and dry the cilantro. Remove the leaves. Gather the leaves into small bunches and chop them with a chef's knife. Preheat the oven to 210°C – 400°F (gas mark 6–7) on the convection setting. Rub the bottom of a baking dish with the other half of the garlic.
Use a pastry brush to grease the dish with 1 tablespoon of olive oil. Add the chopped onion scraps. Add the cilantro and crushed garlic.

4 Place the core and skins of the tomatoes and the onion cores in the food chopper. Season with salt and pepper, and add 1 1/2 teaspoons of olive oil.
Add 1 tablespoon of water. Add the tomato paste. Blend. Pass the sauce through a strainer (sieve), pushing through with the back of a spoon.

5 Pour the sauce into the dish. Make a row of slightly overlapped zucchini slices around the perimeter of the dish. Make small bundles containing one tomato petal, one onion petal, and one slice of mozzarella. Lean them against the zucchini. Finish with the remaining zucchini slices in the center. Pack the row of zucchini slices tightly. Drizzle the vegetables with olive oil. Season with salt and pepper. Bake for 30 minutes. Serve hot.

1

2

TIPS FROM OUR CHEFS

BUFFALO MOZZARELLA
Choose buffalo mozzarella, a more fragrant and flavorful product than cow's milk mozzarella.

TEMPERATURE
If you don't have a convection (fan-assisted) setting in your oven, cook the tian at 210°C – 410°F (gas mark 6–7).

EGGS EN COCOTTE WITH SALMON AND SPINACH

Serves 4

Preparation time 25 minutes
Cooking time 4 minutes

EQUIPMENT

Pressure cooker

200 g – 7 ounces (7 cups) spinach
1 clove garlic
1 tablespoon olive oil
Salt
25 g – 0.88 ounce (2 tablespoons) very soft butter
120 g – 4.23 ounces smoked salmon (scraps or trimmings)
4 eggs
1/4 cup light (single) cream
1/2 ficelle loaf (thin baguette)

1 Fold the spinach leaves in half and remove the central ribs (page 520). Wash, drain, and let dry on a cloth. Peel the garlic clove. Prick the clove with a fork and leave it on the end. Heat the oil in the pressure cooker on high heat. Add the spinach and season with salt. Stir for a few seconds with the fork containing the garlic clove until the spinach wilts. Transfer the spinach to another container.

2 Heat 750 ml – 3 cups of water in the pressure cooker on high heat. Use a pastry brush to grease four 8-cm- – 3 1/8-inch-diameter ramekins with butter. Dice half of the salmon. Arrange the cooked spinach leaves flat in a single layer. Set a few leaves aside. Line the ramekins with spinach leaves, letting them stick out over the sides. Lightly season the bottom of each ramekin with salt. Distribute the diced salmon among the ramekins. Break the eggs, one at a time, and gently slide one into each ramekin.

3 Arrange the four ramekins in a line. Stretch out a length of heat-resistant plastic wrap (cling film) over them. Cut the plastic between the ramekins and wrap tightly around each. Place the ramekins in a steamer basket for use with a pressure cooker. Place in the pressure cooker, over simmering water. Place the lid on the pressure cooker and lock. Program the cooker for 4 minutes (page 508). Once cooking has finished, open the pressure cooker and take out the basket. Remove the plastic wrap from the ramekins.

4 Pour the cream over the eggs. Fold the spinach leaves over. Pass a knife blade around the contents of each ramekin to loosen.

5 Spread plastic wrap tightly over a plate. Turn the plate upside down over a ramekin and turn both over, keeping the ramekin firmly in place. Gently remove the ramekin. Place a serving plate upside down over the egg en cocotte.

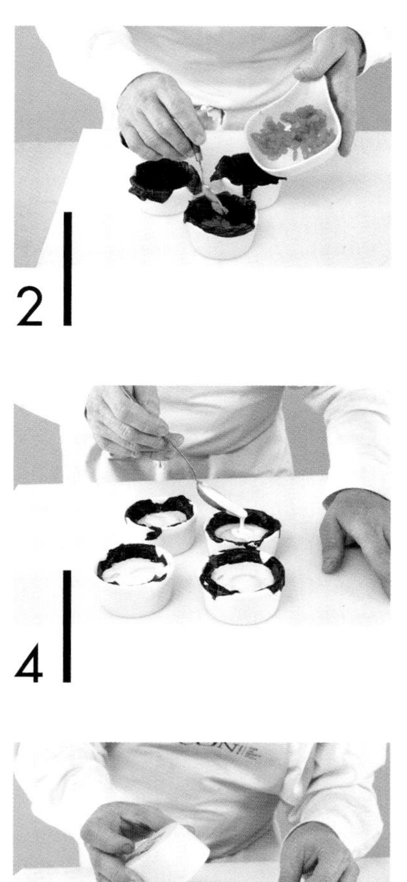

2

4

5

6 Turn both over: The egg en cocotte should be the right way up on the serving plate. Do the same for the other three ramekins. Cut the bread on a diagonal into eight slices. Place under the broiler (grill) for 30 seconds. Cut the remaining salmon and spinach into pieces. Place the spinach on the bread. Cover with a piece of salmon. Place two canapés on each plate. Serve.

TIPS FROM OUR CHEFS

UNWELCOME INTRUDERS

Wash the spinach in warm water with a drop of vinegar added to bring out any undesirable snails or slugs.

AT ROOM TEMPERATURE

For even cooking, take the eggs out of the refrigerator a little before starting to prepare this dish; they should be at room temperature when cooking begins.

SALMON TARTARE

Serves 4

Preparation time 25 minutes
Cooking time 3 minutes per blini

EQUIPMENT

10-cm- – 4-inch-diameter cake ring
10–12-cm – 4–4 3/4-inch blini pan

Salmon

500 g – 1 pound 2 ounces skinless salmon tail fillet
1 red onion
1 lime
2 sprigs basil
1/4 cup olive oil, divided
Fleur de sel
Freshly Ground Pepper
100 g – 3.5 ounces salmon roe
1 tablespoon lemon juice
150 g – 5.3 ounces mesclun

Blinis

150 ml – 2/3 cup whole milk
25 g – 0.88 ounce (1 1/2 tablespoons) butter
200 g – 7 ounces (1 cup) mashed potatoes (page 555)
80 g – 2.82 ounces (2/3 cup) flour, sifted
2 medium (UK small) eggs
3 egg whites
Salt

TIPS FROM OUR CHEFS

OIL
Here's a chef's trick: Oil the knife so that the salmon you are slicing doesn't stick.

SIFT
Be sure to sift the flour through a fine sifter (sieve) or drum sifter to stop lumps from forming.

WITHIN REACH
Keep a little bowl of cold water beside the stovetop. When shaping the blinis, dip the spoons in the water frequently to prevent the batter from sticking.

1 Make the tartare: Cut the fillet in half lengthwise. Cut three horizontal slices from each piece.
Cut into thin strips, then dice. Put into a bowl.

2 Peel the onion and cut off the root. Make four evenly spaced cuts through the first layer and detach the pieces. Stack and cut lengthwise into strips. Next, dice by cutting across. Add to the salmon. Supreme the lime and cut into segments (page 514).
Then dice. Add to the salmon.

3 Wash and pat dry the basil. Remove the stems (stalks). Chop the basil by moving the blade forward continuously in the same direction. Add to the salmon.

4 Make the blinis: Warm the milk with 15 g – 0.52 ounces (1 tablespoon) of butter. Put the mashed potatoes into a saucepan and pour the warmed milk and butter over the top.
Add the flour. Stir until the mixture forms a ball. Add one egg and mix vigorously. Add the second egg, and incorporate carefully.
Beat the three egg whites to relatively stiff peaks (page 565). Fold into the batter. Season with salt.

5 Heat the blini pan. Melt a bit of the remaining butter. Use two spoons to drop about one-quarter of the batter into the pan. Spread the batter out using the back of a wet spoon and cook for 1 minute 30 seconds. Turn the blini over with a wide spatula (slotted turner) and cook for another 1 minute 30 seconds. Cook the four blinis in this way, adding butter before cooking each one. Place on paper towels.

6 Season the tartare with 2 tablespoons of olive oil and fleur de sel. Mix. Sprinkle with freshly ground pepper. Mix again. Arrange the blinis on a dish. Place a cake ring over one and fill with the tartare. Press well with the back of the spoon. Remove the ring and repeat with remaining blinis and tartare. Cover the tartare with the salmon roe. Whisk the remaining 2 tablespoons olive oil with lemon juice and fleur de sel. Dress the mesclun with this mixture and serve it alongside the blinis.

1

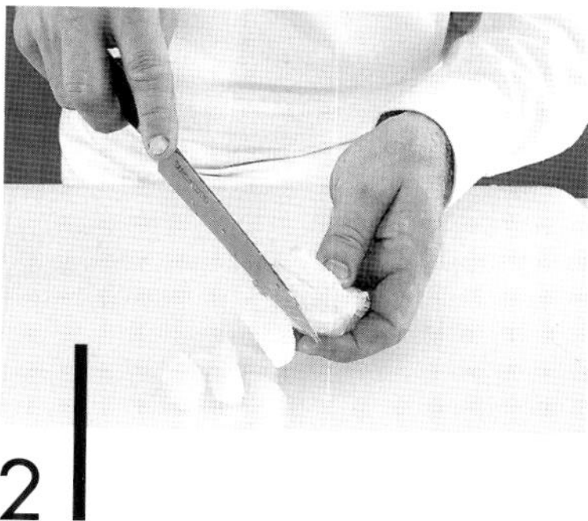

2

4

MARINATED COD APPETIZERS WITH FRAGRANT RICE

Serves 4

Fragrant rice
Preparation time 15 minutes
Cooking time 15 minutes
Resting time 10 minutes

Cod
Preparation time 20 minutes
Cooking time 15 minutes

TIPS FROM OUR CHEFS

TRIVIA
Cod fillet is also labeled cod loin and is called coeur ("heart") of cod by some French fish dealers.

SCALLIONS
Small, thin, long, green onions with a very fine flavor, scallions (spring onions) are produced in the south of France.

DON'T REFRIGERATE
Let the rice rest at room temperature. Don't put it into the refrigerator or it will dry out.

CLEAN CUTTING
To make cutting the fish easier, put it in the freezer for 15 minutes.

RAW OR COOKED?
If you prefer to cook the fish, place the assembled appetizers under the broiler (grill) for 2 minutes.

Fragrant rice

1 stick cinnamon
1 sprig thyme
2 scallions (spring onions)
1 teaspoon olive oil
80 g – 2.82 ounces (1/3 cup plus 1 tablespoon plus 1 teaspoon) short-grain rice
Fine salt

Cod

2 limes
20 g – 0.7 ounce (about 3 tablespoons grated) fresh ginger
1 teaspoon fleur de sel
Freshly ground pepper
1/4 cup olive oil
450g – 1 lb cod loin

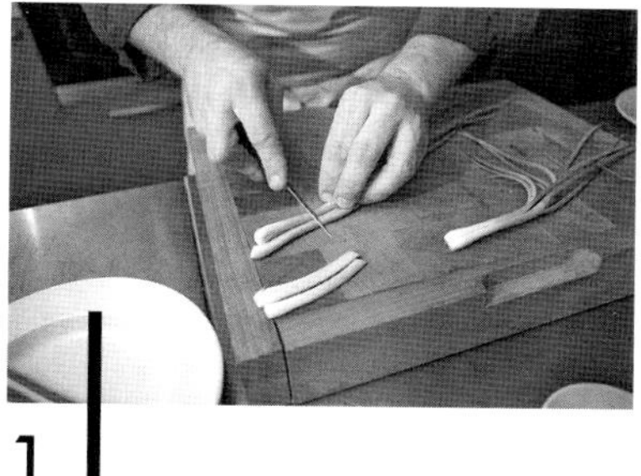
1

3

5

1 Prepare the rice: Bring 300 ml – 1 1/4 cups of water to a boil with the cinnamon and thyme. Cover, remove from heat, and let infuse for 10 minutes. Cut off the roots and remove the outer layer of skin from the scallions. Cut off the white bulb end at the bottom of the leaves. Rinse the bulbs, pat dry, and finely slice.

2 Heat the olive oil in another saucepan. Cook the scallions for 2 minutes over medium heat until soft.
Add the rice and a pinch of salt, and mix. Strain the infused water over the rice and simmer for 15 minutes. Mix well, cover, and remove from heat. Let stand for 15 minutes for the rice to swell. Transfer to a bowl, cover with plastic wrap (cling film), and set aside.

3 Wash and dry the limes. Finely grate their zest onto a plate (page 514).
Peel the ginger with a vegetable peeler. Finely grate over the zest.
Add 1 teaspoon of fleur de sel, add a generous amount of black pepper (18 turns of the peppermill). Squeeze one lime over a bowl to obtain 2 tablespoons of juice. Stir in the olive oil.

4 Cut 5-mm – 1/4-inch slices of fish. Slide the knife between the skin and the flesh to detach the slices as you cut them.
Arrange the slices on the plate in a single layer. Marinate for 5 minutes in the ginger and lime marinade.
Turn all of the slices over. Drizzle with half of the lime juice and olive oil mixture.
Cover with plastic wrap and refrigerate for 10 minutes.

5 Cut out a small piece of plastic wrap. Place 1 teaspoon of rice in the middle and make a small bundle. Twist the plastic to shape into a ball. Tighten as much as possible until the plastic bursts and releases the ball of rice. Check that there is no plastic left on the rice. Do the same with the rest of the rice.

6 Place a slice of fish over each ball of rice. Divide the remaining lime juice and olive oil mixture among individual dipping bowls. Place the bowls on plates and arrange the rice balls beside them.

APPLES IN SYRUP

Serves 4

Preparation time 20 minutes
Cooking time 8 minutes
Resting time 10 minutes

750 ml – 3 cups hard dry cider
150 g – 5.3 ounces (3/4 cup) sugar
Juice of 1/2 lemon, strained
1 organic, unwaxed orange
40 ml – 2 tablespoons plus 2 1/4 teaspoons Calvados
4 Golden Delicious apples

1 Pour the cider into a deep skillet or frying pan (sauteuse).
Add the sugar and the lemon juice. Mix.
Put over high heat.

2 Wash and dry the orange. Use a vegetable peeler to remove five strips of zest (page 514) and add to the cider.
Add the Calvados. Bring the syrup to a boil while stirring constantly. Remove from heat and let infuse for 10 minutes.

3 In the meantime, peel the apples. Halve and core them (page 512). Cut each half into four relatively thick pieces.
Immerse the apple pieces in the hot syrup. Bring to a boil over medium heat, then poach over low heat.

4 Cook until apples are tender but firm when pierced with a knife, 3–5 minutes, then remove from heat.
With a slotted spoon, transfer the poached apple pieces to a plate in a single layer and allow to cool, reserving the cooking liquid. Serve the apples cold with some of the syrup and a strip of orange zest.

1

2

3

TIPS FROM OUR CHEFS

BE CAREFUL OF SPLASHING
Be careful when placing the apple pieces in the hot syrup. Use a long-handled spoon if necessary.

NOTHING GOES TO WASTE
Reuse the syrup to make a delicious granita (page 122), and use any leftover apple pieces for the shortbread barquettes that accompany the granita.

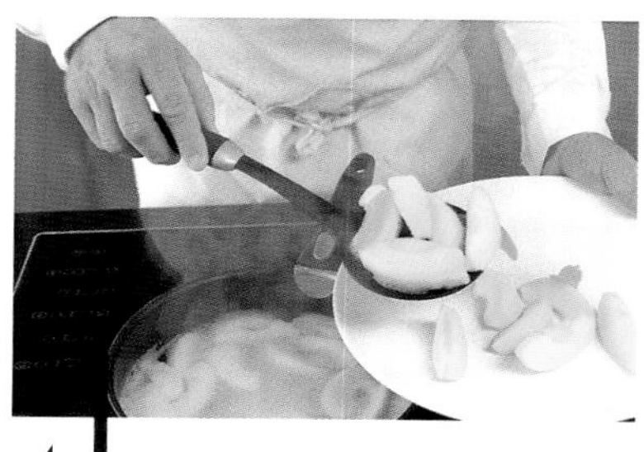

4

STEWED APPLES

Makes 300 ml – 1 1/4 cups stewed fruit

Preparation time 15 minutes
Cooking time 15 minutes

600 g – 1 pound 5 ounces apples
100 g – 3.5 ounces (1/2 cup) sugar
1 stick cinnamon

1 Peel the apples. Core (page 512).

2 Cut into thick slices.
Cut the slices into batons, and then dice (page 513).

3 Put into a stewpot over medium heat. Add the sugar and mix. Add the cinnamon. Cook the apples, stirring frequently, until the apples begin to release their liquid.

4 Cover and let soften completely over low heat.
When the apple pieces are very soft, turn off the heat.
Let cool.
Crush the apples coarsely with a fork. Serve with toast or use these stewed apples to make the apple tiramisu (page 70).

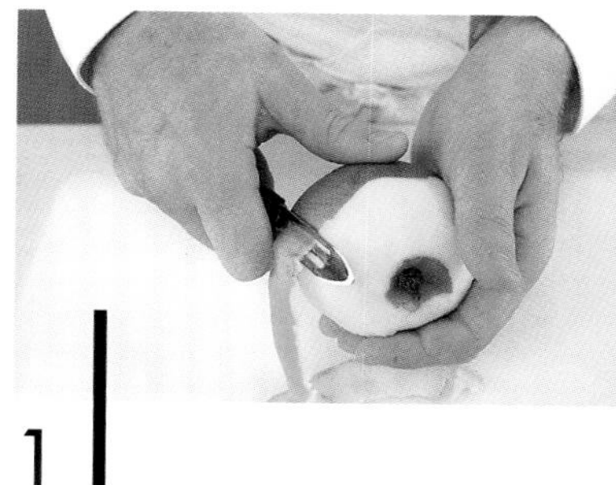

1

3

TIPS FROM OUR CHEFS

NOT A JAM AND NOT A COMPOTE
With less than 20% added sugar, this isn't a jam. It also differs from compote (page 82), because the apples aren't poached in added liquid.

STORAGE
Like a compote, stewed apples can keep for 8 days in the refrigerator. For longer periods, preserve in sterilized jars using appropriate canning methods.

1

2

3

CONFITURE DE LAIT (CARAMEL)

Makes enough to fill 2 280-g – 10-ounce jars

Preparation time 15 minutes
Cooking time 55 minutes + 5 minutes

EQUIPMENT

8- or 10-liter – 8.5- or 10.5-quart pressure cooker
2 sterilized 280-g – 10-ounce jars

1 vanilla bean (pod)
350 g – 12.35 ounces (1 3/4 cups) sugar
1 liter - 4 1/4 cups whole milk

1. Split the vanilla bean lengthwise to about 2 cm – 3/4 inches from the end. Pour the milk into the pressure cooker. Add the sugar, followed by the split vanilla bean.
2. Heat for 3–4 minutes over medium heat until the sugar has dissolved. Bring to a boil on high heat. Place the lid on the pressure cooker and lock. Set the timer for 55 minutes of cooking time and reduce the heat to medium.
3. After cooking, bring down the pressure quickly by running cold water over the lid. Open the pressure cooker and remove the vanilla bean. Stir with a spatula (scraper) to compact the milk particles and thicken the jam. Scrape the bottom well to detach any caramel. Clean the sides of the pressure cooker pot with a wet pastry brush.
4. Scrape the vanilla bean to recover any remaining seeds. Add them to the jam.
5. Use a handheld immersion blender to blend. Cook over medium heat for 10 minutes, uncovered, to reduce, stirring from time to time with a wooden spoon.
6. Pour the jam into the jars and seal tightly. Turn upside down and let cool.

4

5

6

TIPS FROM OUR CHEFS

WARNING
This recipe isn't recommended for a 4.5-liter – 4.75-quart pressure cooker, and if you have a 6-liter – 6.35-quart pressure cooker, make sure you halve the amounts.

A WORD OF CAUTION
During the cooking process, the milk and sugar mixture reduces, forming large bubbles that stick to the sides of the pot. Some of these may escape through the steam vent. Be very careful; they burn.

ABOUT THE JARS
Sterilize the jars (and lids) while the jam is cooking, and leave them in the heat source without drying them. Stand them upright only when it is time to fill them with jam.

APPLE TIRAMISU

Serves 4

Preparation time 20 minutes
Cooking time 2 hours

1 batch stewed apples (page 66)
1 egg
25 g – 0.88 ounces (2 tablespoons) sugar
125 g – 4.41 ounces mascarpone cheese
1 tablespoon Calvados
150 ml – 2/3 cup whipping cream

1 Prepare the stewed apples and refrigerate. All of the ingredients should be very cold.
Break the egg and separate the yolk from the white.
Beat the yolk with the sugar until thick and pale.
Incorporate the mascarpone and the Calvados.

1

2 Whip the cream by hand or use an electric mixer (page 567). Incorporate into the yolk mixture, whisking by hand or with the electric mixer.

2

3 Make a 1-cm – 1/2-inch layer of stewed apples at the bottom of a glass. Use a ring mold for this if necessary (page 504).
Cover with some of the mascarpone mixture, pressing lightly to form an even layer.

3

4 Add another layer of stewed apples.
Repeat the process to the top of the glass, finishing with the apple. Repeat with remaining apples and mascarpone mixture in 3 additional glasses.
Refrigerate the tiramisu for 2 hours before serving.

TIPS FROM OUR CHEFS

CHILL

Cream must be very cold in order to be whipped. Refrigerate the bowl you are going to use to whip the cream for 30 minutes for best results.

MORE CHILLING

Remember to put the glasses in the refrigerator at least 10 minutes before filling them. This will make plating easier.

PANNA COTTA WITH PEACHES AND CARAMELIZED ALMONDS

Serves 6

Preparation time 25 minutes
Cooking time 10 minutes + 15 minutes
Resting time 1 hour

2 g – 0.07 ounce sheet (leaf) gelatin (1 sheet)
250 ml – 1 cup light (single) cream
1/2 vanilla bean (pod)
90 g – 3.17 ounces (1/4 cup plus 3 tablespoons) sugar
20 g – 0.71 ounce (1/4 cup) slivered (flaked) almonds
2 yellow peaches

TIPS FROM OUR CHEFS

NO BOILING
Don't let the cream and vanilla boil. The mixture should only simmer. Then let the vanilla bean infuse the mixture off the heat.

REHEAT
Let the cream reheat for just a few seconds before adding the gelatin. The liquid must be sufficiently hot to melt the gelatin, but not at a boil.

ITALIAN-STYLE CREAM
In Italian, panna cotta literally means "cooked cream"
Adding a little gelatin lends this cream enough substance that it can support the weight of the stewed peaches.

1 Soak the gelatin in cold water for 5 minutes. Pour the cream into a small saucepan. Split the vanilla bean half and scrape the seeds into the cream. Add the vanilla bean. Add 40 g – 1.41 ounces (3 tablespoons) sugar. Heat without bringing to a boil, then remove from the heat and let infuse for 5 minutes. Lightly reheat the cream. Squeeze the gelatin with your fingers and add to the cream. Mix until the gelatin dissolves.

2 Transfer to a measuring cup. Remove the vanilla bean. Use a silicone spatula (scraper) to retrieve the seeds. Mix well. Pour the cream into ramekins. Let stand until the cream reaches room temperature.
Place in the refrigerator for at least 1 hour to set.

3 In the meantime, preheat the oven to 170°C – 325°F (gas mark 3). Boil 50 ml – 3 tablespoons plus 1 teaspoon water with the remaining 50 g – 1.76 ounces (1/4 cup) of the sugar. Add the almonds. Let boil for 1 minute. Drain the almonds. Set the syrup aside. Line a baking sheet (tray) with parchment (baking) paper. Reserve 2 tablespoons of the syrup and brush the parchment with the remaining syrup. Place the almonds on the baking sheet one at a time so that they are flat and there is room between them. Bake in the preheated oven until caramelized, about 10 minutes, then cool.

4 Bring water to a boil. Immerse the peaches for 10 seconds in boiling water. Drain. Peel the peaches. Halve and pit. Cut into slices, then batons, and then dice. Place in a saucepan.

5 Add the reserved 2 tablespoons of the almond syrup. Cook for 15 minutes over low heat, stirring from time to time. Transfer to another container. Let cool.
Just before serving, cover the panna cotta with the stewed peaches. Top with caramelized almonds.

THREE-CHOCOLATE PANNA COTTA

Serves 6

Preparation time 20 minutes
Cooking time 6 hours

Dark chocolate panna cotta

125 g – 1/2 cup whole milk
125 g – 1/2 cup light (single) cream
2.5 g – 0.09 ounce sheet (leaf) gelatin (1 1/4 sheets)
15g – 0,53 oz dark chocolate (70 percent cocoa)

Milk chocolate panna cotta

150 g – 2/3 cup whole milk
75 g – 1/3 cup light (single) cream
2.5 g – 0.09 ounce sheet (leaf) gelatin (1 1/4 sheets)
30g – 1.06 oz milk chocolate (40 percent cocoa)

White chocolate panna cotta

150 g – 2/3 cup whole milk
50 g – 3 tablespoons plus 1 teaspoon light (single) cream
2.5 g – 0.09 ounce sheet (leaf) gelatin (1 1/4 sheets)
45g – 1.59 oz white chocolate

1 Make each panna cotta the same way: Pour the milk into a saucepan. Add the cream. Heat over medium heat. Soak the gelatin in cold water for 5 minutes.
Remove milk mixture from the heat and add the chocolate. Mix with a whisk.

2 Drain the gelatin in a small strainer (sieve). Add to the milk and chocolate. Mix well. Transfer to a bowl.

3 Let cool to room temperature.

4 Pour the dark chocolate cream to one third the height of the glasses. Let set in the refrigerator for 2 hours. Pour the milk chocolate cream over the dark chocolate to two thirds the height. Let set in the refrigerator for 2 hours.
Finish with the white chocolate cream. Let set in the refrigerator for another 2 hours. Serve very cold.

TIPS FROM OUR CHEFS

GELATIN
Most sheet (leaf) gelatin found in stores comes in sheets weighing 2 g – 0.7 ounce (check on the package). Cut one sheet into quarters and add a quarter to a whole sheet to make 2.5 g – 0.09 ounces.

COLOR
The difference in color is not as striking as you might expect. Using more of the dark chocolate would result in a darker color, but the texture of the dark chocolate panna cotta would be unpleasantly tough.

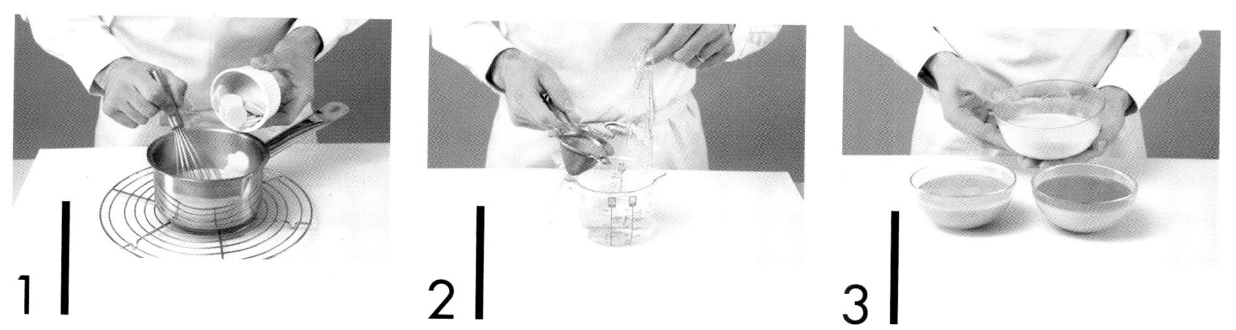
1
2
3

THREE-CHOCOLATE POTS DE CRÈME

Serves 4

Preparation time 10 minutes
Cooking time 20–40 minutes
Resting time at least 2 hours

Dark chocolate cream

250 g – 1 cup whole milk
60 g – 1/4 cup light (single) cream
1/2 vanilla bean (pod)
40 g – 1.41 ounces (3 tablespoons plus 1 teaspoon) sugar
60 g – 2.12 ounces (about 4) egg yolks
20g – 0.71 oz dark chocolate (66 percent cocoa)

Milk chocolate cream

250 g – 1 cup whole milk
60 g – 1/4 cup light (single) cream
1/2 vanilla bean (pod)
35 g – 1.23 ounces (3 tablespoons) sugar
60 g – 2.12 ounces (about 4) egg yolks
25g – 0.88 oz milk chocolate (40 percent cocoa)

White chocolate cream

250 g – 1 cup whole milk
60 g – 1/4 cup light cream
1/2 vanilla bean
30 g – 1.06 ounces (2 1/2 tablespoons) sugar
60 g – 2.12 ounces (about 4) egg yolks
30g – 1.06 oz white chocolate

1 Preheat the oven to 110–120°C – 225–250°F (gas mark 1/4–1/2). Make each cream the same way: Combine the milk and cream in a saucepan. Scrape out the seeds from the vanilla bean half. Add to the mixture. Bring to a boil while stirring.

2 Put the sugar into a bowl. Add the egg yolks. Mix. Remove the pan from the heat. Add the chocolate to the boiling liquid. Return the pan to the heat. Bring to a boil while stirring.

3 Pour the contents of the pan over the sugar mixture while stirring gently with a whisk.
Skim off any froth with a spoon.

4 Fill the pots. Cook for 20–40 minutes in the preheated oven. Let cool, then cover with plastic wrap (cling film) and refrigerate for at least 2 hours.

TIPS FROM OUR CHEFS

NO NEED FOR BAIN-MARIE
There's no point in preparing a bain-marie when the pots de crème will be cooked at a maximum of 120°C – 250°F (gas mark 1/2), because there is no danger that they will boil at that temperature. If necessary, use an oven thermometer to check the precise temperature of your oven.

COOKING TIME?
The range for cooking time is wide because it depends greatly on the capacity and shape of the pans used (small pots, tall pots, wide ramekins, and so on.) Check how the pots de crème are doing from time to time; they should still wobble slightly when they come out of the oven.

VERY COLD
These little pots de crème should be served chilled, but not ice-cold.

THREE-CHOCOLATE CRÈME BRÛLÉE

Serves 6

Preparation time 10 minutes
Cooking time 20–25 minutes
Resting time at least 3 hours

EQUIPMENT

Chef's torch

Dark chocolate crème brûlée

190 g – 6.7 ounces (3/4 cup plus 1 tablespoon) whole milk
190 g – 6.7 ounces (3/4 cup plus 1 tablespoon) light (single) cream
75g – 2.65 oz egg yolks (about 5)
35 g – 1.23 ounces (3 tablespoons) sugar
60g – 2.12 oz dark chocolate (70 percent cocoa)
1/4 cup plus 2 tablespoons superfine (caster) sugar

Milk chocolate crème brûlée

190 g – 6.7 ounces (3/4 cup plus 1 tablespoon) whole milk
190 g – 6.7 ounces (3/4 cup plus 1 tablespoon) light (single) cream
75g – 2.65 oz egg yolks (about 5)
30 g – 1.06 ounces (2 tablespoons plus 1 1/2 teaspoons) sugar
60g – 2.12 oz milk chocolate (40 percent cocoa)
1/4 cup plus 2 tablespoons superfine (caster) sugar

White chocolate crème brûlée

290 g – 10.23 ounces (1 1/4 cups) whole milk
90 g – 3.17 ounces (1/3 cup plus 1 tablespoon plus 1 teaspoon) light cream
75g – 2.65 oz egg yolks (about 5)
20 g – 0.71 ounces (1 tablespoon plus 2 teaspoons) sugar
75g – 2.65 oz white chocolate
1/4 cup plus 2 tablespoons superfine (caster) sugar

1 Preheat the oven to 110–120°C – 225–250°F (gas mark 1/4–1/2). Make each crème brûlée the same way : Pour the milk into a saucepan. Add the cream. Bring to a boil over high heat.

2 Put the egg yolks into a bowl. Add the sugar. Mix gently with a whisk. Remove the pan from the heat. Add the chocolate to the boiling liquid. Mix until it melts. Return the pan to the heat and bring to a boil while stirring. Pour the contents of the pan over the sugar mixture while stirring gently with the whisk. Skim off the froth with a tablespoon.

3 Pour each type of chocolate mixture into a liquid measuring cup with a spout, then pour equal amounts into ramekins, cleaning off the rims if necessary. Bake in the preheated oven until set but still wobbly in the center, 20–25 minutes.

4 Let cool to room temperature. Rest for at least 3 hours in the refrigerator. Take the cold crèmes brûlées out of the refrigerator. Dust each one with 1 tablespoon of superfine sugar. Shake to distribute evenly. Tip out the excess. Use your finger to scrape off any sugar sticking to the rims. Caramelize the sugar with a chef's torch or place under the broiler (grill) for a few minutes.

1

3

4

TIPS FROM OUR CHEFS

WEIGHING ESSENTIAL

Weighing the egg yolks is essential if your crème brûlée is to turn out perfectly. Use a digital scale.

WATCH CLOSELY

Avoid boiling the crème brûlée mixture at all costs; it should not happen at 120°C – 250°F (gas mark 1/2). If necessary, check the temperature of your oven with a thermometer. If the oven temperature is higher than indicated, bake the crèmes brûlées in bain-marie.

WOBBLY

The cooking time can be longer or shorter, depending on the amount of mixture in the ramekins. When cooked, the crèmes brûlées should still wobble slightly. They will firm up in the refrigerator.

CHOCOLATE ÎLES FLOTTANTES

Serves 2

Preparation time 15 minutes
Cooking time 3 hours

EQUIPMENT

Stand mixer

Crème anglaise

50 g – 1.76 ounces (about 3 1/2) egg yolks
250 g – 8.82 ounces (1 cup) whole milk
30 g – 1.06 ounces (2 tablespoons plus 1 1/2 teaspoons) sugar
30g – 1.06 oz dark chocolate (70 percent cocoa) or 45g - 1.59 oz milk chocolate (40 pecent cocoa) or 60g - 2.12 oz white chocolate

Îles flottantes

3 egg whites
60 g – 2.12 ounces (1/4 cup plus 1 tablespoon) sugar
40 g – 1.41 oz dark, milk, or white chocolate

TIPS FROM OUR CHEFS

COATING THE SPATULA
Run your finger over the spatula; if some of the crème anglaise sticks to it without falling off, then it's good. Don't ever let a crème anglaise boil, because it will curdle (egg yolks coagulate at 70°C – 158°F). If yours curdles, put an ice cube in it, then smooth it out in a blender.

NO MICROWAVE
If you don't have a microwave, mold the meringue in a ladle and cook for 5 minutes in simmering milk.

1 Make the crème anglaise: Break three eggs and separate the yolks from the whites. Weigh out the egg yolks. Set aside the whites for the îles flottantes. Pour the milk into a saucepan. Bring to a boil over medium heat. Put the sugar into a bowl. Add the egg yolks. Mix gently with a whisk. Pour about 60 ml – 1/4 cup of boiling milk over the egg mixture while stirring.

2 Return the rest of the milk to a boil over medium heat. Add the egg mixture to the pan while stirring with a silicone spatula (scraper), then reduce the heat to low. Cook the mixture, stirring constantly with the silicone spatula, until it is thick enough to coat the spatula. Remove from heat. Immediately add the chocolate in pieces. Mix. Transfer to a bowl. Cover with plastic wrap (cling film) in direct contact with the crème anglaise. Rest in the refrigerator for about 2 hours.

3 In the meantime, prepare the egg whites: Beat the previously set aside egg whites in a stand mixer (page 565). When they form soft peaks, add the sugar. Continue to beat until stiff. Use a knife to chop up the chocolate. Fold the chocolate into the beaten egg whites.

4 Transfer to two evenly shaped glass containers. Scrape away the egg white from the sides near the rim. Cook each meringue in the microwave for 15 seconds at 900 W. Cool in the refrigerator for at least 1 hour.

5 Pour the chocolate crème anglaise into the wells of two shallow soup plates. Loosen the meringues from the sides of the container. Use a knife if necessary. Turn each container over in the middle of one of the plates. Unmold.

1

2

3

4

APPLE COMPOTE

Serves 4

Preparation time 25 minutes
Cooking time 15 minutes

250 g – 8.82 ounces (1 1/4 cups) sugar
1 vanilla bean (pod)
3–4 Belchard, Gala, or Reinette Grise du Canada apples (600 g – 1 pound 5 ounces)

1 Combine the sugar with 500 ml – 2 cups water in a saucepan and bring to a boil over high heat.
Use a paring knife to split the vanilla bean. Scrape out the seeds. Add to the pan. Immerse the bean in the syrup.

2 Peel the apples. Core (page 512).
Dice the apples (page 513). Add to the boiling syrup.
Cover and let soften for 15 minutes over low heat.

3 Cut out a rectangle of parchment (baking) paper (the width being that of the roll).
Fold the paper in half. Fold it in half again.
Fold it diagonally. Fold the paper to join the two sides of the triangle.

4 Place the paper triangle over the saucepan and position the tip at the center. Use a pencil to trace the curve of the pan. Cut along the pencil line.
Cut off the tip to make a small hole. This will serve as a vent.

5 Unfold the paper. Place the circle over the apples. Let cool away from the heat.

6 Drain the apple pieces without crushing.
Serve with a little syrup, and decorate with the vanilla bean.

TIPS FROM OUR CHEFS

WHY?
By placing the parchment paper directly on the apples, you protect their flesh from the air. This will stop their surface from turning dark as they cool.

REUSE
You can use the rest of the syrup to soak a sponge, for a fruit salad, or to make an instant apple jelly (page 564). You can also reuse the vanilla bean after drying it to flavor sugar or rum.

1
2
3
4
5

EXOTIC APPLE SALAD

Serves 6

Preparation time 25 minutes
Cooking time 5 minutes
Resting time 10 minutes

150 g – 5.29 ounces (3/4 cup) sugar
1 bunch mint
1 organic, unwaxed lemon
8 organic, unwaxed apples of different varieties
3 passion fruits

3

1 Pour 500 ml – 2 cups of water into a saucepan and place over high heat. Add the sugar and mix well.
Pluck the leaves from two sprigs of mint. Add the leaves to the syrup.
Use a vegetable peeler to remove three strips of zest from the lemon (page 514). Add to the pan. Bring to a boil, then let reduce for 3 minutes. Turn off the heat and let infuse for 10 minutes.

2 Wash and dry the apples. Use a melon baller to scoop out uniform balls of apple (page 512).
Put the apple balls into a bowl as they are made. Squeeze the lemon over them to keep them from turning brown.

3 Strain the cool syrup through a conical or fine strainer (sieve) over the apple balls, being careful to avoid drenching them.

4 Halve the passion fruits. Empty them out over the apple balls. Mix gently.
Pluck the rest of the mint leaves. Cut the leaves into thin strips with a chef's knife. Sprinkle them over the apple salad.

TIPS FROM OUR CHEFS

A FEAST FOR THE EYES
Choose apples with bright colors to enliven this fruit salad. Impact guaranteed.

NO BACK AND FORTH
To chop mint into narrow strips, lay four leaves flat, one on top of the other. Make one cut (without sawing back and forth) to avoid tearing.

BAKED APPLES

Serves 4

Preparation time 25 minutes
Cooking time 40 minutes

Almond cream

50 g – 1.76 ounces (3 tablespoons) butter
100 g – 3.53 ounces *tant pour tant* mixture – a mixture of confectioners' (icing) sugar (1/3 cup plus 1 tablespoon plus 1 teaspoon) and almond meal (ground almonds) (1/2 cup)
1 egg
10 g – 0.35 ounce (1 tablespoon) flour

Apples

4 large Golden Delicious apples
2 vanilla beans (pods)
25g - 0.88 oz (1 3/4 tbsp) butter
25g - 0.88 oz (2 tbsp) sugar
25 ml – 2 tbsp Calvados

Crème fraîche for serving

TIPS FROM OUR CHEFS

VANILLA ARROWS
The vanilla beans have to be cut on a diagonal so that they can pierce the apples easily. If possible, freeze them to harden them.

NO WASTE
If you have any leftover almond cream, you can use it to make a Bourdaloue-style tart; fill a tart shell (base) with the almond cream and cover with pear segments.

A TRICK FROM THE PROS
If you have a pastry (piping) bag, don't hesitate to use it to fill the apples. You'll save time and gain precision.

1

2

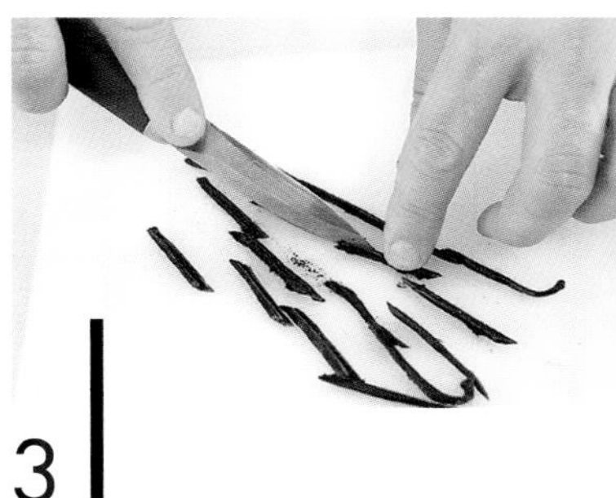

3

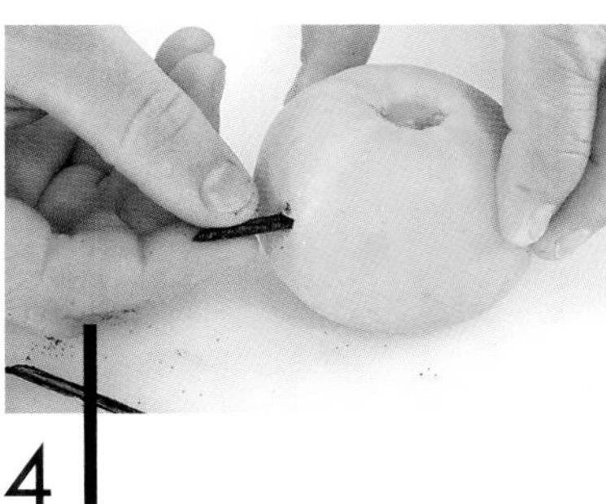

4

5

1 Make the almond cream: Cut the 50 g – 1.76 ounces (3 tablespoons) of butter into cubes. Put into a bowl. Beat until pale. Add the *tant pour tant*. Mix with a silicone spatula (scraper). Break the egg and incorporate. Sprinkle in the flour. Mix well, then let stand at room temperature.

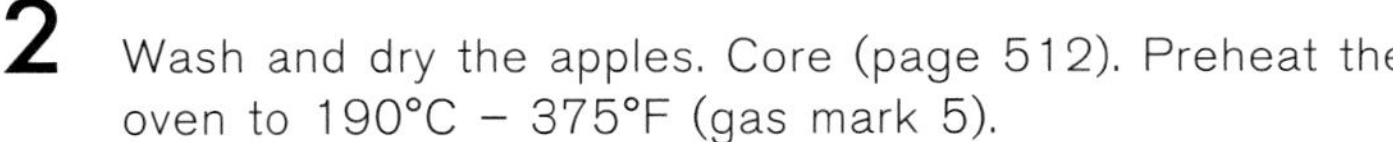

2 Wash and dry the apples. Core (page 512). Preheat the oven to 190°C – 375°F (gas mark 5).

3 Use a paring knife to split the vanilla beans. Cut each half diagonally into four lengths.

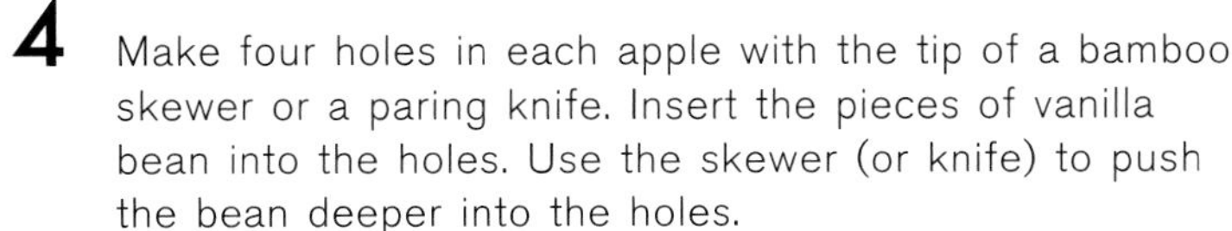

4 Make four holes in each apple with the tip of a bamboo skewer or a paring knife. Insert the pieces of vanilla bean into the holes. Use the skewer (or knife) to push the bean deeper into the holes.

5 Use a melon baller (page 512) to widen the holes at the top of the apples to make them easier to fill. Cut the 25 g – 0.88 ounces (2 tablespoons) butter into cubes. Put into an ovenproof dish. Use the back of a tablespoon to spread the butter well over the bottom and sides of the dish. Sprinkle with the sugar. Place the apples in the dish. Use a demitasse spoon to fill the apples with almond cream. Press down well with the back of the spoon. Bake for 40 minutes. Once the apples come out of the oven, deglaze the dish with the Calvados. Serve the apples hot or warm with crème fraîche.

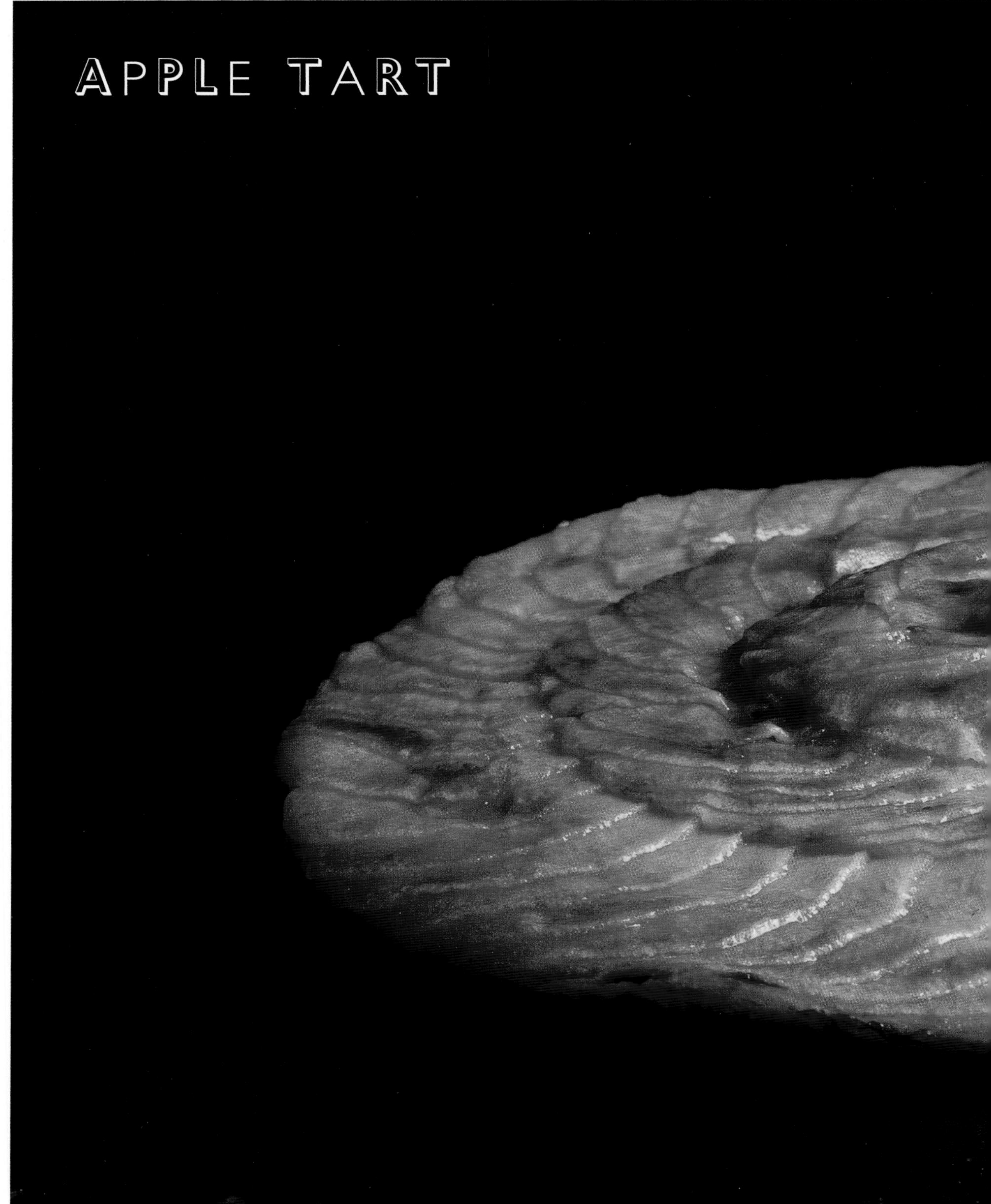

APPLE TART

APPLE TART

Serves 6

Preparation time 20 minutes
Cooking time 35 minutes

20 g – 0.75 ounces (1 tablespoon) butter
1 roll puff pastrySugar for sprinkling
4 Golden Delicious apples
Apple jelly, homemade (page 564) or store bought
300 g - 10.5 oz homemade apple compote (page 82) or store bought

1 Clarify the butter (page 546). Lay a sheet of parchment (baking) paper over the work surface.
Roll the puff pastry on top of the parchment paper to a thickness of 3 mm – 1/8 inch. Brush with some of the clarified butter. Sprinkle with sugar.

2 Slide the dough onto a rack and place a baking sheet (tray) upside down on top. Turn everything over. Preheat the oven to 210°C – 400°F (gas mark 6–7).

3 Remove the parchment paper from the pastry. Wash and dry the apples. Core (page 512).
Slice very finely with a mandoline slicer (page 513).

4 Cover the pastry with a thin layer of compote. Spread the compote to the edge.

5 Arrange the apple slices in a rosette pattern over the pastry, overlapping. Finish by sliding the last slice under the first. Fill the center of the tart.

6 Brush the tart with the remaining butter. Sprinkle with additional sugar. Place a sheet of parchment paper on top, then cover with a rack or baking sheet (tray).
Bake for 30–35 minutes. Slide the tart onto a rack or a serving dish. Glaze the tart with apple jelly. There's nothing left to do but enjoy it, either hot or cold.

1

2

3

4

TIPS FROM OUR CHEFS

RIGHT TO THE EDGE

The compote coating will help keep the puff pastry in check. In order to keep the tart shell (base) thin and flat, the entire surface of the pastry has to be covered. If you love the crispy edges of a crust, you're out of luck!

WEIGHING DOWN

The rack or baking sheet placed over the tart weighs down the shell to keep it from puffing so that it will be very, very thin.

CRUNCH

Covering the tart shell with clarified butter and sugar allows it to caramelize lightly.

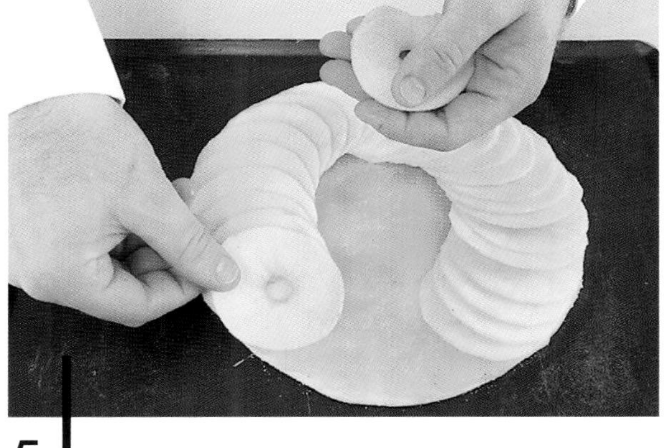

5

APPLE CRISP

Serves 4

Preparation time 10 minutes
Cooking time 12–15 minutes
Resting time 30 minutes

125 g – 4.41 ounces (1 stick) butter, plus more for buttering dish
125 g – 4.41 ounces (2/3 cup) sugar
125 g – 4.41 ounces (1 cup) flour
100 g – 3.53 ounces (1 cup) almond meal (ground almonds)
2 Nashi, Gala, or Pink Lady apples

1 Lay a large sheet of parchment (baking) paper on the work surface.
Cut the 125g – 4.41 ounces butter into cubes.

2 Place the sugar, flour, and almond meal on the parchment paper. Mix together with your hands.
Rub the butter together with the dry ingredients.
The mixture should form small clumps between your palms.

3 Crumble with your fingers, then repeat the operation.
When you have coarse crumbs of a uniform size, refrigerate for 30 minutes. Preheat the oven to 200°C – 400°F (gas mark 6).

4 Peel and core the apples (page 512).
Then dice (page 513).
Grease an ovenproof dish with butter. Spread the diced apples evenly in the dish. Cover with the crumble topping. Bake until topping is golden and crisp, 12–15 minutes.

TIPS FROM OUR CHEFS

VARIATION
The granulated sugar can be replaced with brown sugar. The resulting crisp will be a darker brown.

DELIGHT YOUR TASTE BUDS
Accompany the hot or warm crisp with fruit sorbet or vanilla ice cream.

1

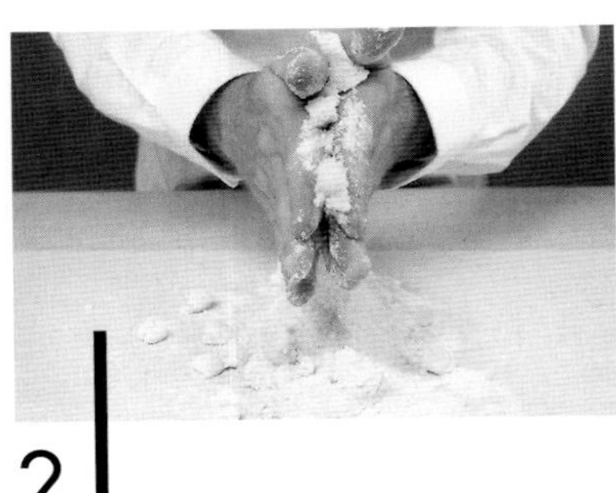
2

BROWNIES

Serves 4

Preparation time 30 minutes
Cooking time 30 minutes

EQUIPMENT

Square stainless steel cake mold 12 x 12 x 3.5 cm – 4 3/4 x 4 3/4 x 1 3/8 inches

60 g – 2.12 oz (2/3 cup) pecans
145 g – 5.12 ounces (1/2 cup plus 3 tablespoons plus 2 teaspoons) sugar, divided
100 g – 3.53 oz dark chocolate (70 percent cocoa)
100 g – 3.53 oz (7 tbsp) butter, softened
2 (60-g – 2.12-ounce) eggs (weight with shell)
50 g – 1.76 ounces (1/3 cup plus 1 tablespoon plus 1 teaspoon) flour

1

2

3

1 Preheat the oven to 170°C – 325°F (gas mark 3).
Use a chef's knife to chop the pecans.

2 Pour 1 tablespoon of water into a saucepan. Add 100 g – 3.53 ounces (1/2 cup) of the sugar. Bring to a boil. Remove from heat and add the pecans. Mix with a silicone spatula (scraper).
Bake for 10 minutes, moving them around every 2–3 minutes. Take out of the oven and let cool.

3 Turn the oven up to 195°C – 375°F (gas mark 5–6). Melt the chocolate in the microwave for 1 minute 30 seconds (600 W). Place the butter in a bowl.
Add the remaining 45 g – 1.59 ounces (3 tablespoons plus 2 teaspoons) sugar. Whisk vigorously.
Add the eggs. Whisk until the fat separates slightly from the eggs.
Add the flour. Whisk vigorously.
Add the melted chocolate. Whisk vigorously.
Fold in the caramelized pecans, working gently with the silicone spatula to avoid breaking them.

4 Line a baking sheet with parchment paper and place the buttered cake mold on top of it. Pour in the batter. Bake for 20 minutes.
Check that the brownies are cooked by inserting the tip of a knife. You should see a slight residue of batter on the blade. A light crust should form on top, but the interior should remain slightly creamy.
Transfer to a cooling rack and remove the cake mold. Cut into individual brownies and serve.

TIPS FROM OUR CHEFS

SUBSTITUTE
If pecans aren't available, use Grenoble walnuts for a continental touch. Make sure they are fresh, because nuts with a high fat content can turn rancid quickly.

MOLDING
If you don't have a square stainless steel cake mold, bake the brownie in a square baking pan with the same dimensions, but don't line the pan with parchment paper.

ADDITIONAL OPTIONS
To make mini brownies, use a silicone mold with 15 cavities. Bake for 10 minutes. Let stand for 5 minutes, then unmold.
To make cannelés, fill four 80-ml – 1/3-cup cannelé molds. Bake for 15 minutes, let stand for 5 minutes, then unmold. Drizzle with chocolate sauce.

TIRAMISU-STYLE CHARLOTTE

Serves 8

Preparation time 20 minutes
Resting time 12 hours

30 dry ladyfingers (boudoir) biscuits
400 g – 14 ounces (1 2/3 cups) strong coffee, warm
150 g – 5.3 ounces (3/4 cup) sugar, divided
250 g – 9 ounces (1 cup) whipping cream, very cold
250 g – 9 ounces mascarpone cheese
20 g – 0.71 ounce (1 tablespoon plus 1 teaspoon) unsweetened cocoa powder

1 Make the syrup for soaking the ladyfingers the previous night by mixing the warm coffee with 100 g – 3.5 ounces (1/2 cup) of the sugar. The next day, place a rack over a large plate. Quickly dip the flat side of the ladyfingers in the coffee syrup. Let them drain on the rack.

2 Line the sides of a charlotte mold with some of the ladyfingers, keeping their soaked sides facing outward. Use kitchen shears to trim the ends of the ladyfingers that stick out over the sides of the mold.

3 Make the mascarpone cream: Pour the whipping cream into the bowl of a stand mixer. Add the mascarpone and the remaining 50 grams – 1.76 ounces (1/4 cup) of the sugar. Beat on medium speed. Stop the mixer when the mixture is firm.

4 Fill a pastry (piping) bag with mascarpone cream (page 507). Cover the bottom of the mold with a layer of the cream.

5 Add a layer of ladyfingers. Add another layer of cream. Finish with a layer of ladyfingers (soaked side facing upward against the cream).

6 Cover the charlotte and refrigerate for 12 hours. Take off the cover. Unmold the charlotte. Dust with the cocoa. You can also pipe a light layer of any leftover mascarpone cream over the charlotte, sprinkle with crumble, and dust with cocoa.

TIPS FROM OUR CHEFS

SIMPLIFY

Use cornflakes or cookie crumbs for a simple garnish.

BACK TO FRONT

Always soak the flat sides of the ladyfingers in the liquid. Here the soaked sides face outward (against the sides of the mold) so that the cream is not flavored.

DRY

Ladyfingers have a tendency to expel liquid, so place dry ladyfingers on the bottom. This way, they will soak up the excess.

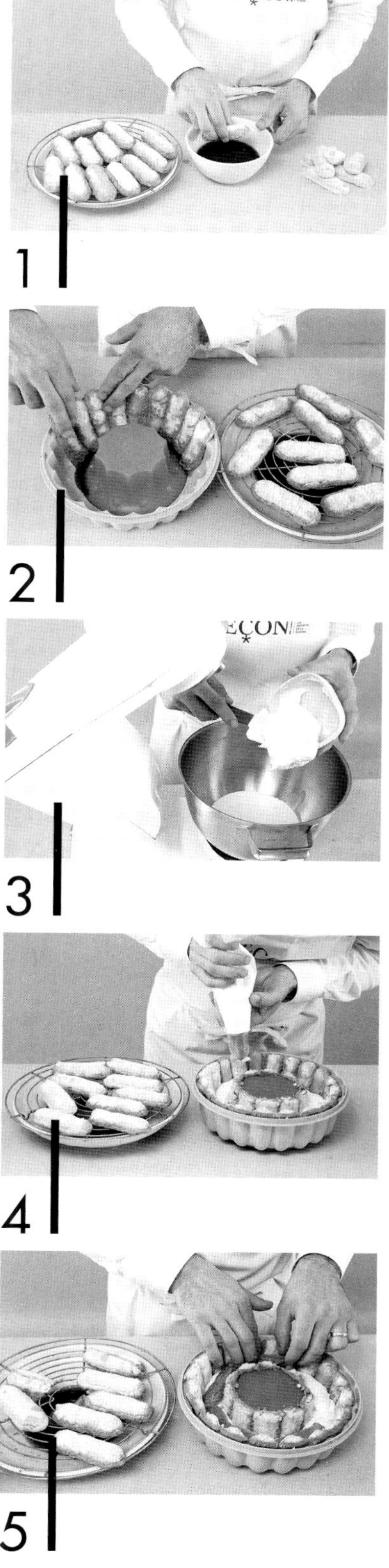

RASPBERRY MUFFINS

Makes 6 muffins

Preparation time 15 minutes
Cooking time 25 minutes
Resting time 5 minutes

EQUIPMENT

Silicone muffin pan with six 7-cm- – 2 3/4-inch-diameter cavities

175 g – 6.17 ounces (1 1/3 cups plus 1 tablespoon) flour
20 g – 0.71 ounces (1/4 cup) hazelnut meal (ground hazelnuts)
1/2 teaspoon vanilla powder
70 g – 2.47 ounces (1/3 cup) sugar
6 g – 0.21 ounces (1 1/2 teaspoons) baking powder
1 (60-g – 2.12-ounce) egg (weight with shell)
30 g – 1.06 ounces (2 tablespoons) roasted hazelnut oil
115 g – 4.06 ounces (1/2 cup) whole milk
18 raspberries
30 g – 1.06 ounces (1/4 cup) raw hazelnuts

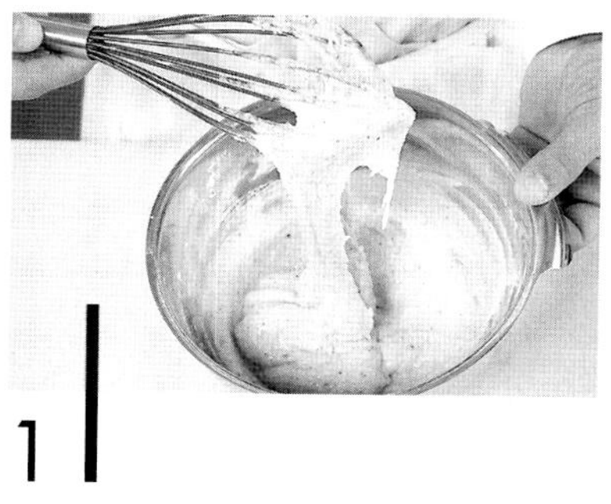

1

2

3

1 Preheat the oven to 200°C – 400°F (gas mark 6).
In a bowl combine the dry ingredients: the flour, hazelnut meal, vanilla powder, sugar, and baking powder. Break the egg into another bowl. Whisk in the oil. Add the milk and mix. Mix the dry ingredients.
Make a well in the center. Pour the liquid ingredients into the well. Scrape the sides of the bowl with a silicone spatula (scraper) to make sure no dry ingredients cling to the sides. Mix with a whisk, starting in the middle and gradually incorporating the dry ingredients. The batter should be elastic but not runny.

2 Use a tablespoon to fill the cavities of the muffin pan to one third their depth. Push three raspberries into each cavity, without letting them touch the bottom. Finish filling the cavities, covering the raspberries fully with additional batter.

3 Break up a hazelnut with the flat side of the blade of a chef's knife by hitting on it with your hand. Repeat with remaining hazelnuts. Coarsely chop the larger pieces with the knife.
Scatter the chopped hazelnuts over the muffins.

4 Bake in the preheated oven for 25 minutes. Turn the pan around halfway through. Rest for 5 minutes; the muffins will shrink slightly, making them easy to unmold. Unmold onto a rack and let cool completely.

TIPS FROM OUR CHEFS

THE REAL MCCOY

Real vanilla powder, sold in small jars, is very dark, almost black. Don't confuse it with beige-colored vanilla powder, which is mixed with sugar. If you can't find vanilla powder, scrape out the seeds from a vanilla bean (pod).

A USEFUL TIP

6 g – 0.21 ounces of baking powder is equivalent to half of an envelope (sachet).

ALL-CHOCOLATE MUFFINS

Makes 6 muffins

Preparation time 15 minutes
Cooking time 25 minutes
Resting time 5 minutes

EQUIPMENT

Silicone muffin pan with six 7-cm – 2 3/4-inch-diameter cavities

6 g – 0.21 ounces (1 1/2 teaspoons) baking powder
70 g – 2.47 ounces (1/3 cup) sugar
20 g – 0.71 ounces (3 tablespoons plus 1 1/2 teaspoons) almond meal (ground almonds)
155 g – 5.47 ounces (1 1/4 cups) flour
20 grams – 0.71 ounce (1 tablespoon plus 1 teaspoon) unsweetened cocoa powder
1 (60-g – 2.12-ounce) egg (weight with shell)
30 g – 1.06 ounces (2 tablespoons) peanut oil
115 g – 4.06 ounces (1/2 cup) milk
40 g – 1.4 ounces dark chocolate (70% cocoa)
3 tablespoons chocolate mini pearls

1 Preheat the oven to 200°C – 400°F (gas mark 6). Combine the baking powder, sugar, almond meal, and flour in a bowl. Place the cocoa in a small strainer (sieve) and shake gently to sift into the bowl. Mix together with a whisk. Break the egg into another bowl. Whisk in the oil. Add the milk while stirring.
Make a well in the center of the dry ingredients. Pour in the liquid ingredients while stirring.
Mix with a whisk, starting in the middle.
The batter should be thick and slightly runny.

2 Use a chef's knife to chop the dark chocolate. Add to the batter.

3 Place the silicone muffin pan on a baking sheet (tray). Use a tablespoon to fill the cavities to one-third their depth. Sprinkle the chocolate mini pearls over the muffins.

4 Place in the oven. Bake for 15 minutes. Turn the pan around and bake for another 10 minutes. Take the muffins out of the oven and let rest for 5 minutes. Unmold onto a rack and let cool completely.

TIPS FROM OUR CHEFS

SIFTING ESSENTIAL
Cocoa powder clumps together easily, making it difficult to incorporate into a batter. It's better to sift than to risk less-than-perfect results.

PISTOLES?
Professional pastry chefs buy their chocolate in the form of pistoles or pastilles—flat rounds of chocolate. It's absolutely fine to use a chocolate bar and chop it up with a knife.

1
2
3
4

COOKIES

Makes about 20 cookies

Preparation time 20 minutes
Cooking time 30 minutes
Resting time 3 hours

Candied Hazelnuts

100 g - 3.53 oz (3/4 cup) raw hazelnuts
50 g - 1.76 oz (1/4 cup) sugar

Cookie dough

70 g – 2.47 ounces (5 tablespoons) butter, softened
75 g – 2.65 ounces (1/3 cup packed) brown sugar.
10 g – 0.35 ounce (2 teaspoons) chestnut honey
1 (60-g – 2.12-ounce) egg (weight with shell)
100 g – 3.5 ounces (3/4 cup plus 1 tablespoon) flour
5 g – 0.18 ounce (1 teaspoon) baking powder
1 g – 0.03 ounce (2 generous pinches) salt
85 g – 3 ounces dark chocolate

1 Preheat the oven to 170°C – 325°F (gas mark 3). Make the candied hazelnuts. Break up a hazelnut with the flat side of the blade of a chef's knife by hitting on it with your hand. Repeat with remaining hazelnuts.

2 Place the sugar in a saucepan and add 20 ml – 1 tablespoon plus 1 teaspoon water. Bring to a boil. Remove from heat and add the hazelnuts. Mix with a silicone spatula (scraper) to coat well. Line a baking sheet (tray) with parchment (baking) paper. Place the hazelnuts on top. Spread them out with the spatula. Bake for 15 minutes, moving them around every 2–3 minutes to help the sugar crystallize faster.

3 In the meantime, combine the butter and brown sugar in a bowl. Add the honey. Mix together with a whisk. Break the egg into a small bowl and add. Mix. Add the flour, baking powder, and salt. Mix. Use a chef's knife to chop up the chocolate. Add to the bowl. Add the hazelnuts. Mix with the silicone spatula.

4 Turn the dough out onto a sheet of plastic wrap (cling film). Wrap the plastic around the dough. Shape the dough into an even log with a diameter of about 4 cm – 1 1/2 inches. Pinch and twist the ends of the plastic closed. Roll back and forth to even out. Rest for 3 hours in the refrigerator or 1 hour in the freezer. Preheat the oven to 190°C – 375°F (gas mark 5). Unwrap the dough. Cut into disks 1 cm – 3/8 inch-thick. Line a baking sheet with parchment paper. Arrange the disks of dough on top of it, leaving at least 4 cm – 1 1/2 inches between them on all sides.

5 For uniform cookies, place a ring mold around each one. Bake for 15 minutes.

6 Take the cookies out of the oven and let cool on a rack; they should be soft on the inside and crisp on the outside.

TIPS FROM OUR CHEFS

BREAK
Break up the hazelnuts without crushing them to make good-sized pieces. And don't use a food processor or chopper, because either one will grind the nuts to a coarse powder.

COOKIES ON HAND
You can store the cookie dough in the freezer. You can also slice and bake as few or as many cookies as you want and leave the rest of the dough in the freezer.

ORANGE-LAVENDER SCONES

Makes 6 scones

Preparation time 1 hour
Cooking time 15 minutes
Resting time 6 hours

EQUIPMENT

7-cm – 2 3/4-inch plain round cookie cutter (page 503)

1

2

Scone dough

1 organic, unwaxed orange
100 g – 3.5 ounces (1/3 cup plus 1 tablespoon plus 1 teaspoon) whole milk
2 g – 0.07 ounce lavender pistils, plus more for decoration
120 g – 4.23 ounces (1 cup) cake flour or pastry (plain) flour
10 g – 0.35 ounce (1 3/4 teaspoons) baking powder
15 g – 0.53 ounce (1 tablespoon plus 1 teaspoon) sugar
50 g – 1.76 ounces (3 tablespoons) butter, softened
50 g – 1.76 ounces (3 tablespoons plus 1 teaspoon) lavender honey

Orange marmalade

1 (about 300-g – 10.58-ounce) organic, unwaxed juice orange
75 g – 2.65 ounces (1/3 cup plus 1 tablespoon) sugar
100 ml – 1/3 cup plus 1 tablespoon plus 1 teaspoon orange juice

Glaze

20 g – 0.71 ounce (1 tablespoon plus 1 teaspoon) honey
1 egg

1 Weigh out all the ingredients for the scone dough. Wash and dry the orange. Grate half of its zest onto a sheet of parchment (baking) paper (page 514).

2 Pour the milk into a saucepan. Add the 2 g – 0.07 ounces lavender pistils and slowly bring to a boil. Remove from heat. Cover the pan with plastic wrap (cling film) and let infuse for about 15 minutes, until the milk is cold. Strain the fragrant milk through a sieve, pushing with a spoon to recover all of the liquid. Combine the flour, baking powder, and sugar in a food processor fitted with the metal blade. Add the butter. Add the grated orange zest and lavender honey. Replace the lid. Pour in the milk through the feed tube while blending on the highest speed.

3 Use a silicone spatula (scraper) to compact the dough; it should have a texture like mayonnaise, with the butter thoroughly mixed through. Turn the dough out onto a sheet of plastic wrap. Scrape the bowl and blades to recover all the dough. Fold the plastic over the dough. Spread out the dough with your hands, pressing down to remove any air. Wrap the dough completely. Refrigerate for 6 hours.

4 Make the orange marmalade: Wash and dry the juice orange. Use a chef's knife to cut it into 2–3-mm – 1/8-inch slices. Put into a saucepan. Cover with cold water and bring to a boil. Drain and rinse in cold water. Return to the saucepan. Cover with water. Bring to a boil again. Drain. Rinse. Repeat one more time. Put the orange slices into a food processor fitted with the metal blade. Add the sugar and orange juice and blend for about 15 seconds. The orange slices should be finely chopped.

5 Put into a saucepan. Bring to a boil. Cook over low heat for about 30 minutes, stirring occasionally, until all the liquid has evaporated. Transfer to a plate. Cover with plastic wrap (cling film) in direct contact with the marmalade. Let cool, then refrigerate.

6 Preheat the oven to 200°C – 400°F (gas mark 6). Lightly dust the work surface and the scone dough with flour. Roll out the dough to a thickness of 1 cm – 3/8 inch. Use the cookie cutter to cut out 6 disks. Gently remove the excess dough. Line a baking sheet (tray) with parchment paper. Use a wide spatula to transfer the dough disks to the baking sheet. Make the glaze: Heat the honey for 10 seconds in the microwave (800 W). In a small bowl, beat the egg. Pour the honey into the egg. Brush the tops of the disks with the mixture. Sprinkle about 1 teaspoon lavender pistils on top of the glazed dough. Bake for 7 minutes. Turn the baking sheet around and bake for another 5 minutes. Take the scones out of the oven. Let cool completely. Use a serrated knife to cut the scones in half horizontally. Spread about 1 teaspoon of orange marmalade over the bottom of each scone. Replace the top halves on the bottoms and serve.

APRICOT AND LAVENDER MACARONS

Makes about 35 cookies

Apricot and lavender macaron shells
Makes about 70
Preparation time 15 minutes
Cooking time 12 minutes + 12 minutes
Crust formation 1 hour

Apricot jam
Preparation time 15 minutes
Cooking time 20 minutes
Resting time 2 hours

EQUIPMENT

Food processor fitted with metal blade
Stand mixer
Pastry (piping) bag
Size 8 plain pastry tip (nozzle)

Apricot and lavender macaron shells

110 g – 3.88 ounces (1 cup plus 2 tablespoons) almond meal (ground almonds)
225 g – 8 ounces (1 3/4 cups plus 1 tablespoon) confectioners' (icing) sugar
120 g – 4.23 ounces (about 4) egg whites, room temperature
50 g – 1.76 ounces (1/4 cup) superfine (caster) sugar
10 drops red food coloring
20 drops yellow food coloring
1 tablespoon culinary lavender

Apricot jam

125 g – 4.4 ounces very ripe apricots
1/2 vanilla bean (pod)
3 g – 0.11 ounce (1/2 teaspoon) lemon juice (equivalent to about 1/2 lemon)
25 g – 0.88 ounce (2 tablespoons) superfine sugar
2.5 g – 0.09 ounce (1/2 teaspoon) pectin NH

1

Weigh out all the ingredients individually. Make the macaron batter: Blend the almond meal and confectioners' sugar for about 2 minutes on high speed to a very fine powder. Transfer to a drum sifter (sieve) and sift over a sheet of parchment (baking) paper.

2

Break the eggs (they should be at room temperature) and separate 120 g – 4.23 ounces (1/2 cup) of egg whites. Beat the egg whites on the highest speed until they form soft peaks (page 565). Add the superfine sugar, a little at a time, while beating constantly. Continue to beat the egg whites until they form stiff peaks, about 3 minutes. Add the almond meal and confectioners' sugar mixture to the beaten egg whites. Fold in gently.

TIPS FROM OUR CHEFS

A GOOD TEST
To check whether the macaron batter is ready, lift out a little batter with a spatula. It should flow back and quickly become reincorporated into the rest of the batter.

LAVENDER?
Use culinary lavender with a light hand, as too much can overwhelm. Lavender flowers can be found in organic supermarkets.

COOKING DOUBLE
If your oven is large enough, you can bake two batches of macaron shells at the same time; make sure the baking sheets are at least 15 cm – 6 inches apart to allow the air to circulate well.

NO PROBLEM
When you take macaron shells off parchment paper, small pieces may stick to the paper and break off. Don't worry. Once the macarons are filled, you won't even notice.

3

Take 2 tablespoons of the batter and mix with both types of food coloring until well dissolved. Pour the colored portion back into the batter. Mix a little more briskly. The batter should be smooth, shiny, and elastic, but not runny.

4

Fill a pastry bag with the batter. Pipe evenly sized macaron shells onto two baking sheets (trays) lined with parchment paper (page 507). Sprinkle with lavender, then shake each baking sheet to remove any excess. Let sit at room temperature until a crust forms and the batter no longer sticks to your finger, about 1 hour. Preheat the oven to 170°C – 325°F (gas mark 3).

5

Bake for 12 minutes, rotating halfway through. Take the macaron shells out of the oven and let cool.

6

Make the apricot jam: Wash, pit, and quarter each apricot. Use a paring knife to scrape out the seeds from the vanilla bean half. Heat the apricot pieces with the vanilla seeds and lemon juice in a saucepan for 5 minutes over medium heat. Add the sugar and pectin and cook for about 15 minutes while stirring constantly; the apricots should be completely soft.
Let the apricots cool, then blend. Cover with plastic wrap (cling film) and refrigerate.

7

Turn the cooled macaron shells upside down (flat side up) on a large sheet of parchment paper.
Fill the pastry bag with the apricot jam. Pipe a small ball of jam in the middle of every other macaron shell (page 507). Top the filled shells with the unfilled shells (flat side down), pressing lightly to bind them.

RASPBERRY MACARONS

Makes about 35 cookies

Raspberry macaron shells
Makes about 70
Preparation time 15 minutes
Cooking time 12 minutes + 12 minutes
Crust formation 1 hour

Raspberry jam
Preparation time 10 minutes
Cooking time 10 minutes
Resting time 2 hours

EQUIPMENT

Food processor fitted with metal blade
Stand mixer
Pastry (piping) bag
Size 8 plain pastry tip (nozzle)
Cooking thermometer

Raspberry macaron shells

110 g – 3.88 ounces (1 cup plus 2 tablespoons) almond meal (ground almonds)
225 g – 8 ounces (1 3/4 cups plus 1 tablespoon) confectioners' (icing) sugar
120 g – 4.23 ounces (about 4) egg whites, room temperature
50 g – 1.76 ounces (1/4 cup) superfine (caster) sugar
30 drops red food coloring

Raspberry jam

225 g – 8 ounces (1 cup) frozen raspberry puree
225 g – 8 ounces (1 cup) frozen crumbled raspberries
365 g – 13 ounces (1 3/4 cups plus 1 tablespoon) superfine sugar

TIPS FROM OUR CHEFS

COLOR PALETTE
You can easily make variations on the raspberry macaron recipe by playing with the colors and the filling: orange, strawberry, lemon, tropical fruits—the only limit is your imagination.

THERMOMETER
The thermometer should never touch the bottom of the pan, otherwise the temperature reading will be wrong. If you don't have a thermometer, place a teaspoon of the jam on a plate to check whether it is properly cooked. The jam should set, not run.

1

Weigh out all the ingredients individually. Blend the almond meal and confectioners' sugar for about 2 minutes on high speed to a very fine powder. Sift the mixture over a sheet of parchment (baking) paper. Break the eggs (they should be at room temperature) and separate 120 g – 4.23 ounces (1/2 cup) of egg whites.

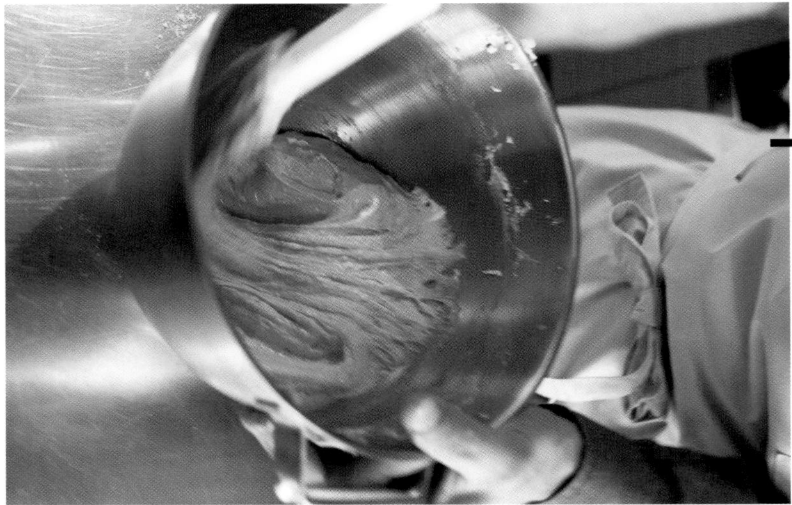

2

Beat the egg whites on the highest speed until they form soft peaks (page 565). Add the superfine sugar, a little at a time, while beating constantly. Continue to beat the egg whites until they form stiff peaks, about 3 minutes. Add the almond meal and confectioners' sugar mixture to the beaten egg whites. Fold in gently. Take 2 tablespoons of the batter and mix with the food coloring until well dissolved. Pour the colored portion back into the batter. Mix a little more briskly. The batter should be smooth and shiny, but not runny.

3

Fill a pastry bag with the batter. Pipe evenly sized macaron shells on two baking sheets (trays) lined with parchment paper (page 507). When your pastry bag is nearly empty, use a spatula (scraper) to push the rest of the batter toward the tip.

4

Let stand at room temperature until a crust forms and the batter no longer sticks to your finger, about 1 hour. Preheat the oven to 170°C – 325°F (gas mark 3). Bake for 12 minutes, rotating halfway through. Take the macaron shells out of the oven and let cool.

5

Make the raspberry jam: Combine the raspberry puree, crumbled raspberries, and sugar in a saucepan. Stir with a silicone spatula to make sure the raspberry pieces are well coated in sugar. Cook over high heat, stirring constantly with a whisk, until the temperature reaches 105°C – 220°F, about 10 minutes. The raspberries should be very soft. Transfer the raspberry jam to a dish. Let cool, then cover with plastic wrap (cling film) and refrigerate for 2 hours.

6

Turn the cooled macaron shells upside down (flat side up) on a large sheet of parchment paper. Fill a pastry bag with the raspberry jam. Pipe a small ball of filling in the middle of every other macaron shell (page 507). Top the filled shells with the unfilled shells (flat side down), pressing lightly to bind them.

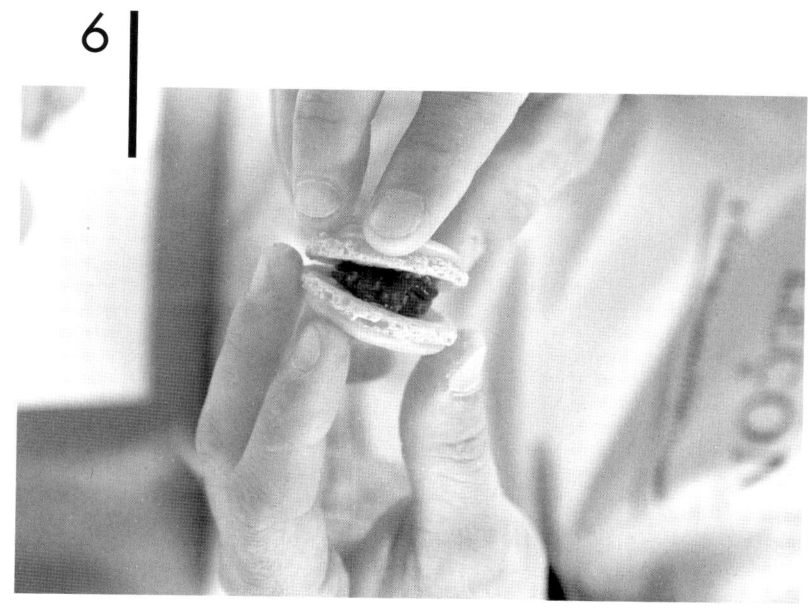

CHOCOLATE MACARONS

CHOCOLATE MACARONS

Makes about 35 cookies

Chocolate macaron shells
Makes about 70
Preparation time 20 minutes
Cooking time 12 minutes + 12 minutes
Crust formation 1 hour

Chocolate ganache
Preparation time 10 minutes
Cooking time 1 minute
Resting time 24 hours

EQUIPMENT

Food processor fitted with metal blade
Stand mixer
Pastry (piping) bag
Size 8 plain pastry tip (nozzle)
Candy thermometer

Chocolate ganache

30 g – 1 ounce (2 tablespoons) heavy (double) cream
125 g – 4.4 ounces (1/2 cup) whole milk
125 g – 4.4 ounceschocolate (preferably 53% cocoa), roughly chopped

Chocolate macaron shells

120 g – 4.23 ounces (about 4) egg whites
50 g – 1.76 ounces (1/4 cup) superfine (caster) sugar
110 g – 3.88 ounces (1 cup plus 2 tablespoons) almond meal (ground almonds)
225 g – 8 ounces (1 3/4 cups plus 1 tablespoon) confectioners' (icing) sugar
25 g – 0.88 ounce (3 tablespoons plus 1 1/2 teaspoons) unsweetened cocoa powder
30 drops red food coloring
1 tablespoon chocolate sprinkles

TIPS FROM OUR CHEFS

MACA-SHAPE
While traditionally macarons are round, they can be made in different shapes: strips, squares, hearts. Use your imagination.

1 Make the ganache: Combine the cream and milk in a saucepan and bring to a boil. Then add the chopped chocolate.
Whisk the mixture and return to a boil. Transfer the ganache to a dish. Cover with plastic wrap (cling film) while still hot and let cool. Refrigerate the ganache until it crystallizes, approximatively 24 hours.

2 Blend the almond meal, confectioners' sugar, and cocoa powder for about 2 minutes on high speed to a very fine powder. Spread the mixture out evenly over a baking sheet (tray) lined with parchment (baking) paper. Heat in the oven for 5 minutes. Sift the mixture.

3 Break the eggs (they should be at room temperature) and separate 120 g – 4.23 ounces (1/2 cup) of egg whites. Beat the egg whites on the highest speed until they form soft peaks (page 565). Add the superfine sugar, a little at a time, while beating constantly. Continue to beat the egg whites until they form stiff peaks, about 3 minutes. Add the almond meal, cocoa powder and confectioners' sugar mixture to the beaten egg whites. Fold in gently. Take 2 tablespoons of the batter and mix with the food coloring until well dissolved. Pour the colored portion back into the batter. Mix a little more briskly. The batter should be smooth and shiny, but not runny.

4 Let stand at room temperature until a crust forms and the batter no longer sticks to your finger, about 1 hour. Preheat the oven to 170°C – 325°F (gas mark 3). Bake for 12 minutes, rotating halfway through. Take the macaron shells out of the oven and let cool.

5 Turn the cooled macaron shells upside down (flat side up) on a large sheet of parchment (baking) paper.
Fill the pastry bag with the ganache (page 507).
Pipe a small ball of filling in the middle of every other macaron shell (page 507). Top the filled shells with the unfilled shells (flat side down), pressing lightly to bind them.

3

4

CHOCOLATE MACALONGS

Makes about 20

Preparation time 20 minutes + 5 minutes
Cooking time 12 minutes + 12 minutes + 1 minute
Crust formation 1 hour
Resting time 24 hours

EQUIPMENT

Size 10 plain pastry tip (nozzle)

Chocolate ganache (page 116)

Chocolate macaron shells (page 116)

Chocolate sprinkles

1 Make the chocolate ganache (page 116).

2 Make the chocolate macaron shells (page 116).
Pipe macaron shells about 5 cm – 2 inches in length onto two baking sheets lined with parchment paper.
Cover with chocolate sprinkles.
Shake each baking sheet to remove the excess sprinkles.
Let stand at room temperature until a crust forms and the batter no longer sticks to your finger, about 1 hour.

3 Preheat the oven to 170°C – 325°F (gas mark 3). Bake for 12 minutes, rotating halfway through.
Take the macaron shells out of the oven and let cool.

4 Turn the cooled macaron shells upside down (flat side up) on a large sheet of parchment (baking) paper.
Fill the pastry bag with the ganache. Pipe a small ball of filling in the middle of every other macaron shell (page 507).
Top the filled shells with the unfilled shells (flat side down), pressing lightly to bind them.

1

2

APPLE SORBET

Serves 6

Preparation time 15 minutes
Cooking time 3 minutes
Churning time 45 minutes

EQUIPMENT

Juicer
Ice cream maker

90 g – 3.17 ounces (1/3 cup) glucose syrup
1 kg – 2 pounds 2 ounces Granny Smith apples
1 lemon

1 Combine the glucose syrup with 500 ml – 2 cups of water. Heat in a saucepan over low heat to dissolve. Let cool.

2 Wash and dry the apples. Quarter (without peeling or coring).

3 Squeeze lemon juice over the apple pieces to prevent them from changing color.
Place in a bowl and then process with a juicer.

4 Strain the juice through a conical strainer (sieve). Weigh the juice (or use a measuring cup).
Pour into a bowl and add the same amount of cold syrup by weight.
Churn for 45 minutes in the ice cream maker. Freeze to firm up.
Serve in attractive glasses or bowls, with Breton shortbread cookies (page 565).

TIPS FROM OUR CHEFS

VELVETY
Glucose syrup is the secret to a creamy sorbet. This translucent syrup can be bought in specialty grocery stores or online.

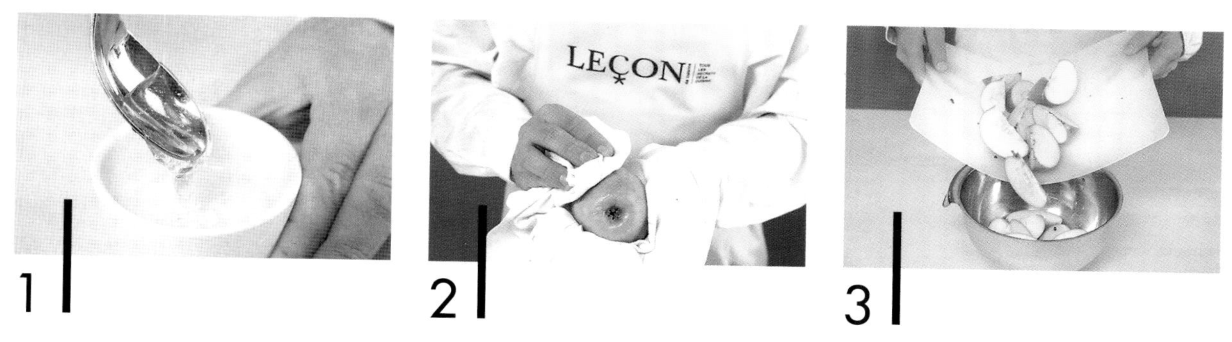
LEÇON
1
2
3

APPLE SHORTBREAD BARQUETTES AND GRANITA

Serves 4

Preparation time 15 minutes
Cooking time 10 minutes

Apples in syrup (page 64)
1 batch shortbread dough (page 565), refrigerated
Sugar for sprinkling

1 Make apples in syrup (page 64).

2 Pour the cold syrup into a rectangular dish (strain if necessary), then let set in the freezer for 4 hours.
Let the apple pieces drain on a plate. Preheat the oven to 200°C – 400°F (gas mark 6).
Roll out the shortbread dough. Place one piece of apple on top and cut around it, leaving a 4–5-mm – 1/8-inch space around it. Repeat with remaining apple pieces.

3 Place the barquettes on a baking sheet (tray) lined with parchment (baking) paper (or use a nonstick one). Sprinkle with sugar. Bake until deep golden, about 10 minutes. Meanwhile, chill the serving glasses in the freezer.

4 Break the syrup into crystals by scraping with a fork. The crystals will gradually separate.

5 Take the barquettes out of the oven when they are deep golden.
Serve the granita in the chilled glasses, with the warm barquettes.

TIPS FROM OUR CHEFS

LEAVE A MARGIN
Leave a 4–5-mm – 1/8-inch margin of dough around the apples on all sides when cutting out the shortbread dough because the dough will shrink when baked.

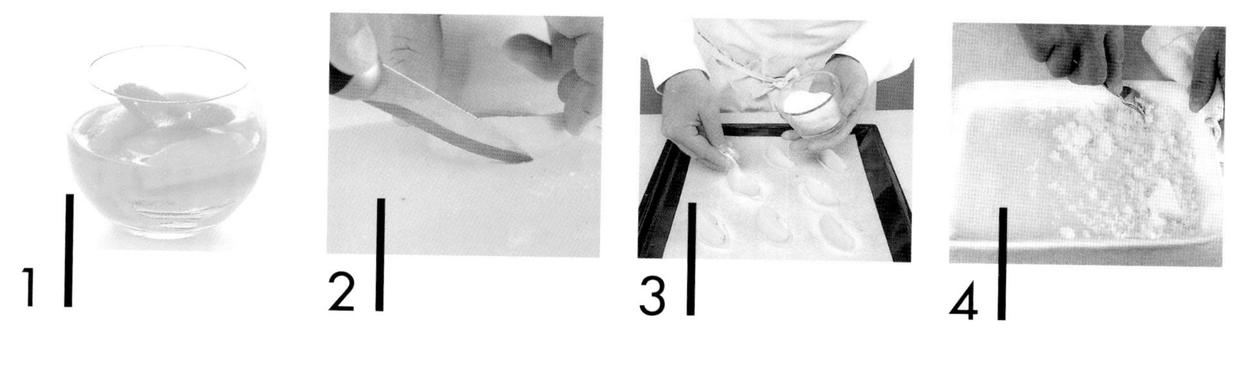
1
2
3
4

MINT PASTILLES

Makes about 30 candies

Preparation time 20 minutes
Resting time 24 hours

1 packet Frisk® mint candies
100 g – 3.5 ounces (3/4 cup plus 1 tablespoon) confectioners' (icing) sugar
1 g – 0.04 ounce sheet (leaf) gelatin (1/2 sheet)
6 g – 0.21 ounce (1 teaspoon) lemon juice

1 Put the Frisk® mints into the food chopper attachment for an immersion (stick) blender or in a blender. Blend to a very fine powder. Transfer to a bowl and combine with the confectioners' sugar. Mix well.

2 Soak the gelatin in a bowl filled with ice water. When soft, drain in a strainer (sieve).

3 Strain the lemon juice into a small saucepan. Heat over low heat. Remove from heat, add the gelatin, and let it melt. Pour the liquid over the candy mixture. Mix to combine. Work to a very soft paste. Knead with your hands to make a large ball of dough.

4 Shape into small balls: Break off a small piece of the dough that weighs about 3 g – 0.11 ounce (it's best to weigh each one to make uniform pastilles), and roll between your palms to make a round and even ball. Place the ball on a baking sheet (tray) lined with parchment (baking) paper. Repeat with remaining dough, then squash the balls with your thumb to give them a characteristic pastille shape. Dry the pastilles uncovered at room temperature for 12 hours, then flip them over and dry for 12 more hours.

TIPS FROM OUR CHEFS

COLD
The water must be cold to keep the gelatin from dissolving.

PATIENCE
The time it takes for the pastilles to dry will vary depending on the temperature of the room and the humidity level. Test one after 24 hours and let them dry a little longer, if necessary.

1
2
3

VANILLA MARSHMALLOWS

Makes about 30 knots or 32 cubes

Preparation time 40 minutes
Cooking time 5 minutes
Resting time 2 hours

EQUIPMENT

Stand mixer
Square stainless steel cake mold
Candy thermometer
Pastry bag
Plain pastry tip (nozzle) 10 mm - 3/8-inch diameter

250 g – 9 ounces (1 1/4 cups) sugar
12 g – 0.42 ounce sheet (leaf) gelatin (6 sheets)
1/2 vanilla bean (pod)
90 g – 3.17 ounces (about 3) egg whites
5 g – 0.18 ounce (1 teaspoon) vanilla extract
50 g – 1.76 ounces (1/3 cup plus 1 tablespoon) confectioners' (icing) sugar
40 g – 1.4 ounces (1/3 cup) starch (cornstarch/cornflour, potato starch, or rice starch)

TIPS FROM OUR CHEFS

NO STIFF PEAKS
Be careful when beating the egg whites. Beat them to soft peaks, not stiff peaks. Overbeaten egg whites will produce a grainy texture.

EXPERIMENT
You can add drops of food coloring or flavorings other than vanilla, such as orange flower water, to this paste.

TAKE A BREAK
The 2-hour resting time allows for the marshmallow to harden and dry without drying out. (They will break if too dry.) Cover with plastic wrap (cling film) to retain some moisture.

STORAGE
You don't need to eat all of the marshmallows at once. These marshmallows will keep for a week in an airtight jar; dust with the coating and place sheets of parchment paper between layers.

1

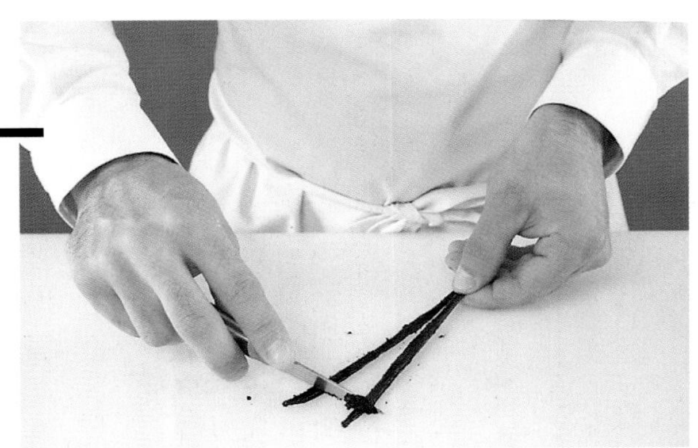

Put the sugar in a saucepan. Add 80 ml – 1/3 cup of water. Cook over medium heat until the liquid comes to a simmer. Bring to 130°C – 265°F, using the candy thermometer to keep an eye on the temperature. In the meantime, soak the gelatin in a bowl of cold water (page 543). Use a paring knife to split the vanilla bean. Scrape out the seeds.

2

Separate the egg whites from the yolks. Weigh out 90 g – 3.17 ounces (about 6 tablespoons) egg white and put into the bowl of the mixer. Beat to soft peaks. Drain the gelatin and squeeze out the water. When the syrup reaches 130°C – 265°F, remove from heat. Pour in the egg whites, beating constantly, and add the vanilla seeds, followed by the gelatin and the vanilla extract.

3

Make the coating: Mix the confectioners' sugar with the starch in a bowl. Line a baking sheet (tray) with parchment (baking) paper. Place the cake mold over one half of the sheet. Dust the bottom with the coating. Dust the other half of the sheet.

4

Stop the mixer: The paste should be thick and still warm. Fill the cake mold with part of the mixture. Fill it right to the top and edges with a spatula (palette knife). Smooth the surface.

5

Fit a pastry (piping) bag with a 10-mm – 3/8-inch tip (nozzle) and fill with the rest of the mixture (page 507). Pipe even strips lengthwise over the other half of the sheet, holding the bag with one hand and gently pressing with the other hand to push out the paste. Dust the strips and the mixture in the cake mold with the coating. Let stand at room temperature for 2 hours to set.

6

Use a knife with a wide blade to cut the strips in half. Shape the half strips into knots, without pulling tight to avoid breaking them. Dust with the coating. Use your fingertips to dust off excess coating, then place the knots on a baking sheet.

7

To unmold the marshmallow in the cake mold, soak a paring knife in hot water and run the tip around the sides. Lift off the cake mold with one hand while keeping the marshmallow in place with the other. Use a chef's knife with a wide blade to cut the square in half. Wet the blade. Cut each half in two. Turn the baking sheet around and make perpendicular cuts to obtain cubes. Dust with the coating. Use your fingertips to remove excess coating, then place the cubes on a baking sheet.

DESERT ROSES IN THREE CHOCOLATES

Makes 30 roses (10 of each kind)

Preparation time 20 minutes per batch
Resting time 10 minutes per batch

White Chocolate

100 g – 3.53 oz white chocolate couverture
30 g – 1.06 oz (2 cups) puffed rice
10 g – 0.35 oz (1 tbsp) raw pistachio nuts, shelled
10 g – 0.35 oz (1 tbsp) Zante (dried) currants

Milk Chocolate

50 g – 1.76 oz (1 3/4 cups) unsweetened cornflakes
100 g – 3.53 oz milk chocolate couverture (40 percent cocoa)
1 organic, unwaxed lemon

Dark Chocolate

100 g – 3.53 oz dark chocolate couverture (70 percent cocoa)
40 g – 1.41 oz (1 cup) sugar-coated cornflakes
10 g – 0.35 oz (1 tbsp) candied orange peel (page 388)

1 Make the white chocolate desert roses: Melt the white chocolate in the microwave or over a bain-marie. The temperature should be 50–55°C – 122–131°F. Place the bowl with the chocolate inside a bowl filled with ice water. Mix, taking the bowl of chocolate out and returning it to the water, until the temperature falls to 26–27°C – 79–80°F. Microwave again for 5 seconds or place over the bain-marie to raise the temperature to 28–29°C – 82–84°F. Add the puffed rice to the chocolate, followed by the pistachios and currants. Mix well. Line a baking sheet (tray) with parchment (baking) paper.

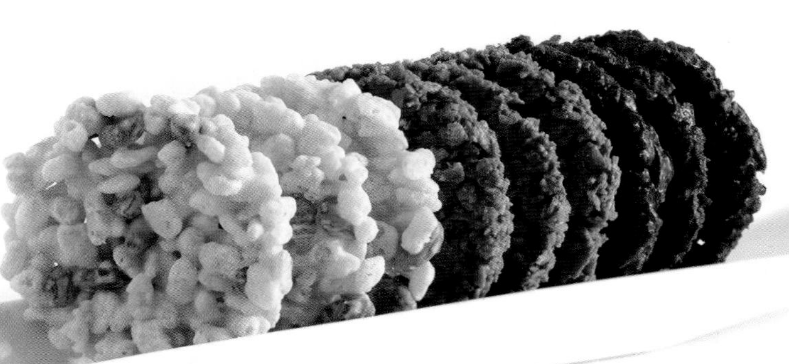

2 Place about 1 tablespoon of the mixture in a 7-cm- – 2 3/4-inch-diameter ring mold with 3–4-mm- – 1/8-inch-tall sides. Press down with a fork, being careful not to crush the rice. Carefully remove the mold. Do the same to make the other roses. Let harden for about 10 minutes.

1

3 Make the milk chocolate roses: Crush the cornflakes with a rolling pin. Press lightly to avoid reducing to a powder.

4 Temper the milk chocolate: melt it at 50–55°C – 122–131°F. Cool to 27–28°C – 80–82°F. Then reheat to 29–30°C – 84–86°F. Finely grate the zest of the lemon over the chocolate (page 556). Incorporate the cornflakes. Mix gently. Make the roses following the same steps as for the white chocolate ones. Let harden for about 10 minutes.

3

5 Make the dark chocolate roses: Temper the chocolate: melt it at 55–60°C – 131–140°F. Cool to 28–29°C – 82–84°F. Reheat to 30–31°C – 86–88°F. Crush the sugar-coated cornflakes with a rolling pin. Press lightly to avoid reducing to a powder. Dice the candied orange peel very finely and add to the chocolate. Incorporate the sugar-coated cornflakes. Mix gently. Make the roses following the same steps as for the white and milk chocolate ones. Let harden for about 10 minutes.

4

TIPS FROM OUR CHEFS

TEMPERING

This is a very important step because it keeps the roses glossy. Chocolate that is not tempered may "bloom" or develop white blotches.

DON'T RUSH

If the mixture starts to harden before you finish molding the roses, microwave it for 5 seconds or soften it in a bain-marie.

5

CHOCOLATE TRUFFLES

Makes 50 truffles

Preparation time 1 hour
Resting time 24 hours + 1 hour

EQUIPMENT

Pastry (piping) bag
Plain pastry tip (nozzle)
14-mm- – 1/2-inch-diameter opening

Chocolate ganache (page 116)

100 g – 3.5 ounces chocolate
Cocoa powder

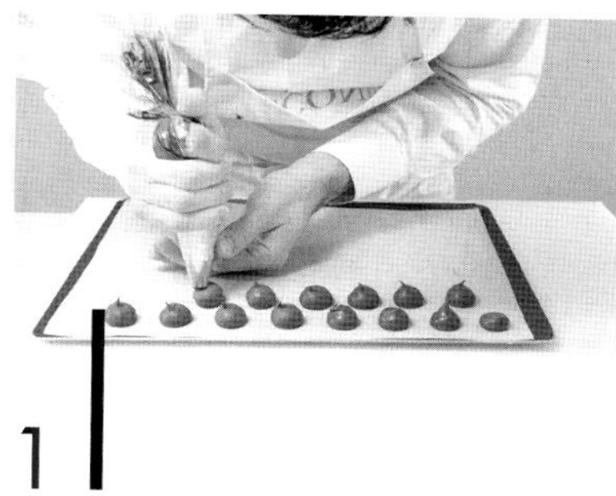

1

1 Fill the pastry bag with the ganache. Pipe small balls on a baking sheet (tray) lined with parchment (baking) paper (page 507). Refrigerate until firm.

2 Melt the chocolate until it reaches 33–35°C – 92–95°F.
Put on a pair of latex gloves. Place a small amount of melted chocolate in the palm of one hand.

3 Roll one of the balls of ganache between your palms to coat with the chocolate.

4 Transfer to a large plate filled with the cocoa powder and roll in the cocoa with a fork. Repeat with remaining ganache balls and chocolate.

5 Let the truffles harden for 1 hour in the refrigerator. Place in a drum strainer (sieve) and shake gently to remove the excess cocoa powder.

2

3

4

PRALINES AND CARAMELIZED HAZELNUTS

Preparation time 15 minutes
Cooking time 25 minutes

250 g – 9 ounces (1 1/4 cups) sugar
2 vanilla beans (pods)
300 g – 10.5 ounces (2 1/4 cups) blanched hazelnuts
40 g – 1.4 ounces (3 tablespoons) butter, cut into cubes
1 g – 0.04 ounce (1/4 teaspoon) fleur de sel

TIPS FROM OUR CHEFS

RAW OR BLANCHED
You can use raw hazelnuts to make the caramelized hazelnuts—they will have a sharper flavor. However, always use pale blanched hazelnuts to make the pralines so that the golden color of the caramel will be highlighted.

A LOT OF SPACE
Use a wide and relatively shallow saucepan so that all of the hazelnuts come into contact with the caramel. Make wide sweeping movements to cover the entire surface of the pan. Don't overlook any of the hazelnuts; they all have to be completely coated.

1 Make the pralines: Put the sugar into a saucepan. Add 100 ml – 1/3 cup plus 1 tablespoon plus 1 teaspoon water. Place over high heat. Use a thermometer to monitor the temperature and bring to 115°C – 239°F. In the meantime, use a paring knife to split the vanilla beans. Scrape out the seeds. When the syrup reaches 115°C – 239°F, add the hazelnuts. Remove from heat. Use a spatula (palette knife) to toss the hazelnuts in the syrup to coat.

2 The syrup will turn white and crystallize around the hazelnuts. Place the pan over medium heat and mix until the sugar melts and begins to caramelize. When the nuts turn a light golden color, transfer some of them to a baking sheet (tray) lined with parchment (baking) paper and let cool.

3 Make the caramelized hazelnuts: Return the rest of the nuts to the heat. Let caramelize while stirring constantly with the spatula. When they start to brown, add the vanilla bean seeds. Mix well, then turn off the heat. Add all the butter. Add the fleur de sel. Mix. Keep stirring until the caramel coats the hazelnuts completely. Transfer to a baking sheet lined with parchment paper.

4 Use two spoons to separate the hazelnuts so that they do not form clusters. Let cool.
Serve the caramelized hazelnuts with the pralines so that the contrasting colors and flavors can be enjoyed.

1

2

INTERMEDIATE

CHEESE PUFFS

Makes 45 puffs

Choux puffs
Preparation time 30 minutes
Cooking time 35 minutes

Béchamel sauce
Preparation time 20 minutes
Cooking time 5 minutes

EQUIPMENT

Choux puffs
Pastry (piping) bag
Size 10 plain pastry tip (nozzle)

Béchamel sauce
Size 2 plain pastry tip (nozzle)
Pastry (piping) bag
Size 7 plain pastry tip (nozzle)

TIPS FROM OUR CHEFS

2 OPTIONS
If you prefer plain cheese puffs, stop at step 2 of this recipe.

NO SIZE 2 TIP?
You can also pierce the bottoms of the puffs with a thick trussing needle.

VARIATION
You can vary these using almost any cheese you like.

Choux puffs

300 g – 10.5 ounces choux paste (page 602)
1 egg
40 g – 1.4 ounces (1/2 cup) grated young (fresco) Parmesan cheese

Béchamel sauce

300 ml – 1 1/4 cups whole milk
100 ml – 1/3 cup plus 1 tablespoon plus 1 teaspoon light (single) cream
30 g – 1.06 ounces (2 tablespoons) butter
30 g –1.06 ounces (2 tablespoons) all-purpose (plain) flour
Fine salt
Freshly ground pepper
Ground nutmeg

1 Preheat the oven to 170°C – 350°F (gas mark 3). Fit the tip to the pastry bag and fill with the choux paste (page 507).
Pipe puffs 3 cm – 1 1/4 inches in diameter on a baking sheet (tray), spacing them 2 cm – 3/4 inch apart.

1

2 Break the egg into a bowl and beat with a fork. Gently brush the tops of the puffs with the beaten egg.
Sprinkle the Parmesan generously over the puffs.
Shake the baking sheet over a sheet of parchment (baking) paper to remove the excess cheese. Set aside for the béchamel sauce. Bake for 30 minutes.

3 In the meantime, make the béchamel sauce. Heat the milk and cream in a saucepan. Melt the butter in another saucepan. Whisk the flour into the butter. Whisk for 40 seconds without letting the mixture turn brown. Add the milk mixture while stirring constantly over medium heat.
Season with three large pinches salt, four turns of the peppermill, and two pinches nutmeg. Mix.
Add 10 g – 0.35 ounce (2 tablespoons) of the excess grated Parmesan from the puffs. Mix.
Transfer the béchamel sauce to a dish, cover with plastic wrap (cling film), and let cool.

3

4 Detach the puffs from the baking sheet with the back of a spatula (turner). Pierce the bottom of each puff with the size 2 pastry tip.
Fit the size 7 tip on the pastry bag and fill the bag with the béchamel sauce. Fill the puffs with the sauce.
Reheat the puffs in the oven for 5 minutes at 190°C – 375°F (gas mark 5). Serve warm as an appetizer.

POTATO AND TAPENADE FRITTERS

Serves 4

Preparation time 10 minutes
Cooking time 5 minutes

2 large Mona Lisa potatoes
1 egg yolk
1 tablespoon potato starch
1 batch tapenade (page 11)

1 Wash, brush, and peel the potatoes. Slice into chips (crisps) with a mandoline slicer (page 519). Heat the oil in a fryer to 180°C – 350°F.
Arrange the slices in rows in a single layer on a sheet of paper towel and cover with another sheet. Repeat to make several layers.

2 Mix the egg yolk with the potato starch in a bowl.
Brush the mixture on every other potato slice.
Put a little tapenade in the center of the brushed slices.
Cover with the unbrushed slices.

3 Seal the edges well by pressing firmly with your thumbs all around the perimeters of the slices.
Fry the fritters in the oil at 180°C – 350°F until golden.
Turn them if necessary.

1

2

TIPS FROM OUR CHEFS

ALL STARCH

Contrary to the standard advice for making fries (chips), don't soak the potatoes before slicing. You actually have to conserve the starch so that the two pieces will stick together.

VARIATIONS

Vary the filling for these fritters by using mushroom duxelles, fish livers, glazed tomato skins, crushed anchovies, or other savory items.

ROSEVAL POTATOES, SMOKED SALMON, AND LEMON CREAM

1 Wash and brush the potatoes. Put into a stockpot. Measure in enough water to cover the potatoes completely, then add 12 g – 0.42 ounces (2 1/4 teaspoons) kosher salt for every 1 liter – 4 1/4 cups of water added. Add the whole garlic and herbs. Cook for 15–20 minutes.

2 In the meantime, make the cream. Pour the crème fraîche into a bowl, add the pepper (four turns of the peppermill) and the salt. Add the lemon juice and stir well. Chop half of the chives. Add to the cream. Drain the potatoes. Let cool. Without peeling, cut into 4-mm – 1/8-inch slices.

3 Arrange the potato slices on a dish. Place a tablespoon of sour cream on top of each. Cover with slices of smoked salmon and decorate with the whole chives, cut into shorter lengths if desired.

TIPS FROM OUR CHEFS

CHOOSING WELL

Potato varieties Charlotte, Ratte, and Belle de Fontenay combine flavorful skin with firm flesh, but Roseval has the added advantage of a pretty pink color.

Serves 4

Preparation time 8 minutes
Cooking time 15–20 minutes

Potatoes and salmon

600 g – 1 pound 5 ounces Roseval potatoes of the same size
Kosher (coarse) salt
1 clove garlic
3 sprigs rosemary
2 sprigs thyme or 2 bay leaves
200 g – 7 ounces sliced smoked salmon

Lemon cream

1/4 cup crème fraîche
Freshly ground pepper
1/2 teaspoon fine salt
Juice of 1/2 lemon
1/2 bunch chives

1

2

3

POTATO ROLLS

Serves 4

Preparation time 20 minutes
Cooking time 25 minutes
Resting time 30 minutes

EQUIPMENT

Food Mill

350 g – 12.35 ounces Charlotte potatoes
Kosher (coarse) salt
1/2 teaspoon fine salt
70 g – 2.47 ounces (1/2 cup plus 1 tablespoon plus 1 teaspoon) all-purpose (plain) flour, divided
100 ml – 1/3 cup plus 1 tablespoon plus 1 teaspoon milk
1 envelope (sachet) active dry yeast or 15 g – 0.53 ounce fresh compressed yeast

2

1 Wash, brush, and peel the potatoes. Cut into medium-size pieces.
Fill a stockpot with water. Season with kosher salt. Add the potato pieces and cook over high heat. Skim off and discard any foam. After 10 minutes, check that the potatoes are cooked through; the tip of a knife should pierce a potato easily.
Transfer the potatoes to a large colander. Drain well. If necessary, put into the oven for 5 minutes to dry out.

2 Put a few potato pieces into a food mill fitted with a disk with medium holes and mash. Repeat with remaining potato pieces, working in batches. Collect 200 g – 7 ounces (1 cup) mashed potatoes in a large bowl.
Mix with the fine salt and 60 g – 2.12 ounces (1/2 cup) of the flour. Pour in the warm mashed potatoes around the sides of the bowl. Warm the milk. Dissolve the yeast in a small bowl with a little warm milk. Pour the yeast mixture over the mashed potatoes. Gradually add the remainder of the milk to the bowl and mix in with your fingers. Knead the dough by hand until smooth. Roll into a ball.

3 Roll the ball into a long cylinder.
Cut into uniform lengths with a knife. Roll in the remaining 10 g – 0.35 ounce (1 tablespoon plus 1 teaspoon) flour.
Lightly press each piece between your thumb and index finger to flatten two of the sides and to round the top.
Moisten a baking sheet (tray) with water and arrange the pieces of dough evenly spaced on it.
Let the dough rise (proof) for 30 minutes at room temperature or in a warm (not hot) spot.
Preheat the oven to 230°C – 450°F (gas mark 8).
Bake until golden, about 15 minutes.

DUCK ROULADE WITH APPLE CHUTNEY

Serves 4

Preparation time 30 minutes
Cooking time 25 minutes

EQUIPMENT

2 wooden skewers

Apple chutney makes 250 ml – 1 cup

2 (300 g – 10.5 ounces) Belle de Boskoop or Reinette Grise du Canada apples
40 g – 1.4 ounces (about 1/2 small) white onion
20 walnut halves
50 g – 1.76 ounces (1/4 cup) sugar
100 ml – 1/3 cup plus 1 tablespoon plus 1 teaspoon cider vinegar
Salt
Freshly ground pepper
1 tablespoon olive oil

Duck roulade

2 Belle de Boskoop or Reinette Grise du Canada apples
4 duck tenderloins (fillets)
Fleur de sel
Freshly ground pepper
1 tablespoon olive oil

TIPS FROM OUR CHEFS

HISTORY

Chutney is a British specialty with Indian influences. Derived from the Hindi word chatni, meaning "strong spices," it is a sweet-and-sour condiment made from fruits or vegetables cooked in vinegar with sugar and spices.

PERFECT MATCHES

Chutney is a wonderful accompaniment to game dishes, broiled or grilled (barbecued) meats, and even hard cheeses. Don't be afraid to play around with the ingredients. For instance, you can replace the sugar with honey, or add Zante (dried) currants.

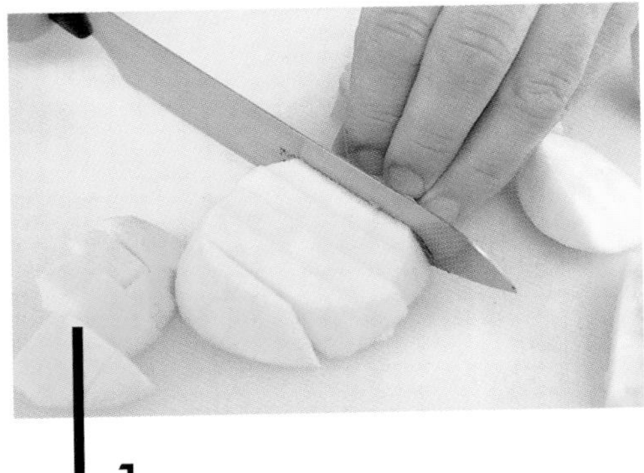

1

Make the chutney: Peel the apples and core whole. Cut into batons, and then in large dice (page 512).

2

Peel the onion, halve, and thinly slice (page 525). Chop the walnuts. Roast for 5–6 minutes in the oven at 200°C – 400°F (gas mark 6). Heat a saucepan over high heat. Add the sugar and caramelize. Deglaze with the vinegar. Add the sliced onion and sauté while stirring constantly. Add the diced apple, cover, and simmer over low heat for 15 minutes, stirring from time to time. Season with salt and pepper, then drizzle with the olive oil. Mix. Add the roasted walnuts and mix well. Continue cooking until the apples are soft. Transfer to a bowl and let cool.

3

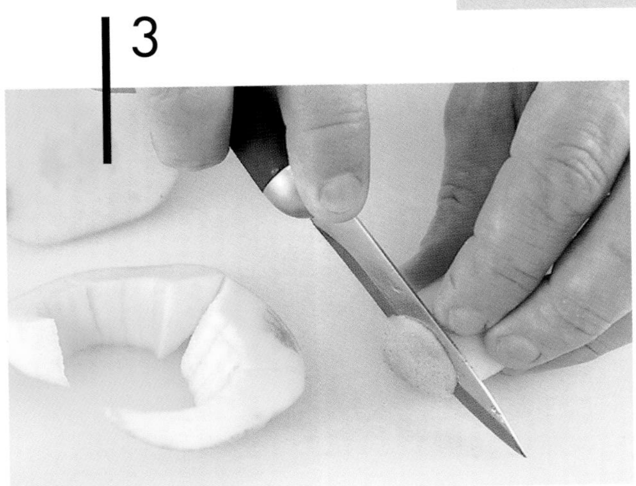

Make the roulades: Wash and dry the apples. Cut off one side of an apple just next to the core.
Use a paring knife to peel off the skin from the piece, then carve off the flesh gradually while turning the piece. Continue turning to make a cylinder (3 cm – 1 1/4 inches high and about 2 cm – 3/4 inch in diameter). Trim, if necessary, until even.
Remove any traces of skin left on the cylinder. Repeat this process to make four cylinders.

4

Lay the duck tenderloins flat. Place an apple cylinder at one third of the length of a tenderloin. Roll the meat around it. Repeat with remaining tenderloins and apple cylinders.

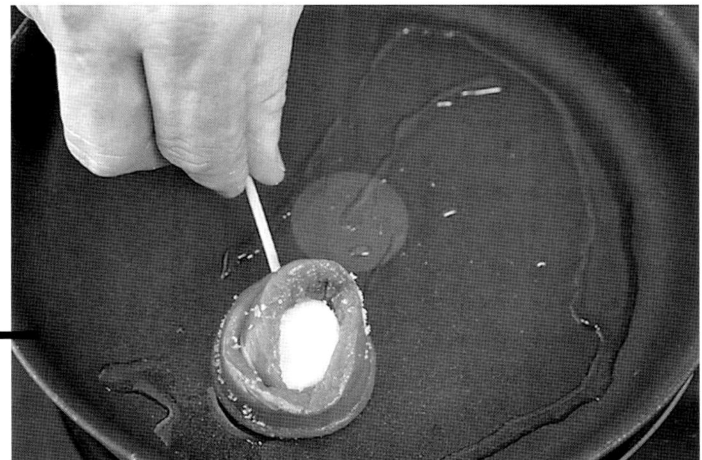

5

Use half a skewer to hold each roulade closed. Season with fleur de sel and pepper.
Brown the flat sides of each roulade for 2 minutes on each side in the olive oil. Cook for 2 minutes at 170°C – 350°F (gas mark 5). Serve with the chutney.

BEEF CARPACCIO PEARLS

Serves 4

Preparation time 45 minutes
Cooking time 10 minutes

2 organic, unwaxed lemons
2 Breton artichokes
1 tablespoon olive oil, plus more for drizzling
Salt
Freshly ground pepper
2 small poivrade artichokes
Fleur de sel
20 slices of beef for the carpaccio
100 g – 3.5 ounces sylvetta (wild arugula/rocket)
2 scallions (spring onions)
50 g – 1.76 ounces aged (*vecchio*) Parmesan cheese
1 pinch all-purpose (plain) flour

TIPS FROM OUR CHEFS

ARUGULA AND SYLVETTA
Arugula (rocket) is a cultivated salad green (leaf), while sylvetta is the wild version of the same plant. Its leaves are thinner and more serrated than those of arugula, and its flavor is more pungent.

RUB WITH LEMON
Rubbing the artichoke hearts with lemon as you are slicing them will stop them from turning brown.

YOUNG OR AGED
For this recipe, you should use aged Parmesan, which will add more flavor and make tasty tuiles.

1

Cut one lemon in half and set aside one half. Cut one of the halves in half. Squeeze the juice of the two lemon quarters into a bowl of cold water. Pull the stems (stalks) off the Breton artichokes. To trim the base, hold a Breton artichoke upside down and use your knife to pare around the base toward the left, making two rotations (page 516).

Next, hold the artichoke upright and pare toward the right, making two rotations. Rub the heart with the remaining lemon half. Cut off the leaves to 2 cm – 3/4 inch from the heart. Remove the rest of the leaves, then scoop out the choke with a melon baller. Scrape well. Immerse the heart immediately in the water and lemon juice. Repeat with remaining Breton artichoke.

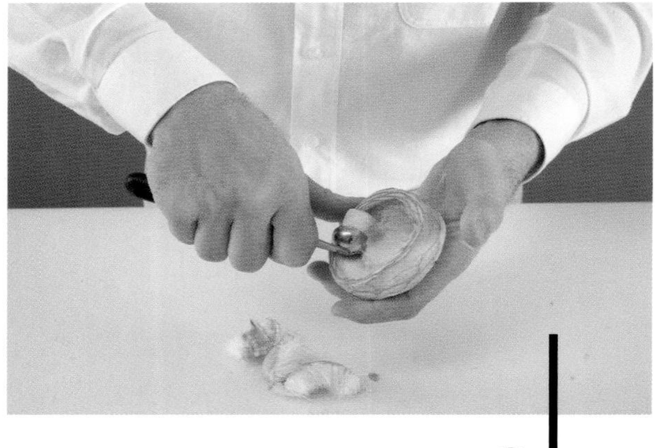

2

3

Drain the hearts, then cut them into 5-mm – 1/4-inch slices, then into batons, and finally into small dice. Heat 1 tablespoon of oil in a copper saucepan. Add the diced artichokes. Season with salt and pepper. Cook for 5–6 minutes, shaking the pan one or two times. Cut the stem from one of the poivrade artichokes 3 cm – 1 1/4 inches from the bottom. Remove the leaves one by one, leaving the heart. Cut off the top to 2 cm – 3/4 inch from the heart.
Pare the heart and peel the stem right up to the heart with a vegetable peeler (page 516). Immerse immediately in the water and lemon juiceRepeat with remaining poivrade artichoke. Transfer the sautéed artichokes to a dish. Let cool. Trim, wash, and dry the sylvetta.

4

Cut the roots off the scallions. Cut the entire white part into thin slices. Chop three-quarters of the sylvetta. Add to the scallions. Add the sautéed artichokes. Shave 20 g – 0.7 ounce of Parmesan over the mixture. Grate the zest of the remaining lemon half over the top. Drizzle with olive oil and lemon juice. Add a little fleur de sel. Season with pepper. Toss.

5

Spread plastic wrap (cling film) over the work surface. Lay the beef slices over it, spaced 5 cm – 2 inches apart. Lightly brush the slices with oil. Put 1 teaspoon of the sautéed artichoke mixture in the center of each slice. Cut the plastic around the slices. Pull the plastic up, around the meat and filling.

6

Twist the plastic as if it were a candy wrapper until it bursts and the pearl is released. Repeat with remaining meat.

7

Put the rest of the sylvetta into a bowl. Slice the poivrade artichokes using the finest mandoline slicer setting (page 504) and add to the bowl. Season with salt and pepper and drizzle with olive oil. Mix.

8

Place a little of the greens in the bottom of an individual serving dish, then a few artichoke slices, three beef pearls, a little more sylvetta, a few more artichoke slices, and another two beef pearls. Drizzle with a little olive oil. Repeat with remaining items. Preheat the oven to 220°C – 425°F (gas mark 7). Grate the remaining 30 g – 1.06 ounces Parmesan into a bowl (you should have about 1/3 cup). Add the pinch of flour. Mix. Line a baking sheet (tray) with parchment (baking) paper. Make bands of the grated Parmesan mixture. Place in the oven. Let melt for 3–4 minutes without browning. Detach the Parmesan tuiles from the paper as soon as they come out of the oven. Let harden for a few minutes, then garnish each serving with one or more tuiles.

CRISPY SALAD WITH FLASH-SEARED TUNA

Serves 4

Preparation time 10 minutes
Cooking time 1 minute

6 sucrine (small butterhead) lettuce heads
1 clove garlic
100 g – 3.5 ounces sun-dried tomatoes in oil
1 sprig basil
2 tablespoons plus 1 teaspoon olive oil, divided, plus more for drizzling
2 vine tomatoes
300 g – 10.5 ounces tuna loin
25 g - 0.88 oz (1/4 cup) pitted black olives
1 organic, unwaxed lemon
3 scallions (spring onions)
Fine salt
Freshly ground pepper
Ground Espelette pepper
Fleur de sel

TIPS FROM OUR CHEFS

SWEET SUCRINES
Sucrine, Boston, Bibb, and Little Gem are all small and sweet varieties of butterhead lettuce. They may be sold already washed.

DON'T OVERCOOK
The tuna should not be cooked for too long. This fish can even be eaten raw. Here it is "flash-seared," meaning it is seared over high heat on all sides for a few seconds so that it remains very tender on the inside.

BE UNCOMPROMISING
Because you will be using the zest, it is essential that you purchase an organic, unwaxed lemon. This should be specified on the packaging. If it isn't, ask the seller.

1 Tear off the large outer leaves to expose the lettuce hearts. Cut off the stems (stalks). Halve the hearts.

2 Peel and halve the garlic clove and remove any green core. Scrape out the seeds from the sun-dried tomatoes with a knife.
Use a handheld immersion (stick) blender with food chopper attachment to chop the tomatoes and garlic. Add three basil leaves and a teaspoon of oil. Blend. Transfer to another dish.
Remove the stems from the fresh tomatoes and cut each tomato into eight sections (segments). Peel them by passing the knife blade between the skin and the flesh (page 521).
Remove the cores and seeds. Cut the tomato sections into strips, then into small dice. Set aside in a bowl.

3 Cut the tuna into 4 pieces. Season with salt and pepper. Heat 1 tablespoon oil in a deep nonstick skillet or frying pan.
Lay the fish in the pan. Cook for 10 seconds. Turn the pieces on their sides and cook for 10 seconds. Do the same for the remaining two sides, then transfer to a plate. Let cool.

4 Halve the olives. Wash and dry the lemon. Finely grate the zest (page 514) and sprinkle over tuna. Squeeze the lemon and set aside the juice. Cut the roots off the scallions. Slice the white part and 3 cm – 1 1/4 inches of green into fine rounds. Add to the diced tomato. Season with salt and pepper. Add a pinch of Espelette pepper. Drizzle with 1 tablespoon of olive oil and 1 1/2 teaspoons of lemon juice.

5 Cut the tuna into 5-mm – 1/4-inch slices.
Put a tablespoon of sun-dried tomato puree on each lettuce heart. Place a piece of tuna on each one. Add the diced tomato.
Garnish with a few basil leaves. Drizzle with oil and season with a little fleur de sel.

1

2

3

SUMMER TIAN

Serves 4

Avocado, shrimp, grapefruit
Preparation time 30 minutes
Cooking time 11 minutes

Cocktail (marie rose) sauce
Cooking time 5 minutes

EQUIPMENT

Wooden toothpick

A WORD FROM OUR SOMMELIER

Pair with a Provençal white wine (e.g., Coteaux de Pierrevert).

TIPS FROM OUR CHEFS

SHOPPING LIST
Choose very large shrimp (prawns) for this dish; it will look much more appealing, and you'll save precious time making it. Purchase very ripe avocados or let the avocados ripen at room temperature for a few days.

AN EASY REMEDY
You can brown the avocados in the skillet to correct their color.

Tian

8 very large cooked shrimp (prawns)
4 (200-g – 7-ounce) avocados
Juice of 1/2 lemon
2 pink grapefruits
1 onion
3 tablespoons olive oil, divided
Fine salt
White pepper
Fleur de sel
Coarsely ground pepper

Cocktail (marie rose) sauce

1 egg
Fine salt
White pepper
4–5 drops Tabasco® sauce
1 teaspoon Dijon mustard
1 tablespoon ketchup
1 tablespoon lemon juice
100 ml – 1/3 cup plus 1 tablespoon plus 1 teaspoon grapeseed oil
1 teaspoon cognac

1 Remove the heads from the shrimp. Peel (page 541). Make a 2-mm- – 1/8-inch-deep and 1.5-cm – 3/4-inch-long incision into the back of each shrimp. Use the wooden toothpick to lift up and draw out the small black "vein" (intestine).

1

2 Use a chef's knife to cut the avocados in half lengthwise. Stick the heel of the knife blade into the pits (stones) to remove them without damaging the avocado flesh. Use a paring knife to peel the avocados. Drizzle with lemon juice. Cut into 5–6-mm – 1/4-inch slices.

2

3 Supreme the grapefruits: Cut off the ends, then cut the skin in vertical strips following the curve of the fruit to expose the flesh. Slide the knife between the membrane and flesh of each section (segment) to detach (page 514). Squeeze the peels over a bowl to recover any juice.

4 Peel and halve the onion. To chop, cut each half lengthwise without cutting through the root, then cut horizontally, and, finally, slice across (page 525). Heat 1 tablespoon of oil in a deep skillet or frying pan. Sauté the avocado slices for 1 minute 30 seconds over high heat. Season with salt and white pepper, then transfer to a plate. Preheat the oven to 230°C – 425°F (gas mark 8).

5 Put the diced onion in the same skillet with 1 tablespoon of oil. Season with salt and white pepper, and brown for 1 minute over high heat. Transfer to the plate with the avocado slices. Heat 1 tablespoon of oil in the same skillet. Drain the grapefruit sections and sauté for 30 seconds over high heat. Transfer to another plate. Arrange three avocado slices together with a sprinkling of the onion in a baking dish. Add a grapefruit section and one shrimp. Continue in the same way until the dish is filled. Drizzle with the grapefruit juice from step 3. Cook in the preheated oven for 8 minutes.

6 Make the sauce: Break the egg and separate the yolk into a bowl. Season the yolk with salt and white pepper and mix. Add the Tabasco sauce. Add the mustard and ketchup. Mix. Incorporate the tablespoon of lemon juice. Mix together with a whisk. Pour in the grapeseed oil, a drop at a time, while whisking briskly. Finally, mix in the cognac.
Take the tian out of the oven. Sprinkle with fleur de sel and coarsely ground pepper. Serve warm or cold with the sauce.

PISSALADIÈRE

Serves 4–6

Preparation time 30 minutes
Cooking time 1 hour
Resting time 1 hour +
15 minutes

3 cloves garlic
700 g – 1 pound 8 ounces)
yellow onions, about 4
2 tablespoons olive oil, plus
more for drizzling
10 anchovy fillets in oil, drained
3 sprigs thyme
1 bay leaf
Freshly ground pepper
80 g – 2.82 ounces Niçoise
black olives

TIPS FROM OUR CHEFS

NO SALT
Don't add salt to the topping because the anchovies already provide enough.

GOOD POSITIONING
Push the dough down well around the edge of the pan. If the dough hangs over the edges, cut off the excess by passing the rolling pin over the rim of the pan.

1 Make the pizza dough and let rise for 1 hour (page 548). Cut the garlic cloves in half. Peel and remove the green cores, if any. Peel the onions. Cut them in half. Use the tip of a knife to cut off the roots, then thinly slice (page 525).

2 Heat 2 tablespoons of olive oil in a deep skillet or frying pan. Soften the anchovies for 1 minute over low heat. Add the garlic and mix it in with the anchovies. Cook for 1 additional minute.
Add the onions, thyme, and bay leaf. Season with pepper. Mix. Soften for 30 minutes over low heat, stirring from time to time.
Remove the bay leaf and thyme. Taste and adjust the seasoning with pepper. Transfer to a container and let cool.

3 Lightly dust your fingers, the pizza dough, and a rolling pin with flour. Turn the dough out onto the work surface and flatten with your fingers. Knead it lightly and shape it into a ball again.
Roll it out, regularly changing the direction of the rolling pin to make a disk measuring 28–29 cm – 11–11 1/2 inches in diameter.

4 Line a pizza pan with parchment (baking) paper. Fold the dough in half along the diameter and then in half again. Place it on the pan with the point in the center.

5 Unfold the dough to fill the pan. Let rise at room temperature (about 15 minutes). Meanwhile, preheat the oven to 210°C – 400°F (gas mark 6–7).
Spread the onion mixture over the dough. Top with the olives. Drizzle a little olive oil over the edge of the dough to stop it from drying out. Bake for 25 minutes. Take the pissaladière out of the oven. Slide it off the pan and the paper. Slice and serve.

2
3
4

BARIGOULE ARTICHOKES

Serves 4

Preparation time 30 minutes
Cooking time 20 minutes

1/2 lemon
16 poivrade artichokes
2 onions
1 stalk celery
1 carrot
1 (80-g – 2.82-ounce) slice country bacon
1 tablespoon olive oil, plus more for drizzling
1 clove garlic, unpeeled
Salt
Freshly ground pepper
2 sprigs thyme
1 bay leaf
1 teaspoon coriander seeds
120 ml – 1/2 cup dry white wine
330 ml – 1 1/3 cups chicken broth or stock
2 sprigs basil
125 g – 4.4 ounces (about 1 tablespoon plus 1 teaspoon) Brousse sheep's milk cheese

1 Fill a large bowl with water. Squeeze the 1/2 lemon into the bowl. Cut the stems (stalks) from the artichokes 2 cm – 3/4 inch from the bottom.
Remove the harder outer leaves from the artichokes, leaving the tender leaves. Pare around the artichokes with a knife, following the curve of the heart, and peel the stems (page 516). Cut the leaves to one third of their length. Immerse the artichokes one by one in the water as you finish them.

2 Peel the onions. Thinly slice (page 525). Peel the celery stalk with a vegetable peeler. Cut in half. Cut each piece into 4 batons, then into very small dice.

3 Peel the carrot. Trim off the top and bottom ends. Cut into 2–3-mm – 1/2-inch slices. Cut the slices into batons, and then into very small dice (brunoise).

4 Cut the slice of bacon into four equal pieces.
Heat 1 tablespoon of oil in a deep skillet or frying pan over low heat. Add the bacon, onion, celery, carrot, and the unpeeled garlic.

5 Drain the artichokes. Add to the pan. Season with a pinch of salt and four turns of the peppermill. Cook for 3 minutes to soften. Stir several times to coat well with the oil and bacon fat. Add the thyme, bay leaf, and coriander seeds. Pour in the white wine.
Wipe down the sides of the pot with a wet pastry brush to detach any caramelized juices. Reduce for 3 minutes over medium heat to let the liquid evaporate completely. Add the broth. Pluck the basil leaves and add them to the pot, reserving a few for garnish. Cover the pot and cook for 10 minutes over medium heat. Check that the artichokes are cooked through by piercing with the tip of a paring knife. They should be tender. Transfer the artichokes to a plate. Drizzle a little olive oil into the cooking liquid. Stir. Reduce for 1–2 minutes. Distribute the artichokes, vegetables, and bacon on plates. Place 1 teaspoon of cheese on each plate. Pour sauce over the artichokes and garnish with reserved basil.

2

3

4

DARPHIN POTATOES

Makes 4 cakes

Preparation time 7 minutes
Cooking time 12 minutes

EQUIPMENT

2 blini pans

1.2 kg – 2 pounds 10 ounces Charlotte potatoes
80 g – 2.82 ounces (5 3/4 tablespoons) butter
Leaves of 3 sprigs thyme
Leaves of 5 sprigs chervil
1/2 bunch chives
1/2 teaspoon fine salt
Freshly ground white pepper

1 Wash, brush, and peel the potatoes.
Slice with a mandoline or coarsely grate into thin straws (page 519).
Transfer to a dish.
Clarify the butter (page 546). Finely chop the herbs.
Add the herbs and 3 tablespoons of clarified butter to the grated potatoes.

1

2 Season with the salt and pepper. Mix well. Grease the two blini pans with a sheet of paper towel dipped in the clarified butter.
Heat the pans over medium heat. Put a thick layer of the potato mixture in each pan.

2

3 Press well with the back of a spoon. Fill the pans to the rim.
Cook until the edges are golden, 5–6 minutes. Turn the cakes over.
Cook the other sides 5–6 minutes. Transfer the potato cakes to paper towels to drain. Make another two potato cakes.

TIPS FROM OUR CHEFS

VARIATION

Incorporate zucchini (courgette), mushrooms, onions, or other vegetables for a little variety. Be sure the mixture is always at least 70% potato.

IN THE OVEN

If the potatoes aren't perfectly cooked, finish the process in the oven. (If you prefer you can make one large potato cake with all of the mixture, and in that case you will definitely need to finish it in the oven.) You can also make the cakes in small molds and bake them for 20 minutes at 180°C – 375°F (gas mark 6).

POTATOES ANNA

Makes 4 cakes

Preparation time 15 minutes
Cooking time 45 minutes

1 kg – 2 pounds 3 ounces
Belle de Fontenay potatoes
120 g – 4.23 ounces
(8 tablespoons/1 stick) butter
Fine salt
Freshly ground white pepper

1

2

1 Wash, brush, and peel the potatoes. Cut into cylinders with a cookie cutter (page 519). Cut into 2–3-mm – 1/12-inch slices (page 518). Salt the slices as soon as they are cut to soften them a little.
Lay the slices on paper towels. Cover with paper towels to soak up the moisture. Preheat the oven to 170°C – 350°F (gas mark 3).

2 Clarify the butter (page 546). Reserve 1 tablespoon of clarified butter. Brush four small molds with some of the butter.

3 Put the potato slices in a dish with the rest of the clarified butter. Coat well with the butter. Season with salt and pepper. Mix.
Arrange the slices in a rosette pattern in the bottom of the molds. Make a total of four layers, reversing the direction of the slices in each layer, to fill the molds completely.
Drizzle with the reserved tablespoon of clarified butter.
Bake in the preheated oven for 45 minutes.
Before serving, place the potato cakes on paper towels to soak up excess butter.

TIPS FROM OUR CHEFS

INVERTED ROSETTES
Start the first rosette by overlapping the slices in a clockwise direction. Arrange the following layer in the opposite direction, continuing in this way to the top of the mold.

FIRMLY ATTACHED
For the dish to hold its shape, the slices have to stick to one another well. Flatten each layer by pressing on it before making the next one.

POTATOES MAXIM'S

1 Wash, brush, and peel the potatoes. Cut into cylinders with a cookie cutter (page 519). Slice into very fine rounds with a mandoline slicer. Salt the slices as soon as they are cut to soften them a little.

2 Lay the slices on paper towels and cover with more paper towels to soak up the moisture. Preheat the oven to 210°C – 400°F (gas mark 6–7).
Clarify the butter (page 546). Brush four small molds with clarified butter.
Place the first potato slice in the middle of the mold. Make a single layer of slices, overlapped to form a rosette.

3 Place the last slice over the first to finish the rosette. Season with salt and pepper.
Brush the top of each potato cake with clarified butter. Bake for 15 minutes. Before serving, place the potato cakes on paper towels to soak up any excess butter.

Makes 4 cakes

Preparation time 10 minutes
Cooking time 15 minutes

500 g – 1 pound 2 ounces Belle de Fontenay potatoes
50 g – 1.76 ounces (3 1/2 tablespoons) butter
Fine salt
Freshly ground white pepper

1

2

TIPS FROM OUR CHEFS

AS THIN AS POSSIBLE

The potato slices for potatoes Maxim's are thinner than those needed for potatoes Anna. Overlap the slices more, leaving smaller gaps, so that they stick to each other.

POTATO GNOCCHI WITH POIVRADE ARTICHOKES

Serves 6

Preparation time 30 minutes
Cooking time 50 minutes + 5 minutes

Gnocchi

Kosher (coarse) salt
1.4 kg – 3 pounds 1.4 ounces Mona Lisa potatoes
Freshly grated nutmeg
Fine salt
2 eggs
3 tablespoons olive oil
120 g – 4.23 ounces (1 cup) all-purpose (plain) flour, plus more for dusting the work surface
200 ml – 3/4 cup plus 1 tablespoon white chicken broth or stock

Garnish

1 bunch poivrade artichokes
2 small scallions with their green leaves
400 ml – 1 2/3 cups olive oil, plus more for dressing spinach
1/4 teaspoon fine salt
Freshly ground pepper
50 g – 1.76 ounces (1 2/3 cups) baby spinach

TIPS FROM OUR CHEFS

QUICKLY DOES IT
When mashing the potatoes, work quickly while they are hot, because the potatoes become sticky as they cool. Never use a blender.

VARIATIONS
You can make lemon gnocchi with finely grated lemon zest; black gnocchi with cuttlefish ink; or green gnocchi with blended and strained spinach.

PROPER TEXTURE
Gnocchi dough should be very dry; add the flour gradually so that it incorporates well. The dough should come away from the bowl and form a ball.

TIPS FROM OUR CHEFS

LIKE A PRO
Shape gnocchi with a fork.
Place a ball of dough on the concave side of a fork. Press in the middle with your thumb to make an indentation and to elongate the ball. Push on the dough with your thumb to roll it, then let it fall onto the baking sheet. The dumpling will have a concave side with an indentation, and a convex side with raised ridges left by the fork.

1

Line a baking sheet (tray) with parchment (baking) paper. Reserve 12 g – 1 tablespoon of the kosher salt. Spread the remaining kosher salt over the sheet to a thickness of 1 cm – 3/8 inch. Preheat the oven to 200°C – 400°F (gas mark 6). Wash, brush, and dry the potatoes. Arrange them on top of the salt in a single layer. Bake for 45 minutes. Check that the potatoes are cooked through by piercing with a knife.

2

As soon as the potatoes are cool enough to handle, peel them. Place one in a fine strainer.
Use a bowl scraper (or a pestle or wooden spoon) to press the potato through the mesh. Use only an up-and-down movement, without turning. Repeat with remaining potatoes. Collect the hot mashed potatoes in a bowl. Grate a little nutmeg into the bowl. Season with salt. Break the eggs and separate the whites from the yolks. Add the white of one egg and two yolks to the bowl. Add the olive oil. Gradually sprinkle in the flour while stirring with the bowl scraper (or a wooden spoon).

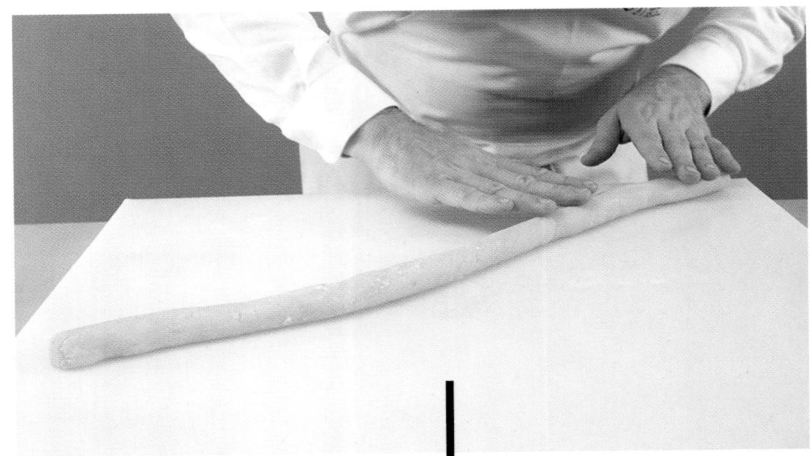

3

Mix the dough well, working the dough quickly from the top down. It will dry out as you add the flour. When the dough is firm enough to roll into a ball, transfer to the work surface. Roll the ball into a cylinder. Cut the cylinder into three pieces. Cover two pieces with a cloth to keep warm. Roll the third piece into a long and even cylinder of dough (about 1.5 cm – 5/8 inch in diameter).

4

Cut into pieces weighing about 12 g – 0.5 ounce each. Line a baking sheet with parchment paper. Dust your hands, particularly your palms, with flour and roll the pieces of dough into small balls. Put them onto the parchment paper.

5

Make an indentation in each one with your thumb. Shape by rolling them over a gnocchi board or pressing on a fork. Dust with flour. Repeat with the remaining two cylinders of dough. In the meantime, bring water to a boil. Add the reserved kosher salt.

6

Slide the gnocchi into the boiling water. If the gnocchi are sticking to the parchment paper, put them in the water with the paper. Take the paper out immediately. The gnocchi should be very lightly poached (1–2 minutes); wait until they float to the surface, then take them out quickly with a skimmer.
Pour the chicken broth into a large skillet or frying pan. Reduce well. Add the gnocchi. Shake the pan gently to coat the gnocchi well in the sauce. Set aside in a warm place.

7

Make the garnish: Prepare the artichokes by removing the largest leaves. Use a vegetable peeler to pare from the stems to the leaves, removing all the green and hard parts (page 516). Use a paring knife to cut off all the leaves by paring the artichokes to a cup shape. Cut off the tops. Slice vertically into six or eight pieces. Peel the scallions. Halve lengthwise.

8

Heat the 400 ml – 1 2/3 cups olive oil in a skillet or frying pan. Add the artichokes and scallions. Lightly brown. Add the salt and a generous amount of pepper (four or five turns of the peppermill). Mix well. Cook for 5 minutes over medium heat. The artichokes and onions should remain crisp. Transfer to a bowl. Serve the gnocchi with the artichoke sauce on plates. Toss the baby spinach leaves with a few drops of olive oil. Season with salt. Arrange over the gnocchi. Serve immediately.

PLAIN RISOTTO

Serves 4

Preparation time 10 minutes
Cooking time 25 minutes

2 liters – 8 1/2 cups chicken broth or stock
30 g – 1.06 ounces (2 tablespoons) butter
40 g – 1.4 ounces (about 1/2 small) white onion
40 g – 1.4 ounces (1/2 cup grated) young (fresco) Parmesan cheese, plus several shavings of cheese
100 g – 3.5 ounces (1/2 cup) whipping cream (for 30 g – 1.06 ounces/1/4 cup whipped cream)
1 tablespoon olive oil
180 g – 6.35 oz (3/4 cup plus 3 tbsp) Arborio rice
Fine salt
80 ml – 1/3 cup dry white wine

TIPS FROM OUR CHEFS

100% WOOD
Always stir risotto with a wooden spoon to avoid breaking the grains.

MEASURES
It is impossible to whip only 30 g – 1.06 ounces (1/4 cup) of whipping cream. You have to whip at least 100 g – 3.5 ounces (1/2 cup) and then use the required amount. Serve the extra cream on the side, or reserve for another use.
Keep the mixing bowl in the refrigerator beforehand or chill for a few minutes in the freezer to make the cream easier to whip.

CORRECTING
If you realize while you are cooking that the broth is too strongly seasoned or salty, finish cooking the risotto with boiling water in place of the broth. This will balance out the flavors.

1. Bring the chicken broth to a boil.
In the meantime, weigh out all the ingredients. Cut the butter into cubes. Peel and chop the onion. Grate the Parmesan (except for the shavings).
Half-whip the cream until slightly velvety.

2. Melt about one third of the butter with the olive oil in a deep skillet or frying pan for 1 minute over low heat. Sauté the onion in the pan for 1 minute, without browning.
Increase the heat to medium, then add the rice (page 556).

3. Season lightly with salt. Stir the rice constantly for 2 minutes to coat well with the fat. The rice should be shiny and translucent.
Moisten with the white wine and let reduce completely.

4. Add enough hot broth to cover the rice. Cook, stirring constantly, for 18 to 20 minutes.
Each time the broth you've added is almost fully absorbed, add additional broth to cover. The rice should always be kept moist.
Check whether the rice is cooked by cutting a grain in half. It should have a small white filament in the center.
Remove from the heat, add the remaining two thirds of the butter, and briskly stir to incorporate.

5. Stir in the grated Parmesan to thicken.
Add 30 g – 1.06 ounces (1/4 cup) of the half-whipped cream and mix well. Taste and adjust the seasoning.
Serve immediately, garnished with the Parmesan shavings and accompanied by the remaining half-whipped cream, if desired. Serve immediately.

1

2

3

4

RISOTTO WITH CRISPY VEGETABLES

RISOTTO WITH CRISPY VEGETABLES

Serves 4

Garnish
Preparation time 15 minutes
Cooking time 1 minute

Risotto
Preparation time 10 minutes
Cooking time 25 minutes

Garnish

1 carrot
1 large button mushroom
1 poivrade artichoke
1 slice lemon
1 tomato
3 tablespoons plus 1 teaspoon olive oil, divided
Fleur de sel
1/2 fennel bulb
1/2 zucchini (courgette)
Leaves of 1 sprig parsley, chopped
3 chive leaves, chopped

Risotto

180 g – 6.35 oz (1 cup) Arborio rice
2 liters – 8 1/2 cups vegetable broth or stock
30 g – 1.06 ounces (2 tablespoons) butter
40 g – 1.4 ounces (about 1/2 small) white onion
40 g – 1.4 ounces (1/2 cup grated) young (*fresco*) Parmesan cheese
100 g – 3.5 ounces (1/2 cup) whipping cream (for 30 g – 1.06 ounces/1/4 cup whipped cream)
3 tablespoons olive oil
Fine salt
80 ml – 1/3 cup dry white wine

2

3

1. Wash all the vegetables in running water. Peel the carrot and mushroom (page 516).

2. Remove the dark outer leaves from the artichoke, leaving only the lighter ones. Peel the artichoke stem with a vegetable peeler and cut the leaves to the level of the heart. Remove the choke. Immerse in cold water together with the lemon slice.

3 Blanch and peel or simply peel the tomato (page 572). Seed and chop the flesh.
Press through a strainer (sieve) and mix the juice with 1 teaspoon olive oil and a little fleur de sel, reserve.

4 Make the risotto: Bring the broth to a boil.
In the meantime, cut the butter into pieces. Peel and chop the onion. Grate the Parmesan. Half-whip the cream (slightly velvety). Melt one third of the butter in a saucepan with 1 tablespoon of olive oil for 1 minute over low heat. Sauté the onion for 1 minute without browning.
Increase the heat to medium, then add the rice.

4

5 Season lightly with salt. Stir the rice constantly for about 2 minutes to coat well with the fat. The rice should be shiny and translucent. Moisten with the white wine and let reduce completely. Add enough hot broth to cover the rice. Cook, stirring constantly, for 18 to 20 minutes. Each time the broth you've added is almost fully absorbed, add additional broth to cover. The rice should always be kept moist.
Check whether the rice is cooked by cutting a grain in half. It should have a small white filament.
Remove from the heat. Briskly incorporate the remaining two thirds of the butter and 2 tablespoons of olive oil. Stir in the Parmesan to thicken. Add 30 g – 1.06 ounces (1/4 cup) of half-whipped cream and mix well. Taste and adjust the seasoning.

6

6 Slice the carrot, mushroom, artichoke heart, fennel, and zucchini with the mandoline slicer.

7 Heat a deep skillet, frying pan, or wok and add the sliced vegetables.
Drizzle with 2 tablespoons of olive oil, season with fleur de sel, and brown the vegetables for 1 minute.
Plate the risotto, arrange the crispy vegetables on top, and sprinkle with chopped parsley and chives.
Drizzle with the tomato juice and the remaining 1 tablespoon olive oil. Serve immediately.

7

TOMATO RISOTTO

Serves 4

Fondue
Preparation time 6 minutes
Cooking time 21 minutes

Risotto
Preparation time 10 minutes
Cooking time 25 minutes

Fondue

1.2 kg – 2 pounds 8 ounces vine tomatoes
1 clove garlic
40 g – 1.4 ounces (about 1/2 small) white onion
4–5 sprigs fresh thyme
1 tablespoon olive oil, plus more for drizzling
Pepper
Fine salt
Sugar
40 g – 1.4 ounces (1/2 cup grated) young (*fresco*) Parmesan cheese

Risotto

2 liters – 8 1/2 cups vegetable broth or stock
30 g – 1.06 ounces
2 tablespoons) butter
40 g – 1.4 ounces (about 1/2 small) white onion
40 g – 1.4 ounces (1/2 cup grated) young (fresco) Parmesan cheese
100 g – 3.5 ounces (1/2 cup) whipping cream (for 30 g – 1.06 ounces/1/4 cup whipped cream)
3 tablespoons olive oil
180 g – 6.35 oz (1 cup) Arborio rice
Fine salt
80 ml – 1/3 cup dry white wine

TIPS FROM OUR CHEFS

COVERED TOMATOES
Cover the tomatoes while they cook. You can use a sheet of parchment (baking) paper placed directly on top of the tomatoes instead of a lid. Remove when their liquid has evaporated.

1

Weigh out all the ingredients.
Make the tomato fondue: Blanch and peel or simply peel the tomatoes (page 521), then seed.

2

Peel and crush the garlic clove (page 523). Peel and chop the onion (page 525). Tie sprigs of thyme together with kitchen twine. Remove and chop a few thyme leaves and reserve. Sauté the onion and garlic for 1 minute in a saucepan with 1 tablespoon of olive oil. Add the tomatoes, thyme bouquet, a little pepper, and a pinch of salt and sugar. Cover the pan and let soften for 30 minutes over low heat, stirring from time to time.

TIPS FROM OUR CHEFS

TOTAL DEDICATION
Once you start cooking the risotto, you have to devote yourself completely to the task and stir without stopping.

GOOD BALANCE
When you are plating a risotto, be sure to use appropriate amounts of rice and garnish. Once you have assembled a plate, you can't undo it.

3

Make the risotto: Bring the broth to a boil. In the meantime, cut the butter into pieces. Peel and chop the onion. Grate 80 g – 2.82 ounces (1 cup grated) of Parmesan (for both the risotto and garnish). Sift half to reduce to a very fine powder (for the garnish).

4

Half-whip the cream (slightly velvety). Melt one third of the butter in a deep skillet or frying pan with 1 tablespoon of olive oil for 1 minute over low heat. Sauté the onion for 1 minute without browning. Increase the heat to medium, then add the rice. Season lightly with salt. Stir the rice constantly for about 2 minutes to coat well with the fat. The rice should be shiny and translucent.

5

Moisten with the white wine and let reduce completely. Add enough hot broth to cover the rice. Cook, stirring constantly, for 18 to 20 minutes. Each time the broth you've added is almost fully absorbed, add additional broth to cover. The rice should always be kept moist. Check whether the rice is cooked by cutting a grain in half. It should have a small white filament. Remove from heat. Briskly incorporate the remaining two thirds of the butter and 2 tablespoons of olive oil. Stir in the unsifted Parmesan to thicken. Add 30 g – 1.06 ounces (1/4 cup) of half-whipped cream and mix well. Taste and adjust the seasoning.

6

Make Parmesan tuiles with the sifted Parmesan (page 555). Plate the risotto, alternating the tomato fondue, rice, and tomato fondue. Drizzle with olive oil. Garnish with reserved chopped thyme and Parmesan tuiles. Serve immediately.

SQUASH RISOTTO WITH CRISPY BACON

Serves 4

Risotto
Preparation time 10 minutes
Cooking time 25 minutes

Garnish
Preparation time 10 minutes
Cooking time 15 minutes + 4 minutes

Risotto

2 liters – 8 1/2 cups vegetable broth or stock
30 g – 1.06 ounces (2 tablespoons) butter
40 g – 1.4 ounces (1/2 cup grated) young (fresco) Parmesan cheese
40 g – 1.4 ounces (about 1/2 small) white onion
Fine salt
6 tablespoons olive oil
180 g – 6.35 oz (1 cup) Arborio rice
80 ml – 1/3 cup dry white wine
Freshly ground pepper

Garnish

250 g – 9 ounces winter squash
8 thin slices bacon
1 tablespoon olive oil
Leaves of 1 sprig fresh thyme
1 clove garlic
Meat jus or vinegar

TIPS FROM OUR CHEFS

VARIATION

You can replace the bacon with cured duck breast (magret) or cured ham. You can also replace the squash with diced tomatoes mixed with tomato paste, artichokes, or button mushrooms.

REDUCTION

Reducing the wine completely enhances the acidity of the dish while preserving the flavor. Of course, you can also use red wine, or even Champagne.

1

Preheat the oven to 190°C – 375°F (gas mark 5) and grease a baking sheet (tray) with oil. Bring the broth to a boil. In the meantime, cut the butter into pieces. Grate the Parmesan. Peel and chop the onion. Slice each half lengthwise without cutting through the root, then make three horizontal cuts. Finish chopping by slicing across (page 525).

2

Make the garnish:
Peel the squash with a vegetable peeler. Then slice vertically.
Cut each slice into batons, then dice. Set aside 50 g – 1.76 ounces (1/3 cup) for garnish.

3

Continue with the risotto: Melt one third of the butter in a deep skillet or frying pan with 1 tablespoon of olive oil for 1 minute over low heat. Sauté the onion for 1 minute without browning.
Add the diced squash and brown for 1 minute. Mix to coat the squash in the fat. Increase the heat to medium and add the rice. Season lightly with salt.
Stir the rice constantly for about 2 minutes to coat well with the fat. The rice should be shiny and translucent. Moisten with the white wine and let reduce completely.

4

Continue with the garnish: Lay the bacon slices on the prepared baking sheet and bake in the preheated oven for 15 minutes.

5

Finish the risotto: Meanwhile, add enough hot broth to the skillet to cover the rice. Cook, stirring constantly, for 18 to 20 minutes. Each time the broth you've added is almost fully absorbed, add additional broth to cover. The rice should always be kept moist. Check whether the rice is cooked by cutting a grain in half. It should have a small white filament.
Remove from heat, add the remaining two thirds of the butter, and briskly incorporate. Add the remaining 1/4 cup plus 1 tablespoon olive oil. Stir in the Parmesan well to thicken. Taste and adjust the seasoning.

6

Take the bacon out of the oven. It should be very crispy.
Lay the bacon on paper towels. Take the diced squash previously set aside and pan-fry for 4 minutes in 1 tablespoon of olive oil with the thyme and the crushed unpeeled garlic clove.
Use a spoon to plate the risotto. Sprinkle pan-fried squash over the top. Decorate with crispy bacon. Drizzle with a little meat jus or vinegar. Serve immediately.

VEGETARIAN COUSCOUS

Serves 4

Vegetables
Preparation time 30 minutes
Cooking time 20 minutes

Plain couscous
Preparation time 6 minutes
Cooking time 10 minutes
Resting time 20 minutes

Vegetables

1 yellow bell pepper
2 young carrots
4 young turnips
1 fennel bulb
1 celery heart
4 large button mushrooms
1 zucchini (courgette)
2 tomatoes
100 g – 3.5 ounces flat (runner) beans
4 scallions (spring onions)
100 g – 3.5 ounces green beans
2 tablespoons olive oil, plus more for drizzling
Grated zest of 1/2 organic, unwaxed lemon
2 cloves young garlic unpeeled
500 ml – 2 cups vegetable broth (page 549)
100 g – 3.5 ounces (2/3 cup) shelled petits pois young peas
100 g – 3.5 ounces (2/3 cup) shelled and peeled fava beans (broad beans)
60 g – 2.12 ounces (1/3 cup) cooked chickpeas
3 sprigs cilantro (coriander)
Salt
Fleur de sel

Plain couscous

400 g – 14 ounces (2 1/3 cups) fine- or medium-grain couscous
4 g – 0.14 ounces (2/3 teaspoon) salt
60 ml – 1/4 cup olive oil
500 ml – 2 cups vegetable broth (page 549)

TIPS FROM OUR CHEFS

NO LID
Never cover vegetables cooking in a liquid—they will turn gray.

WINTER VERSION
This spring couscous can also be made in winter using vegetables in season then, such as squash, cardoons, and Chinese artichokes (crosnes). Use your imagination, and remember to adjust the cooking times accordingly.

1

Slice off the top and bottom of the bell pepper. Stand upright on a cutting board and cut along the ribs to separate the pieces.
Remove the core, seeds, and membrane. Peel the lobes with a vegetable peeler (page 513). Cut into even rectangles, then halve each piece along the diagonal.
Peel the carrots. Cut diagonally into 2-cm – 3/4-inch slices.

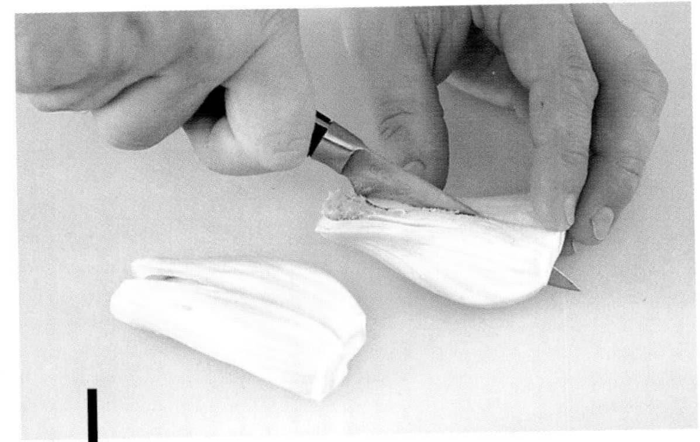

2

Trim the turnip tops, keeping only 1 cm – 3/8 inch. Peel the turnips by paring around them with a paring knife. Cut the turnips in half.
Remove the outer layer from the fennel bulb. Quarter the fennel, then remove the core with tip of a knife (page 515).

3

Do the same with the celery heart.
Cut off the bottoms of the mushroom stems. Peel the caps with a paring knife, starting from the base (page 516). Quarter the mushrooms.
Slice off the top and bottom ends of the zucchini. Halve, then remove the core by cutting along the four sides around it (page 522). Cut these slices in half along the diagonal.

TIPS FROM OUR CHEFS

UNIFORM PIECES
For consistent cooking to a tender-crisp stage, the vegetables must be cut in equal-sized pieces.

ZUCCHINI CORE
When you cut the zucchini (courgette) into rectangles, you will be left with the core; don't throw it away. If it doesn't contain too many seeds, you can cut it into cubes and use them in a ratatouille or to thicken a vegetable soup.

4

Remove the stems (stalks) from the tomatoes. Cut each into 12 sections (segments). Peel by passing the blade of a paring knife between the skin and flesh (page 521). Seed. Cut the flat beans diagonally into 4 equal pieces. Chop the scallions. Trim the green beans. Blanch the flat and green beans for 1 minute in boiling salted water (page 551). Immediately plunge into ice water.

5

Prepare and steam the couscous (page 552) with the salt, olive oil, and vegetable broth. Cover with plastic wrap (cling film) to keep warm.

6

Continue with the vegetables: Heat 2 tablespoons of olive oil in a stockpot over high heat. Add the bell pepper, carrot, turnip, fennel, and celery, followed by the lemon zest. Add the salt to retain the color of the vegetables.

7

Then add the mushroom, zucchini, and tomato, along with the unpeeled garlic cloves. Season with salt. Sauté for 5 minutes over medium heat. Add the broth, bring to a boil, and cook for 10 minutes over medium heat.
Add the scallions and peas. Bring back to a boil, then cook for 2 minutes. Add the fava beans and chickpeas. Bring back to a boil, then cook for 2 minutes. Add the flat and green beans. Cook for 3 minutes. Remove from heat. Rinse, dry, and pluck the cilantro. Add the leaves. Drizzle the vegetables with olive oil and season with fleur de sel. Accompany with the couscous.

ARTICHOKE TIANS

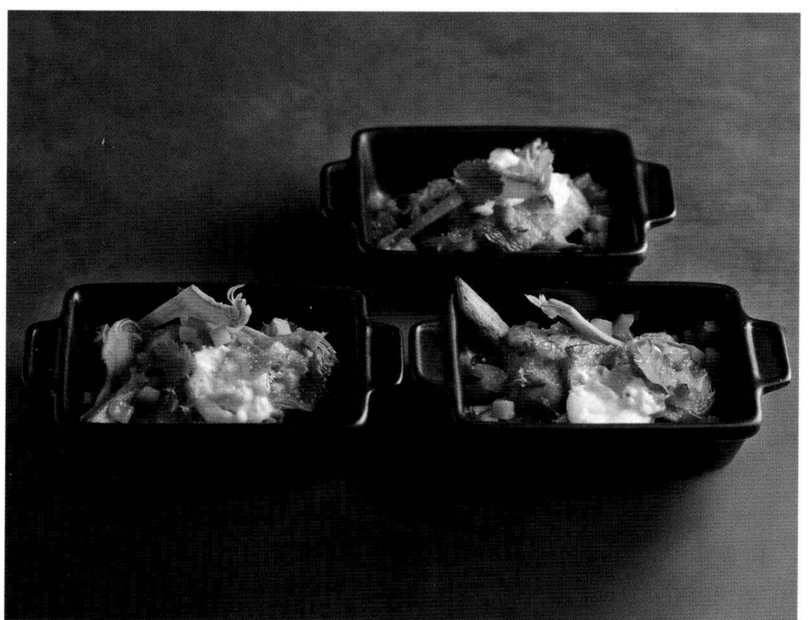

Makes 4 tians

Preparation time 15 minutes
Cooking time 18 minutes +
5 minutes

1 lemon
9 poivrade artichokes
Fine salt
1 carrot
1 red onion
White pepper
12 slices bacon
1 clove garlic unpeeled
30 ml – 2 tablespoons white wine
250 ml – 1 cup chicken broth or stock
1/4 cup mascarpone cheese
30 g – 1.06 ounces (1/3 cup grated) Parmesan cheese
2 sprigs cilantro (coriander)
Fleur de sel

TIPS FROM OUR CHEFS

KEEP THE COLOR
Brown the cut sides of the artichokes first to preserve their color.

1 Quarter the lemon. Squeeze two of the quarters into a bowl containing cold water and then add the squeezed quarters to the bowl. Set aside the remaining half.
Remove the three first rows of leaves from one artichoke by pulling them downward while pressing on the base with your thumb (page 516).

2 Cut off the stem 2 cm – 3/4 inch from the bottom of the artichoke with a paring knife. Peel the stem. Use a vegetable peeler to remove the few remaining small threads. Immerse in the water with lemon juice. Repeat with remaining artichokes.
Remove the green covering of the remaining attached stems and the base of each artichoke with a vegetable peeler, peeling upward from the bottom. Cut off the top two thirds of the leaves (this part is bitter).
Repeat with remaining artichokes.
Immerse the artichokes one by one in the water with lemon as you finish them. Repeat with remaining artichokes.

3 Peel the carrot. Use a chef's knife to cut into batons, then dice (brunoise). Peel the onion, halve, and chop (brunoise).

4 Drain eight artichokes and pat dry with paper towels. Cut them in half. Cut the stems into 2-mm – 1/16-inch slices.

5 Heat 1 tablespoon of olive oil in a deep, wide skillet or frying pan. Add the artichokes halves. Brown for 1 minute 30 seconds over medium heat. Add a light sprinkling of salt and season with white pepper.
Turn over. Add the bacon and cook for 1 minute 30 seconds. Add the diced carrot and onion, the unpeeled garlic clove, and the artichoke stems.
Cook for 2 minutes over low heat while stirring constantly. Moisten with the white wine and let reduce completely. Add the chicken broth, then bring to a boil. Cover the pan and cook for 13 minutes over medium heat. Check that the artichokes are cooked through by piercing with the tip of a knife. Remove the garlic clove from the pan.
Preheat the oven to 230°C – 450°F (gas mark 8). Line each of four individual baking dishes with three slices of bacon. Top with some of the vegetable mixture. Add 1 tablespoon of mascarpone cheese to each. Place four artichoke halves in each dish.
Distribute the rest of the vegetables in the baking dishes. Grate the Parmesan and sprinkle over the dishes. Bake in the preheated oven for 5 minutes.
In the meantime, drain the last artichoke. Cut in half and thinly slice with a mandoline slicer. Squeeze 1 tablespoon of lemon juice from the remaining lemon quarters and whisk with the remaining 1 tablespoon olive oil. Dress the sliced artichokes with this mixture. Wash and dry the cilantro. Pluck the leaves over the artichoke slices, reserving a few for garnish. Season with fleur de sel and white pepper.
Garnish the tians with the artichoke slices.
Sprinkle with reserved cilantro and serve.

1

3

4

TIPS FROM OUR CHEFS

STAINING

Artichokes have an annoying tendency to blacken your fingers when peeled due to oxidation, so rub your fingers with lemon juice or wear gloves when peeling them. You soak the artichoke hearts in water with lemon juice for the same reason.

SALMON NIGIRI SUSHI

Makes 8 pieces

Preparation time 20 minutes

1 (160-g – 5.64-ounce) fillet smoked salmon
Wasabi (page 558)
160 g – 5.64 ounces vinegared rice (page 559)

TIPS FROM OUR CHEFS

NO COOKING
Don't keep your fingers on the fish for too long; the warmth of your hands will begin to "cook" it.

AERATE
Don't press the fish too hard against the rice—you want the dimple you made to remain intact and aerate the rice so it stays soft.

STORAGE
Never store sushi in the refrigerator. The rice grains will harden and lose their flavor.

1 Prepare the salmon fillet by trimming to a width of about 4 fingers on a cutting board.
Use a very sharp and wet knife to cut the salmon on the diagonal into eight very thin slices weighing about 25 g – 0.88 ounce each, cutting from left to right (page 540).

2 Prepare the wasabi and rice, a bowl of water, and a small, very clean, damp towel.
Wet the fingertips of one hand. Make light circular movements with your wet fingertips to moisten the entire surface of that palm.
Place a slice of salmon over the fingers of your other hand. Use the tip of your index finger to spread a little wasabi over the middle of the salmon.

3 Make a 20-g – 0.75-ounce rice ball (page 560) and place it on top of the slice of salmon.

4 Wet your fingers again, wiping off excess water on the towel.
Use your index finger to make a dimple in the middle of the rice ball. Gently spread the rest of the rice over the surface of the salmon.

5 Press the salmon against the rice using your thumb and middle finger. Holding the nigiri firmly, turn it over. Position it on your fingers.

6 Press delicately against the sides, pressing the nigiri into the correct shape with your thumb and your fingertips, if necessary.
Repeat with the remaining slices of salmon and rice.

1

2

3

4

5

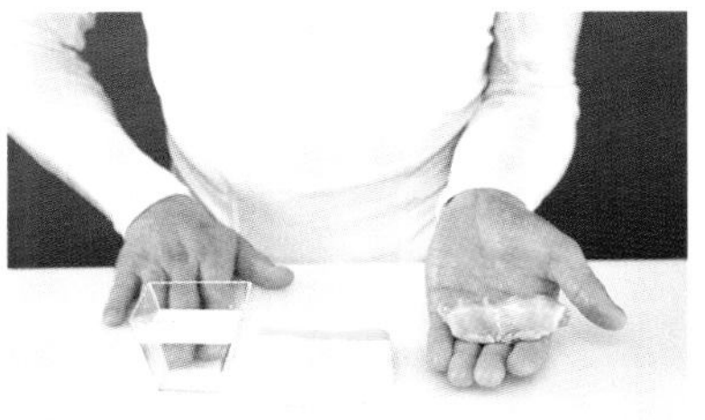

SHRIMP NIGIRI SUSHI

Makes 8 pieces

Preparation time 30 minutes
Cooking time 5 minutes

EQUIPMENT

8 short bamboo skewers

8 medium jumbo shrimp (tiger prawn) tails (size 21/25)
Wasabi (page 558)
160 g – 5.64 ounces vinegared rice (page 559)

TIPS FROM OUR CHEFS

TAKE YOUR TIME
Wait until the cooked shrimp cool before taking out the skewers so that the shrimp don't curl up again.

A USEFUL TIP
Because the shrimp and rice do not stick to each other easily, dry the shrimp thoroughly after cooking.

JUMBO SHRIMP
Crustaceans such as shrimp are a symbol of longevity in Japan. Shrimp cook in an instant, which is why they are scalded here but not boiled. Overcooked shrimp are bland and rubbery.

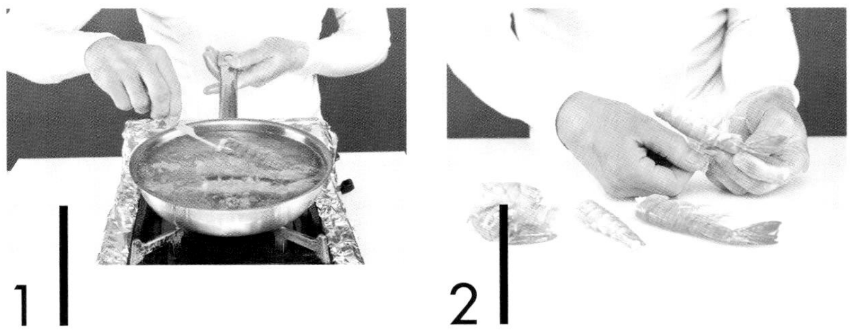

1 2

3

4

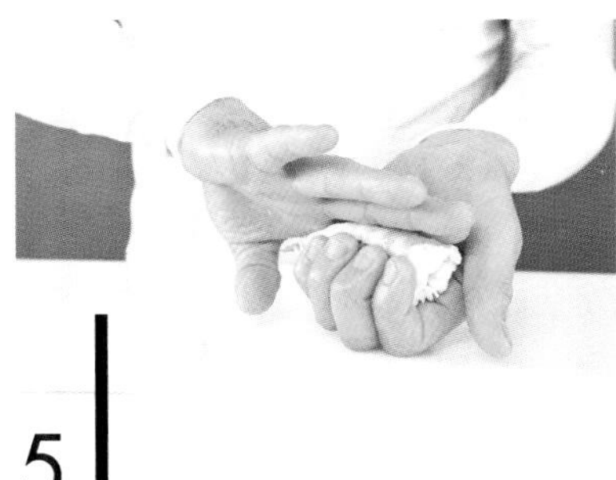

5

1 Lay out the shrimp, skewers, and a saucepan on the work surface. Insert a skewer down the back of each shrimp tail to keep it straight. Fill the pan with water. Bring to a boil. Don't add salt. Add all the shrimp at the same time, then turn off the heat. Let the shrimp cook for 2–3 minutes.

2 Remove the shrimp from the water. Let cool. Remove the skewers. Peel the tails completely, removing the tail fins (page 541). Prepare the wasabi and rice.

3 Butterfly the shrimp by cutting down the middle with a very sharp knife and opening (like a book) without cutting all the way through.

4 If the shrimp are not completely clean, devein them. Prepare a bowl of water and a small, very clean, damp towel. Wet the fingertips of one hand.
Use the tip of your index finger to place a little wasabi in the middle of a shrimp.

5 With your wet fingertips, make a 20-g – 0.75 ounce rice ball (page 560) and place it over the shrimp. Use your index finger to make a dimple in the middle of the rice ball. Turn the nigiri over and press on it lightly with your thumb. Hold it in your palm. Press lightly with the index finger of your other hand.

6 Press on the sides of the nigiri with your thumb and middle finger. Turn it around. Lightly press the rice into shape. Press again gently, holding the nigiri with your thumb and your fingertips to maintain the shape, if necessary. This will give your nigiri an elegant shape. Repeat with the remaining seven shrimp and rice.

AVOCADO MOUSSE WITH CRAYFISH

Serves 6

Preparation time 20 minutes
Cooking time 17 minutes
Resting time 1 hour

EQUIPMENT

Funnel
Siphon
Gas chargers

2 (about 225-g – 8-ounce) avocados
150 ml – 2/3 cup milk
1/4 teaspoon fine salt, plus more for seasoning
Freshly ground pepper
100 ml – 1/3 cup plus 1 tablespoon plus 1 teaspoon light (single) cream
20 g – 0.70 ounce (1 tablespoon) pine nuts
1 red bell pepper
1 tablespoon olive oil, plus more for drizzling
2 scallions (spring onions)
100 g – 3.5 ounces (18 pieces) cooked crayfish, shelled but left whole
1 lime
Fleur de sel

1 Preheat the oven to 220°C – 425°F (gas mark 7). Cut the avocados and remove the pits (stones). Scoop out the flesh with a soupspoon. Put the flesh in the jar of a blender. Add the milk. Blend to a puree. Pass the puree through a strainer (sieve), pressing down firmly with a silicone spatula (scraper). Add the 1/4 teaspoon salt and a generous amount of pepper (five or six turns of the peppermill). Add the cream and mix gently.

2 Use a funnel to transfer the mixture to the siphon. Insert a gas charger and screw halfway into the port on the lid of the siphon. Screw it in fully. Insert a second charger. Shake the siphon two or three times. Rest for at least 1 hour in the refrigerator.

3 Spread out the pine nuts on a baking sheet (tray). Toast in the preheated oven for 1 minute 30 seconds. Let cool.

4 Cut the top off the bell pepper. Cut along the grooves. Remove the seeds and white ribs. Cut into strips, then into small dice (page 513). Heat 1 tablespoon of olive oil in a small copper saucepan over medium heat. Add the diced pepper. Season with salt and pepper. Add 50 ml – 3 tablespoons plus 1 1/2 teaspoons of water. Cover. Cook for 15 minutes.

5 Thinly slice the scallions. Combine with the crayfish. Squeeze the lime juice over the top.
Drizzle with olive oil, and season with a pinch of fleur de sel and two turns of the peppermill. Mix.

6 Transfer the diced bell pepper to a fine strainer over a bowl. Press well with the back of the spoon. Let cool. Pipe the avocado mousse on the bottom of 6 individual serving dishes. Add 1 tablespoon of red bell pepper coulis to each. Arrange three crayfish and some of the scallions in each dish. Garnish with the pine nuts. Serve immediately.

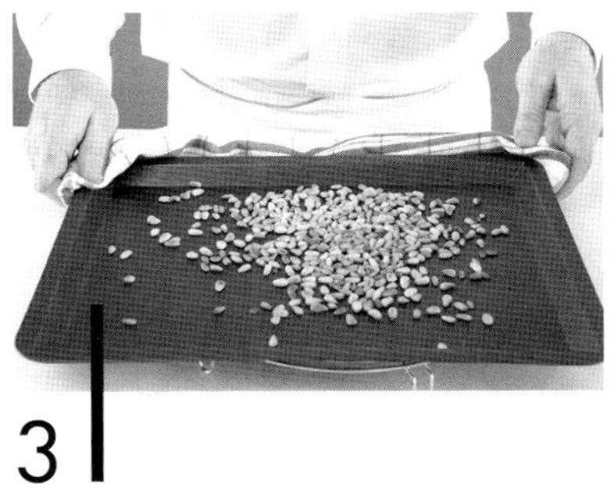

3

4

5

TIPS FROM OUR CHEFS

CHARGERS ON HAND
For best results, use two chargers and a large siphon, though you may be able to get away with one charger, depending on the size of your siphon. It's always a good idea to have a few extra chargers on hand.

A WORD OF ADVICE
Never whip cream before putting it in a siphon. Just mix it gently with a whisk.

DECONSTRUCTED RICE WITH MUSSELS AND SAFFRON SAUCE

Serves 4

Preparation time 45 minutes
Cooking time 30 minutes

EQUIPMENT

Funnel
Siphon
Gas chargers

3 small shallots
10 g – 0.35 ounce (3/4 tablespoon) butter
Fine salt
150 g – 5.29 oz (3/4 cup) Camargue rice
1.5 kg – 3 pounds 4 ounces Bouchot mussels
2 tablespoons olive oil
300 ml – 1 1/4 cups white wine
1 tablespoon pastis
Freshly ground pepper
400 ml – 1 2/3 cups whole milk
1 fennel bulb
100 ml – 1/3 cup plus 1 tablespoon plus 1 teaspoon light (single) cream
2 g – 0.07 ounce (1 teaspoon) saffron powder

TIPS FROM OUR CHEFS

PREPARATION
Before cooking the rice, measure it out, then add one-and-a-half times its volume in water.

THE RIGHT TEMPERATURE
If you serve this dish cold, the rice will become crunchy. To prevent this, cover the rice with plastic wrap (cling film) and keep the siphon in a bain-marie at 75°C – 165°F until plating.

1

Peel 2 shallots. Slice vertically, then horizontally, and finely dice (page 525).
Melt the butter in a saucepan. Add the shallots and sauté for 2 minutes. Add the rice; add two pinches of salt. Stir until the rice becomes translucent. Add 375 ml – 1 1/2 cups of water (or one and a half times the volume of the rice: see note). Bring to a boil. Cover. Cook for 18 minutes over medium heat.

2

In the meantime, peel the remaining shallot and slice. Scrape the mussels. Wash in abundant water. Discard any open ones. Heat 1 tablespoon of oil in a stockpot. Add the sliced shallot and stir for several seconds. Add the mussels. Pour in the white wine. Cover. Cook over high heat. Stir after 1 minute 30 seconds. Cook, covered, for another 1 minute 30 seconds. As the mussels open, transfer to a colander placed over a bowl. Let drain. Set aside their cooking liquid.

3

When the rice is cooked, stir gently. Take out 120 g – 4.23 ounces (1/2 cup) rice and set aside. Add the pastis to the remaining rice and mix well. Season with pepper. Cover with plastic wrap (cling film).
Put the 120 g – 4.23 ounces (1/2 cup) of rice into a saucepan with the milk. Cook for 5 minutes over low heat. Remove the mussels from their shells. Discard any that remain closed.

4

Remove the outer layer from the fennel bulb. Cut off the stems and leaves, reserving a few fennel fronds. Halve the bulb (page 515).
Cut the fennel into thin slices, then dice (brunoise). Heat 1 tablespoon of oil in a saucepan. Add the diced fennel. Season with salt and pepper. Cook for 5 minutes over low heat.

5

Transfer the rice cooked with the milk to a blender. Blend. Add the light cream. Blend again. Pass through a fine strainer (sieve), pressing with a small ladle.

6

Toss the fennel with the mussels. Sprinkle the reserved fennel fronds over the top. Season with pepper. Use a funnel to transfer the rice puree to a siphon. Screw on the lid, then insert two gas chargers. Shake the siphon. Keep warm.

7

Line a strainer with paper towels. Strain the cooking liquid from the mussels. Heat the liquid. When it comes to a boil, add the saffron. Mix. Make a bed of pastis rice in each of the serving dishes. Pipe a thin layer of rice cream on top. Add 2 tablespoons of mussels with fennel to each dish, then cover with the remaining rice cream. Pour a little of the saffron sauce into the dishes, then transfer the rest of the saffron sauce to individual glass pitchers. Serve immediately.

SARDINE TIAN WITH MINT PESTO

Serves 4

Preparation time 35 minutes
Cooking time 30 minutes
Resting time 1 hour

EQUIPMENT

Dutch oven or flameproof casserole dish

10 (35-g – 1.23-ounce) sardines
3 sprigs mint
1 lemon
1/2 cup plus 1 tablespoon olive oil, divided
Fine salt
White pepper
2 eggplants (aubergines)
2 red bell peppers
2 onions
1 clove garlic
25 g – 0.88 ounce (1/2 cup) fresh breadcrumbs
Mint pesto (page 604)

1 Scale the sardines by rubbing gently under cold running water. Use a filleting knife to cut off the head under the gills, and slice along the backbones. Detach the fillets.

2 Turn the sardines over and remove the bones by sliding the knife from the tail toward the head. Dry the fillets on paper towels. Transfer to a plate. Rinse the three sprigs of mint, pat dry, and pluck the leaves. Gather the leaves into small bunches and chop them with a chef's knife. Squeeze the lemon into a bowl. Pour half of the lemon juice and 2 tablespoons of olive oil into a dish. Season with salt and pepper and add half of the mint. Arrange the sardine fillets head-to-tail in the dish, skin side up. Drizzle with the rest of the lemon juice and an additional 2 tablespoons of olive oil. Season with salt and pepper. Sprinkle the rest of the mint over the top. Cover with plastic wrap (cling film) and marinate in the refrigerator for at least 1 hour.

3 Wash and slice off the top and bottom ends of the eggplants. Use a vegetable peeler to remove alternating bands of skin. Use a chef's knife to cut the eggplants in half lengthwise, then cut the halves into rounds 4–5 mm – 1/8 inch thick.

4 Wash and halve the bell peppers. Remove the stems, seeds, and membranes. Cut each piece in half. Lay the pieces flat and peel with a vegetable peeler (page 513). Cut into 5-mm – 1/4-inch slices with a chef's knife.

5 Peel and halve the onions. Cut off the roots. Thinly slice (page 525). Peel the garlic clove, cut in half, and remove the green core. Preheat the oven to 230°C – 425°F (gas mark 8) in a static (conventional) oven. Heat 3 tablespoons of olive oil in the Dutch oven or casserole dish. Brown the bell peppers and onions over high heat. Add the eggplant, garlic clove, and 2 tablespoons of oil. Stir well. Season with salt and pepper, and mix. Clean the sides of the dish with a wet brush. Let cook for 15 minutes over medium heat, stirring from time to time.

6 Spread out the vegetables in an ovenproof dish. Sprinkle with breadcrumbs. Bake for 15 minutes.
Make the mint pesto (page 548). Take the dish out of the oven. Arrange the sardine fillets head-to-tail in the dish over the vegetables, skin side up. Accompany with the pesto.

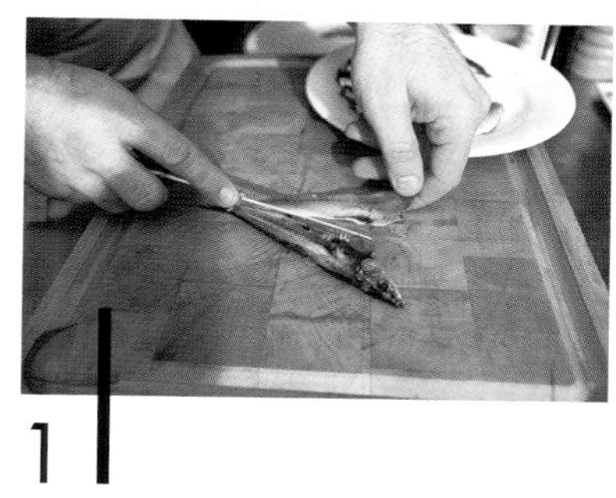

1

4

6

FISH STEW WITH SAFFRON COUSCOUS

Serves 4

Preparation time 30 minutes
Cooking time 35 minutes
Resting time 20 minutes

EQUIPMENT

Couscoussier

Fish

500 g – 1 pound 2 ounces scorpion fish or Atlantic perch fillets
400 g – 14 ounces monkfish fillets
300 g – 10.5 ounces sea robin (gurnard) fillets
Fillets from **1** (500-g – 1 pound 2-ounce) sea bass
2 tomatoes
2 zucchini (courgettes)
1 white onion
30 g – 1.06 ounces (about 1/4 cup plus 1 tablespoon) fresh ginger
1 clove garlic
3 tablespoons olive oil, divided
Salt
600 ml – 2 1/2 cups fish stock
2 teaspoons cumin
1 teaspoon saffron threads
Fleur de sel
120 g – 4.23 ounces (3/4 cup) cooked chickpeas

Saffron couscous

400 g – 14 ounces (2 1/3 cups) fine- or medium-grain couscous
4 g – 0.14 ounce (2/3 teaspoon) salt
60 ml – 1/4 cup olive oil
500 ml – 2 cups fish stock
0.5 g – 0.02 ounce (1/4 teaspoon) saffron powder

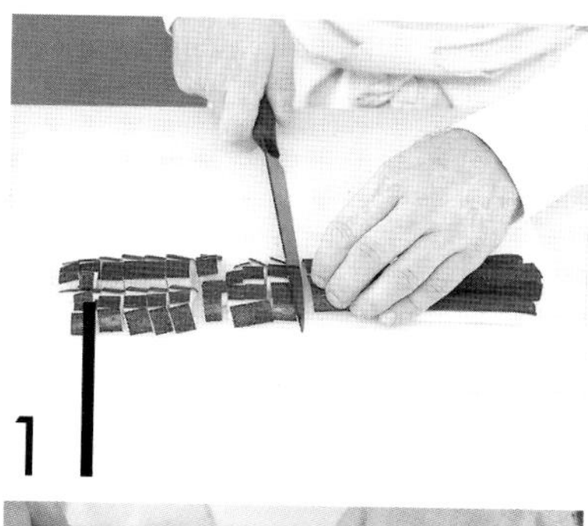

1

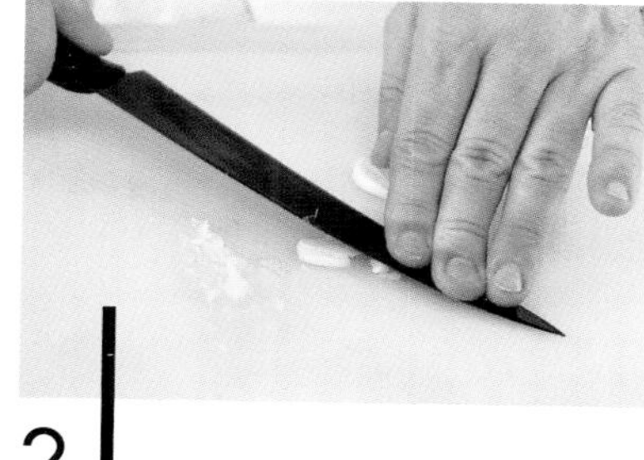

2

3

4

5

1 Cut each fillet into four pieces of equal size. Wash all the vegetables. Remove the stems (stalks) from the tomatoes. Cut each into eight sections (segments). Peel with a knife (page 521) Seed. Cut off the top and bottom ends of the zucchini. Halve, then seed by cutting around the four sides of the core (page 522). Cut the slices into batons, and then a 1-cm – 3/8-inch dice.

2 Peel and thinly slice the onion (page 525). Peel the ginger and cut into 2-mm – 1/16-inch slices (julienne). Peel the garlic and remove the green core. Crush to a puree with the flat side of a knife (page 523).

3 Heat 2 tablespoons of olive oil in a stockpot over medium heat. Add the onion, ginger, and garlic, and sauté for 1 minute. Add the tomatoes and a pinch of salt. Let soften for 15 minutes. In the meantime, heat 1 tablespoon of olive in a skillet or frying pan over high heat. Sear the zucchini and season with salt. Brown for 3 minutes. Pour the fish stock into the stockpot, bring to a boil, and cook for 10 minutes over low heat.

4 In the meantime, generously sprinkle the skin side of the fish fillets with cumin. Sprinkle uniformly with the saffron. Sprinkle with two pinches of fleur de sel. Add the zucchini and chickpeas to the stockpot. Bring to a boil, then gently immerse the fish fillets in it. Bring back to a boil. Reduce the heat and cook for 3 minutes.

5 Prepare the saffron couscous without cooking (page 552). Transfer the accompaniment to the couscoussier pot. Put the couscous into the steamer and place over the pot at a boil. Cover the couscoussier and cook for 10 minutes.

TIPS FROM OUR CHEFS

THE VIRTUES OF SALT

When salted vegetables begin to cook, their residual water is released. This enables them to soften without browning (sometimes called sweating).

DELICATE SEA BASS

The sea bass is the most delicate of the fish used. Immerse the pieces of sea bass in the sauce last, because they will need less time to cook.

COUSCOUSSIER

If you don't have a couscoussier, line a steamer basket with wet cheesecloth (muslin) to stop the couscous grains from falling through the holes. You should at least double the cooking time.

SCALLOP AND FENNEL TIAN

Serves 2

Preparation time 20 minutes
Resting time 30 minutes +
2 minutes

EQUIPMENT
Mandoline slicer
2 bamboo stewers

2 fennel bulbs
1 small onion
1 organic, unwaxed lemon
1 vanilla bean (pod)
1 tablespoon olive oil, plus more for brushing, drizzling, and sautéing
Salt
White pepper
80 ml – 1/3 cup chicken broth or stock
2 tablespoons light (single) cream
4 large sea scallops, only meat
Almond meal (ground almonds)

1 Wash the fennel bulbs, halve, and use a paring knife to remove the cores (page 515). Cut three bulb halves into slices 2–3 mm- – 1/8 inch thick with a chef's knife. Set aside the fourth half. Peel and halve the onion, and cut off the roots. Slice each half. Wash and dry the lemon. Use a vegetable peeler to pare around the fruit, taking off the zest without removing any of the white pith (page 514). Cut the zest into fine strips (julienne).

2 Halve the vanilla bean lengthwise and scrape out the seeds. Heat 1 tablespoon of oil in a saucepan. Add the sliced fennel, onion, lemon zest, and vanilla bean and seeds. Season with salt and white pepper, and let soften for 13 minutes over medium heat. Moisten with the chicken broth and stir. Cover the pan and cook for 10 minutes over low heat, stirring from time to time. In the meantime, slice the remaining half fennel bulb with a mandoline slicer over a bowl filled with ice water.

3 Preheat the oven to 230°C – 425°F (gas mark 6–7) in a static (conventional) oven. Remove the vanilla bean from the pan, cut each half in half again, and set aside. Add the cream and mix. Brush the two round dishes with oil. Distribute the cooked vegetables into the dishes and bake for 15 minutes.

1

2

3

4 In the meantime, remove and discard the small white muscles (adductor muscles) from the scallops. Rinse the scallops and pat dry with paper towels.
Spread the almond meal on a plate and dredge both sides of the scallops.

5 Drain the fennel slices, then dry, put in a bowl, and drizzle with olive oil. Squeeze 1 tablespoon of lemon juice and add to the fennel. Season with salt and pepper. Mix well.

6 Heat a little oil in a skillet or frying pan. Brown the scallops over medium heat, 1 minute per side.
Cut the scallops in half horizontally. Thread four scallop halves on a skewer, then remove the skewer. Replace the skewer with a vanilla bean quarter. Repeat with remaining scallop halves and vanilla bean pieces.
Place the skewered scallops on the tians and serve with the fennel slices.

4

5

COD TIAN WITH SPINACH AND POTATO

Serves 4

Preparation time 1 hour
Cooking time 50 minutes
Resting time 30 minutes

EQUIPMENT

Ring mold

Kosher (coarse) salt
600 g – 1 lb 5 oz cod loin
1 clove garlic
2 teaspoons olive oil, divided, plus more for brushing and drizzling
2 tomatoes
600 g – 1 pound 5 ounces potatoes
250 ml – 1 cup chicken broth or stock
Fine salt
200 g – 7 ounces (7 cups) spinach
White pepper
3 tablespoons light (single) cream
1 egg
Ground Espelette pepper

2

1 Sprinkle the bottom of a dish with kosher salt, lay the fish over it, and cover with kosher salt. Roll the fish a little to cover the sides with salt. Cover with plastic wrap (cling film) and refrigerate for 30 minutes.

2 Peel the garlic clove, cut in half, and remove the green core. Rub the inside of an ovenproof dish with one half of the garlic clove. Grease the dish by brushing with oil. Wash the tomatoes, halve, and remove the stems (stalks). Thinly slice each half.

3

3 Wash and peel the potatoes. Cut into 2-mm – 1/16-inch round slices with a chef's knife (page 518). Put into a deep skillet or frying pan. Add the chicken broth, season with salt, and drizzle with olive oil. Bring to a boil and cook for 3 minutes. Transfer the potato slices and cooking liquid to a dish.

4 Fold the spinach leaves in half and remove the stems and ribs. Immerse in water and stir gently. Change the water and repeat the process until the leaves are free of any soil. Drain (page 520).

4

5 Heat 1 teaspoon of oil in a stockpot and wilt the spinach for 2 minutes over medium-high heat, stirring with the other half garlic clove on the end of a fork. Season with salt and white pepper. Add the cream and mix. Reserve. Break the egg into a bowl. Beat with a fork, pour over the spinach, and spread using the back of the fork. Preheat the oven to 180°C – 350°F (gas mark 4) in a static (conventional) oven. Rinse the cod under cold running water. Transfer to a plate. Heat 1 teaspoon of olive oil in a skillet or frying pan. Brown the fish on one side for 2 minutes over medium heat. Turn with a wide spatula (slotted turner) and brown the other side for 2 minutes.

6 Transfer the fish to a dish. Using a spoon, gently detach the sections. Make a layer of potato slices, then spread the spinach evenly over them. Alternate a row of tomato slices with a row of cod. Drizzle with the potato cooking liquid. Season each row with a pinch of Espelette pepper. Place on the bottom shelf of the preheated oven and bake for 40 minutes. Take the tian out of the oven and drizzle with olive oil. For a more elegant presentation, use a ring mold to plate individual portions.

5

COD STICKS WITH RED BELL PEPPER SAUCE

Serves 4–5

Red bell pepper sauce
Preparation time 15 minutes
Cooking time 25 minutes

Cod
Preparation time 30 minutes
Cooking time 10 minutes

EQUIPMENT

Red bell pepper sauce
Handheld immersion (stick) blender

Cod
15 wooden skewers

Red bell pepper sauce

1 tomato
1 red bell pepper
1/2 onion
2 tablespoons olive oil
1 sprig thyme
Salt

Freshly ground pepper

Cod

40 g – 1.4 ounces (3 tablespoons) butter, cut into cubes
500 g – 1 lb 5 oz cod tail-end fillet
60 g – 2.12 ounces (2/3 cup) almond meal (ground almonds)
Fine salt
5 sheets brick (brik) pastry

TIPS FROM OUR CHEFS

CLARIFIED BUTTER
This butter, gently melted and separated from the milky residue, is able to withstand high temperatures and will not turn black when cooked (page 546).

SLIDE
To skin the fish, make a small incision at the end. While holding the fish firmly with one hand, slide the knife blade between the flesh and the skin, working it back and forth.

ROLL, ROLL
Brick pastry can't wait. The rolling process has to be brisk or the sheets will dry out and crack. Cook the cod fingers as soon as you have finished rolling them.

1

Make the red bell pepper sauce: Wash the tomato and bell pepper. Peel the onion and slice with a chef's knife (page 525).
Remove the stem (stalk) from the tomato, quarter, then thinly slice. Remove the stem, white ribs, and seeds from the bell pepper. Cut into strips (page 513). Heat 2 tablespoons of oil in a saucepan. Add the onion and thyme, and let soften for 30 minutes over low heat. Add the tomato and bell pepper. Season with two pinches of salt and a generous amount of pepper (ten turns of the peppermill). Mix, cover the pan, and cook for 25 minutes over low heat, stirring from time to time.

2

Make the clarified butter: Melt the butter in a saucepan over low heat. Transfer to a dish, leaving the bottom residue in the saucepan (page 546).
Make an incision in the narrow end of the fillet and slide a filleting knife between the flesh and skin. Discard the skin.

3

Preheat the oven to 240°C – 475°F (gas mark 9) in a static (conventional) oven. Cut the cod flesh into uniform batons 1.5 cm – 5/8 inch wide.
Spread an even layer of almond meal on a plate. Season the cod batons with salt. Place the cod batons in the almond meal and roll them over to coat.

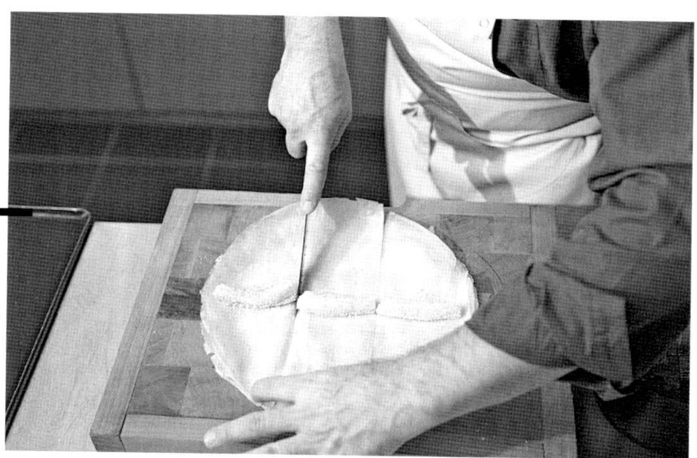

4

Stack the pastry sheets. Brush the first sheet with clarified butter. Place three batons end-to-end in the center of the top pastry sheet. Cut the sheets between the batons, slicing through all the layers. Roll each baton in the top piece of pastry underneath it.

5

Trim the ends of the pastry. Lay the cod sticks on a baking sheet (tray). As the sheets are stacked, they will all be cut at the same time as the first. Roll each baton in a piece of pastry. Brush the rolled cod sticks with melted butter. Bake for 10 minutes.

6

Remove the thyme sprig from the pan with the bell pepper. Transfer the vegetables to a deep container. Place a handheld blender in the container, then wrap the container and handheld blender with plastic wrap (cling film) to protect from splashing.
Blend. To stop the container from moving while blending the sauce, fold a dishcloth and place it under the container to steady it (page 502). Pass the sauce through a fine strainer (sieve), pressing with a spoon. Take the cod fingers out of the oven. Insert a skewer into each one. Transfer the cod sticks to paper towels to soak up excess oil. Serve the red bell pepper sauce in the center of a dish. Arrange the cod sticks around it and serve immediately.

PAN-FRIED COD WITH SPRING VEGETABLES

Serves 4

Spring vegetables
Preparation time 15 minutes
Cooking time 15 minutes

Cod
Preparation and cooking time
15 minutes

EQUIPMENT

Spring vegetables
10-cm – 4-inch-diameter ring mold

TIPS FROM OUR CHEFS

KEEP THE FENNEL
Store the fennel sticks (large stems) in the vegetable crisper drawer of the refrigerator. You can also tie them into small bundles and hang them in the kitchen to dry. You can use them to stuff whole fish or to flavor a fish soup.

USING A WOK
The ingredients are added to the wok in sequence, starting with the ones that require the longest cooking time. Stir after each addition, then push the contents of the wok to the side before putting the next ingredient in the middle.

Spring vegetables

1 red bell pepper
1 yellow bell pepper
2 small zucchini (courgettes)
4 small fennel bulbs with fronds
1 onion
Fine salt
Freshly ground pepper
1 tablespoon olive oil

3–4 basil leaves

Cod

4 (160-g – 5.65-ounce) cod supremes, with skin
Fine salt
4 basil leaves
Olive oil
1 clove garlic, unpeeled
15 g – 0.53 ounce (1 tablespoon) butter, cut into cubes

1

3

1 Wash the bell peppers, zucchini, and fennel bulbs. Remove the stems (stalks) and base from the fennel and cut off the top and bottom ends of the zucchini. Peel the onion. Remove the stems from the bell peppers and cut into quarters. Remove the white membranes and seeds. Peel the bell pepper lobes with a vegetable peeler (page 513). Cut into uniform strips with a chef's knife.

2 Halve the zucchini and remove the core by slicing around it (page 522). Cut the slices into batons. Halve the fennel bulbs, then cut into batons. Halve the onion and remove the core. Slice each half. Season the vegetables with salt and pepper. Heat 1 tablespoon of oil in a wok. Add the onion and let soften for 30 seconds while stirring with a spatula (stir-fry). Push the onion to the side, add the fennel, and let brown for 1 minute over high heat. Push the fennel to the side. Add the bell peppers and brown for 3 minutes. Finally add the zucchini. Mix. Cover and cook for 15 minutes. Add a few basil leaves to the wok and adjust the seasoning. Remove from heat.

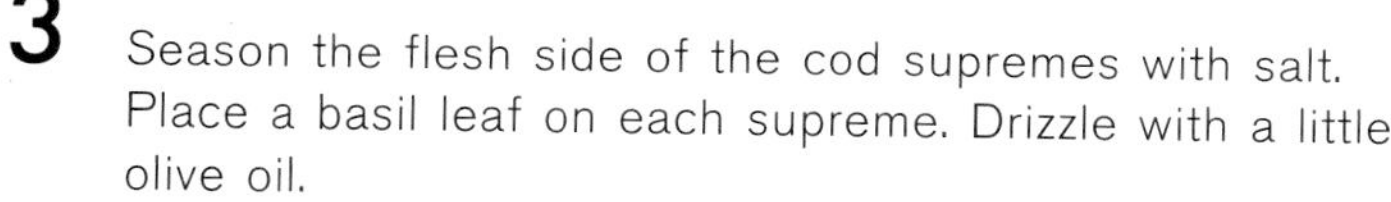

3 Season the flesh side of the cod supremes with salt. Place a basil leaf on each supreme. Drizzle with a little olive oil.
Heat 1 teaspoon of olive oil in a skillet or frying pan. Place the cod supremes skin side down in the pan.

4 Add the whole, unpeeled garlic clove and one third of the butter. Cook for 7–8 minutes over medium heat. Add the rest of the butter and cook for 3–4 minutes, basting the fish often with the melted butter. Cover and cook for 1 additional minute.
Use a wide spatula (slotted turner) to remove the cod from the pan.
Divide the vegetables among four plates and set a piece of fish on top. Serve immediately.

TIPS FROM OUR CHEFS

THE RIGHT SIDE

Avoid salting the skin side of a fish fillet or supreme, because it causes the juice to be released and tends to dry out the flesh.

PAN-FRIED COD WITH SPINACH AND ALMONDS

Serves 4

Cod
Preparation time 15 minutes
Cooking time 8 minutes
Resting time 30 minutes

Spinach and condiment
Preparation time 20 minutes
Cooking time 10 minutes
Resting time 15 minutes

Cod

25 g – 0.88 ounce (1 tablespoon plus 2 1/4 teaspoons) kosher (coarse) salt
4 (**180-g** – 6.35-oz) cod supremes, skinless
Olive oil
20 g – 0.71 ounce (1 tablespoon plus 1 teaspoon) butter, cut into cubes

Spinach and condiment

100 ml – 1/3 cup plus 1 tablespoon plus 1 teaspoon milk
40 g – 1.4 ounces (1/3 cup) blanched almonds
3 sprigs flat-leaf parsley
1/4 cup olive oil, divided
Fine salt
2 tablespoons capers
1 lemon
400 g – 14 ounces (13 cups) spinach
1 clove garlic
25 g – 0.88 ounce (1 3/4 tablespoons) butter, cut into cubes

TIPS FROM OUR CHEFS

BLANCHED?
In professional speak, blanched almonds (from the French blanchir–to whiten) are peeled almonds.

FLAT-LEAF OR CURLY
Curly parsley is more decorative, but flat-leaf parsley has more flavor. It can be fried easily in a little oil.

PROPERLY COOKED
To test that the parsley is fried correctly, take a leaf out of the pan and place it on a paper towel. It should dry completely.

1

Sprinkle the bottom of a dish with about half the kosher salt. Lay the cod supremes on top and cover with the rest of the kosher salt.
Cover with plastic wrap (cling film) and refrigerate for 30 minutes.

2

In the meantime, start to make the condiment: Bring the milk to a boil. Add the almonds and simmer for 5 minutes over low heat. Cover the pan, remove from heat, and let infuse for 15 minutes. Drain in a small strainer (sieve). Let the almonds rest on paper towels to continue to drain, then set aside in a bowl.

3

Wash the parsley and pat dry. Pluck the leaves one at a time. Heat 2 tablespoons of olive oil in a deep skillet or frying pan. Add the parsley leaves and cook for 3 minutes over medium heat. Season with salt. Transfer to a triple thickness of paper towels and let drain. Rinse and drain the capers. Cut both ends off the lemon, then peel. Remove the skin and pith (supreme), following the curved shape of the fruit (page 514). Pass the blade of a paring knife between the flesh and membrane of each section (segment), then pivot the blade under the section. Transfer the flesh and juice to a bowl.

Fold each spinach leaf in half and remove the rib from the entire length, starting from the stem (stalk). Wash the spinach in water, then drain and dry. Peel the garlic clove and insert the tines of a fork into it. Heat 1 tablespoon of olive oil in another deep skillet or frying pan. Add half of the spinach and cook for 3–4 minutes on high heat, stirring with the fork with the garlic clove. Season with salt. Transfer to a plate, then do the same with the remaining spinach. Cover the cooked spinach with plastic wrap to keep hot.

4

5

Preheat the oven to 200°C – 400°F (gas mark 6). Rinse the cod supremes under cold running water. Pat dry with paper towels. Heat 1 tablespoon of olive oil in a skillet or frying pan. Add the cod and half of the butter. Cook for 4 minutes over medium-high heat. Baste with the melted butter and cook for another 2 minutes. Turn the fish over with a wide spatula (slotted turner). Add the remaining butter, baste the fish, and cook for 1 minute.

6

With the wide spatula, transfer the fish to a rack to drain. Add the almonds to the pan with the butter. Let toast lightly for 1 minute 30 seconds while shaking the pan. Add the capers and brown for 1 minute. Finally, add the lemon sections. Reheat the cod in the oven for 1 minute. Divide the spinach among the individual serving plates and lay a piece of fish on top. Garnish with the almonds, capers, and lemon. Finish with the fried parsley leaves. Serve immediately.

GRAVLAX-STYLE COD WITH MANGO SAUCE

Serves 8–10

Cod
Preparation time 15 minutes
Resting time 48 hours

Sauce
Preparation time 15 minutes
Cooking time 7 minutes
Resting time 10 minutes + 15 minutes

EQUIPMENT

Cod
Mortar and pestle

Sauce
Handheld immersion (stick) blender
Mandoline slicer

Cod

5 g – 0.18 ounce (2 teaspoons) black peppercorns
4 g – 0.14 ounce (2 teaspoons) fennel seeds
45 g – 1.6 ounces (3 tablespoons plus 2 teaspoons) superfine (caster) sugar
60 g – 2.12 ounces (1/4 cup) kosher (coarse) salt
1 (**640 g** – 1 lb 6-oz) cod loin
2 teaspoons paprika

Sauce

1/2 mango
1 small onion
2 tomatoes
Fine salt
2 tablespoons plus 1 teaspoon olive oil, divided, plus more for drizzling
Freshly ground pepper
1 fennel bulb
1 tablespoon lemon juice

TIPS FROM OUR CHEFS

NO IMPERFECTIONS
Check that there are no scales left on the fish. Check for bones and use tweezers to remove any that you find.

RESTING
You salt the tomato scraps and let them rest before blending so that they release their tasty liquid.

1

Two days prior to serving this dish, put the peppercorns and fennel seeds into the mortar. Pound lightly. Add the sugar and kosher salt. Pound without crushing completely.

2

Carefully dry the fish. Sprinkle the bottom of a dish with half of the salt mixture, lay the fish over it, and cover with the remainder. Cover with plastic wrap (cling film) and refrigerate for 12 hours. Turn the fish over, and drizzle with the juices that it has released. Cover with plastic wrap and refrigerate for another 12 hours. Repeat this step another two times. (See page 554 for additional information on this technique.)

3

On the day you plan to serve the dish, make the sauce: Cut the mango half into two quarters. Peel (page 515). Cut the two pieces into slices, then into batons, and finally into small dice (brunoise). Peel the onion and chop: Make several cuts lengthwise, then horizontally. Finally cut across to obtain small dice (page 525).

4

Wash the tomatoes and remove the stems (stalks). Cut each into quarters, then halve the quarters to make eight wedges. Peel them by passing the knife blade between the skin and the flesh (page 521). Remove the seeds. Cut the tomato flesh into small dice. Put the skin and seeds (scraps) into a bowl with 2 pinches of salt. Let stand for 15 minutes.

5

Transfer the tomato scraps to a deep container. Insert the handheld blender. Wrap the container and blender with plastic wrap to prevent splashing, then blend. Heat 1 teaspoon of olive oil in a saucepan. Add the onion and let soften for 1 minute without browning. Strain the blended scraps into the pan and reduce for 5 minutes over medium heat. Add the mixture to the diced tomato and mango. Season lightly with salt and a generous sprinkling of freshly ground pepper, and drizzle with olive oil. Mix well. Remove from heat and transfer to a small bowl. Cut off the stems and the bottom of the fennel bulb. Remove the outer layer. Halve the bulb. Remove the core (page 515). Slice the fennel with a mandoline slicer into a bowl filled with ice water so that the slices become firm.

6

Rinse the fish under cold running water.
Lay it on a clean cloth and carefully pat dry. Sprinkle the flesh side with the paprika. Cover with plastic wrap and refrigerate for 15 minutes.

7

In the meantime, drain the fennel slices in a strainer (sieve). Dry gently. Transfer to a bowl with the lemon juice and 2 tablespoons of olive oil. Season with salt and pepper, and mix gently.

8

Use a filleting knife to cut the fish diagonally into thin slices. Place 1 tablespoon of sauce in the bottom of an individual glass bowl. Add a few fennel slices, then fish slices. Repeat with remaining sauce, fish, and fennel.

POACHED COD BRANDADE

Serves 6–8

Preparation time 20 minutes
Cooking time 40 minutes
Resting time 1 hour

EQUIPMENT

Food processor fitted with a metal blade

40 g – 1.4 ounces (3 tablespoons) kosher (coarse) salt
500 g – 1 lb 2 oz fresh cod (belly or tail fillets)
750 ml – 3 cups whole milk
1 clove garlic, unpeeled
1 star anise
1 stalk fresh fennel
1 bay leaf
300 g – 10.5 ounces potatoes
5 sprigs flat-leaf parsley
Salt
1/4 cup olive oil, plus more for brushing
10 slices baguette

1 Sprinkle the bottom of a dish with one third of the kosher salt. Lay half of the fillets on top, skin side down, and cover with another third of the salt. Lay the remaining fillets on top, skin side up, and cover with the remaining salt. Cover with plastic wrap (cling film) and refrigerate for 1 hour.

2 Combine the milk with the unpeeled garlic clove, star anise, fennel, and bay leaf in a saucepan and place over low heat. Once the milk begins to form bubbles, cover and remove from heat.

3 Rinse the fish under cold running water to remove salt. Return the pan with the milk to the heat and bring to a simmer. Immerse the fish in the simmering milk. Cover and cook for 15 minutes over low heat. In the meantime, peel the potatoes with a vegetable peeler, then wash and cut into small chunks. Wash the parsley, pat dry, and pluck the leaves. Gather the leaves into small bunches and chop them with a chef's knife (page 524). Remove the fish from the milk with a wide spatula (slotted turner), then place on paper towels. Add the potatoes to the milk. Taste and adjust the salt. Cover and cook for 15 minutes.

4 Check that the potatoes are cooked through by piercing them with a fork, then transfer to a colander to drain over a bowl. Set aside the milk. Discard the fennel, bay leaf, and star anise. Retrieve the garlic clove, cut in half lengthwise, and remove the skin and green core. Add the garlic to the potatoes. Preheat the oven to 210°C – 425°F (gas mark 6–7).

5 Remove the skin from the fish. Check for bones by flaking the flesh. Blend the fish in the food processor. Scrape down the sides of the bowl with a spatula. Add the potatoes and garlic. Blend and scrape down the sides of the bowl with the spatula.
Add a tablespoon of the reserved milk and blend again. Add 1/4 cup olive oil. Scrape down the sides of the bowl with the spatula. Blend. Finally, add the chopped parsley leaves and blend one last time. Arrange the slices of bread in a single layer on a baking sheet (tray). Lightly brush with oil. Toast in the preheated oven for 4 minutes. Serve the brandade on tasting spoons or plates. Accompany with toast.

2

3

4

COD CONFIT WITH CRANBERRY BEAN PUREE

Serves 4

Cranberry bean puree
Preparation time 15 minutes
Cooking time 1 hour 30 minutes
Resting time 12 hours

Cod
Preparation time 15 minutes
Cooking time 12 minutes
Resting time 30 minutes

EQUIPMENT

Food processor fitted with a metal blade

Cranberry bean puree

150 g – 5.3 ounces (3/4 cup) dried cranberry (borlotti) beans
1 sprig parsley
1 leek leaf
1 sprig rosemary
1 sprig thyme
1 bay leaf
1/2 carrot
1/4 onion
1 clove garlic, unpeeled
1/2 teaspoon kosher (coarse) salt
1 tablespoon grapeseed oil
1 tablespoon balsamic vinegar

Olive oil

Cod

1 (650-g – 1 pound 7-ounce) center cut cod
25 g – 0.88 ounce (1 tablespoon plus 2 1/4 teaspoons) kosher (coarse) salt
1 romaine (cos) lettuce heart
2 cloves garlic
1 liter – 4 1/4 cups grapeseed oil
1 sprig rosemary
Ground Espelette pepper
1 1/2 teaspoons olive oil

TIPS FROM OUR CHEFS

SOAKING ESSENTIAL

All dry legumes (pulses) except lentils have to be soaked in cold water to hydrate. Let stand for 8–12 hours (depending on the age of the legumes). Fermentation begins after 12 hours.

ONE OF GRANDMA'S TRICKS

Adding a pinch of baking (bicarbonate of) soda to the cooking liquid for dry legumes speeds up the cooking process while preserving their color.

AT THE RIGHT TIME

Don't add salt to beans at the beginning of the cooking process. This will harden their skins. Ideally, add a little fleur de sel 15 minutes before they finish cooking.

1 Soak the beans for 12 hours in a bowl filled with cold water. Drain the beans. Put into a saucepan and cover with cold water. Cut the parsley stem (stalk). Wrap in the leek leaf with the rosemary, thyme, and bay leaf. Tie the bouquet garni (page 544). Peel the carrot half with a vegetable peeler and cut into four batons. Peel the onion quarter. Leave the garlic clove unpeeled. Put into the saucepan together with the bouquet garni. Bring to a boil, then cover the pan and simmer for 1 hour 15 minutes. Season with the kosher salt and cook for an additional 15 minutes.

2

In the meantime, cut the cod loin into 4 equal-sized supremes. Sprinkle the bottom of a dish with about half of the kosher salt. Lay the cod supremes on top and cover with the rest of the kosher salt. Cover with plastic wrap (cling film) and refrigerate for 30 minutes. Separate the lettuce heart into individual leaves. Use a paring knife to cut off the bottom of the leaves. Cut the leaves in half, remove the ribs, and trim the ends lightly to resemble arrowheads.
When the beans are cooked, remove the bouquet garni, carrot, and garlic. Drain the beans in a colander over a bowl, reserving their cooking liquid.

3

Blend the beans with about 1/2 cup of their liquid. Add 1 tablespoon of grapeseed oil and 1 tablespoon of balsamic vinegar. Transfer to a bowl, taste, and adjust the seasoning. Cover with plastic wrap.

4

Peel 1 garlic clove with a paring knife and thinly slice. Use a toothpick (cocktail stick) to remove the green core pieces from the slices. Heat 1 liter – 4 1/4 cups of grapeseed oil to 100°C – 212°F in a deep skillet or frying pan. Fry the garlic slices with the whole unpeeled garlic clove in the oil together with the rosemary and a pinch of Espelette pepper for 3 minutes.

5

Rinse the fish under cold running water and dry carefully. Remove the garlic slices from the pan. Drain on paper towels. Check the temperature of the oil. It should be at 80°C – 176°F. Place the fish in the oil, skin side down, and brown for 3 minutes. Use a wide spatula (slotted turner) and a fork to turn over the fish. Cook for 6 minutes.
Take out the fish with the spatula and lay on paper towels to drain. Reduce 4–5 tablespoons of cooking liquid from the beans in another saucepan for 2 minutes. Add 1 tablespoon of balsamic vinegar. Thicken the sauce with 1 1/2 teaspoons of olive oil.

6

Carefully remove the skin from the fish.
Use a spoon to place a little bean puree on the side of a plate. Lift the spoon abruptly to create a large comma shape.
Gently lay a piece of cod in the center of the plate. Pour a little sauce over the fish.
Season with a pinch of Espelette pepper. Add a few garlic chips (crisps). Accompany with lettuce leaves. Repeat with remaining servings.

ONE-SIDED SALMON

Serves 4

Preparation time 50 minutes
Cooking time 15 minutes

2 carrots
2 small leeks
1 fennel bulb
1 celery heart
1 globe turnip
4 small fresh white onions
1.2 liters – 5 cups vegetable broth or stock
4 (160-g - 5.65-oz) salmon supremes, with skin
Salt
1 tablespoon plus 1/2 teaspoon olive oil, divided
4 sprigs chervil
3 sprigs flat-leaf parsley
3 sprigs dill
3 sprigs basil
1 tablespoon balsamic vinegar
Finely ground pepper
Coarsely ground pepper

1 Wash the carrots, leeks, fennel, celery heart, and turnip. Peel the carrot with a vegetable peeler and cut off the ends. Slice on a diagonal, then cut each slice in half.

1

2 Remove the outer leaf from the leeks. Cut off the very green part of the leeks on a diagonal.
Cut off the roots and stems (stalks) from the fennel bulb. Make a vertical cut in the outer layer and remove. Halve the bulb. Remove the hard core at the bottom. Cut each half into quarters (page 515).
Trim the celery heart. Cut it into quarters.
Trim the crown of the turnip, leaving the leaves attached. Peel around the turnip with a vegetable peeler. Cut into quarters. Lightly round off the sharp angles.
Cut off the green leaves from the onions on a diagonal. Cut off the roots.
Bring the broth to a boil. Add the vegetables. Cook, uncovered, for 7 minutes.
Remove the vegetables with a skimmer and drain. Reserve the cooking liquid.

3 Season the flesh side of the fish with salt. Heat a deep skillet or frying pan over high heat.
Add 1/2 teaspoon of olive oil to the pan. Heat for a few seconds. Use a wide spatula (slotted turner) to place the fish in the pan, skin side down.
Cook for 3 minutes. Reduce the heat. Remove the fat with a spoon and reserve. Cook for another 5 minutes on the skin side.

3

4 Wash and dry the chervil, parsley, dill, and basil. Pluck off the leaves.
Chop the leaves using a chef's knife, cutting in only one direction. Turn the cutting board 90 degrees and chop in the other direction. Mix 1 teaspoon of cooking liquid from the vegetables with the balsamic vinegar in a bowl. Add the remaining 1 tablespoon olive oil. Season with salt and finely ground pepper. Add the herbs. Drizzle the fish with its fat. Drain on paper towels. Arrange the fish on a warm dish. Add the vegetables. Drizzle with vinaigrette. Season with coarsely ground pepper. Serve hot.

PAN-FRIED CRUSTED SALMON WITH BLACK RICE

Serves 4

Preparation time 20 minutes
Cooking time 25 minutes
Resting time 15 minutes

Crust and vinaigrette

6 jumbo shrimp (tiger prawns), cooked
1 stalk fresh lemongrass
1 organic, unwaxed lemon
50 g – 1.76 ounces (1/2 cup) almond meal (ground almonds)
3 tablespoons plus 1 teaspoon olive oil, divided

Salt

Salmon

4 (125-g – 4.4-ounce) square-cut salmon fillets, skinless
Kosher (coarse) salt
Salt
1 tablespoon olive oil
Freshly ground pepper
150 g - 5.29 oz (3/4 cup) black rice

1 Make the crust: Remove the head from one of the shrimp. Split the underside. Detach from the shell and gently pull out the flesh. Cut along the middle of the back. Lift up the intestine with the tip of a knife (or a toothpick/cocktail stick) and remove (page 514). Repeat with remaining shrimp. Finely chop the shrimp flesh with a knife. Transfer to a bowl.

2 Cut off the lemongrass root. Cut a 10-cm – 4-inch length of the stalk into slices, reserving some for garnish. Mix with the shrimp.
Grate the zest of half the lemon over the mixture (page 514). Add the almond meal. Drizzle with 1 teaspoon olive oil. Add a pinch of salt and mix well. Place fillets in a single layer on a large plate. Spread a thin layer of the crust mixture over each salmon square. Spread evenly with a knife. Refrigerate for 15 minutes.

3 Bring water to a boil in a saucepan. Add kosher salt, tip in the rice, and cook for 18 minutes.

4 Lay a sheet of parchment (baking) paper over the salmon. Place a plate upside down on top.
Hold both plates and turn over. Remove the top plate. Season the fish with salt.

5 Heat 1 tablespoon of oil in a skillet or frying pan. Slide the fish from the paper into the pan. Cook for 3 minutes over medium heat. Use a wide spatula (slotted turner) to turn the fish over. Cook for 1 additional minute. Lift the salmon squares out of the pan and lay on paper towels.

6 Squeeze half of the lemon into a bowl. Add a pinch of salt and 2 tablespoons of olive oil. Drain the rice. Heat the remaining 1 tablespoon of olive oil in a skillet or frying pan. Add the rice and stir. Sauté for 2 minutes. Make a bed of rice on each of 4 serving plates. Place a salmon square on each bed of rice. Drizzle with vinaigrette. Garnish with the remaining lemongrass and serve.

2

3

4

5

GRILLED SALMON

Serves 4

Béarnaise sauce
Preparation time 20 minutes
Cooking time 18 minutes

Salmon
Preparation time 5 minutes
Cooking time 4 minutes

Béarnaise sauce

1 (50-g – 1.76-ounce) shallot
1 tomato
1/2 bunch chervil
1/2 bunch tarragon
1/2 bunch flat-leaf parsley
150 ml – 2/3 cup white wine vinegar
1 teaspoon coarsely ground pepper
100 ml – 1/3 cup plus 1 tablespoon plus 1 teaspoon chicken stock
1 tablespoon olive oil

Salmon

4 (175-g - 6.17-oz) salmon supremes, with skin
Olive oil for brushing
Fleur de sel
150 g – 5.3 ounces (about 5 cups) mesclun

1 Make the béarnaise sauce: Peel, halve, and chop the shallot (page 525).

2 Remove the stem (stalk) from the tomato. Cut into eight wedges. Peel by passing the knife blade between the skin and the flesh (page 521). Remove the core and seeds. Cut the wedges into strips, then dice. Wash and dry the herbs, then pluck the leaves. Chop the leaves with a knife, cutting in one direction without crushing. Turn the cutting board 90 degrees and chop in the other direction. Set aside. Combine the chopped shallot and diced tomato in a saucepan. Add the vinegar. Add the coarsely ground pepper. Bring to a boil, reduce the heat, and cook for 15 minutes over medium heat.

3 For the salmon: Heat a cast-iron grill pan over high heat. Brush the flesh side of the fish with oil. Season with fleur de sel.
Place the salmon flesh side down on the hot grill, on the diagonal in relation to the ridges in the pan. Sear for 30 seconds.

4 Turn the fish 90 degrees. Sear for 30 seconds. The flesh should have a scored pattern. Turn the fish over, skin side down. Reduce the heat and cook for 3 minutes. Remove the fat released as the fish cooks.
Pour the chicken jus into the béarnaise sauce. Infuse for 3 minutes. Lay the grilled salmon pieces on paper towels.

5 Select and wash the best salad greens. Wrap in a clean cloth and shake to dry. Make a bed of some of the mesclun on a serving dish. Arrange the salmon pieces on top. Add the oil and herbs to the béarnaise sauce. Serve the salmon with the sauce and the rest of the mesclun.

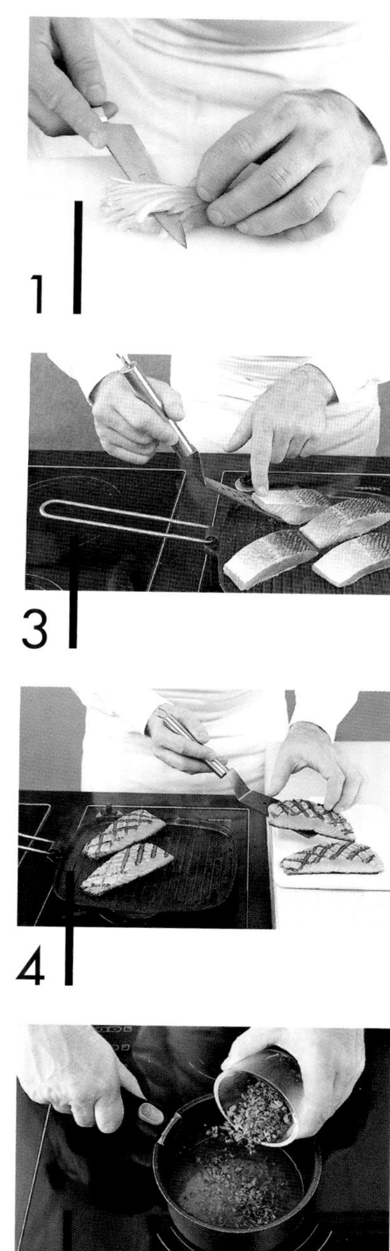

TIPS FROM OUR CHEFS

FIRM BUT RIPE

If the tomato is very ripe but still firm, it should be easy to peel the wedges. If not, immerse the whole tomato in boiling water for 1 minute, refresh in ice water, and peel.

PAN-FRIED SALMON WITH NUTS

Serves 4

Preparation time 20 minutes
Cooking time 4 minutes

2 (250-g – 9-ounce) skin-on salmon tail fillets
300 g – 10.5 ounces (10 cups) spinach
100 g – 3.5 ounces (about 1 cup) nuts, such as almonds, peanuts, and/or walnuts
Fleur de sel
1 egg yolk
1 small onion
2 tablespoons olive oil, divided
Salt
10 g – 0.35 ounce (2/3 tablespoon) butter, cubed
150 ml – 2/3 cup barbecue sauce

1. Cut each salmon fillet in half lengthwise without cutting through the skin.
Slide the knife between the flesh and the skin to remove the skin. Remove any fatty or bloody parts from the skin side of the fillets.
Fold each spinach leaf in half and remove the rib in the center (page 520). Wash, drain, and let dry on a cloth.

2. Put the nuts on a large sheet of parchment (baking) paper. Fold one side of the paper over the nuts. Fold the opposite side over. Fold the ends over. Hit the parchment paper envelope with a rolling pin to crush the nuts without grinding them to a powder. Transfer to a plate.

3. Season the salmon on both sides with fleur de sel.
Beat the egg yolk. Brush the egg over both sides of the fish. Dredge the fish on both sides in the crushed nuts, pressing gently for better adhesion.

4. Peel, halve, and chop the onion (page 525).
Heat 1 tablespoon of olive oil in a saucepan. Add the onion. Let soften for 1 minute over medium heat.
Add the spinach. Season with salt. Let wilt for 1 minute while stirring. Transfer to a dish.

5. Heat 1 tablespoon of olive oil in a deep skillet or frying pan over high heat. Put the fish pieces in the pan. Add half of the butter cubes. Cook for 1 minute. Gently turn the fish over with a wide spatula (slotted turner).
Add the rest of the butter cubes. Cook for 1 minute, then transfer the fish pieces to paper towels. Slice the fish and arrange on plates. Use a ring mold to shape the spinach into disks. Serve with the barbecue sauce.

1
3
4

PARIS-STYLE SALMON

Serves 4

Preparation time 20 minutes
Cooking time 6 minutes

EQUIPMENT

Mortar and pestle

Salmon

600 g – 1 pound 5 ounces skin-on salmon fillet cut from center back
1.5 liters – 6 1/3 cups fish stock
1 bunch scallions (spring onions)
10 g – 0.35 ounce (1 tablespoon plus 1 teaspoon) pickled capers in vinegar
Coarsely ground pepper

Green mayonnaise

2 sprigs tarragon
3 sprigs flat-leaf parsley
1 egg yolk
1 tablespoon mustard
Freshly ground pepper
Salt
250 ml – 1 cup grapeseed oil

1 Cut the fillet in half lengthwise. Cut each piece in half to make four pieces. Pour the stock into a deep skillet or frying pan. Place the pieces in the pan, skin side down. Cook for 6 minutes over medium heat. Turn off the heat when the stock comes to a simmer. Let cool. Use a wide spatula (slotted turner) to remove the fish from the pan. Drain on paper towels.

2 Make the green mayonnaise: Wash and dry the tarragon and parsley, then pluck the leaves into the mortar. Pound thoroughly.

3 Put the egg yolk into a bowl. Add the mustard. Sprinkle with freshly ground pepper (four or five turns of the peppermill). Add a large pinch of salt. Add the pounded herbs. Surround the bowl with a rolled-up dishcloth to steady it (page 502). Mix the contents with a whisk. Pour in the grapeseed oil in a thin stream while whisking.

4 Lift one corner of the skin on each piece of salmon and pull gently to remove without damaging the flesh. Gently scrape off the brown layer of flesh with a spoon.

5 Cut the roots off the scallions. Cut into rounds.
Use a spoon to spread a little green mayonnaise over each piece of salmon. Spread evenly with a knife.
Top with the scallion slices. Rinse the capers and spread them over the salmon pieces. Sprinkle with coarsely ground pepper.

2

3

4

5

TIPS FROM OUR CHEFS

IMMERSION
Make sure the pieces of fish are totally immersed in the stock. If they are not quite covered with liquid, baste them occasionally.

GENTLY DOES IT
Don't whisk the green mayonnaise for too long. If it's too firm it won't coat the salmon pieces properly.

SIMMER
Don't let the stock boil. This will cause the fish to dry out and crumble.

POACHED SALMON WITH GREEN BEANS AND BUTTON MUSHROOMS

Serves 4

Preparation time 15 minutes
Cooking time 20 minutes

EQUIPMENT

Tea infuser

Salmon

200 g – 7 ounces extra thin green beans
Kosher (coarse) salt
250 g – 9 ounces small button mushrooms
1.5 liters – 6 1/3 cups cold fish stock
4 (175-g – 6.17-oz) salmon supremes, with skin
1 tablespoon plus 1 teaspoon green tea or smoked black tea (or 4 tea bags)

Sauce

1 shallot
1 tablespoon balsamic vinegar
Salt
Pepper
2 tablespoons toasted sesame oil
Fleur de sel

1 Trim the green beans, removing only the part holding the bean to the stem (stalk). Immerse in ice water. Bring water to a boil in a saucepan. Add kosher salt.Immerse the green beans and cook for 3 minutes, counting from when the water comes back to a boil. Drain, plunge in ice water, then drain in a colander. Cut the stems off the mushrooms. Peel the caps (page 516). Place the stock in a saucepan. Immerse the salmon pieces, skin side down, in the cold stock. Put the tea into the infuser and add to the saucepan. Cook for 7 minutes over medium heat. The fish will be poached when the liquid reaches 60°C – 140°F. Remove the supremes with a wide spatula (slotted turner), reserving the stock. Transfer the fish to a dish. Cover with plastic wrap (cling film) to keep hot. Bring the stock back to a boil and immerse the mushrooms. Cook 7–8 minutes.

2 In the meantime, make the sauce: Chop the shallot (page 525). Mix the chopped shallot with the vinegar. Add 1 tablespoon of stock from the pan. Season with salt and pepper and add the sesame oil. Mix well.

3 Just before the mushrooms are finished cooking, add the green beans to reheat for 30 seconds. Drain the vegetables.

4 Carefully remove the skin from the fish.

5 Use a spoon to scrape off the brown layer of flesh, starting in the center and working your way to the sides. Use a spatula to transfer the salmon pieces to the plates. Season with fleur de sel. Arrange the vegetables around the fish. Drizzle with sauce and serve.

2
3
4

SHALLOW-BRAISED SALMON WITH POTATOES AND SORREL SAUCE

Serves 4

Preparation time 15 minutes
Cooking time 40 minutes
Resting time 30 minutes

400 g – 14 ounces waxy potatoes
Kosher (coarse) salt
600 g – 1 lb 5.16 oz salmon, skinless and cut into 4 scallops (escalopes)
Fleur de sel
1 shallot
1 bunch sorrel
3 tablespoons olive oil, divided, plus more for drizzling
200 ml – 3/4 cup plus 1 tablespoon fish stock
50 ml – 3 tablespoons plus 1 1/2 teaspoons white wine
2 tablespoons crème fraîche

TIPS FROM OUR CHEFS

VARIATION
You can also rub the fish with olive oil and a dried herb of your choice and refrigerate for 30 minutes before cooking.

1 Wash the potatoes. Immerse in a saucepan filled with cold water. Add kosher salt. Bring to a boil and cook for 25 minutes. In the meantime, sprinkle the fish with fleur de sel to firm the flesh. Cover with plastic wrap (cling film) and refrigerate for 30 minutes.

2 Peel the shallot. Halve and chop (page 525).
Wash the sorrel and pat dry. Fold each leaf in half and remove the stem (stalk) and rib. Lay the leaves one on top of the other. Cut into strips (chiffonade) with a chef's knife.

3 Drain the potatoes. Peel with a paring knife while still hot. Cut into 5-mm – 1/4-inch slices. Transfer to a bowl. Drizzle with a generous stream of olive oil. Season with fleur de sel.

4 Heat 1 tablespoon of olive oil in a skillet or frying pan. Use a wide spatula (slotted turner) to place the salmon scallops in the pan. Sear for 10 minutes over medium heat. Pour in enough stock to come halfway up the sides of the salmon. Boil for 1 minute.

5 Use a wide spatula (slotted turner) to turn the salmon pieces over. Cook for 1 additional minute. Transfer to a plate. Cover to keep hot. Heat 2 tablespoons of olive oil in a saucepan. Add the chopped shallot. Sauté (soften) for 2 minutes over low heat. Add the white wine and reduce until the liquid has evaporated. Add 40 ml – 2 tablespoons plus 2 teaspoons of cooking liquid from the fish and three quarters of the sorrel. Add the crème fraîche. Mix and cook for 8 minutes over low heat.

6 Blend the sauce with a handheld blender, then pass through a fine strainer (sieve). Pour the remaining cooking liquid from the fish over the potatoes. Arrange the fish on a warm serving dish with the potatoes. Season with fleur de sel and serve with the rest of the sorrel and the sauce.

STEAMED SALMON WITH SHIITAKE MUSHROOMS AND SEA BEANS

Serves 2

Preparation time 30 minutes
Cooking time 18 minutes

EQUIPMENT
Steamer

Salmon

400 g – 14 ounces skin-on salmon fillets cut from center back
150 g – 5.3 ounces shiitake mushrooms
1 shallot
3 sprigs flat-leaf parsley
1 tablespoon olive oil
5 g – 0.18 ounce (1 teaspoon) salted butter
Salt
125 g – 4.4 ounces sea beans (samphire)

Beurre blanc

30 g – 1.06 ounces (2 tablespoons) salted butter
100 ml – 1/3 cup plus 1 tablespoon plus 1 teaspoon white wine
1/2 organic, unwaxed lime, zest and juice

1 Cut the fillet in half across. Halve again. Arrange the pieces in pairs. Fit inversely with their flesh sides pressed together snugly to form "steaks." Wind kitchen twine around each steak. Knot and cut off the excess twine.

1

2 Cut the stems (stalks) off the mushrooms. Wash the caps under cold running water. Pat dry with paper towels. Peel the shallot, cut in half. Thinly slice one half (page 525). Reserve the other half for the beurre blanc. Wash the parsley, pat dry, and pluck the leaves. Chop the leaves in one direction. Turn the cutting board 90 degrees and chop in the other direction (page 524). Heat 1 tablespoon of olive oil and the butter in a skillet or frying pan. Add the mushrooms and season with salt. Cook for 4 minutes over high heat. Add the sliced shallot. Mix and cook for 2 minutes. Add the parsley. Mix and cook for 1 additional minute. Transfer to an ovenproof dish. Cover with aluminum foil and keep warm in the oven, on a low temperature.

3

3 Make the beurre blanc: Chop the remaining shallot half. Melt 5 g – 0.18 ounce (1 teaspoon) of semi-salted butter in a saucepan. Add the shallot. Let soften for 2 minutes over low heat without browning.
Add the white wine and let reduce over low heat until only about 1 teaspoon of liquid is left, about 3 minutes. Add 15 g – 0.53 ounce (1 tablespoon) butter cut into cubes and stir with a whisk. Add 10 g – 0.35 ounce (2 teaspoons) of butter cut into cubes. Stir again. Bring to a simmer in order to stabilize the butter.

4 Add a pinch of lime zest and 1 teaspoon of juice. Rinse the sea beans. Cut off the twigs and discard the hard base. Line a steamer basket with the sea bean twigs. Bring water to a boil in the steamer pot. Season the salmon steaks with salt on both sides. Lay them over the sea beans.

4

5 Set the basket in the steamer, over the boiling water. Cover and cook for 3 minutes. Check that the fish is cooked by pressing with your finger; when you press, your finger should leave an imprint and then the tender flesh should spring back. Remove the steamer basket. Arrange the steaks on warm plates. Remove the twine. Divide up the sea beans and mushrooms and arrange on the plates. Serve with the beurre blanc.

SALMON EN PAPILLOTE WITH MANGO CHUTNEY

Serves 4

Preparation time 20 minutes
Cooking time 45 minutes

Salmon

4 (160-g – 5.65-ounce) skin-on salmon supremes
2 carrots
4 stalks celery
1 red bell pepper
1 leek
2 tablespoons olive oil, plus more for drizzling
Salt
1 egg white, beaten

Mango chutney

5-cm – 2-inch length of fresh ginger
1 white onion
1/2 mango
2 tablespoons olive oil
1 tablespoon sugar
100 ml – 1/3 cup plus 1 tablespoon plus 1 teaspoon sherry vinegar
3 drops Tabasco® sauce

TIPS FROM OUR CHEFS

GINGER
Use fresh ginger, not the ground variety. Their flavors are different.

EASY
If the mango is very ripe, you only have to pull on one end of the skin for it to come away from the flesh. Otherwise, use a knife to peel it.

AIRTIGHT
The packages have to be closed very tightly. En papillote dishes are cooked by the steam released by the food, which inflates the package. You should not wait to serve the packages, as they will deflate. Serve them straight from the oven.

1 Remove the skin from the fish: Cut into the flesh very close to the thinnest end of the supreme, without cutting through the skin. Slide the blade of your knife under the flesh, holding up the end with your other hand, to detach the flesh from the skin.

2 Wash the vegetables. Peel the carrots and celery stalks with a vegetable peeler. Cut up and seed the bell pepper (page 513). Remove the skin from each lobe with a vegetable peeler. Cut off the roots and leaves from the leek. Cut the white part across into two halves. Stand the pieces and halve vertically. Separate the core from the outer layers. Cut the outer layers into thin strips. Cut the other vegetables into pieces of the same length as the leek strips, then into thin strips. Heat 2 tablespoons of olive oil in a saucepan or deep skillet or frying pan. Add the vegetables. Add a pinch of salt. Cover the pan. Cook for 10 minutes over low heat, stirring occasionnaly.

3 Make the chutney: Remove the skin from the ginger with a vegetable peeler. Cut into slices, then batons, and then into very small dice (brunoise). Transfer to a plate. Halve and chop the onion (page 525). Remove the skin from the mango half (page 515).
Cut the flesh into 3-mm – 1/8-inch slices, then into thin strips. Cut the strips into a small dice.

4 Combine 1 tablespoon of olive oil in a saucepan with the diced ginger, onion, and mango. Mix gently and sauté for 3 minutes over low heat. Add the sugar and vinegar. Cover the pan and let soften for 25 minutes over low heat.

5 Prepare four rectangles of parchment (baking) paper measuring about 40 x 50 cm – 16 x 20 inches each. Put the vegetables in the center, covering the same surface area as the salmon pieces. Preheat the oven to 250°C – 475°F (gas mark 9). Lay the pieces of salmon over the vegetables. Season the fish with salt. Drizzle with a little olive oil. Brush egg white around the edges of the paper and fold each piece into a pouch (page 505). Use a wide spatula (slotted turner) to transfer the pouches to a baking sheet (tray). Bake for 5 minutes. Add 1 tablespoon of olive oil and 3 drops of Tabasco® sauce to the chutney.
Take the pouches out of the oven. Place on plates. Cut the pouches diagonally in a cross to open. Serve immediately with the chutney.

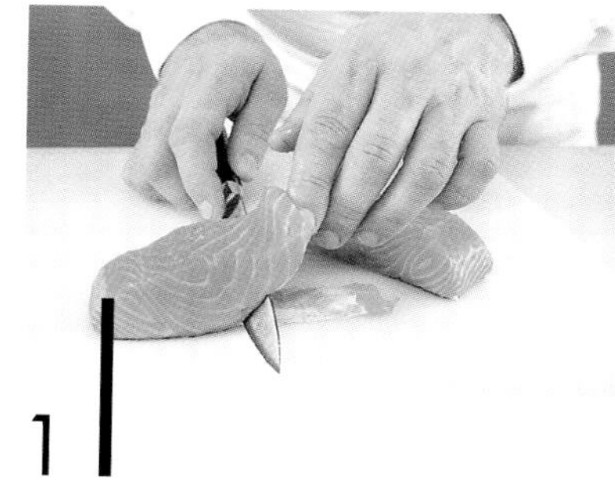
1

2

4

SALMON PIES WITH ENDIVES AND ORANGES

Serves 4

Preparation time 30 minutes
Cooking time 30 minutes
Resting time 30 minutes

Salmon

- **4** (160-g – 5.65-ounce) skin-on salmon supremes
- **2** heads Belgian endive (chicory)
- **2** oranges
- **1** tablespoon olive oil
- Salt
- **1** pinch saffron threads
- **1** pinch sugar
- **1** egg yolk
- **8** (15-cm – 6-inch) squares puff pastry

Orange sauce

- **80 ml** – 1/3 cup fresh orange juice
- **100 ml** – 1/3 cup plus 4 tsp chicken broth or stock
- **2** tablespoons olive oil
- Salt
- Freshly ground pepper

1. Remove the skin from the fish: Cut into the flesh very close to the thinnest end of the supreme, without cutting through the skin. Slide the blade of your knife under the flesh, holding up the end with your other hand, to detach the flesh from the skin.

2. Remove the outer leaves from the endive. Discard the less attractive leaves. Trim the ends of several leaves so that they resemble arrowheads. Slice the rest of the endives into rounds.

3. Cut off the top and bottom of each orange. Stand upright, supreme, and cut into sections (page 514).

4. Put 1 tablespoon of olive oil in a deep skillet or frying pan. Add the sliced endive. Season with salt and heat over medium heat. Sauté the endive 2–3 minutes, stirring from time to time. Sprinkle the saffron threads over the orange sections. Add to the endive. Simmer for 10 minutes, then let cool.

5. For the sauce: Combine the orange juice and chicken broth in a saucepan and reduce by three quarters. To make a glaze, mix 1 teaspoon of water with a pinch of salt, a pinch of sugar, and the egg yolk. Lay the four pastry squares on parchment (baking) paper. Brush the glaze over the edges; reserve remaining glaze. Divide up the endive mixture and place on the squares. Cut the paper between the squares.

6. Preheat the oven to 230°C – 450°F (gas mark 8). Season the salmon pieces on both sides with salt. Lay over the vegetables. Cover with the remaining four squares. Press on the edges to seal well.

7. Press around the fish with the back of a knife blade to leave a light mark. Trim the pastry to 5 mm – 1/4 inch from the mark to even out the edges. Refrigerate 30 minutes. Brush reserved glaze over the top of the pies. Slide the pies onto a baking sheet (tray). Bake for 10 minutes.

8. Transfer the orange reduction to a bowl. Whisk in the olive oil a thin stream. Taste the sauce. Adjust the seasoning with salt and pepper. Take the pies out of the oven. Serve hot with the orange sauce.

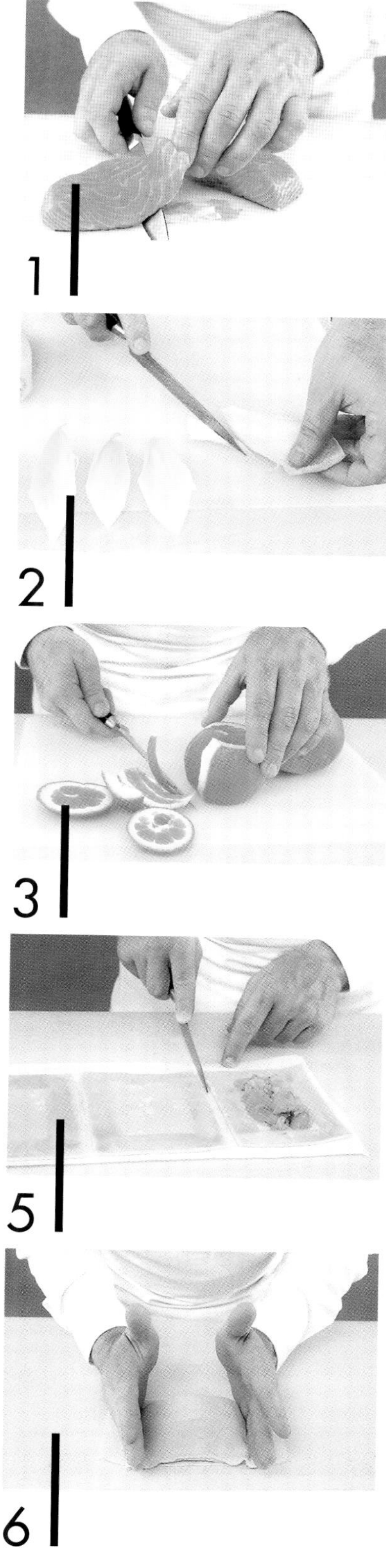

BOUILLABAISSE

Serves 6

Preparation time 1 hour
Cooking time 1 hour 30 minutes

EQUIPMENT

Handheld blender
Mortar and pestle
Garlic press

Bouillabaisse

1 large onion
1 fennel bulb
2 tomatoes
1 organic, unwaxed orange
2 tablespoons olive oil
1 teaspoon fennel seeds
5 cloves garlic, unpeeled
1 heaping tablespoon tomato paste (purée)
400 g – 14 oz conger eel in large pieces
1 (1.2-kg - 2 lb 10-oz) John Dory, filleted, with the head and bones separate
1.1 kg – 2 lb 7 oz monkfish, skinned, filleted, and cut into pieces, with the cartilage separate
1 (800-g – 1 pound 12-ounce) sea robin (tub gurnard), filleted, with the head and bones reserved
2 (300-g – 10.5-ounce) weevers, filleted, with the heads and bones separate
120 ml – 1/2 cup white wine
1 star anise
1 teaspoon saffron threads, divided
Salt
600 g – 1 pound 5 ounces small potatoes

Rouille

1 (60-g – 2.12-ounce) potato
5 cloves garlic
1 egg yolk
1 pinch saffron threads
Salt
70 ml – 1/3 cup olive oil
Tabasco® sauce

1

Peel the onion. Cut it in half, then into 3-mm – 1/8-inch slices. Halve the fennel bulb (page 515). Then cut it into slices. Cut the tomatoes into eight wedges each, then cut each piece in half crosswise. Wash the orange. Dry. Use a vegetable peeler to take off five strips of zest 2–3 cm – 3/4–1 1/4 inches in length, being careful not to remove any of the pith (page 514). Put 2 tablespoons of oil into a stockpot with the onion, fennel, and fennel seeds. Sauté the vegetables for 3 minutes over low heat without browning. Add the tomatoes, unpeeled garlic, and tomato paste. Mix for 1 minute.

2

Add the conger eel and the fish heads, bones, and cartilage to the stockpot. Stir. Add the white wine and enough water to cover the contents of the pot. Add the orange zest, star anise, and 1/2 teaspoon saffron threads. Season with salt. Bring to a boil. Skim off any impurities and cook for 20 minutes. Meanwhile, cook the potato for the rouille in its skin in salted water for 25 minutes.

3

Cut the sea robin fillets into three pieces and the John Dory, monkfish, and weever fillets in half. Set aside.

4

Pass the soup through a strainer (sieve). Remove and discard the larger bones at the same time.

5

Pass the solid ingredients left in the strainer through a food mill several times, using a bottom plate with large holes.
Add the resulting puree to the strained soup. Blend with a handheld blender and pass through a fine strainer, pressing with a ladle.

6

Make the rouille: Use the boiled unpeeled potato. Drain. Peel while still hot. Pound in a mortar. Cut the garlic cloves in half. Peel and remove the green cores from inside. Crush through a garlic press into a mortar. Pound. Add the egg yolk. Mix well with the pestle. Incorporate 2 tablespoons of fish soup. Continue to pound. Add a pinch of saffron threads. Pound again. Season with salt. Gradually stir in 70 ml – 1/3 cup of oil. Add a few drops of Tabasco sauce. The rouille is ready when the pestle can stand upright in it. Season the fish pieces with salt. Place half of them in a deep skillet or frying pan with 1 liter – 4 1/4 cups of soup. Add 1/2 teaspoon saffron. Cover and bring to a boil over high heat. Reduce the heat and let simmer for 7–8 minutes. Take out the thinnest pieces first. Cook the rest of the fish the same way. Peel and wash the potatoes for the soup. Put them into a saucepan with the rest of the soup (500 ml – 2 cups). Bring to a boil. Cover. Cook for 20 minutes. Mix the soup used to cook the fish and that from cooking the potatoes and blend, adding gradually. Distribute the fish, potatoes, and soup into warm bowls. Serve the rouille separately.

POTTED RABBIT

Serves 6–8

Preparation time 30 minutes
Cooking time 45 minutes
Resting time 1 hour

EQUIPMENT
Stand mixer

1 (1.2-kg – 2 pound 10-ounce) rabbit, head removed
2 yellow onions
1/4 cup plus 3 tablespoons olive oil, divided, plus more for drizzling
Salt
Freshly ground pepper
5 cloves garlic, unpeeled
1 sprig rosemary
100 ml – 1/3 cup plus 1 tablespoon plus 1 teaspoon white wine
100 ml – 1/3 cup plus 1 tablespoon plus 1 teaspoon chicken broth
1 loaf pain de campagne

1 Preheat the oven to 190°C – 350°F. Cut up the rabbit (page 538). Save the liver for another purpose. Peel the onions. Cut them in half. Use the tip of a knife to cut off the roots, then thinly slice (page 525). Heat 2 tablespoons of olive oil in a deep oven-proof skillet or frying pan over high heat. Add the rabbit pieces. Season with salt and pepper. Brown for 2 minutes.

2 Turn the pieces of rabbit over. Season with salt and pepper. Brown for another 2 minutes, shaking the pan from time to time. Add the onions, unpeeled garlic, and rosemary. Drizzle with a little olive oil.
Cook in the preheated oven for 20 minutes. Turn the pieces over. Cook for an additional 20 minutes.
Take the pan out of the oven. Add the white wine and reduce for 1 minute over high heat. Add the chicken broth. Cover and let cool off the heat.

3 Transfer the contents of the pan to a colander over a bowl.

4 Bone the rabbit. Remove the pulp from the garlic cloves by pressing on their skins. Add the pulp to the rabbit. Strip the rosemary leaves from the sprig, chop with a knife, and add them to the rabbit. Transfer everything to a stand mixer. Add the cooking liquid and 3 generous tablespoons of olive oil. Blend. Taste and adjust the seasoning. Add 2 tablespoons of oil. Blend. Transfer to a container.

5 Cover with plastic wrap (cling film) and refrigerate. Serve with toasted slices of pain de campagne.

1

3

4

5

TIPS FROM OUR CHEFS

WATCH FOR SPLINTERS

When cutting up a rabbit, be careful not to create splinters. Cut the flesh only as far as the bone, then dislocate the joint with your hands. Finally, cut at the joint.

FOIE GRAS ON TOAST WITH APPLES

Serves 4

Preparation time 15 minutes
Cooking time 30 minutes

1 Golden Delicious apple
1/4 teaspoon sugar
4 (90-g - 3.17-oz / 1.5-cm - 5/8-inch-thick) slices of raw foie gras
Fine salt
Freshly ground white pepper
1 loaf pain de campagne
120 ml – 1/2 cup port
1 Granny Smith apple
Fleur de sel
Coarsely ground pepper

1 Peel the Golden Delicious apple with a vegetable peeler. Halve and core (page 512). Cut into uniform slices, then into a small dice. Put into a saucepan with the sugar and 2 tablespoons of water. Cover and let soften for 15 minutes over low heat.

1

2 In the meantime, season the slices of foie gras on both sides with a little fine salt and white pepper.
Cut four slices of bread with the same diameter as the slices of foie gras, but with half the thickness.

2

3 Put the slices of foie gras, two at a time, into a hot skillet or frying pan. Pan-fry for 1 minute on each side over high heat. When you turn the foie gras over, add the slices of bread to the pan and toast just one side. When the foie gras has finished cooking, place the slices of pan-fried foie gras on the untoasted sides of the bread; the bread will stay soft. Drain on paper towels.

3

4 Pour the port into another saucepan. Reduce over high heat until it reaches a syrupy consistency, being careful not to let it burn, about 10 minutes.

4

5 Wash the Granny Smith apple and cut into uniform slices. Cut each slice into matchsticks. Remove the foie gras from the bread. Spread the stewed apple over the slices of bread, then return the pan-fried slices of foie gras to the bread. Drizzle with the port reduction and season with fleur de sel and coarsely ground pepper. Decorate with the Granny Smith matchsticks.

TIPS FROM OUR CHEFS

PROPERLY COOKED
The foie gras should be a beautiful golden color on both sides, but be careful not to overcook it because it can turn bitter. It is normal for the foie gras to give off some fat, but it should be pan-fried over high heat or it will become too soft.

PROPER TEXTURE
Reducing the port allows the alcohol to evaporate and the sugar to thicken. For a successful reduction, it should be syrupy (almost like a gel) and coat a spoon.

FOIE GRAS TERRINE WITH PEARS

Serves 6

Preparation time 20 minutes
Cooking time 2 minutes +
4 minutes
Resting time 12 hours

EQUIPMENT

Terrine dish (dimensions 12 x 9 x 6 cm – 4 3/4 x 3 1/2 x 2 1/2 inches)
Small board
Weight (page 509)

1 Bartlett (Williams) pear
1 (about 500-g - 1 lb 2-oz) foie gras
8 g – 0.28 ounce (1 1/4 teaspoons) fine salt
2 g – 0.07 ounce (1 teaspoon) Freshly ground pepper
30 ml – 2 tablespoons port
Fleur de sel
Coarsely ground pepper
1 loaf sourdough bread
1 small very firm pear for grating

1. Peel the Bartlett pear with a vegetable peeler. Cut in half and remove the core and seeds. Cut the bottom off each pear half to provide a stable base and cut into 5-mm – 1/4-inch slices. Use a paring knife to scrape off the ball of fat and any bile found under the liver. Separate the foie gras into two lobes by hand and cut the small vein holding them together.

2. Slice the foie gras diagonally into scallops (escalopes) about 1 cm – 3/8 inch thick. Season the scallops of foie gras on both sides with the fine salt and white pepper. Pan-fry the scallops for 1 minute on each side over very high heat. Drain on paper towels. Collect the fat released when cooking the scallops and pass through a strainer (sieve). Discard the residue from the bottom of the pan. Put 1 tablespoon of the strained fat into the pan. Brown the pear slices on both sides for 4 minutes over low heat. They should be cooked. Deglaze the pan with the port and let reduce. This will color the slices.

3. Line the terrine dish with plastic wrap (cling film). Start assembling the terrine by making a layer of pan-fried foie gras in the terrine dish. Continue by alternating the pear with the foie gras, finishing with the foie gras. Press down firmly with the back of a spoon from time to time so that the filling is spread out. Pull the plastic wrap tightly over the terrine.

4. If you don't have a small board and weight on hand, you can make them yourself (page 509). Lay the board over the terrine. Press down firmly. Place the weight over the terrine in order to make the foie gras and pear stick together. Refrigerate for at least 12 hours.

5. Take the terrine out of the refrigerator. Remove the weight and board. Open the plastic wrap and lift gently so that the terrine will come away from the dish. Slice the terrine. Pass a hot knife over the slices to smooth before serving. Sprinkle with fleur de sel and coarsely ground pepper. Serve with toasted slices of sourdough bread and a little grated raw pear.

1

4

TRADITIONAL FOIE GRAS TERRINE

TRADITIONAL FOIE GRAS TERRINE

Serves 6

Preparation time 30 minutes
Cooking time 50 minutes
Resting time 12 hours + 5–6 hours + 2–3 days

EQUIPMENT

Small terrine dish with lid
Cooking thermometer
Small board
Weight

1 (approximatively 500-g – 1 pound 2-ounce) foie gras
8 g – 0.28 ounce (1 1/4 teaspoons) fine salt
2 g – 0.07 ounce (1 teaspoon) freshly ground white pepper
1 g – 0.04 ounce (1/4 teaspoon) sugar
2 tablespoons cognac or Madeira
1 loaf pain de campagne
Fleur de sel
Coarsely ground pepper

1 Devein the foie gras (page 531). Set aside the veins.

2 Mix the fine salt with the white pepper and sugar. Use half of this mixture to season the inside of the two deveined lobes. Fold the smaller lobe closed. Press gently on it. Turn it over. Do the same for the larger lobe. Season the two lobes on their skin side.

3 Start assembling the terrine by placing the larger lobe at the bottom of the dish, skin side down. Fold the parts that don't fit on the bottom over the top so that the lobe is firmly compacted.
Add the smaller lobe, skin side up. The pieces should overlap a fair amount and be spread out over the dish. Press down well to fill all the sides of the terrine dish. Dry the edges of the dish with paper towels. Drizzle with cognac and let marinate for a few minutes. Place the lid on the terrine dish and cover with plastic wrap (cling film). Refrigerate for at least 12 hours.

1

3

4 The next day, take the terrine dish out of the refrigerator, remove the plastic wrap, and let stand at room temperature for 30 minutes. Heat water to 80°C – 176°F for a bain-marie. Preheat the oven to 140°C – 275°F (gas mark 1).
Line the bottom of a baking pan with paper towels. Place the terrine dish over them and add enough water to fill the pan halfway. Bake for about 50 minutes.
Use a thermometer to check the temperature of the terrine. It should reach a core temperature of 48°C – 118.4°F.

4

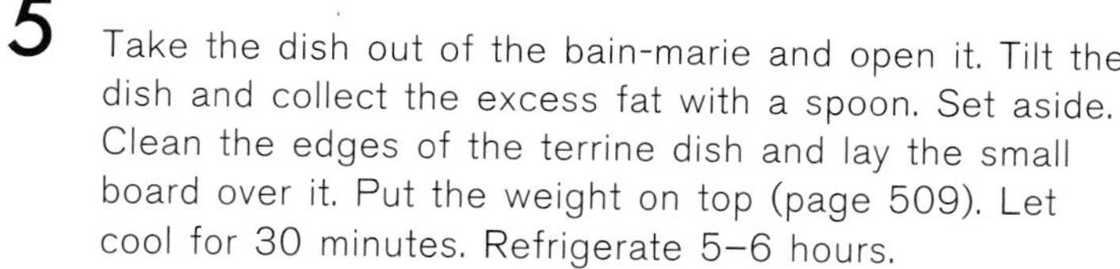

5 Take the dish out of the bain-marie and open it. Tilt the dish and collect the excess fat with a spoon. Set aside. Clean the edges of the terrine dish and lay the small board over it. Put the weight on top (page 509). Let cool for 30 minutes. Refrigerate 5–6 hours.

5

6 Remove the weight. Lift off the board and clean off the fat. Do the same with the top of the terrine dish.
Mix the fat taken from the terrine dish and board with the fat previously set aside (step 5). Spread evenly over the foie gras to cover completely.
Clean the edges of the dish with paper towels. Place the lid on the terrine dish and cover with plastic wrap. Refrigerate for 2–3 days.
Open the dish and cut the terrine into uniform slices with a hot knife.
Serve with toasted slices of pain de campagne, a little fleur de sel, and coarsely ground pepper.

STEAMED FOIE GRAS WITH GREEN LENTILS

STEAMED FOIE GRAS WITH GREEN LENTILS

Serves 4

Green lentils
Preparation time 5 minutes
Cooking time 20–25 minutes

Foie gras
Preparation time 5 minutes
Cooking time 8 minutes
Soaking time 2 hours

Green lentils

120 g – 4.23 ounces (2/3 cup) green lentils
1/2 onion
1 small carrot
Leek leaves
1 sprig fresh thyme
1 bay leaf
Several parsley stems (stalks)
10 g – 0.35 ounce (2/3 tablespoon) butter
600 ml – 2 1/2 cups vegetable broth or stock (page 549), hot
Fine salt
Aged wine vinegar

Olive oil

Foie gras

4 (90-g – 3.17-ounce) slices raw foie gras
Fine salt
Freshly ground white pepper
Fleur de sel
Coarsely ground pepper

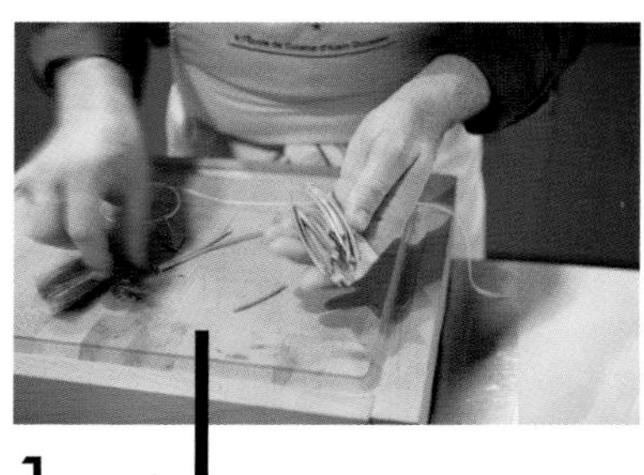
1

1 Wash the lentils by soaking in cold water for 2 hours, then rinse.
Peel and chop the onion (page 525). Peel the carrot with a vegetable peeler and cut into small dice (brunoise).
Make a bouquet garni with the leek leaves, thyme, bay leaf, and parsley stems (page 544).

2

2 Melt the butter in a saucepan and sauté the onion and carrot for 2 minutes.
Add the lentils to the pan and mix. Moisten with the hot vegetable broth. Add the bouquet garni and bring to a boil.
Cook for 20–25 minutes. Skim off any impurities.

3

4

5

3 Cook the foie gras: bring water to a boil in a stockpot. Season the slices of foie gras on both sides with a little fine salt and white pepper.
Lay a slice of foie gras on a square of plastic wrap (cling film).
Wrap three times in the plastic, then fold over the sides to seal the foie gras well in a package. Repeat the process for the other slices.

4 Put the slices of foie gras in a steamer basket. Place the basket over the stockpot. Cover the pot and cook for 8 minutes.
Check that the foie gras is cooked with your finger. It should be soft. Remove the packages from the stockpot. Set aside.

5 Continue with the lentils: Remove the bouquet garni 5 minutes before the lentils finish cooking, and season with salt. Finish cooking.
Remove the lentils with a slotted spoon or skimmer, reserving the cooking liquid, and distribute among four bowls. Reduce the cooking liquid over medium heat to a syrupy consistency.
Lift up the folded sides of one of the foie gras packages. Cut off one side with a paring knife.
Drain off the fat into a bowl. Repeat with remaining foie gras packages. (Discard the fat when cold.)
Unwrap the foie gras slices and slide onto a plate lined with paper towels. Keep hot by covering with plastic wrap.

6 Drizzle the lentils with a little of the reduced cooking liquid, a dash of vinegar, and a little olive oil.
Lay one slice of foie gras over the lentils in each of the plates. Sprinkle with fleur de sel and coarsely ground pepper.

FOIE GRAS EN PAPILLOTE WITH FIGS AND PORCINI

Serves 4

Preparation time 20 minutes
Cooking time 15 minutes

4 fresh figs
4 porcini (ceps)
1 shallot
4 (100-g - 3.53-oz) slices of raw foie gras
Fine salt
Freshly ground white pepper
1 egg white, beaten
Fleur de sel
Coarsely ground pepper
Sherry vinegar

1 Preheat oven to 230°C – 450°F (gas mark 8). Wash the figs and cut each into five slices. Use a paring knife to cut off the part of the mushrooms covered in soil. Scrape off the brown skin from the stem (stalk). Clean the mushrooms with a damp brush. Cut them in half. Cut off a part of each stem and cut into small dice (brunoise). Peel and chop the shallot (page 525). Season the mushrooms, fig pieces, and the slices of foie gras on both sides with a little fine salt and white pepper.

2 Start assembling the first package by laying a rectangle of parchment (baking) paper over a rectangle of aluminum foil (page 505). Spread one-quarter of the diced mushroom and chopped shallot over the middle of one-half of the rectangle. Arrange two mushroom halves head-to-tail on top. Add a slice of foie gras. Surround the foie gras with five fig pieces. Brush a little egg white over the edges of the rectangle.

3 Fold to make an airtight package. Repeat with remaining ingredients to make 4 packets.

4 Bake in the preheated oven for 15 minutes. When they come out of the oven, the packages should be fully inflated. Use a knife to pierce the center of the aluminum foil, then use scissors to cut the diagonally in a cross. Do the same for the parchment paper. Sprinkle with fleur de sel and coarsely ground pepper, and drizzle with a dash of vinegar. Serve immediately.

1

2

3

TIPS FROM OUR CHEFS

TIME SAVING

The packages can be prepared ahead of time. In this case, sauté the shallots with the diced mushroom for 3 minutes over high heat to stop them from altering the flavor of the foie gras. Store the prepared pouches in the refrigerator and cook just before serving.

DUCK TIAN WITH ORANGES AND TURNIPS

Serves 2

Preparation time 1 hour
Cooking time 40 minutes

EQUIPMENT

2 (15-cm- – 6-inch-diameter) earthenware dishes
Citrus squeezer
Grill (griddle) pan
2 large toothpicks (cocktail sticks)

3 organic, unwaxed oranges
1 large turnip
1 medium onion
2 tablespoons olive oil, plus more for brushing dishes
Fine salt
Freshly ground white pepper
1 teaspoon honey
60 ml – 1/4 cup veal broth or stock
About 80 ml – 1/3 cup chicken broth or stock
1 tablespoon sugar
1 (about 300-g - 10.5-oz) duck breast
Five-spice powder

TIPS FROM OUR CHEFS

AT ROOM TEMPERATURE

Never cook meat straight out of the refrigerator. Take the duck fillet out at least 10 minutes beforehand.

HOMEMADE SPICE BLEND

To make your own five-spice powder, mix cinnamon with pepper, grated nutmeg, ground clove, and ground ginger (or star anise).

1

Wash and dry one of the oranges. Use a vegetable peeler to take off six strips of zest (page 514). Remove the pith.
Cut the pieces of zest into thin strips with a chef's knife.
Preheat the oven to 200°C – 400°F (gas mark 6).
Supreme and section (segment) the two remaining oranges over a bowl (page 514). Squeeze the peels into the bowl to collect the juice.

2

Peel the turnip with a vegetable peeler, starting at the bottom, then cut off the top and bottom ends. Cut into rounds 3–4-mm – 1/8-inch thick, starting at the bottom. Peel and chop the onion (page 525). Heat 1 tablespoon of olive oil in a deep skillet or frying pan. Brown the turnip slices for 1 minute over medium heat. Add the onion and cook for 5 minutes while stirring. They should color lightly. Use a wet pastry brush to push the onions off the sides of the pan. Season with salt and white pepper. Incorporate the honey. Clean the sides of the pan with the damp brush.

3

Add the orange juice to stop the cooking process. Cook until the juice reduces completely, about 5 minutes. Transfer the turnip mixture to a plate.
Heat 1 tablespoon of olive oil in the same pan, then add the orange sections. Sauté for 30 seconds, shaking the pan. Transfer to a bowl.

4

Brush the two ovenproof dishes with oil. Arrange the turnip slices overlapped in a row over the bottom of each dish. Make a second layer, overlapping in the opposite direction. Alternate every two turnip slices with an orange section. Divide the veal broth between the two dishes. Add enough chicken broth to fall just short of covering the contents of the dishes. Place on the middle shelf of the preheated oven and bake for 40 minutes.

5

Put the orange zest strips in a saucepan and cover with cold water. Bring to a boil. Drain. Repeat the process another two times. Return the zest to the pan. Squeeze the zested orange and add 100 ml – 1/3 cup plus 1 tablespoon plus 1 teaspoon of juice to the pan. Add the sugar and cook for 30 minutes over very low heat. Heat the grill pan over high heat. Peel off any muscle membrane from the duck breast by sliding the blade of a boning knife underneath. Pull and cut. Remove the excess fat from around the breast. Score the breast in a diamond pattern: Make diagonal incisions about 12 mm – 1/2 inch apart in one direction, and then in the other. Season both sides with salt and white pepper and dust with the five-spice powder.

6

Place the breast on the grill pan, skin side down. Reduce the heat and cook for 5 minutes. Pour off the fat. Turn the breast 90 degrees and cook for 5 minutes to create a crisscross pattern. Turn the breast over. Cook for 1 minute 30 seconds, turn 90 degrees, and cook for 1 minute 30 seconds. Transfer the breast to a dish. Cover tightly with aluminum foil and let rest for 6 minutes. Check that the turnips and oranges are cooked through by piercing with the tip of a paring knife. They should be tender. Lay the breast on a cutting board and cut in half. Fold each half and secure with a toothpick. Sprinkle with cooked zest. Serve the duck very hot with the turnips and oranges. For a more stylish presentation, take the turnips and oranges from the dish and serve directly on plates.

DUCK BREAST WITH BIGARADE SAUCE

Serves 4

Preparation 1 hour 45 minutes
Cooking time 1 hour 5 minutes

EQUIPMENT

Citrus squeezer
12 large toothpicks (cocktail sticks)

Bigarade sauce

1 organic, unwaxed orange
1 organic, unwaxed lemon
40 g – 1.6 ounces (3 tablespoons plus 1 teaspoon) superfine (caster) sugar
2 tablespoons sherry vinegar
About 80 ml – 1/3 cup chickent broth or stock

Mushroom duxelles

250 g – 9 ounces button mushrooms
1/2 lemon
1 small white onion
1 shallot
15 g – 0.53 ounce (1 tablespoon) butter, cut into cubes
Fine salt

Asparagus and duck breast

1 (about 400-g - 14-oz) magret (breast)
12 spears asparagus
1 tablespoon kosher (coarse) salt
Fine salt
Freshly ground pepper
Fleur de sel
Coarsely ground pepper

TIPS FROM OUR CHEFS

BLANCHING AND BITTERNESS
Blanching citrus zests, which involves bringing it to a boil in water, refreshing it, and repeating the process another two times, removes the natural bitterness from the zest.

DOUBLE SHOCKING
The thermal shocks that the asparagus receives as it goes straight from ice water to boiling water, then back into ice water, preserve its color. In addition, the second immersion in ice water immediately stops the cooking process.

1

Make the bigarade sauce: Wash and dry the orange and lemon. Use a paring knife to cut 5-cm / 2-inch ribbons of zest (page 514). Set aside. Cut the orange and lemon in half and squeeze them separately. Strain the juice after squeezing. Measure out 80 ml – 1/3 cup of orange juice and 50 ml – 3 tablespoons plus 1 1/2 teaspoons of lemon juice.

2

Combine the sugar with 2 tablespoons of water in a saucepan. Place over high heat for about 3 minutes to make a dark caramel. Pour in the vinegar, guarding against splatters, and swirl the pan. Add the orange and lemon juices. Clean the sides of the pan with a damp brush. Cook until reduced by half, about 9 minutes. Bring 100 ml – 1/3 cup plus 1 tablespoon plus 1 teaspoon water to a boil. Add the cube of duck jus. Pour the jus into the caramel. Cook over low heat until thickened, about 20 minutes. Put the zests into a saucepan with cold water. Bring to a boil. Drain. Refresh in ice water. Repeat this blanching process another two times.

3

Peel the asparagus spears (remove the scales from the stems/stalks). Trim to uniform length. Wash the asparagus. Tie into two bundles of 6 spears each: With the tips facing downward, twist the twine around a bundle three times, then push the twine down and twist the string around the bundle another two or three times 10 cm – 4 inches higher up. Secure with a knot. Immerse the asparagus in ice water. Bring water to a boil in a small stockpot. Add 1 tablespoon of kosher salt to the boiling water. Immerse the asparagus in the boiling water. Leave the pot uncovered. Cook for 3 minutes over medium heat. Check that they are cooked through. Remove the bundles from the water with a skimmer. Immediately immerse them in ice water and let stand for about 2 minutes. Cut the twine. Drain on paper towels.

TIPS FROM OUR CHEFS

BY HAND

Using a food processor to chop mushrooms turns them dark. It is better to cut them by hand to make light-colored duxelles. The term "duxelles" refers to a finely chopped mixture of mushrooms, onion, and shallots that is used in different preparations.

4 Make the duxelles: Cut the stems off the mushrooms. Peel the caps (page 516) and dice. Drizzle with lemon juice. Peel the onion. Halve and chop (page 525). Drizzle with lemon juice. Peel, halve, and chop the shallot (page 525). Melt the butter in a saucepan. Add the onion and shallot. Season lightly with salt. Cook for 1 minute 30 seconds to soften. Add the mushrooms and two pinches of salt. Mix. Cover the pan. Cook for 15 minutes over low heat.

5

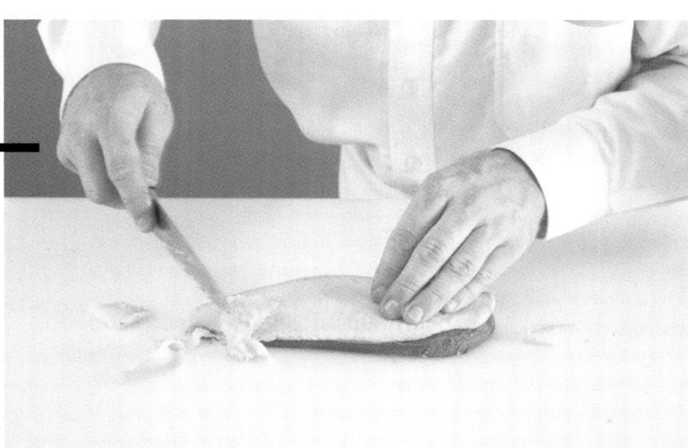

Prepare the duck: Remove the muscle membrane and fat from the flesh side of the duck breast, then trim off the excess fat from around the meat. Trim off a little of the fat from the skin side. Score the fat side in a diamond pattern. Carefully season this side with salt and pepper. Heat a deep skillet or frying pan. Place the duck breast in the pan fat side down. Cook for 4 minutes over high heat. Use a spoon to remove fat from the pan from time to time. Continue to cook for 4 minutes over medium heat. Season the flesh side of the breast with salt and pepper. Turn the breast over. Cook for 4 minutes over medium heat.

6

Place the duck breast on paper towels to absorb the fat. Cut off the asparagus tips. Cut the stems into 3-mm – 1/8-inch slices. Mix them with the duxelles. Reheat the tips for a few seconds. Reheat the bigarade sauce over low heat. Cut the breast into twelve 5-mm – 1/4-inch slices. Fold each slice in half and secure with a toothpick (cocktail stick). Put 2 tablespoons of duxelles into the bottom of each individual serving bowl. Arrange five asparagus tips and three duck slices on top. Immerse the citrus zests in the bigarade sauce. Mix. Let infuse for a few seconds. Add the zests to the bowls, then cover with the sauce. Sprinkle with a little fleur de sel and coarsely ground pepper. Serve immediately.

CARAMELIZED VEAL SPARERIBS WITH MASHED POTATOES

Serves 4

Preparation time 50 minutes
Cooking time 50 minutes
Resting time 12 hours

EQUIPMENT

Citrus squeezer
Mortar and pestle
Pressure cooker
Steamer basket
5-cm- – 2-inch–diameter cookie cutter (page 503)
Wooden skewers

Veal spareribs

100 g – 3.5 ounces (1/2 cup) sugar
100 ml – 1/3 cup plus 1 tablespoon plus 1 teaspoon sherry vinegar
2 lemons
1 orange
2 sprigs rosemary
1 tablespoon peppercorns
4 (350-g - 12.35-oz) slices veal breast, bone in
2 tablespoons olive oil
100 ml - 1/3 cup plus 4 tsp white veal broth or stock
Salt
Freshly ground pepper
Fleur de sel

Mashed potatoes

800 g – 1 pound 12 ounces potatoes
50 g – 1.76 ounces (3 1/2 tablespoons) butter, softened
Salt

TIPS FROM OUR CHEFS

DON'T TOUCH
Don't stir the sugar when making the caramel. It is enough just to shake or swirl the pan.

QUICK STOCK
Make a stock quickly by dissolving 1 tablespoon of veal bouillon (stock) powder in 100 ml – 1/3 cup plus 1 tablespoon plus 1 teaspoon hot water.

BONELESS
Remove the bones after you take the ribs out of the pressure cooker for pieces as close to the same size as possible.

BROIL OR BURN
Slide the ribs as closely as possible to the broiler (grill) element or burner, keep the door ajar, and watch closely, because the meat can burn in one second.

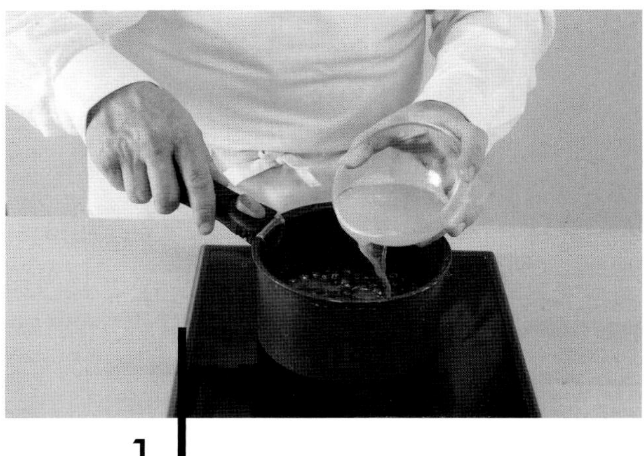

1

Put the sugar into a very dry saucepan. Heat over high heat to make a dark caramel (page 566). Pour the vinegar over the caramel and swirl the pan. Halve the lemons and orange. Squeeze with a citrus squeezer. Mix the juices. Add the juice to the caramel. Reduce by half to a slightly syrupy consistency. Let cool.

2

Pluck the rosemary. Chop the leaves with a knife. Coarsely grind the peppercorns in the mortar. Set aside 1 teaspoon of coarsely ground pepper for finishing.

3

Combine half of the rosemary and half of the remaining pepper in the bottom of a dish. Arrange the veal ribs in the dish. Cover with the rest of the rosemary and pepper. Drizzle the ribs with the citrus syrup. Cover the dish with plastic wrap (cling film). Marinate in the refrigerator for 12 hours.

4

When ready to cook, heat 2 tablespoons of olive oil in a pressure cooker pot over medium heat. Brown half of the meat for 3 minutes, turning the pieces over.
Remove the well-browned ribs, then brown the rest of the ribs in the same way. Return all the meat to the pressure cooker. Add the remaining marinade from the dish. Clean the sides of the pressure cooker with a damp brush. Add the veal broth. Season with salt and pepper. Place the lid on the pressure cooker and lock. Program the timer for 24 minutes of cooking time, starting on high heat. When the timer sounds, reduce the heat (page 508).

In the meantime make the mashed potatoes: Peel the potatoes. Cut in half, then into chunks. Put into a steamer basket. Season with salt. Place a rack in the drip pan. Brush with oil. When the ribs are cooked, turn off the heat and timer. Open the pressure cooker. Turn on or light the oven broiler (grill). Transfer the ribs to the rack. Strain the cooking liquid into a saucepan. Reduce by half over high heat. Pour 750 ml – 3 cups of water into the pressure cooker. Put the steamer basket with the potatoes inside. Pressure-cook for 9 minutes, starting on high heat.

5

6 Slide the ribs under the broiler. Cook for 2 minutes. Baste with the reduced cooking liquid. Place under the broiler for 30 seconds. Take the ribs out of the broiler. Sprinkle with fleur de sel and the reserved coarsely ground pepper.

7 When the potatoes are cooked, open the pressure cooker. Transfer to a bowl. Mash with a fork. Incorporate the butter, followed by a little fleur de sel. Cut each rib into three pieces. Thread three rib pieces onto a 15-cm – 6-inch wooden skewer. Repeat with remaining ribs and skewers.

8 To plate, place a 5-cm- – 2-inch-diameter cookie cutter on a plate. Fill with mashed potatoes and remove. Repeat with remaining mashed potatoes. Add the skewers. Serve immediately.

CHICKEN COUSCOUS WITH ALMONDS, RAISINS, AND SAFFRON

Serves 4

Preparation time 25 minutes
Cooking time 55 minutes
Resting time 12 hours

EQUIPMENT

Stockpot
Couscoussier

Chicken

1 (1.5 kg – 3 pounds 4 ounces) organic chicken
1 white onion
2 cloves garlic
60 g – 2.12 ounces (about 2/3 cup grated) fresh ginger
1 g – 0.04 ounce (1/2 teaspoon) saffron powder
1/4 cup plus 1 tablespoon olive oil, divided
1 tomato
1 bay leaf
Salt
Freshly ground pepper
700 ml – 3 cups chicken broth or stock
60 g – 2.12 ounces (1/3 cup plus 2 tablespoons) golden raisins (sultanas)
80 g – 2.82 ounces (1/2 cup plus 1 tablespoon) blanched almonds

Plain couscous

recipe on page 552

1 The day before you plan to serve the dish, cut up the chicken (page 527). Peel and finely chop the onion (page 525). Put half into a bowl. Peel and crush the garlic, remove green core. Add half to the bowl. Add half the grated ginger and half of the saffron. Arrange the pieces of chicken on top of the ingredients in the bowl.

2 Cover with the remaining onion, garlic, ginger, and saffron. Drizzle with 60 ml – 1/4 cup of olive oil. Cover with plastic wrap (cling film) and refrigerate for 12 hours.

3 On the day you plan to serve the dish, cut the tomato into 12 wedges. Peel by passing the blade of a paring knife between the skin and flesh (page 521). Seed.
Heat 1 tablespoon of olive oil in a stockpot and brown the chicken pieces. Add the tomato and bay leaf.
Season with salt and pepper.
Add the cold broth, mix, and bring to a boil. Cover the pan and simmer for 45 minutes.

4 In the meantime, make and steam the plain couscous (page 522). Cover with plastic wrap to keep hot.
Soak the raisins for 10 seconds in a bowl of hot water to swell. Drain.

5 Toast the almonds in a very hot skillet or frying pan without adding oil. Add the raisins and toast for 2 minutes while stirring constantly. Transfer to a plate to stop the cooking process. When the chicken is cooked, add the raisins and almonds. Simmer for 5 minutes. Serve immediately with the couscous.

TIPS FROM OUR CHEFS

WISHBONE

The wishbone is the forked bone between the neck and breast. When boning a chicken, always start by removing the wishbone.

BEST BAY LEAF

Use dried bay leaf to avoid the sharp bitterness of fresh bay leaf.

COUSCOUS WITH PAPRIKA AND SPICED MEATBALLS

Serves 4

Meatballs
Preparation time 40 minutes
Cooking time 35 minutes
Resting time 1 hour

Couscous with paprika
Preparation time 6 minutes
Cooking time 10 minutes
Resting time 10 minutes

EQUIPMENT

Couscous with paprika
Stockpot
Couscoussier

Meatballs

1 red bell pepper
1 bunch flat-leaf parsley
1 bunch cilantro (coriander)
1 white onion
600 g - 1 lb 5 oz ground (minced) beef, 15 percent fat
40 g – 1.4 ounces (1 cup) fresh breadcrumbs soaked in 100 ml – 1/3 cup plus 1 tablespoon plus 1 teaspoon whole milk
1 egg, beaten
Salt
1 1/2 teaspoons paprika
1 teaspoon ground cumin
1 pinch ground cinnamon
Freshly ground pepper
Flour
3 tomatoes
Olive oil
500 ml – 2 cups beef broth or stock

Couscous with paprika

400 g – 14 ounces (2 1/3 cups) medium-grain couscous
4 g – 0.14 ounce (2/3 teaspoon) salt
60 ml – 1/4 cup olive oil
1 tablespoon paprika
500 ml - 2 cups beef broth or stock
Harissa

TIPS FROM OUR CHEFS

SHAKE

Don't squeeze your herbs to dry them. Hold them upside down and shake off the excess water, or use a salad spinner.

BETTER WITH TWO

Using two forks allows you to crush the breadcrumbs thoroughly to bind the meatball mixture better. You achieve effective mixing and a softer texture in a single action.

1

Wash, then cut up and seed the bell pepper (page 513). Cut into strips, and then 2-mm – 1/16-inch dice (brunoise). Wash, dry, and pluck the parsley and cilantro. Gather the leaves into small bunches and finely chop (page 524). Peel and finely chop the onion (page 525). Combine the ground beef with the diced bell pepper and chopped onion in a bowl. Drain the breadcrumbs and add to the mixture. Add the beaten egg and 2 teaspoons of salt. Sprinkle the mixture with 1 teaspoon of the paprika, then with the cumin and cinnamon. Season with freshly ground pepper (two turns of the peppermill). Add the chopped herbs. Use two forks to mix. Taste and adjust the seasoning.

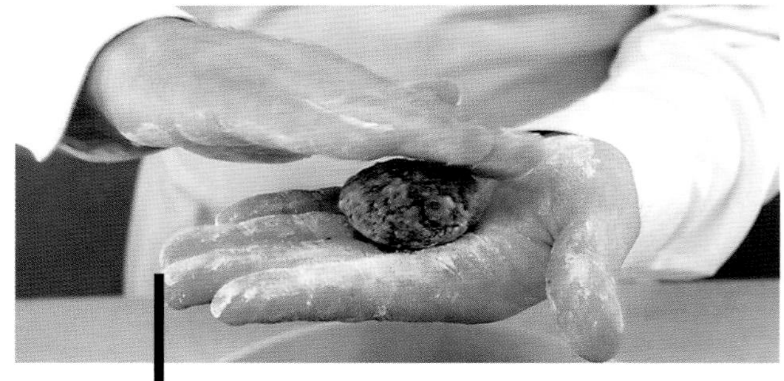

2

Fill a plate with flour. Cover your hands with flour by laying them flat on the plate. Make the meatballs by rolling 1 tablespoon of the mixture between your palms. Put the meatballs on a plate. Continue making meatballs until you use up all of the mixture. Cover with plastic wrap (cling film) and refrigerate for 1 hour.

TIPS FROM OUR CHEFS

PAPRIKA RED

If you can find paprika flakes, don't hesitate to use them in place of the powder. They will add a brighter color to your couscous.

USE HARISSA WITH CARE

For lovers of strong flavors, dissolve a teaspoon of harissa in a bowl of broth and serve on the side.

3

Bring water to a boil in a saucepan. Remove the stem (stalk) and core from the tomatoes by cutting out a cone-shaped plug from each. Cut a cross in the bottom of each one (page 521). Immerse each tomato for 10 seconds in boiling water, then plunge immediately in ice water. Peel, halve, and seed the tomatoes (page 521). Chop with a chef's knife. Heat a little olive oil in a stockpot. Brown the meatballs for 3 minutes while shaking the pan constantly. Transfer to a plate.

4

Add the chopped tomatoes to the pan. Add two pinches of salt, freshly ground pepper (two turns of the peppermill), and the remaining 1/2 teaspoon paprika. Cook for 5 minutes over high heat. Add the broth and let reduce for 15 minutes over medium heat. Transfer the sauce and meatballs to the bottom pot of the couscoussier.

5

Prepare the couscous: Rinse and roll the couscous with the salt and olive oil (page 552). Dissolve the paprika in the broth and bring to a boil in a saucepan. Pour the broth over the couscous and let swell. Transfer the couscous to the top pot of the couscoussier. Place the top pot over the bottom pot, the meatballs and the sauce will be at a boil. Cover the couscoussier and cook for 10 minutes.
Serve immediately with harissa (page 553).

LAMB TAGINE WITH COUSCOUS AND NUTS

Serves 4

Lamb tagine
Preparation time 30 minutes
Cooking time 1 hour 40 minutes
Resting time 2 hours

Couscous
Preparation time 20 minutes
Cooking time 10 minutes

EQUIPMENT

Lamb tagine
Tagine pot

Couscous
Couscoussier

Lamb tagine

900 g – 2 pounds boneless lamb shoulder (neck)
1/4 teaspoon ground cinnamon
1/4 teaspoon ground ginger
12 saffron threads
Fine salt
Freshly ground pepper
3 tablespoons olive oil, plus more for drizzling
1 onion
300 ml – 1 1/4 cups chicken broth or stock
1 stick cinnamon
40 g – 1.4 ounces (1/4 cup) raisins
16 dried apricots
30 g – 1 ounce (3 tablespoons plus 1 1/2 teaspoons) blanched almonds
30 g – 1 ounce (1/4 cup) pine nuts

Plain couscous

recipe on page 552

1

3

4

1 Remove the yellow nerve from the lamb. Use a boning knife to cut off the fat, then cut the meat into chunks about 2 x 5-cm – 3/4 x 2 inches.
Put the meat into a bowl with the cinnamon, ginger and saffron threads.
Add three pinches of salt and a generous amount of pepper (ten turns of the peppermill). Add 2 tablespoons of olive oil. Mix well.
Cover with plastic wrap (cling film) and marinate for at least 2 hours at room temperature.

2 Peel, halve, and chop the onion (page 525).
Heat 1 tablespoon of oil in the tagine pot. Lightly cook the meat over medium-high heat without browning too much, while stirring constantly.
Add the onion, mix, and cook for 2 minutes.
Add 250 ml – 1 cup of broth (the liquid should come halfway up the meat) and bring to a boil. Break the cinnamon stick in half and add.
Cover the pot and cook for 1 hour 15 minutes over low heat. Add a little broth, if necessary, after the tagine has been cooking for 30–45 minutes. In the meantime, prepare the couscous (page 552).

3 Rinse the raisins and apricots and put into a small saucepan. Cover with cold water, bring to a boil, then let cool. Drain in a strainer (sieve).

4 Add the dried fruit to the tagine pot (after the tagine has cooked for 1 hour 15 minutes). Cover and cook for 10 additional minutes. Heat a skillet or frying pan. Lightly toast the almonds without adding oil. Add the pine nuts and toast for 2 minutes. Add the nuts to the tagine pot. Cover the pot and simmer for another 5 minutes. When cooked, drizzle with olive oil to add shine. Cover (to keep hot) and serve with the couscous.

TIPS FROM OUR CHEFS

TAGINE POT

If you don't have a tagine pot, you can use a stockpot or a deep skillet or frying pan with a lid.

SHOPPING LIST

You can use golden raisins (sultanas), which are less sweet than other raisins, and try to find large soft dried apricots. Your best bet is usually to buy them in bulk from a specialty fruit and vegetable dealer or supplier.

LAMB CURRY WITH COCONUT RICE

Serves 4

Lamb curry
Preparation time 30 minutes
Cooking time 1 hour 35 minutes
Resting time 12 hours

Coconut rice
Preparation time 30 minutes
Cooking time 20 minutes
Resting time 15 minutes

EQUIPMENT

Coconut rice
Citrus squeezer
10-cm- – 4-inch–diameter ring mold

Lamb curry

800 g – 1 pound 12 ounces boneless lamb (shoulder, neck, breast)
1 (125 g – 4.40 ounces) container plain (greek) yogurt
1 organic, unwaxed lemon, plus extra juice for drizzling
Fine salt
Freshly ground pepper
5 g – 0.17 ounce (2 1/4 teaspoons) curry powder
1/2 onion
1 celery stalk
1 tablespoon peanut (groundnut) oil
50 ml – 3 tablespoons plus 1 1/2 teaspoons dry white wine
200 ml – 3/4 cup plus 1 tablespoon veal broth or stock

Coconut rice

1 coconut
600 ml – 2 1/2 cups whole milk
1 carrot
1/2 onion
1 tablespoon olive oil
200 g – 7 ounces (1 cup) basmati rice
Fine salt

1

Cut the meat into 25-g – 0.88-ounce cubes (about 3 cm – 1 1/4 inches). Place in a bowl.

2

Put the yogurt into a bowl. Wash the lemon. Finely grate its zest over the yogurt (page 514). Halve the lemon and squeeze with the citrus squeezer. Add 1 tablespoon of juice to the yogurt. Add 1 teaspoon of salt and season with pepper. Add the curry powder.

3

Mix gently. Pour over the meat. Peel the onion and slice with a chef's knife (page 525). Add the onion slices to the meat. Mix gently. Cover with plastic wrap (cling film) and marinate for 12 hours in the refrigerator.

4

When ready to cook the meat, remove the leaves from the celery. Peel the stalk with a vegetable peeler and cut into 5 mm – 1/4 inch matchsticks, then into small dice (brunoise).
Drain the meat, discard the marinade. Heat 1 tablespoon of oil in a deep skillet or frying pan. Add the meat and cook for 2 minutes over high heat while stirring constantly. Add the celery and mix well. Add the white wine and let reduce for 2 minutes. Add the broth and bring to a boil. Mix. Cover the pan and cook for 1 hour 30 minutes over low heat, stirring from time to time.

5

In the meantime, pierce the soft "eye" of the coconut with a corkscrew; screw in, then pull out a plug of pulp.

6

Shake well to collect all of the coconut water in a glass. Wrap the coconut in a cloth and hit hard against the work surface four or five times to break the shell. Use a paring knife to scrape off all of the coconut pulp. Rinse under running water.

7

Use a vegetable peeler to take a few shavings of pulp for the decoration. Finely grate half of the pulp. Heat the milk. Incorporate the grated pulp into the hot milk, then bring to a boil. Cover the pan, remove from heat, and let infuse for 15 minutes. Pass the infused milk through a fine strainer (sieve), pressing on the coconut pulp with the back of a spoon. Wash and peel the carrot. Use a chef's knife to cut it into very thin rounds on a diagonal. Finely chop the onion. Heat 1 tablespoon of olive oil in a deep skillet or frying pan. Lightly cook the carrot and onion for 1 minute over medium heat while stirring with a spatula (turner). Add the rice and two pinches of salt and mix. Add the coconut-infused milk. Cover the pan with a circle cut out of parchment (baking) paper and cook for 20 minutes over medium heat, stirring from time to time. When cooked, mix well. Taste and adjust the seasoning.

8

Use the ring mold to shape the rice. Drizzle the lamb with a little lemon juice, adjust the seasoning, and place a serving on the rice. Decorate with a few coconut shavings and drizzle a line of sauce around the plate.

BROILED LAMB SKEWERS, RED BELL PEPPER COULIS, AND PAN-FRIED SUCRINE LETTUCE

Serves 4

Broiled lamb skewers
Preparation time 20 minutes
Cooking time 10 minutes

Red bell pepper coulis
Preparation time 20 minutes
Cooking time 30 minutes
Resting time 3 minutes

EQUIPMENT

Broiled lamb skewers
4 (30-cm – 12-inch) skewers

Red bell pepper coulis
Carving fork
Handheld immersion (stick) blender

A WORD FROM OUR SOMMELIER

Pair with a red wine from the southwest region of France (e.g., Coteaux du Languedoc).

Broiled lamb skewers

1 long green zucchini (courgette)
160 g – 5.64 ounces small white onions (the size of an egg)
600 g - 1 lb 5 ounces lamb leg or loin, boneless, cut into 3-cm - 1 1/4-inch cubes
Fine salt
Freshly ground pepper
Olive oil
4 heads sucrine (Boston, Bibb, or Little Gem) lettuce
Sherry vinegar

Red bell pepper coulis

1 red bell pepper
20 g – 0.71 ounce (10 small) black olives, pitted
3 tablespoons olive oil
Fine salt
Freshly ground pepper
Sugar
1 tablespoon sherry vinegar

TIPS FROM OUR CHEFS

MORE THAN ONE WAY TO COOK
If you don't have a gas stove, cook the bell pepper under the broiler (grill). And if you don't have a broiler, you can cook your skewers on a grill (barbecue), in a skillet or frying pan, or on a cast-iron grill (griddle) pan.

ALL METAL
If you use metal skewers, oil them before threading them. Be careful when taking them out of the oven because they'll be very hot.

DON'T WAIT
If the pan-fried sucrine lettuce is left to stand it will lose its lovely color. As soon as it's cooked, serve it.

1

Secure the bell pepper on the tines of carving fork and grill for 3 minutes 30 seconds over a gas flame, while turning regularly. Transfer the bell pepper to a plate, cover with plastic wrap (cling film), and let rest for 3 minutes. Use a chef's knife to slice the olives.

2

Wash the zucchini and with a chef's knife cut into six slices 3-cm – 1 1/4-inch thick. Slice around the core (page 522) to make 24 squares (about 5-mm – 1/4-inch thick). Discard the cores. Peel the onions, separate the layers, and cut them into squares the same size as the zucchini squares, set aside for the skewers.

3

Continue with the coulis: Chop up the onion scraps (trimmings) and cores. Peel the grilled bell pepper by scraping with a paring knife. Rinse. Split the bell pepper open and remove the seeds, ribs, and stem (stalk; page 513). Use a chef's knife to cut the bell pepper into large strips, then dice. Heat 1 tablespoon of olive oil in a saucepan. Add the chopped onion scraps and diced bell pepper. Season with salt and pepper, add a pinch of sugar, and mix. Cover the pan and cook for 30 minutes over low heat, stirring from time to time. Add a little water if the mixture cooks too quickly. When cooked, add half of the sliced olives. Add 1 tablespoon of vinegar. Incorporate 2 tablespoons of olive oil and mix well.

4

Transfer to a deep container and blend to a coulis with the handheld blender. Add the remainder of the sliced olives. Set aside.

5

Turn on the oven broiler (grill). Prepare the skewers by alternating the lamb with onion and zucchini pieces six times, finishing with a piece of lamb. Season both sides of the skewers with salt and pepper. Drizzle with a generous stream of olive oil. Brush an oven rack with oil. Place the skewers on the rack near the broiler (about 15 cm – 6 inches away from the burner or element), and cook for 3 minutes. Turn over and cook for another 3 minutes.

6

In the meantime, wash, dry, and halve the sucrine lettuce heads. Drizzle the cut sides with olive oil and season with salt and pepper. Cook for 2 minutes in a hot skillet or frying pan. Season the uncooked side with salt and pepper and drizzle with oil. Turn the lettuce over and cook for an additional 2 minutes.

7

Transfer the lettuce to a serving dish and drizzle with vinegar. Take the skewers out of the broiler and serve immediately with the red bell pepper coulis and pan-fried sucrine lettuce.

PROVENÇAL-STYLE GRILLED LAMB CHOPS WITH VEGETABLE MILLEFEUILLE

Serves 2

Preparation time 20 minutes
Cooking time 8 minutes

EQUIPMENT

Mortar and pestle
Wooden toothpicks (cocktail sticks)
Grill (griddle) pan

Lamb chops

1 large bunch flat-leaf parsley
1 small clove garlic
10 g – 0.35 ounce (5 small) black olives, pitted
20 g – 0.71 ounce (3 tablespoons plus 1 teaspoon) dry breadcrumbs
6 lamb chops from the loin end
Olive oil
Fleur de sel
Freshly ground pepper

Vegetable millefeuille

2 large button mushrooms
2 tomatoes
1 long eggplant (aubergine)
1 onion
Fine salt
Freshly ground pepper
Olive oil

1 Wash, dry, and pluck the parsley, then chop the leaves with a chef's knife (page 524). Peel the garlic clove with a paring knife. Cut in half and remove the green core. Crush the garlic in the mortar. Add the parsley and pound gently. Slice the olives into thin rings. Add to the mortar and crush lightly. Add the breadcrumbs. Mix well.

2 Make the millefeuille: Cut off the parts of the mushrooms covered in soil. Scrape the stems (stalks) and peel the caps (page 516). Wash the tomatoes and eggplant and remove the stems. Peel the onion. Cut all the vegetables into rounds 5-mm – 1/4-inch thick. Pierce each onion round horizontally with a toothpick to keep whole. Arrange the vegetable slices on a dish. Season with salt and pepper, then drizzle with olive oil. Heat the grill pan. Place the onion and eggplant slices in the pan. Cook for 15 seconds over high heat. Turn them over with tongs and cook for another 15 seconds. Repeat this process working in batches. Transfer to a plate.

3 Cook the tomatoes and mushrooms for 40 seconds on each side. Assemble the first millefeuille on a spatula (turner): Alternate slices of tomato, onion, eggplant, and mushroom. Remove the toothpicks from the onion slices. Finish with a tomato slice. Slide onto a plate. Assemble the second millefeuille the same way.

4 Transfer the breadcrumb mixture to a dish. Dredge the chops in the mixture (except the bone side). Lightly coat with oil.

5 Cook the chops in the grill pan on one side for 1 minute 30 seconds over medium-high heat. Turn over and cook the other side for 1 minute 30 seconds. Stand the chops on end and cook for 1 minute 30 seconds. Turn them over onto the bone side, then remove immediately. Arrange the chops on plates. Season with fleur de sel and pepper. Place the millefeuilles to one side and serve.

1

2

3

4

ROASTED LEG OF LAMB AND GARLIC BONBONS

Serves 6

Preparation time 30 minutes
Cooking time 20 minutes per 1 kg – 2 pounds 3 ounces of meat + 10–12 minutes
Resting time 1 hour

3 heads garlic
300 ml – 1 1/4 cups milk
1 (1.4–1.6-kg - 3–3-lb 8-oz) whole leg of lamb
Fine salt
Freshly ground pepper
3 tablespoons olive oil, plus more for drizzling
25 g – 1.4 ounces (1 3/4 tablespoons) butter, cut into cubes
3 sprigs thyme

TIPS FROM OUR CHEFS

BONBONS OR PALETS

You can replace the garlic bonbons with palets (disks)*: Immerse 125 g – 4.4 ounces (about 1 cup) peeled garlic in cold water and bring to a boil. Drain and cook for 15 minutes in milk with added salt over very low heat. Drain and cool, then blend with 50 g – 1.76 ounces (3 1/2 tablespoons) of butter and the crushed yolks of 5 hard-boiled eggs. Roll into a cylinder in plastic wrap (cling film) and refrigerate for 30 minutes to harden. Cut into 1-cm- – 3/8-inch–thick disks. Dredge in flour, beaten egg, and dried breadcrumbs, then fry in a pan for 1 minute on each side.*

1 Preheat the oven to 190°C – 375°F (gas mark 5). Separate the individual garlic cloves by pressing down firmly on the heads with both hands. Peel the cloves carefully with a paring knife. Leave the last layer of skin on.

2

Combine the milk and garlic cloves in a saucepan, bring to a boil over medium heat, then simmer for 5 minutes over low heat. Drain the garlic cloves in a strainer (sieve).
Remove any traces of paper, the stamp, and unwanted fat from the leg with a boning knife. Tie the sirloin (chump) with twine. Season with salt and pepper on all sides. Heat 3 tablespoons of olive oil in a roasting pan. Place the leg on its rounded side and brown for 1 minute 30 seconds. Turn the leg onto its cut side and brown for 1 minute while holding it steady with your hand.

TIPS FROM OUR CHEFS

SOMETHING FOR EVERYBODY
Because the leg is irregularly shaped, the sections will have cooked differently: well-done, rare, medium. So everybody will find something they like.

ACCOMPANIMENTS
Accompany the leg with a puree made using the milk from cooking the garlic or with spring vegetables: new onions, baby carrots, purple artichokes, mushrooms.

3

Turn the leg onto its flat side. Brown for 1 minute 30 seconds, basting with the fat in the pan, then brown the other cut side for 1 minute. Turn the leg back onto its rounded side and drizzle with a generous stream of olive oil. Place in the preheated oven and cook for 12 minutes. Without taking the leg out of the oven, baste the meat with the juices in the pan, then cook for another 12 minutes. Add the butter, let melt, and baste the leg with the melted butter. Add the thyme and garlic cloves. Cook for another 6 minutes. Check whether the lamb is cooked by piercing it with the thermometer. It should show 55°C – 131°F. Take the pan out of the oven. Wrap the bone with a sheet of aluminum foil folded in half. Transfer the cooked leg to a dish, cover with aluminum foil, and rest for at least half as long as it took to cook.

4

Put the thyme and garlic cloves into a bowl. Remove any pieces of skin that have come away from the garlic. Degrease the cooking juices. Place the roasting pan over the heat, add 100 ml – 1/3 cup plus 1 tablespoon plus 1 teaspoon of water, and bring to a boil. Stir well to dissolve the caramelized juices. Add the thyme and garlic cloves, and mix well.
Return the thyme, garlic, and jus to the bowl. Remove the foil from the leg. Remove the twine from the sirloin. Place the leg in a hot oven for 5 minutes, then carve (page 537). Serve with the garlic bonbons.

ROASTED SHOULDER OF LAMB

Serves 4

Preparation time 25 minutes
Cooking time 35 minutes

1 (1.3-kg – 2 pound 14-ounce) lamb shoulder
Fine salt
Freshly ground pepper
1 1/2 (50 g – 1.76 ounces) white onions
1 tablespoon grapeseed oil
10 g – 0.35 ounce (2/3 tablespoon) butter, cut into cubes
1 sprig fresh savory
80 ml – 1/3 cup dry white wine
80 ml – 1/3 cup chicken broth or stock or water
Olive oil

TIPS FROM OUR CHEFS

CONCENTRATION
It is important to sear the meat on all sides over the heat in order to start the cooking process. This causes a crust to form that will hold the juices inside the muscle fibers.

TRIVIA
To let the heat penetrate better, dislocate the joint at the shoulder blade with a quick jab of a knife.

RECTIFYING
If the meat browns too quickly in the oven, add a little broth or water. Add only a little at a time, because the shoulder should not be bathed in liquid.

1

Trim the shoulder: Remove the stamp by cutting around it, then trim off the excess fat with a boning knife. Remove any muscle membrane and nerves.
Lift up any thin and flat parts of the flesh that hang off the shoulder. Cut them off. They will provide scraps (trimmings) for later use. Wrap the bone with aluminum foil. Season both sides of the shoulder with salt and pepper.

2

Preheat the oven to 200°C – 400°F (gas mark 6). Move an oven rack to the bottom slot. Chop up the scraps into small pieces. Peel, halve, and chop the onions (page 525). Heat 1 tablespoon of oil in a skillet or frying pan. Brown the shoulder on its rounded side for 2 minutes over high heat. Use a wide spatula (slotted turner) to turn the meat over. Add the butter to one side and let melt. Baste the shoulder with the melted butter for 2 minutes. Transfer the shoulder from the pan to a plate.

3

Add the scraps and onions to the pan. Brown for 3–4 minutes over high heat while stirring constantly. Add the savory. Pour in the white wine. Wipe the sides of the pan with a wet pastry brush to detach any caramelized juices. Transfer the contents of the pan to a roasting dish and spread out evenly. Place the shoulder in the dish, rounded side up. Place on the bottom rack and cook for 35 minutes.

4

When cooked, take the dish out of the oven. Remove the shoulder from the roasting dish. Cover with aluminum foil and let rest for 18 minutes.
Transfer the contents of the dish to a saucepan. Clean the dish well with the wet brush to collect all of the caramelized juices. Add the chicken broth to the saucepan and simmer for 5 minutes while stirring to let the gravy thicken. Add a little olive oil. Pour into a strainer (sieve) over a deep container. Press down on the solid pieces with the back of a spoon to extract all of their liquid.

5

Place the shoulder in a hot oven for 5 minutes, then transfer to a cutting board. Carve the shoulder (page 535). Serve immediately with the strained gravy.

NAVARIN OF LAMB WITH SPRING VEGETABLES

Serves 4

Preparation time 45 minutes
Resting time 1 hour

EQUIPMENT

Round Dutch oven or flameproof casserole dish with lid, 28 cm – 11 inches diameter

Navarin of lamb

1 clove garlic
1 small white onion
800 g - 1 lb 12 oz lamb shoulder (neck), boneless
Fine salt
Freshly ground pepper
1 tablespoon grapeseed oil
1 bay leaf
20 g – 0.7 ounce (1 tablespoon) tomato paste (puree)
80 ml – 1/3 cup dry white wine
150 ml – 2/3 cup veal broth or stock

Spring Vegetables

6 thin baby carrots, with greens
5 round turnips, with greens
300 g – 10.58 ounces Ratte or other waxy potatoes
20 pearl (baby) onions
Fine salt

TIPS FROM OUR CHEFS

PRECIOUS VITAMINS

The vegetables should be covered with damp paper towels to keep them fresh. If exposed to the air, they will dry out, and if immersed in water, they will lose their vitamins.

COOKING SEPARATELY

If your pan isn't big enough, cook the vegetables separately with 10 g – 3.5 ounces (2/3 tablespoon) of butter and two pinches of sugar.

1

Peel the garlic and onion. Halve the garlic clove and remove the green core. Halve and chop the onion (page 525). Cut the meat into 3-cm – 1 1/4-inch dice. Season with salt and pepper. Heat 1 tablespoon of oil in the Dutch oven. Add the diced meat. Brown for 5–6 minutes over high heat while stirring with a spatula (turner). Add the garlic, onion, 1 sprig of thyme, and the bay leaf. Cook everything for 1 minute.

2

Add the tomato paste and cook for 1 minute while mixing gently. Clean the sides of the pot with a wet pastry brush. Add the white wine. Preheat the oven to 180°C – 350°F (gas mark 4). Loosen the caramelized juices by scraping with a spatula, and let the wine reduce for 3–4 minutes to remove the acidity. Only 2–3 tablespoons should remain in the pot. Add the veal broth. Bring to a boil, then cover the Dutch oven. Place in the oven and cook for 1 hour.

3

In the meantime, prepare the vegetables: Wash and peel the carrots and turnips. Cut the carrots on a diagonal into 3-cm – 1 1/4-inch pieces. Quarter the turnips. Scrub the potatoes. Peel the onions. Arrange the vegetables in rows on a dish and cover with damp paper towels.

4

After the lamb has been cooking for 1 hour, take the pot out of the oven, open, and mix. Season the vegetables with salt. Add all of the vegetables to the pot. Mix well. Add a little water if there isn't enough liquid. Clean the sides of the pot with a wet brush.

5

Cover the Dutch oven again, return to the oven, and cook for 30 additional minutes. Check that the vegetables are cooked through by piercing with the tip of a knife. Arrange the meat and vegetables on well-heated plates, and drizzle with a little cooking liquid. Taste and adjust the seasoning. Serve immediately.

SEVEN-HOUR LEG OF LAMB SERVED WITH A SPOON

Serves 6

Dead dough
Preparation time 5 minutes
Resting time 1 hour

Leg of lamb
Preparation time 30 minutes
Cooking time 7 hours

EQUIPMENT

Dead dough
Food processor fitted with the dough blade

Leg of lamb
Oval Dutch oven or flameproof casserole dish with lid, 32 cm – 12 1/2 inches diameter

Dead dough

300 g – 10.58 ounces (2 1/3 cups plus 1 tablespoon) all-purpose (plain) flour, plus more for dusting
Fine salt
1 egg

Leg of lamb

1 (1.4-kg – 3-pound) whole bone-in leg of lamb
Fine salt
Freshly ground pepper
1 head pink garlic
1 onion
1 carrot
2 tablespoons olive oil
2 (2-mm- – 1/16-inch–thick) slices bacon
100 ml – 1/3 cup plus 1 tablespoon plus 1 teaspoon dry white wine
250 ml – 1 cup veal broth or stock
1 sprig thyme
1 bay leaf

TIPS FROM OUR CHEFS

TOO LONG A LEG
A leg weighing any more than 1.4 kg – 3 pounds will be too large to fit in the Dutch oven. Ask your butcher to trim it by cutting off the bone, or by cutting off the shank or sirloin, depending on the piece. Brown the cut-off piece for 3 minutes after adding the leg.

GARLIC, GARLIC, GARLIC
If you are a garlic fan, stud the lamb leg with garlic: Make incisions in the fleshiest part and gradually insert pieces of garlic (slices or whole cloves), pushing them in with the tip of a paring knife.

LE CREUSET

1

Make the dead dough: Combine the 300 g – 10.58 ounces (2 1/3 cups plus 1 tablespoon) flour with a pinch of salt in the food processor. Break the egg into a ramekin and add. Measure out 150 ml – 2/3 cup of water and add to the food processor. Process to obtain a soft dough. Spread plastic wrap (cling film) over the work surface, dust lightly with flour (about 1 tablespoon), and place the dough on top. Fold the plastic wrap over the dough, wrapping completely. Rest for at least 1 hour in the refrigerator.
Prepare the meat: Remove any traces of paper, the stamp, and unwanted fat from the leg of lamb with a boning knife. Tie the sirloin (chump) in two or three places to hold in place. Generously season both sides of the meat with salt and pepper.

2

Separate the garlic cloves. Peel the onion and carrot. Wash the carrot, quarter lengthwise, then cut into dice (mirepoix). Halve and chop the onion (page 525).
Heat 2 tablespoons of olive oil in the Dutch oven over high heat. Add the leg on its rounded side. Brown for 5 minutes on all sides, basting with the oil. Transfer the lamb to a dish.

3

Put the garlic cloves, onion, and carrot in the Dutch oven and season with salt. Add the bacon and brown for 1 minute over low heat while stirring constantly. Add the white wine, mix, and reduce completely over medium heat, without burning.

4

Return the leg to the pot, rounded side up, over the vegetables. Pour the veal broth around it. Add the thyme and bay leaf. Clean the sides of the pot with a wet pastry brush and bring to a boil.

5

Lightly dust the work surface with flour (about 1 tablespoon) and knead the dough to form a 2-cm– 3/4-inch–diameter cylinder. Preheat the oven to 140°C – 275°F (gas mark 1). Cover the Dutch oven and pass a wet brush around the edge of the lid. Place the dough over the edge of the lid, pressing down to seal the pan well. Place the pan in the oven and cook for 7 hours. After cooking, take the pot out of the oven. Dust the lid with a little flour (about 1 tablespoon), which is the method used by chefs to show that the pot is very hot. Pry (prise) off the dough with a knife, open the pan, and pass a wet brush over the edges. Remove the twine from the leg and serve with a spoon.

TIPS FROM OUR CHEFS

TRIVIA

Garlic should be used only for long cooking techniques. With short cooking times, there isn't enough time for the garlic to flavor the meat, and it will remain practically raw.

UNWANTED FAT

"Unwanted" fat refers to areas of dark or reddish fat that should be removed from the meat. However, be sure to leave the white fat, which will "nourish" the meat as it cooks.

SOFT

Having cooked for so long, this very tender leg of lamb can be cut using a spoon. Bring the pot to the table and serve it there. Impact guaranteed.

DEAD DOUGH

This is used to form an airtight seal on the lid of the pan, letting the food cook in its own juices without any evaporation. This type of dough, known as "dead dough," contains only flour, water, and sometimes egg and isn't meant to be eaten.

DAUBE DE BOEUF À L'ORANGE (BRAISED BEEF WITH ORANGE)

Serves 4

Preparation time 45 minutes
Cooking time 4 hours

Daube

1 large onion
2 carrots
150 g – 5.3 ounces bacon
2 organic, unwaxed oranges
1.3 kg - 2 lb 14 oz paleron (cut of beef chuck or stewing steak)
4 chunks oxtail
1 tablespoon grapeseed oil
Salt
Freshly ground pepper
3 cloves garlic, unpeeled
750 ml – 3 cups (1 standard bottle) red wine
1 teaspoon black peppercorns
1 clove
5 juniper berries
75 g – 2.65 ounces (1/3 cup plus 2 teaspoons) sugar

Bouquet garni

5 sprigs parsley
1 stalk celery
1 sprig thyme
1 bay leaf
3–4 leeks green part only (10-cm – 4-inch lengths)

TIPS FROM OUR CHEFS

NO RIND
Remove the rind and any excess fat from the bacon. If you find any cartilage in the bacon while you are dicing it, remove and discard that as well.

BRUSHING
After browning ingredients, clean the sides of the pot with a wet brush to remove stuck-on food. If left in place it will burn as you are cooking the dish and will give it an unpleasant flavor.

OLIVE OIL
The locals in Provence cook with a lightly fruity olive oil, but mild-flavored grapeseed oil is more appropriate to certain dishes. Save your very fruity oils for dressing and drizzling, not for cooking.

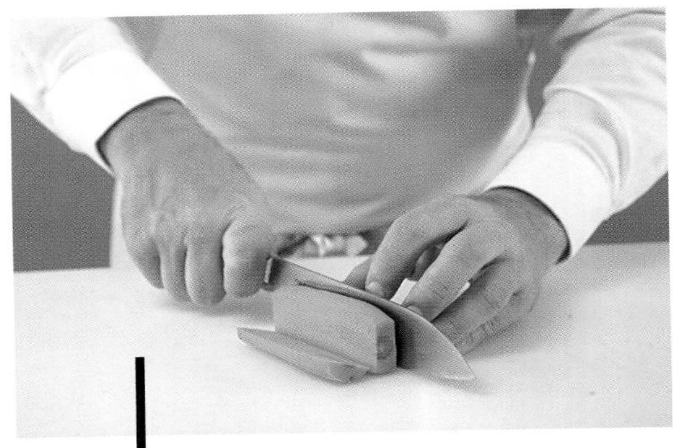

1 Peel the onion. Cut it in half. Cut off the root with the tip of a knife. Cut each half into 1-cm – 3/8-inch vertical slices, then cut once horizontally. Finally, chop into large dice (page 525). Peel the carrots. Cut them into three pieces lengthwise, then cut into two batons, except for the largest piece, which should be cut into three batons. Finally, cut into large dice.

2 Make the bouquet garni: Wrap the parsley, celery, thyme, and bay leaf in the leek leaves and tie (page 544).

3 Trim the rind from the bacon. Cut the bacon into 1-cm – 3/8-inch dice. Wash and dry the oranges. Remove the zest with a vegetable peeler, being careful not to remove any of the pith (page 514). Cut off the top and bottom of the oranges. Stand upright, supreme, and cut into sections (segments; p. 514). Do this over a container to collect the juice.

4 Trim off the muscle membrane from the beef. Cut the meat into 3-cm- – 1 1/4-inch–thick slices. Cut each slice again into three pieces.

5

Heat 1 tablespoon of grapeseed oil in a stockpot over high heat. Season the oxtail with salt and pepper. Brown for 2–3 minutes, then remove. Season the beef with salt and pepper. Brown for 3-4 minutes on all sides, then remove. Put the bacon, onion, carrot, and unpeeled garlic into the pot. Clean the sides of the pot with a wet brush to detach the caramelized juices. Cook the contents of the pot for 3 minutes while stirring constantly.

6

Return the oxtail to the pot. Mix. Add the beef. Pour in the wine. Add enough water to cover the contents (about 750 ml – 3 cups). Add the bouquet garni, 1 teaspoon of peppercorns, the clove, and the juniper berries. Clean the sides of the pot again with the wet brush. Bring to a boil. Skim to remove any foam that forms on the surface.

7

Add the orange sections and juice. Cover the pot and cook for 3 hours over low heat. Stir halfway through cooking and brush the sides of the pot again. Combine the pieces of orange zest with cold water in a saucepan. Bring to a boil. Drain. Refresh in ice water. Repeat. Put 400 ml – 1 2/3 cups of water and the sugar in the pan where you blanched the zest. Return the zest to the pan. Bring to a boil. Simmer for 30 minutes uncovered.

8

After cooking, clean the sides of the pan with the wet brush to detach any caramelized juices. Drain the orange zest. Add to the cooked daube. Cover and let infuse for 5 minutes. Adjust the seasoning. Remove the bouquet garni. Serve the meat on individual plates accompanied by noodles, gnocchi, or mashed potatoes.

EGGS FLORENTINE

Serves 4

Preparation time 30 minutes
Cooking time 25 minutes

EQUIPMENT

4 (200-ml – 7-ounce) latch-top canning jars fitted with rubber seal rings

400 g – 14 ounces (13 cups) spinach leaves
4 large button mushrooms (250 g – 9 ounces)
1 clove garlic
1 tablespoon olive oil
Fine salt
Freshly ground pepper
1 large shallot
30 g – 1.06 ounces (2 tablespoons) butter
100 ml – 1/3 cup plus 1 tablespoon plus 1 teaspoon light (single) cream
Nutmeg
4 eggs

1 Fold the spinach leaves in half and remove the stems and ribs. Wash and drain (page 520).

2 Peel the mushroom caps (page 516). Slice, trimming off the bottom and the stem (stalks). Cut the slices into batons.

3 Peel the garlic clove, removing green core. Prick the clove with a fork and leave it on the end. Heat 1 tablespoon of olive oil in a large saucepan. Add the spinach by the handful. Season lightly with salt. Season with pepper. Stir for 2 minutes using the fork with the garlic clove to wilt the spinach. Transfer to a bowl. Peel the shallot. Halve and slice (page 525). Heat a saucepan over high heat. Add one third of the butter and the shallot. Soften for 1 minute while stirring constantly. Add the mushrooms. Season with salt and pepper. Mix. Cook for 5 minutes on high heat. Pour the cream over the mushrooms. Add a little grated nutmeg. Let boil for 1 minute. Remove from heat. Transfer to a bowl.

4 Melt the remaining two thirds butter. Use a brush to grease the inside of the jars with melted butter. Divide the spinach among the jars. Add the mushrooms and their sauce. Press down on the mushrooms with the back of a spoon to form a well in the center of each jar.

5 Break each egg into a separate ramekin. Tip them, one at a time, into the wells made in the mushrooms. Seal the jars.

6 Place the jars in a stockpot filled halfway with cold water. Heat over medium heat. When the water begins to simmer, cover the pot and cook for 13–14 minutes. With your hands protected from both heat and moisture, carefully take the jars out of the pot. Open them, taking care to keep your face out of range, as they will give off a blast of steam. Lightly season the eggs with salt and pepper. Serve.

TIPS FROM OUR CHEFS

VARIATION

You can replace the mushrooms with smoked salmon or ham, or add oven-roasted nuts.

WILT WITHOUT BREAKING

The spinach should be wilted, meaning the volume of the leaves will be reduced and they will release the water they naturally contain.

DOUBLE ADVANTAGE

The sealed jars keep the flavors from evaporating, while the moisture released via cooking accumulates inside the lid and keeps a skin from forming.

PASSION FRUIT AND MANGO WITH A CRUMB TOPPING

Serves 6

Preparation time 20 minutes
Cooking time 25 minutes

Crumb topping

1/2 vanilla bean (pod)
50 g – 1.76 ounces (1/3 cup plus 1 tablespoon) all-purpose (plain) flour
25 g – 0.88 ounce (1/4 cup) almond meal (ground almonds)
50 g – 1.76 ounces (1/4 cup) sugar
50 g – 1.76 ounces (3 1/2 tablespoons) butter, melted

Mangoes + cream

1 mango (about 600 g – 1 pound 5 ounces)
1 passion fruit
1 vanilla bean (pod), cut in half
30 g – 1 ounce (2 tablespoons) sugar
100 g – 3.5 ounces (1/3 cup plus 2 tablespoons) passion fruit puree
200 g – 7 ounces (3/4 cup plus 1 tablespoon plus 1 1/2 teaspoons) light (single) cream, very cold
10 g - 0.35 ounces (1 tablespoon plus 3/4 teaspoon) confectioners' (icing) sugar plus more for dusting
50 g – 1.76 ounces (1/3 cup plus 2 tablespoons) red currants, loose

1 Make the crumb topping: Preheat the oven to 180°C – 350°F (gas mark 4). Weigh out all the ingredients for the crumb topping (crumble) dough. Split the vanilla bean half. Scrape out the seeds. Combine the flour with the almond meal in a bowl. Add the sugar and vanilla seeds. Mix with a silicone spatula (scraper). Add the melted butter. Mix well. Line a baking sheet (tray) with parchment (baking) paper. Coarsely crumble the mixture over it. Bake for 20 minutes.

2 Make the mango: Peel the mango with a vegetable peeler. Cut the mango in half, guiding the chef's knife along the pit (stone). Remove the flesh from around the pit (page 515). Slice the flesh horizontally. Slice lengthwise. Dice the flesh.

3 Halve the passion fruit. Use a small spoon to scoop out the contents into a small bowl.

4 Split a vanilla bean half. Scrape out the seeds. Heat a skillet or frying pan over high heat. Add the sugar and vanilla seeds. Let caramelize. Add the diced mango. Caramelize for about 5 minutes, shaking the pan from time to time. Add the passion fruit puree. Let boil for 1 minute, stirring a little. Transfer to a bowl. Scrape the pan well to get everything out. Cover with plastic wrap (cling film), making direct contact with the mango mixture. Let cool.

5 Make the soft whipped cream: Split the remaining vanilla bean half. Scrape out the seeds. Combine the vanilla seeds, very cold light cream, and confectioner's sugar in a bowl. Whisk until the cream is foamy and soft. Refrigerate.

6 Add the red currants to the mixture mango. Add the passion fruit. Mix gently to avoid crushing the fruits. Divide the fruit mixture among six glasses. Add 2–3 tablespoons of cream to each glass. Cover with the crumb topping. Dust with confectioners' sugar and decorate with a few fruits.

3

TROPICAL FRUIT VACHERIN

Serves 4

Preparation time 30 minutes
Cooking time 40 minutes

Strawberry sauce

200 g – 7 ounces strawberries
2 heaping tablespoons superfine (caster) sugar

Vacherin

1 mango
1 small Victoria pineapple
2 tablespoons confectioners' (icing) sugar, divided, plus more for dusting
1 organic, unwaxed lime
500 ml – 1 pint coconut sorbet
500 ml – 1 pint mango and passion fruit sorbet
150 ml – 2/3 cup whipping cream, very cold
40 g – 1.4 ounces meringue formed into batons (page 569 and note opposite)
4 Cape gooseberries (physalis)

1 Heat water in a saucepan. Rinse, hull, and halve the strawberries. Put into a small heat-proof mixing bowl. Sprinkle 2 heaping tablespoons of superfine sugar over the strawberries. Cover with plastic wrap (cling film). Place the bowl over the pan of simmering water. Cook for 30 minutes over low heat.
Set aside a few strawberry halves for garnish. Pass the others through a strainer (sieve), pressing with a spoon. Return the strained juice to the saucepan. Reduce until the sauce becomes slightly syrupy. Let cool.

2 Cut the mango in half (page 515), guiding the knife along the pit (stone). Peel it. Cut into thin slices, then batons, and then into very small dice (brunoise).

3 Cut off the top and bottom of the pineapple. Cut it in half. Slice off the skin. Cut the pineapple into thin slices, then batons, and then into very small dice (brunoise).

4 Mix the diced mango and pineapple together. Sprinkle with 1 tablespoon of the confectioners' sugar. Grate the lime zest (page 514). Add to the mango mixture. Refrigerate.

5 Press 1 heaping tablespoon of coconut sorbet into the bottom of each of the serving dishes, followed by 1 tablespoon of mango and passion fruit sorbet. Place in the freezer.

6 Pour the cream into a bowl. Add the remaining 1 tablespoon confectioners' sugar. Whip (page 567). Make a layer of whipped cream in the serving dishes. Divide the diced fruits and place on top. Add more whipped cream. Make another layer of diced fruits. Pour strawberry sauce over the top. Add more whipped cream. Garnish with a few meringue batons. Garnish each serving with a few small pineapple leaves, the reserved strawberries, and a Cape gooseberry. Dust with a pinch of confectioners' sugar. Serve immediately.

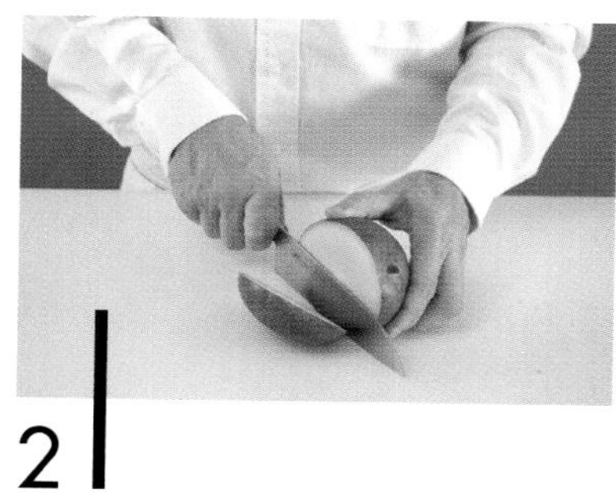

2

3

4

5

TIPS FROM OUR CHEFS

FIND ALL THE EYES

Don't forget to remove any eyes from the pineapple with the tip of a chef's knife after skinning.

HOMEMADE MERINGUES

Beat the whites of 2 eggs with 1 drop of lemon juice, 50 g – 1.76 ounces (1/4 cup) of superfine (caster) sugar, and 50 g – 1.76 ounces (1/3 cup plus 1 tablespoon) of confectioners' (icing) sugar. Pipe batons of meringue over parchment (baking) paper with a pastry (piping) bag fitted with a 3-mm – 1/8-inch pastry tip (nozzle). Let dry overnight in the oven at 100°C – 200°F *(page 569)*.

CAPE GOOSEBERRY

The Cape gooseberry (Physalis alkekengi), also known as Chinese lantern, physalis, or ground cherry, has a slightly acidic flavor, close to that of a gooseberry. Lift the lobes of the corolla from the fruit and twist before placing in the glass.

SHORTBREAD COOKIES WITH CHOCOLATE CHANTILLY CREAM

Serves 6

Preparation time 45 minutes
Resting time 2 hours

EQUIPMENT

Handheld immersion (stick) blender
3 disposable pastry (piping) bags
Size 17 fluted pastry tip (nozzle)

Chantilly cream (select two of three)

90 g – 3.17 ounces dark chocolate (66% cocoa), 100 g – 3.5 ounces milk chocolate (40% cocoa), or 110 g – 3.88 ounces white chocolate
170 g – 6 ounces (2/3 cup plus 1 tablespoon) whipping cream

Shortbread cookie (one flavor of your choice)

6 shortbread cookies (page 368)

1 Make each type of Chantilly cream the same way: Weigh out the chocolate and the cream. Place the chocolate in a heat-proof bowl.
Pour the cream into a saucepan. Scrape the container well with a silicone spatula (scraper) to collect all of the cream. Bring to a boil over high heat.
Pour about half of the cream over the chocolate while stirring with the spatula.

2 Stir briskly, starting in the middle, until smooth.
Pour the rest of the hot cream over the chocolate. Mix until the chocolate is fully melted.
Transfer the mixture to a deep container. Blend with the handheld blender for about 10 seconds.
Transfer the mixture to a large bowl. Cover each of the creams with plastic wrap (cling film), making direct contact with the surface. Let thicken for 2 hours in the refrigerator.

3 Whip one thickened cream until firm peaks form but don't allow it to turn grainy.
Whip the second cream the same way.

4 Transfer both creams to separate pastry bags with their points still intact. Twist the ends of the bags closed. Cut off the points of the bags.
Use a bowl scraper to scrape the cream to the bottoms of the bags, washing it in between uses.
Fit the pastry tip onto a third bag and cut off the point. Place the two cream-filled bags side by side. Place them into the third bag.

5 Bring the tops of the bags together, twist to close, then pipe a cone-shaped swirl of cream over each of the six shortbread cookies. Serve.

TIPS FROM OUR CHEFS

USE WHIPPING CREAM
Whipping cream is a type of light (single) cream. However, it has a minimum butterfat content of 30%. Use it to ensure the Chantilly cream holds its shape successfully.

SAME TEXTURE
It is important that the two creams have the same texture so that they flow uniformly when piped.

VARIETY
Flavor your Chantilly creams with coffee beans, lemon verbena, peppercorns, basil, mint, or other flavors. Bring the whipping cream to a boil with the chosen flavoring ingredient, cover with plastic wrap, and let infuse for 15 minutes off the heat. Strain when cold. Bring back to a boil and pour over the chocolate.

CHOUX STICKS WITH HAZELNUT AND CHOCOLATE CREAM

Makes 15 sticks

Hazelnut and chocolate cream
Preparation time 10 minutes
Cooking time 15 minutes

Choux sticks
Preparation time 20 minutes
Cooking time 30 minutes
Resting time 20 minutes

EQUIPMENT

Hazelnut and chocolate cream
Food processor fitted with metal blade

Choux sticks
Pastry (piping) bag
Size 7 plain pastry tip (nozzle)

Hazelnut and chocolate cream

100 g – 3.5 ounces (3/4 cup) hazelnuts
70 g – 2.47 ounces milk chocolate (40% cocoa)
10 g – 0.35 ounces (1 tablespoon plus 3/4 teaspoon) confectioners' (icing) sugar
20 ml – 1 tablespoon plus 1 teaspoon neutral oil, such as grapeseed oil

Choux sticks

30 g – 1 ounce (1/4 cup) hazelnuts
2 tablespoons sanding or caliber 10 pearl (nib) sugar

1 Make the hazelnut and chocolate cream: Preheat the oven to 180°C – 350°F (gas mark 4). Spread the hazelnuts in a single layer on a baking sheet (tray) lined with parchment (baking) paper and place in the oven. Toast for 15 minutes. Take out of the oven and let cool.

2 Put the hazelnuts into a food processor fitted with the metal blade and process for 3–4 minutes to a smooth and runny hazelnut paste. Transfer to a bowl.
Break the chocolate into pieces. Melt in the microwave for about 1 minute on 600 W. Mix the chocolate gently. Add the confectioners' sugar and stir. Add the oil and mix to incorporate. Mix the hazelnut paste into the chocolate. Cover with plastic wrap (cling film) and refrigerate for 20 minutes.

3 Make the choux sticks: Put the hazelnuts on a cutting board. Crush with the flat side of the blade of a chef's knife, then finely chop.

4 Preheat the oven to 170°C – 350°F (gas mark 3–4) and prepare one recipe of the choux paste (page 545). Fit the tip to the pastry bag and fill with the choux paste (page 501). Pipe 25-cm – 10-inch sticks on a nonstick baking sheet.

5 Sprinkle the choux sticks with sanding sugar. Sprinkle with chopped hazelnuts. Shake the baking sheet over a sheet of parchment paper to remove the excess sugar and hazelnuts. Bake in the preheated oven for 30 minutes. Serve with the hazelnut and chocolate cream at room temperature.

1

2

4

TIPS FROM OUR CHEFS

ADJUST AS NEEDED

Watch the chocolate carefully in the microwave; you may have to heat it a little at a time, mixing each time. The chocolate should be melted but only warm. This consistency is essential for combining it with the hazelnut paste.

STICKING

If you don't have a nonstick baking sheet, grease your baking sheet lightly with butter to prevent the choux sticks from sticking.

CHOCOLAT LIÉGEOIS

Serves 2

Preparation time 10 minutes
Cooking time 15 minutes
Resting time 24 hours +
2–4 hours

EQUIPMENT

Ice cream maker
Pastry (piping) bag
Size 8 fluted pastry tip (nozzle)

TIPS FROM OUR CHEFS

BAIN-MARIE
Use a saucepan that can hold the bowl without it coming into contact with the boiling water.

WEIGHING OUT
The amount of egg yolk is crucial when making ice cream. Weigh them to be sure of successful results.

INSULATION
When transferring the ice cream, place the cold bowl on a rack to prevent it from heating up in contact with the work surface.

Ice cream (select one of the following three)

Dark chocolate

2 g – 0.07 ounce sheet (leaf) gelatin (1 sheet)
60 g – 2.12 ounces (about 4) egg yolks
110 g – 3.88 ounces (1/2 cup plus 1 tablespoon) sugar
50 ml – 1.76 ounces (3 tablespoons plus 1 teaspoon) light (single) cream
40 g – 1.4 (2 tablespoons plus 2 teaspoons) glucose syrup (page 543) or light corn syrup
500 ml – 2 cups milk
260 g - 9.2 oz dark chocolate (66 percent cocoa)

Milk chocolate

2 g – 0.07 ounce sheet (leaf) gelatin (1 sheet)
60 g – 2.12 ounces (about 4) egg yolks
100 g – 3.5 ounces (1/2 cup) sugar
50 ml – 1.76 ounces (3 tablespoons plus 1 teaspoon) light (single) cream
40 g – 1.4 (2 tablespoons plus 2 teaspoons) glucose syrup (page 543) or light corn syrup
500 ml – 2 cups milk
280 g - 10 oz milk chocolate (40 percent cocoa)

White chocolate

2 g – 0.07 ounce sheet (leaf) gelatin (1 sheet)
70 g – 2.47 ounces (about 5) egg yolks
80 g – 2.82 ounces (1/3 cup plus 1 tablespoon) sugar
50 ml – 1.76 ounces (3 tablespoons plus 1 teaspoon) light (single) cream
40 g – 1.4 (2 tablespoons plus 2 teaspoons) glucose syrup (page 543) or light corn syrup
500 ml – 2 cups milk
320 g - 11 oz white chocolate

Chantilly cream (page 626)

200 g – 7 ounces (3/4 cup plus 2 tablespoons) whipping cream
10 g – 0.35 ounce (1 1/4 tablespoons) confectioners' (icing) sugar

Frosting

1/2 cup plus 2 tablespoons frosting

Desert roses (one flavor of your choice)

2 desert roses (page 130)

1

4

5

1 Make the chocolate ice cream: Soak the gelatin for 5 minutes in cold water (page 542). Weigh out the egg yolks and put into a bowl. Add the sugar and mix without beating.

2 Pour the cream over the eggs. Scrape the container well with a silicone spatula (scraper) to collect all of the cream. Add the glucose syrup (page 543). Mix in the milk without beating. Add the chocolate. Drain the gelatin in a small strainer (sieve). Add to the mixture. Place the bowl over a bain-marie at a boil. Cook for 10 minutes at 85°C – 185°F. Transfer to a plate. Cover with plastic wrap (cling film), making direct contact with the surface of the cream. Let cool, then refrigerate for 24 hours.

3 Transfer to the ice cream maker. Churn according to the manufacturer's instructions. Chill a bowl in the freezer. Place the bowl on a rack. Transfer the ice cream to the bowl. Return the bowl to the freezer for 2–4 hours.

4 When it is time to serve, make the Chantilly cream: Whip the cream with the confectioners' sugar.

5 Fill the pastry bag fitted with the fluted tip with the Chantilly cream. Pipe a swirl in the bottom of each serving glass, using about one third of the cream. Drizzle with 1 tablespoon of frosting (icing).

6 Place a scoop of ice cream on top of each, using about half of the ice cream. Add more Chantilly cream, 1 tablespoon of frosting, and another scoop of ice cream. Finish with the remaining Chantilly cream. Chop up the desert roses with a knife. Sprinkle over the glasses. Serve immediately.

PROFITEROLES

Serves 4

Choux puffs
Preparation time 30 minutes
Cooking time 40 minutes

EQUIPMENT

Chocolate sauce
Pastry (piping) bag
Size 10 plain pastry tip (nozzle)
Size 8 fluted pastry tip

Choux puffs

400 g – 14 ounces choux paste (page 545)
1 egg
500 ml – 1 pint vanilla ice cream
Gold leaf

Chocolate sauce

30 g – 1 ounce (1/3 cup) unsweetened cocoa powder
70 g – 2.47 ounces (1/3 cup) superfine (caster) sugar
80 ml – 1/3 cup light (single) cream
100 g – 3.5 ounces dark chocolate couverture (70% cocoa)

TIPS FROM OUR CHEFS

GLAZED
Brushing the tops of the choux puffs with beaten egg is known as glazing. Be careful not to let the egg run down the sides of the puffs or they won't puff up.

REUSE
If your pastry brush is worn out, don't throw it away. Just cut off the tips and it will be like new.

TIMING
Warning: Don't let the chocolate sauce boil in the microwave. The same goes for the remaining sauce that is heated before serving.

1

Preheat the oven to 150°C – 300°F (gas mark 3) in a convection (fan-assisted) oven or 170°C – 350°F (gas mark 3–4) in a static (conventional) oven and prepare the choux paste (page 545). Fit the plain tip to the pastry bag and fill with the choux paste (page 507). Pipe twelve 4-cm – 1 1/2-inch-diameter puffs on a baking sheet (tray) with 3 cm – 1 1/8 inches between them on all sides.

2

Break the egg into a bowl and beat with a fork. Gently brush the tops of the puffs with beaten egg. Bake for 40 minutes. In the meantime, make the chocolate sauce: Put the 100 ml – 1/3 cup plus 1 tablespoon plus 1 teaspoon water into a saucepan. Add the cocoa powder. Add the sugar and bring to a boil over high heat, mixing constantly with a whisk. Let boil for 1 minute over low heat. Remove from heat. Heat the cream in another saucepan. Put the chocolate couverture into a heatproof bowl and pour half of the cream over it. Stir the middle of the bowl with a silicone spatula (scraper). Pour the rest of the cream into the bowl and continue to stir until smooth.

3

Transfer to another bowl. Add half of the chocolate–cream mixture to the cocoa powder mixture and mix with the spatula. Add the rest of the cream mixture. Continue to mix gently without incorporating any air. Cover with plastic wrap (cling film), making direct contact with the surface.

4 When it is time to fill the profiteroles, heat half of the chocolate sauce for 30 seconds in a microwave (600 W) to melt. Dip the tops of the puffs in the heated sauce, let any excess sauce drip off, then stand the puffs on the work surface, dipped sides up. Let dry.

5 Use a serrated knife to cut the dry puffs horizontally at one third their height.

6 Work the vanilla ice cream with a spatula to soften. Fit the fluted tip on the pastry bag and fill with the softened ice cream. Fill the bottom of each puff with a generous amount of ice cream.

7

Replace the dipped tops. Decorate with a little gold leaf. Heat the remainder of the chocolate sauce for 50 seconds in the microwave (600 W). Coat the bottom of serving plates with the very hot sauce. Arrange three profiteroles on each plate and serve immediately.

COFFEE ÉCLAIRS

Makes 10 éclairs

Coffee pastry cream
Preparation time 10 minutes
Cooking time 5 minutes
Resting time 1 hour

Choux puffs and frosting
Preparation time 1 hour
Cooking time 50 minutes

EQUIPMENT

Choux puffs and frosting
Pastry (piping) bag
Size 15 fluted pastry tip (nozzle)
Size 2 plain pastry tip
Size 7 plain pastry tip

Coffee pastry cream

250 ml – 1 cup milk
6 g – 0.21 ounce (1 tablespoon) ground Arabica coffee
4 g – 0.14 ounce (scant 1 teaspoon) coffee extract
3 egg yolks
50 g – 1.76 ounces (1/4 cup) superfine (caster) sugar
10 g – 0.35 ounce (1 tablespoon plus 1 teaspoon) all-purpose (plain) flour
10 g – 0.35 ounce (1 tablespoon plus 1 teaspoon) cornstarch (cornflour)
25 g – 0.88 ounce (1 3/4 tablespoons) butter, cut into cubes

Choux puffs and frosting

500 g – 1 pound 2 ounces choux paste (page 545)
8 g – 0.28 ounce (1 2/3 teaspoons) coffee extract
400 g – 14 ounces white fondant
Yellow food coloring

2

1 Make the coffee pastry cream: Pour the milk into a saucepan. Add the ground coffee. Add the coffee extract, mix, and bring to a boil. Remove from the heat and let infuse for 5 minutes.

2 Put the egg yolks into a bowl. Add the superfine sugar and beat until thick and pale. Incorporate the flour and cornstarch. Strain the milk through a fine strainer (sieve) over the saucepan. Empty the strainer and strain the milk a second time over the saucepan. Bring to a boil again.

3 Pour a little boiling milk over the egg yolks and mix. Pour the egg yolk mixture into the remaining milk in the saucepan and bring to a boil for 1 minute while stirring constantly. Remove from heat. Add the butter and mix.

Line a bowl with plastic wrap (cling film). Pour the pastry cream into the bowl and cover with plastic wrap. Let cool, then refrigerate for at least 1 hour.

4 Preheat the oven to 150°C – 300°F (gas mark 3) in a convection (fan-assisted) oven or 170°C – 350°F (gas mark 3–4) in a static (conventional) oven and prepare a choux paste (page 545). Fit the size 15 fluted tip to the pastry bag and fill with the choux paste (page 507). Pipe ten 15-cm – 6-inch éclairs on a baking sheet (tray), spacing them 2 cm – 3/4 inch apart.

5 Bake for 50 minutes. Take the éclairs out of the oven and let cool. Take the coffee pastry cream out of the refrigerator and whisk. Pierce three holes in the bottom of each éclair with the size 2 pastry tip. Fit the size 7 plain tip to the pastry bag and fill with the coffee pastry cream (page 507). Fill the éclairs through each of the holes.

6 Make the coffee frosting (icing): Put 1 tablespoon plus 1 teaspoon of water into a saucepan. Add the coffee extract. Add the fondant. Melt over low heat, then stir until warmed through. Add a few drops of yellow food coloring, mix well, and transfer to a bowl. Use an offset spatula (palette knife) to spread the coffee frosting over the éclairs. Use your finger to make the frosting on and around the éclairs even. Let any excess frosting fall back into the bowl. Let dry.

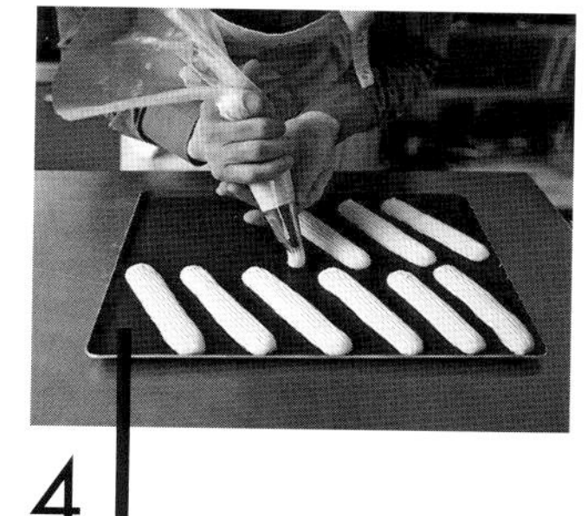

4

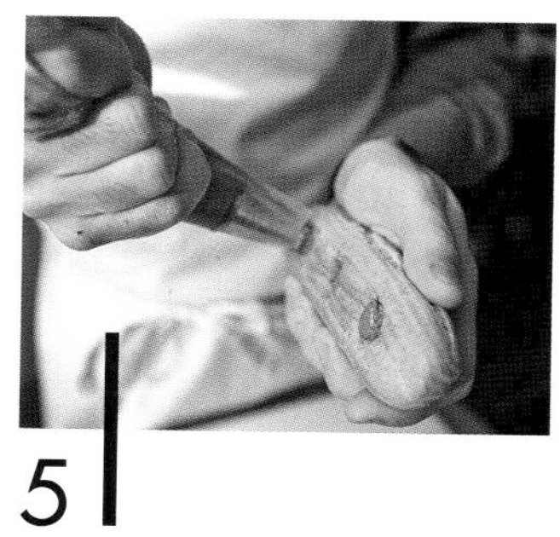

5

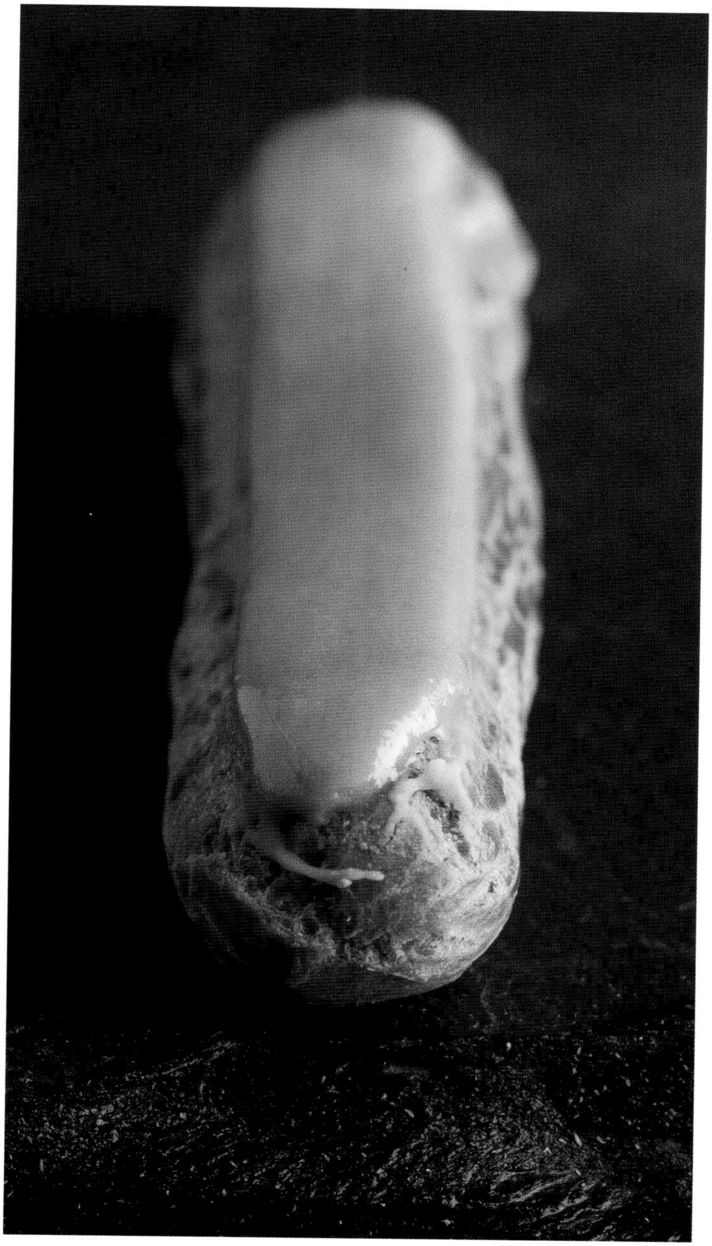

STRAWBERRY ÉCLAIRS

Makes 10 éclairs

Preparation time 45 minutes
Cooking time 1 hour 20 minutes
Resting time 1 hour

EQUIPMENT

Filling
Pastry (piping) bag
Size 10 fluted pastry tip (nozzle)

Choux puffs
Pastry (piping) bag
Size 15 fluted pastry tip (nozzle)

Filling

4 g – 0.14 ounce sheet (leaf) gelatin (2 sheets)
125 g – 4.4 ounces (1/2 cup) frozen crumbled raspberries
40 g – 1.4 ounces (3 tablespoons) frozen raspberry puree
40 g – 1.4 ounces (3 tablespoons plus 1 teaspoon) superfine (caster) sugar
30 Gariguette strawberries
200 g – 7 ounces (3/4 cup plus 1 tablespoon) light (single) cream, very cold
15 g – 5.3 ounces (2 tablespoons) confectioners' (icing) sugar, plus more for dusting
300 g – 10.5 ounces (2 cups) mousseline cream (page 570)

Choux puffs

500 g – 1 pound 2 ounces choux paste (page 545)
3 tablespoons sanding or caliber 6 pearl (nib) sugar
3 tablespoons chopped almonds

1 Make a raspberry jelly: Soak the gelatin in cold water for 5 minutes (page 542). Put the crumbled raspberries into a saucepan and add the raspberry puree. Add the superfine sugar. Bring to a boil, stirring from time to time. Drain the gelatin in a fine strainer (sieve), then pat dry with paper towels. Add the gelatin to the raspberry mixture, remove from heat, and mix carefully. Transfer to a bowl, cover with plastic wrap (cling film), and let cool. Refrigerate until it's cold.

2 Make the choux puffs: Preheat the oven to 150°C – 300°F (gas mark 3–4) in a convection (fan-assisted) oven or 170°C – 350°F (gas mark 3–4) in a static (conventional) oven and prepare a choux paste (page 545). Fit the size 15 fluted tip to the pastry bag and fill with the choux paste (page 507). Pipe ten 15-cm – 6-inch éclairs on a baking sheet (tray), spacing them 2 cm – 3/4 inch apart on all sides.

3 Sprinkle with sanding sugar. Sprinkle with chopped almonds. Shake the baking sheet over a sheet of parchment paper to remove the excess sugar and almonds. Bake for 50 minutes.

4 Prepare the strawberries: Wash and pat dry with paper towels. Hull them and cut in half. Pour the cream into a bowl, add the 15 g – 5.3 ounces (2 tablespoons) confectioners' sugar, and whip to a Chantilly cream with a mixer (page 567). Use a serrated knife to cut off the tops of the éclairs. Spread raspberry jelly over the bottoms of the éclairs.

5 Fit the size 10 tip to the pastry bag. Fill with the mousseline cream and pipe a line of cream back and forth to cover two thirds of each bottom lengthwise. Dust the tops with confectioners' sugar. Empty the pastry bag, and rinse both bag and tip. Fill the bag with Chantilly cream and pipe a line over the remaining third of the bottom. Top with strawberry halves, overlapping them. Pipe a line of Chantilly cream over one side of the tops. Place the tops of the éclairs over the strawberries, with the Chantilly cream lines on the tops over the Chantilly cream lines on the bottoms, pressing lightly and leaving the strawberries exposed.

6 Finish the inside of the tops with a line of Chantilly cream to add volume. You can also embellish the éclairs with additional piped Chantilly cream. Refrigerate for 1 hour.

2

3

4

5

CHOCOLATE MOUSSE

Serves 4

Preparation time 30 minutes
Resting time 4 hours +
15 minutes

EQUIPMENT

Food processor fitted with a metal blade
4 (5-cm- – 2-inch–diameter) ring molds
Chef's torch or hair dryer
1 acetate sheet

Mousse

2.5 g – 0.09 ounce sheet (leaf) gelatin (1 1/4 sheets)
125 ml – 1/2 cup whipping cream
90 ml – 1/3 cup plus 1 tablespoon plus 1 teaspoon whole milk
90 g - 3.17 oz dark chocolate (70 percent cocoa), or 110 g - 3.88 oz milk chocolate (40 percent cocoa), or 120 g - 4.23 oz white chocolate

Desert roses (one flavor of your choice)

4 desert roses (page 130)

Decoration

100 g – 3.5 ounces dark chocolate couverture (70% cocoa)
Gold leaf

1. Make the chocolate mousse: Soak the gelatin for 5 minutes in cold water (page 542). Pour the cream into the food processor. Whip until foamy and soft. Pour the milk into a saucepan. Heat without bringing to a boil. Drain the gelatin in a small strainer (sieve). Add to the milk and mix until it melts.
2. Put the chocolate into a heatproof bowl. Pour the milk over the chocolate. Starting in the middle, mix until it melts. Check the temperature of the mixture. It should be about 35°C – 95°F. Fold in the whipped cream. Transfer to a measuring cup.
3. Trim the desert roses with four ring molds. Transfer the ring molds with the desert roses still in them to a plate.
4. Fill the molds with the mousse. Refrigerate until set, about 4 hours.
5. Unmold the individual portions: Place one ring mold (desert rose on the bottom) on top of an overturned glass whose bottom has a diameter smaller than that of the ring mold. Heat the mold for a few seconds with the chef's torch or a hair dryer. Slide the mold off. Repeat with remaining portions. Return the mousse to the refrigerator.
6. Make the decoration: Cut the acetate sheet into four right (right-angled) triangles measuring 8 cm – 3 1/8 inches high by 14 cm – 5 1/2 inches long. Temper the dark chocolate: Melt it at 55–60°C – 131–140°F. Cool to 28–29°C – 82–84°F. Reheat to 30–31°C – 86–88°F. Pour chocolate over one of the triangles. Spread smooth with an offset spatula (palette knife). Do the same for the remaining three triangles and chocolate. Take the mousse out of the refrigerator. Lift up a chocolate triangle together with the acetate.
7. Place the triangle around one portion of mousse, acetate side facing outward. Repeat with remaining triangles and portions. Firm up in the refrigerator for at least 15 minutes. To serve, use a spatula (turner) to transfer each portion of mousse to an individual serving plate. Peel off the acetate. Place a little gold leaf in the middle of each mousse.

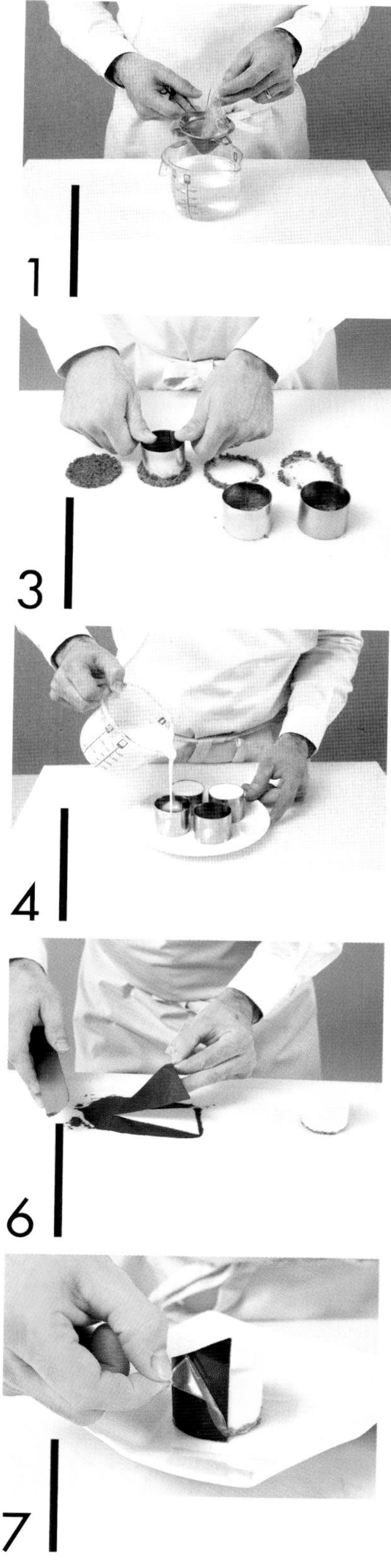

RICE PUDDING AND PAN-FRIED FRUIT

Serves 4

Rice pudding
Preparation time 3 minutes
Cooking time 25 minutes

Pan–fried fruit
Preparation time 8 minutes
Cooking time 3 minutes

EQUIPMENT

Accompaniment
4 wooden skewers
4 dry vanilla beans

Rice pudding

1.2 liters – 5 cups low-fat (semi-skim) milk
1 vanilla bean (pod)
80 g – 2.82 ounces (1/3 cup plus 1 tablespoon) superfine (caster) sugar
5 g – 0.18 ounce (1/3 tablespoon) butter
180 g - 6.35 oz (1 cup) Arborio rice
2 egg yolks

Pan-fried fruit

1 vanilla bean (pod)
1 kiwi
1/4 pineapple
1 fig
1/2 pear
1/2 apple
1/2 banana
20 g – 0.71 ounce (1 1/2 tablespoons) butter
20 g – 0.71 ounce (1 tablespoon plus 2 teaspoons) sugar
Juice of 1/2 orange

TIPS FROM OUR CHEFS

PIANISSIMO!
Be careful: Letting the milk be absorbed into the rice for rice pudding is a slightly slower process than incorporating the broth (stock) in a savory risotto.

FIRM VANILLA BEANS
To harden the vanilla beans, dry them out in the oven or put them in the freezer.

1

Bring the milk to a boil. In the meantime, split the vanilla bean lengthwise. Use a paring knife to scrape out the seeds. Add the vanilla seeds and bean and the sugar to the boiling milk. Mix well.

2

Melt the butter for 1 minute in a deep skillet or frying pan over low heat. Increase the heat to medium, then add the rice. Stir the rice constantly for about 2 minutes to coat well with the fat. The rice should be shiny and translucent. Add enough of the milk to cover the rice and add the vanilla bean. Cook, stirring constantly, for 20–22 minutes. Each time the milk is almost fully absorbed, add a little more milk. Remove from heat and let cool a little while stirring constantly. Remove the vanilla bean and add the egg yolks. Mix briskly to combine yolks without cooking them. Transfer to a bowl. Cover with plastic wrap (cling film) and let cool to room temperature.

3

Prepare the fruit: Split the vanilla bean lengthwise. Use a paring knife to scrape out the seeds; reserve. Peel the kiwi. Halve lengthwise. Cut each half into four pieces. Remove the skin from the pineapple and cut into slices. Quarter the fig. Core the pear half. Cut the pear half, apple half, and banana half into four pieces each. Use the wooden skewers to make fruit skewers, alternating in the following order: fig, apple, pineapple, kiwi, banana, pineapple, kiwi, pear.

4

Carefully remove the wooden skewers, keeping the fruit in place, and replace with the dry vanilla beans. Make a caramel by heating the butter and sugar for 1 minute 30 seconds in a skillet or frying pan (page 566). Use a spatula (turner) to gently lay the fruit skewers in the pan.

TIPS FROM OUR CHEFS

REVIVING WITH MILK

Your rice pudding may stiffen while cooling. Mix in a little cold milk and soft (semi-) whipped cream and it will regain its soft and shiny texture.

MAGIC SPATULA

Cooking the fruit skewered with the vanilla beans is a very delicate process, so be sure to use a spatula large enough to turn the skewers. If you don't have one, wait and replace the wooden skewers with the vanilla beans after cooking the fruit.

5

Add the vanilla seeds and bean. Cook the skewers for 1 minute on each side. Transfer to a plate and deglaze the pan with the orange juice. Pour the orange juice and caramel mixture into a bowl. Divide the rice pudding among four small bowls. Accompany each one with a skewer drizzled with the orange and caramel sauce. Serve immediately.

STRAWBERRY TIAN

Makes 4 individual tarts

Preparation time 30 minutes
Cooking time 10 minutes
Resting time 30 minutes

EQUIPMENT

10-cm- – 4-inch–diameter ring mold

1 tablespoon flour
250 g - 9 oz shortbread dough (recipe on p. 604)
500 g – 1 pound 2 ounces strawberries
1 vanilla bean (pod)
50 g – 1.76 ounces (1/4 cup) sugar
3 tablespoons balsamic vinegar
200 ml – 3/4 cup plus 1 tablespoon light (single) cream

4

1 Dust the work surface with the flour. Roll the dough out to a thickness of 2 mm – 1/16 inch. Use the ring mold to cut out four 10-cm – 4-inch disks. Transfer to a baking sheet (tray) and rest for 30 minutes in the refrigerator.

2 Wash and dry the strawberries and hull with a paring knife. Cut into quarters. Transfer to a bowl.

3 Halve the vanilla bean lengthwise and scrape out the seeds from one half, set aside. Preheat the oven to 180°C – 350°F (gas mark 4). Heat a skillet or frying pan. Put the sugar in the pan. Caramelize for 2 minutes (page 566). Add the unscraped vanilla bean half. Add the strawberries and mix gently for 1 minute 40 seconds. Add the balsamic vinegar. Mix for 20 seconds to coat the strawberries thoroughly. Return the strawberries and any cooking liquid to the bowl, let cool, then refrigerate.

4 Bake the dough disks in the preheated oven until light golden all over, about 10 minutes. In the meantime, combine the cream and reserved vanilla seeds in a bowl. Whip the cream by whisking briskly (page 567). Refrigerate. Take the disks out of the oven when they are a light golden all over. Slide onto a cold work surface. Let cool. Place the mold on a sheet of parchment (baking) paper. Arrange the strawberries inside with their tips pointing toward the center. Reserve any liquid in the bowl.

5 Fill the middle with 2 heaping tablespoons of whipped cream and spread using the back of the spoon. Place a shortbread disk on top. Press down lightly. Repeat with remaining portions. Gently slide the mold onto a plate using the parchment paper. Place an overturned plate over the mold. Hold both plates well with both hands and turn them over. Remove the top plate. Carefully remove the parchment paper. Slide an offset spatula (palette knife) under the mold. Unmold. Transfer the tian to an individual serving plate. Repeat the process to make the remaining three tians. Drizzle with the strawberry cooking liquid.

TARTE TATIN WITH APPLES

Serves 6

Preparation time 20 minutes
Cooking time 1 hour 15 minutes

EQUIPMENT

Baking pan (tin) for use on stovetop (hob)

8 Reinette, Cox, or Boskoop apples
25 g - 0.88 oz (1 3/4 tbsp) butter
250 g - 9 oz (1 1/4 cups) sugar
1 vanilla bean (pod)
1 roll puff pastry or basic pastry dough, rolled into circle to fit the pan (see note)

Crème fraîche or vanilla ice cream

TIPS FROM OUR CHEFS

THE PERFECT SIZE
If possible, choose apples of the same size. This is important for both appearance and even cooking. If necessary, you can cheat by cutting off the bottoms of the apples to make them all the same height.

WATCH CLOSELY
Don't take your eyes off the caramel. It can turn dark very quickly and acquire a burned taste. And remember that it will continue to cook once it's off the heat.

1 Preheat the oven to 190°C – 375°F (gas mark 5). If possible, set for use with only the bottom element or burner. Peel the apples (page 512). Halve and core the apples (page 512). Cut the butter into 25 cubes. Reserve 10 cubes.

2 Use a paring knife to split the vanilla bean. Scrape out the seeds. Heat the baking pan over high heat. Add the the sugar and make a dry caramel (page 566). Tilt the pan in all directions to cook the sugar evenly.

3 Add 15 butter cubes to the caramel one at a time. Let melt. Remove the pan from the heat when the caramel is golden. Add the vanilla seeds and bean.
Arrange the apple halves upright around the pan. Place an apple half in the middle, cut side up.

4 Cut any remaining apples into chunks and fill in the gaps. Sprinkle with sugar. Sprinkle with the 10 reserved cubes of butter. Place the pastry over the apples, pressing down on the edges to seal. Bake for 1 hour 15 minutes.

5 After taking the tart out of the oven, wait until it is no longer piping hot and get ready to unmold it.
Put the pan on a cooling rack and place the serving plate over the pan. Hold the rack, plate, and pan firmly and turn over very quickly. Remove the rack and lift off the pan. If any apple pieces stick to the pan, simply return them to their spot on top of the tart. Serve the tart hot. Accompany with crème fraîche or vanilla ice cream.

TIPS FROM OUR CHEFS

MADE-TO-MEASURE PASTRY
To make the pastry fit the pan perfectly, use a paper template. Turn the pan over onto a sheet of parchment (baking) paper. Trace out a circle with a pencil. Cut it out with scissors. Place the paper circle on the work surface. Roll the pastry out over it. Cut out the pastry using the tip of a knife by following the outline of the paper.

1
2
3
4

APPLE AND VANILLA CHARLOTTE

Serves 6

Preparation time 30 minutes
Cooking time 15 minutes
Resting time 1 hour + 12 hours

EQUIPMENT

Charlotte mold

Fruit and bavarois filling

450 g – 1 pound apples (Royal Gala or Jonagold)
50 g – 1.76 ounces (3 1/2 tablespoons) butter
50 g – 1.76 ounces (1/4 cup packed) brown sugar
50 ml – 1.76 ounces (3 tablespoons plus 1 teaspoon) Calvados
7 g – 0.24 ounce sheet (leaf) gelatin (3 1/2 sheets)
80 ml – 2.82 ounces (1/3 cup) milk
2 vanilla beans (pods)
7 eggs
50 g – 1.76 ounces (1/4 cup) sugar
300 ml – 10.5 ounces (1 1/4 cups) whipping cream, very cold

Ladyfingers and Finishing

1 75 cl-size bottle hard dry cider
100 g – 3.5 ounces (1/2 cup) sugar
20 ml – 0.71 ounce (1 tablespoon plus 1 teaspoon) Calvados
60 dry ladyfingers (boudoir biscuits)
1 apple
Juice of 1 lemon
20 g – 0.71 ounce (2 tablespoons plus 1 1/2 teaspoons) confectioners' (icing) sugar

1

Make the charlotte the day before serving: Start by peeling the apples with a vegetable peeler. Cut them in half. Use a melon baller to core (page 512). Cut each half into eight slices. Melt the butter in a skillet or frying pan over medium heat. When the butter turns a nut brown color (beurre noisette), add the apple slices. Brown the apples lightly, stirring regularly. Add the brown sugar. Let the apples caramelize a little. Drizzle with Calvados. Light a match and flambé. Drain the apples and refrigerate for 10 minutes.

2

Make the vanilla bavarois: Soak the gelatin for 5 minutes in cold water to soften (page 542). Heat the milk in a saucepan over medium heat. Use a paring knife to split the vanilla beans. Scrape out the seeds. Add the vanilla beans and seeds to the milk. Separate the eggs. Weigh out 130 g – 4.59 ounces of egg yolk. (Reserve whites and any excess yolk for another use.) Add the sugar to the yolks and mix immediately.

3

When the milk comes to a boil, pour a little hot milk over the egg yolks. Mix with a whisk. Place the pan back on very low heat. When the milk comes back to a boil, pour the yolk mixture into the pan while stirring with the whisk. Heat over low heat while stirring constantly. When the cream is thick enough to coat a silicone spatula (scraper) or spoon, remove from heat.

4 Drain the gelatin. Add it to the cream off the heat. Mix to dissolve well. Pass the cream through a conical or fine strainer (sieve). Immediately cover with plastic wrap (cling film), pressing it against the surface of the cream to prevent a skin from forming. Let set in the refrigerator for 1 hour. In the meantime, make the soaking syrup for the ladyfingers: Pour the hard cider into a bowl. Add the sugar while mixing with a whisk. Pour in the Calvados and mix well. Pour the whipping cream into the bowl of a stand mixer and whip. It should be foamy but not too firm.

TIPS FROM OUR CHEFS

BEURRE NOISETTE

When butter melts, the milk solids that sink to the bottom of the pan begin to caramelize and give the butter a subtle nutty taste. Once the butter browns, add the apple slices immediately, because it can burn and turn black.

BEATING EGG YOLKS

There is no point to beating the egg yolk and sugar mixture until it turns thick and pale. The more it is beaten, the fluffier it becomes, which makes cooking difficult to control.

5 Briefly soak the ladyfingers in the syrup. Drain on a rack. Line the sides of the mold with the ladyfingers, keeping their sugared sides facing outward. Also line the bottom of the mold. Fill any gaps with small pieces of ladyfinger.

6 Take the cream out of the refrigerator and pour into a bowl. Whisk until soft and smooth. Fold in the whipped cream. Spread a layer of cream over the bottom ladyfingers. Arrange apple pieces overlapped in a layer. Set aside the remaining apples in the refrigerator. Cover with another layer of ladyfingers. Add another layer of cream. Finish with a layer of ladyfingers. Fill in any gaps with small pieces of ladyfinger. Cover the mold and refrigerate for 12 hours. On the day you want to serve the dessert, place the serving dish upside down over the mold. Hold the dish and mold firmly and turn over. Unmold. Arrange the reserved caramelized apples on top of the charlotte. Slice the raw apple, toss with the lemon juice, and use to decorate the charlotte. Dust with the confectioners' sugar and serve.

STRAWBERRY CHARLOTTE

Serves 6

Preparation time 25 minutes
Cooking time 10 minutes
Resting time 12 hours

EQUIPMENT

Charlotte mold
Electric mixer

Strawberry gelatin and mousse

30 g – 1 ounce (2 tablespoons plus 1 teaspoon) sugar
160 g - 5.64 oz strawberries
5 g – 0.46 ounces sheet (leaf) gelatin (2 1/2 sheets), divided
12 g – 0.42 ounce (2 tablespoons) lemon juice (or juice of 1 lemon)
250 g – 9 ounces (1 cup plus 1 tablespoon) cream cheese (40% fat)
1 egg (for 25 g – 0.88 ounce of egg white)
25 g – 0.88 ounce (2 tablespoons) sugar

Biscuits and Finishing

350 g – 12 ounces (1 cup) glucose syrup (page 543)
125 g – 4.4 ounces (1/2 cup) strawberry puree
40 dry ladyfingers (boudoir) biscuits
About 20 strawberries
Prepared strawberry jelly
Chantilly cream (page 567)

TIPS FROM OUR CHEFS

WATCH FOR LUMPS
Add the sugar to the frying pan a little at a time. This will allow it to melt well. If you put all the sugar in at once, you may end up with lumpy caramel.

SHAKE THE PAN
Shake the strawberries in the caramel and they will release their juices quickly as they soften—and this way they won't get crushed. Stop the cooking process when they start to soften without cooking them completely. They should still hold their shape.

NOT TOO STIFF
When making mousse, it's important that the egg whites aren't too stiff so that the mixture will be smooth.

1 The day before you plan to serve the dessert, put the sugar into a skillet or frying pan and make a dry caramel while constantly swirling the pan (page 566). Hull, wash, and drain the strawberries. Cut into pieces. When the caramel is a dark golden color, add the strawberries. Let soften and release their juice, then transfer to a bowl. Soak 1 g – 0.04 ounces (1/2 sheet) gelatin in cold water (page 542). Drain the gelatin and add to the strawberries, stirring to dissolve. Cover with plastic wrap (cling film) and refrigerate until set (or freeze for 5 minutes).

2 Make the syrup for the biscuits by mixing the glucose syrup with the strawberry puree. Dip the biscuits in the syrup, leaving them immersed only long enough for them to become soaked through. Line the mold with the biscuits, starting with the sides and keeping their sugared sides facing outward. Finish by covering the bottom.

3 Make the cream cheese mousse: Soak the remaining 4 g – 0.42 ounces (2 sheets) gelatin to soften. Heat the lemon juice in a saucepan over medium heat. Drain the gelatin and add to the lemon juice off the heat. Stir to dissolve. Put the cream cheese into a bowl and add the lemon juice mixture. Mix well. Transfer to a large bowl. Beat the egg white in the electric mixer (or by whisking) to firm peaks (page 565). Whisk in the sugar. Fold the beaten egg white into the cream cheese mixture.

4

Make an even layer of about half the cream cheese mousse over the bottom of the charlotte mold. Take the strawberry mixture out of the refrigerator. Pour it over the mousse.

5

Add a layer of biscuits, sugared side facing outward. Add another layer of the remaining cream cheese mousse. Finish with a layer of biscuits. Fill in any gaps with small pieces of biscuit. Cover the charlotte and refrigerate for 12 hours.

6

Unmold onto a serving dish. Wash and drain the strawberries for finishing. Cut them in half. Melt the prepared strawberry jelly. Glaze the entire surface of the charlotte by brushing with the jelly. Arrange strawberry halves on top and around the charlotte. Serve with Chantilly cream (page 567).

RASPBERRY CHARLOTTE

RASPBERRY CHARLOTTE

Serves 4–6

Preparation time 40 minutes
Cooking time 5 minutes

Freezing time

2 hours + 12 hours

EQUIPMENT

14-cm- – 5 1/2-inch–diameter cake ring
Hair dryer
16-cm- – 6 1/4-inch–diameter cake ring

Gelatin

13 g – 0.46 ounce sheet (leaf) gelatin (6 1/2 sheets)
200 g – 7 ounces (3/4 cup plus 1 tablespoon) raspberry puree
300 g – 10.5 ounces (2 1/3 cups) whole raspberries, plus 26 whole raspberries (pick the prettiest ones)
125 g – 4.4 ounces (2/3 cup) sugar

Ladyfingers and soaking syrup

10 g - 0.35 oz (2 tsp) raspberry schnapps
500 g – 1 pound 2 ounces (2 cups) glucose syrup (page 543)
20 dry ladyfingers (boudoir) biscuits

Mousse

9 g – 0.32 ounce sheet (leaf) gelatin (4 1/2 sheets)
200 g - 7 oz (3/4 cup plus 1 tbsp) raspberry puree
20 g – 0.71 ounce (1 tablespoon plus 1 teaspoon) sugar
6 g – 0.21 ounce (1 1/4 teaspoons) raspberry schnapps
250 ml – 8 ounces (1 cup) whipping cream, very cold

1 Make the charlotte the day before serving. Start by soaking the gelatin in cold water (page 542). Pour the raspberry puree into a saucepan. Add the 300 g – 10.5 ounces (2 1/3 cups) whole raspberries and the sugar. Place over medium heat and stir constantly to stop the contents from sticking to the bottom of the pan.

2 Drain the gelatin and add to the pan off the heat. Mix well with a whisk to dissolve. Place the 14-cm – 5 1/2-inch cake ring on a baking sheet (tray) lined with plastic wrap (cling film). Pour 200 g – 7 ounces (about one third) of the raspberry gelatin inside the ring. Set the remainder aside in the refrigerator.

2

3 Stand 12 whole raspberries upright in the gelatin, pressing well. Let set in the freezer for 2 hours. Make the soaking syrup for the ladyfingers by mixing the schnapps with the glucose syrup. Take the disk of raspberry gelatin out of the freezer. Peel off the plastic wrap. To make unmolding easy, heat the sides of the cake ring with a hair dryer.

3

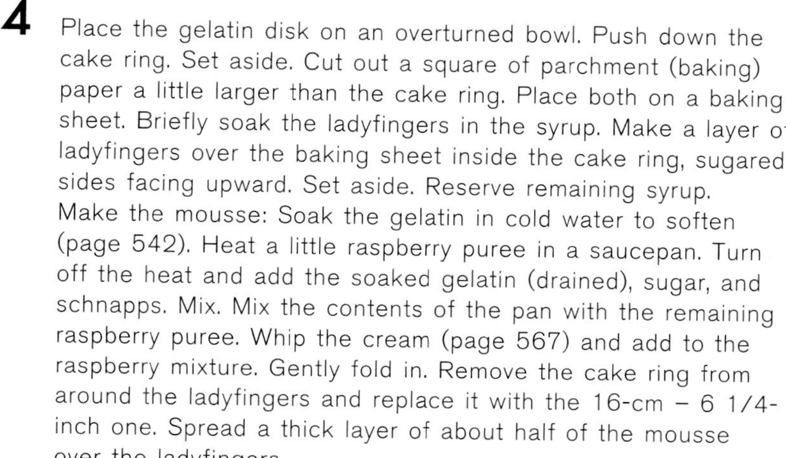

4 Place the gelatin disk on an overturned bowl. Push down the cake ring. Set aside. Cut out a square of parchment (baking) paper a little larger than the cake ring. Place both on a baking sheet. Briefly soak the ladyfingers in the syrup. Make a layer of ladyfingers over the baking sheet inside the cake ring, sugared sides facing upward. Set aside. Reserve remaining syrup. Make the mousse: Soak the gelatin in cold water to soften (page 542). Heat a little raspberry puree in a saucepan. Turn off the heat and add the soaked gelatin (drained), sugar, and schnapps. Mix. Mix the contents of the pan with the remaining raspberry puree. Whip the cream (page 567) and add to the raspberry mixture. Gently fold in. Remove the cake ring from around the ladyfingers and replace it with the 16-cm – 6 1/4-inch one. Spread a thick layer of about half of the mousse over the ladyfingers.

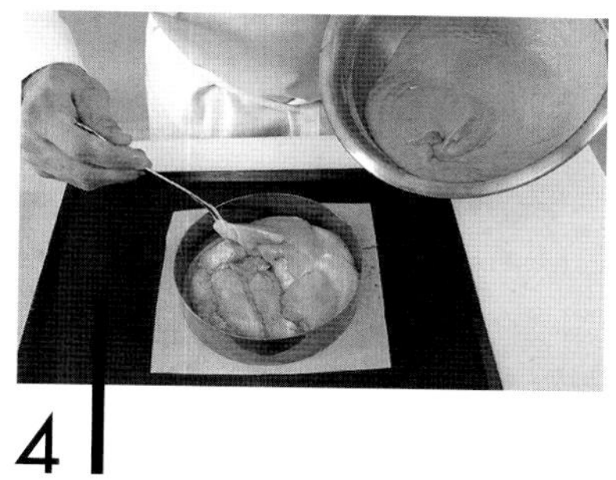

4

5 Use a spatula (palette knife) or spoon to push down in the center, spreading the mousse out to the edges. Take the disk of frozen raspberry gelatin, turn it upside down, and place over the mousse, with the raspberries facing downward. Press to push it down into the mousse. Cover the disk with the remaining mousse. Fill the cake ring evenly to the very top. Smooth the surface with an offset spatula (palette knife) or a large knife. Cover with plastic wrap and freeze for 12 hours.

5

6 On the day you plan to serve the dessert, about 6 hours before serving, take the charlotte out of the freezer. Peel off the plastic wrap. Heat the sides of the cake ring with a hair dryer. Place the charlotte on an overturned bowl. Push the cake ring down. Transfer to a rack placed over a plate. Take the remaining raspberry gelatin out of the refrigerator. Heat it just enough to be liquid (but still cold). Pour it over the charlotte. Transfer the charlotte to a serving dish. Take the remaining soaking syrup out of the refrigerator. Very briefly soak the unsugared sides of the biscuits roses de Reims, then lay them on a flat plate. Cut the biscuits to the height of the charlotte. Attach them to the outside, sugared sides facing outward. The gelatin will hold them in place as it cools. Garnish the top with the 14 remaining whole raspberries. Let the charlotte thaw completely. Serve.

CITRUS CHARLOTTE

Serves 6

Preparation time 30 minutes
Cooking time 3 minutes
Resting time 1 hour + 12 hours

EQUIPMENT

Ring mold
Charlotte mold

Gelatin and ladyfingers

6 organic, unwaxed oranges
10 g – 0.35 ounce sheet (leaf) gelatin (5 sheets)
45 g – 3 tablespoons lemon juice (juice of about 2 lemons)
180 g – 6.35 ounces (3/4 cup plus 2 tablespoons plus 1 1/2 teaspoons) sugar
30 dry ladyfingers (boudoir) biscuits

Lemon mousse and finishing

2 g - 0.07 oz sheet (leaf) gelatin (1 sheet)
1 organic, unwaxed lemon
35 g – 1.23 ounces (3 tablespoons) sugar
150 g – 5.3 ounces (2/3 cup) cream cheese (40% fat)
150 ml – 5.3 ounces (2/3 cup) whipping cream, very cold
100 g – 3.5 ounces (1/4 cup) apricot or apple glaze
1 organic, unwaxed lime

TIPS FROM OUR CHEFS

MORE AROMA
Infuse the juice with the zest for at least one hour for a more intense aroma. When straining, use a spatula to crush the zest inside the strainer.

EASY UNMOLDING
Line the bottom of the gelatin mold with plastic wrap, with a little excess hanging over the sides. To unmold, pull lightly on the plastic to lift up the bottom.

ADD SHEEN
A fine coating of apricot or apple glaze makes the orange pieces shine.

1

The day before you plan to serve the dessert, make the gelatin: Grate the zest of two oranges (page 514). Squeeze five oranges (for 400 ml – 14 ounces or 1 3/4 cups of juice). Soak the gelatin in cold water to soften (page 542).

2

Pour a little orange juice into a saucepan. Place the pan over medium heat to heat but don't let it boil. Drain the gelatin. Add it to the pan off the heat. Mix with a whisk to dissolve well. Transfer the mixture to a bowl. Add the remaining orange juice. Mix well. Add the orange zest. Squeeze the lemon juice into the bowl. Finally, add the sugar. Mix well. Let stand at room temperature for 1 hour to infuse. Strain the orange gelatin through a fine strainer (sieve).

3

Cut off the top and bottom of the two oranges for the finishing. Stand upright on the work surface. Cut the skin from its flesh, beginning at the top and following the curves down. Use a paring knife to cut out each section (page 514). Slice each section (segment) in half. Line the bottom of a ring mold a little smaller than the charlotte mold with plastic wrap (cling film). Cover the bottom with orange section halves. Set the remaining orange section halves aside in the refrigerator. Pour most of the gelatin mixture over the supremed orange halves in the mold to cover, reserving a little gelatin for soaking the ladyfingers. Cover with plastic wrap and freeze for 1 hour to set.

4

Briefly soak the ladyfingers in the remaining gelatin. Let drain on a rack.

5

If the charlotte mold has deep indentations, mold the soaked ladyfingers by pressing lightly to give them a rounded shape. Line the sides of the mold with the ladyfingers, keeping their sugared sides facing outward. Line the bottom, with the sugared sides of the ladyfingers facing upward. Fill in any gaps with small pieces of ladyfinger. If necessary, use scissors to trim the ends of the ladyfingers that stick out over the sides of the mold. Make the lemon mousse: Soak the gelatin to soften (page 542). Grate the zest of the lemon (page 514) and squeeze to obtain 20 g – 0.71 ounce (1 tablespoon plus 1 1/2 teaspoons) of juice. Heat the juice over medium heat. Drain the gelatin. Add it to the pan off the heat. Mix with a whisk to dissolve well. Add the sugar. Add the lemon zest. Mix.

6

Put the cream cheese into a bowl. Add the lemon gelatin. Mix gently with a silicone spatula (scraper). Whip the cream in a stand mixer. Fold into the lemon mixture. Take the orange gelatin disk out of the freezer. Remove the plastic wrap and unmold. Spread a layer of about half the lemon mousse in the charlotte mold.

7

Place the orange gelatin disk on top. Cover with a layer of the remaining mousse. Finish with a layer of ladyfingers (sugared sides facing downward against the mousse). Fill in any gaps. Cover the mold and refrigerate for 12 hours. On the day you plan to serve the dessert, unmold the charlotte. Arrange the reserved orange section halves on top. Melt the apricot glaze in a saucepan. Brush over the orange section halves. Grate lime zest over the charlotte.

CHOCOLATE AND BANANA CHARLOTTE

Serves 6

Preparation time 1 hour
Cooking time 10 minutes
Resting time 15 minutes + 12 hours

EQUIPMENT

Ring mold
Charlotte mold
Electric mixer
Pastry bag
Size 14 tip (nozzle)

Banana filling, crust, and ladyfingers

1 large or 2 small bananas
20 g – 0.71 ounce (1 1/2 tablespoons) butter
10 g – 0.35 ounce (1 tablespoon) sugar
20 g – 1 tablespoon plus 2 teaspoons rum
35 g – 1.23 ounces gavottes (crêpe dentelle cookies)
40 g – 1.4 ounces (1 1/3 cups plus 2 tablespoons) cornflakes
35 g – 1.23 ounces milk chocolate (44% cocoa)
85 g – 3 ounces (1/3 cup) hazelnut spread
300 g – 10.58 ounces (1 cup) glucose syrup (page 543)
30 plain ladyfingers

Chocolate mousse and sauce

5 eggs
60 g – 2.11 ounces (1/4 cup plus 1 tablespoon) sugar, divided
150 g – 5.3 ounces dark chocolate (70% cocoa)
120 ml – 4.24 ounces (1/3 cup plus 3 tablespoons plus 1 teaspoon) whipping cream, very cold, divided
15 g – 0.53 ounce (1 tablespoon) unsweetened cocoa powder
45 g – 1.6 ounces dark chocolate (66% cocoa)

TIPS FROM OUR CHEFS

SAME TEXTURES
Before mixing the beaten egg whites with the chocolate, you first incorporate a little beaten egg white into the chocolate so that they have the same foamy texture and combine easily.

NO RUNNING
To stop lines of sauce from running over the serving dish, leave the charlotte in the freezer instead of the refrigerator. On the day you plan to serve it, when it is still hard, put it on a rack, pour the sauce over it, then transfer it to a serving dish. Allow enough time for it to thaw out.

1

Make the charlotte the day before serving. Start by cutting the bananas into fairly thick slices. Cut the butter into cubes and put into a hot skillet or frying pan. The butter should turn amber in color and take on a nutty flavor. Add the banana slices. Brown, then sprinkle with sugar. Turn the banana slices. Add the rum, light a match, and flambé. Drain the fruit and set aside on a plate.

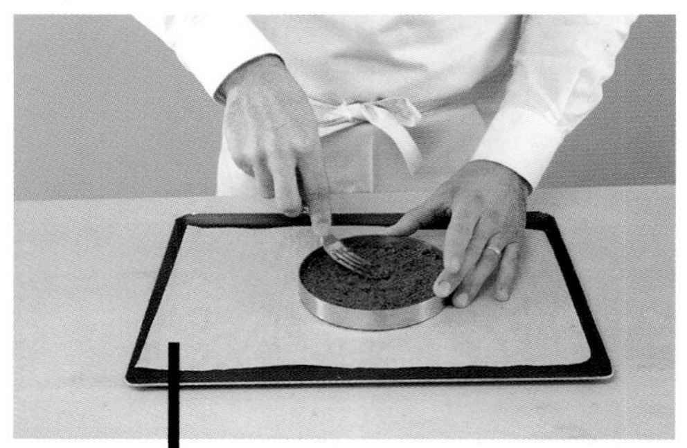

2

Make the crust (base): Crumble the gavottes and cornflakes. Melt the chocolate (without adding water). Mix the chocolate with the hazelnut spread. Add the crumbled cookie–cornflakes mixture while stirring. The paste should be smooth. Place a ring mold smaller than the charlotte mold on a baking sheet (tray) lined with parchment (baking) paper. Pour the mixture into the mold to a thickness of 1 cm – 3/8 inch. Spread evenly without pressing. Refrigerate until hard, about 15 minutes.

3

Pour the glucose syrup into a large bowl. Place a rack over a plate. Soak the ladyfingers briefly and let drain on the rack. Line the sides of the charlotte mold with the ladyfingers (sugared sides facing outward), then line the bottom (sugared sides facing upward). If necessary, use scissors to trim the ends of any ladyfingers that stick out past the sides of the mold.

4

Make the chocolate mousse: Break the eggs and weigh out 100 g – 3.5 ounces of whites and 30 g – 1 ounce of yolks. Beat the whites on high speed (page 565). When soft peaks form, reduce the speed to medium. Add 25 grams – 0.88 ounce (2 tablespoons) of the sugar. Melt the 70% dark chocolate in the microwave or over a bain-marie without adding water. Mix in 75 grams – 2.65 ounces (1/3 cup) of the cream. Add the egg yolks. Mix. Fold a little of the stiff beaten egg white into the chocolate mixture to dilute. Then pour the chocolate mixture over the beaten egg whites. Fold in gently to prevent the egg whites from collapsing. Use a pastry (piping) bag (page 507) to spread a layer of about one third of the chocolate mousse in the mold (or use a spoon). Arrange the cooked banana slices on top of the mousse. Cover with another layer of mousse. Add a layer of ladyfingers. Finish with a layer of mousse. (Store any leftover mousse in an airtight container in the refrigerator.)

5

Remove the chocolate disk from the refrigerator and unmold. Place it on top of the charlotte. When turned over, it will be the crust. Cover the charlotte and refrigerate for 12 hours.

6

On the day you plan to serve the dessert, make the chocolate sauce: Put 45 g – 3 tablespoons of water into a saucepan. Heat over medium heat. Add the remaining 35 grams – 1.23 ounces (3 tablespoons) sugar and the cocoa powder. When it boils, let thicken for 30 seconds. Transfer to a bowl. Heat the remaining 45 grams – 1.6 ounces (3 tablespoons plus 1 teaspoon) cream in a saucepan over medium heat. Melt the 66% chocolate in pieces in the microwave or over a bain-marie without adding water.When the cream comes to a boil, pour it over the melted chocolate. Mix well. The mixture will thicken into a ganache. Gradually pour the cocoa mixture into the ganache and mix well. If necessary, blend with a electric mixer. The sauce should be perfectly smooth.

7

Let cool to room temperature. Unmold the charlotte onto a rack placed over a plate. Decorate with the chocolate sauce and with chocolate shavings made using a vegetable peeler.

MONT BLANC–STYLE CHARLOTTE

Serves 6

Preparation time 50 minutes
Cooking time 1 hour 30 minutes
Resting time 12 hours

EQUIPMENT

Charlotte mold
Pastry (piping) bag
Size 14 plain pastry tip (nozzle)
Stand mixer

Ladyfingers and chantilly cream

400 g – 14.11 ounces (1 1/4 cups) glucose syrup (page 543)
250 ml - 0.88 oz (1 3/4 tbsp) dark rum
30 plain ladyfingers
1/2 vanilla bean (pod)
200 g – 7 ounces (3/4 cup plus 1 tablespoon plus 1 teaspoon) whipping cream, very cold
10 g – 0.35 ounce (1 1/4 tablespoons) confectioners' (icing) sugar
150 g – 5.3 ounces (2/3 cup) chestnut cream

Meringue

80 g – 2.82 ounces (about 4) egg whites
80 g – 2.82 ounces (1/3 cup plus 1 tablespoon) sugar
80 g – 2.82 ounces (2/3 cup) confectioners' sugar, plus more for dusting
8 chestnuts candied in the syrup

1 Make the syrup for soaking the ladyfingers the previous night by mixing the glucose syrup with the rum. Place a rack over a large plate. Briefly dip the ladyfingers in the syrup. Let drain on the rack.

2 Line the sides of the charlotte mold with the ladyfingers, keeping their sugared sides facing outward. Line the bottom, with the sugared sides of the ladyfingers facing upward.

3 Make the Chantilly cream: Scrape the seeds out the vanilla bean half and mix with the whipping cream. Whip by hand or with a mixer (page 567). Sift the confectioners' sugar over the cream. Mix gently with a whisk.

4 Fit the pastry bag with the tip and fill with the cream (page 507). Spread a layer of a little less than half of the Chantilly cream in the bottom of the mold. Spread the chestnut cream in a layer over it. Smooth the top.

5 Add a layer of ladyfingers. Add another layer of Chantilly cream, reserving some for decorating the finished charlotte. Set the remainder aside in the refrigerator.

6 Chop three candied chestnuts into small pieces. Sprinkle over the chantilly cream. Finish with a layer of ladyfingers, sugared sides facing downward. Fill in any gaps. Cover the charlotte and refrigerate for 12 hours. Preheat the oven to 120°C – 250°F (gas mark 1/2). Make meringue with the egg whites, sugar and confectioners' sugar (page 569). Pipe strips of meringue the same length as the height of the charlotte onto a baking sheet (tray) lined with parchment (baking) paper.

1

2

6

Bake in the preheated oven until dry and hard, 1 hour to 1 hour 30 minutes. Set aside. On the day you plan to serve the dessert, take the charlotte out of the refrigerator and remove the lid. To unmold, place the serving plate over the mold. Hold the plate and mold firmly and turn over. Lift off the mold.

7 With the remaining Chantilly cream, pipe a ring on top of the charlotte. Pipe vertical lines of Chantilly cream on the sides in each of the spaces between the ladyfingers. Place the meringue strips vertically over the Chantilly cream. Dust with confectioners' sugar. Top with the remaining candied chestnuts.

SHORTBREAD COOKIES IN THREE CHOCOLATES

Makes 50 cookies

Preparation time 15 minutes
Cooking time 10 minutes

EQUIPMENT

Silicone mat with holes
Cookie cutter (page 503)

Dark chocolate shortbread cookies

50 g – 1.76 ounces dark chocolate (66% cocoa)
90 g – 3.17 ounces (6 1/3 tablespoons) butter, softened
40 g – 1.4 ounces (1/3 cup) confectioners' (icing) sugar
40 g – 1.4 ounces (1/3 cup plus 1 tablespoon plus 1 teaspoon) almond meal (ground almonds)
15 g - 0.53 oz (about 1 large/UK medium) egg yolk
80 g – 2.82 ounces (2/3 cup) all-purpose (plain) flour
2 g – 0.07 ounce (1/2 teaspoon) fleur de sel

Milk chocolate shortbread cookies

55 g – 1.94 ounces milk chocolate (40% cocoa)
85 g – 3 ounces (6 tablespoons) butter, softened
30 g – 1 ounce (1/4 cup) confectioners' (icing) sugar
40 g – 1.4 ounces (1/3 cup plus 1 tablespoon plus 1 teaspoon) almond meal (ground almonds)
15 g - 0.53 oz (about 1 large/UK medium) egg yolk
80 g – 2.82 ounces (2/3 cup) all-purpose (plain) flour
2 g – 0.07 ounce (1/2 teaspoon) fleur de sel

White chocolate shortbread cookies

60 g – 2.12 ounces white chocolate
80 g – 3 ounces (5 2/3 tablespoons) butter, softened
30 g – 1 ounce (1/4 cup) confectioners' (icing) sugar
40 g – 1.4 ounces (1/3 cup plus 1 tablespoon plus 1 teaspoon) almond meal (ground almonds)
15 g - 0.53 oz (about 1 large/UK medium) egg yolk
80 g – 2.82 ounces (2/3 cup) all-purpose flour
2 g – 0.07 ounce (1/2 teaspoon) fleur de sel

1 Make each kind of shortbread cookie (biscuit) in the same way: Melt the chocolate for 40 seconds in the microwave (800–900 W). Mix. Microwave for another 40 seconds.

2 Place the softened butter in a bowl. Add the sugar, almond meal, egg yolk, and flour in that order. Mix gently.
Incorporate the melted chocolate. Mix. Add the fleur de sel. Mix. Preheat the oven to 170°C – 350°F (gas mark 3).

3 Set silicone mat on top of a piece of parchment (baking) paper. Spread a thick layer of dough over the mat with a silicone spatula (scraper). Smooth with an offset spatula (palette knife). Peel off the mat, leaving behind the shaped cookies.

4 Instead of using a silicone mat, you can spread the dough over the work surface and use a cookie cutter to shape the cookies, then put them on the parchment paper.
Slide the parchment paper onto a cookie sheet (tray). Bake in the preheated oven for 10 minutes. Let cool, then transfer to the serving dish.

TIPS FROM OUR CHEFS

NO WASTE
Combine any dough scraps (trimmings), roll them out, and cut out more cookies. Repeat until you've used up the dough (or impatient food lovers have gobbled it up).

SO, SO SOFT
These soft shortbread cookies don't store well, because they become mushy quickly. Make them on the day you want to eat them.

MICROWAVE MAGIC
Don't set the timer for too long. Start by setting the microwave for 40 seconds, then mix and repeat the process until the chocolate is melted. Never add water. You can also melt the chocolate over a bain-marie at a simmer.

SHORTBREAD SANDWICH COOKIES
Fit a pastry (piping) bag with a 10-mm – 3/8-inch plain tip (nozzle) and fill with ganache or buttercream. Pipe a line around the edge of the flat side of half of the cookies and fill the center. Cover each topped cookie with a plain cookie, flat side against the filling, and press lightly.

1

2
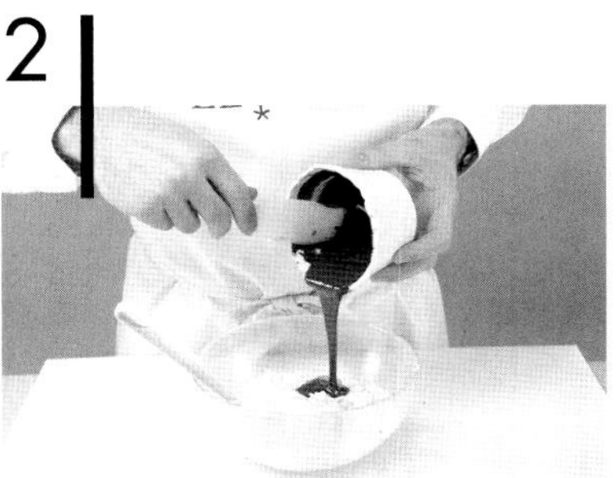

3

PLAIN CHOUQUETTES

Makes about 30 puffs

Preparation time 30 minutes
Cooking time 30 minutes

EQUIPMENT

Pastry (piping) bag
Size 10 plain pastry tip (nozzle)

300 g – 10.5 ounces choux paste (page 545)
1 egg
200 g – 7 ounces (1 cup) sanding or caliber 10 pearl (nib) sugar

1 Preheat the oven to 170°C – 350°F (gas mark 3). Fit the tip to the pastry bag and fill with the choux paste (page 545).
Pipe 3.5-cm- – 1 1/2-inch–diameter puffs on a baking sheet (tray), 3 cm – 1 1/8 inches apart.

2 Break the egg into a bowl and beat with a fork.
Gently brush the tops of the puffs with beaten egg.

3 Sprinkle generously with sanding sugar.
Shake the baking sheet over a sheet of parchment (baking) paper to remove the excess sugar.

4 Bake in the preheated oven for 30 minutes.
Detach the puffs from the baking sheet with an offset spatula (palette knife) and let cool.

TIPS FROM OUR CHEFS

AIR
Pipe the chouquettes in staggered rows in order to let air circulate around them when baking. This is important for even distribution of heat.

GENTLY DOES IT
When brushing the puffs with beaten egg, be sure not to let any drip onto the baking sheet. This will stop the beads of sanding sugar from falling off the baking sheet when you shake it and they'll burn when baked.

INVERSE
Decorative sanding sugar, also called pearl or nib sugar, comes in different sizes. The higher the number, the smaller the beads.

1

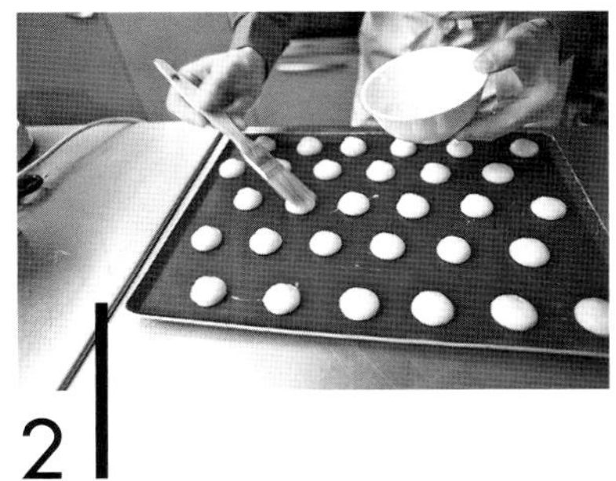

2

3

4

CHOCOLATE CHOUQUETTES

Makes about 80 puffs

Preparation time 30 minutes
Cooking time 30 minutes

EQUIPMENT
Pastry (piping) bag
Size 10 plain pastry tip (nozzle)

125 ml plus 1 teaspoon – 1/2 cup plus 1 teaspoon milk
120 ml – 1/2 cup cold water
125 g – 4.4 ounces (1 stick plus 1 tablespoon) butter, cut into cubes
4 g – 0.14 ounce (2/3 teaspoon) fine salt
4 (60-g – 2-ounce) eggs
110 g – 3.88 ounces (3/4 cup plus 2 tablespoons) all-purpose (plain) flour
30 g – 1 ounce (1/3 cup) unsweetened cocoa powder
200 g – 7 ounces (1 cup) sanding or caliber 6 pearl (nib) sugar
1/4 cup chocolate sprinkles

TIPS FROM OUR CHEFS

LEND A HAND
When the milk is boiling, whisk the preparation to make sure the butter is thoroughly melted.

TECHNIQUE
Get into the habit of breaking eggs into small bowls or ramekins one at a time before adding them to the rest. If one of them isn't fresh, you won't have to waste the whole lot.

1 Preheat the oven to 150°C – 300°F (gas mark 3) in a convection (fan-assisted) oven or 170°C – 350°F (gas mark 3) in a static (conventional) oven. Pour the milk into a saucepan. Add the cold water, followed by the butter. Add the salt and slowly bring to a boil while stirring occasionally.

2 In the meantime, break three eggs separately. Break the last egg and beat with a fork, leaving the rest untouched. Sift the flour and cocoa powder over a sheet of parchment (baking) paper.

3 When the milk is boiling, remove the pan from the heat and add all of the flour and cocoa powder mixture. Mix with a silicone spatula (scraper). Place the pan over medium heat and continue to mix for 1 minute to dry the paste. Transfer to a bowl. Add the three unbeaten eggs, one at a time, stirring briskly. Add the beaten egg, a little at a time, to obtain a smooth paste.

4 Fit the pastry bag with the tip and fill with the chocolate choux paste (page 545). Pipe 3.5-cm- – 1 1/2-inch–diameter puffs on a baking sheet (tray), 3 cm – 1 1/8 inches apart.

5 Sprinkle generously with sanding sugar. Sprinkle with chocolate sprinkles. Shake the baking sheet over a sheet of parchment paper to remove the excess sugar and sprinkles. Place one baking sheet on the top shelf and the other on the bottom shelf of the preheated oven. Bake for 30 minutes, switching them top to bottom and front to back about halfway through. Detach the puffs from the baking sheet with the back of an offset spatula (palette knife) and allow to cool.

1

2

3

4

PETS-DE-NONNE ("NUN'S FARTS")

Makes about 60 puffs

Preparation time 20 minutes
Cooking time 25 minutes

EQUIPMENT

Pastry (piping) bag
Size 16 pastry tip (nozzle)

400 g - 14 oz choux paste (recipe on p. 545)
125 g - 4.41 oz (1/2 cup) vanilla pastry cream
500 ml – (2 cups) frying oil
Confectioners' (icing) sugar

1 Preheat the oven to 150°C – 300°F (gas mark 3) in a convection (fan-assisted) oven or 170°C – 350°F (gas mark 3) in a static (conventional) oven.
Pour the oil into a saucepan and heat to 170°C – 350°F over medium heat.
In the meantime, mix the pastry cream with the choux paste.

2 Fit the tip to the pastry bag and fill with the choux paste mixture (page 545).
Dip the blade of a paring knife into the hot oil.
Rest the metal tip (not the bag) on the edge of the pan and tilt it downward toward the oil. Squeeze the bag to push out the choux paste mixture and cut the paste every 2 cm – 3/4 inch with the knife.

3 Make about 20 puffs in each batch (three batches) to avoid crowding the pan.
Cook for 6–8 minutes, shaking the pan from time to time.

4 Drain the pets-de-nonne on paper towels and dust with confectioners' sugar. Repeat with remaining mixture.
Serve hot.

TIPS FROM OUR CHEFS

SPREAD OUT
Use a pan that is large enough to hold 6–7 cm – 2 1/2–2 3/4 inches of oil. The puffs need room to expand.

FRY AHEAD
You can also fry the pets-de-nonne ahead of time and reheat them in the oven at 200°C – 400°F (gas mark 6) in a conventional oven.

1

2

3

4

APPLE TURNOVERS

Makes 8 small turnovers

Preparation time 20 minutes
Cooking time 12 minutes

EQUIPMENT

Cookie cutter or glass (8-cm – 3 1/4-inch diameter)

Apple compote, homemade (page 82) or store–bought
1 roll puff pastry
1 pinch sugar
1 pinch salt
1 egg yolk

TIPS FROM OUR CHEFS

RESTING
After rolling out the dough, let it rest for at least 30 minutes in the refrigerator to make it easier to handle.

ADD SHEEN
Adding a pinch of sugar and a pinch of salt to the beaten egg yolk for the egg wash makes the baked turnovers shiny and golden.

1 Make the apple compote. Refrigerate. Preheat the oven to 230°C – 450°F (gas mark 8). Roll the dough out on a floured work surface.
Cut out a rectangle measuring 20 x 15 cm – 7 3/4 x 6 inches. Place an overturned glass on top and press down to mark two circles next to each other on one half of the rectangle.
Make a thick layer of compote in the center of the first circle, then do the same with the second.
Moisten the edges of the circles with a pastry brush dipped in cold water.

2 Pick up the unmarked side of the rectangle. Fold over the mounds of compote.
Use your hands to locate the circle marks and seal the pastry well.

3 Place the overturned glass over the sealed disks. Press down firmly to cut the dough.
Remove the scraps (trimmings). Repeat this process with the rest of the dough. Reuse the scraps each time.

4 Use the blade of a knife to detach the turnovers from the work surface. Use a spatula (turner) to transfer the turnovers to a baking sheet (tray) lined with parchment (baking) paper.
Use the tip of a knife to make a decorative edge around each turnover; hold the turnover with one hand and with your other hand lightly notch around the edge, holding the blade at a slight slant.

5 Add the sugar and salt to the egg yolk and beat with a fork. Brush this egg wash over the turnovers.
Bake in the preheated oven until puffed and golden, about 12 minutes.

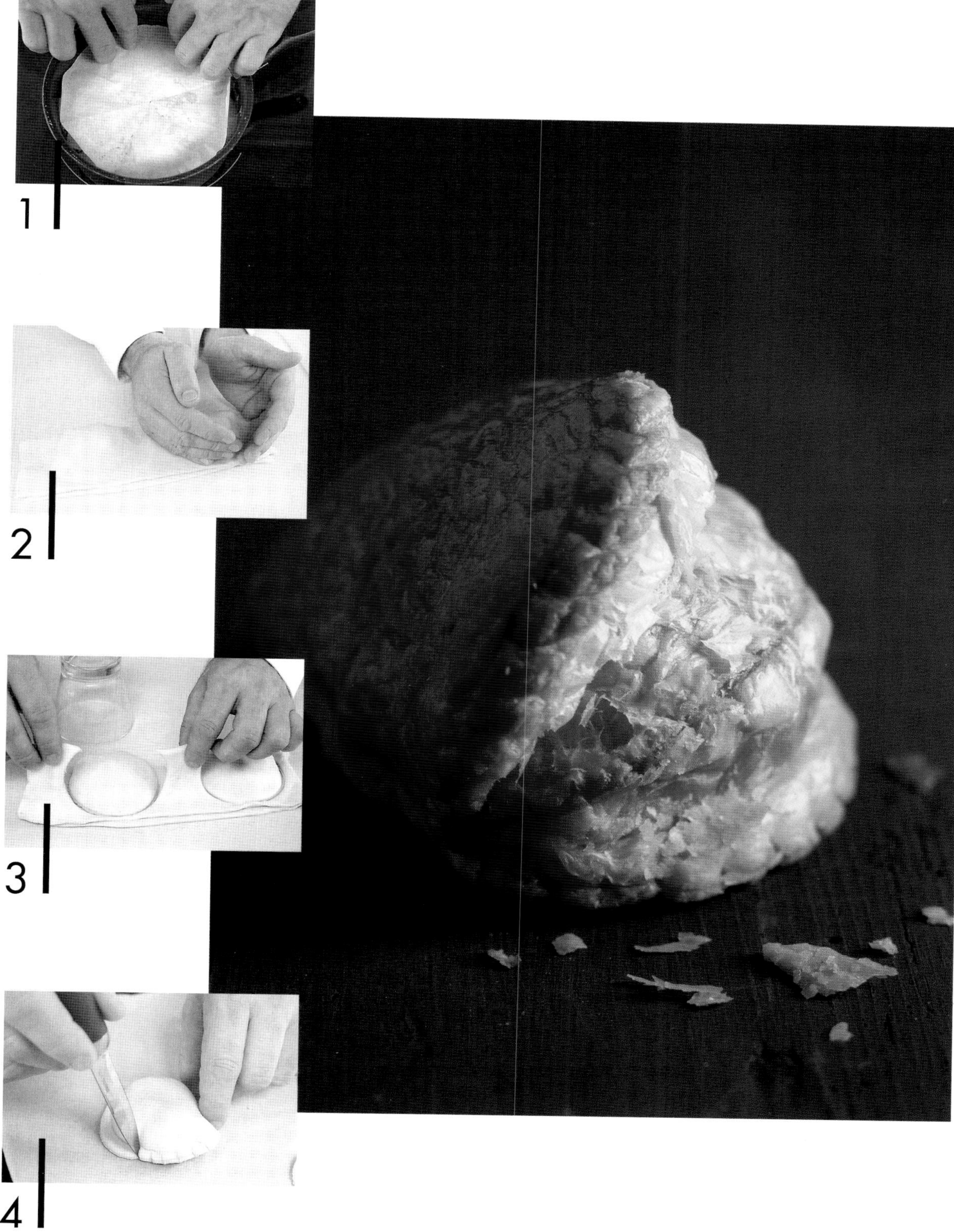
1
2
3
4

VANILLA MACARONS

Makes about 35 cookies

Vanilla macaron shells makes about 70
Preparation time 15 minutes
Cooking time 12 minutes + 12 minutes
Crust formation 1 hour

Vanilla buttercream
Preparation time 20 minutes

EQUIPMENT

Vanilla buttercream
Food processor fitted with metal blade
Stand mixer
Pastry (piping) bag
Size 8 plain pastry tip (nozzle)

Vanilla macaron shells

110 g – 3.88 ounces (1 cup plus 2 tablespoons) almond meal (ground almonds)
225 g – 8 ounces (1 3/4 cups plus 1 tablespoon) confectioners' (icing) sugar
120 g – 4.23 ounces (about 4) egg whites (at room temperature)
50 g – 1.76 ounces (1/4 cup) superfine (caster) sugar
1/2 vanilla bean (pod)

Vanilla buttercream

125 g – 4.4 ounces (1/2 cup) plain buttercream (page 565)
3 g – 0.11 ounce (about 1/2 teaspoon) natural vanilla extract

1

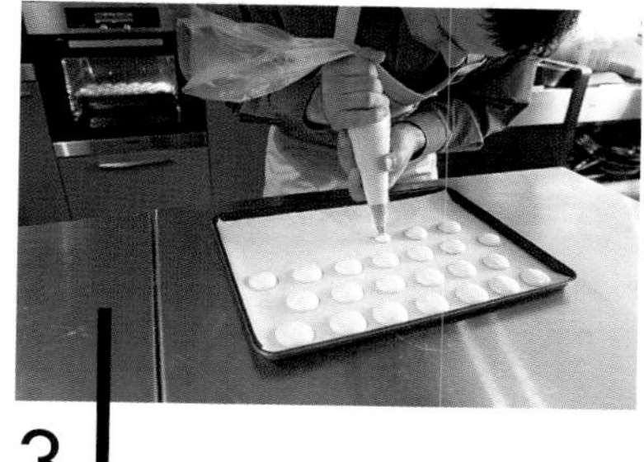

3

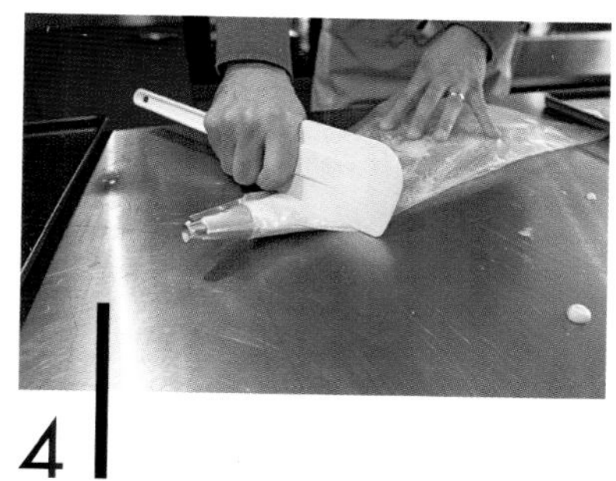

4

1 Preheat the oven to 170°C – 350°F (gas mark 3). Blend the almond meal and confectioners' sugar for about 2 minutes on high speed to a very fine powder. Sift the mixture. Break the eggs and separate 120 g – 4.23 ounces (about 1/2 cup) of egg whites.

2 Beat the egg whites on the highest speed until they form soft peaks (page 565). Add the superfine sugar, a little at a time, beating constantly. Continue to beat the egg whites to form stiff peaks, about 3 minutes. Pour all of the almond meal mixture over the egg whites and fold in using a silicone spatula (scraper). Use a paring knife to scrape out the seeds from the vanilla bean half. Add them to the mixture. Mix a little more briskly. The batter should be smooth, shiny, and elastic, but not runny.

3 Fill the pastry bag with the batter. Pipe evenly sized macaron shells onto two baking sheets (trays) lined with parchment (baking) paper (page 507).

4 When the pastry bag is nearly empty, use a spatula to push the rest of the batter toward the tip.

5 Let stand at room temperature until a crust forms and the batter no longer sticks to your finger, about 1 hour. Bake in the preheated oven for 12 minutes, rotating halfway through. Take the macaron shells out of the oven and let cool. Make the vanilla buttercream: Take 125 g – 4.4 ounces (1/2 cup) of plain buttercream (page 565). Add the natural vanilla extract. Whisk until smooth. Turn the cooled macaron shells upside down (flat sides up) on a large sheet of parchment paper. Fill the pastry bag with the buttercream (page 507). Pipe a small ball of filling in the middle of every other macaron shell. Cover the filled shells with the unfilled shells, flat sides down, pressing lightly to bind them.

TIPS FROM OUR CHEFS

CONDENSATION
Avoid boiling water during the crust formation process so that the air in the kitchen stays quite dry. To heat the air in the kitchen, open the door of your hot oven.

READY TO PIPE
To pipe successfully, hold the pastry bag 1–2 cm – 3/8–3/4 inch away from the baking sheet. Use one hand to squeeze the bag and the other to guide it. Don't forget to use a quarter twist to cut the flow of batter.

PISTACHIO MACARONS

Makes about 35 cookies

Pistachio macaron shells makes about 70
Preparation time 15 minutes
Cooking time 12 minutes + 12 minutes
Crust formation 1 hour

Pistachio buttercream
Preparation time 20 minutes

EQUIPMENT

Pistachio buttercream
Food processor fitted with metal blade
Stand mixer
Pastry (piping) bag
Size 8 plain pastry tip (nozzle)

Pistachio macaron shells

110 g – 3.88 ounces (1 cup plus 2 tablespoons) almond meal (ground almonds)
225 g – 8 ounces (1 3/4 cups plus 1 tablespoon) confectioners' (icing) sugar
120 g – 4.23 ounces (about 4) egg whites (at room temperature)
50 g – 1.76 ounces (1/4 cup) superfine (caster) sugar
30 drops green food coloring
1 tablespoon chopped pistachios

Pistachio buttercream

125 g – 4.4 ounces (1/2 cup) plain buttercream (page 565)
35 g – 1.23 ounces (2 tablespoons plus 3/4 teaspoon) pistachio paste

1 Preheat the oven to 170°C – 350°F (gas mark 3). Blend the almond meal and confectioners' sugar for about 2 minutes on high speed to a very fine powder. Sift the mixture.

2 Break the eggs and separate 120 g – 4.23 ounces (about 1/2 cup) of egg whites.
Beat the egg whites on the highest speed until they form soft peaks (page 565). Add the superfine sugar, a little at a time, while beating constantly. Continue to beat the egg whites for about 3 minutes to form stiff peaks.
Pour all of the almond meal mixture over the egg whites and fold in using a silicone spatula (scraper).
Take 2 tablespoons of the batter and mix with the food coloring until well dissolved.
Pour the colored portion back into the batter. Mix a little more briskly. The batter should be smooth, shiny, and elastic, but not runny.

3 Fill the pastry bag with the batter. Pipe evenly sized macaron shells onto two baking sheets (trays) lined with parchment (baking) paper (page 507).
When your pastry bag is nearly empty, use the spatula to push the rest of the batter toward the tip.
Sprinkle with chopped pistachios. Remove excess pistachio pieces and let the shells stand at room temperature until a crust forms and the batter no longer sticks to your finger, about 1 hour.
Bake in the preheated oven for 12 minutes, rotating halfway through. Take the macaron shells out of the oven and let cool.

4 Make the pistachio buttercream: Take 125 g – 4.4 ounces (1/2 cup) of plain buttercream (page 565). Add the pistachio paste. Whisk until smooth.

5 Turn the cooled macaron shells upside down (flat sides up) over a large sheet of parchment paper.
Fill the pastry bag with the pistachio buttercream (page 507).
Pipe a small ball of filling in the middle of every other macaron shell.
Cover the filled shells with the unfilled shells, flat sides down, pressing lightly to bind them. Your macarons are ready.

2

4

TIPS FROM OUR CHEFS

TOO GREEN
A touch of yellow food coloring will tone down a green that is too intense.

SPRINKLE
Don't try to place the pistachio pieces individually on each of the cookies; just sprinkle them evenly all over the baking sheet.

LOW-FAT VERSION
If you don't want to fill the macarons, pour a little water between the parchment paper and the baking sheet when it comes out of the oven. The steam produced will make slightly sticky shells that will stay together without a filling.

COCONUT MACARONS

Makes about 35 cookies

Coconut macaron shells makes about 70
Preparation time 15 minutes
Cooking time 12 minutes + 12 minutes
Crust formation 1 hour

Coconut buttercream
Preparation time 20 minutes

EQUIPMENT

Food processor fitted with metal blade
Stand mixer
Pastry (piping) bag
Size 8 plain pastry tip (nozzle)

Coconut macaron shells

110 g – 3.88 ounces (1 cup plus 2 tablespoons) almond meal (ground almonds)
225 g – 8 ounces (1 3/4 cups plus 1 tablespoon) confectioners' (icing) sugar
120 g – 4.23 ounces (about 4) egg whites (at room temperature)
50 g – 1.76 ounces (1/4 cup) superfine (caster) sugar
2 tablespoons shredded coconut

Coconut buttercream

100 g – 3.5 ounces (1/3 cup) plain buttercream (page 565)
15 g – 0.53 ounce (about 1 tablespoon) Malibu® coconut rum
20 g – 0.71 ounce (about 1 tablespoon plus 1 teaspoon) unsweetened coconut milk

1 Preheat the oven to 170°C – 350°F (gas mark 3).
Blend the almond meal and confectioners' sugar for about 2 minutes on high speed to a very fine powder. Sift the mixture.
Break the eggs and separate 120 g – 4.23 ounces (about 1/2 cup) of egg whites.
Beat the egg whites on the highest speed until they form soft peaks (page 565). Add the superfine sugar, a little at a time, beating constantly.
Continue to beat the egg whites until stiff peaks form, about 3 minutes.

2 Pour the almond meal mixture over the egg whites. Gently fold in using a silicone spatula (scraper). Mix a little more briskly.
The batter should be smooth, shiny, and elastic, but not runny.
Fill the pastry bag with the batter (page 507). Pipe evenly sized macaron shells onto two baking sheets (trays) lined with parchment (baking) paper.

3 When the pastry bag is nearly empty, use the spatula to push the rest of the batter toward the tip.
Sprinkle with shredded coconut. Shake the baking sheets over a sheet of parchment paper to remove the excess coconut.
Let stand at room temperature, until a crust forms and the batter no longer sticks to your finger, about 1 hour.
Bake in the preheated oven for 12 minutes, rotating halfway through. Take the macaron shells out of the oven and let cool.

4 Make the coconut buttercream: Take 100 g – 3.5 ounces (1/3 cup) of plain buttercream (page 565). Add the Malibu.
Add the coconut milk. Whisk until smooth.

5 Turn the cooled macaron shells upside down on a large sheet of parchment paper.
Fill the pastry bag with the coconut buttercream (page 507). Pipe a small ball of filling in the middle of every other macaron shell.
Cover the filled shells with the unfilled shells, flat sides down, pressing lightly to bind them. Your macarons are ready.

2

TIPS FROM OUR CHEFS

SPRINKLING

Coconut macarons are sprinkled with coconut instead of incorporating this ingredient into the batter. That way the coconut flavor is more pronounced.

DON'T LET ANYTHING BURN

Tilt the baking sheet after sprinkling coconut over the macaron shells and remove any coconut that falls off of the shells. That way you will prevent any excess coconut from burning while baking.

HAZELNUT MACARONS

Makes about 35 cookies

Hazelnut macaron shells makes about 70
Preparation time 15 minutes
Cooking time 12 minutes + 12 minutes
Crust formation 1 hour

Hazelnut praline cream
Preparation time 30 minutes
Cooking time 15 minutes

EQUIPMENT

Hazelnut praline cream
Food processor fitted with metal blade
Stand mixer
Pastry (piping) bag
Size 8 plain pastry tip (nozzle)

Hazelnut macaron shells

110 g – 3.88 ounces (1 cup plus 2 tablespoons) hazelnut meal (ground hazelnuts)
225 g – 8 ounces (1 3/4 cups plus 1 tablespoon) confectioners' (icing) sugar
120 g – 4.23 ounces (about 4) egg whites (at room temperature)
50 g – 1.75 ounces (1/4 cup) superfine (caster) sugar

Hazelnut praline cream

100 g – 3.5 ounces (3/4 cup) unskinned hazelnuts
100 g - 3.53 oz (1/3 cup) plain buttercream (recipe on p. 565)

1

2

4

5

1 Preheat the oven to 170°C – 350°F (gas mark 3).
Blend the hazelnut meal and confectioners' sugar for about 2 minutes on high speed to a very fine powder. Sift the mixture.

2 Break the eggs and separate 120 g – 4.23 ounces (about 1/2 cup) of egg whites. Beat the egg whites on the highest speed until they form soft peaks (page 565). Add the superfine sugar, a little at a time, while beating constantly. Continue to beat the egg whites until stiff peaks form, about 3 minutes. Pour all of the hazelnut mixture over the egg whites and fold in using a silicone spatula (scraper). Mix a little more briskly. The batter should be smooth, shiny, and elastic, but not runny.

3 Fill the pastry bag with the batter (page 507). Pipe evenly sized macaron shells onto two baking sheets (trays) lined with parchment (baking) paper. When your pastry bag is nearly empty, use the spatula to push the rest of the batter toward the tip.

4 Let stand at room temperature, until a crust forms and the batter no longer sticks to your finger, about 1 hour.
Bake in the preheated oven for 12 minutes, rotating halfway through. Take the macaron shells out of the oven and let cool.

5 Make the hazelnut praline cream: Spread the hazelnuts for the cream in a single layer on a baking sheet lined with parchment paper. Bake for 15 minutes to toast. Let cool, then blend to a smooth and runny paste. Transfer to a bowl, cover with plastic wrap (cling film), and refrigerate until it's cold. Take 100 g – 3.5 ounces (1/3 cup) of plain buttercream (page 565). Add 30 g – 1 ounce (2 tablespoons) of the hazelnut paste. Whisk until smooth. Turn the cooled macaron shells upside down over a large sheet of parchment paper. Fill the pastry bag with the hazelnut praline buttercream (page 507). Pipe a small ball of filling in the middle of every other macaron shell. Cover the filled halves with the unfilled shells, flat sides down, pressing lightly to bind them.

TIPS FROM OUR CHEFS

HAZELNUT MEAL
Hazelnuts are just as good as almonds for making macaron batter. They can be used to make the starter base for other macarons as well.

FREEZING MACARONS
Macarons freeze very well. You can make a very large batch of them and thaw out a few at a time.

THAWING MACARONS
To thaw macarons, take them out of the freezer 24 hours before you want to serve them and put them in the refrigerator. Keep them in an airtight container or covered with plastic wrap to prevent them from absorbing odors in the refrigerator.

RASPBERRY AND CHOCOLATE-RASPBERRY PÂTE DE FRUIT (FRUIT JELLIES)

Makes 32 squares

Preparation time 20 minutes
Cooking time 8 minutes
Resting time 2 hours

EQUIPMENT

Candy thermometer
2 square stainless steel cake molds (20-cm by 20-cm)

180 g – 6.35 ounces (3/4 cup) frozen raspberry puree
80 g – 2.82 ounces (2/3 cup) fresh or frozen whole raspberries
275 g – 9.88 ounces (1 1/4 cups plus 2 tablespoons) sugar, divided, pus extra for finishing
8 g – 0.28 ounce (about 1 tablespoon) HM pectin powder (available at gourmet specialty stores)
5 g – 0.18 ounce (1 teaspoon) lemon juice
25 g – 0.88 ounce dark chocolate (64% cocoa)

1 Pour the raspberry puree into a saucepan. Add the whole raspberries.

1

2 Add 250 g – 9 ounces (1 1/4 cups) of the sugar and stir with a whisk. Heat over medium heat.
In the meantime, put the remaining 25 g – 0.88 ounce (2 tablespoons) sugar into a bowl. Add the pectin. Mix well.
When the raspberries are hot (don't allow them to boil), very gradually sprinkle in the sugar and pectin mixture while whisking.
Increase the heat to high and continue to whisk. Use a thermometer to monitor the temperature, which should reach 104°C – 219°F.

3 At 104°C – 219°F, add the lemon juice and mix well. Remove from heat. Place the two cake molds on a baking sheet (tray) lined with parchment (baking) paper. Pour half of the mixture into the first cake mold to form a fairly thin layer (about 6 mm – 1/4 inch).
Break the chocolate into small pieces and add to the pan off the heat. Whisk until perfectly smooth.
Pour the mixture into the second cake mold to form a fairly thin layer (about 6 mm – 1/4 inch). Let cool for 2 hours at room temperature.

3

4 Slide the blade of a knife around the edge of each cake mold to detach the pâte de fruits and unmold by lifting off.
Use a wide chef's knife to cut each square of pâte de fruits in half. Cut each half in two.
Turn the baking sheets and cut the pieces in half perpendicularly.
Halve again to make uniform squares. Separate the raspberry squares using a knife tip.
Put sugar into a bowl and dip the raspberry squares. Coat well with the sugar.
Separate the raspberry-chocolate squares. Enjoy them just as they are.

CANDIED ORANGE AND ORANGETTES

Makes 10 orange slices and 12 orangettes

Preparation time 20 minutes
Cooking time 5 x 10 minutes + 5 minutes
(48 HOURS IN ADVANCE)
Resting time 5 x 8 hours

10 g – 0.35 ounce (1 3/4 teaspoons) fine salt
2 organic, unwaxed oranges
750 g – 1 pound 10.53 ounces (3 3/4 cups) sugar
400 g – 14 ounces chocolate coating (page 567)

1 Starting 48 hours in advance, pour 1 liter – 4 1/4 cups water into a large saucepan. Add the salt. Take one orange and cut a slice from two opposite sides. Then cut ten 5-mm – 1/4-inch slices.

2 Trim off the top and bottom of the other orange, stand, and cut off a strip of peel together with the pith. Supreme the orange (page 514). Use a paring or filleting knife to trim the strips into uniform rectangles. Slightly thin the strips by removing any flesh still attached to the pith. Put the orange slices, supremes, and peels into the cold salted water. Bring to a boil over high heat, then simmer for 10 minutes. Transfer to a strainer (sieve). Discard the cooking water. Refresh the blanched orange pieces under a gentle stream of running water.

3 Drain and return to the pan. Add 650 g – 1 pound 7 ounces (3 1/4 cups) of sugar. Add 500 ml – 2 cups of water. Place over medium heat and bring to a simmer, then simmer for 10 minutes. Turn off the heat. Cover with heatproof plastic wrap (cling film) and seal tightly. Let cool. Let stand for at least 8 hours at room temperature. After 8 hours, take off the plastic wrap and add the remaining 100 g – 3.5 ounces (1/2 cup) of sugar. Place over medium heat and bring to a simmer, then simmer for 10 minutes. Cover with heatproof plastic wrap and let stand for 8 hours. Repeat the process of heating, simmering and resting another three times. Preheat the oven to 130°C – 250°F (gas mark 1/2). Drain the candied orange pieces and peel. Transfer to a baking sheet (tray) lined with parchment (baking) paper. Place in the oven for 5 minutes. Take the orange pieces and peel out of the oven and let cool. Use a chef's knife to cut one strip of orange peel into 4-mm- – 1/8-inch–wide matchsticks. Do the same for the rest of the peel. Leave the orange slices and supremes whole.

4 Make the chocolate coating (page 567). Immerse the orange matchsticks completely. Wipe off excess chocolate on the side of the bowl and place the orangettes on a sheet of parchment paper. Gently reheat the chocolate while stirring well. Dip half of each candied orange slice and supreme in the chocolate. Drain well. Place the chocolate-coated candied orange pieces on a sheet of parchment paper and let cool. Enjoy.

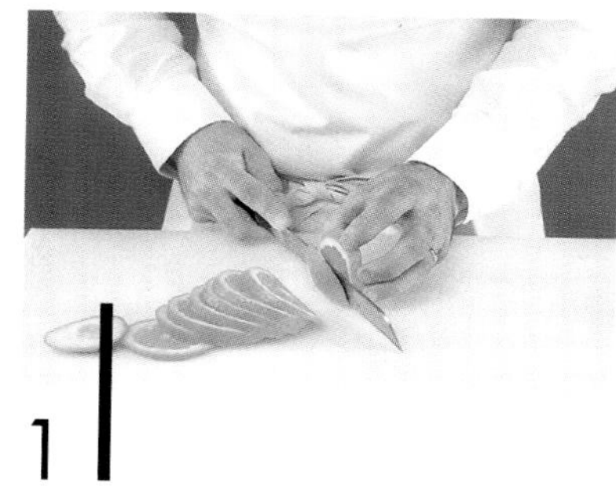

1

2

TIPS FROM OUR CHEFS

SALT TO COUNTER THE BITTERNESS
The oranges are blanched for 10 minutes in salted water because salt neutralizes the bitterness of the orange peel.

IN A CORNER
During the eight-hour resting periods, leave the oranges in the saucepan at room temperature. Don't refrigerate. If cooled too quickly, their delicate flesh may break.

NO SUGAR
When draining the orange pieces, remove excess syrup with your fingers. If the syrup is extremely thick, quickly rinse the pieces under a thin stream of cold water and then drain thoroughly.

FRUITS DÉGUISÉS (DRIED FRUIT WITH MARZIPAN)

Makes 36 pieces of fruit

Preparation time 50 minutes
Cooking time 5 minutes

EQUIPMENT

18 wooden skewers
Candy thermometer
Kitchen scissors

Fruits déguisés

1/2 organic, unwaxed orange
75 g – 2.65 ounces (3/4 cup) almond meal (ground almonds)
75 g – 2.65 ounces (1/2 cup plus 2 tablespoons) confectioners' (icing) sugar
1/2 organic, unwaxed lemon
1 vanilla bean
1 egg
12 pitted (stoned) prunes
12 candied (glacé) cherries
12 dates

Coating

250 g – 9 ounces (1 cup plus 2 tablespoons) superfine (caster) sugar
80 g – 2.82 ounces (3 tablespoons) glucose syrup (page 543) or light corn syrup

TIPS FROM OUR CHEFS

STORAGE
The citrus marzipan can be stored for quite a long time in an airtight container in the refrigerator, but use up the vanilla marzipan in short order because it contains egg white.

IN THE CENTER
Poke the skewer into the center of the fruit, because the weight of the sugar can cause it to become unsteady and fall off.

ALWAYS LIQUID
As you are dipping the fruit, the syrup will cool and thicken. If it becomes too thick to use, reheat by placing the saucepan over very low heat. The more liquid the syrup, the finer the coating.

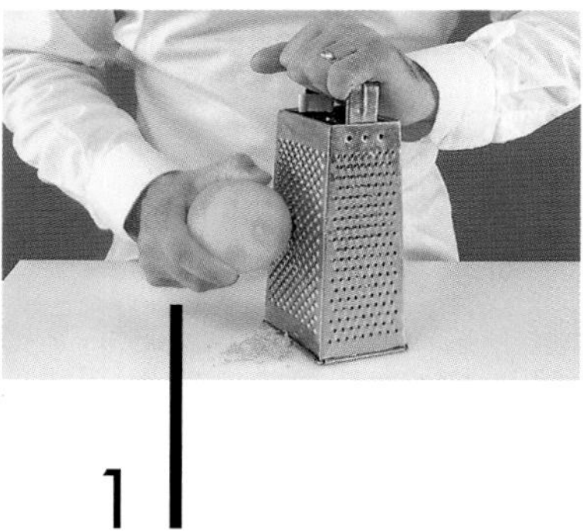

1

Finely grate the zest of the orange half (page 514). Squeeze and weigh out 6 g – 0.21 ounce (about 1 1/4 teaspoon) of juice.

2

Divide the almond meal into three equal portions (25 g – 0.88 ounce/1/4 cup each) and place in three different bowls. Divide the confectioners' sugar into three equal portions (25 g – 0.88 ounce/3 tablespoons plus 1 teaspoon each) and add to the bowls with the almond meal. Mix. Add the orange zest to the first bowl. Stir well. Add the orange juice. Mix to a smooth paste. Finely grate the zest of the lemon half (page 514). Squeeze and weigh out 6 g – 0.21 ounce (about 1 1/4 teaspoon) of juice. Add the lemon zest to the second bowl. Stir well. Add the lemon juice. Mix to a smooth paste. Split the vanilla bean lengthwise and scrape out the seeds from one half. Add to the third bowl. Stir well. Separate the egg. Weigh out 6 g – 0.21 ounce (about 1 teaspoon) of egg white. Add the egg white to the bowl with the vanilla. Mix to a smooth paste.

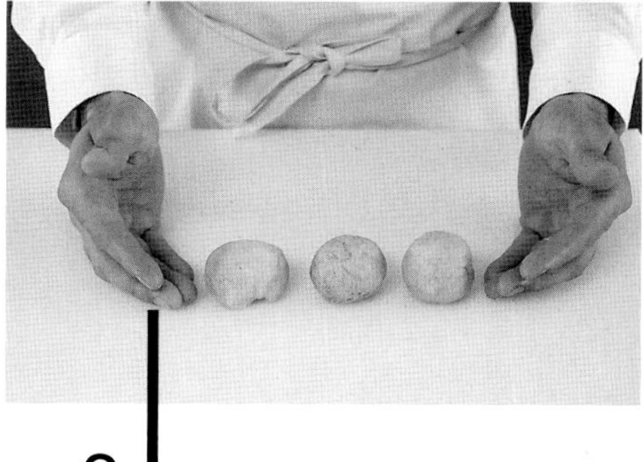

3

Use your hands to roll the three different pastes into balls.

4

Use a paring knife to cut the prunes and cherries in half. Halve the dates. Remove the pits (stones) with the knife tip. Roll the orange marzipan into a cylinder with a 1.5-cm – 3/4-inch diameter. Cut into 12 uniform pieces weighing 3–5 g – 0.11–0.18 ounce each. Roll into ovals. Place a piece over a prune half. Cover with the other half of the fruit. Repeat the process with remaining ovals of marzipan and prunes. Press to bind, without crushing. Roll the lemon marzipan into a cylinder with a 1.5-cm – 3/4-inch diameter. Cut into 12 uniform pieces weighing 3–5 g – 0.11–0.18 ounce each. Roll into ovals. Insert a piece between the halves of each date. Press to bind, without crushing.

5

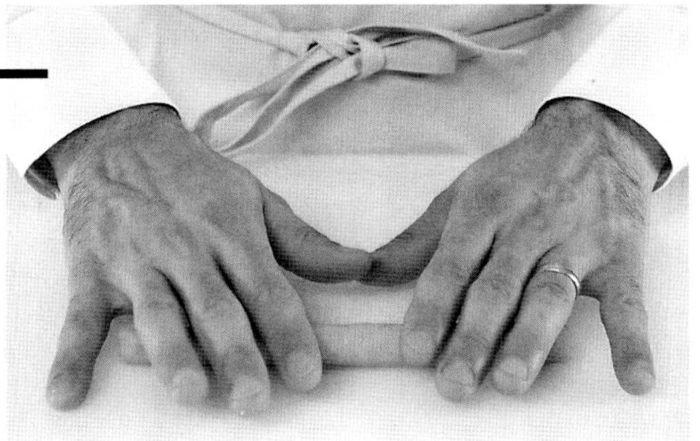

Roll the vanilla marzipan into a cylinder with a 1.5-cm – 3/4-inch diameter. Cut into 12 uniform pieces weighing 3–5 g – 0.11–0.18 ounce.

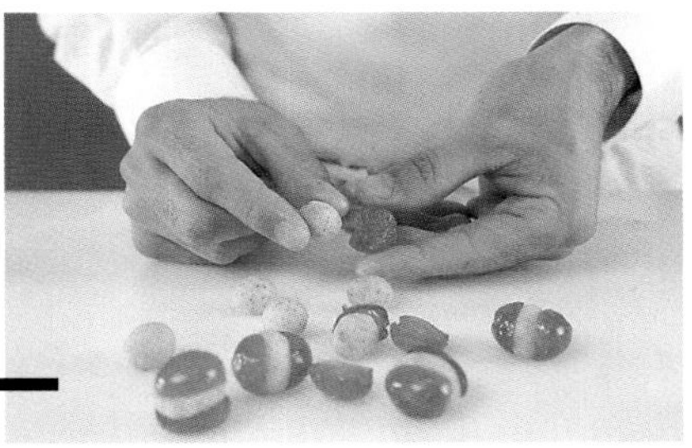

6

Roll into little balls. Insert a piece between the halves of each cherry. Press to bind, without crushing.

7

Pierce a fruit on each end of a wooden skewer. Handle the fruit gently without squeezing to avoid deforming. Make the coating: Put the sugar in a saucepan. Add 80 ml – 1/3 cup of water. Add the glucose syrup. Mix. Place over high heat. Use a thermometer to monitor the temperature and bring it to 115°C – 239°F. Dip a prune into the syrup while tilting the pan. Then dip the prune on the other end of the same skewer. Rest this skewer on an overturned box. Repeat with the remaining prunes. Let cool. Cut off the sugar threads with scissors and set aside on a plate. Dip the dates in the hot syrup in the same way as the prunes. Rest the skewers on the box and let cool. Cut off the sugar threads with scissors and set aside on a plate. Dip the cherries in the hot syrup. Rest on the box. Let cool.

8

Cut off the sugar threads with scissors and set aside on a plate. Carefully remove the prunes from the skewers, followed by the dates. Finally, do the same for the cherries. Be sure not to squeeze the fruit, because you may break the coating.

MONTÉLIMAR NOUGAT

Makes 32 large squares

Preparation time 40 minutes
Cooking time 20 minutes
Resting time 4 hours

EQUIPMENT

Candy thermometer
Stand mixer
Square stainless steel cake mold (20- cm by 20- cm)

250 g – 9 ounces (3/4 cup) orange flower honey
200 g – 7 ounces (1 cup) sugar
200 g – 7 ounces (1 3/4 cups) almonds, with skin
2 eggs (for 50 g - 1.76 oz of egg white)
50 g – 1.76 ounces (1/3 cup plus 1 tablespoon) pistachio nuts, peeled
100 g – 3.5 ounces (1/2 cup) candied orange peel matchsticks (page 389)
Oil

1 Pour the honey into a saucepan. Heat to 135°C – 275°F. Use a thermometer to monitor the temperature. Combine the sugar with 80 ml – 1/3 cup of water in another saucepan. Heat to 145°C – 293°F. Preheat the oven to 190°C – 375°F (gas mark 5). Spread the almonds on one half of a baking sheet (tray) lined with parchment (baking) paper. Place in the oven and roast for 5 minutes. In the meantime, separate the eggs. Weigh out 50 g – 1.76 ounces (about 3 tablespoons plus 1 1/2 teaspoons) of egg white. Beat the egg whites to soft peaks in the mixer.

2 Spread the pistachios on the baking sheet next to the almonds. Place in the oven and roast for 5 minutes. Use a chef's knife to cut the candied orange peel matchsticks (page 389) into very small dice. Take the nuts out of the oven and put the diced orange peel on the baking sheet to heat. Let stand at room temperature.

3 When the honey reaches 135°C – 275°F, remove the sauce pan from the heat. Pour the honey over the beaten egg whites with the mixer running. Be careful not to pour the boiling liquid directly over the whisk attachment. When the sugar syrup reaches 145°C – 293°F, remove the pan from the heat. Add to the mixer by pouring down the side of the bowl. Continue to beat at low speed. Lightly grease the inside of the cake mold by brushing with oil. Set on a baking sheet lined with parchment paper. Use a hair dryer to heat the mixture (to remove moisture) by blowing air into the bowl for 2 minutes while the mixer continues to beat. Then heat the outside of the bowl by blowing air around it for 2 minutes. Lift up the whisk and add the nuts and candied peel.

4 Immediately mix the nougat with a spatula (scraper). Work fast, because it will begin to harden. Spread the mixture inside the cake ring, filling right to the top. Push down with the spatula to fill in the corners. Lay a sheet of parchment paper over the nougat and press with a rolling pin. Allow to set for at least 4 hours at room temperature. Remove the parchment paper. Insert the tip of a knife vertically against one side of the mold. Slide the knife blade along all the sides of the mold to detach the nougat. With the nougat flat, lift off the mold. Use a serrated knife to cut off a strip and cut horizontally to a 1–1.5-cm – 3/8–5/8-inch thickness.
Cut all of the nougat into uniform strips. Cut each strip into squares. Enjoy.

1

2

TIPS FROM OUR CHEFS

FLAVOR OF THE SOUTH
If you don't have orange flower honey, you can add orange flower water to it. Just a few drops are enough to give it a subtle flavor.

PALE
Watch the almonds carefully when toasting. They should remain pale. If they darken, their flavor will be too strong. Stir them as they cook to move them around, because the ones at the edges will toast more quickly.

FRAGILE
It is important to let the candied orange peel heat up on the baking sheet with the nuts. That way you'll avoid thermal shock when adding it to the egg whites, which would make the pieces clump together.

LEMON CANDIES

Makes 40 candies (or 15 lollipops)

Preparation time 15 minutes
Cooking time 10 minutes
Resting time 1 hour

EQUIPMENT

Candy thermometer
Silicone mold with small cavities

Lemon syrup

250 g – 9 ounces (1 1/4 cups) sugar
50 g – 1.75 ounces (3 tablespoons) glucose syrup (page 543) or light corn syrup
15 drops yellow food coloring
8 g – 0.28 ounce (1 2/3 teaspoons) lemon extract
10 g – 0.35 ounce (2 teaspoons) lemon juice, strained

Effects

Confectioners' (icing) sugar
or
Superfine (caster) sugar

1 Pour 100 ml – 1/3 cup plus 1 tablespoon plus 1 teaspoon of water into a small saucepan and add the sugar. Add the glucose syrup. Heat over medium heat.

2 Clean the sides of the pan with a wet pastry brush. Insert a candy thermometer into the syrup when it boils and keep an eye on the syrup as the temperature rises to 140°C – 284°F. In the meantime, place the silicone mold with small cavities on a baking sheet (tray) lined with parchment (baking) paper. When the syrup reaches 140°C – 284°F, add the yellow food coloring. Stir to even out the color. Continue to heat to 150°C – 302°F.

3 At 150°C – 302°F, add the lemon extract. Add the lemon juice. At 160°C – 320°F, remove the pan from the heat and transfer the mixture to a heatproof bowl.

4 Pour the syrup into the mold cavities. Let harden at room temperature. Unmold the candies when cool.

5 For an iced effect, fill a bowl with confectioners' sugar. Add the candies. Cover with the confectioners' sugar and let sit in the sugar for at least 1 hour for the sugar to adhere well. Take the candies out of the bowl and rub them very gently with your finger to remove the excess. For a crystallized effect, fill a bowl with superfine sugar. Add the candies. Cover with the superfine sugar. Take the candies out of the bowl and rub them very gently with your finger to remove the excess.

1

2

3

4

TIPS FROM OUR CHEFS

NOT DARK

Unlike caramel, which cooks slowly and gradually darkens to a brown color, sugar cooked more quickly without exceeding 170° – 338°F will stay white and harden as it cools. This technique is used for making candies, lollipops, and coating fruits déguisés (dried fruit with marzipan, page 390).

BRUSHING

Bubbles of sugar syrup can burst and splash particles over the sides of the saucepan, so you have to clean the sides of the very hot pan every 2–3 minutes after starting to cook (more often if you are cooking with gas).

SALTED BUTTER CARAMELS

Makes about 40 candies

Preparation time 30 minutes
Cooking time 10 minutes
Resting time 2 hours

EQUIPMENT

2 square stainless steel cake molds (20-cm x 20-cm)
Candy Thermometer

80 g – 2.82 ounces (2/3 cup) heavy (full-fat) whipping cream
1 vanilla bean (pod)
250 g – 9 ounces (1 1/4 cups) sugar
80 g – 2.82 ounces (5 1/2 tablespoons) semi-salted butter, cut into cubes
2 g – 0.07 ounce (1/2 teaspoon) fleur de sel

1

1 Pour the cream into a saucepan. Place over low heat and heat until it comes to a simmer. Don't let it boil. Remove from heat.

2

2 Use a paring knife to make an incision in the vanilla bean. Split lengthwise. Keep only one half. Scrape out the seeds with a knife tip, reserve.
Lightly caramelize a little of the sugar in another saucepan (page 566). Mix with a spatula (palette knife). Add a little more sugar while stirring constantly. Cook until it melts.
Add the rest of the sugar and stir well. The caramelized sugar should be runny, never pasty or lumpy.
Use a thermometer to check the temperature, which should reach 180°C – 356°F. Add the vanilla seeds. Stir well.
Add the hot cream. Stir. Heat over medium heat to 140°C – 284°F while stirring constantly.

3

3 At 140°C – 284°F, remove from the heat. Add the butter.
Stir briskly to stop the caramel from cooking any further. Add the fleur de sel.

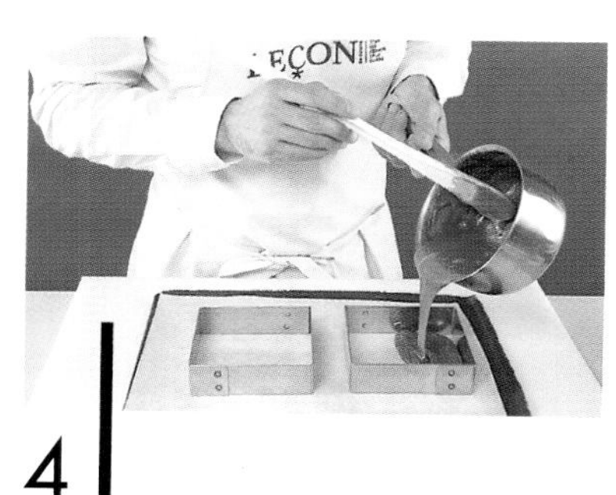

4

4 Place the two cake molds on a baking sheet (tray) lined with parchment (baking) paper. Pour the caramel halfway up the molds.

5 Let cool for 2 hours at room temperature. Check the hardness of the caramel by pressing with your finger. Once the caramel is hard, lift off the molds.
Use a serrated knife to cut each block of caramel in half with a back-and-forth movement.
Cut each half in half. Turn the baking sheet around and make perpendicular cuts to obtain squares.
Separate the caramels and wrap in cellophane.

CHOCOLATE CARAMEL LOLLIPOPS

Makes about 15 lollipops

Preparation time 20 minutes
Cooking time 15 minutes

EQUIPMENT

Silicone mold with large oval cavities
Candy Thermometer
15 lollipop sticks

Chocolate caramel (page 567), very hot

Chocolate coating (page 567)
50 g – 1.76 ounces (1/4 cup) chocolate chips
Hairdryer
1/2 bar white chocolate

1 Set aside a little of the chocolate caramel. Pour the remaining caramel to a depth of 6–8 mm – 1/4 inch into the large oval cavities of the silicone mold. Let harden, then unmold by pushing up on the bottom of the mold. Transfer to a sheet of parchment (baking) paper with the shiny sides facing down.

2 Make the chocolate coating (page 567).

3 Check the thermometer to be sure the temperature falls to 27°C – 81°F. Use a hair dryer to increase the temperature to 30°C – 86°F, while stirring constantly.

4 Gently reheat the reserve chocolate caramel. Dip the lollipop sticks, one at a time, into the slightly tilted saucepan. Immediately stick them to the caramel and hold in place until the caramel hardens completely.

5 Put the chocolate chips into a bowl. Dip half of the lollipops halfway into the chocolate coating. Immediately dip them a quarter of the way into the chocolate chips to create a textured effect.
Coarsely chop the white chocolate and put into a bowl. Dip the rest of the lollipops halfway into the chocolate coating. Immediately dip the top edge of those lollipops into the chopped white chocolate to create arches around the tops of those lollipops.

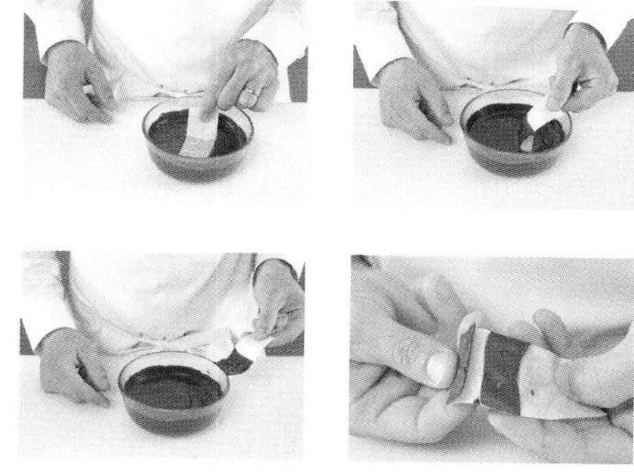

TESTING TEMPERED CHOCOLATE

Cut out a small rectangle of parchment paper. Dip it in the chocolate at 30°C – 86°F (step 3), drain on the rim of the bowl. Cool quickly (in the refrigerator, if necessary because the kitchen is hot). Snap it in half.

The chocolate should break cleanly, and it should be shiny and not have any streaks.

It is now ready to use for coating.

DIFFICULT

STUFFED VEGETABLES

STUFFED VEGETABLES

Serves 4

Preparation time 1 hour
Cooking time 40 minutes

4 (40-g – 1.4-ounce) vine tomatoes
8 (40-g – 1.4-ounce) round zucchini (courgettes)
4 (40-g – 1.4-ounce) fresh onions
4 zucchini flowers
2 long green zucchini
1 large white onion
2 large tomatoes
1/4 cup olive oil, divided, plus more for greasing dish and drizzling
2 sprigs thyme
Salt
Freshly ground pepper
2 sprigs mint
2 sprigs basil
40 g – 1.4 ounces (about 1/2 cup grated) Parmesan cheese
300 ml – 1 1/4 cups chicken broth or stock
Fleur de sel

1 Wash the vegetables. Cut the tops off the vine tomatoes and reserve. Cut a thin slice from the bottom of each to form a base. Use a melon baller to core the tomatoes (page 521). Trim the tops of the round zucchini to neaten and cut them off. Reserve tops. Also cut off the bottom of each to form a base. Hollow out the round zucchini with a melon baller.

2 Cut off the leaves of the small onions 1.5 cm – 3/4 inch from the bulb. Cut off the tops and reserve. Cut off the bottom of each onion to form a base. Hollow out the onions with a melon baller. Open the zucchini flowers. Grasp the pistil with your fingers and pull it out (page 522).

3 Slice off the tops and bottoms of the long zucchini. Cut in half. Slice them around the core to remove the seeds (page 522). Cut them into batons, and then into very small dice (brunoise). Peel the large onion. Halve and chop (page 525). Remove the stems (stalks) from the large tomatoes and cut in eight wedges. Peel by passing the knife blade between the skin and the flesh (page 521). Remove the cores and seeds by passing the blade over the flesh. Cut the flesh into strips, then cut into large dice. Pour 1 tablespoon plus 1 1/2 teaspoons of olive oil into a saucepan with the chopped onion and 1 sprig of thyme. Season with salt and pepper. Mix. Sauté for 8 minutes over medium heat uncovered. Pour 1 tablespoon of olive oil into a deep skillet or frying pan with the diced zucchini. Season with salt. Season with plenty of pepper. Pluck the mint leaves into the pan. Cook for 8 minutes over medium heat, stirring from time to time.

4 Wash the basil. Gently pat dry. Pluck the leaves. Gather the leaves into small bunches and chop them with a knife (page 524). Pour 1 tablespoon plus 1 1/2 teaspoons of olive oil into a saucepan and add the diced tomatoes. Add the basil. Season with salt and pepper. Mix. Cook over medium heat until the tomatoes release their liquid, about 2 minutes. Bring water to a boil in a saucepan. Add salt. Immerse the round zucchini and their tops in the water for 2 minutes. Pour some cold water with ice cubes into a bowl. Drain the zucchini with a skimmer and refresh in the ice water.

5 Immerse the onions and their tops in the same boiling water for 2 minutes. Drain with a skimmer. Preheat the oven to 210°C – 400°F (gas mark 6–7). Lightly grease an ovenproof dish with oil. Stand the zucchini and onion shells in it. Season lightly with salt. Season with pepper. Drizzle with a little olive oil. Grate the Parmesan. Pluck the leaves of 1 sprig of thyme and scatter over the Parmesan. Combine a tablespoon of the cheese–thyme mixture with the chopped onion. Fill each of the onion shells with this stuffing. Place their tops over them. Mix the rest of the cheese mixture with the diced zucchini. Fill the zucchini shells with some of this stuffing.

6 Drizzle a little olive oil over their tops. Season with salt and pepper. Place the tops on the zucchini. Open the zucchini flowers. Fill one flower with 2 teaspoons of the zucchini filling. Bring the tips of the petals together. Twist them to form a package. Fold them back over the stuffed flower. Repeat with remaining flowers. Place the zucchini flowers in the dish, arranging them with the folded sides down. Drizzle the vegetables with the broth. Drizzle on a little olive oil. Bake for 25 minutes. Mix the rest of the onion stuffing (about 1 teaspoon) with the diced tomatoes. Fill the tomatoes to overflowing with this stuffing. Place their tops over them. Drizzle with a little olive oil. Set aside in the refrigerator. Arrange the baked stuffed vegetables on a dish, together with the tomatoes. Reduce the cooking liquid and pour over the vegetables. Sprinkle with fleur de sel and serve.

POTATO RAVIOLI

Serves 4

Preparation time 1 hour
Cooking time 4 minutes
Resting time 1 hour

EQUIPMENT

Pasta machine
Cookie cutters (page 503)

TIPS FROM OUR CHEFS

PLANNING
Make your ravioli dough ahead of time. Cover it with plastic wrap (cling film) and store in the refrigerator. It will keep for several days in the refrigerator. You can store it for a longer time in the freezer. If you make it the same day you are going to use it, factor in the resting time.

MACHINE SETTINGS
Roll out the dough a first time so that the dough can fit into the pasta machine on the widest setting. Each successive time that you run the dough through the machine, adjust the setting to make the space between the rollers more narrow.

Ravioli dough

150 g – 5.3 ounces (3/4 cup plus 1 tablespoon plus 1 1/2 teaspoons) finely ground semolina flour
150 g – 5.3 ounces (1 cup plus 3 tablespoons plus 1 1/2 teaspoons) all-purpose (plain) flour, sifted, plus flour for dusting the work surface
5 eggs
1/2 teaspoon salt
1 tablespoon olive oil

Filling

50 g – 1.76 ounces (3 1/2 tablespoons) butter
500 g - 1 lb 2 oz (2 1/3 cups) hot Mashed potatoes (page 555)
1/2 teaspoon salt
3 eggs
3 sage leaves
150 g - 5.29 oz cured ham

Finishing

1 tablespoon Kosher (coarse) salt
120 ml – 1/2 cup veal jus
1 sage leaf
50 g – 1.76 ounces (1 2/3 cups) baby spinach

1

Make the ravioli dough: Mix the ingredients and knead into a ball. Rest for 1 hour in the refrigerator. Make the filling: Add the butter to the hot mashed potatoes. Season with the salt (keeping in mind that the ham is already salted). Break the eggs. Separate the eggs. Add the white of 1 egg and 3 yolks to the still hot potato mixture. Mix well. Remove the ribs in the center of the sage leaves. Stack the leaves. Finely chop with a chef's knife. Cut the ham into slices, then batons, and then dice. Weigh out 350 g – 12.35 ounces (about 1 2/3 cups) of mashed potatoes. Incorporate the ham. Add the sage. Mix.

TIPS FROM OUR CHEFS

THE DAY BEFORE

If you prefer, you can make ravioli a day in advance. They keep very well in the refrigerator arranged in a single layer (not overlapping) on a dish dusted with flour. Note: Don't cover them with plastic wrap.

2

Dust the work surface with flour. Use a rolling pin to flatten the dough ball.

3

Run the dough through the pasta machine a first time (or roll it out with the rolling pin). Run the dough through the machine several times (or roll out) to a long strip of very thin pasta.

4

Cut the strip into two bands of the same length, with one being a little wider (1 cm – 3/8 inch) than the other. Lay the narrower band in front of you. Make two rows of small mounds of filling with space in between them. If you have a 4-cm – 1 1/2-inch ring mold, use it to make the mounds of filling neat. Use a pastry brush dipped in water to moisten the entire surface of the second band. Lay the moistened band over the first, moistened side down. Adjust so that they are well aligned.

5

Press lightly with a 5-cm – 2-inch cookie cutter (or small glass) around the mounds of filling in the first row to remove any air bubbles. (Do not cut through the dough.) Seal the edges around the mounds well by pressing with your fingers. Place the cookie cutter (or glass) around the mounds of filling in the second row without pressing too firmly.

6

Use a 6-cm – 2 1/2-inch cookie cutter (or a glass that is a little larger than the first) to press firmly on the dough, turning to cut. Lift off the excess pasta to separate the ravioli disks. Dust a baking sheet (tray) with flour. Lay the ravioli on it.

7

Boil water in a large stockpot. Add 1 tablespoon of kosher salt. Put the ravioli into the boiling water. Reduce the heat and poach until al dente, 3–4 minutes. In the meantime, heat the veal jus with the sage leaf in a large skillet or frying pan. Drain the ravioli and transfer to the pan. Gently toss to coat in the veal jus. Arrange the ravioli on a serving dish. Drizzle with very hot jus. Garnish with baby spinach. Serve immediately.

AVOCADO MAKI ROLLS

Makes 8 pieces

Preparation time 15 minutes

EQUIPMENT

Bamboo rolling mat

1 very ripe avocado
1/2 sheet toasted nori seaweed
1 (70-g – 2.47-ounce) ball of vinegared sushi rice (page 559)
A little wasabi to taste (page 558)

1 Cut the avocado in half. Run the blade of a very sharp knife around the pit (stone). Separate the two halves by twisting lightly. To dislodge the pit, strike it hard enough with a knife to embed the blade. The pit will remain attached to the blade when it is pulled away.

2 On a cutting board, cut each avocado half into four slices. Carefully peel the pieces. Prepare two avocado slices and the remaining ingredients; set up the bamboo mat and a bowl of water. Place the nori on the mat, shiny side up. Use your fingertips to spread the rice over the nori, starting on the left and gradually progressing toward the right, without crushing the grains.

3 Make sure the rice completely covers the sheet of nori, including the corners. Gently lift up the rice-covered nori sheet so that it can be turned over. Dip your fingertips in the bowl of water and moisten the surface of the mat to stop the rice from sticking. Quickly turn the nori sheet over and put it back on the mat. Use the tip of your index finger to spread a small amount of wasabi over the middle of the middle of the nori along its entire length. Place a slice of avocado on top, touching one side of the sheet. Add a second slice, continuing the line.

4 Carefully lift the bottom end of the mat. Roll tightly to the top of the nori sheet. Lift up the mat and roll forward gently.

5 Press with your fingers to tighten the roll, without crushing its contents. Unroll the mat. Transfer the roll to a cutting board. Cut in half. Line up the two pieces on the board. Cut in half again. Separate the pieces completely. Cut in half one last time. Serve the eight avocado maki rolls on their side.

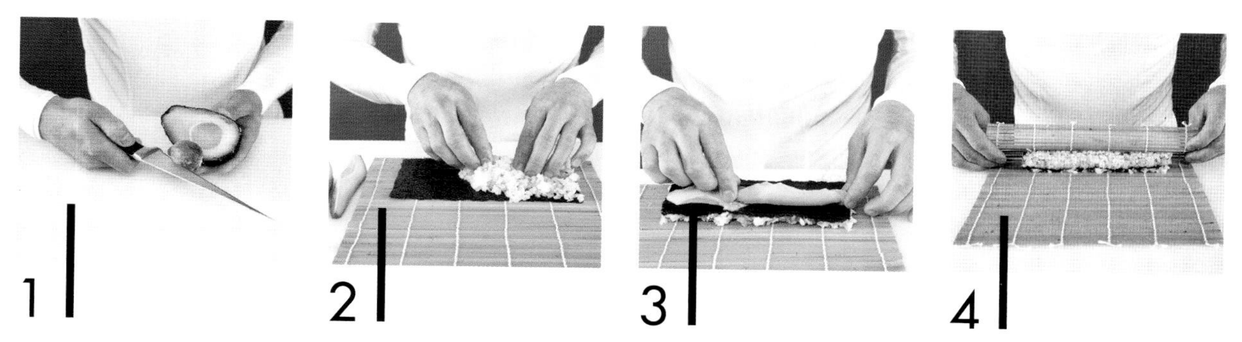
1
2
3
4

CALIFORNIA ROLL

Makes 8 pieces

Preparation time 25 minutes

EQUIPMENT

Bamboo rolling mat

1 (40-g – 1.4-ounce) salmon supreme
1/2 sheet toasted nori seaweed
1 (70-g – 2.47-ounce) ball of vinegared sushi rice (page 559)
A little wasabi to taste (page 558)
40 g - 1.41 oz (1/4) avocado
A little mayonnaise to taste
1/4 cup toasted sesame seeds

TIPS FROM OUR CHEFS

MAKI ROLLS MADE EASY
Did you know that there are tube-shaped molds for making maki rolls (page 509)? Just put in a sheet of nori, then add the rice and the filling of your choice. Fold the nori over, close the mold, and press, and there you have it.

SESAME SEEDS
Sesame seeds toasted over low heat have a light nutty flavor. They can be bought in stores already toasted, or you can make them yourself by gently heating white sesame seeds in a skillet or frying pan until they begin to color and turn fragrant.

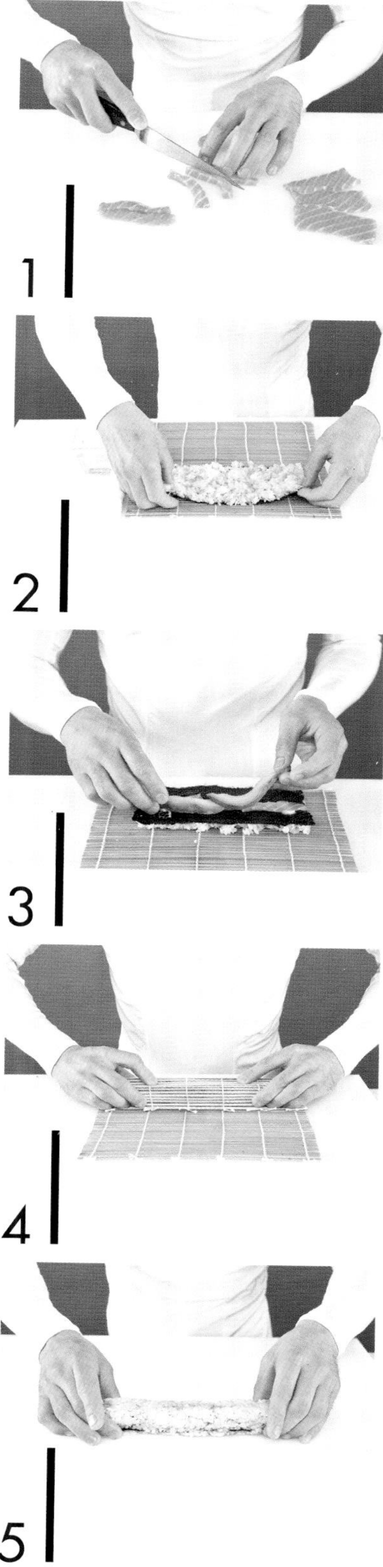

1 Prepare the ingredients and set up the bamboo mat and a bowl of water. Use a very sharp knife to cut four slices of salmon 3–5 mm – 1/8–1/4 inch thick (page 540). Cut the slices into quarters.

2 Lay the half sheet of nori on the mat, shiny side up. Place the rice ball on top.
Use your fingertips to spread the rice out over the whole sheet, starting on the left and gradually progressing toward the right, without crushing the grains.

3 Gently lift up the rice-covered nori sheet so that it can be turned over and rolled toward the top of the mat. Dip your fingertips in the bowl of water and moisten the surface of the mat to stop the rice from sticking. Quickly turn the nori sheet over and put it back on the mat. Use the tip of your index finger to make a line of wasabi over the nori. Spread it across the entire length in a continuous movement. Add a little mayonnaise following the same line. Arrange pieces of salmon along the middle of the sheet. Peel and slice the avocado (page 412). Add one or two slices of avocado along the same line.

4 Roll tightly to the top of the nori sheet.
Lift up the mat and roll forward gently.
Press with your fingers to tighten the roll, without crushing its contents. Carefully lift the bottom end of the mat.

5 Lift up the roll and transfer to a cutting board.
Prepare a bowl of sesame seeds and set it in front of you. Gently turn the roll in the seeds to coat well.
Return the roll to a cutting board.

6 Cut in half a first time. Dry the knife blade well. If it sticks a little, moisten it. Line up the two pieces and cut in half. Cut each piece in half again. Serve the eight California rolls on their side.

FUTOMAKI ROLLS

Makes 6 pieces

Preparation time 15 minutes
Resting time 30 minutes

EQUIPMENT

Bamboo rolling mat

2 sheets toasted nori seaweed
2 deveined shrimp (prawns), cooked
1/2 cucumber
100 g – 3.5 ounces Japanese omelet (page 561)
250 g – 8.76 ounces vinegared sushi rice (page 559)
A little wasabi to taste (page 558)

TIPS FROM OUR CHEFS

GENTLY DOES IT
It is important when making maki rolls not to crush the rice. Work lightly with your fingertips to spread the rice out over the nori sheet.

TIGHTLY PACKED
When you are placing the filling ingredients on the rice, try to pack them tightly against each other. This will make rolling the futomaki easier.

HANDLING
Because the futomaki is very thick, use your fingers to hold the filling in place when rolling.

PATIENCE
Let the futomaki rest for about 30 minutes before cutting it. This will allow the ingredients to settle into place.

FUTOMAKI ART
In Japan, futomaki rolls are sometimes made in very complex figurative designs, such as flowers, animals, and emblems.

1

Prepare the ingredients and set up the bamboo mat and a bowl of water. Fold one of the nori sheets in half lengthwise between your thumb and index finger. Cut in half. You will need one full sheet and one half-sheet. Reserve the extra half-sheet for another use. Butterfly the shrimp by cutting open down the middle with a thin sharp knife. Slice off the end of the cucumber. Cut in half lengthwise. Cut each piece in half again.

2

Cut a slice of the japanese omelet 1 cm – 3/8 –inch thick. Cut the entire omelet into slices of the same size.

3

Lay the full sheet of nori on the mat, shiny side down. Wet the fingers of one hand. Take a large ball of vinegared rice (about 200 g – 7 ounces) in your right hand. Pat on a small, very clean, damp towel to remove excess moisture. Use your fingertips to spread the rice out over the sheet, starting on the left and gradually progressing toward the right, without crushing the grains and leaving a 3-cm – 1 1/4-inch uncovered margin at the top. Make sure the sides are well covered with rice. Extend by overlapping the half-sheet of nori over the uncovered band.

4

Press lightly to hold the added piece in place. Take a 50-g – 1.76-ounce ball of rice. Place it over the newly added surface. Spread this rice layer in the same way as previously, quickly and lightly, completely covering the corners. Prepare the desired amount of wasabi (page 558). Use the tip of your index finger to make a line of wasabi over the middle of the first nori sheet. Spread it out over its entire length.

5

Place a slice of omelet over the wasabi, then add two slices of cucumber, flesh side down, over the rice. Press the cucumber tightly against the omelet. Arrange the two butterflied shrimp over the cucumber. Lift up the mat by its two bottom corners. Holding the inside of the mat with your three largest fingers, quickly roll it over as far as the top of the first nori sheet.

6

Press tightly on the mat to make the rice and nori stick to the filling. This is the most crucial step. Bring the roll up to the additional band of rice. Leave this part unrolled for the time being. Lift the mat up again. Check that all of the ingredients are in place. Roll right to the end of the nori, holding it firmly in place. Squeeze gently along its entire length with your hand to tighten. Roll the futomaki completely in the mat. Squeeze gently along its entire length.

7

Unroll the mat. Cut the roll in half. Cut one half into three uniform pieces. Repeat with the other half.

RISOTTO WITH RED MULLET AND SAFFRON

Serves 4

Fish
Preparation time 12 minutes
Cooking time 2 minutes

Risotto
Preparation time 10 minutes
Cooking time 25 minutes

Fish

2 (150-g – 5.3-ounce) red mullets, scaled (or 4 red mullet or red snapper fillets)
1 clove garlic, unpeeled
1 teaspoon olive oil, plus more for frying basil leaves
Fleur de sel

4 basil leaves, plus more for garnish

Risotto

30 saffron threads or 0.5 g – 0.02 ounce (1/4 teaspoon) saffron powder
2 liters - 8 1/2 cups strained fish soup
40 g – 1.4 ounces (about 1/2 small) white onion
1/2 fennel bulb
1/4 cup plus 2 tablespoons olive oil
180 g - 6.35 oz (1 cup) Arborio rice
Fine salt
80 ml – 1/3 cup dry white wine

TIPS FROM OUR CHEFS

LIGHT SOUP
This recipe calls for light fish soup, meaning it is strained so that it is brothy and clear.

NO SOUP
If you don't have fish soup, use a stock with the bones from the fish added to it.

PERFECTLY COOKED FISH
The fish fillets are barely cooked because when they are placed over the risotto, the heat from the rice will finish cooking them.

1 Rinse the fish. Slide your knife under the fin. Pass the blade over the backbone between the head and the tail. Lift out the first fillet. Remove the bones with tweezers. Check that there are no bones left by running a finger over the fillet. Turn the fish over and proceed in the same way, starting at the tail. Repeat with remaining fish. Set aside the fillets.

2 Make the risotto: Add the saffron to the soup and bring to a boil. In the meantime, peel and chop the onion (page 525). Chop the fennel. Heat 2 tablespoons of olive oil in a deep skillet or frying pan over low heat. Add the onion. Sauté the onion and fennel for 1 minute, without browning.
Increase the heat to medium, then add the rice. Season lightly with salt. Stir the rice constantly for about 2 minutes to coat well with the fat. The rice should be shiny and translucent.
Moisten with the white wine and let reduce completely.

3 Add enough hot soup to cover the rice. Cook, stirring constantly, for 18 to 20 minutes. Each time the broth is almost fully absorbed, add additional broth to cover. The rice should always be kept moist.
Check whether the rice is cooked by cutting a grain in half. It should have a small white filament. Off the heat, add the remaining 1/4 cup olive oil. Mix well and adjust the seasoning.

4 Crush the unpeeled garlic clove. Put the fish fillets skin side down into a hot skillet or frying pan with 1 teaspoon of olive oil. Season the fillets with a little fleur de sel. Place one basil leaf over each fillet, add the garlic clove, and cook for 1 minute 30 seconds. Turn each of the fillets over with its basil leaf, then remove immediately from the pan. Discard the garlic clove and drizzle the fillets with oil from the pan. Plate the risotto, then place one fish fillet on top of each portion, accompanied by basil leaves lightly fried in olive oil. Sprinkle with fleur de sel.

1

2

3

STUFFED SARDINES

Serves 4

Preparation time 1 hour
Cooking time 15 minutes

12 medium sardines
150 g – 5.3 ounces (5 cups) spinach
1 onion
2 cloves garlic
50 g – 1.75 ounces (2 slices) white bread
600 ml – 2 1/2 cups light (single) cream
50 g – 1.75 ounces (1/3 cup prepared) sun-dried tomatoes in oil (page 547)
1 tablespoon olive oil, plus more for sautéing and drizzling
Salt
Freshly ground pepper
40 g – 1.4 ounces (1/2 cup grated) Parmesan cheese
1 egg

TIPS FROM OUR CHEFS

MAKE HASTE

Scale, clean, and bone the sardines as soon as you get them home. Keep them in the refrigerator until it is time to prepare the dish.

A WORD OF WARNING

If you scale the sardines in the sink, do it over a colander to collect the scales; otherwise they can clog the drain. Wash the sardines over a colander for the same reason.

1

Scale a sardine with the back of a knife, starting at the tail and moving toward the head. Rinse to remove any remaining scales. Repeat with remaining sardines. Cut open the belly of a sardine, cutting from the tail toward the head. Clean out the insides of the sardine with your finger. Use your finger to remove the gills.

2

Push down on the spine with your thumb to detach. Snip it with scissors at the tail. Pull it up starting at the tail. Snip it again at the bottom of the head. Use a knife blade to scrape out any little bones and the belly membrane from one side. Do the same on the other side. Repeat with remaining sardines.

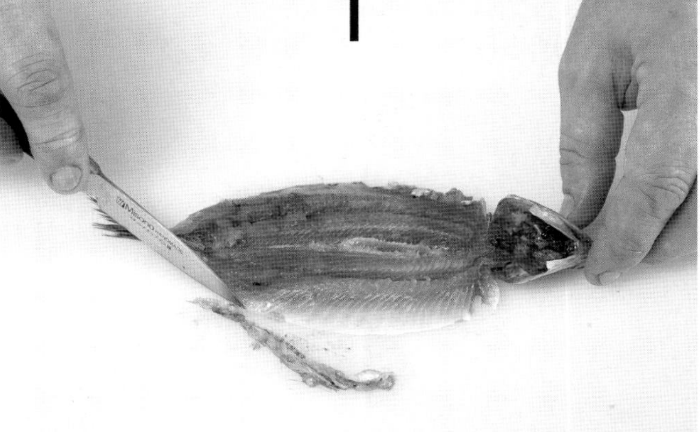

3

Fold the spinach leaves in half and remove the stems (stalks) and ribs (page 520). Wash. Drain. Peel the onion. Halve and chop (page 525). Peel the garlic cloves. Cut one of them in half and remove the green core from inside. Crush the two halves with the flat side of a knife blade. Prick the other clove with a fork and leave it on the end. Cut the crust off the bread. Cut it into slices 1-cm – 3/8-inch thick and then into cubes. Pour the cream over the bread in a bowl. Let stand.

4

Scrape the seeds from the sun-dried tomatoes with a knife. Cut into strips, then chop by cutting in the other direction. Put 1 tablespoon of oil into a saucepan. Add the spinach. Season lightly with salt. Season with pepper. Wilt the spinach over high heat, stirring with the fork containing the garlic clove. Transfer to a plate. Add a little oil to the same pan. Add the onion, tomatoes, and crushed garlic. Let soften for 3 minutes, stirring constantly. Do not allow to brown.

5

Chop up the spinach with a knife. Transfer to a bowl. Add the contents of the pan. Grate the Parmesan. Crush the bread with a fork. Add both ingredients to the bowl along with the egg. Mix gently. Preheat the oven to 220°C – 450°F (gas mark 8). Line a baking sheet (tray) with parchment (baking) paper. Lay the sardines in a single layer on the work surface. Season lightly with salt. Place 1 tablespoon of the stuffing at the bottom of the head of each sardine.

6

Pick up the tail and fold both tail fins together. Pull them through the mouth of the fish. Push the head down until it rests on the stuffing. Place the stuffed sardines on the baking sheet. Drizzle with olive oil. Cook in the preheated oven for 8 minutes. Arrange the sardines on plates. Serve hot or cold.

STEAMED SHRIMP, SPICED BROTH, AND APPLESAUCE

Serves 4

Preparation time 30 minutes
Cooking time 17 minutes

EQUIPMENT

Mandoline slicer
Pressure cooker
4 (15-cm – 6-inch) wooden skewers

Shrimp and broth

16 medium shrimp (prawns)
1 shallot
2 tomatoes
1 fennel bulb
1/2 head napa cabbage (Chinese leaves)
3 tablespoons olive oil, divided
1 clove garlic, unpeeled
1 tablespoon tomato paste (puree)
100 ml – 1/3 cup plus 1 tablespoon plus 1 teaspoon white wine
1 tablespoon cognac
1 star anise
1 organic, unwaxed lemon
1 teaspoon fleur de sel
2 long pepper catkins
Salt
Freshly ground pepper

Applesauce

1/2 green apple
125 g – 4.4 ounces (1/2 cup) plain (natural) yogurt
1 tablespoon lemon juice
Salt
Freshly ground pepper

TIPS FROM OUR CHEFS

A STAR

Star anise is the seed pod of the Chinese star anise tree, a relative of the magnolia. Its name comes from the fact that the pod is shaped like an eight-pointed star. Each star anise houses a brown seed with a taste very similar to that of aniseed, but longer lasting.

LONG PEPPER

Long pepper (also known as Java long pepper) is a different species than the ordinary round peppercorn. It comes in the forms of catkins some 3 cm – 1 1/4 inches in length. Its slightly sweet flavor is quite pronounced. If unavailable, it can be replaced with ten black peppercorns in this recipe.

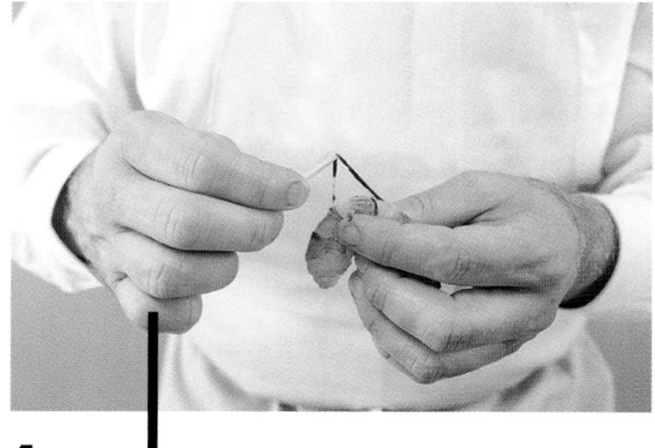

1

Separate the shrimp heads from the tails. Set aside the heads. Peel the tails (page 541). Make a cut along the back of each shrimp. Lift up the intestines with a toothpick (cocktail stick) and pull out (page 541).

TIPS FROM OUR CHEFS

NAPA CABBAGE

Napa cabbage (also known as Chinese leaves) is a variety of Chinese cabbage that is shaped like a loaf of bread some 30–40 cm – 12–16 inches in length. It has very light-colored leaves that cook quickly.

TIPS FROM OUR CHEFS

TURNING RED

Brown the shrimp heads for about 2 minutes until they change color and turn red.

2

Peel the shallot. Cut into slices, then into large pieces. Remove the stem (stalk) from the tomatoes. Cut into slices, then into pieces. Cut off the bottom of the fennel bulb (page 515). Peel off the first three layers. Cut off any remaining stems and leaves. Cut the outer layers in half, then cut into strips. Cut the bulb in half, then slice very finely with the slicing surface of a grater or a mandoline slicer; reserve the slice for garnish.

3

Cut out the core of the cabbage half. Remove four large leaves and trim the ends of the ribs. Cut the rest of the cabbage into strips. Line the pressure cooker steamer basket with the four large cabbage leaves. Heat 1 tablespoon of olive oil in the pressure cooker pot. Add the shrimp heads. Stir and cook for 2 minutes over medium heat. Add the shallot, tomatoes, fennel strips, unpeeled garlic, and tomato paste. Stir until browned, about 5 minutes. Add the white wine, cognac, and star anise. Reduce it completely. Wash the lemon. Use a vegetable peeler to remove five strips of zest (page 514). Add to the pot. Add 650 ml – 2 3/4 cups of water. Increase the heat to high, then add the fleur de sel and the long pepper.

4

When the pot comes to a boil, cover. Program 8 minutes of cooking time. When the timer sounds, reduce the heat. Thread four shrimp onto each wooden skewer. Season generously with salt and pepper. Drizzle the cabbage strips with 2 tablespoons of olive oil. Season with salt. Spread out in the steamer basket. Set the skewers on top.

5

When the broth is cooked, open the pressure cooker and place the steamer basket inside. Program the timer for 2 minutes of cooking time, starting on high heat. When the timer sounds, reduce the heat. Take the steamer basket out of the pot and stand on a plate. Allow to drain briefly. Strain the broth. Taste and adjust seasoning.

6

For the applesauce, peel the apple half. Cut into slices, then batons, and then into small dice (page 512). Mix with the yogurt. Add the lemon juice, 1 pinch of salt, and season generously with pepper (five turns of the peppermill). Mix again.

7

Place the cabbage on the plates. Lay the skewers on top. Garnish with thinly sliced raw fennel. Serve the broth and sauce on the side.

GRAVLAX CANNELLONI

Serves 4–6

Preparation time 20 minutes
Resting time 12 hours +
36–60 hours + 2 hours

EQUIPMENT

Mortar and pestle
Slicing knife

A WORD FROM OUR SOMMELIER

Pair with a dry white Alsatian wine (e.g., Riesling).

Salmon

1 (1.5-kg – 3 pound 5-ounce) salmon fillet
200 g – 7 ounces (3/4 cup plus 2 tablespoons) kosher (coarse) salt
160 g – 5.64 ounces (3/4 cup plus 1 tablespoon) sugar
15 g – 0.53 ounce (2 tablespoons) fennel seeds
10 g – 0.35 ounce (1 tablespoon) black peppercorns

Filling

150 g – 5.3 ounces (5 cups) baby spinach
2 small onions
1 tablespoon olive oil
Fleur de sel
1/4 cup Brousse (cream cheese)

TIPS FROM OUR CHEFS

BITE-SIZE VARIATION

RUSSIAN-STYLE HORS D'OEUVRES

Slide your knife between the skin and flesh at the thickest part of the fillet, at the head end. Cut it into strips 2–3 cm – 1 inch wide. Cut into 1.5-cm – 1/2-inch cubes. Insert a toothpick (cocktail stick) into the center of each cube. Drizzle with one small glass of vodka. Sprinkle with coarsely ground pepper. Grate the zest of one lime over them. Serve as an appetizer.

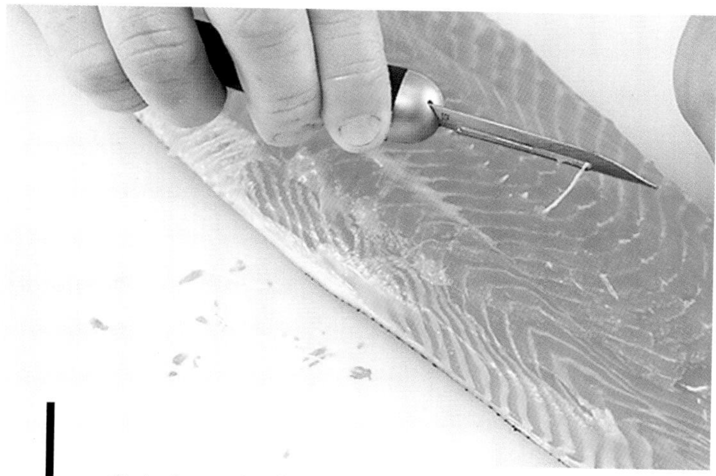

1 Cut along the fillet to remove any belly bones (page 540). Remove any fatty (whitish) parts from the belly. Remove the small piece of fat from the loin. Remove any bones by scraping with the tip of a vegetable peeler. Catch them in the slot in the blade, turn the peeler toward you, then pull straight out.

2

Weigh out the salt, sugar, and fennel seeds. Coarsely crush the peppercorns in the mortar. Weigh out. Add to the mixture. Mix. Cover the bottom of a baking pan with half of the mixture. Place the salmon over it, skin side down. Cover with the rest of the mixture. Cover the pan with plastic wrap (cling film). Marinate in the refrigerator for 12 hours. After 12 hours, turn the fish over. Drizzle with liquid collected in the pan. Cover with the plastic wrap. Refrigerate for another 36–60 hours, turning the fish and drizzling with its liquid every 12 hours.

TIPS FROM OUR CHEFS

NO NEED TO WASTE

You can use all the fatty parts of the belly and loin to make tartare.

A SMALL PAN

If you don't have a big enough pan, cut the fillet in half and arrange one piece on top of the other, flesh against flesh, sprinkling with the seasoning in between as well.

3

Rinse the salmon under cold running water. Pat dry with paper towels. Use the slicing knife to cut slices from the tail. Reserve for another use. Cut four to six large, thin, fairly horizontal slices from the center of the fish. Set aside.

4

Wash the baby spinach. Fold in half and remove the stems (stalks) and ribs from the entire length of the leaves. Lay on a clean cloth. Dry gently without crushing the leaves. Cut off the roots of the onions. Leave 4 cm – 1 1/2 inches of stem. Halve and chop the onions (page 525). Make small piles with half of the spinach leaves and cut into strips (chiffonade); the other half of the leaves remain whole. Combine the strips of spinach with the onions in a bowl. Drizzle with the olive oil and season with fleur de sel. Mix. Add the Brousse cheese and mix well.

5

Lay one slice of salmon over plastic wrap and make a line of filling over it.

Roll in the plastic. Continue to roll to wrap completely. Twist the ends.

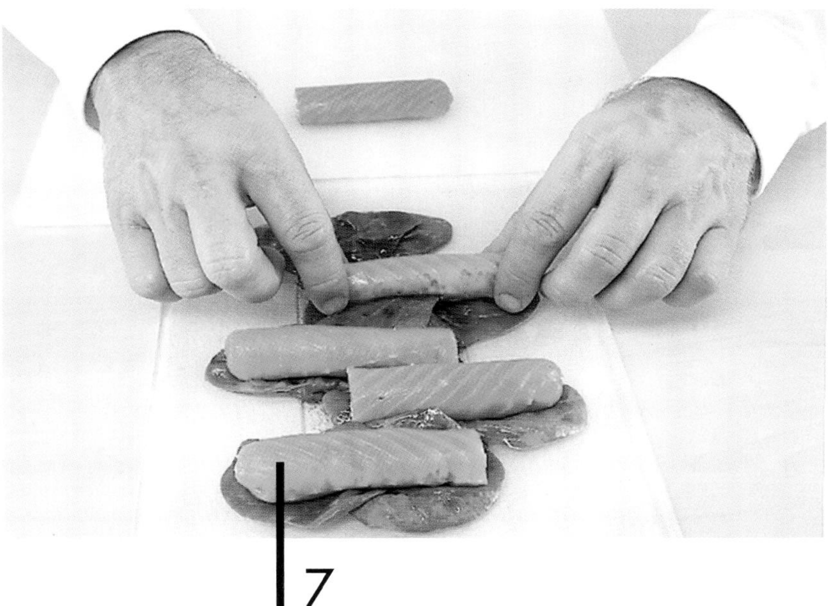

Repeat the process with the other slices and the filling. Let firm in the refrigerator for about 2 hours. Cut off the ends of the plastic wrap. Cut the rolls in half. Slip the salmon cannelloni out of the plastic. Arrange each piece on two of the reserved whole baby spinach leaves. Serve the rest of the spinach separately.

TIPS FROM OUR CHEFS

SWIRL

To wash spinach leaves, swirl the water with your finger; centrifugal force causes impurities to sink to the bottom, collecting in the middle of the basin.

STEAMED COD WITH SOCCA AND CITRUS

Serves 4

Socca
Preparation time 5 minutes
Cooking time 5 hours
Resting time 5 hours

Cod
Preparation time 1 hour
Cooking time 8 minutes

EQUIPMENT

Steamer
Handheld immersion (stick) blender
Cookie cutter (page 503)

Socca

70 g – 2.5 ounces (3/4 cup) chickpea (besan or gram) flour
30 ml – 2 tablespoons olive oil, divided, plus more for greasing
Fine salt
Freshly ground pepper
1 grapefruit
1 orange
Fleur de sel
Coarsely ground pepper

Cod

2 (300-g – 10.5-ounce) cod fillets
2 large leeks (only white part)
Olive oil
Fine salt
Freshly ground pepper
Fleur de sel

1

Make the socca batter (page 556): Put the chickpea flour into a bowl. Pour in the 200 ml – 3/4 cup plus 1 tablespoon water while stirring with a whisk. Add 15 ml – 1 tablespoon of olive oil, two large pinches of salt, and five twists of the peppermill. Cover with plastic wrap (cling film) and rest in the refrigerator for 5 hours. Prepare the cod: Make an incision in the narrow end of one of the cod fillets and slide a filleting knife between the flesh and skin to remove the skin. Repeat with the second fillet. Lay one fillet head-to-tail over the other, leaving the side where the skin was on the outside. Cut into four tournedos.

2

Bring water to a boil in the steamer pot. Fill a bowl with cold water and ice cubes. Cut off the roots and remove the first layer from one leek. Make an incision lengthwise into the next layer of each leek. Peel off. Repeat with the second leek. Wash the four leek layers. Immerse in the boiling water for 1 minute. Drain with a skimmer, then plunge in the ice water for 1 minute. Spread flat on paper towels and pat dry. Trim the leek layers to an even length. Place one cod tournedo lengthwise on each layer. Trim the width of each layer to match the size of the fish. Roll the tournedos in the leek layers, starting on one side. Stand the tournedos on their cut sides, wrap each bundle twice with kitchen twine, and tie in a loose knot. Cut off excess twine. Transfer to a dish. Cover with plastic wrap and refrigerate for 10 minutes.

3

Wash the rest of the leeks and cut diagonally into pieces with a paring knife. Put 1 teaspoon of olive oil into a saucepan. Add the leeks, season with salt and pepper, and let soften for 5 minutes over medium heat. Transfer to a bowl. Prepare the fruit: Cut off the top and bottom of the fruit with a paring knife. Supreme the fruit: Cut off the peel, following the curved shape of the fruit with the knife over a bowl (page 514), pass the blade of a paring knife between the flesh and membrane of each section (segment), then pivot the blade under the section (page 514). Collect the flesh and juice in the bowl.

4

Preheat the oven to 230°C – 450°F (gas mark 8). Use a brush to grease a baking sheet (tray) with oil. Drain the sections, one at a time, and lay on the baking sheet. Divide into four groups, alternating orange and grapefruit sections. Sprinkle with a little fleur de sel and coarsely ground pepper. Let stand. Meanwhile season the tournedos flesh on both sides with fleur de sel. Brush the steamer basket with oil. Place the tournedos in the steamer, flesh sides up and down. Brush the tops of the tournedos lightly with oil. Place the basket over the steamer pot, cover with the lid, and steam for 3 minutes. Return the softened leeks to the pan and heat for a few minutes over low heat. Use a wide spatula (slotted turner) to turn the tournedos over, then cover and steam for another 3 minutes. Use a wide spatula to transfer the tournedos to a dish. Transfer the leeks to another dish. Blend the socca batter quickly with a handheld blender. Heat 1 teaspoon of olive oil in a skillet or frying pan. Pour in a ladle of batter (about half of the total amount). Spread out evenly. When the edges have set, transfer the pan to the preheated oven and cook for 3 minutes.

5

Lift the socca out with a wide spatula (slotted turner) and flip it over onto the work surface. Sprinkle with a few twists of freshly ground pepper. Repeat the process to make a second socca.

6

Heat the citrus sections in the oven for 5 minutes. Remove the twine from the cod tournedos. Use a cookie cutter to cut the socca into disks. Plate one cod and leek bundle with a few socca circles and a few pieces of leek on each individual serving plate. Next, arrange the citrus sections on the plates. Combine the juice from the fruit and 1 teaspoon of olive oil in a saucepan, mix well, and reduce for a few seconds. Pour a little of this warm vinaigrette over the tournedos. Sprinkle the tournedos with fleur de sel and serve immediately.

POACHED COD IN A MILLEFEUILLE

Serves 4

Cod
Preparation time 20 minutes
Cooking time 6 minutes
Resting time 30 minutes

Millefeuille, arugula and pesto
Preparation time 30 minutes
Cooking time 30 minutes

EQUIPMENT

Millefeuille, arugula salad, and pesto
Mandoline slicer
Handheld immersion (stick) blender

Cod

30 g – 1 ounce (2 tablespoons) kosher (coarse) salt
1 (450-g - 1-lb) cod loin, skinless
800 ml – 3 1/3 cups whole milk
1 star anise
1 clove garlic
2 tablespoons olive oil

Millefeuille, arugula salad, and pesto

2 large potatoes
2 tablespoons plus 1 1/2 teaspoons olive oil, divided, plus more for brushing
Fine salt
150 g – 5.3 ounces (7 1/2 cups) arugula (rocket)
1 clove garlic
Freshly ground pepper
Fleur de sel
Lemon juice

TIPS FROM OUR CHEFS

LIKE A PRO
Professionals use a mortar and pestle to make pesto.

1

Sprinkle the bottom of a dish with half of the kosher salt. Arrange the fish on top. Cover with the remainder of the kosher salt. Cover with plastic wrap (cling film) and refrigerate for 30 minutes.

2

Preheat the oven to 190°C – 375°F (gas mark 5). Wash the potatoes and peel with a vegetable peeler. Set the mandoline slicer to a 1-mm – 1/32-inch setting and cut a dozen fine slices (chips) from each potato (page 518). Line a baking sheet (tray) with parchment (baking) paper and brush with oil. Sprinkle with a large pinch of salt. Arrange the potato slices on the baking sheet, placing them very close together. Brush with olive oil. Season lightly with fine salt. Cover with parchment paper. Place another baking sheet on top. Bake in the preheated oven until crisp, 25–30 minutes. Drain the cooked potato slices on paper towels to absorb excess oil.

3

Rinse the fish under cold running water. Transfer to a double thickness of paper towels and carefully pat dry. Combine the milk and star anise in a saucepan. Heat to 70°C – 158°F (start of a simmer). Add the fish. Remove from heat, cover the pan, and let stand.

4

Remove the stems (stalks) from the arugula leaves: Gather in groups of five leaves and cut off their stems. Set the stems aside. Wash the leaves in ice water. Drain. Bring salted water to a boil in a saucepan. Add the arugula stems and less attractive leaves. Boil for 5 minutes. Remove from the pan with a skimmer, then refresh for 2 minutes in the ice water. Drain in a colander. Peel the garlic clove for the pesto and the one for the cod and remove their green cores. Crush one clove firmly with the blade of a chef's knife to reduce to a puree. Place in a small and deep bowl. Add the blanched arugula, one pinch of salt, and a generous amount of pepper (five twists of the peppermill). Add 1 tablespoon of olive oil. Wrap the container and handheld blender with plastic wrap (cling film) to protect from splashing. Blend to a pesto. Crush the remaining garlic clove by pressing firmly on the blade of a knife with your hand (page 523).

5

Use a wide spatula (slotted turner) to drain the fish. Transfer to triple thickness of paper towels. Gently pat dry. Heat 2 tablespoons of olive oil in a deep skillet or frying pan over medium-high heat. Brown the crushed garlic for just 1 minute. Remove the garlic and put the fish in the pan. Baste with the hot oil and brown for 3 minutes. Turn over with a spatula and brown the other side for another 2 minutes 30 seconds. Gradually remove any small pieces of cooked fish and transfer to a dish. Transfer the remaining fish to the dish. Cover with plastic wrap.

6

Season the arugula with one pinch of fleur de sel, a little lemon juice, and 1 tablespoon plus 1 1/2 teaspoons of olive oil. Mix well. Brush a wide line of pesto on each individual serving plate. Over each line arrange two arugula leaves, one potato slice on top of them, and another arugula leaf. Flake the cod into sections. Assemble the first layer with one cod section, one arugula leaf, and one potato slice. Do the same to make another three layers. Serve the rest of the greens and pesto separately.

LOBSTER AND FAVA BEANS WITH COLD SOUP

Serves 4

Preparation time 1 hour
Cooking time 55 minutes
Resting time 1 hour

TIPS FROM OUR CHEFS

ROASTING
Coffee, nuts, and seeds are all roasted to bring out their flavor. Here, the pieces of shell are lightly roasted in oil for the same purpose.

DISJOINTING
To extract the tail flesh, instead of disjointing the shell, you can cut the softer shell of the belly with kitchen shears and peel off the shell.

SKINNING FAVA BEANS
This process involves removing the skin from the beans after cooking. Remove the top of the bean, open the widest side by removing the black part, then press on the base to push out the bean.

Lobster

2 teaspoons kosher (coarse) salt
1 teaspoon peppercorns
1 (800-g - 1-lb 12-oz) live lobster
1 small onion
Olive oil
Fleur de sel
Freshly ground pepper
1 organic, unwaxed lemon

Soup

1 (60-g – 2.12-ounce) small onion
1/2 (130 g – 4.6 ounces) fennel bulb
1 stalk celery
1 tomato
1 clove garlic
20 g – 0.71 ounce (about 1/4 cup sliced) fresh ginger
Olive oil
20 g – 0.71 ounce (1 tablespoon plus 1 1/2 teaspoons) tomato paste
50 ml – 3 tablespoons plus 1 1/2 teaspoons cognac
4 tarragon leaves
500 ml – 2 cups vegetable broth or stock (page 549)
2 g – 0.07 ounce (leaf) gelatin (1 sheet)

Bean puree

800 g – 1 pound 12 ounces fresh fava (broad) beans
1 teaspoon kosher (coarse) salt
500 ml – 2 cups vegetable broth or stock
Salt
Freshly ground pepper
Tabasco® sauce

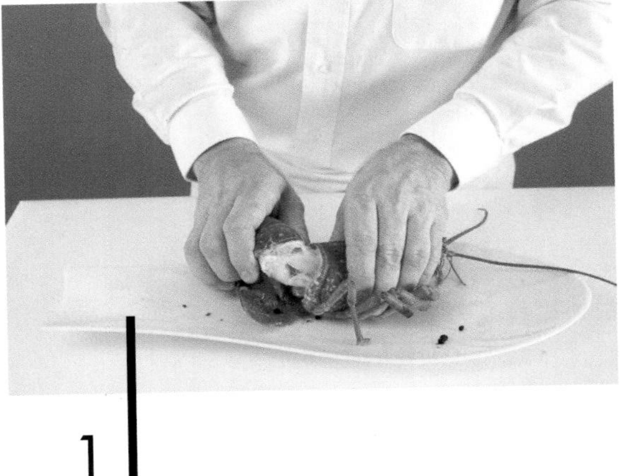

1

For the lobster, bring water to a boil in a large saucepan. Add the kosher salt and peppercorns. Use rubber bands to remove the claws from the lobster. Immerse the lobster and claws in the boiling water. Cook the body for 4 minutes. Drain. Cook the claws for another 2 minutes. Drain the claws. Cover the body and claws with a damp cloth or damp paper towels. Let cool. Remove the rubber bands keeping the claws closed. Dislocate the tail at the bottom of the head and pull to separate the two parts.

2

Lift up the shell of the head and detach by pulling it back. Use a spoon to collect the tomalley and any coral (roe) contained in the shell. Remove the stomach sac containing grit and sand. Set aside the antennae. Scoop out the flesh and tomalley remaining inside the head. Make the soup: Cut the head into small pieces. Chop up the legs into small pieces. Cut up the shell from the head.

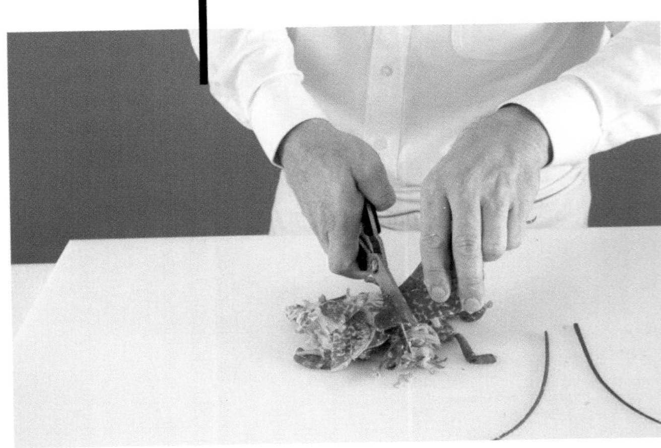

3

Peel and slice the onion (page 525). Cut the fennel into strips, then into small dice (brunoise). Cut the celery into large pieces, then into batons, and finely dice. Slice the tomato, then cut into strips, and finely dice. Halve the garlic clove and remove the green core. Slice the ginger. Heat 1 tablespoon of oil in a small stockpot. Add the pieces of shell. "Roast" for 3 minutes over high heat while stirring constantly. Add the onion, fennel, tomato, and garlic. Mix. Incorporate the tomato paste. Reduce the heat. Cook for 8 minutes over medium heat. Clean the sides of the pot from time to time with a wet brush. Add the cognac and flambé. Add the tarragon and ginger. Add enough of the broth to cover the contents of the pot by a few inches. Reserve remaining broth. Simmer for 25 minutes, uncovered.

4

Split open the lobster tail in the middle by disjointing the shell. Detach the segments, one at a time, and take out the flesh. Cut the tail in half lengthwise. Remove the intestine with the tip of a knife. Slice the flesh. Transfer to a plate. Lay the claws on a cloth. Break the claws in half at the joint, Remove the thinnest part. Fold the cloth over the claws and hit with a rolling pin to break up the shell. Peel the claws and extract the flesh. Use a lobster scraper if necessary. Put the flesh from the claws on another plate.

5

Continue with the soup: Soak the gelatin for 5 minutes in cold water. Pour the soup into a strainer (sieve) lined with paper towels. Let strain thoroughly. Measure out the soup. Take out about half for immediate use. Drain the gelatin between your fingers, squeeze, and add to this soup. Mix to dissolve. Pour a little soup with added gelatin into the bottom of serving dishes. Refrigerate together with the rest of the soup (in separate bowls). Refrigerate for about 1 hour to set. Make the puree: Bring water to a boil in a saucepan. Shell the fava beans. Season with 1 tablespoon of kosher salt. Cook the beans for 5 minutes, uncovered. Take the beans out with a skimmer and immerse in ice water. Let cool. Set aside the cooking liquid. Drain the beans. Peel off their skins. Set aside a few of the smallest beans. Use a bowl scraper to crush the remaining beans to a puree. Dilute the puree with a little of the reserved vegetable broth. Mix gently. Transfer to a blender to make smooth (process in several batches if necessary). Season with salt. Season with pepper. Add a few drops of Tabasco®.

6

Finish the lobster: Cut off the leaves of the onion at about 15 cm – 6 inches from the bulb. Thinly slice the leaves and chop the bulb (page 525). Add three quarters of the onion to the lobster slices and reserve the rest. Cut the claw flesh in half across. Drizzle a little oil over the two plates of lobster flesh. Add a little fleur de sel. Season with pepper. Grate the zest of the lemon over the lobster slices and claw pieces (page 514). Place a few lobster slices over the soup in the serving dishes. Cover with a layer of bean puree. Place the claw flesh on top. Add a spoonful of the soup that was not combined with the gelatin. Garnish with the reserved small fava beans, the antennae cut in half, and the reserved onion.

CRISP AND TENDER CHICKEN WITH HERBS

Serves 4

Preparation time 1 hour
Cooking time 1 hour 30 minutes
Resting time 1 hour

EQUIPMENT

Small chef's torch
Demitasse spoon

Chicken

2 (300-g – 10.5-ounce) chicken thighs
1 sprig thyme
Salt
Freshly ground pepper
250 ml – 1 cup chicken broth or stock
8 chicken wings
3 small shallots
4 sprigs chervil
1 sprig flat-leaf parsley
1 sprig marjoram
1 sprig tarragon
2 sprigs basil
2 sage leaves
2 tablespoons Olive oil
2 heads sucrine (Boston, Bibb, or Little Gem) lettuce
Fleur de sel

Barbecue sauce

1 white onion
1 clove garlic
2 tomatoes
20 g – 0.71 ounce (1 tablespoon plus 1 teaspoon) sugar
1 tablespoon honey
30 ml – 2 tablespoons sherry vinegar
Fine salt
Freshly ground pepper
150 ml - 2/3 cup chicken stock
1 tablespoon Meaux mustard
Juice of 1/2 lime

TIPS FROM OUR CHEFS

SMALLER
Smaller than a teaspoon, the demitasse spoon is more suitable for widening the opening in the winglets. A teaspoon will probably tear the flesh.

WEIGH IT DOWN
Place a ramekin, saucer, or small plate on the winglets to keep them immersed in the water while cooking.

1

Use the chef's torch to singe the thighs. Remove any remnants of feathers by scraping the skin with a knife against the direction of the feathers.

2

Make an incision along each side of the bone, pushing aside the flesh. Remove the bone and the small vein. Put the thighs, side by side, in a small stockpot. Add the sprig of thyme. Season with salt and pepper. Add the broth and bring to a boil. Cover the pan. Simmer for 15 minutes. Turn the thighs over. Simmer for another 15 minutes. Cut the wings at the joint to separate the drumettes from the winglets. Cut off the wing tips. Use the chef's torch to singe both sides of the winglets. Remove any remnants of feathers by scraping with a knife. Cut off the two ends with scissors. Hold a winglet upright and push down the flesh to expose the bone. Turn over and do the same. Remove the two small bones. Return the winglet to its original shape. Repeat for the remaining winglets. Take the thighs out of the pot and transfer to a dish. Let cool to room temperature, then refrigerate for at least 1 hour.

3

Peel the shallots. Chop (page 525). Pluck the leaves from the sprigs of herbs. Add the sage leaves and chop finely. Heat 1 tablespoon of oil in a small saucepan. Add the shallots and season with salt and pepper. Let soften for 2 minutes over medium heat. Add the herbs and mix for 1 minute. Transfer to a bowl. Use the demitasse spoon to widen the openings in the winglets, then fill with the herb mixture.

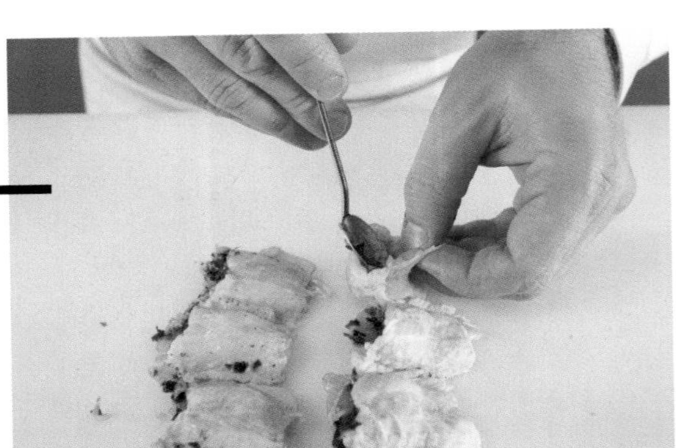

4

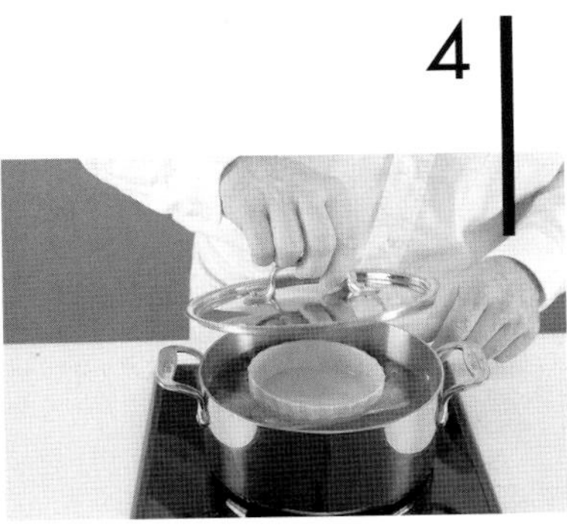

Spread out plastic wrap (cling film). Place four winglets on it. Season with salt and pepper. Lift up the plastic to turn the winglets over. Stretch the plastic wrap out to smooth. Season the other side of the winglets with salt and pepper. Wrap the winglets twice in the plastic wrap. Cut the plastic. Roll to pack tightly. Fold over the ends of the roll. Place the roll in the center vertically in front of you over a new sheet of plastic wrap, 10 cm – 4 inches away from the end. Cut the plastic at the same distance on the top side of the roll. Fold one side over to the other. Roll up the winglets. Fold over the top and bottom of the plastic, then roll in the opposite direction. Do the same for the other winglets. Heat water in a stockpot. Immerse the rolls in the simmering water. Place a ramekin on top to keep submerged. Cover the pot. Cook for 20 minutes.

5 Heat the remaining 1 tablespoon of oil in a deep skillet or frying pan. Put the thighs in the pan, skin side down. Cover the thighs with parchment (baking) paper, then place a saucepan filled halfway with water on top. Cook for 3 minutes over high heat, then for 12 minutes over low heat. Separate the lettuce leaves. Wash and drain them. Take the winglet rolls out of the pot and transfer to a dish. Remove the saucepan and parchment paper from the pan. Turn the thighs over and let cook for another 3 minutes. Transfer the thighs to paper towels to drain. Season with salt and pepper.

6 Make the barbecue sauce: Peel, halve, and chop the onion (page 525). Halve the garlic clove and remove the green core. Crush with a knife (page 523). Remove the stems (stalks) from the tomatoes. Cut into six wedges each. Peel them by passing the knife blade between the skin and the flesh (page 521). Remove the cores and seeds. Cut the flesh into slices, then dice. Put the sugar in a small saucepan. Add the honey and vinegar. Bring to a boil over medium heat. Let thicken for 2 minutes. Add the onion, garlic, and diced tomato. Season with salt. Season with plenty of pepper. Add the stock. Thicken for 20 minutes over medium heat. Stir from time to time.

TIPS FROM OUR CHEFS

A PAN FILLED WITH WATER

Placing a pan filled with water on top of the thighs keeps them flat and ensures that their skin will turn golden. Start off with the heat on high, but don't forget to reduce it later to prevent the skin from burning.

7 Cut one end off the winglet rolls. Push the winglets out by squeezing on the other ends. Place the thighs skin side down. Cut in half, then cut each half into three pieces. Take the sauce off the heat. Add the mustard and mix to incorporate. Add the lime juice.
Fill the serving dishes with the lettuce leaves. Add one winglet and three thigh slices to each dish.
Add another winglet. Cover with the sauce. Add a little more lettuce and season with fleur de sel.

RABBIT AND POTATO TIAN

Serves 4

Preparation time 1 hour
Cooking time 55 minutes
Resting time 5 minutes

800 g – 1 pound 12 ounces potatoes
2 cloves garlic
2 white onions
50 g – 1.76 ounces (about 1/2 cup) black olives
1 sprig rosemary
3 tablespoons olive oil, divided, plus more for drizzling
Fine salt
White pepper
500 ml – 2 cups white chicken broth or stock
50 g – 1.76 ounces (1/2 cup plus 1 tablespoon grated) Parmesan cheese
1 (300g – 10 1/2 ounces approximately) saddle of rabbit
Leaves of 2 sprigs basil

TIPS FROM OUR CHEFS

TWO IN ONE
It is more efficient to cut the olive flesh around the pit (stone) than to pit the olives first and then slice: one step instead of two.

WHITE PEPPER
You should use white pepper for light-colored dishes. Black specks of pepper can sometimes spoil the appearance of a dish.

GENUINELY GOOD
Grated or shredded Parmesan sold in packages doesn't always state its origin. Nothing beats a good, authentic Parmigiano-Reggiano freshly grated.

1

Preheat the oven to 200°C – 400°F (gas mark 6). Peel and wash the potatoes. Cut into rounds 2 mm – 1/16 inch thick with a knife.

2

Peel one garlic clove, cut in half, and remove the green core. Slice the onions (page 525). Use a knife to slice the olives. Remove and discard their pits. Peel the other garlic clove, cut in half, and remove the green core. Crush by pressing firmly with the flat side of the blade of a chef's knife (page 523). Rinse and dry the rosemary, then pluck the leaves.

3

Heat 2 tablespoons of olive oil in a deep skillet or frying pan. Add the onion, crushed garlic clove, and rosemary leaves. Add the olives. Brown for 2 minutes over low heat while stirring with a spatula (palette knife). Add the potatoes. Season with two large pinches of salt, add white pepper, and mix. Pour in the chicken broth, bring to a boil, and simmer for 2 minutes. Prick half a clove of garlic with a fork and leave it on the end. Rub it over an earthenware dish. Pour in 1 tablespoon of olive oil and swirl to spread out the oil. Transfer the potatoes to the dish. Finely grate Parmesan over the top. Place on the bottom shelf of the preheated oven and cook for 45 minutes.

4

Put the saddle on a cutting board, flesh side up. With a boning knife, cut down the middle on both sides of the backbone. Gently lift up the flesh, then pass the knife underneath, following the curve of the bone.

5

Lift out the tenderloins. Place them beside each saddle half. Rub the meat with the remaining garlic clove half. Season with salt and pepper. Completely cover the flesh of the saddle with basil leaves. Reserve any remaining leaves. Drizzle with a little olive oil. Roll up each saddle half, starting with the fleshy side. Season all sides with salt and pepper.

6

Cut out two 40-cm – 15 3/4-inch squares of aluminum foil. Lay each saddle half 2 cm – 3/4 inch away from the edge and roll in the foil. Crumple the ends and twist. Cook the rolls in a hot skillet or frying pan over medium heat for 2 minutes on each of the four sides. Let rest for 5 minutes.

7

Check that the potatoes are cooked through by piercing with a knife. Put the rolls in the oven with the potatoes and cook for another 4 minutes. Take the potatoes and rolls out of the oven. Unwrap the saddle rolls and cut in half on a diagonal. Cut off the ends, then cut the rolls on a diagonal into 8-mm – 3/8-inch slices. Arrange the rabbit pieces over the potatoes. Chop the remaining basil leaves. Drizzle with olive oil and sprinkle with a little chopped basil. Serve hot or cold.

RISOTTO AL SALTO

Serves 4

Preparation time 10 minutes
Cooking time 10 minutes

Risotto
Preparation time 10 minutes + 5 minutes
Cooking time 25 minutes
Resting time 12 hours

EQUIPMENT

Chicken
Grill (griddle) pan
12 wooden toothpicks (cocktail sticks)

Risotto

180 g – 6.35 oz (1 cup) Arborio rice
2 liters – 8 1/2 cups chicken broth or stock
30 g – 1 ounce (2 tablespoons) butter
40 g – 1.4 ounces (about 1/2 small) white onion
40 g – 1.4 ounces (1/2 cup grated) young (*fresco*) Parmesan cheese
100 g – 3.5 ounces (1/2 cup) whipping cream (for 30 g – 1.06 ounces 1/4 cup whipped cream)
Fine salt
80 ml – 1/3 cup dry white wine

Chicken and finishing

2 (130-g – 4.6-ounce, approximately) chicken breasts
Olive oil
Fine salt
Freshly ground pepper
20 g – 0.71 ounce Parmesan cheese, ground to a powder
Chicken jus

1 The day before you plan to serve the dish, make a plain risotto (page 168) with the ingredients listed. When finished, transfer to a square dish lined with parchment (baking) paper.
Use a silicone spatula (palette knife) to spread it out into a cake of even thickness. Cover with plastic wrap (cling film) and refrigerate for 12 hours.

2 On the day you plan to serve the dish, drizzle the chicken breasts generously with olive oil. Season only one side with salt and pepper.
Place on the grill pan, seasoned side down, and cook for 4 minutes over high heat. Season the top with salt and pepper. Use a wide spatula (slotted turner) to turn the breasts over.
Cook for another 4 minutes. Transfer to a plate and cover with aluminum foil to keep hot.

3 Sprinkle a large sheet of parchment (baking) paper with half of the ground Parmesan. Take the risotto cake out of the refrigerator and place on top.
Turn the cake over, being careful not to break it. Fold the parchment paper over the top and press down well to enable the cheese to stick. Lift the sheet off the top. Sprinkle with the rest of the cheese.
Fold the parchment paper back over. Run a rolling pin over the top to make sure the cheese adheres well to the rice.

4 Remove the paper from the top. Cut the risotto cake into 12 rectangles.
Transfer the risotto pieces to a hot skillet or frying pan with a little olive oil and brown for 1 minute. Turn over with a spatula and let brown for 1 additional minute.

5 Cut the chicken breasts across into six pieces. Insert a toothpick in each piece.
Place on the risotto rectangles and serve immediately as an hors d'oeuvre or appetizer (starter), drizzled with a little chicken jus.

1

3

4

TIPS FROM OUR CHEFS

COMPACT RISOTTO
For this recipe, the risotto should be somewhat compact so it can be cut and pan-fried easily.

CRISPY
The Parmesan powder should form a light crust on the cold risotto that will keep the risotto from softening while adding a touch of crispiness.

FOIE GRAS POACHED IN BROTH

Serves 4

Preparation time 40 minutes
Cooking time 30 minutes
Refrigeration 12 hours + 2–3 days

EQUIPMENT

Cooking thermometer
Meat thermometer

1 (about 500-g – 1 pound 2-ounce approximately) raw foie gras
8 g – 0.28 ounce (1 teaspoon plus 1 heaping 1/4 teaspoon) fine salt
2 g – 0.07 ounce (heaping 1/4 teaspoon) freshly ground white pepper
1 g – 0.04 ounce (1/4 teaspoon) sugar
30 ml – 2 tablespoons port
2 liters – 8 1/2 cups chicken broth or stock
Fleur de sel
Coarsely ground pepper
4 fresh figs

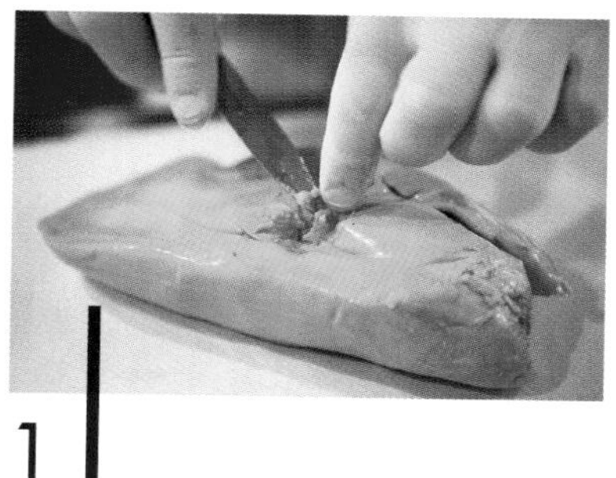

1

4

1 Use a paring knife to scrape off the ball of fat and any bile found under the liver (page 531).

2 Mix the fine salt with the white pepper and sugar. Season the foie gras on both sides with the mixture and press well for the seasoning to penetrate well. Transfer to a dish and drizzle with port. Tightly cover the foie gras with plastic wrap (cling film). Marinate for 12 hours in the refrigerator. Take the foie gras out of the refrigerator 30 minutes in advance of cooking and remove the plastic wrap.

3 Bring the broth to 80°C – 176°F in a stockpot fitted with a thermometer. Immerse the liver and cook for 15 minutes at 75°C – 167°F without covering the pot. Adjust the heat to keep the temperature constant. Turn the foie gras over and cook for an additional 15 minutes at 75°C – 167°F. Check that the foie gras is cooked using a meat thermometer. It should have a core (internal) temperature of 45°C – 113°F. Drain, covered in plastic wrap, on a rack for 30 minutes to bring out any blood.

4 Spread a large sheet of plastic wrap over the work surface and lay the foie gras over it. Roll like a candy (sweet) in the plastic wrap and let cool completely. Refrigerate the poached foie gras for two or three days. Take the foie gras out of the refrigerator. Remove the plastic wrap.

5 Cut the poached foie gras into slices and sprinkle with fleur de sel and coarsely ground pepper. Cut up the figs. Serve the foie gras slices with pieces of fresh fig.

TIPS FROM OUR CHEFS

EFFECTIVE MARINADE
The time the foie gras spends marinating in the refrigerator allows the seasoning to penetrate so that it doesn't dissolve in the broth. A chilled foie gras won't become overly soft when cooked.

A GOOD BROTH
The broth used for this dish should be intensely flavored. If you like, you can infuse it with fresh verbena, saffron, or anything else you like.

PLASTIC WRAP
Never skimp on plastic wrap. It stops the foie gras from oxidizing in the refrigerator.

WHOLE BRAISED FOIE GRAS

Serves 4

Preparation time 20 minutes
Cooking time 30 minutes
Resting time 10 minutes

EQUIPMENT

Dutch oven or flameproof casserole dish
Meat thermometer

Foie gras

1 (about 500-g – 1 pound 2-ounce, approximately) raw foie gras
8 g – 0.28 ounce (2 teaspoons) fleur de sel
2 g – 0.07 ounce (heaping 1/4 teaspoon) freshly ground white pepper

Garnish

2 slices pain de campagne
12 chestnuts, peeled (fresh or frozen)
Fine salt
8 green grapes
8 black grapes
100 ml – 1/3 cup plus 1 tablespoon plus 1 teaspoon dessert wine or muscatel
100 ml – 1/3 cup plus 1 tablespoon plus 1 teaspoon chicken broth or stock
4 grape (vine) leaves
Fleur de sel
Coarsley groud white pepper

1 Season the foie gras on both sides with the fleur de sel and white pepper. Brown the rounded side for 2 minutes over medium heat in the Dutch oven. Turn over and brown for 1 minute. Cook each side for 30 seconds while holding down with a wide spatula (slotted turner).

2 Transfer to paper towels. Remove the fat released during cooking, keeping only a little in the pot. Cut the bread into cubes. Brown in the pot for 2 minutes over medium heat. The bread will absorb the fat. Transfer to a plate.

3 Season the chestnuts with fine salt and brown for 2 minutes in the pot. Add the green grapes, followed by the black grapes, and also brown for 2 minutes.

4 Take the grapes out of the pot (leave the chestnuts). Return the foie gras to the pot on its rounded side. Moisten with the wine and let it reduce completely over medium heat. Drizzle with two thirds of the chicken broth. Cover and cook for 7 minutes on medium heat. Take off the lid. Use a spatula to turn the foie gras. Cover the pot again and cook for another 7 minutes. Transfer the foie gras to a plate. Cover with plastic wrap and let rest for 10 minutes.

5 Remove the excess fat from the pan, add the remaining broth, and continue to cook the chestnuts.
Check whether the chestnuts are cooked by piercing with a knife. They should be tender. Return the grapes to the pan. Add the grape leaves. Mix gently and cook for 2 minutes uncovered. Finally, add the bread so that the slices can soak up a little of the liquid. Place the foie gras on a serving dish. Arrange the garnish around it and drizzle with the cooking liquid. Sprinkle with fleur de sel and coarsely ground white pepper. Serve immediately.

TIPS FROM OUR CHEFS

HANDLING

Halfway through the cooking process (step 4), lightly separate the two lobes to allow the heat to penetrate well. Always use a silicone spatula that won't damage the foie gras.

2

3

TIPS FROM OUR CHEFS

FOIE GRAS COOKED TO THE CORE

To check that the foie gras is cooked, press lightly on the top. It should spring back into shape. If you have a meat thermometer, use it: The foie gras should have a core temperature of 48–50°C – 118–122°F.

DOUBLE COOKING

Braising is a technique that involves two processes: cooking by concentration (searing) and cooking by expansion (the liquid brings out the flavors).

RACK OF LAMB WITH HERB CRUST

Serves 2

Rack of lamb
Preparation time 10 minutes
Cooking time 12 minutes
Resting time 4 minutes

Herb crust
Preparation time 20 minutes

EQUIPMENT

Herb crust
Mini food processor

Rack of lamb

1 rack of lamb (8 ribs) prepared by a butcher
Fine salt
Freshly ground pepper
1 clove garlic
1 tablespoon grapeseed oil, plus more for drizzling
10 g – 0.35 ounce (2/3 tablespoon) butter, cut into cubes
1 sprig thyme

Herb crust

25 g – 0.88 ounce (1/2 cup) dry breadcrumbs
1 anchovy fillet
1/2 clove garlic
5 sprigs parsley

TIPS FROM OUR CHEFS

INSTANT GRAVY

To make gravy, degrease the liquid remaining after cooking the rack. Remove the thyme and garlic and add 1 tablespoon of veal broth or stock and 1 tablespoon of water to the dish. Place over heat and bring to a boil while stirring.

HOMEMADE BREADCRUMBS

For really white breadcrumbs, dry stale white bread for about 30 minutes in an oven at 100°C – 200°F (gas mark 1/4). Then use a rolling pin to crush the bread and store the breadcrumbs in an airtight container.

1 Use a boning knife to trim the fat off the rack of lamb. Tie each chop with twine, starting from the center of the rack and making a loose double knot. Season both sides of the rack with salt and pepper. Crush the garlic clove (page 523). Preheat the oven to 200°C – 400°F (gas mark 6).

2 Heat 1 tablespoon of oil in an ovenproof skillet or frying pan on the stovepot. Sear the meat for 1 minute on its rounded side, basting the concave side with oil. Turn the meat over and sear the other side for 1 minute. Add the butter and baste the meat once it has melted. Finally, turn the meat on its "heel" (ribs in the air) and sear for 1 minute. Add the garlic and thyme. Turn the meat onto its concave side. Cook in the preheated oven for 4 minutes. Turn the meat over, baste, and cook for another 4 minutes. Transfer to a dish, cover with aluminum foil, and let rest for at least 4 minutes.Preheat the broiler (grill).

3 Put the breadcrumbs in the bowl of the mini food processor with the anchovy fillet. Slice the garlic half and add. Wash and dry the parsley, then pluck the leaves into the food processor. Blend.

4 Take the foil off the meat and remove the twine. Drizzle the top of the rack (rounded side) with a little oil. Cover the top with the seasoned breadcrumbs. Hold the back of a knife against the rack to stop the crumbs from falling over the rest of the meat.

5 Wipe out the pan and return the rack to it, or transfer to a roasting dish. Broil for 1 minute. Watch carefully to guard against burning. Transfer the rack to a cutting board and carve into chops.

TIPS FROM OUR CHEFS

FIND THE NERVE

If the butcher hasn't already done so, remove the small yellow nerve from the side of the rack to prevent the meat from contracting when cooked.

PROPERLY COOKED

Check that the rack is cooked by pressing on the two ends with your fingers. The meat should spring back into shape immediately.

ROASTED LOIN OF LAMB STUFFED WITH SPINACH AND ALMONDS

Serves 4

Preparation time 30 minutes
Cooking time 15 minutes

EQUIPMENT

Cooking thermometer
Carving knife

Spinach and almond stuffing

1 clove garlic
100 g –3.5 ounces (3 1/2 cups) spinach
1 tablespoon olive oil
Fine salt
Pepper
10 g - 0.35 oz (1 tbsp) blanched almonds
2 sprigs basil
1 egg

Loin of lamb

1/2 (600-g – 1 pound 5-ounce, approximately) loin of lamb, boned
1 sprig thyme
Fine salt
Freshly ground pepper
2 tablespoons olive oil, divided
50 ml – 3 tablespoons plus 1 1/2 teaspoons dry white wine
Fleur de sel

TIPS FROM OUR CHEFS

ASK YOUR BUTCHER

Don't forget to ask your butcher to save the scraps from trimming the loin for you. You will be using them for cooking the meat and making the sauce. Also have the butcher score the skin on the loin (if the butcher fails to take care of this, follow the instructions on page 534) so that the fat will run off better when cooked.

1

Make the stuffing: Peel the garlic clove and prick with a fork, leaving it on the end. Fold the spinach leaves in half to remove the ribs in the center (page 520). Immerse in water and stir gently. Change the water and repeat until the leaves are free of any soil. Drain. Heat 1 tablespoon of olive oil in a stockpot. Wilt the spinach for 2 minutes over medium-high heat, stirring with the garlic clove on the end of the fork. Season with salt and pepper, then remove from the pot with a skimmer. Finely chop. Use a chef's knife to cut the almonds into small pieces.

2

Heat a skillet or frying pan. Toast the almonds lightly for 3 minutes over medium heat, shaking the pan from time to time. Pluck the basil leaves, group together in piles, and chop by rocking the knife blade back and forth (page 524). Mix the spinach with the basil and almonds in a bowl. Make a well in the center, add the egg, and season lightly with salt and pepper. Mix.

3

Spread out the loin. Set the tenderloin to one side. Pluck the thyme over the meat, and season with salt and pepper, including the belly flaps and both sides of the tenderloin. Place the tenderloin next to the meat, over the belly flap (page 534). Cover with the stuffing.

Cover the meat tightly with the belly flap. Preheat the oven to 200°C – 400°F (gas mark 6).
Tie the stuffed loin with twine every 5 cm – 2 inches, starting at the middle.

4

5

Season the top (flesh side) with salt and pepper; season the underside (stuffing side) more lightly. Cut the lamb scraps into small pieces. Heat 1 tablespoon of olive oil in a roasting dish. Brown the flesh side for 2 minutes over high heat, then brown for 1 minute on the cut side, holding in place with a spoon. Do the same for the bottom (stuffing side), while basting. With the loin on its bottom, add the scraps and the garlic clove used with the spinach. Roast in the preheated oven for 7 minutes. Stir the scraps, baste the meat, and cook for another 7 minutes. Check whether the meat is cooked. The thermometer should show a core (internal) temperature of 52°C – 126°F.

6

Transfer the meat to a dish, cover with aluminum foil, and rest for at least half as long as the cooking time. Degrease the roasting dish. Place the dish over high heat. Add the white wine and cook until the liquid has reduced completely. Add 50 ml – 3 tablespoons plus 1 1/2 teaspoons of water, reduce the heat, and mix. Simmer for 10 minutes over low heat. Strain through a small strainer (sieve). Taste and adjust the seasoning. Add 1 tablespoon of olive oil and mix well. You should have a thick and shiny sauce. Place the meat on a cutting board and remove the twine. Cut the loin in half with the carving knife. Cut each half on a diagonal into two pieces. Season with fleur de sel and pepper. Serve immediately with the sauce.

CHOCOLATE AND COCONUT PUFFS

Makes 12 pastries

Preparation time 1 hour 15 minutes
Cooking time 1 hour 35 minutes
Resting time 2 hours

EQUIPMENT

Pastry (piping) bags
Size 16 plain pastry tip (nozzle)
Size 10 plain pastry tip
Size 2 plain pastry tip
Size 7 plain pastry tip
Plastic wrap (cling film)
Silicone spatula (scraper)

TIPS FROM OUR CHEFS

Immediately cover the hot creams with plastic wrap, making direct contact with the surface, to prevent a skin from forming.

PATIENCE
Don't bake the large and small puffs at the same time. The small ones will cook first and you will have to open the oven, which will affect the way the large ones turn out.

Coconut cream

4 g – 0.14 ounce sheet (leaf) gelatin (2 sheets)
125 ml – 1/2 cup light (single) cream
30 g – 1 ounce (2 tablespoons plus 1 1/2 teaspoons) superfine (caster) sugar
125 ml – 1/2 cup coconut milk

Chocolate pastry cream

250 ml – 1 cup whole milk
3 egg yolks
50 g – 1.76 ounces (1/4 cup) superfine (caster) sugar
8 g – 0.28 ounce (1 tablespoon) all-purpose (plain) flour
8 g – 0.28 ounce (1 tablespoon) cornstarch (cornflour)
45 g – 1.6 ounces dark chocolate (70% cocoa)
50 g – 1.76 ounces (3 1/2 tablespoons) butter, cut into cubes

Choux puffs

500 g – 1 pound 2 ounces choux paste (page 545)
1 egg

Frosting and finishing

300 g – 10.5 ounces white fondant, divided
50 g – 1.76 ounces cocoa paste
Red food coloring
50 g – 1.76 ounces (1/2 cup) shredded coconut
3 tablespoons chocolate sprinkles

1

Make the coconut cream: Soak the gelatin in cold water for 5 minutes. Pour the cream into a saucepan and bring to a boil while stirring with a whisk. Remove from heat. Drain the gelatin in a strainer (sieve), add to the cream, and stir with the whisk. Add the superfine sugar and mix well. Add the coconut milk and stir again. Transfer to a bowl, cover with plastic wrap, and let stand for at least 1 hour in the refrigerator. In the meantime, make the chocolate pastry cream: Put the milk into another saucepan and bring to a boil. Put the egg yolks into a bowl, add the superfine sugar, and whisk until thick and pale. Incorporate the flour and cornstarch. Add a little boiling milk and mix. Pour the egg mixture into the rest of the milk.

2

Bring to a boil for 1 minute while stirring. Remove from heat and add the chocolate in pieces. Mix gently for a long time until the cream is smooth. Incorporate the butter.

3

Line a bowl with plastic wrap. Pour in the chocolate pastry cream. Cover with plastic wrap in direct contact with the surface of the cream. Let cool, then refrigerate for at least 1 hour.

4

Preheat the oven to 150°C – 300°F (gas mark 3) in a convection (fan-assisted) oven or 170°C – 325°F (gas mark 3) in a conventional (static) oven. Make the choux paste (page 545). Fit the size 16 tip to the pastry–bag and fill with the choux paste (page 507). Pipe twelve 5-cm- – 2-inch–diameter puffs on a baking sheet (tray), spacing them 3–4 cm – 1 1/4 inches apart on all sides. Beat the egg with a fork and brush over the tops of the puffs. Dip the back of a fork in the beaten egg and press against the top of each puff in perpendicular positions to create a grid pattern. Place in the middle of the oven and bake until golden, 50–60 minutes.

Use the size 10 tip to pipe twelve 3.5-cm- – 1 1/2-inch–diameter puffs on another baking sheet, spacing them 3–4 cm – 1 1/4 inches apart. Gently brush the tops of the puffs with beaten egg. Take the first batch of puffs out of the oven and let cool. Place the second batch in the middle of the oven and bake until golden, 30–35 minutes. Pierce the bottoms of the larger puffs with the size 2 pastry tip.

5

6 Take the chocolate pastry cream out of the refrigerator and whisk. Fit the size 7 plain tip to a clean pastry bag and fill with the chocolate pastry cream. Fill the large puffs with the cream. Make the chocolate frosting (icing): Melt 200 g – 7 ounces of fondant in a saucepan over low heat with 2 tablespoons of water. Melt the cocoa paste for 30 seconds in the microwave (600 W) and add to the fondant. Mix well. Add a few drops of red food coloring and mix gently. Transfer the chocolate frosting to a bowl. Dip the tops of the large puffs in the frosting, covering them halfway. Smooth with your finger. Let dry.

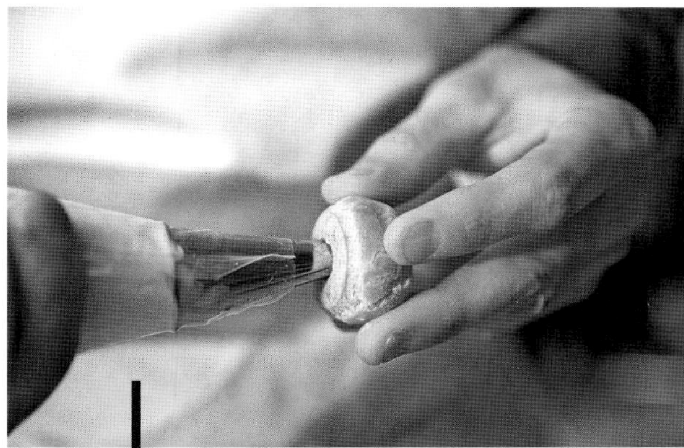

7 Pierce the bottoms of the small puffs with the size 2 pastry tip. Take the coconut cream out of the refrigerator and whisk. Fit the size 7 plain tip to a clean pastry bag and fill with the coconut cream. Fill the smaller puffs.

8

Make the coconut frosting: Melt 100 g – 3.5 ounces of fondant in a saucepan over low heat with 1 tablespoon of water. Transfer to a bowl and dip the tops of the small puffs in the frosting. Immediately dip in the shredded coconut. Spread a little chocolate frosting around the puffs with a spatula. Immediately dip in the chocolate sprinkles. Place the small puffs on top of the large ones.

TIPS FROM OUR CHEFS

PREPARING AHEAD

You can bake the choux puffs the day before. Put them on a baking sheet, cover with plastic wrap, and store in the freezer. Heat them in the oven at 200°C – 375°F for 3 minutes when you're ready to proceed with the recipe.

CHEESECAKE

Serves 6

Preparation time 1 hour
Cooking time 1 hour
Resting time 12 hours

EQUIPMENT

26-cm- – 10 1/4-inch–diameter cake ring
Food processor fitted with metal blade

Cheesecake batter

3 (75-g – 2.65-ounce) eggs (weight with shell)
560 g – 1 pound 4 ounces cream cheese
150 g – 5.3 ounces (3/4 cup) sugar
25 g – 0.88 ounce (3 tablespoons plus 1 1/2 teaspoons) flour
50 g – 1.76 ounces (3 tablespoons plus 1 1/2 teaspoons) light (single) cream

Frosting

4 g – 0.14 ounce sheet (leaf) gelatin (2 sheets)
1 vanilla bean (pod)
320 g – 11.3 ounces (1 1/3 cups) light cream
30 g – 1.06 ounces (2 tablespoons) sugar

Shortbread dough and decoration

1 egg
60 g – 2.12 ounces (1/4 cup plus 1 tablespoon) sugar
130 g – 4.59 ounces (1 stick plus 1 tablespoon) butter
130 g –4.59 ounces (1 cup plus 1 tablespoon) all-purpose (plain) flour, plus more for dusting
60 g – 2.12 ounces (2/3 cup) almond meal (ground almonds)
3–4 strawberries
5–6 raspberries
Confectioners' (icing) sugar

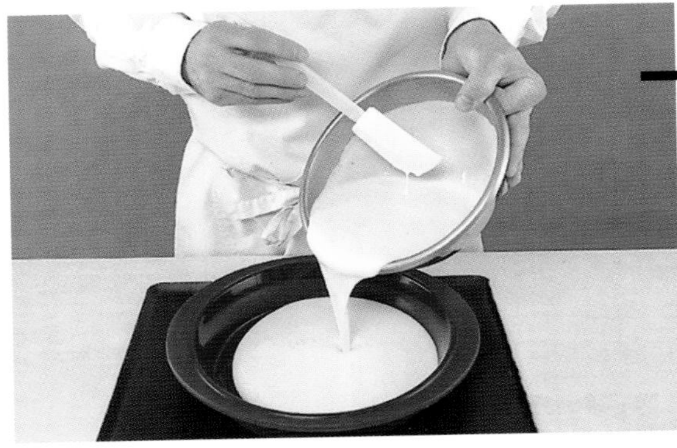

1

Make the cheesecake batter: Break one egg and separate the white from the yolk. Beat the yolk with a fork until smooth. Weigh out the cheese, sugar, flour, cream, and 20 g – 0.71 ounce (about 1 tablespoon plus 1 1/2 teaspoons) beaten egg yolk. Preheat the oven to 115°C – 200°F (gas mark 1/4–1/2). Put the cheese into a bowl and mix with a silicone spatula (scraper) until smooth. Add the sugar and flour. Mix. Incorporate the cream, the egg yolk, and two whole eggs. Mix. Place the cake ring on a baking sheet (tray). Fill with the batter. Bake for 30 minutes. Let rest for 15 minutes. Freeze until hard, about 8 hours.

2

Make the frosting (icing): Soak the gelatin in cold water for 5 minutes. Halve the vanilla bean lengthwise and scrape out the seeds. Pour the cream into a saucepan. Add the vanilla bean and seeds. Whisk the cream to break up the seeds and distribute evenly. Bring to a boil over low heat.

3

Remove the vanilla bean. Drain the gelatin in a small strainer (sieve). Add to the hot cream and mix until it dissolves. Add the sugar. Mix. Pass through a strainer into a bowl. Cover with plastic wrap (cling film), making direct contact with the surface and pressing lightly with your hand. Let stand for 2 hours in the refrigerator.

4

In the meantime, weigh out the ingredients for the shortbread dough. Break the egg, beat, and weigh out 20 g – 0.71 ounce (about 1 tablespoon plus 1 teaspoon). Put into a bowl. Add the sugar. Whisk briskly until the mixture turns pale and frothy. Combine the butter, flour, and almond meal in a food processor fitted with the metal blade. Blend until crumbly. Add the sugar mixture, scraping down the bowl of the food processor well with a silicone spatula. Blend until the dough forms a ball. Put the dough on a sheet of plastic wrap. Spread out with the spatula.

TIPS FROM OUR CHEFS

WHIPPING CREAM
Whipping cream is the name given to cream with a high enough fat content to be whipped. It can be whole (full fat) or heavy (double), light (single) cream with 30% fat, or low-fat cream with about 25% fat. For best results, use heavy cream.

STEP IT UP
Beat the sugar and egg mixture thoroughly so the mixture turns thick and pale when the sugar melts. And use it immediately if you don't want to see its pretty color turn orange.

GENTLY DOES IT
In this recipe, the shortbread dough is baked at low temperature so that it cooks and dries out at the same time. At a higher temperature, only the edges would cook and the pastry would end up sinking.

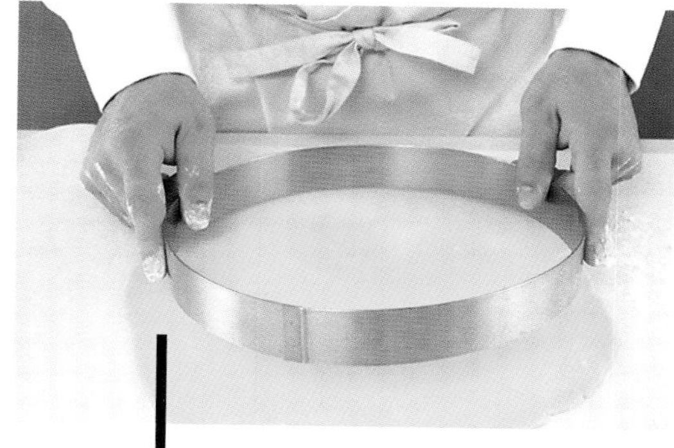

5 Fold the plastic over the dough. Press the dough with your hand until it has a thickness of 1 cm – 3/8 inch. Wrap well and refrigerate for 1 hour. Preheat the oven to 170°C – 350°F (gas mark 3). Place a sheet of parchment (baking) paper on the work surface and dust lightly with flour. Roll out the dough to a disk 3 mm – 1/8 inch thick and slightly larger than the cake ring. Push the cake ring down over the dough. Gently remove the excess dough. Remove the ring.

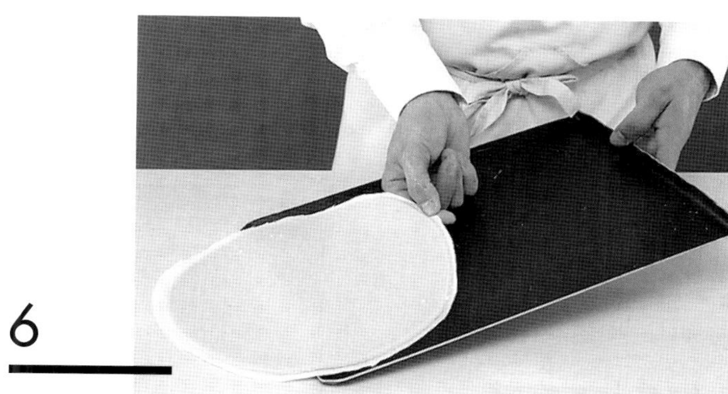

6 Cut the paper around the dough disk, leaving a margin of about 2 cm – 3/4 inch. Turn the sheet as you cut. Slide the dough on the paper onto a baking sheet (tray). Bake for 20 minutes.

7 Pour the frosting into a bowl and whisk lightly. Warm in the microwave for 30 seconds (800 W). Unmold the frozen cheese disk. Transfer to a rack. Use a ladle to coat with frosting. Place the shortbread disk on the serving dish. Carefully lift the cheesecake with a very large offset spatula (palette knife), supporting the bottom with one hand, and smooth off the excess frosting with the spatula. Place on top of the shortbread disk. Arrange the strawberries and raspberries on top of the cheesecake. Dust with confectioners' sugar. Let stand for 1 hour at room temperature or 3–4 hours in the refrigerator.

MACAFRAISE

Serves 4

Preparation time 30 minutes
Cooking time 14 minutes
Crust formation 1 hour

EQUIPMENT

Pastry (piping) bag
Size 14 plain pastry tip

Macaron shells

1 batch raspberry macaron shell batter (page 110)

Filling

100 g – 3.5 ounces (1/3 cup) plain buttercream (page 565)
3 g – 0.11 ounce (1/2 teaspoon) natural vanilla extract
100 g – 3.5 ounces strawberries, washed and hulled
10 small whole strawberries, washed and hulled
5 large whole strawberries, washed

1 Make a raspberry macaron batter, but mix it a little less briskly (page 110).

2 Draw two 14-cm- – 5 1/2-inch–diameter circles on a sheet of parchment (baking) paper. Place on a baking sheet (tray). Cover the template with another clean sheet of parchment. Pipe the two shells over the circles (page 507). Let crust form for 1 hour at room temperature. Preheat oven to 170°C – 350°F (gas mark 3–4). Bake the shells for 14 minutes. Turn the baking sheet around halfway through. Take the macaron shells out of the oven and let cool.

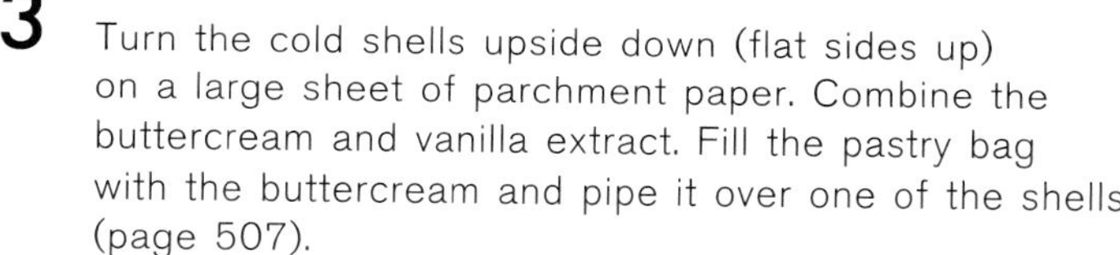

3 Turn the cold shells upside down (flat sides up) on a large sheet of parchment paper. Combine the buttercream and vanilla extract. Fill the pastry bag with the buttercream and pipe it over one of the shells (page 507).

4 Crush the 100 g – 3.5 ounces of strawberries to make a puree and drain in a strainer (sieve). Spread the strawberry puree over the buttercream.
Cut the small strawberries in half and arrange over the puree, around the perimeter of the shell.
Cover with the other shell (flat side down) and garnish with the large strawberries.

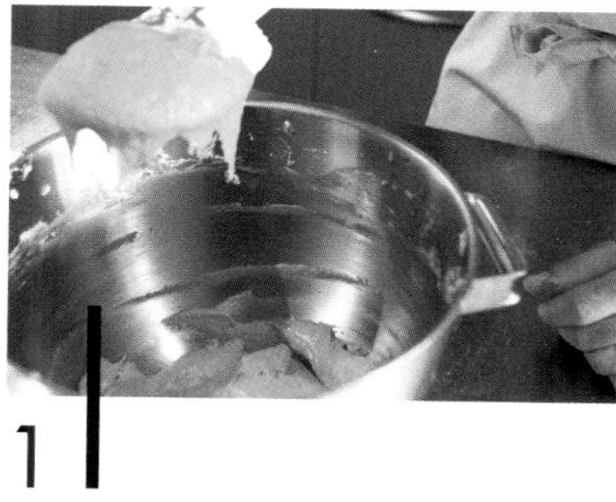

1

3

TIPS FROM OUR CHEFS

ECONOMIZE
Keep the sheet of paper with the circles drawn on it. You can reuse it each time you want to make this recipe.

ANOTHER TRICK
Pipe the large shells in a spiral on the parchment paper, leaving a 5-mm – 1/4-inch margin between the two circles and between their edges and the sides of the pan (the batter will spread out when cooking). Slide the parchment template out from underneath before baking.

SAINT HONORÉ CAKE

Serves 4–6

Mousseline cream, caramel, and chantilly cream
Preparation time 30 minutes
Cooking time 5 minutes

Choux puffs
Preparation time 1 hour
Cooking time 45 minutes
Resting time 40 minutes

EQUIPMENT

Mousseline cream, caramel, and chantilly cream
Stand mixer
Pastry (piping) bag
Size 9 plain pastry tip
Size 10 plain pastry tip
Size 7 Saint-Honoré pastry tip

Choux puffs
Pastry (piping) bag
Size 10 plain pastry tip (nozzle)
18-cm- – 7-inch–diameter stainless steel ring mold
Size 16 plain pastry tip
Size 2 plain pastry tip

Mousseline cream, caramel, and chantilly cream

300 g – 10.5 ounces vanilla pastry cream (page 571)
100 g – 3.5 ounces (7 tablespoons) butter, in cubes
250 g – 8.82 ounces (1 1/4 cups) superfine (caster) sugar
200 g – 7 ounces (3/4 cup plus 1 tablespoon) light (single) cream, very cold
15 g – 0.53 ounce (2 tablespoons) confectioners' (icing) sugar

Choux puffs

200 g - 7 oz puff pastry
200 g – 7 ounces choux paste (page 545)
1 egg
Flour

TIPS FROM OUR CHEFS

IN ADVANCE
The pastry cream should rest for at least 1 hour in the refrigerator, because a thermal shock between the cold cream and the softened butter is required for the proper emulsion of the mousseline cream.

TEXTURE
Try to find a good balance with a caramel that is neither too runny nor too thick. If it hardens as it cools, reheat gently.

RIGHT ANGLE
To make the small cream peaks in the center of the Saint-Honoré, hold the pastry bag at a 45-degree angle.

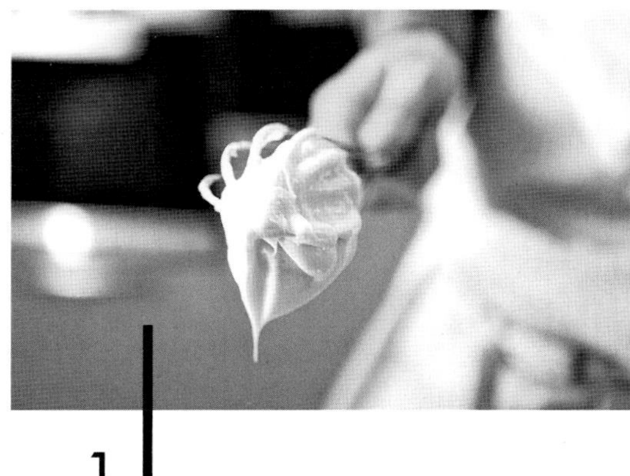

Preheat the oven to 170°C – 350°F (gas mark 3) and make the choux paste (page 545). Fit the size 10 tip to the pastry bag and fill with half of the choux paste (page 507). Pipe fifteen 3-cm- – 1 1/4-inch-diameter puffs on a baking sheet (tray), spacing them 2–3 cm – 3/4–1 1/4 inches apart on all sides.

1

Whisk the pastry cream until smooth. It should have the consistency of mayonnaise. Add the butter to make mousseline cream (page 570).

2

3

Beat the egg with a fork. Gently brush the tops of the puffs with beaten egg. Bake for 35 minutes. Lightly dust the work surface with flour and roll out the puff pastry to a thickness of 2 mm – 1/16 inch. Place the stainless steel ring mold in the center and push down firmly. Remove the excess dough. Brush another baking sheet with water. Place the pastry disk on the baking sheet and prick with a fork. Let stand for 20 minutes.

4

Fit the size 16 tip to the pastry bag and fill with the rest of the choux paste. Pipe a line of choux paste over the puff pastry 2–3 mm – 1/12 inch from the edge and another line 3 cm – 1 1/4 inches from the edge. Bake at 170°C – 350°F (gas mark 3) for 45 minutes. Check whether the disk is cooked by lifting it. The underside of this choux pastry–puff pastry crown should be golden.

5

Pierce the bottoms of the 12 best-formed puffs with the size 2 pastry tip. Fit the size 9 plain tip to the pastry bag and fill with the mousseline cream (page 507). Fill the puffs.

6

Make the caramel (page 566): Put the superfine sugar into a saucepan. Add 75 ml – 1/4 cup plus 1 tablespoon of water. Bring to a boil while cleaning the sides of the pan from time to time with a wet brush. Cook to a deep golden caramel.

7

Dip the pan into a container filled with cold water to stop the caramel. Wait until there are no more bubbles in the caramel, then apply it with a frosting spatula (palette knife). Cover the two choux pastry–puff pastry crowns with it.

8

Prick the bottom of a filled puff and dip the top in the caramel. Let the excess drip off. Turn the puff over. Place on parchment paper. Hold it in position by leaning against another puff. Do the same for the remaining 11 filled puffs and let dry. Once dry, dip the bottom of 11 puffs in the caramel and drain carefully on the rim of the pan.

9

Attach immediately to the outside crown, spacing them 1 cm – 3/8 inch apart. Fit the size 10 tip to the pastry bag and fill with the mousseline cream. Pipe the cream over the center, including over the smaller crown. Use a frosting spatula to shape the cream into a flattened dome. Make the Chantilly cream: Whip the cream with the confectioners' sugar (page 567). Pipe a little over the mousseline cream, giving it the shape of a slightly taller dome. Fit the special size 7 Saint-Honoré tip to a bag and fill with the Chantilly cream. Pipe a sliver of cream between each of the puffs. Pipe small peaks in horizontal rows over the center. Place the last puff in the center of the Saint-Honoré.

PARIS-BREST WITH HAZELNUTS

Serves 6–8

Nougatine and hazelnut mousseline cream
Preparation time 30 minutes
Cooking time 30 minutes

Choux pastry
Preparation time 30 minutes
Cooking time 45 minutes

EQUIPMENT

Nougatine and hazelnut mousseline cream
Food processor fitted with metal blade
Pastry (piping) bag
Size 15 fluted pastry tip (nozzle)

Choux pastry
20-cm- – 7 3/4-inch–diameter stainless steel ring mold
Pastry bag
Size 16 plain pastry tip
18-cm- – 7-inch–diameter stainless steel ring mold

Nougatine and hazelnut mousseline cream

25 g – 0.88 ounce (1/4 cup) chopped almonds
90 g – 3.17 ounces (1/3 cup plus 2 tablespoons) superfine (caster) sugar
50 g – 1.76 ounces (1/3 cup) hazelnuts
400 g – 14.11 ounces mousseline cream (page 570)

Choux pastry

300 g – 10.58 ounces choux paste (page 545)
Flour
80 g – 2.82 ounces (1/2 cup plus 1 tablespoon) hazelnuts
1 egg
Confectioners' (icing) sugar

TIPS FROM OUR CHEFS

TOO HARD
If the nougatine hardens too quickly, slide the parchment paper onto a baking sheet and put into the oven for 2–3 minutes to soften.

A HEAD START
You can make the nougatine ahead of time. Store it in an airtight container in a dry place, such as a cupboard, but not in the refrigerator.

PREPARING AHEAD
You can make the hazelnut paste ahead of time. It will keep for fifteen days in the refrigerator in an airtight container.

NO RING MOLD
If you don't have a stainless steel ring mold, use an overturned bowl.

BAKING
Bake the large ring on the top shelf of the oven and the small ring on the bottom shelf.

1

Make the nougatine: Preheat the oven to 150°C – 300°F (gas mark 3) in a convection (fan-assisted) oven or 170°C – 350°F (gas mark 3) in a conventional (static) oven. Spread the almonds in a single layer on a baking sheet (tray) and toast lightly in the oven for 15 minutes. Put 1 tablespoon of the sugar in a saucepan over high heat. When it melts, very gradually add the rest of the sugar. Stir over medium heat to make a deep golden caramel (page 566). Remove from heat, add the almonds, and mix with a spatula (palette knife). Pour onto parchment (baking) paper and let cool for 2 minutes.

2

Fold the almond paste in half, then in half again to form a ball. Use a rolling pin to roll out the nougatine to a thickness of 5 mm – 1/4 inch.

3

Turn the oven temperature up to 160°C – 325°F (gas mark 4). Spread 50 g – 1.76 ounces (1/3 cup) hazelnuts in a single layer on a baking sheet lined with parchment paper. Toast for 15 minutes (to enhance their flavor). Let cool. Put the hazelnuts into the food processor and blend for 3–4 minutes to a smooth and runny hazelnut paste.

TIPS FROM OUR CHEFS

NO CONVECTION OVEN
If you don't have a convection (fan-assisted) setting in your oven, bake one ring at a time.

WHAT IS IT FOR?
The lines of cream piped in the center of the Paris-Brest (step 7) let the dessert keep its volume without overloading the balls of cream.

4

Add the hazelnut paste to the mousseline cream and mix gently. Refrigerate. Preheat the oven to 150°C – 300°F (gas mark 3) in a convection (fan-assisted) oven or 170°C – 350°F (gas mark 3) in a conventional (static) oven. Make the choux paste (page 545). Dust the work surface with a little flour. Place the 20-cm- – 7 3/4-inch–ring mold in the flour. Press the mold firmly on a baking sheet to make a circle of flour and remove. Fit the size 16 tip to the pastry bag and fill with the choux paste (page 507). Pipe two concentric rings of choux paste, following the outline of the flour circle.

5

Put the hazelnuts on a cutting board. Crush with the flat side of the blade of a chef's knife, then coarsely chop. Beat the egg with a fork. Gently brush the larger choux paste ring with beaten egg. Sprinkle generously with chopped hazelnuts. Shake the baking sheet over a sheet of parchment paper to remove excess hazelnuts.

6

Place the 18-cm – 7-inch ring mold in the flour. Press the mold firmly on another baking sheet and remove. Pipe a ring of choux paste inside the flour circle. Put both baking sheets in the oven. Bake the smaller ring for 35 minutes and the larger one for 45 minutes. Chop up the nougatine with a chef's knife. Cut the large ring in half horizontally. Fit the fluted tip to the pastry bag and fill with the hazelnut mousseline cream (page 507).

7

Pipe balls of cream over the outer edge of the bottom half of the large ring by making a continuous up and down motion with the pastry bag. Pipe a line of cream over the inner edge of the ring. Place the whole small ring inside the large one. Slide onto a dish. Pipe balls of cream over the small ring. Pipe a line of cream all around it. Sprinkle with chopped nougatine. Dust the top of the large ring with confectioners' sugar. Place it on the Paris-Brest and press lightly. Refrigerate before serving.

FONDANT CAKE IN THREE CHOCOLATES

Serves 10

Cooking time 1 hour 30 minutes
Resting time 16 hours + 8–12 hours

EQUIPMENT

Candy thermometer
Pastry (piping) bag
Size 4 plain pastry tip (nozzle)

TIPS FROM OUR CHEFS

CHOICE OF MOLD
If you don't have a silicone mold, use a standard loaf pan and line it with plastic wrap to make unmolding easy. Don't put it in the freezer.

SET, BUT NOT TOO MUCH
Each layer of ganache must be just set before the next layer is added.

THE RIGHT WEIGHT
It's better to weigh the food coloring as it is added to the mixture. If you weigh it out separately, then add it, some will be lost, and it can make a difference when working with such a small amount.

White chocolate ganache

300 g – 10.5 ounces white chocolate
2 g – 0.07 ounce sheet (leaf) gelatin (1 sheet)
150 g – 5.3 ounces (2/3 cup) whipping cream

Milk chocolate ganache

300 g – 10.5 ounces milk chocolate (40% cocoa)
2 g – 0.07 ounce sheet (leaf) gelatin (1 sheet)
150 g – 5.3 ounces (2/3 cup) whipping cream

Dark chocolate ganache

225 g – 8 ounces (3/4 cup plus 3 tablespoons) whipping cream
190 g - 6.7 ounces dark chocolate (66 percent cocoa)

Frosting

230 g – 8.11 ounces (1 cup plus 2 tablespoons plus 1 1/2 teaspoons) superfine (caster) sugar
3 g – 0.11 ounce (1/2 teaspoon) red food coloring
10 g – 0.35 ounce sheet (leaf) gelatin (5 sheets)
150 g – 5.3 ounces (2/3 cup) whipping cream
80 g – 2.82 ounces (1/3 cup) glucose syrup (page 543) or light corn syrup
90 g – 3.17 ounces (1 cup) unsweetened cocoa powder

Shortbread dough (one flavor of your choice)

Enough shortbread dough to make 50 cookies (page 565)

1

Make the white chocolate ganache: Put the white chocolate into a heatproof bowl and melt over a saucepan filled with simmering water for 2–3 minutes. Remove from the bain-marie and mix gently. Soak the gelatin for 5 minutes in cold water. Bring the cream to a boil in a saucepan over high heat. Drain the gelatin in a small strainer (sieve). Add to the hot cream and stir. Pour half of the cream over the chocolate. Mix in the center to create an emulsion. Add the rest of the cream. Mix until the ganache has an elastic consistency and is smooth and glossy. Pour the ganache into a silicone mold. Put in the refrigerator to set for about 2 hours (or 30 minutes in the freezer).

2

Make the milk chocolate ganache: Melt the chocolate halfway over a simmering bain-marie. Stir from time to time. Soak the gelatin for 5 minutes in cold water. Bring the cream to a boil over high heat. Drain the gelatin in a small strainer. Add to the hot cream and stir. Pour half of the cream over the chocolate. Mix in the center to create an emulsion. Reheat the rest of the cream. Pour over the chocolate. Mix until the ganache has an elastic consistency and is smooth and glossy. Pour the milk chocolate ganache over the white ganache. Put the mold in the refrigerator to set for about 2 hours (or 30 minutes in the freezer).

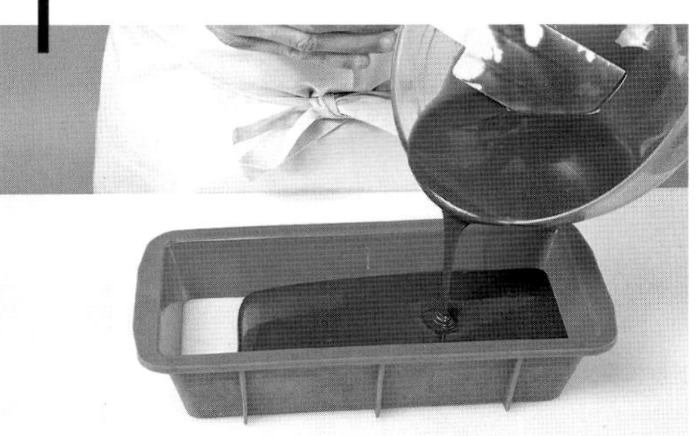

3

Make the dark chocolate ganache: Put the cream into a saucepan. Bring to a boil over high heat. Pour half of the cream over the dark chocolate. Mix in the center to create an emulsion. Reheat the rest of the cream. Pour over the chocolate. Mix gently. Pour the dark chocolate ganache over the milk chocolate ganache. Refrigerate for 2 hours, then transfer the mold to the freezer for 8–12 hours.

4

Make the frosting (icing): Put 70 g – 1/4 cup plus 2 teaspoons water into a saucepan. Add the sugar. Put the pan on the scale. Add 3 g – 0.11 ounce red food coloring. Place the pan over high heat and use a thermometer to monitor the temperature as you bring it to 110°C – 230°F (3–5 minutes). Remove from heat.

5

Soak the gelatin for 5 minutes in cold water. Pour the cream into a saucepan. Add the glucose syrup. Bring to a simmer over medium heat. Add the cocoa powder while stirring with a whisk. Remove the pan from the heat. Finish by mixing the paste until smooth. Add the colored sugar syrup while stirring. Whisk until smooth. Transfer to a deep bowl. Drain the gelatin and add. Blend. Transfer to another bowl. Cover with plastic wrap (cling film), making direct contact with the frosting. Let stand for about 2 hours in the refrigerator.

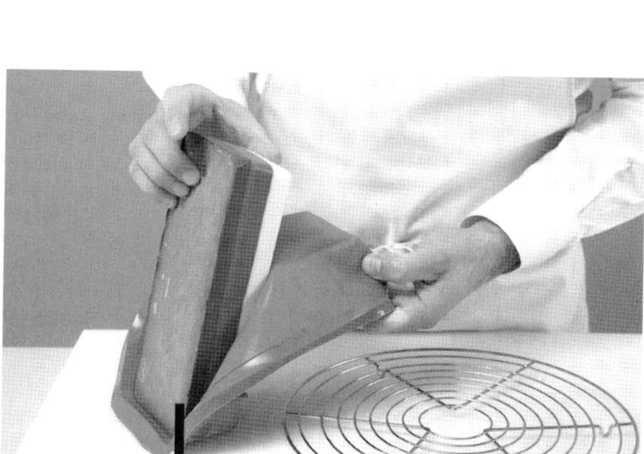

6

Make the shortbread dough. Preheat the oven to 170°C – 350°F (gas mark 3). Trace around the top of the mold on parchment (baking) paper. Place on a baking sheet (tray). Fill the pastry bag fitted with the size 4 tip with the dough (page 507). Pipe the dough in parallel strips inside the rectangle. Put the baking sheet into the oven and bake for 15 minutes, then let cool. Place a rack over the work surface. Unmold the frozen layers of ganache onto the rack.

7

Place the rack over a large plate. Reheat the frosting in the microwave or over a bain-marie at 40–50°C – 104–122°F. Transfer the frosting to a liquid measuring cup. Pour over the cake. Smooth twice with an offset spatula (palette knife) to remove the excess. Place the shortbread on a dish. Use a wide offset frosting spatula to position the frozen ganache over the shortbread. Refrigerate until firm, at least 8 hours. Dip a large non-serrated knife in hot water, drain without drying, and cut 1–2-cm – 1/3–3/4-inch slices.

CRISPY CHOCOLATE TART

Serves 6

Preparation time 30 minutes
Cooking time 20 minutes
Resting time 5 hours
15 minutes

EQUIPMENT

Food processor fitted with metal blade
Square cake mold with 15-cm – 6-inch sides
Candy thermometer

Chocolate cream (one flavor of your choice)

150 g – 5.3 ounces (2/3 cup) milk
100 g – 3.5 ounces (1/2 cup) whipping cream
50 g – 1.76 ounces (about 3 1/2) egg yolks
30 g – 1.06 ounces (2 tablespoons) sugar
120 g - 4.23 oz dark chocolate (70 percent cocoa), 160 g - 5.64 oz milk chocolate (40 percent cocoa), or 185 g - 6.53 oz white chocolate

Chocolate tart shell

50 g – 1.76 ounces (1/4 cup) sugar
1 (60-g – 2.12-ounce) egg
75 g – 2.65 ounces (5 1/3 tablespoons) very cold butter, cut into small cubes
15 g – 0.53 ounce (2 tablespoons) all-purpose (plain) flour, plus more for dusting
1/8 teaspoon salt
10 g - 0.35 oz (2 tbsp) unsweetened cocoa powder

Desert roses (one flavor of your choice)

3 desert roses (page 130)

Decoration

100 g – 3.5 ounces dark, milk, or white chocolate
1 tablespoon unsweetened cocoa powder
Gold leaf

TIPS FROM OUR CHEFS

GENTLY DOES IT
Don't knead the dough, as that will make it tough. And don't roll it into a ball, because it won't chill evenly.

1 Make the chocolate cream: Combine the milk and cream in a saucepan. Bring to a boil over medium heat. Mix the egg yolks with the sugar without beating. Pour about 1/4 cup of boiling milk over the yolk mixture while stirring with a whisk. Return the rest of the milk to a boil over medium heat. Pour the yolk mixture into the milk while stirring. Reduce the heat to low. Cook the mixture, a crème anglaise, stirring constantly with a silicone spatula (scraper), until it is thick enough to coat the spatula.

2 Put the chocolate into a bowl. Pour half of the very hot crème anglaise over the chocolate. Mix in the center with the silicone spatula to create an emulsion. Reheat the rest of the crème anglaise. Pour over the chocolate. Mix gently until the chocolate has melted and the mixture is smooth. Blend if necessary. Cover with plastic wrap (cling film) in direct contact with the surface of the chocolate cream. Refrigerate for about 2 hours.

3

Make the tart shell: Put the sugar into a bowl. Break the egg into a small bowl and beat. Pour half of the beaten egg over the sugar. Beat until thick and pale. Put the butter in the food processor fitted with the metal blade. Add the flour, salt, and cocoa powder. Pulse briefly until the mixture is crumbly. Add the yolk mixture. Mix again for a few seconds, but don't blend thoroughly. Stop when the dough begins to form a ball.

4

Transfer to a sheet of plastic wrap. Lightly flatten the dough. Wrap in the plastic wrap and refrigerate for 2 hours. Preheat the oven to 170°C – 350°F (gas mark 3). Dust the work surface with flour. Unwrap the dough. Lightly dust with flour. Roll out the dough, rotating it to keep it even, to a thickness of 2–3 mm – 1/12 inch. Place the square cake mold over the dough. Cut the dough around it, leaving a margin twice as long as the height of the mold. Trim off the excess.

5

Roll the dough around the rolling pin. Place it on top of the baking ring, centering it evenly. Push the dough down, being careful not to wrinkle or fold it. Carefully cover the mold, keeping the corners very straight. Fold the edges over the mold. Pass a rolling pin over the top of the mold in both directions to trim off excess dough. Press on the edges with your thumb and index finger to adhere the dough to the mold. Transfer the tart shell to a baking sheet (tray) lined with parchment (baking) paper. Place in the oven. Bake for 20 minutes. Take the tart shell out of the oven. Unmold and place on the work surface with the bottom resting on the surface. Chop up the three desert roses with a knife. Sprinkle the pieces over the bottom of the tart shell. Fill with the cream. Be careful not to crush the tart shell while pushing the cream down gently to the bottom of the tart shell so that the cream fills the space between the cookie crumbs.

6

Smooth with a frosting spatula. Rest for 1 hour in the refrigerator.

7

Make the decoration: Melt the chocolate over a bain-marie at 55–60°C – 131–140°F. Cool to 28–29°C – 82–84°F, then reheat to 30–31°C – 86–88°F. Lay a sheet of soft plastic over the work surface. Pour the chocolate over it. Smooth with a frosting spatula to a thickness of 1 mm – 1/16 inch.

TIPS FROM OUR CHEFS

NO BUTTER

The dough contains enough butter that there is no need to grease the baking mold. Place the side dusted with less flour against the frame so that it will adhere to it well.

PLASTIC

You need light transparent plastic film to make the chocolate decorations. You can also use flexible Rhodoïd® (cellulose acetate) or clear cellophane.

8

Touch the chocolate with your finger. It should no longer stick. Immediately cut one or more 7-cm – 2 3/4-inch squares. Leave them there. Place the plastic sheet on an overturned baking sheet. Cover the chocolate with parchment paper. Cover with another overturned baking sheet to keep the chocolate flat. Let stand for at least 15 minutes in the refrigerator. Take the baking sheets out of the refrigerator and turn them over. Peel off the plastic. Use a small fine strainer to dust the tart with cocoa powder. Position the best–looking chocolate square in the center (reserve the others for another use). Decorate with a little gold leaf.

DOUGHNUTS

Makes 12 doughnuts

Preparation time 1 hour
Resting time 3 hours 30 minutes
Cooking time 3 minutes per batch

EQUIPMENT

Stand mixer with a dough hook
Deep fryer (deep-fat fryer)

Starter

3 g – 0.11 ounce compressed fresh yeast
140 g – 4.94 ounces (1 cup plus 2 tablespoons) all-purpose (plain) flour, plus more for dusting

Doughnuts

4 small eggs (for 50 g – 1.76 ounces/about 3 tablespoons plus 1 1/2 teaspoons egg yolk)
15 g – 0.53 ounce (1 tablespoon) milk
20 g – 0.71 ounce compressed fresh yeast
30 g – 1 ounce (2 tablespoons) sugar
125 g – 4.4 ounces (1 cup) all-purpose (plain) flour, plus more for dusting
5 g – 0.18 ounce (1 1/4 teaspoons) fleur de sel
30 g – 1 ounce (2 tablespoons) butter, softened
Oil for deep-frying
400 g – 14 ounces white fondant

TIPS FROM OUR CHEFS

FRESH OR IN GRANULES
If you want to use freeze-dried (active dry) yeast in envelopes or packets (granules), you'll need 2 g – 0.07 ounce (about 2/3 teaspoon) for the starter and 1 1/2 envelopes (1 tablespoon plus 1 1/2 teaspoons) for the dough.

NEITHER HOT NOR COLD
Dough rises best at 20°C – 68°F, as microorganisms develop fastest at that temperature.

SCRAPING
Scraping refers to pushing down dough or gathering together small clumps. It typically involves the use of a bowl scraper.

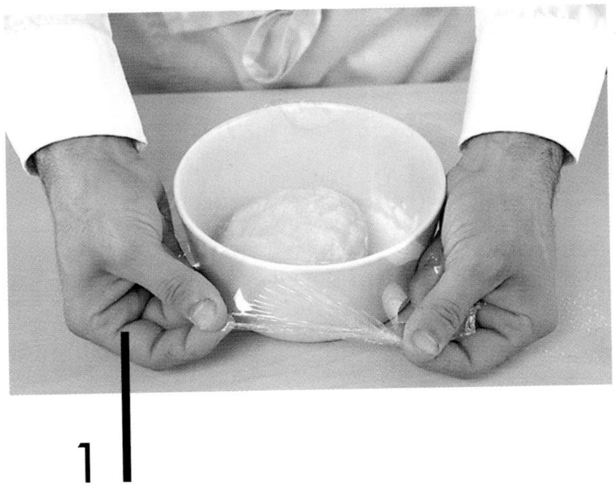

1

Make the starter: Coarsely crumble the yeast into a bowl. Add 140 g – 4.94 ounces (1 cup plus 2 teaspoons) warm (not hot) water. Add the flour and mix with a silicone spatula (palette knife), starting from the middle. Stir well. Finish by beating the dough firmly against the sides of the bowl by hand. Roll into a ball. Dust the bottom of a small bowl and the starter ball with a large pinch of flour. Put the starter into the bowl. Cover with plastic wrap (cling film) and let rise (proof) for 1 hour–1 hour 30 minutes.

2

Make the doughnut dough: Break the eggs and separate the whites from the yolks. Weigh out 50 g – 1.76 ounces (about 3 tablespoons plus 1 1/2 teaspoons) of egg yolks. Put the starter into the bowl of the stand mixer. Add the milk, crumbled yeast, sugar, flour, and egg yolks. Mix on low speed. When the flour is well mixed, add the fleur de sel. Mix, then scrape down the sides of the bowl. Use a silicone spatula (scraper) for this. Increase the speed to medium. Continue mixing until the dough comes away from the sides of the bowl. Scrape the dough hook and bowl with the silicone spatula.

3

Add the softened butter. Knead until the dough is smooth and shiny. Transfer to a bowl. Work the dough a little to shape it into a ball. Dust lightly with flour. Cover with plastic wrap and let rise until doubled in size, about 1 hour. Punch down (knock back) the dough. Dust with flour.

TIPS FROM OUR CHEFS

STICKY

This dough is very sticky. To prevent sticking, dust the work surface, parchment paper, and your fingers, but do this lightly so you don't end up with large clumps of flour in or on the doughnuts. Repeat as needed.

4

Weigh out 40-g – 1.4-ounce portions of dough for 12 doughnuts. Dab your fingers in flour and rub them. Lightly dust the work surface. Flatten each portion of dough with the palm of your hand, turning counterclockwise (anticlockwise).

5

Push in the center of each with a folded index finger and turn to make a hole. Gradually widen the hole in each donut by turning it on its side and rotating it around with your fingers.

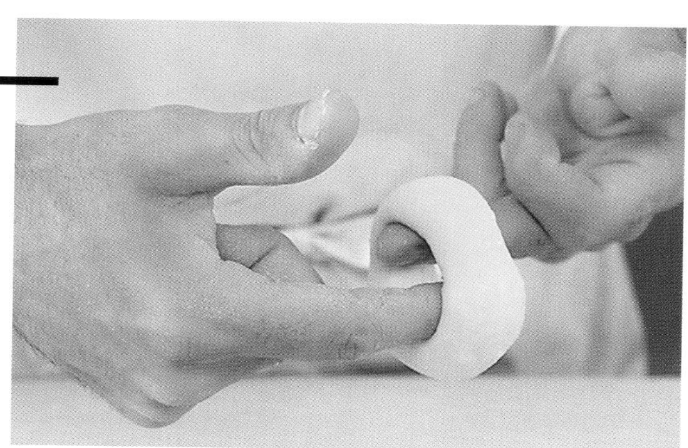

6

Line a baking sheet (tray) with parchment (baking) paper and dust the paper with flour. Lay the doughnuts on it. Let rise for 1 hour. Heat the oil in the fryer to 180°C – 355°F. Fry the doughnuts in batches of three for 2–3 minutes. Turn over and let brown for another 2–3 minutes. Drain. Transfer to a baking sheet lined with paper towels.

7

Mix the fondant with 3 tablespoons of water. Warm in the microwave for a few seconds. Mix. Dip the doughnuts in the fondant frosting (icing). Stir the frosting after each use. Use a knife tip to scrape off the frosting from inside the hole. Smooth the edge with your finger.

PRALINE BONBONS

Makes about 30 square or 40 round bonbons

Preparation time 15 minutes
Cooking time 5 minutes
Resting time 1 hour

EQUIPMENT

2 silicone ice cube trays
Silicone mold with small round cavities
Food processor fitted with metal blade

150 g – 5.3 ounces caramelized hazelnuts (page 152)
20 g – 0.71 ounce gavottes (crêpe dentelle cookies)
15 g – 0.53 ounce (1/2 cup) unsweetened cornflakes
80 g – 2.82 ounces milk chocolate (40% cocoa)
Oil

1 Make the caramelized hazelnuts (page 34) and let cool completely. Weigh out 150 g – 5.3 ounces.

1

2 Put the hazelnuts into the food processor fitted with the metal blade. Blend briefly. Stop the machine and break apart the hazelnut pieces that have clumped together with a spatula (palette knife).
Blend to a praline paste. Put 150 g – 5.3 ounces of the paste into a bowl.

2

3 Crumble the gavottes into another bowl.
Gather the cornflakes into a small mound on a cutting board. Break up with a knife and chop into crumbs. Add to the gavottes.

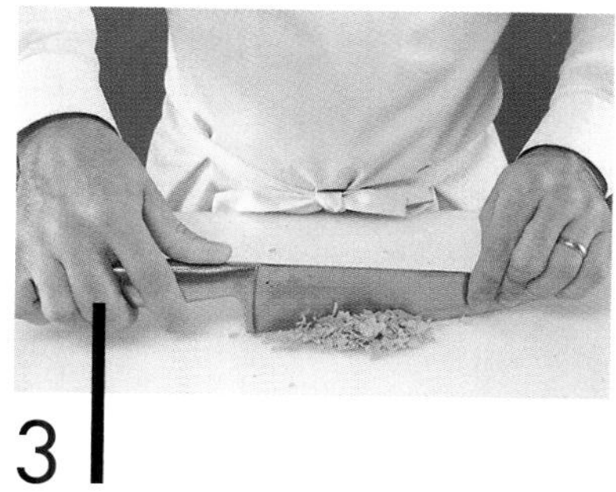

3

4 Warm a heatproof bowl over a bain-marie on medium heat. Add the chocolate.
Mix well with a spatula. Remove from heat before the chocolate is melted.
Off the heat, continue to stir to melt the chocolate completely. Pour over the praline paste. Mix well.
Add the gavotte and cornflake crumbs. Mix to a smooth paste.

4

5 Brush the insides of the ice cube trays with oil.
Fill with part of the mixture. Be careful not to fill more than two–thirds full.
Use the rest of the mixture to fill the silicone mold with small round cavities.
Let cool, then refrigerate for at least 1 hour.
Unmold the bonbons.

CHOCOLATE CARAMEL CHESTNUTS

Serves 4

Preparation time 1 hour
Cooking time 5 minutes

EQUIPMENT

Wire
4 wooden skewers

1 (250 g – 8.80 ounces) can chestnut paste

Chocolate caramel (page 567)

Confectioners' (icing) sugar

1

2

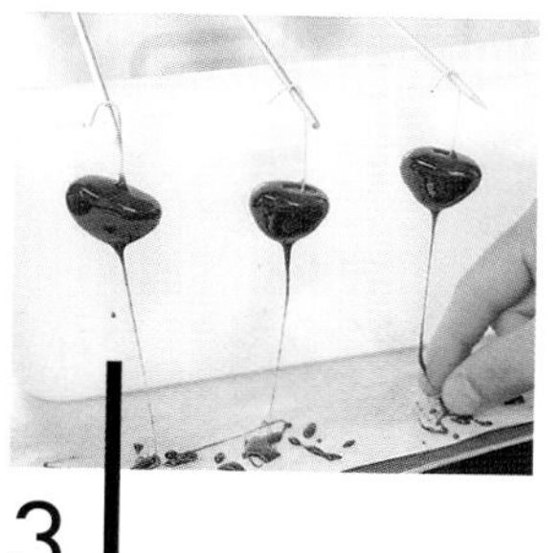
3

4

1 Use your hands to shape small balls of chestnut paste weighing about 5 g – 0.2 ounce each. Mold them into the shape of chestnuts. Cut pieces of wire about 3 cm – 1 1/4 inches in length. Cut as many pieces of wire as you have balls of chestnut paste. Bend one end of each piece of wire to make a hook.
Fold the other end and insert it into a chestnut.

2 Make the chocolate caramel (page 567).
Overturn a deep container on parchment (baking) paper. Arrange the skewers on top of the overturned container, letting their ends extend past both sides. Tilt the saucepan. Holding a chestnut by the hook, dip in a generous amount of chocolate caramel.

3 Holding the chestnut vertically, remove it from the caramel, and immediately hang it by its hook on one of the skewers resting on the container. Repeat the process for the remaining chestnuts. Let cool a little, then pull on the caramel on each chestnut with two fingers to form a tail.

4 Let cool completely, then remove the chestnuts from the skewers. Cut the caramel threads with scissors, leaving a small point on each. Carefully remove the wires.

5 Put a little confectioners' sugar in a bowl. Holding a chestnut by the tip, immerse the bottom into the sugar. Make a back-and-forth movement in the sugar so that it adheres well to the chestnut. Remove any excess sugar. Repeat with remaining chestnuts.

TIPS FROM OUR CHEFS

NEITHER CREAM NOR PUREE
Canned chestnut paste is sweet, unlike chestnut puree, but not as sweet as chestnut cream. You can find it in gourmet grocery stores and certain large retail establishments. It lends itself very well to molding and shaping.

VARIATIONS
Replace the glucose syrup with chestnut honey, which goes very well with the chestnut paste. This recipe can also be made using almond paste formed into chestnuts.

MAGIC
The red food coloring adds intensity to the color of the chocolate, making it richer and more enticing.

APPENDIX

THE CHEF'S TOOLBOX

BAKING SHEET (TRAY)

A metal sheet (tray) with low sides and often covered with a nonstick coating for use in the oven.

It lets you bake several small items

together, such as choux puffs, macarons, and other mignardises.

If the baking sheet does not have nonstick coating, line with parchment (baking) paper or grease with butter and flour.

To bake with two sheets at a time, place them in the oven at evenly spaced heights to let hot air circulate freely.

For mignardises, grease very lightly with melted butter using a pastry brush.

Note: If there is too much butter on the baking sheet, the batter may run. There is no reason to grease a nonstick baking sheet.

BOWL

Make sure you have different-size bowls ready before you start cooking.

Here is a tip to hold your bowl steady if you have to mix a preparation vigorously.

1

2

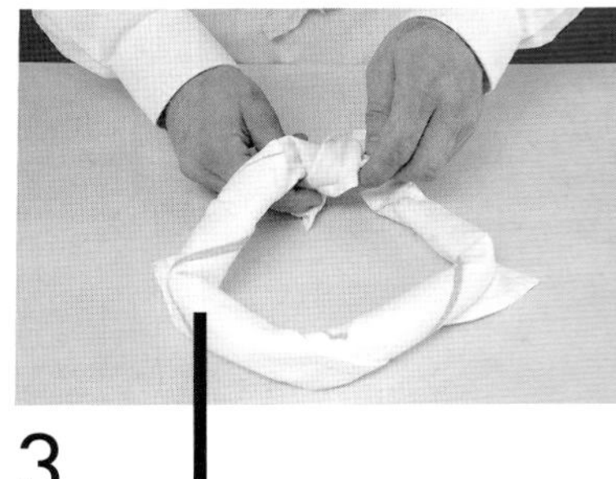

3

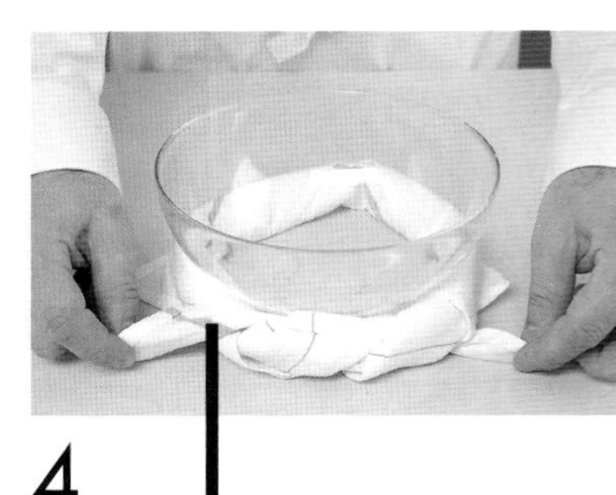

4

To hold your bowl steady, surround it with a dish towel tied as shown. Fold it along the diagonal, roll it up, and tie a knot. Place it around the bowl. Nothing will move now.

CHEF'S KNIFE

This knife has a wide and very sharp non-serrated blade and slices cleanly.

CHEF'S TORCH

Caramelizing a crème brûlée or clafoutis with a chef's torch takes a little longer than doing it in the oven, but yields much more uniform results.

A number of retail outlets sell economical mini butane torches and canister refills for kitchen use. Make sure you have a butane lighter refill handy in case you run out of gas.

If you prefer to use the oven, make sure the dish you are using can withstand high temperatures (300°C – 570°F). Place it as near as possible to the top element or broiler and watch carefully.

CONICAL STRAINER (CHINOIS)

A conical strainer is a fine strainer made from a solid material. It is used to sift powdered ingredients or to separate out liquid. To do this, press down on the contents in the strainer and collect the liquid that comes out.

COOKIE CUTTER

A ring with a sharp edge for cutting dough and other preparations by pressing down firmly over them.

Cookie (biscuit) cutters come in metal and plastic, in different diameters, and with smooth or serrated edges.

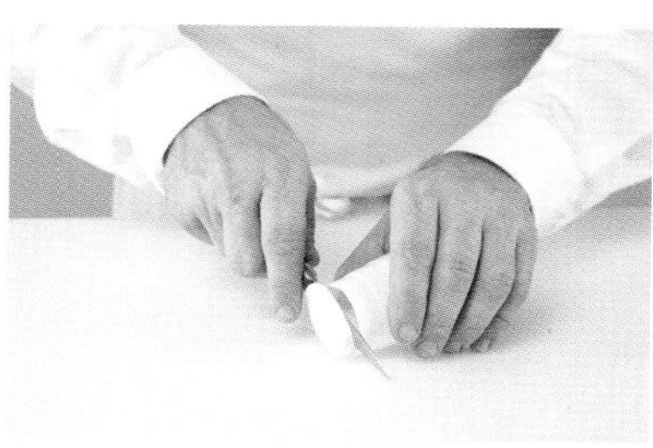

If you don't have a plain cookie cutter, cut the bottom off a plastic cup, then cut the cup into a ring with a height of about 1 cm – 1/2 inch.

(APPLE) CORER

This utensil serves to remove the core from a whole apple with very little wasted flesh.

COUSCOUSSIER

This consists of a perforated basket that lets steam pass through and cook the couscous, a pot to simmer the sauce and accompaniments, and a lid.

MANDOLINE SLICER

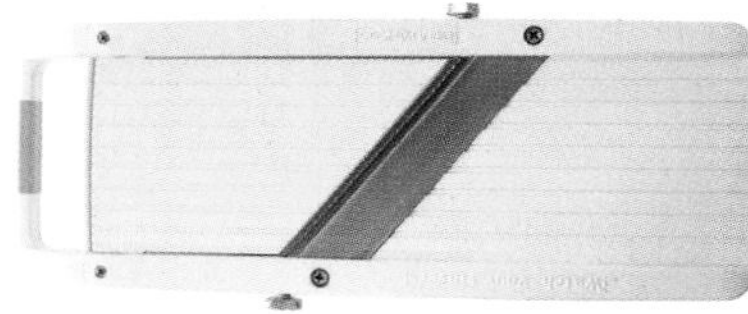

Fitted with either a straight or serrated blade, this accessory is used to cut all kinds of fruits and vegetables uniformly into fine slices, chips, or batons. Adjustable models let you vary the width of the cut.

MELON BALLER

This hemispherical implement lets you scoop balls out of firm fruit and vegetables.

Also known as a Parisienne scoop, it lets you remove the core from apple halves or make balls from their flesh. The sharp edge of the scoop lets you easily remove the choke from raw artichokes.

Melon ballers come with scoops of different diameters, the most common being 25 mm – 1 inch.

MIXING BOWL

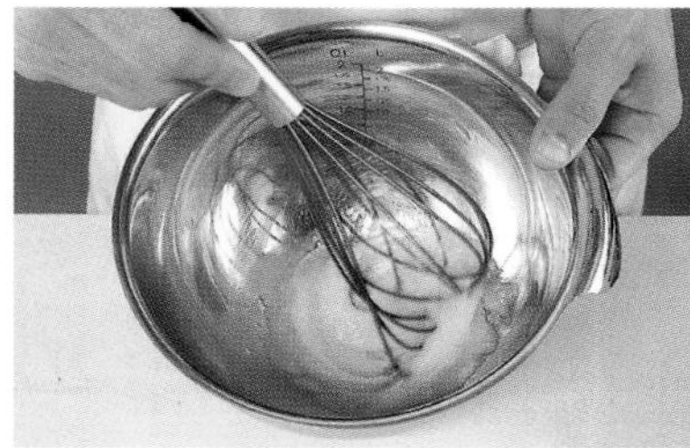

This container with a round bottom and curved rim, designed for pouring without splashing, is ideal for mixing preparations and cooking over a bain-marie. It is generally made from stainless steel, although it also comes in aluminum or brass.

ROUND AND SQUARE (RING) MOLDS

A mold is used to shape a preparation, typically a cold one consisting of different layers.

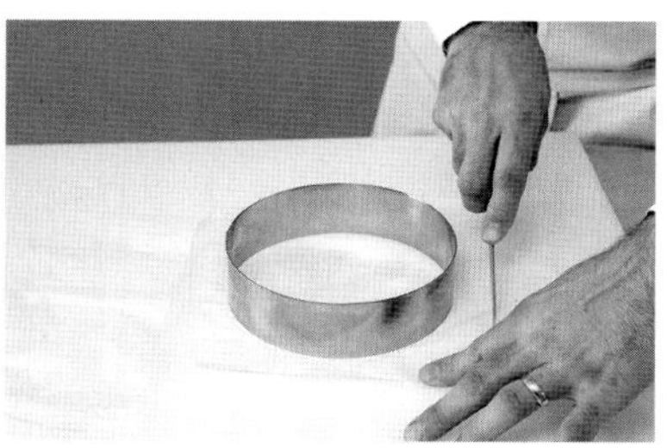

MORTAR AND PESTLE

The mortar and pestle are quintessentially Mediterranean utensils. There is nothing better than a heavy mortar (for steadiness) for use with a likewise heavy pestle (for better pounding) if you want to make a good aïoli, rouille, pesto, or harissa.

OVEN

The temperatures given in this book are for conventional (static) ovens. Reduce the temperature by 20°C – 25°F for a convection (fan-assisted) oven.

Convection ovens circulate the hot air around the food, cooking more efficiently and evenly, but are most often found in professional kitchens.

Calibrate your oven temperature and test often, as older oven models tend to be less powerful. While cooking, don't open the oven door: This will cause the oven temperature to fall.

(EN) PAPILLOTE

In addition to adding interest and appeal, cooking and presenting dishes "en papillote" preserves all the flavors of a product as the result of the gentle cooking process. Pouches made from parchment (baking) paper are the best. This material is impermeable, withstands a certain level of heat, and provides good insulation. For more stylish pouches, line the outside of the parchment paper with aluminum foil (so that the foil does not come into contact with the food). Use enough paper so that when food is placed in the middle, it is not tightly packed, and so that the pouch can puff up when cooking. Closing the pouch well is key to success with this style of cooking.

Instructions

Lay out sheets of parchment paper measuring about 40 x 50 cm – 15 3/4 x 19 1/2 inches. Place the food in the middle of each.

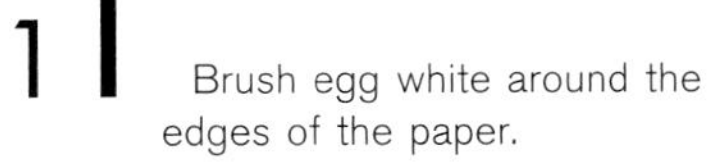

1 Brush egg white around the edges of the paper.

2 Take the side nearest to you and fold over to the other side.

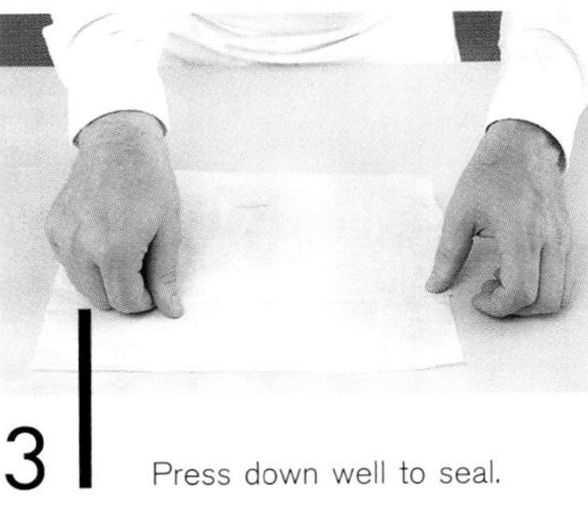

3 Press down well to seal.

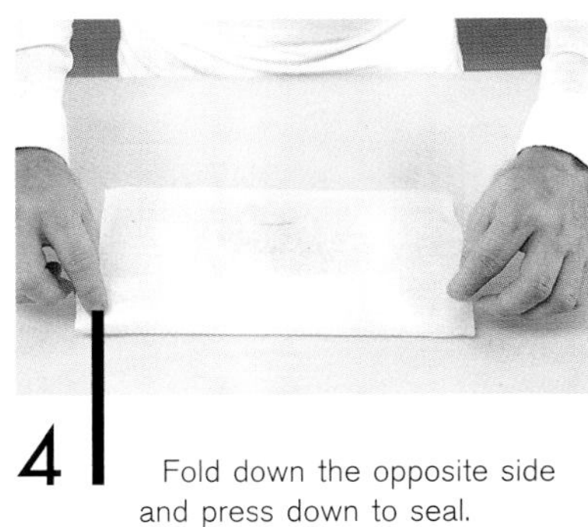

4 Fold down the opposite side and press down to seal.

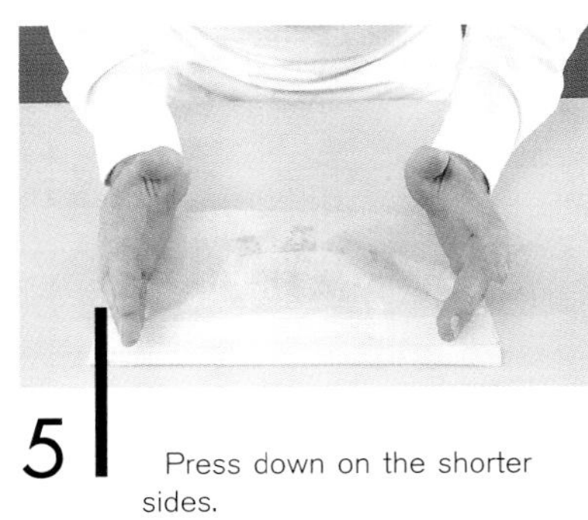

5 Press down on the shorter sides.

6 Brush with egg white along the longer side as well.

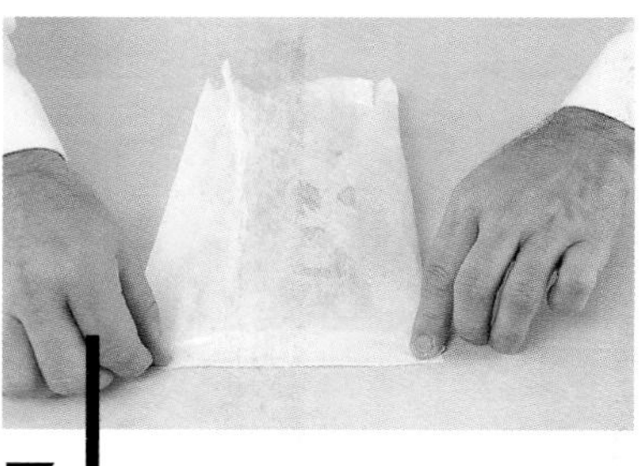

7 Fold the small sides over, brush with egg white, and fold a second time.

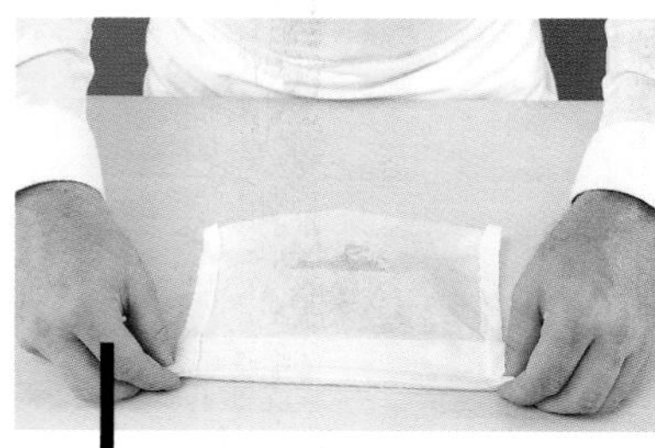

8 Do the same with the longer side.

9 Use a wide spatula (slotted turner) to transfer the pouch to a baking sheet (tray). Your "en papillote" preparation is ready to cook.

Like a pro

Egg white makes an excellent glue for both dough and parchment (baking) paper. Beat lightly with a fork before applying with a pastry brush. Note: Egg white dries very quickly.

PARING KNIFE

This small pointed knife has many uses: cutting, scooping, splitting, and so on. It will become your best friend.

PASTRY (PIPING) BAG

A pastry bag is probably not the first thing you rush out to buy when learning to cook or bake, but once you've gotten one and learned to use it, you won't be able to live without it. It is essential for perfectly preparing and filling choux puffs and éclairs, decorating cakes, spreading cream, and filling certain types of Italian pasta.

More specifically, a pastry (piping) bag is a large flexible and waterproof triangular bag (it can be made from paper, cloth, or a synthetic material), to which a tip (nozzle) is attached. Different tips are used for different purposes.

Choose tips made of chrome-plated stainless steel rather than aluminum ones, which can alter the flavor of certain products, or tips made from synthetic materials (their quality often leaves much to be desired). Pastry bags, either washable or single-use, are sold in most supermarkets. Wash both bag and tip between uses with different preparations, or have several bags handy to save time.

Pastry tips, whether plain or fluted (also known as "star"), are numbered. The number corresponds to the tip's diameter, which is a good indicator of its use.

1

Insert the tip inside the bag. Slide it to the end. Cut off the corner with scissors. Push the end of the tip through the hole. With your finger, push the bag into the tip to block the opening temporarily while you fill the bag.

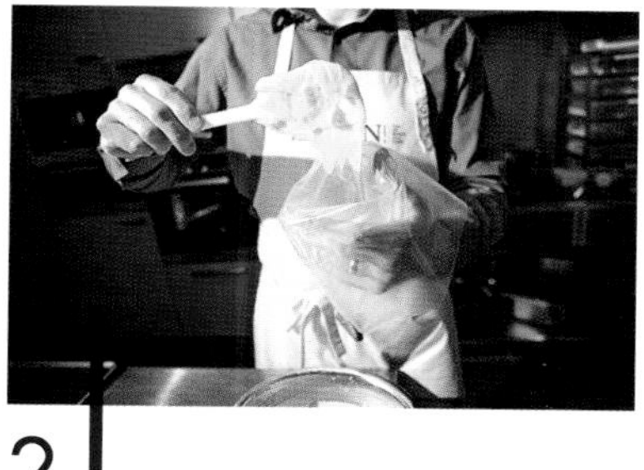

2

Fold 15–20 cm – 6–8 inches of the bag over your hand. Use a silicone spatula or a spoon to fill the bag about one third full.

3

Unfold the open end and twist the bag to contain the filling.

4

Unblock the tip so that the filling can pass through it. Squeeze the bag to push the filling down, pressing firmly so no air enters.

5

Twist the empty part and wrap it around your finger, at the top of the filling.

6

For éclairs, bring the tip very close to the baking sheet and pipe short lines in staggered rows, holding the bag at a 45-degree angle. At the end of each line, straighten the bag vertically and make a quarter twist to the left to cut the flow of batter.

7

For choux puffs, bring the tip very close to the baking sheet and hold the bag upright to pipe the batter. Turn sharply to cut the flow of batter.

8

For macaron shells, finish piping each shell by giving the pastry bag a quarter twist to cut the flow of batter.

9

To fill the bottom of a cream puff or profiterole with ice cream, gently pipe in a circular motion. Take your time. The important thing is that the ice cream cover the entire bottom of the puff so that it won't collapse afterward.

PASTRY BRUSH

An essential utensil for cooking, the pastry or basting brush lets you glaze a preparation with beaten egg yolk so that it will turn a wonderful golden color when cooked, grease oven racks with oil, and remove excess flour or sugar. It is a good idea to have two of them in different sizes with special bristles for cooking (dishwasher safe).

Try brushing down the sides of a pot or pan with a wet brush to dissolve any caramelized juices sticking to them; they can burn and add a bitter taste to your preparation.

PEELER

A must for peeling, a peeler removes just the right amount of peel or skin while leaving the flesh intact. They come in several different sizes. There are peelers with very narrow blades to peel more finely: these are used for carrots, potatoes, and citrus zest. Others have wider blades that can be used for removing the harder skin of asparagus, or for turnips, which have two layers of skin.

PRESSURE COOKER

The famous French physicist Denis Papin is credited with inventing the forerunner to the pressure cooker. In 1679, he invented a pot with a safety valve and a tightly fitting lid locked in place with a bar and screw. He considered his invention, which he named a "Digester," a tool for combating starvation, because it offered, as the title of the treatise he published in 1682 put it, "the means to soften bones and cook all manner of meats in little time and inexpensively; with a description of the machine which is to be used for this purpose, etc." Nevertheless, 250 years would pass before the first pressure cooker reached stores.

To ensure the success of your dish and your safety, it is essential that you follow the instructions for closing, operating, and opening the pressure cooker.

Do not add more liquid than indicated in the recipe, because it does not evaporate off during the cooking process. Never exceed the maximum level indicated inside the pressure cooker.

To prevent food particles from adhering to the pressure cooker and burning, clean the sides of the pot with a brush moistened in hot water when cooking without the lid.

SCALE

This piece of equipment is required for weighing out ingredients. Precise measures are essential in pastry-making if a recipe is to work. Digital scales are preferable because they are much more accurate.

SILICONE SPATULA

This spatula is ideal for stirring a preparation that risks sticking to the bottom of a pan, such as caramel.

This flexible spatula can scrape out all of the contents, leaving nothing behind—no waste. Care is needed when cooking at very high temperatures. Check that the spatula you are using can be used for cooking, or use a wooden spoon.

STRAINER (SIEVE)

An instrument with a very fine mesh that is used to filter a preparation, but also to push through solids to make them creamier or to prevent the formation of lumps. A strainer (sieve) may be round with a handle or flat (drum-shape flour strainer or sieve) for thicker preparations.

SUSHI: SPECIFIC TOOLBOX

– Metal chopsticks for plating.
– Square pan for making rolled omelet.
– Brush for preparing the omelet.
– Rice cooker.
– Flat wooden bowl for preparing the rice.
– Bamboo mat for making maki rolls.
– Sushi molds: These are very popular in Japan and come in different shapes (triangles, circles, and so on). They are used to make the playful and symbolic preparations that are so popular in Japan and are often included in bentos (lunch boxes) to brighten someone's day.

(COOKING) THERMOMETER

A cooking thermometer is a professional tool specifically for use in the kitchen. The most commonly available thermometer is a digital probe thermometer. It enables you to measure the internal temperature of foods accurately, which is particularly helpful when cooking certain delicate foods (such as foie gras).

The thermometer is inserted gently into the center of the preparation. Avoid touching the bottom of the pan or pot, because this will give a false reading. Leave it for several seconds, take it out, and check the temperature immediately. (A candy thermometer, used for measuring the temperature of sugar syrups and oil for deep-frying, is designed to remain in the pot and may have a higher temperature range than an all-purpose thermometer. An oven thermometer, as the name indicates, is used to measure oven temperature accurately and can be left in the oven indefinitely.)

A thermometer is an excellent investment that allows you to work precisely when preparing meat, syrups, and crème anglaise, among other items.

WEIGHT AND SMALL BOARD

These two utensils are essential in order to press a terrine and prevent air bubbles from forming in the fat. You need a small, rigid wooden board or piece of stiff cardboard that fits snugly inside the terrine dish in order to ensure even pressing. The weight should be neither too light nor too heavy – 300 g – 10–11 ounces will be sufficient. It is placed on the board to press the terrine. Use the type of cast iron or brass weight that is used with a traditional scale, or simply use something from the cupboard, such as a jar or can.

1 Cut a piece of cardboard to the size of the terrine dish.

2 Wrap in plastic wrap (cling film), then in aluminum foil.

3 Finish with another layer of plastic wrap.

4 Your board is ready for use.

5 Wrap the weight (which might be a jar or can) as you did the board.

INFORMATION ABOUT BASIC INGREDIENTS

FRUIT AND VEGETABLES

ALMONDS

Preparation

Almonds of all type are used in cooking. Green almonds are especially good to use. They can be opened easily by cutting them in half with a sharp knife (if the shell resists, open very carefully with a nutcracker).

Remove the almond halves from the shell with a knife tip. Detach the skin with a knife tip, starting at the pointed end. Pull the skin off.

Use for any recipe that calls for peeled green almonds.

Tips from our chefs

If you use dried almonds, poach them for 10 minutes in boiling milk before peeling. They will come to be whiter than if poached in water.

APPLE

Varieties

There are thousands of apple varieties on record, some of which are very old, but today many of these are no longer grown. At most, there are about a dozen varieties widely available.

They are traditionally classified as "eating apples" or "cooking apples," but many of them are as good raw as they are cooked. Cider apples have a sour taste that makes them unsuitable for other uses.

- **Golden delicious** is the most common variety. This is the apple of the modern age, and it has expanded its reach with the growth of supermarkets. It originated in North America as a chance seedling, but its adaptability has made it popular all over the world. Its yellow flesh is juicy and very sweet, but perhaps a little bland. It is good for use in pies and tarts, because it stays firm when cooked.

- **Pink lady** is named for its distinctive color. This Golden Delicious hybrid has a stronger flavor.

- **Reine de reinette**, known in English as the King of the Pippins, is one of the oldest French apple varieties. It is also considered to be the best. While biting into its coarse and slightly bitter skin is less inviting, its flesh is very tasty and filled with fresh flavor. It is delicious raw, but equally perfect for making compotes, jams, chutney, and sauces. It is a good choice for pastries, because it softens very quickly.

- **Reinette grise du Canada**, a younger sister to the Reine de Reinette, is increasingly found on the shelves in stores.

- **Chanteclerc** or **belchard**, another relative of the Reine de Reinette, is the result of crossing the Golden Delicious with the Reinette Clochard. Its fine, crisp, and slightly acidic flesh is very aromatic.

- **Gala**, originating in New Zealand, is a somewhat large apple. Its skin is almost completely covered with orange and bright red over a yellow background. Its flesh is juicy and very sweet.

- **Royal gala**, a close relative of the Gala, is redder.

- **Braeburn** is a very round apple, with smooth and shiny skin colored dark red over a pale green background. Sweet and juicy, it is an excellent eating apple.

- **Granny smith** owes its name to the Australian grandmother who grew this variety in her garden in the late nineteenth century. This variety with incomparably shiny, bright green skin is greatly appreciated for its crisp, juicy, and slightly tart flesh. It can be pan-fried in slices or quarters with its skin, or served raw in a salad. Remember to drizzle it with lemon juice, because its white flesh oxidizes particularly fast.

- **Fuji**, as its name indicates, is native to Japan. Its very sweet flesh is crisp and full of juice.

- **Nashi**, also a native of Japan, resembles a cross between an apple and a pear; it looks like the former but tastes like the latter.

- **Cox's orange pippin** has reddish orange skin and sweet yellow flesh that melts in the mouth. It is one of the best eating apples.

- **Starking**, with bright and shiny scarlet skin, has a reputation for flesh that is sometimes mealy.

Perfect matches

- **Sweet apples**
  These combine well with slightly sour fruit. While spices such as cinnamon, nutmeg, and cloves accentuate their flavor, they in turn sweeten certain spicy foods, such as curries.
- **Tart apples**
  These are a perfect accompaniment for strongly flavored meats, such as game, or fatty meats, such as pork and blood sausage (black pudding), which they make easier to digest.
- **Mild apples**
  These tone down the sharp flavors of certain vegetables (celery, red cabbage) or marinated or smoked fish (salmon). They enhance the flavor of certain cheeses: apple stuffed with Camembert is a classic.
- **Cooking apples**
  The best cooking companion for apples is butter; a tablespoon or so is enough to make them even tastier. They also combine well with honey, brown sugar, and caramel, which is essential for tarte Tatin.

Tips from our chefs

Don't miss out on the nutritional goodness of apple skin (vitamins and fiber) or its flavor. Salads with raw apples, baked apples, and tarts are among the many dishes that showcase the entire apple.

Save the skins and wrap them in a small bundle in gauze. Because they are high in pectin, a natural gelling agent, they are useful for making compotes, mousses, and jams.

Apple flesh exposed to air oxidizes quickly and turns an unappealing rust color. If you are not going to cook a peeled apple immediately, drizzle it with lemon juice. For fruit salad, prepare a syrup in advance and pour it cold over the apples.

Preparation

Peeling an apple with a paring knife.

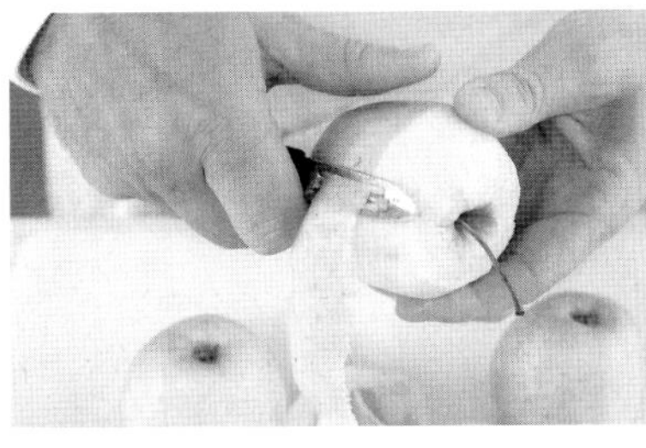

Start from the top, lifting off a thin ribbon of skin. Continue peeling by gradually turning the fruit. Finish at the bottom.

- **Coring an apple with a melon baller.**

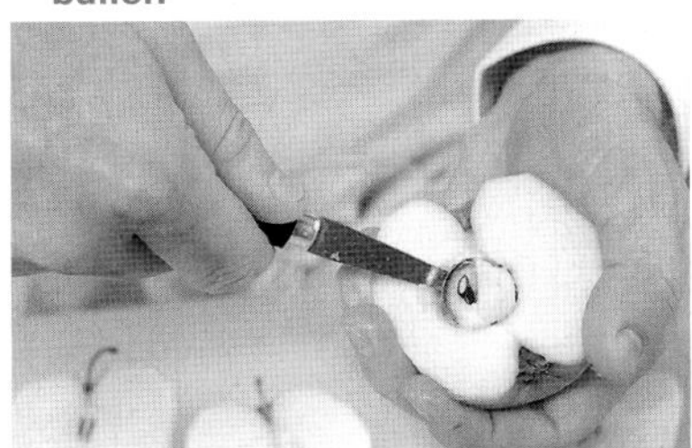

Cut the apple in half with a very sharp knife. Lift out the top and bottom of the core with the melon baller. Lift out the core and seeds by turning the melon baller around.

- **Coring an apple with an apple corer.**

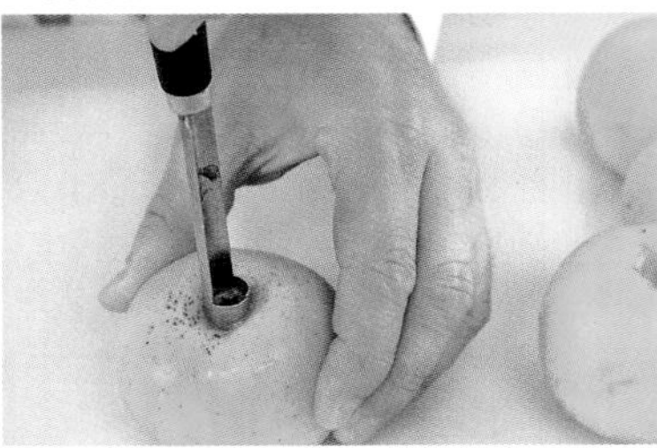

Stand the apple corer upright on top of the apple. Push it right down to the bottom and turn 360 degrees. Pull out the corer; it will be filled with the core and seeds. Remove them from the corer with the tip of a knife. The apple is now ready to be filled with raisins, berries, or even almond cream.

Cutting

- **Balls**

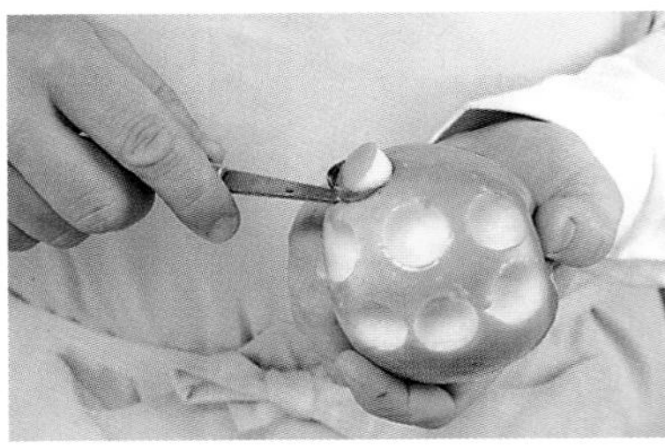

Use a melon baller, making one fast and complete rotation. Remove the ball. Do the same for the rest of the balls.
Use the remainder of the apples (peeled) for jam (page 82).

- **Matchsticks**

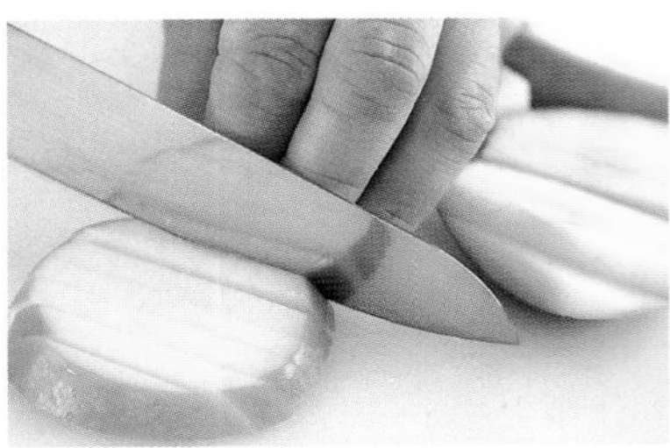

Cut off the bottom to form a base. Cut vertical slices. Before you get to the seeds, start on another side and continue in the same way. You will be left with the core as a rectangular block. Then cut each slice into uniform matchsticks.

- **Diced**

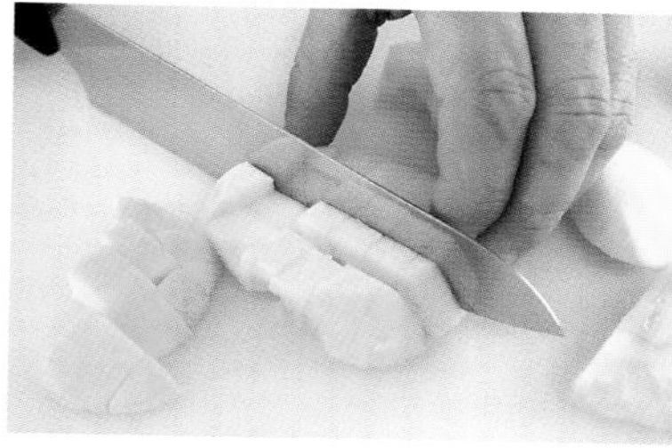

Cut off the bottom to form a base. Cut vertical slices. Cut each slice into uniform batons. Cut across to obtain dice.

- **Fine slices**

Core the apple with an apple corer. Place the apple on a mandoline and cut into fine slices with a back and forth motion, holding the mandoline at an angle.

- **Grated**

Place the apple on a mandoline and grate with a back and forth motion. Just before you reach the seeds, start on another side. Continue to grate. Repeat the process until only the core is left.

- **Flower**
  Cut very thin rounds with the mandoline. Fold each one over without breaking. Hold a folded slice between your thumb and index finger, then place another one next to it, overlapping. Continue until you have a flower.

BELL PEPPER

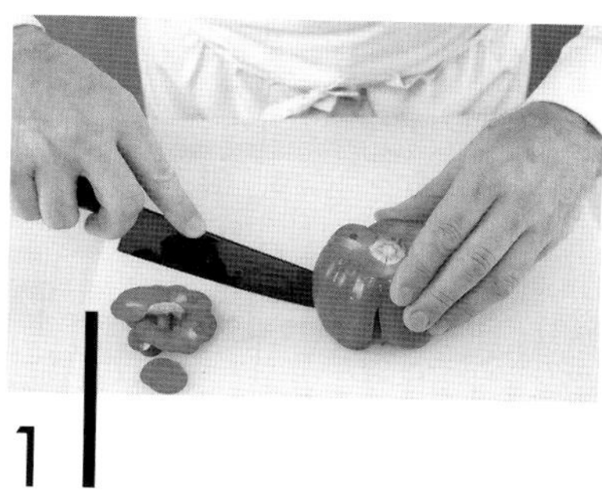

1

2

3

Cutting

The best way to cut a vegetable is to let its shape guide you. In the case of a bell pepper, follow the ribs from the bottom of the stem (stalk)—the thin lines that separate it into lobes—in order to obtain even pieces. Cut the flesh around the core, again following the grooves, then peel the pieces with a peeler.

Peeling a bell pepper

There are two different ways to peel peppers, depending on their shape. If the piece is flat and even, lay it flat on the work surface and pass the knife under the skin; if it is irregular, hold the piece in your hand when peeling.

CITRUS FRUIT

Rolling, squeezing

To get more juice, roll a lime over the work surface before squeezing. If you don't have a lemon squeezer, squeeze the fruit over a fine-mesh strainer (sieve) to catch the seeds.

Zesting

When you need to use the zest, always purchase organic, unwaxed fruit. This should be specified on the packaging. Start by carefully washing and drying the fruit.

To remove the zest from an orange (or other citrus), use a peeler and don't take off any pith (white). To make cutting into fine strips easy, lay the ribbons of zest flat, skin side down, against the work surface.

To remove any bitterness, put into a saucepan, add cold water to cover, and bring to a boil. Drain and let cool. The zest is now "blanched."

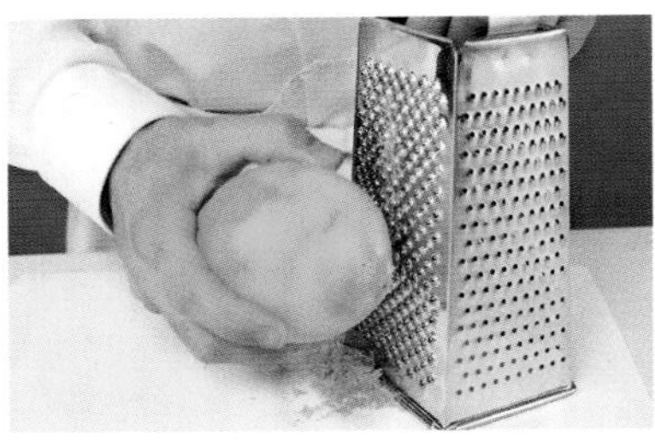

You can find small zesters with or without handles, which are very practical. You can also use a cheese grater or the smallest holes on a box grater. It is often necessary to use a brush to remove the grated zest that gets caught in the holes. Be careful not to skin your fingertips.

Supreming

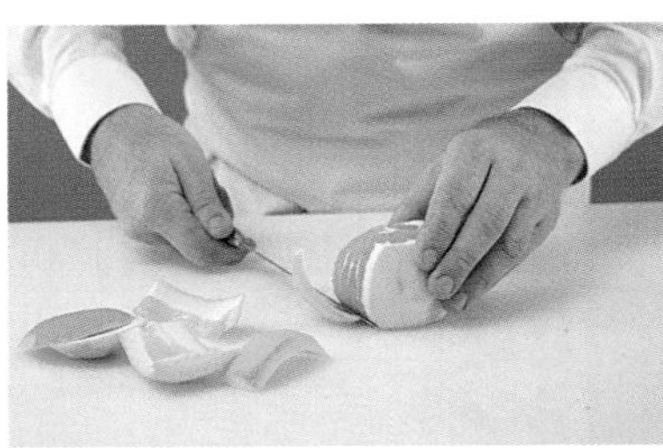

Once the zest has been removed, cut off the top and bottom of the orange. Stand it upright, with the core vertical. Cut off the skin, exposing the flesh.

Sectioning

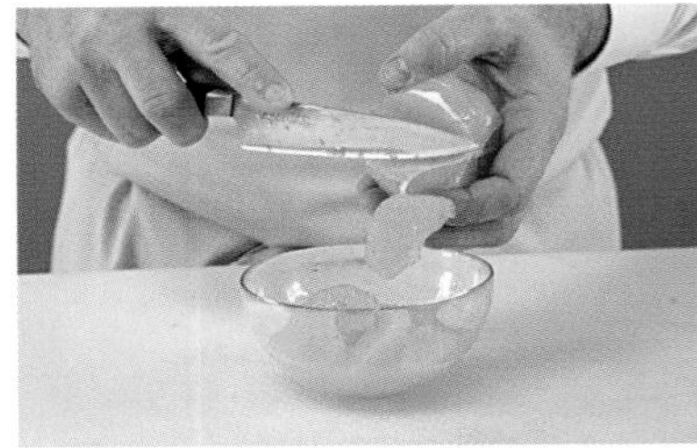

Once the skin has been removed completely, insert the blade of a very sharp paring (or fillet) knife between the section (segment) and the fine membrane surrounding it. Do the same with the remaining membrane, then push outward to completely detach the supremed section.

FENNEL

Characteristics and seasons

Typical of southern France, fennel has a delicate aniseed-like flavor. Its appearance varies depending on the season: a straight, long, and flat bulb sold in bunches in spring; a little fleshier in summer; fully rounded in the fall.

Preparation

The larger the bulbs, the more necessary it is to remove strings from the outer layers. Olive oil, Parmesan cheese, olives, and tomatoes make the best accompaniments for fennel.

Buying

A fennel bulb should always be very white, without stains or blemishes, and its green fronds (the feathery leaves) should be very pungent; they can be used as a substitute for tarragon.

Storing

Fennel keeps for seven days in the crisper drawer of the refrigerator, preferably in an airtight container.

Cutting

1

2

3

4

Cut off the fronds and the bottom of the fennel bulb. Remove the outer layer.

Halve the bulb. Remove the core.

Slice with a mandoline into a bowl.

Fill the bowl with cold water and ice cubes to crisp up the slices.

MANGO

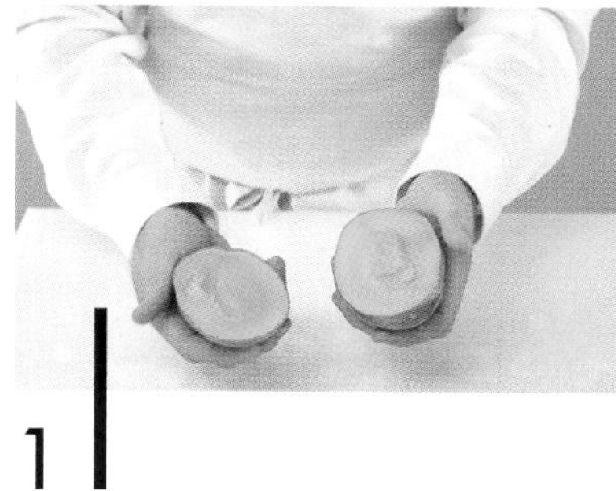

1

2

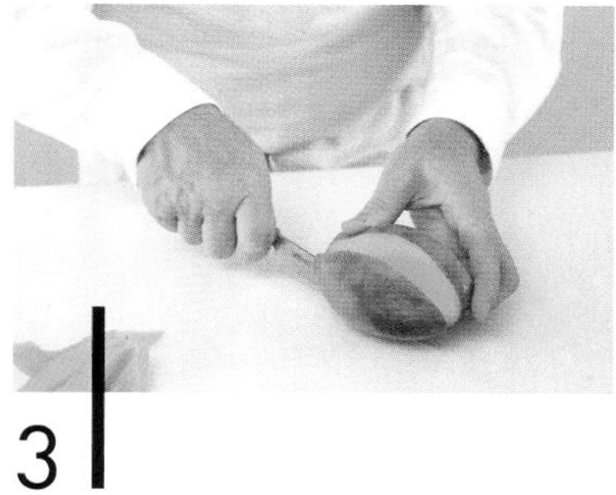

3

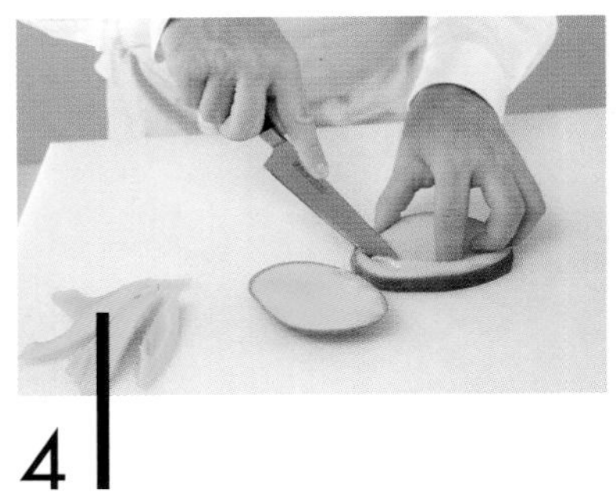

4

Cut the mango in half, guiding the knife along the pit (stone), then cut into slices. Peel the mango slices by passing the knife between the flesh and the skin. Finally, remove the flesh from around the pit.

MUSHROOMS

Rather than washing mushrooms in water, cut off the part of the stem (stalk) covered in soil, then peel the cap; detach the skin with the tip of a paring knife, then gently pull upward from the bottom.

POIVRADE ARTICHOKE

Characteristics

An artichoke is the whole flower of a plant from the thistle family whose fleshy heart is not only edible, but quite tasty. The small Violet de Provence artichoke, grown in the south of France and in Brittany, is known as a poivrade artichoke when it is harvested slightly immature. Its choke is not fully formed.

Season

It is available in French markets from March to May, and again from September to December.

Buying

Choose poivrade artichokes that are compact, with the leaves tightly closed. Also make sure that the cut end of the stem (stalk) is still moist.

Storing

It can be kept for four to five days in the vegetable crisper drawer of the refrigerator.

Preparation

The tops of the leaves need to be cut off, because they are a little too firm to eat. However, the stem is delicious once peeled. French chefs often refer to it as *moelle* (marrow). Like other produce typical of southern France, raw and cooked poivrade artichokes are commonly combined with tomato, Parmesan cheese, and olive oil.

Artichokes tend to turn black when peeled due to oxidation, and that color can rub off on your hands, so rub your fingers with lemon juice or wear gloves when handling them. Soak artichoke hearts in water with lemon juice to avoid discoloration.

Cutting

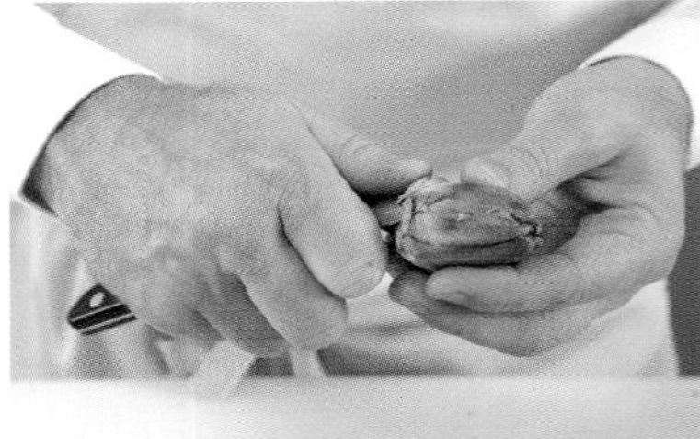

After shortening the stem and removing the tougher leaves by hand, turn (pare) all around the artichoke heart (with a paring knife or peeler), following its outline to remove all the hard and fibrous parts.

POTATO

Varieties

While the first, relatively insipid tubers were scorned, the potato today is the most commonly consumed vegetable. A large range of varieties has been created over time. Whereas some thirty varieties were known in 1800, the list today now includes more than 3,000. However, only about fifteen varieties predominate in French markets. Each variety responds best to a particular cooking method. Before buying, choose the potato that best suits the dish you want to prepare.

- **Agata:** An early variety available beginning in June, this has firm yellow flesh and is perfect for stewed and oven-cooked dishes.

- **Agria:** Available for eating from January to June, this variety is versatile, but its delicious flavor is particularly enhanced by steaming.

- **Belle de Fontenay:** One of the oldest French varieties, this is found as a new potato in June and keeps well until March. Its firm flesh has a nutty flavor.
- **BF 15:** A Belle de Fontenay hybrid, this potato has firm flesh that makes it perfect for roasting, steaming, and frying, among other preparations.

- **Bintje:** The most widely grown variety in France has mealy flesh that makes it perfect for French fries. It is also excellent in purees and thick soups.

- **Charlotte:** Oblong in shape and with a thin skin, this variety holds up well to cooking. It makes a tasty baked (jacket) potato, and is delicious in salads.
- **Estima:** This firm variety has star billing in gratin dauphinois, together with Belle de Fontenay and Mona Lisa.

- **Mona lisa (also known as Monalisa):** Quite similar to the Bintje, but with a better consistency. Like the Bintje, it is perfect for French fries, but also mashed, in soup, and in gratin dishes.

- **Pompadour:** A cross between the Roseval and the BF 15, this potato has flesh suitable for salads, steaming, and pommes rissolées.

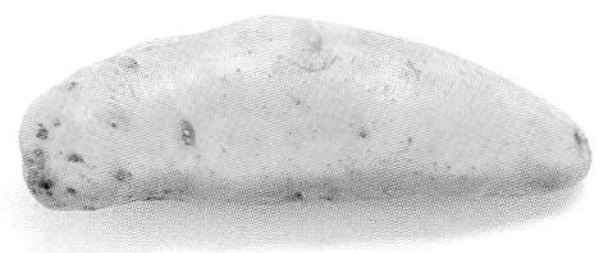

- **Ratte:** Early potato available between August and May. Make use of its firm, melt-in-your-mouth flesh for salads and for steamed or mashed potatoes.

- **Roseval:** The firm pink-striped yellow flesh of this potato has a very sweet flavor and is suitable for any recipe; keep it in its dark red skin if possible.

- **Vitelotte:** This old variety is almost black in color and has firm purple flesh. It makes a spectacular salad.

- **Sweet potato:** Long mistaken for a potato, this vegetable belongs to another South American species. Its soft flesh with a flavor akin to chestnut is delicious in purees, soufflés, and gratin dishes.

Preparation

- **Washing, brushing, peeling**

Potatoes often come covered in soil. Brush them (with a nail brush or vegetable brush) while washing, then rinse well.
Peel them with a paring knife. As a precaution, wear thin surgical gloves to prevent your fingers from turning black.
Immerse in cold water so that they can release their starch (except when otherwise indicated in the recipe). This will also stop them from turning black.

- **With or without starch**
Potatoes that are going to be fried need to lose their starch. Pommes Darphin—the French version of hash browns—on the other hand, need this natural glue in order to hold their shape. You should soak the potatoes in water or prepare them in any other way indicated as soon as they are peeled.

- **Preventing oxidation**
Potatoes oxidize and turn black upon contact with the air. After peeling and cutting, let them soak in water just before cooking. But if you need to wait, blanch them by immersing in boiling water, then refresh or shock them immediately in cold water.

- **Shrinkage**
Potatoes lose water when cooked and shrink. Follow the amounts indicated in your recipe and take this loss into account.

- **Focus on butter**
Potatoes and butter are a perfect combination. But pay close attention when using butter; clarify the butter to stop it from burning in the pan (page 546).

- **Waste nothing**
Use potato scraps (trimmings) to make a soup, and use leftover mashed potatoes to make a soufflé. Have you oversteamed your potatoes? Make them into a salad or serve them in bite-sized pieces as appetizers.

Cutting

- **Uniform slices**

Potato slices need to be of a uniform size in order to cook evenly. First, choose medium potatoes. Round them off a little with a knife, if necessary. Adjust the mandoline blade to make 3–4-mm – 1/8-inch thick round slices or cut the potatoes with a wide chef's knife. In this case, fold your fingertips under so you don't cut yourself.

- **Fries (thick-cut)**

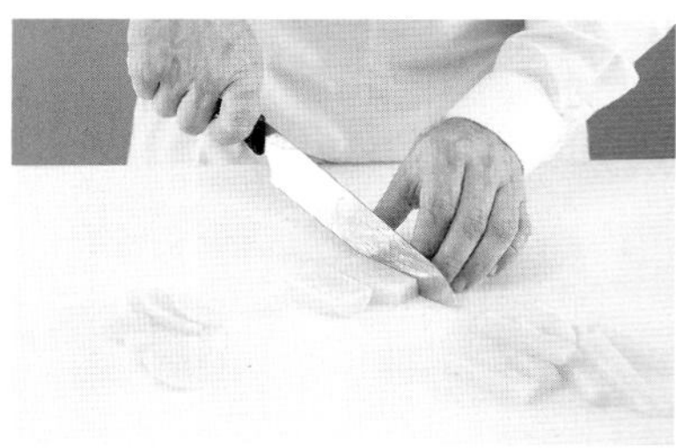

Cut a slice from the four sides of the potato to square it. Cut the potato lengthwise into about 1-cm – 1/2-inch slices. Lay the slices flat and cut into batons.

- **Matchstick potatoes**
Cut a slice from the four sides of the potato to square it. Adjust the mandoline blade to cut matchsticks. Slide the potato over the blade with a back and forth movement.
You can cut matchsticks in different sizes; the largest are appropriate for frying, and the thinnest can be used to make pommes Darphin.

- **Gaufrette potatoes**

Cut a slice from the four sides of the potato to square it. Adjust the mandoline blade. Slide the potato over the blade with a back and forth movement.
Gaufrette potatoes are deep fried like chips (crisps). You can shape them into small baskets by placing slices between two small conical strainers before frying.

- **Pommes noisettes**

Use a melon baller to make small balls.
Let the balls stay in cold water if you plan to pan-fry them, or deep-fry immediately.
If you prepare the potato balls the night before or up to one hour before cooking, blanch them; immerse in boiling water, remove immediately, and place under cold running water.

- **Cylinders/Pommes Anna**

Cut two medium, elongated potatoes in half. Stand the pieces on their flat sides. Place a cookie cutter of the desired diameter on top of each potato half and push down. Push out the resulting potato cylinder. Soak the cookie cutter in water between each cut so that it slides easily.

- **Potato chips (crisps)**

Cut a slice from the two largest sides of the potatoes to flatten. Adjust the mandoline blade. Slide the potato over the blade with a back and forth movement.
If you leave Roseval potatoes unpeeled, your chips will be even prettier.

- **Diced**

Cut a slice from the two largest sides of the potatoes to flatten. Cut the potato lengthwise into thick slices. Cut each slice into batons. Cut again into uniform dice.

- **Château potatoes**

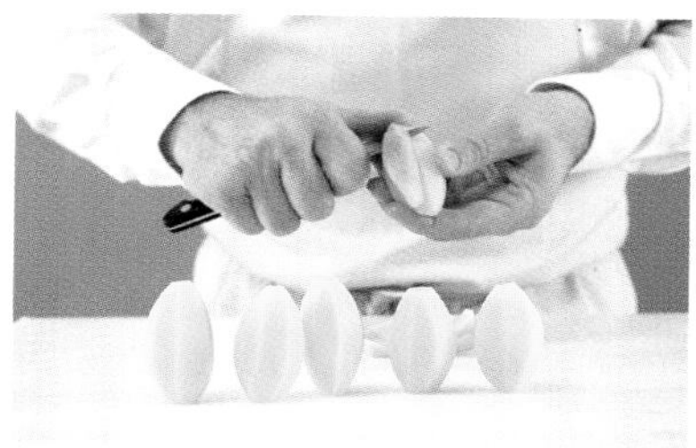

Choose small potatoes (about 5 cm – 2 inches long). Cut off the top and bottom and stand them upright.
Turn the potatoes, trimming into a barrel shape; use a paring knife to round off the flesh starting at the bottom and working your way toward the top.

- **Potato wedges**

Choose large, long potatoes. Cut off the bottom to make a base. Cut into quarters without peeling. Use a peeler to remove a strip of skin from the middle of each wedge to accentuate the rounded form. Remove the skin from the left side while rounding, and do the same on the right side. Remove the inner ridge along the entire length. Pan-fry these boat-shape wedges.

- **For stuffing**

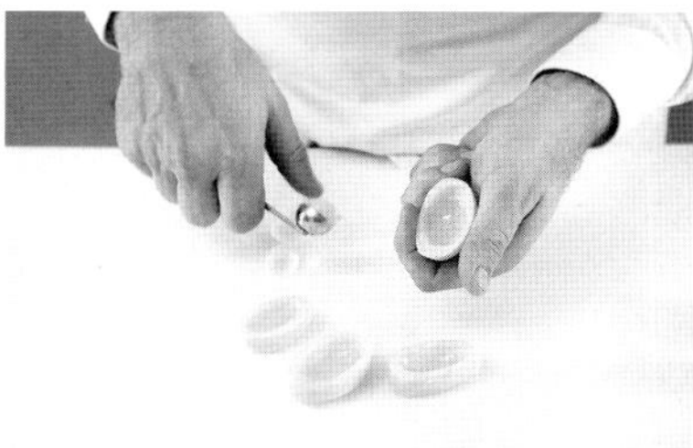

Cut a slice from the two largest sides of the potatoes to flatten. Cut them in half. Start to empty out the insides, using a melon baller.
Hollow them out well. They can be stuffed with meat, herbs, mushrooms, or even snails with parsley butter.

- **Marrow bone potatoes**

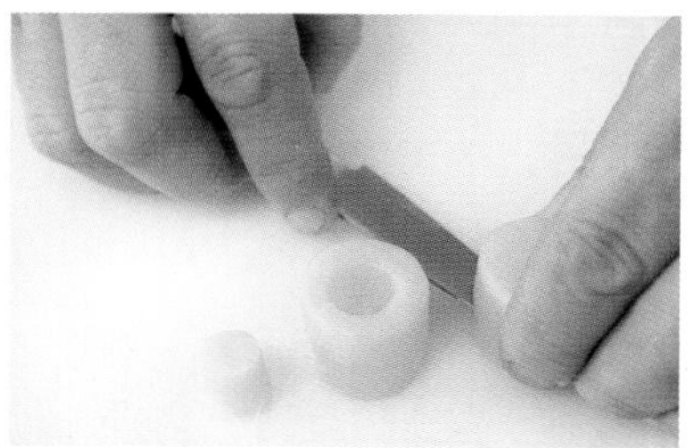

Cut two medium, long potatoes in half. Use a cookie cutter to make cylinders. Place an apple corer over the center of the cylinders. Push down, being careful to go only three quarters of the way through.
Insert a knife tip at the spot where the apple corer stopped in order to detach the base. Use the knife tip to remove the cylinder created by the apple corer.
The potato piece resembles a marrow bone. Fill it with bone marrow, mushroom duxelles, or foie gras.

- **Other cuts:**
  - **Bénédictine:** A spiral.
  - **Chatouillard:** A ribbon.
  - **Cheveu:** Very fine julienne strips.
  - **Delmonico or mirette:** Small dice.
  - **Paysanne:** Thick slices.
  - **Shavings:** Irregular ribbons.
  - **Collerette:** Similar to chips (crisps) but cut from a potato into which grooves have been cut with a knife.

RASPBERRIES AND OTHER BERRIES

Berries are delicate, and raspberries are the most delicate of all. To store, line a dish with paper towels, arrange the fruit on top with a fair amount of space between them and place in the least cold part of the refrigerator.

SPINACH

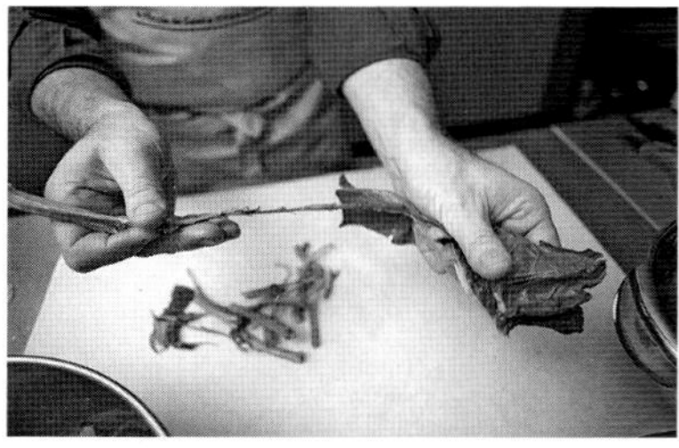

Preparation

Fold spinach leaves in half and remove the entire length of their ribs, starting from the stem (stalk).

To wash spinach leaves, soak them in a generous amount of cold water and swirl the water with your finger; centrifugal force causes the impurities to sink to the bottom, collecting in the middle of the basin. Drain and shake dry.

Tips from our chefs

When wilting the leaves, prick a garlic clove with the tines of a fork and use it to stir. The garlic will imbue the spinach with just enough of its flavor to enhance the preparation.

TOMATO

Peeling a tomato by blanching

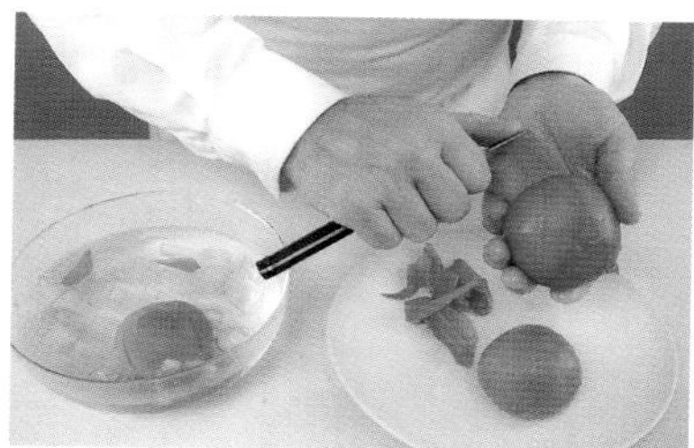

The skin of a tomato cannot withstand a sudden change between hot water and cold. Cut a cross in the tomato skin. Immerse in boiling water, then transfer to ice water. This technique is ideal for peeling a large number of tomatoes. Do not let them stay in the boiling water for more than 20 seconds or they will cook. Do only a few at a time so that the water will stay at the proper temperature.

Peeling a tomato with a knife

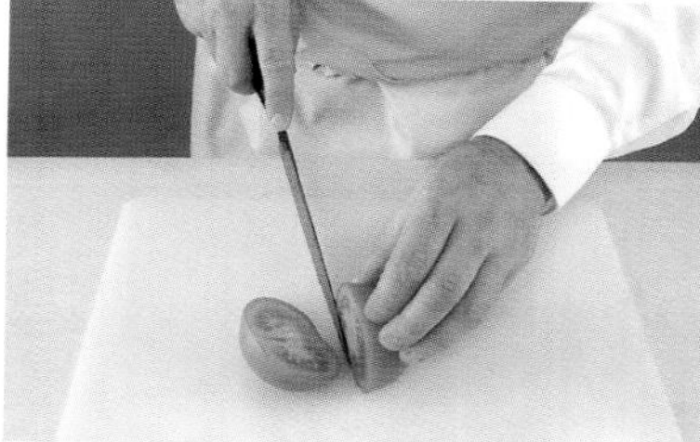

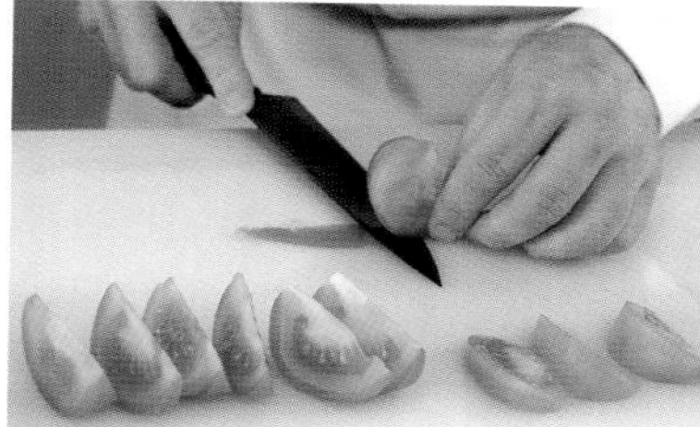

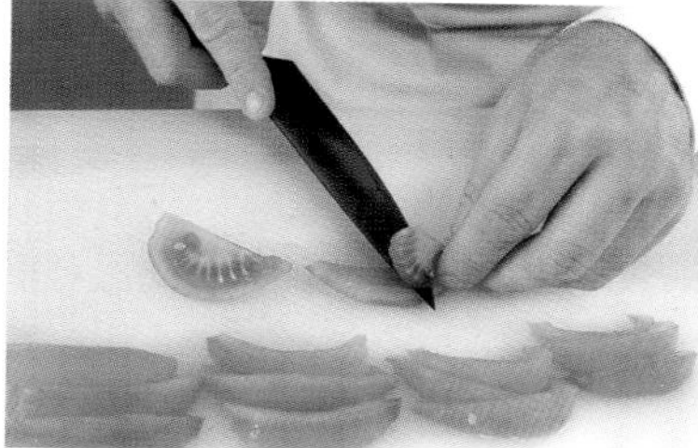

If you only have to peel one or two tomatoes, use this simple and fast method. Cut the tomatoes in half, then cut each half into six pieces. Sharpen your knife well, then slide it between the skin and the flesh, as if peeling a melon. Remove the seeds from each piece.

Hollowing out tomatoes

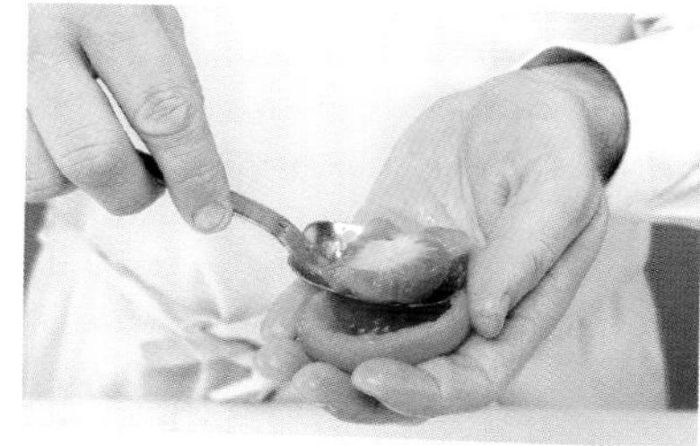

To hollow out tomatoes quickly, cut them in half. Use a soup spoon, turning it to remove the core and seeds without scooping out too much flesh.

If you want to keep the individual sections, use a demitasse spoon to scoop out the flesh.

TURNIP

Characteristics

The turnip is native to eastern Europe, where it grows wild. The ancient Romans were very fond of turnips, but they no longer enjoy the popularity they once had.

Season

Every season. In winter, no good duck dish should be missing caramelized turnips, and every pot-au-feu should be enlivened by the characteristic flavor of turnip. In spring, no jardinière platter is worthy of its name without baby turnips.

Did you know that shredded new turnips eaten raw have the delicate flavor of hazelnuts? And turnip greens are ideal for preparing rustic hearty soups.

Buying

Whatever the variety, color (white, yellow Boule d'Or, or purple), or shape (elongated, round, shaped like a top), this close relative of the cabbage and mustard should be firm and free of blemishes. It should also be heavy in relation to its size; there's nothing worse than a hollow turnip. But be careful: A very large turnip may turn out to be fibrous and unpleasantly spicy.

ZUCCHINI

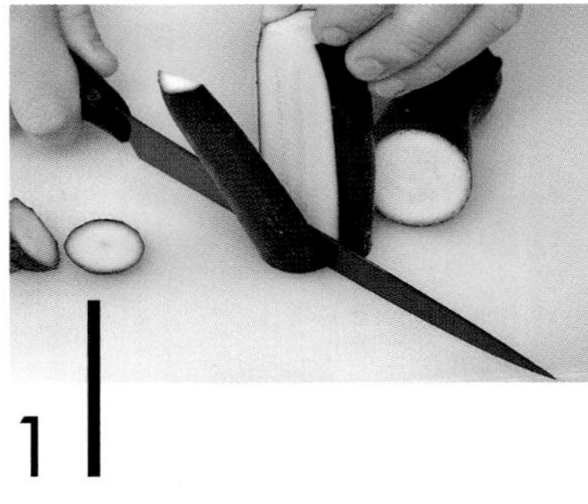

1

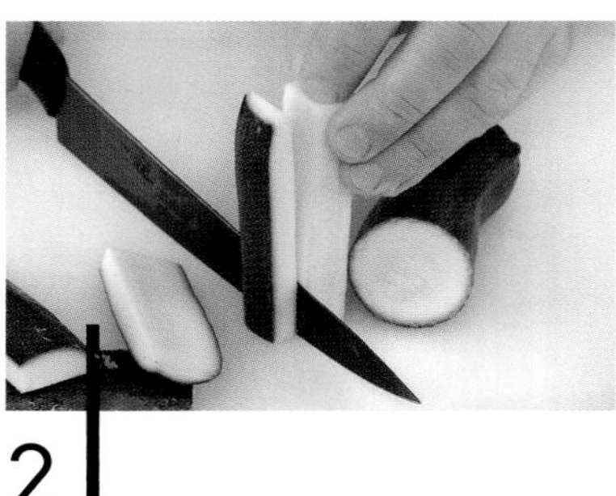

2

3

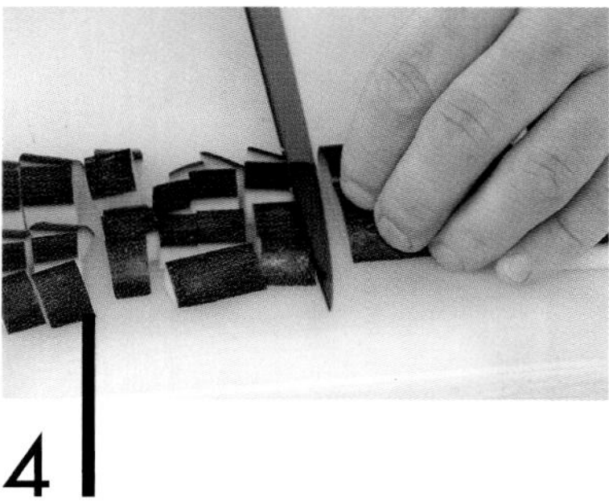

4

To cut a zucchini (courgette) into pieces in the size and shape of your choice, simply cut it in half, then make cuts lengthwise around the seeds. You will be left with the core and four rectangular strips of flesh.

It is then up to you to cut it as you like into batons, dice, slices, and so on.

ZUCCHINI FLOWER

The zucchini (courgette) flower is a particular specialty of the Alpes-Maritimes region of France. It is also proof of Mother Nature's genius. She offers us zucchini flowers in two genders: male and female. The latter can be easily identified by the baby zucchinis attached to them. These flowers are harvested between the month of April and the start of cold weather. Their delicate nature means the process is a fast one; picking takes place in the early morning, and the flowers are left in a cold, dark place with a certain level of humidity.

They should be prepared quickly after picking or purchase, because they are prone to wilting. Both male and female flowers can be enjoyed stuffed or as fritters.

Removing the pistils from zucchini flowers

Zucchini flower pistils should be removed. This is an easy process: Cut off the base of the flowers with a knife; then hold the pistil with your fingers and pull gently.

CONDIMENTS AND AROMATICS

BROTHS AND STOCKS

Characteristics

Liquid obtained by decoction—extraction by boiling—of substances from plants (vegetables, herbs, spices) or animals (meat, poultry). Such liquid is essential for imbuing certain dishes, such as risotto, with flavor. It should, therefore, match the solid ingredients used to make the dish.

Varieties

There are several different types of broths and stocks made from chicken, veal, or vegetables. Apart from homemade broths and stocks (the best kind), you can fine a wide range of concentrates, bouillon (stock) cubes (sometimes low fat), and powdered versions in stores. All concentrated broths and stocks should be diluted in water or wine. Always taste before adding to your dish, because concentrated broths and stocks are very salty.

FISH STOCK

Characteristics

Aromatic liquid prepared with the bones and scraps (trimmings) of chopped up fish, aromatics, and water or white wine. After straining and reducing, it is used as a base for sauces and for cooking fish and rice dishes containing fish or shellfish.

Varieties

Homemade fumets can contain fish, langoustines, mussels, and scallops. Powdered fumet can also be found concentrated; it should be diluted in water or wine.

Buying

Always read the label or packaging carefully to check the type of broth, stock, or fumet contained, and whether salt has been added. The leading brands are available at all grocery stores and supermarkets.

Storing

Concentrated broths and stocks should be stored in their packaging in a dry place. Homemade broths, stocks, and fumets can keep for three days in the refrigerator. They can also be reduced to a concentrate and frozen in tightly sealed containers or in ice cube trays. They should be used within six months.

GARLIC

Identifiable by its fresh skin, young garlic, or green garlic, has a very sweet flavor, letting you use large amounts at a time. Regular garlic, with dry skin, has a stronger flavor. Keep in mind that not all the cloves in one head of garlic are the same size.

Crushing garlic to a puree

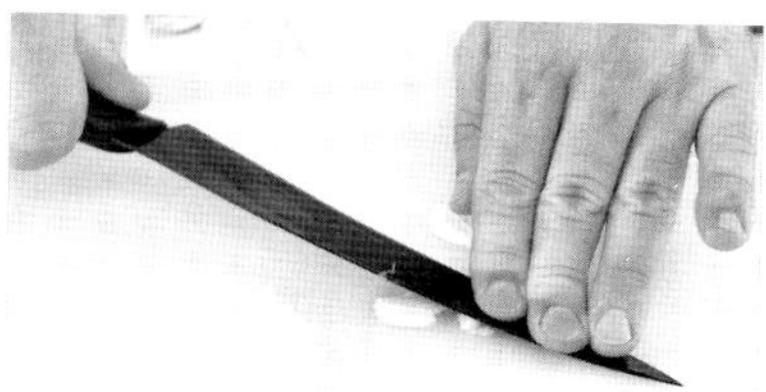

To puree garlic without using a garlic press, lay the flat side of a chef's knife over the clove and crush, then chop finely. Repeat a few times. Alternating the two actions (crushing/chopping) will result in a puree.

Peeling and removing the germ from garlic

Cut the garlic clove in half lengthwise and remove the skin. This makes the process easier. Then use a knife tip to remove the core or germ (this is identified by its pale green color) that is found at the center of each half clove. This way the garlic isn't as strong tasting and is easier to digest.

(FRESH) HERBS

Basil

Treat fresh basil, a noble plant, very gently; it is fragile, so its aroma fades quickly and its leaves bruise if handled roughly.

Mint

To chop fresh mint, in other words to cut fine strips, lay four leaves very flat, one on top of the other. Make one cut (without moving back and forth) to avoid tearing.

Parsley

Pile fresh parsley leaves in little bunches and cut with a chef's knife by rocking the blade from the tip to the rear. Do not do this too far in advance to prevent the fragrance of the parsley from fading.

Curly parsley is more decorative, but flat-leaf parsley has more flavor. It can be fried crisp in a little oil.

OLIVE OIL

The Greeks taught the natives of Provence the art of growing olive trees, harvesting the fruit, and extracting the oil.

Among the best-known varieties of olive grown in Provence, for eating or for making oil, are Berruguette, Cailletier (tiny Nice olives), Grossanne (large fleshy fruit), Lucques (originally from Italy), Picholine (large and fleshy), Salonneque (from Salon-de-Provence), Tanche (from Noyons and the Baronnies), and Verdale, also known as Verdale des Bouches-du-Rhone (fruit of a tree resembling a weeping willow).

The oil content of the fruit increases gradually as it ripens. A ripe olive is black and its oil content varies from 15 to 35%. A large number of olive oil mills are still active, allowing for high-quality oils to be produced—under the extra-virgin olive oil label—a number of which have won medals, and even enjoy *Appellation d'Origine Contrôlée* (Controlled Designation of Origin) or AOC status.

The level of acidity for these oils cannot exceed 1 g per 100 g or 1%. Their colors range from the color of straw to deep green. Their flavor (nutty or spicier) depends on certain parameters: soil and climate, date of harvesting, and the miller's skill. The choice of variety can be made according to preference and intended use.

ONION

Finely slicing an onion

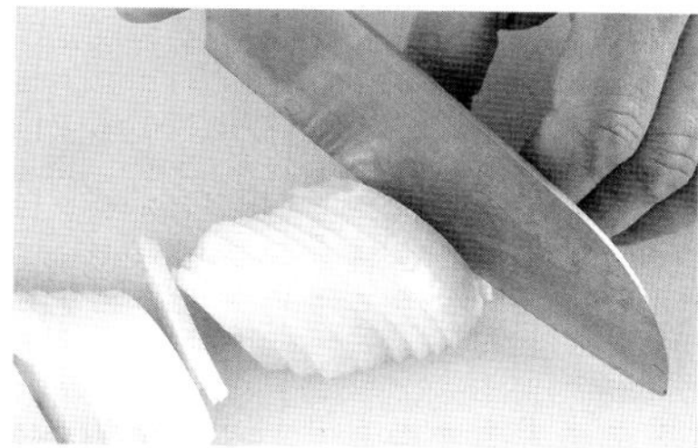

Using a perfectly sharpened knife, cut the onion in half quickly and cleanly to stop the juice, an irritant, from squirting into your eyes. Lay each half on its flat side on the work surface. Slice each half, being careful to fold your fingers inward, out of reach of the knife.

To cut onions without any tears, put the onions into a bowl of cold water before you peel them, or put them in the freezer for 20–30 minutes.

Chopping an onion

Cut the onion in half lengthwise. Put one half on its flat side on the work surface and hold it firmly with your hand. Use a chef's knife to make vertical slices lengthwise, without cutting through the root. Then make three horizontal cuts through the onion half. Finish by slicing crosswise.

Don't make the vertical and horizontal slices to the very end of the onion. Leave a space of about 1 cm – 1/2 inch uncut in order to hold the slices together and make it easier to finely chop the onion.

Do the same with shallots.

MOZZARELLA

A brief history

This cheese has been made in Italy since the Lombards introduced buffaloes from Asia in the sixth century.

Characteristics

This rindless, cooked pasta filata (stretched-curd) cheese has a mild and slightly tart flavor. It is sold in spheres, small braids, pearl-size balls, or knots in salted water or whey.

Buying

In the Latium (Rome) and Campania (Naples) regions only, mozzarella cheese is made with a very particular type of buffalo milk. It contains 52% fat and is protected by its *Denominazione di Origine Controllata* (Controlled Designation of Origin) or DOC status, which explains its creaminess—and its price. Mozzarella is made from cow's milk in the rest of Italy; this cheese is less soft, less fragrant, and slightly rubbery, and is mainly used in cooking, perhaps most famously on pizza, while buffalo mozzarella can be eaten as it is, drizzled with olive oil, seasoned with salt and pepper, or with tomato and basil.

PARMESAN

A brief history

This very old cheese was already being produced in Parma as far back as the Middle Ages. It was probably in 1612 that the mark for Parmesan was developed by the treasurer of the Farnese estates: "Parmigiano Reggiano" in small dots, plus the date of production imprinted in the rind of each wheel. Today, it enjoys *Denominazione di Origine Controllata* (Controlled Designation of Origin) or DOC status, which is strictly enforced.

Characteristics

Parmesan is a cooked pressed cheese with a hard and granular consistency and fruity taste, and with a naturally oily rind. Parmesan is produced in large wheels 35–40 cm – 14–16 inches in diameter and 18–25 cm – 7–10 inches thick and can weigh 24–40 kg – 53–88 pounds. It is made from the milk of cows fed on grass or hay, which is partly skimmed (32–40% fat).

Source

It is produced only in the Emilia-Romagna region (provinces of Parma, Reggio Emilia, Modena, Mantua, and Bologna) of Italy.

Denominations

It is known as *fresco* (young) when aged up to 18 months, *vecchio* (aged) when aged from 18 months to 2 years, *stravecchio* (extra-aged) when aged from 2 to 3 years, and *stravecchione* (long-aged) when aged for a longer time.

Season

Quality Parmesan is available throughout the year.

Buying

It is always preferable to buy Parmesan by the block instead of pre–shredded or grated. It should not be grated until the last minute in order to preserve all of its flavor. Besides, the grated cheese sold in bags in the fresh food aisles of supermarkets is quite often not real Parmesan. The rind should be smooth and the cheese fine, grainy, straw-colored, hard, crumbly, and brittle. Look for it at specialty cheese retailers or shops selling Italian products. This will also allow you to check the age of the cheese with the vendor.

Storing

Keep Parmesan wrapped in a damp cloth in the refrigerator.

RICE

Risotto rice

The development of rice–growing in Italy actually began in the sixteenth century, although there are theories that the ancient Romans were familiar with rice. The plague epidemics and famines of the Middle Ages were factors that led to the emergence of rice. Under the auspices of the monasteries, it was introduced to the Piedmont region, where the climate was particularly suitable. As a result, the Vercelli district became the largest rice-producing area of Italy. The rice paddies in the Po Valley are irrigated in the same way as those in China, making the countryside resemble the Far East.

Risotto rice varieties have round, semihard grains with a high starch content, which is better at absorbing liquid than long-grain varieties. Carnaroli, Arborio, and Vialone, classified as *riso superfino* (high-quality rice), are three varieties used to make a risotto worthy of its name.

Sushi rice

Japanese rice is white and round and becomes slightly sticky when cooked (which allows the sushi to retain its shape). This type of rice, known as Japonica, can be found at Asian grocery stores and is typically grown in California or Spain. (Japanese rice is not currently exported).

The grains should not be broken, and you should purchase the rice from a store with frequent turn-over.

MEAT AND POULTRY

CHICKEN

Cutting up a raw chicken

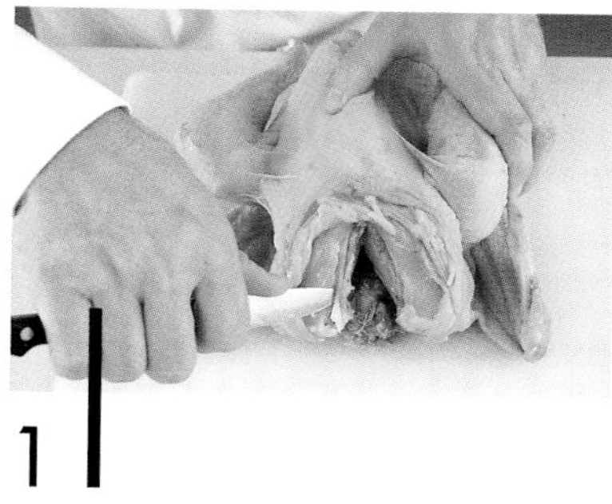

1

Put the chicken on its back on a cutting board. Lift up the skin of the neck and free the wishbone by scraping on one side and then on the other.

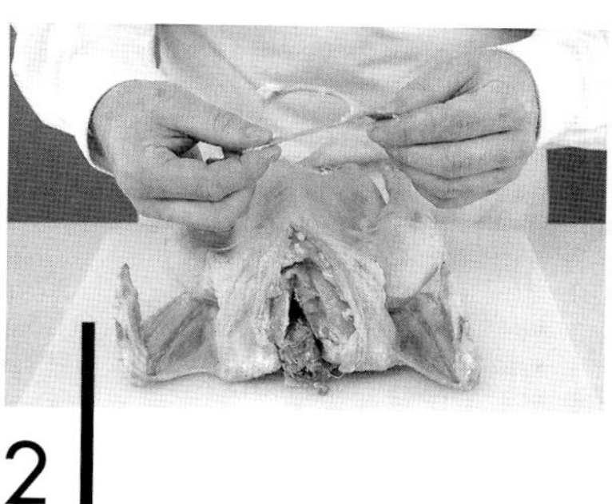

2

Cut along both sides of the wishbone at the neck joint to release the bone. Pull from the base (the bottom of the "V") and take out the bone. Close the chicken by pulling on the neck skin.

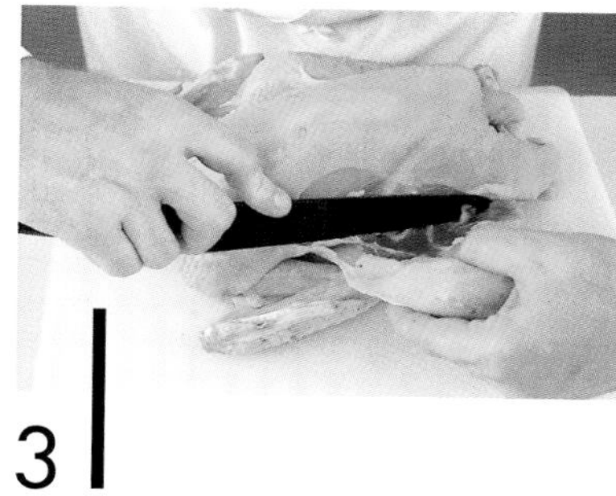

3

Slide the knife between the thigh and the breast to detach the leg quarter.
Dislocate the leg by hand (pull to make the round leg bone appear).

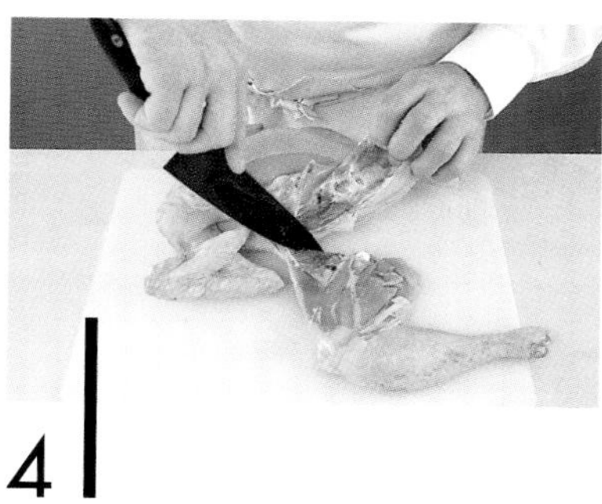

4

Cut at the hip joint and along the back as closely as possible so that you also detach the "oysters."

5

Do the same with the other leg.

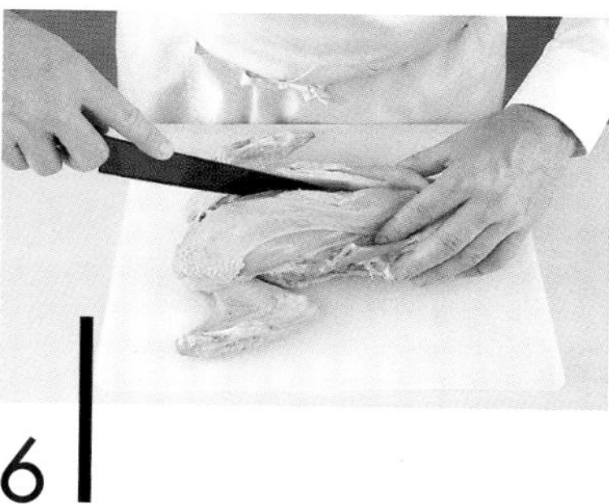

6

Cut along the breastbone to separate the two breast portions.

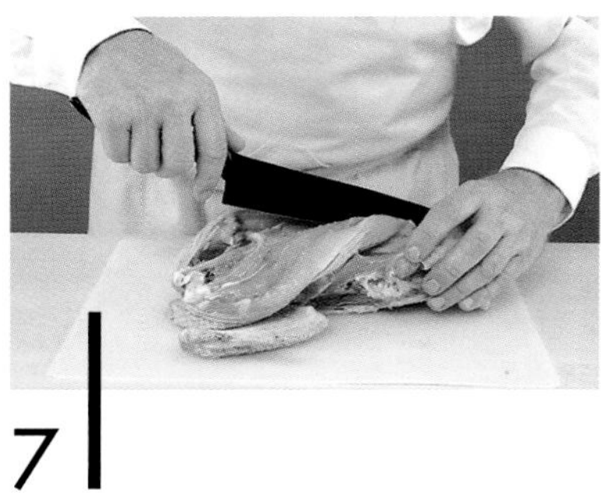

7

Detach one of the breast portions from the wing joint with a knife tip. Slide the knife along the carcass to remove it.

8

Do the same with the other breast portion.

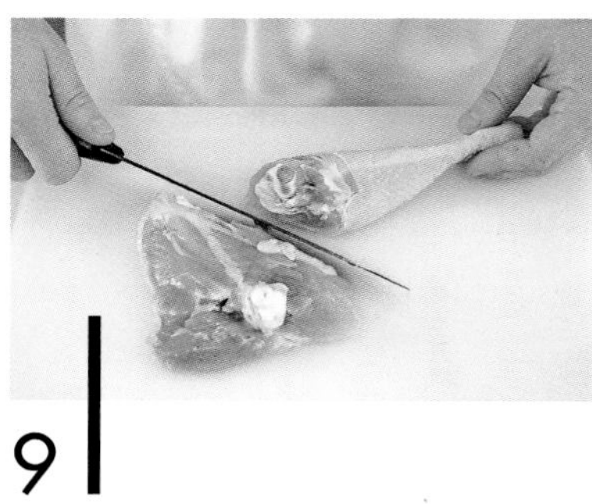

9

Dislocate the thigh from the drumstick and cut at the joint to separate the two.

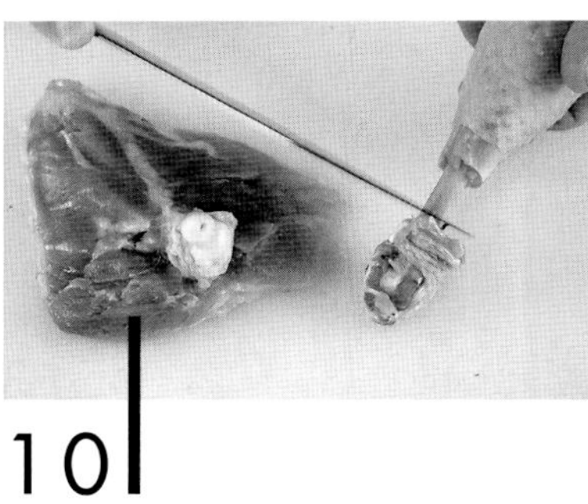

10

Run a knife around the bone of the drumstick to detach the skin. Scrape off the nerves and tendons.

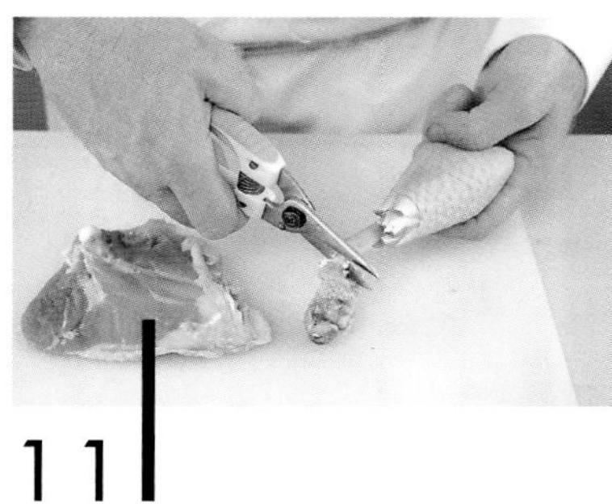

11

Cut off the end of the bone with poultry shears. Do the same with the other leg.

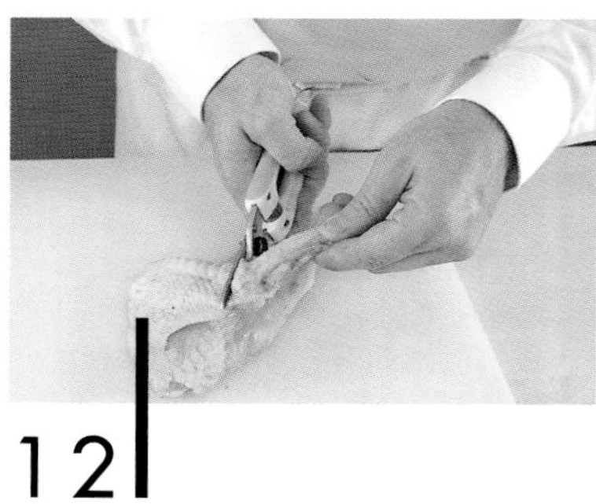

12

Cut off the wing tip at the joint with poultry shears.

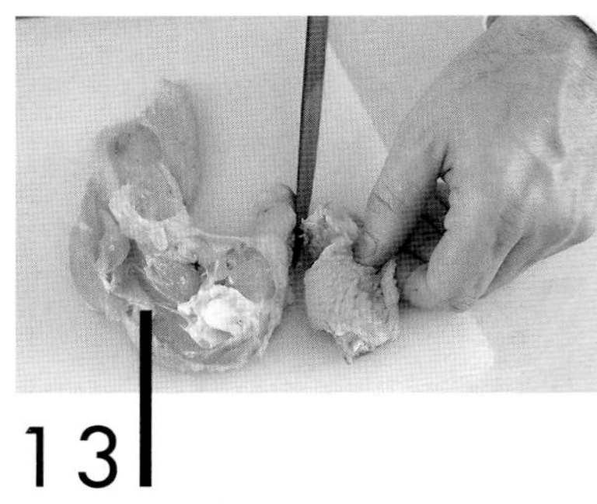

13

Cut the joint between the drumette and winglet.

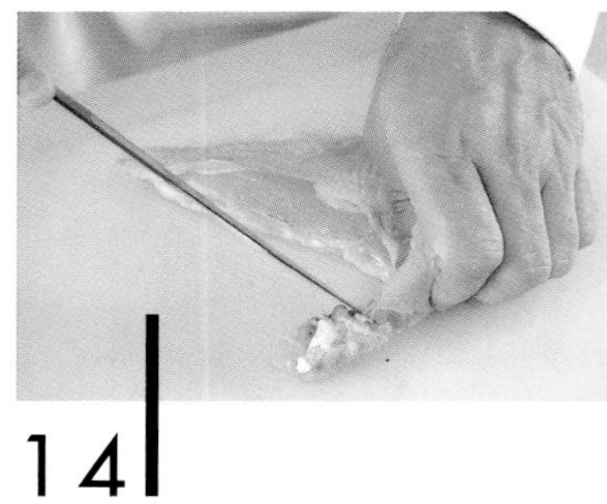

14

Run a knife around the bone of the drumette to detach the skin. Scrape off the nerves and tendons (the same as for the drumsticks).

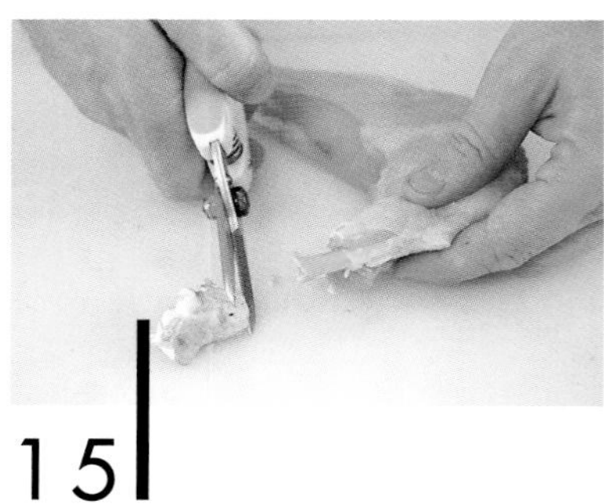

15

Cut off the end of the drumette bone with poultry shears. Do the same with the other wing.

16

Cover and refrigerate until needed.

Carving a chicken

If you have a whole chicken, cut off the thighs by lifting them and dislocating the joint. Cut off the winglets from each side. Scrape the wishbone to expose it, pass the knife behind to catch the bone, then free it, and pull it out. Cut along the breastbone to separate the two breasts.

Cut off the wing tips. Halve the breasts. Cut the legs into thighs and drumsticks at the joint. Scrape ("French") the drumstick bone and cut off the end with scissors. Keep the carcass to make broth or stock.

FOIE GRAS

A brief history

The invention of foie gras has long been attributed to Pompey's father-in-law, the consul Metellus Scipio, who had the custom of fattening his geese with dried figs before eating them. His method was later perfected by Marcus Gavius Apicius, who would immortalize it in one of the oldest gastronomic treatises, *De Re Culinaria*.

About 2,500 years earlier, the inhabitants of the banks of the Nile were already fattening their geese by force-feeding them with figs, as evidenced by numerous ancient Egyptian bas-reliefs. The Jewish diaspora would carry this tradition into the lands around the Mediterranean. These dishes appealed greatly to French cooks after corn, introduced by Christopher Columbus in the fifteenth century, revived the breeding of geese and ducks.

However, it was only during the reign of Louis XVI of France that foie gras would gain its privileged status. In the Southwest of France, the food merchant Courtois, a resident of Périgueux, invented pâté de foie gras with truffles. At the same time, the governor of Strasbourg's cook, Jean-Pierre Clause (or Klotz), invented the recipe for pâté de foie gras encased in pastry.

It was only when Nicolas Appert discovered the principles of preservation by canning in 1795 that this choice delicacy was at last able to travel, making it one of the most famous representatives of French cuisine.

Producing regions

France is the leading producer of foie gras, responsible for 74% of the world's production, followed by Hungary and Israel; Belgium, Romania, and Lithuania follow far behind. The main producing regions in France are the Southwest for goose and duck foie gras, Vendée and Pays de Loire for duck, and Alsace for goose. As much as 97% of foie gras produced comes from ducks.

Goose or duck?

The choice is sometimes difficult, although consumers have their preferences: foie gras from a duck is smaller (400–600 g – 14–21 ounces) than foie gras from a goose (600–900 g – 21–32 ounces). The former is less refined and slightly firmer, with a stronger flavor; the latter, creamier and with a more subtle flavor, is considered to be of higher quality. Duck foie gras is less expensive than goose foie gras.

Read the label carefully

Foie gras is sold in several different forms defined by law. It is sometimes difficult to distinguish the difference, and the term "foie gras" itself can be misleading.

- **100% foie gras**
  Foie gras entier (whole)
  This represents a whole liver or a part of one (depending on the size). It can be raw, *mi-cuit* ("half-cooked"), or cooked, and is sold in different packaging formats (fresh, vacuum-packed, canned, in terrines). We use raw whole foie gras in our recipes.

- **Foie gras**
  This consists of different pieces of liver (no more than three). It can be *mi-cuit* or cooked and is found in different packaging formats.

- **Bloc de foie gras**
  Reconstituted foie gras made from different livers. When the label states *avec morceaux* (with pieces), it should contain 30–50% visible pieces. It can be *mi-cuit* or cooked and is found in different packaging formats.

- **More than 75% parfait de foie gras**
  This should contain at least 75% foie gras.

- **More than 50% mousse de foie gras**
  This should contain at least 50% foie gras.

- **Pâté de foie gras cuit or médaillon**
  This should contain at least 50% foie gras surrounded by forcemeat.

Raw foie gras

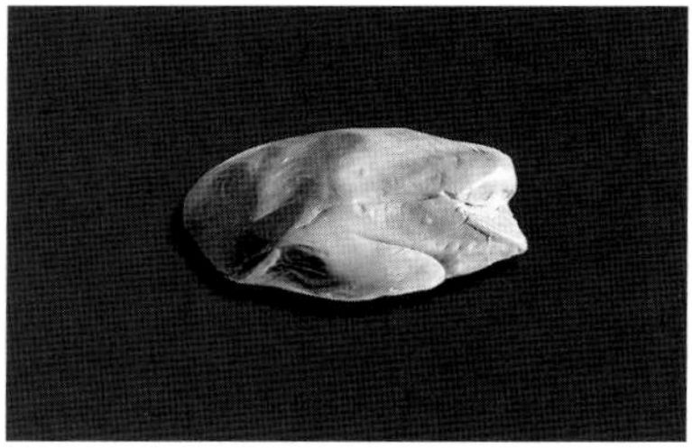

Raw foie gras is used in all the recipes in this book, because it will undergo a cooking process.

There are no legally recognized designations for raw foie gras, but the *Canard à Foie Gras du Sud-Ouest* (duck bred to produce foie gras in the Southwest region of France) enjoys Protected Geographical Indication (PGI) status. Ideally, it should be purchased directly from producers, at markets, or at specialty *"foires au gras"*—fairs specializing in foie gras products—where you will be guaranteed freshness.

However, it can also be found vacuum-packed or frozen at supermarkets.

In the United States, local and imported whole foie gras is readily available from artisanal producers, gourmet retailers, and online.

Different grades

Professionals in France use a classification system to differentiate the different grades of quality.

- **Qualité Foie-A:** This is the liver of a Moulard duck, unbruised, creamy, and a very consistent beige color; it withstands long cooking times without much shrinkage. It is found very rarely and must be purchased from producers at their facilities or at specialty fairs.
- **Qualité extra-B:** The liver of a Moulard or Muscovy duck, firm, beige, yielding very little fat.
- **Première qualité and deuxième qualité:** These livers are reserved for the production of bloc de foie gras and mixtures.
- **Troisième qualité:** This grade is used for livers resulting from an unsuccessful fattening process. They are used to make mousses, parfaits, and pâtés.

In the United States, raw foie gras is similarly classified in three grades according to quality and fat-content. Grade A is typically highest in fat and most suited for low-temperature preparations. Grade B usually contains a higher proportion of protein, making it preferable for higher-temperature preparations, such as searing. Grade C is generally reserved for making sauces or where the liver's higher blood content will not affect the appearance of the final dish.

Buying

A raw foie gras should be of "extra" quality, with a supple and creamy texture—difficult to judge when the liver is very cold—and neither hard nor brittle. The pointed end of the lobe should be firm when pressed with a finger. There should be no grittiness or blemishes, and the liver should have an even color, ranging from pale cream to pinkish beige. Weight can vary, typically 400–500 g – 14–18 ounces for a duck liver (if smaller, there is a risk of being dry; any larger and it will lose a lot of fat), and 450–800 g – 16–28 ounces for a goose liver (any larger and it will lose too much fat when cooked).

Storage

Raw foie gras keeps for about six days in the refrigerator at a temperature of 0–5°C – 32–41°F wrapped in a cloth. If it is vacuum-packed, store it in the refrigerator and check the date on the packaging. It should be used as soon as possible, because its flavor becomes altered if kept cold too long. You can also freeze raw foie gras in a freezer bag or in its packaging if vacuum-packed.

Deveining raw foie gras

The term used here is deveining, and not nerve removal, because the veins that carry blood to the liver have to be removed. For this somewhat delicate process, the foie gras should be at room temperature; take it out of the refrigerator about 90 minutes beforehand. Wear gloves, and spread a large sheet of parchment (baking) paper over the work surface. This is more hygienic and convenient for cooking. The paper will also let you collect the seasoning and any of the foie gras that falls off. It should take about 15 minutes to devein a foie gras.

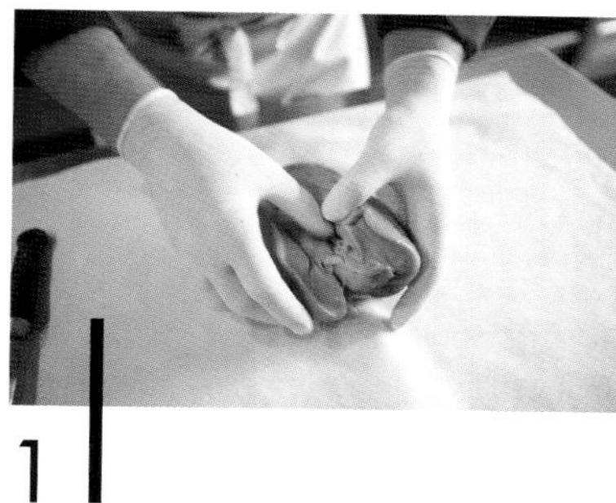

1

Press on the top of the liver with a fingertip to check that it is soft enough. It should spring back by itself. Separate the two lobes by hand, pulling them apart gently.

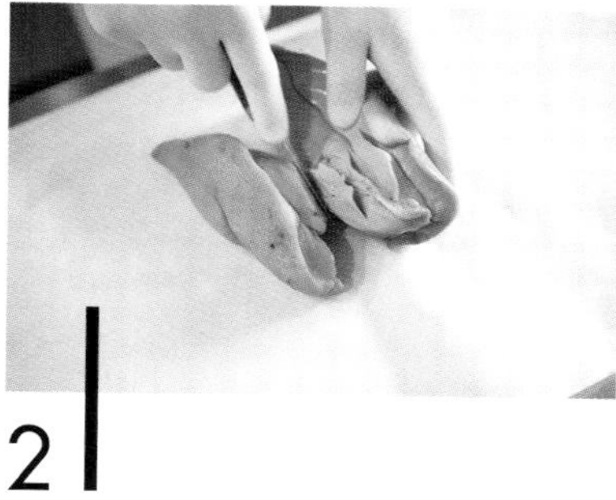

2

They are held together by a vein. Cut the vein with a paring knife.

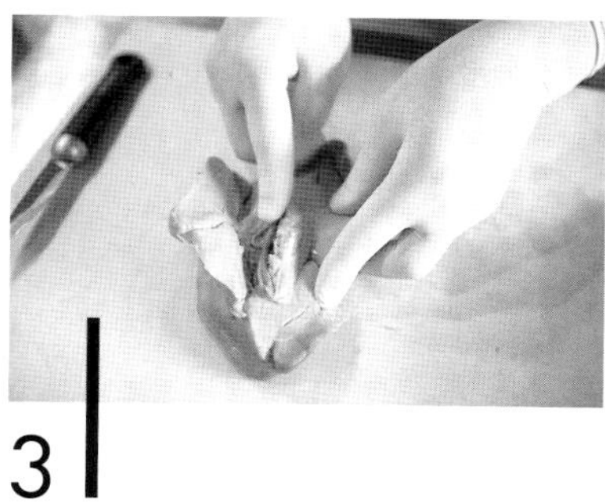

3

Use the back of a spoon to open out the smaller lobe on its skin (rounded) side.

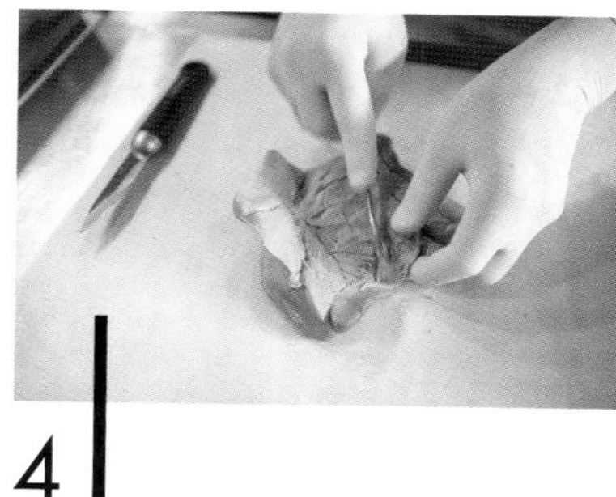

4

Using only the back of the spoon, gently scrape the inside of the liver to expose two main veins.

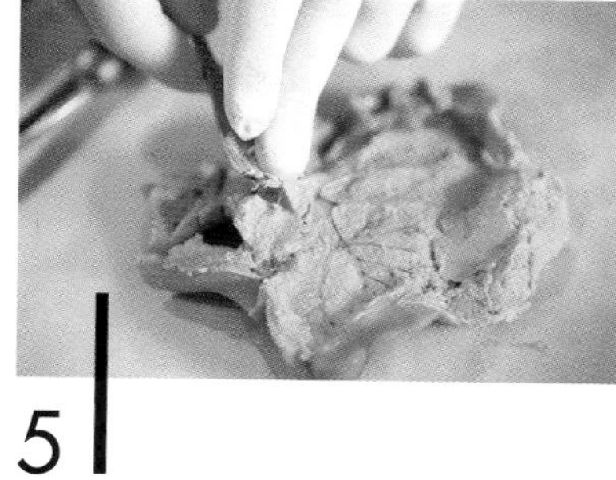

5

Lift up the first vein, using the back of the spoon to help.

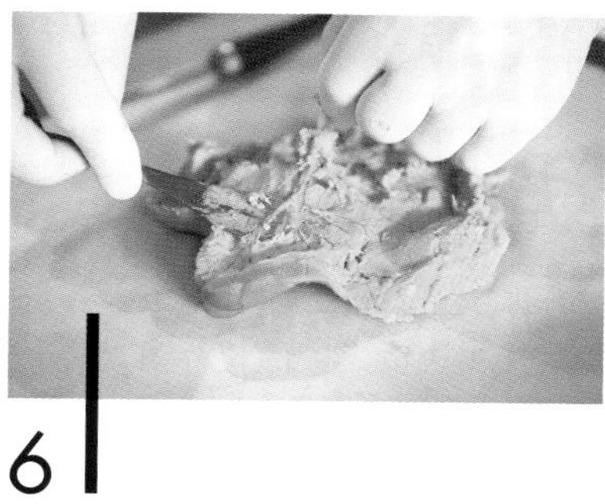

6

Pass the back of the spoon under it. Slide it gradually along the vein, being careful not to break it.

7

Once the vein has become detached, pull it up gently to remove. Scrape the liver again to expose the second vein. Repeat the process.

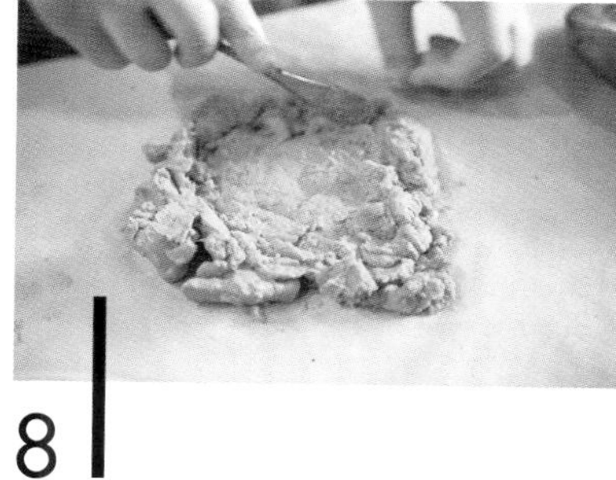

8

Spread out that part that has been scraped to remove the small ends of the vein that may have been overlooked, then mold the lobe into its original shape.

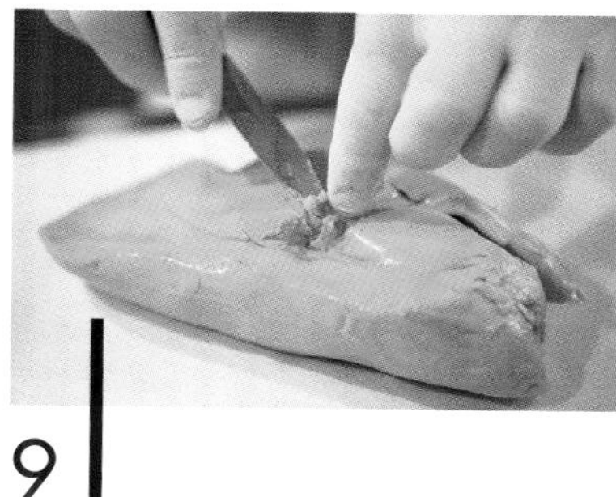

9

To devein the larger lobe, first remove the ball of fat located underneath. Proceed to devein in the same way as you did the smaller lobe, starting with the vein coming out of the liver.

LAMB

Making the right choice

Protected Geographical Indication (PGI) status in Europe or the Label Rouge marking and conformity certifications (CCP) in France can help guide your choice. Each animal sold bears mandatory markings in the form of a stamp showing the slaughterhouse number, numbers identifying the region and municipality, and a veterinarian's mark to certify that the animal is free of disease and fit for eating.

It is not by chance that the best time for lamb is at Easter in spring. Officially, a lamb can be only under one year of age. The season for suckling lamb, fed exclusively on its mother's milk, extends from December to May. Slaughtered before weaning, between 30 and 60 days, a suckling lamb weighs 8–12 kg – 18–26.5 pounds. Its flesh is tender and delicate. As much as 70% of the lamb sold at butcher shops, known in France as *agneau blanc* (white lamb), has pink flesh and very white fat and is slaughtered between 70 and 150 days of age, weighing 15–20 kg – 33–44 pounds. It is raised on hay, grass, or fodder beets.

Weaned lambs, known in French as *agneau gris* (gray lamb) or broutart, is raised on pastureland. These are slaughtered between 6 and 10 months of age and weigh 30-45 kg – 66–100 pounds. When a lamb reaches the age of one year, its meat is sold as hogget and mutton and is redder, with a more pronounced smell.

Lamb cuts

- **Breast**
  The underside of a lamb, the breast comprises bones, muscle layers, and fatty tissue. If bought whole, it can be broiled (grilled); when cut into pieces, it is suitable for broiling (grilling) and stewing.

- **Leg**
  The hind leg of a lamb. The famous medieval French cook Taillevent coined the French word for this cut, *gigot,* in reference to the gigue fiddle, a musical instrument from the period. Whole leg refers to the entire haunch, comprising the leg and sirloin (chump), while a short leg does not include the sirloin. The shank is a small pear-shaped muscle located around the tibia. It is particularly soft and is very popular. The leg is typically roasted in the oven.

- **Loin**
  Known as the saddle when referring to both sides joined together, the loin is located after the loin-end ribs and consists of the full set of loin chops. It can be divided into double or single loin chops. It can be broiled (grilled), pan-fried, or roasted.

- **Neck**
  A tasty cut for broiling or grilling, stewing, making into a tajine, or serving with a navarin jus. Ask your butcher to cut it into pieces, with or without bones.

- **Organ meats (Offal)**
  This term refers to the brain, cheeks, thymus (sweetbreads), tongue, heart, liver, kidneys, stomach (for tripe), testicles (known as lamb fries), and feet.

- **Rack**
  The French word for this cut, *carré*, indicates the set of ribs comprising the five shoulder ribs, four center ribs, and four loin-end ribs. The term *carré couvert*, the traditional rack of lamb as it is known in English-speaking countries, corresponds to the set of center and loin-end ribs. This is an excellent cut for roasting. The *carré découvert* or shoulder rack is less refined. It is typically roasted.

- **Ribs**
  This is the bony and flat part of the ribs that continues on from the chops, with relatively little flesh. They are suitable for stewing.

- **Rib chops or cutlets**
  These are sold separately or together (rack of lamb) and can be roasted, grilled (barbecued), sautéed, or braised. They consist of rib bones and part of the backbone to which they are attached. There are three categories of lamb rib chops:
  – Shoulder chops (1st–5th ribs): Located immediately after the neck, they are quite fatty and are suitable for stewing.
  – Center rib chops (6th–10th ribs): Located between the shoulder chops and loin-end ribs, these have less meat.
  – Loin-end rib chops (11th–14th ribs): Located immediately after the rib chops, these are less fatty than the others and have a good portion of the rib-eye muscle. When well cleaned of meat or "Frenched" by the butcher, their long "handles" give them a certain elegance. The meat detached from the bone is known as a noisette or medallion.

- **Shoulder**
  Once known as the foreleg, the shoulder can be bought whole (with or without the shoulder blade) and is prepared in a manner similar to that used for the leg. It can be boned or cut into pieces, and broiled (grilled), sautéed, or stewed.

Preparation

- **Before you start**
  Take the meat out of the refrigerator in advance so that it comes to room temperature before cooking.

- **Sharpen your knives**
  Working with meat requires perfectly sharpened knives, both for preparation and final carving; you will need a boning knife, a chef's knife, and a carving knife.

- **Have the necessary equipment**
  A meat or probe thermometer will indicate clearly when the meat is cooked. For a leg, shoulder, or loin, the core temperature of the meat should reach 52°C – 126°F.

- **Preheat**
  Always remember to preheat the oven or broiler (grill) to sear the meat; this will concentrate the juices. Preheat any pans used as well.

- **Low heat**
  For perfect stewing, make sure the pieces of meat are all the same size. Don't bring the preparation to a boil; a simmer is enough. Stews are actually better when reheated.

- **Resting**
  A rest period after cooking (this does not apply to stews)—equal to at least half the cooking time—is necessary to let the fibers in the meat relax and to allow the blood, drawn to the surface by the heat, to be reabsorbed.

- **Perfect carving**
  Always put the cooked meat onto a large carving board with a groove for collecting the juices. Don't pierce it with the fork when carving—just hold it steady with the back of the fork.

Preparing a saddle of lamb

Lamb loin is a very tender roasting cut that is perfectly suited to a refined meal. If you buy a whole saddle, bone-in, you should know that it isn't difficult to prepare, but you do need to be meticulous, and have well-sharpened knives at the ready. One loin, or half-saddle, is enough for three or four people, while a whole saddle will serve six or seven guests. It will always be presented as two identical pieces, resembling two small rolled roasts, because one is from each side of the backbone.

1

Use a boning knife to make an incision along the bone down the middle of the saddle.

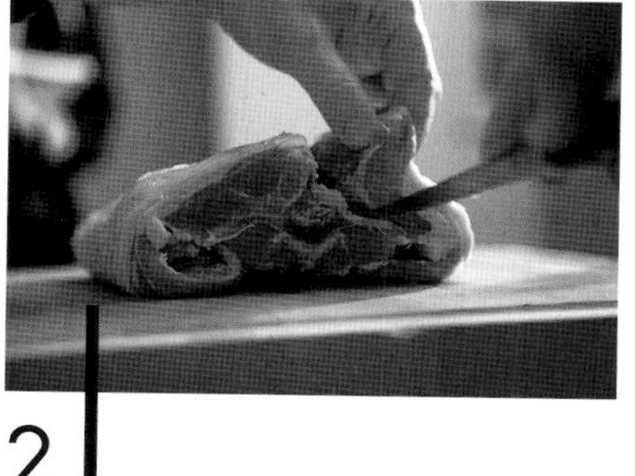

2

Separate the loin meat from the bone. Scrape the round bone.

3

Slide the knife flat along the bone and free the meat. Do the same on the other side.

4

Remove the bone. Turn the saddle over. Slide the knife under the meat. Lift the end and remove the tenderloin. Repeat the process on the other side.

5

Remove the fat and silver skin from the tenderloins.

6

Slide your knife along the meat to separate the triangle of fat, without cutting through the fell (outer membrane).

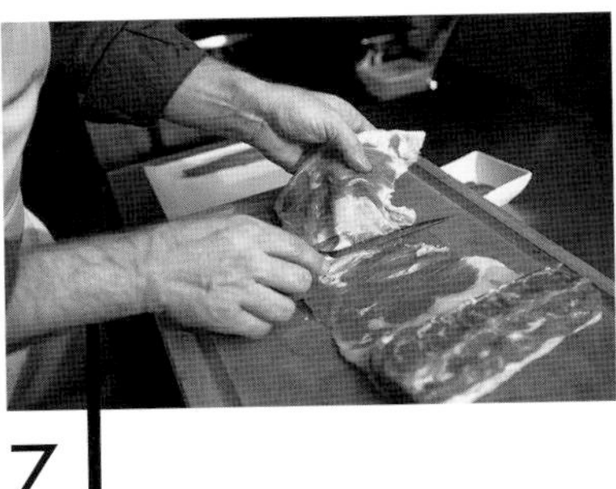

7

Remove the excess (which can be used as scraps or trimmings) and only keep the flaps.

8

Remove surplus fat. Remove the nerve running along the meat.

9

Take off as much fat as possible, leaving only a thin layer.

10

Score the fat left on the meat to enable it to melt and to allow for better heat penetration.

11

Place the tenderloin back on the meat. Sprinkle with thyme.

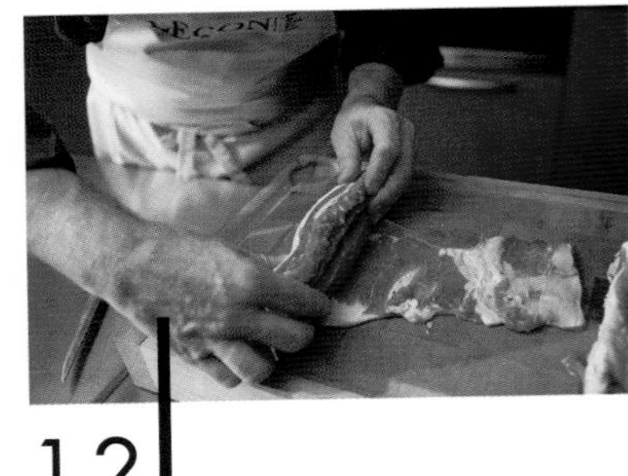

12

Roll to cover the meat completely.

13

Remove the excess fell. Repeat the process with the other half-saddle.

14

Place each half-saddle on a dish. Cover with plastic wrap (cling film) and refrigerate.

15

Cut up the scraps, cover in plastic wrap, and refrigerate.

Carving a shoulder of lamb

When cooked whole, this cut is particularly tasty because its bones give it a lot of flavor. However, it has less prestige than the leg. It is best enjoyed as an informal meal, because its shape doesn't lend itself to elegant carving. Nevertheless, these step-by-step instructions will let you achieve a decent result.

1

Rest the shoulder on the cutting board and cut through at the shoulder joint (shoulder blade).

2

Cut through to the bone, without piercing the meat with your fork.

3

Slide the knife flat along the bone and free the meat.

4

Put the piece onto the cutting board and slice.

5

Turn the shoulder blade over and detach the meat from underneath.

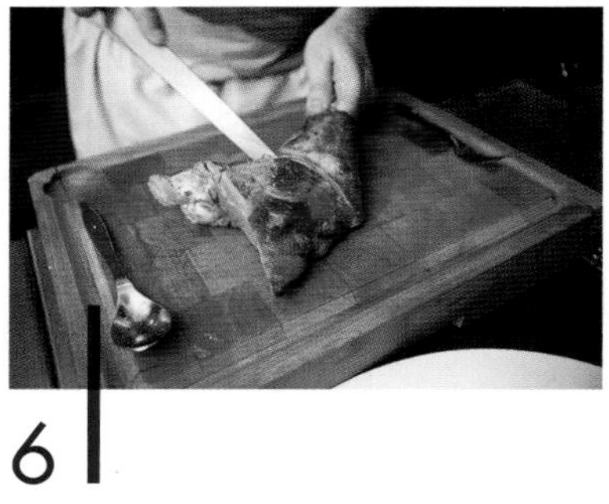

6

Hold the shoulder by the bone and detach the meat from the base of the shank, along the large bone.

7

Carve this piece into slices.

8

Turn the shoulder over and slice the meat from the other side of the large bone, then cut downward with the knife tip.

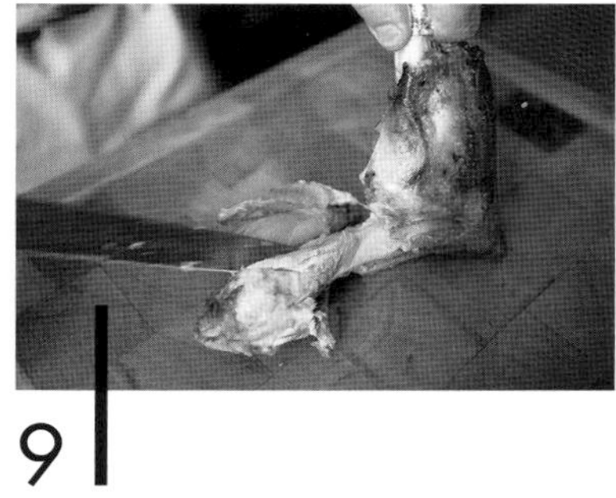

9

Carve along the bone.

10

Detach half of the shank.

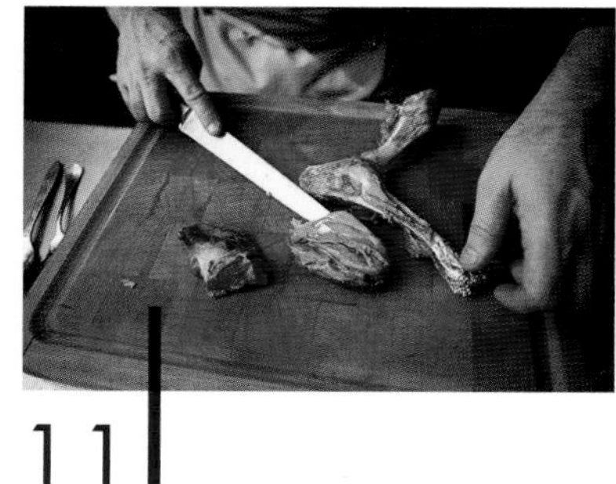

11

Detach the other half.

12

Cut the larger part into three pieces.

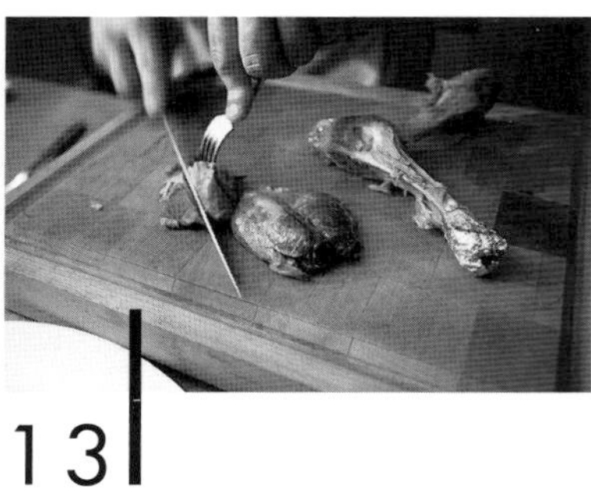

13

Cut the other part into two pieces.

14

Arrange the slices of meat on a warm dish. Season with salt and pepper. Decorate with a sprig of basil.

Carving a leg of lamb

A leg of lamb, long considered a sign of prosperity, has always been carved with special care. This process was once performed with a great deal of solemnity at the table by the master of the household, and the different methods—French and English styles—have had their supporters. The simplest method always gives the best results; here, once the meat is sliced, the bones serve as a guide.

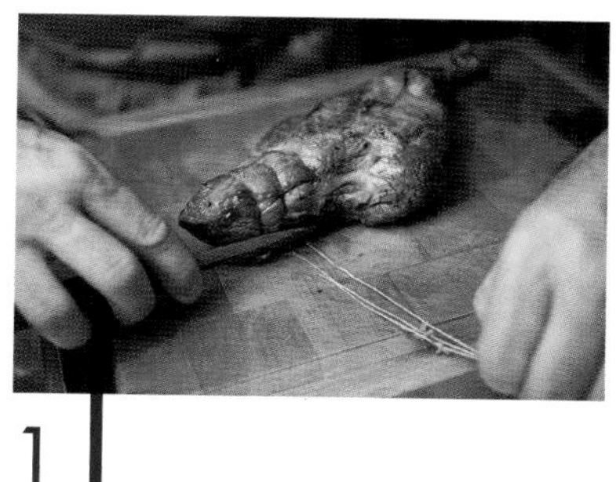

1

Remove the twine holding the muscles in place.

2

Hold the leg by the bone, flat side down on the cutting board. Cut the larger muscle vertically into uniform slices.

Turn the leg over and cut the smaller muscle vertically into slices, perpendicular to the bone. Slide your knife along the bone, away from you, to detach the slices.

3

Remove the small ball of fat from the center of the slices.

4

Cut off the shank.

5

Lay it flat and cut it in half. Cut each half in two.

6

Arrange the slices of meat on a warm serving dish. Season with fleur de sel and a few turns of the peppermill.

RABBIT

Cutting up a raw rabbit

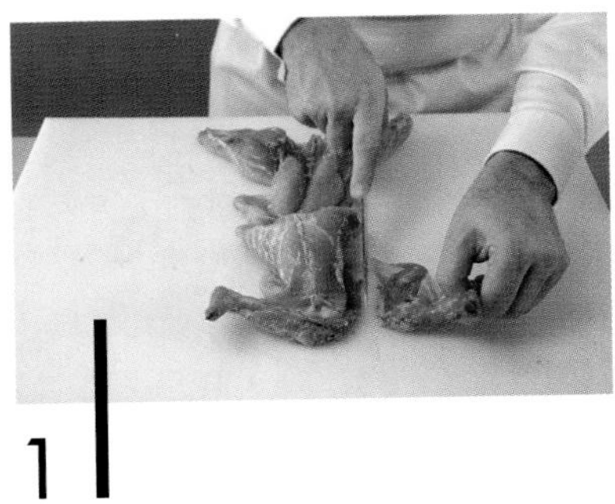

1

Remove the liver from the rabbit. Save it for use in another recipe. Cut off the forelegs.

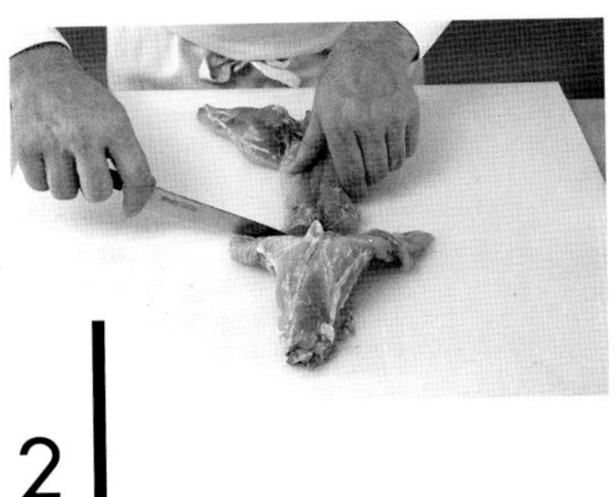

2

Separate the rib cage by cutting it off at the saddle.

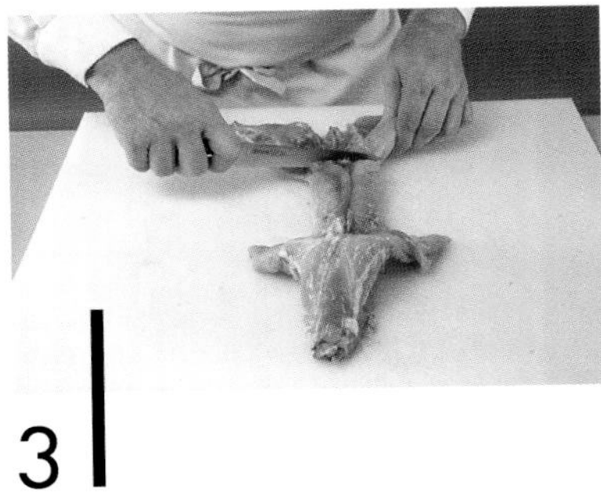

3

Cut the base of the saddle at the thighs.

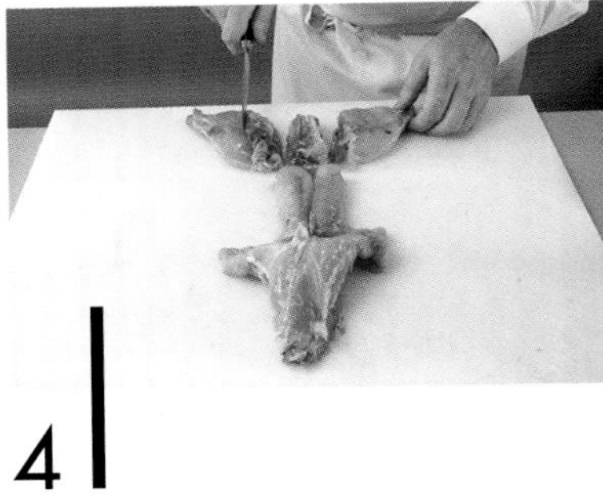

4

Cut the thighs off on each side at the base of the backbone.

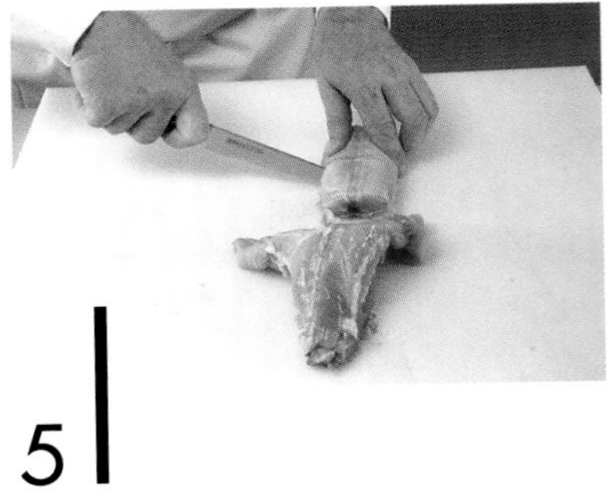

5

Cut the saddle in half.

6

Cut the ribs in half. When cutting up a rabbit, be careful not to create splinters. For this, cut the flesh only as far as the bone, then dislocate the joint with your hands. Finally, cut at the joint.

FISH AND SHELLFISH

COD

Characteristics

This deep-sea fish is caught throughout the year, mainly in the North Atlantic (which includes the English Channel and North Sea, although this is often overlooked).

Cod is also known by the less common name skrei, a variety of cod that migrates once a year from the Arctic Circle to the Lofoten Islands, in Norway, to spawn. Only the large specimens make this journey and acquire their firm, very white, and particularly tasty flesh. They are only caught in February and March.

The French call cod *cabillaud* when it is fresh and large, *moruette* or *doguette* when it is small, and *morue* when it is salted and dried (this is also known as stockfish in the south of France).

Cod can weigh 1–4 kg – 2 1/4–9 pounds and can measure as much as 1.80 m – close to 6 feet in length. Once abundant due to the large number of eggs (roe) it lays, it has now become increasingly rare as a result of overfishing.

Buying

Freshness is an essential quality of all fish. Cod fillets and supremes, also known as pavés, should be clean and evenly colored and have elastic flesh (it should spring back when you press it with your finger). For crosscut steaks, known as darnes, the flesh should be firmly attached to the backbone.

It can be purchased whole (for a large number of guests or if it is to be frozen), or in the form of fillets, supremes, darnes, and so on. Check the recipe. If you can't find cod, you can use pollack or a large hake (the flesh is more delicate) in its place.

The right tools

A fillet knife (long, sharp, and flexible blade) to remove the skin and cut the fish into pieces or slices; tweezers to remove the small bones; a large spatula for handling the cooked fish.

SALMON

Characteristics

After a year at sea, sexually mature young salmon are known as grilse or jacks/jills; after two years, they are known as spring salmon; and after three years large adults are known as winter salmon. This is the typical age for salmon consumption. Kelts, older female salmon that have spawned, are inedible. In keeping with the life cycle of this species, salmon return to the place of their birth to spawn (lay eggs). They typically die there afterward, exhausted.

Today, dams and pollution prevent these great voyagers from swimming up rivers. And while three French towns (Navarrenx in Pyrénées-Atlantiques, Châteaulin in Finistère, and Brioude in Haute-Loire) remain famous for their salmon and the recipes created to showcase them, farmed salmon with its orange flesh (a color enhanced by the feed given to it) has largely overtaken wild salmon, whose very pale pink flesh is less appealing to certain consumers and which is rarer and more expensive.

Buying

Freshness is an essential quality of fish. The fresher the fish, the more its bones adhere to the flesh. Certain types of farmed salmon in France have been granted Label Rouge status for their quality and make a good choice.

You can buy salmon in the form of fillets (center-cut fillets are always thicker), supremes (cut from the back), darnes (crosscut steaks comprising thinner abdomen and the backbone), and tails.

Preparation

Fish has to be cooked to perfection, which in the case of salmon means rare. In other words, it should be pink and tender. Cooked any further, the flesh dries out. Undercooking is better than overcooking; you can always return it to the heat for a few more seconds.

Cutting salmon

1

Lay the fish flat, with the head to your right. Hold the knife at a slant at the base of the head. Make a cut with the knife, turning it around the head.

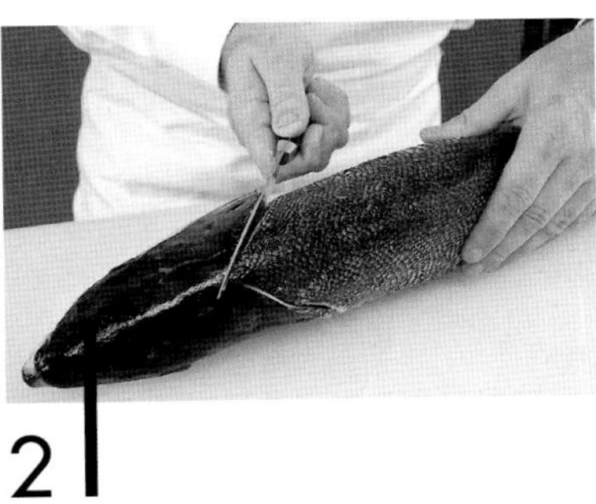

2

Turn the fish over and do the same on the other side. The two cuts should meet at the center. Cut the backbone at the base of the head with a knife or a pair of scissors. Remove the head.

3

Make an incision at the top and slide the knife blade along the length of the backbone.

4

Slide the knife very close to the backbone with a slightly curved motion. Detach the flesh toward the rear (tail) with a circular movement.

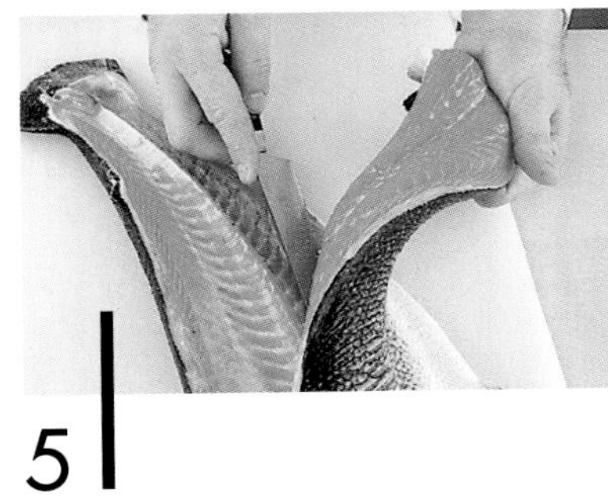

5

Continue to detach the flesh at the rear of the fish by cutting through to the belly side and gradually lifting it up. Come back up toward the top, continuing to detach the flesh.

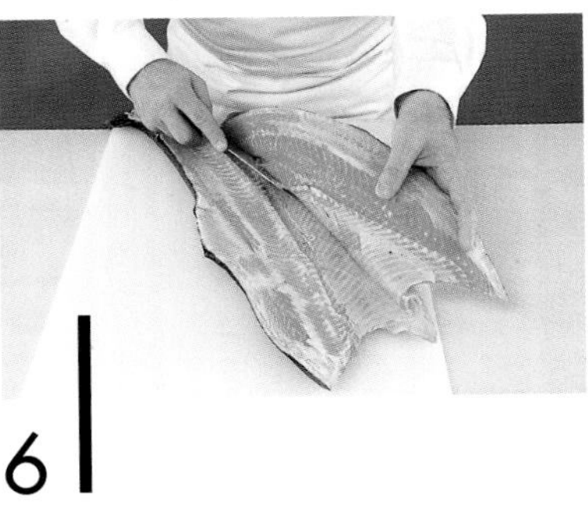

6

Cut through the bones. Lay the first fillet flat on parchment (baking) paper.

7

Scrape the backbone with a spoon to recover any remaining flesh.

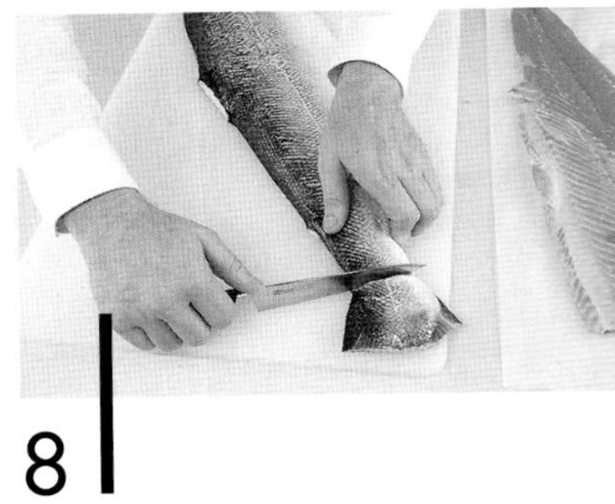

8

Turn the fish over with the top part toward you. Make a cut a few inches from the tail.

9

Cut along the backbone.

10

Cut very close along the backbone to detach the flesh. Continue lifting off the flesh while cutting toward the top.

11

Scrape the backbone with a spoon to recover any remaining flesh.

Shrimp

Prawn is the name given to large shrimp, but in some countries prawn also refers to a smaller shrimp. The shrimp is a symbol of longevity in Japan. Both shrimp and prawns are very flavorful and are considered a delicacy. Be careful not to overcook them or they will become bland and rubbery.

Peeling

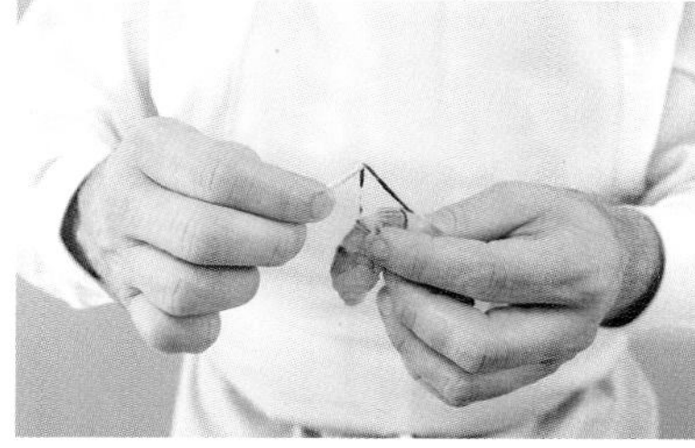

Remove the heads from the bodies, then make a slit along the back. Pinch the tail and pull the body.

Deveining

It is important to remove the little black or transparent "vein" running along the back of the shrimp; this is the intestine. If it is black, it can give this delicious crustacean a bitter taste.

PASTRY MAKING

ALMOND MEAL

Macarons (which are different from macaroons, despite their similar names) and frangipane owe their existence to this princely ingredient in the world of pastry making. Almond meal, or ground almonds, is far better when homemade.

To do this, you only have to peel the almonds (2 minutes in boiling water is enough to detach their skins), toast them in a saucepan for a few minutes, and grind them. You can grind the almonds with their skins; the flavor will be more pronounced, but the gray powder obtained does not lend itself to light-colored preparations.

If you choose to buy almond meal from a store, you should look for a product that is 100% non-defatted and freshly prepared, because its high fat content can turn it rancid very quickly.

To enhance the aroma of store-bought almond meal, you can cheat a little by adding a few drops of bitter almond extract.

CHOCOLATE

A brief history

According to native American legend, chocolate, this food of the gods (*theobroma*), was revealed to mankind by the ants.

So, when did Europe discover its love of chocolate? Christopher Columbus is reported to have thrown the cocoa (cacao) beans presented to him by native Americans overboard (he took them for goat droppings), and it was only in 1519 that the Conquistadors fell under the spell of the magic drink made with the precious beans, called *xocolatl* by the Aztecs and *chacau haa* by the Mayans. Although Spanish caravels had taken the beans back to the Spanish monarchs in 1528, it was only when King Louis XIII of France married a Spanish princess in 1614 that the French court developed a taste for chocolate in beverage form.

With the creation in 1776 of the first mechanized factory, the Chocolaterie Royale in Bayonne, chocolate really developed in France. Its growth would be felt in the following century: Van Houten patented his cocoa powder in 1828; Poulain founded his company in 1848; Menier produced 4,000 metric tons of chocolate in 1853 (before becoming the world's leading producer in 1869); Nestlé built his factory in 1867; the Swiss Tobler developed the first milk chocolate in 1870; and the Italian Caffarel invented gianduja in the 1800s as well. From then on, there would be no stopping the race to see who could make the most delicious chocolate.

Varieties

There are many varieties of cocoa trees, which grow widely throughout the tropics. Different "crus" have been established to denote the origin of the beans: Brazil, Venezuela, Trinidad, Ecuador, French Guiana, Martinique, Java, Ivory Coast, Sri Lanka, and so on. All have specific characteristics: grade of quality, aromatics, cocoa butter content, sourness, and other aspects. The fruit of the tree (cocoa bean), encased in a pod, undergoes a number of processes before reaching the stage known as cocoa: breaking roasting, milling, pressing, and so on.

European Union law recognizes thirteen categories of chocolate, but does not set maximum or minimum cocoa content or maximum sugar content. This explains why the percentage of cocoa stated on labels can vary, ranging from 30 to 99% for dark chocolate. Every chocolate maker or chocolatier creates a unique mixture of crus, with or without the use of a vegetable fat (authorized to a limit of 5%) other than cocoa butter, and incorporating more or less sugar. This explains the very distinct flavors of different chocolates, and particularly, why two chocolates with the same cocoa content do not have the same flavor or "strength."

Buying

The ideal situation is to use the best chocolate possible, depending on what is to be made from it. To make our recipes, choose chocolate with a high cocoa content (mandatory inclusion on packaging).

Formats

– Cocoa powder, pure, unsweetened product (not to be confused with powdered drinking chocolate products).

– Chocolate bars, the most common format.

– Chocolate pistoles (from a French word for "gold coins"), very practical, because there is no need to cut.

– Chocolate blocks, such as couverture chocolate (with a high cocoa butter content, which enhances its fluidity).

Preparation

Always use chocolate in pieces: break it up, cut it, chop it with a knife or in a food processor before melting. You can also use pistoles, sold at specialty chocolate stores.

Follow the instructions given for the temperatures at which the different chocolates should be tempered. Use a cooking or probe thermometer, being careful not to let it touch the bottom of the container.

Testing tempered chocolate

Cut out a small rectangle of parchment (baking) paper. Dip it in the chocolate at 30°C – 86°F, drain on the rim of the bowl.

Cool quickly (in the refrigerator, if necessary, if the kitchen is hot).

Snap it in half. The chocolate should break cleanly, and it should be shiny and without any streaks. It is now ready to use for coating.

GELATIN

Gelatin (gelatine) is most commonly found in stiff, translucent sheets (leaf gelatin). It should always be rehydrated before it is added to a hot preparation.

Completely immerse the sheets whole or cut in half (with scissors) in cold water. Soak for 5–10 minutes.

When soft, pick them up with your fingers and drain them for a few seconds in a small strainer (sieve) to avoid adding excess water to your dish. If necessary, drain the gelatin sheets on paper towels.

Always add gelatin to hot liquid to let it melt completely, but never let it boil.

SUGAR

A brief history

Since the dawn of human history, we have been partial to sweet flavors, starting with honey. This lent itself to a great many culinary uses and was employed to candy different fruits. It was learned that high concentrations of sugar, prepared in different ways, could preserve food.

During the Renaissance, seasoned Italian confectioners arrived in France accompanying Catherine de' Medici, and that led to the appearance of new delicacies.

As sugar was also attributed therapeutic properties, it was dispensed by apothecaries, which used it to sweeten the concoctions made for a privileged minority.

The introduction of sugar cane to the French territories in the Caribbean led to a certain development of confectionery, but it would remain synonymous with luxury until the nineteenth century. It was the discovery of industrial processes for extracting sugar from sugar beets that brought about a genuine revolution. At that point, sugar became available to the masses, and sweet delicacies multiplied and were sold in the streets.

Sugar terminology

Sugar will form a syrup to coat a spoon at 100°C – 212°F; it reaches the "soft ball" stage at 110°C – 230°F, when bubbles form and burst; it reaches the "soft crack" stage at 135°C – 275°F, because it hardens and breaks; it becomes "yellow" at 150°C – 302°F, with the color darkening increasingly until it turns into a caramel at 170°C – 338°F.

Glucose syrup

Often used in pastry making and confectionery, this ingredient is the professionals' secret weapon. Glucose syrup actually complements standard sugar, improving texture, delaying caramelization, preventing crystallization, and improving the ability to store preparations. Glucose gives you an edge in the home kitchen as well. Glucose syrup is made by transforming the starch from corn or maize, wheat, or potato by hydrolysis. Glucose is sold in syrup form (inexpensive) in gourmet grocery stores, certain supermarkets, and online. It can also be found in powdered form; follow the instructions when adding water.

The flavor of glucose syrup is less sweet than that of normal sugar, allowing for the subtle aromas of a preparation to be appreciated. However, it has just as many calories as sugar. Glucose syrup will keep a sponge cake moist longer, add texture to a ganache, and perfectly preserve the creaminess of ice cream or sorbet.

Confectioners' sugar

Praised for its decorative uses and its ability to dissolve instantly, confectioners' sugar (also known as powdered sugar or icing sugar) is made by grinding granulated sugar into an extremely fine powder and then adding a small amount of cornstarch (cornflour) to prevent caking.

Although confectioners' sugar has a long shelf life, it should be stored in an airtight container away from any moisture. It can be used to make frosting or icing and different decorations. You can even make your own confectioners' sugar by processing a few sugar cubes at a time in a food processor fitted with the metal blade (adding a pinch of cornstarch for each cube), but the result will not be of any better quality than commercially available confectioners' sugar.

Confectioners' sugar enhances the velvety texture of creamy preparations. Keep in mind that confectioners' sugar also helps meringues hold their shape during cooking.

BASIC RECIPES AND TECHNIQUES

CONDIMENTS AND BASIC PREPARATIONS

BALSAMIC REDUCTION

A line of balsamic reduction makes a great impression as a final flourish when plating dishes.

Reduce 100 ml – 1/3 cup plus 1 tablespoon plus 1 teaspoon of balsamic vinegar for 3 to 4 minutes.

Stop when the vinegar forms large bubbles and takes on a caramel-like, syrupy consistency.

Mix with a little unreduced balsamic vinegar and transfer to a container.

This reduction can be kept in a small jar or dish.

Reheat for a few seconds in a microwave before use.

BOUQUET GARNI

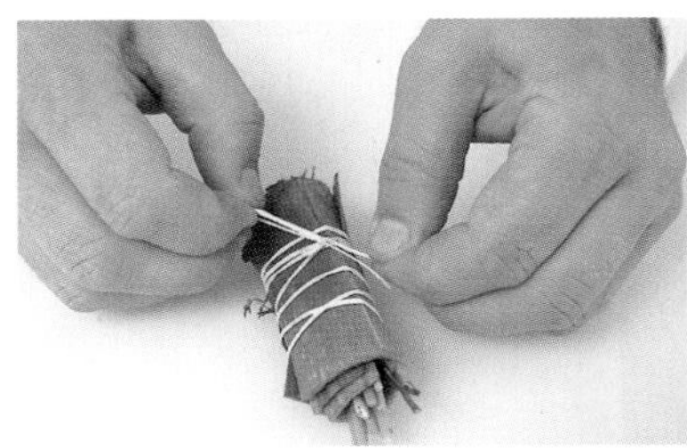

INGREDIENTS

- 4 green leek leaves in 10-cm – 4-inch lengths
- 1 bay leaf
- Several sprigs thyme
- Several celery leaves
- Several parsley leaves

Hold 2 leek leaves flat and one on top of the other in your hand. Place the herbs on top of the leaves in the order given above.

Wrap the bouquet garni in the remaining leek leaves.

Tie it with doubled kitchen twine in several places.

CHOUX PASTE

Before starting

Be aware that not all the recipes require the same amount of choux paste. You can divide up the amounts or freeze surplus uncooked pastry. Simply pipe the choux puffs or éclairs on a baking sheet (tray) lined with parchment (baking) paper and place it in the freezer. To defrost, put into the oven at the required temperature and double the cooking time.

The consistency of choux paste is the most important thing. After it is dried out on the stove, 3 eggs are incorporated, one at a time, to rehydrate. The last egg is beaten so it can be added very gradually until the desired consistency is achieved. If another egg is needed, beat it with a fork and add it in the same way. Preheat the oven to 150°C – 300°F (gas mark 3–4) in a convection (fan-assisted) oven or 170°C – 350°F (gas mark 5) in a conventional (static) oven before starting to prepare the pastry, because it has to be cooked as soon as possible.

Handling the pastry (piping) bag is a little tricky and requires practice (page 507). To make small choux puffs, you can also make do with two teaspoons. For decorating, practice makes perfect.

It is essential that choux puffs and éclairs be cooled before being filled.

Preparing the choux paste

Preparation and cooking time: 20 minutes for 700 g / 1 pound 8 ounces

INGREDIENTS

- 125 ml – 1/2 cup milk
- 125 g – 4.4 ounces (1 stick plus 1 tablespoon) butter, cut into cubes
- 4 g – 0.14 ounce (heaping 1/2 teaspoon) salt
- 140 g – 4.94 ounces (1 1/3 cups) type 45 flour or pastry (plain) flour
- 4 (60-g – 2.12-ounce) eggs

1

Weigh out all the ingredients. Pour the milk into a saucepan. Add 125 ml – 1/2 cup water, followed by the butter.

Add the salt. Bring to a boil over low–medium heat to give the butter time to melt.

2

Sift the flour over a sheet of parchment (baking) paper.

Break the eggs into a small bowl.

3

When the milk is boiling, remove the pan from the heat and add all the flour.

Stir vigorously with a spatula until the flour is fully incorporated.

4

Return the pan to the heat. Dry the dough out for about 1 minute while stirring vigorously until it forms a ball and comes away from the sides of the pan.

5

Transfer the dough to a large bowl. Add 3 eggs, one at a time, stirring vigorously after each addition until they are incorporated.

6

Beat the last egg with a fork. Add it a little at a time until the dough is smooth. It should stick to the spatula before falling off.

A brief history

While there is a certain resemblance between choux puffs and cabbages (*choux*—French for "cabbages"—being the origin of the name), the former is considered to be much tastier than the latter. Most of the creations made using choux paste were given names that are easily explained.

The profiterole takes its name from the French word *profit* or "benefit" (in the sense that the dough "benefits" from cooking). Interestingly, the profiterole was originally savory and was the forerunner of the gougère bourguignonne, which has been in circulation since the eighteenth century.

Pets-de-nonne ("nun's farts"), known as *"beignets venteux"* ("fritters with wind") in the Middle Ages, were most likely invented by the nuns of the abbey of Baume-les-Dames. Those who didn't want to stoop to using that name euphemistically referred to the pastries as *"soupirs de nonne"* ("nun's sighs") instead.

The religieuse (nun), created by the famous pastry chef Frascati in 1856, owes its name both to its shape (profile of a woman in a long skirt with a cinched waist) and its colors, which are reminiscent of the habits worn by the mendicant religious orders.

In 1856, the pastry chef Chiboust, owner of an establishment on the Paris street rue Saint-Honoré, invented Chiboust cream (originally called Saint-Honoré cream) to fill a creation that he named the Saint-Honoré cake. No one knows whether this was in honor of Saint Honoré or Honoratus, the seventh-century Bishop of Amiens and patron saint of bakers and pastry makers, or to satisfy certain delusions of grandeur.

What about the Paris-Brest? It might amuse you to know that in 1891, to mark the first cycling race between Paris and Brest, a pâtissier whose establishment lay along the route created large éclairs in the form of a bicycle wheel and filled them with praline cream.

Making choux paste quenelles

Making beautiful choux paste quenelles with spoons—demonstrated here with Dauphine potatoes (page 49)—is simple if done properly, in two stages.

Take two soup spoons. Fill one with the preparation and shape into a well-rounded oval.

Use the second spoon to detach the quenelle from the first and gently let it drop into the frying oil. Be careful, because the oil may splash.

CLARIFIED BUTTER

Clarifying butter (to make sautéed potatoes or oven fries) prevents it from turning dark or breaking down at high temperatures. Clarified butter hardens again in the refrigerator and can keep for several weeks in a sealed container.

1

Soak the knife blade in cold water before cutting the butter.

2

Keep the butter on its wrapper (so it does not come into contact with the work surface). Cut into dice (to make melting easier).

3

Transfer the butter to a saucepan. Melt over very low heat.

4

The milk serum (white) begins to appear at the bottom as it separates from the butterfat (yellow).

5

Use a spoon or skimmer to remove the froth forming on the surface.

6

Strain the butter through a coffee filter placed inside a conical strainer (sieve). Collect only the yellow liquid. Discard the serum.

DRIED TOMATOES

Make your own dried tomatoes at home with very ripe tomatoes.

INGREDIENTS

- Tomatoes
- Olive oil
- Salt
- Pepper
- Sugar

Peel, quarter, and seed tomatoes.

Roll them in the olive oil with salt, pepper, and sugar.

Lay flat and dry out in the oven for 1 hour 30 minutes to 2 hours at 110°C – 225°F (gas mark 1/4), drizzling one or two times with olive oil during this time.

HERB SACHET

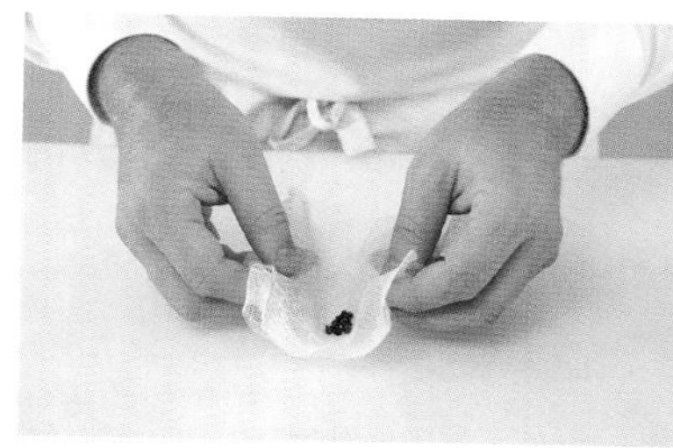

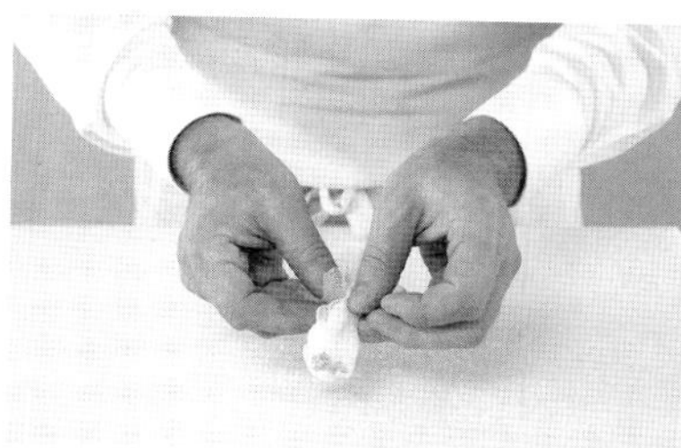

Place the aromatics of your choice (here peppercorns) in a square of cheesecloth.

Bring the sides together, close with two or three twists of kitchen twine, and knot twice. Cut off the excess twine and gauze, and add the sachet to your preparation while cooking. The sachet can be retrieved after cooking, sparing you the task of fishing out the peppercorns and sprigs of herbs, which would not look very attractive on your guests' plates.

PISTOU AND PESTO

Pistou is the Occitan name for Italian pesto, but the basic recipe is the same.

The mortar and pestle are quintessentially Mediterranean utensils. If you don't have one, make this pesto with a hand blender and chopper attachment. The aim is to produce a smooth mixture.

To make mint pesto, substitute 2 sprigs of mint for the basil and don't add any Parmesan. You can vary the recipe to suit your taste.

INGREDIENTS
- 2 cloves garlic
- Salt
- 30 g – 1.06 ounces Parmesan cheese
- 30 g – 1.06 ounces (2 tablespoons) pine nuts
- 2 tablespoons olive oil
- 6 sprigs basil

Peel the garlic cloves, cut in half, and remove the green cores. Pound in the mortar with a pinch of salt. Grate the Parmesan.

Add the pine nuts to the mortar. Pour in 1 tablespoon of oil and pound. Add the grated Parmesan and pound again.

Pluck the basil leaves. Add the leaves to the mortar with 1 tablespoon of oil.

Continue to pound until the sauce is thick and smooth.

PIZZA DOUGH

INGREDIENTS
- 1 (8-g – 0.28-ounce) envelope (sachet) or 2 1/4 teaspoons active dry (easy-blend dried) yeast
- 300 g – 10.5 ounces (2 1/3 cups) flour
- 1 pinch salt
- 1 tablespoon olive oil

1

Dissolve the yeast in 2 tablespoons of warm water. Place the flour on the work surface. Make a well in it. Add the salt and mix.

2

Pour the dissolved yeast into the well, then add the oil.

3

4

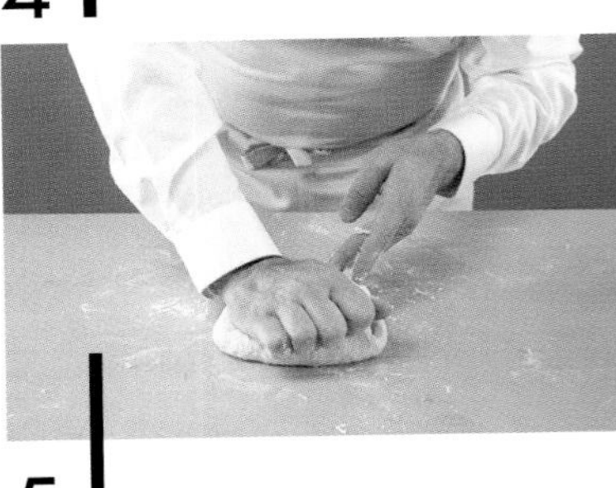

5

Mix with your fingers, gradually bringing the flour in toward the middle and adding a little warm water from time to time to make a soft but not sticky dough.

The amount of water needed depends on how well the flour absorbs water. You will generally require about 150 ml – 2/3 cup water. Lightly dust the work surface with flour and knead the dough by hand to incorporate as much air as possible. You can also use a mixer fitted with a dough hook.

6

Roll the dough into a ball. Put into a bowl. Cover with plastic wrap (cling film). Let the dough rest in a draft-free place until doubled in size, which is known as "rising" or "proofing." For best results, keep the bowl in a place free of drafts (draughts) where the temperature is about 23°C – 73°F. This normally takes 1– hour to 1 hour 30 minutes.

Then, roll out the dough and let rise again at room temperature for about 15 minutes.

RESTING

Many types of dough or batter need to rest. Whether it is cake batter, where resting enhances the chemical action of the yeast, or a tart shell (case), let it rest before baking.

SHORTBREAD DOUGH

INGREDIENTS

- 40 g – 1.4 ounces (3 tablespoons) butter, softened
- 100 g – 3.5 ounces (3/4 cup plus 1 tablespoon) flour
- 25 g – 0.88 ounce *tant pour tant*– a mixture of equal parts confectioners' (icing) sugar and almond meal (ground almonds)
- 25 g – 0.88 ounce (2 tablespoons) sugar
- 1 egg

Put the softened butter into a bowl and beat with a spatula.

Add the flour, the *tant pour tant*, sugar, and egg. Mix well, then roll the dough into a ball.

Rest for 30 minutes in the refrigerator.

Roll the dough on a floured work surface.

VEGETABLE BROTH

Vegetable broth (stock) can be used to make vegetarian risotto or for the long, slow cooking of certain meat dishes, among other things.

You can use all kinds of vegetables to make the broth. If you add green vegetables, be careful to incorporate them toward the end, because they take less time to cook. Avoid using turnips, which give the broth a bitter taste, and beets (beetroot), which change the color.

Save the cooked vegetables as a treat for yourself. Sprinkle with a little fleur de sel and drizzle with olive oil for a vegetable pot-au-feu, or combine with a little broth, butter, olive oil, and vinegar (or lemon juice) for a blanquette of vegetables.

INGREDIENTS

- 3 large button mushrooms
- 4 carrots
- 1 shallot
- 1 white onion
- 1 celeriac
- 2 small leeks
- Black and white peppercorns
- 1 clove
- Kosher (coarse) salt
- Several parsley stems (stalks)
- Several sprigs fresh thyme
- 1 bay leaf
- 1 stem fresh fennel

1

Wash all the vegetables. Peel the mushrooms. Peel the carrots, shallot, and onion. Halve the celeriac. Cut off the leek leaves, setting 3 aside.

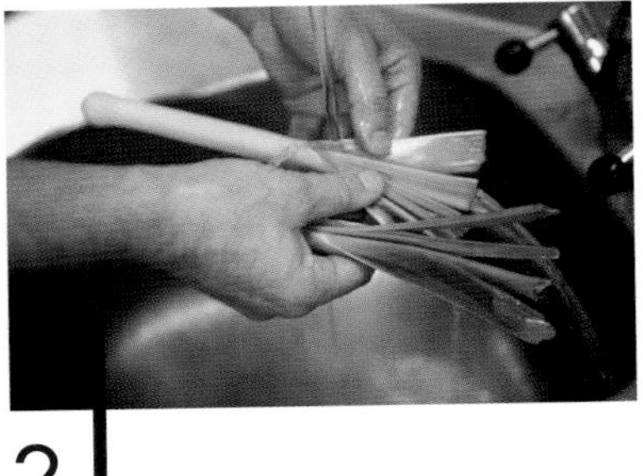

2

Slice the leeks lengthwise, just to where the white part starts, and rinse again under running water, tops down.

Make an herb sachet with a few peppercorns, the clove, and a little kosher salt. Tie it closed with kitchen twine.

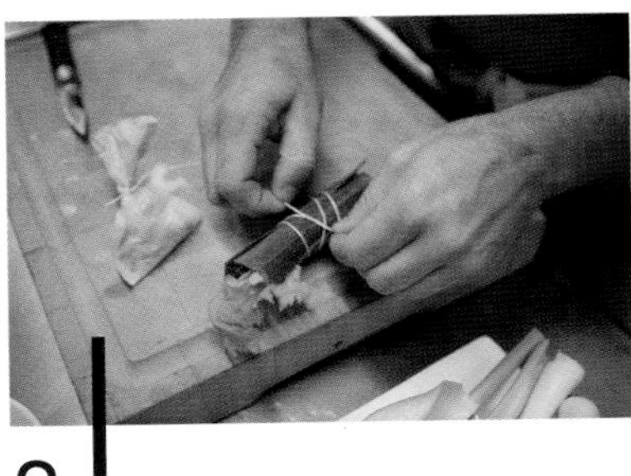

3

Place the parsley stems, thyme, and bay leaf inside 1 reserved leek leaf, along with the fennel stick. Wrap the bouquet garni in the 2 remaining leaves and tie with kitchen twine.

4

Halve the onion and char the cut side of half in a dry skillet or frying pan without oil for 8–10 minutes over high heat.

5

Pour 3 liters – 12 2/3 cups of water into a large stockpot. Add all the vegetables, finishing with the charred onion. Bring to a boil, then cook for 20 minutes over low heat.

Check the vegetables are cooked by piercing. They should be tender.

6

Drain the vegetables and discard the herb sachet.

7

Strain the broth if necessary.

BASIC SAVORY RECIPES AND TECHNIQUES

BLANCHING VEGETABLES

A bath in boiling salted water is followed by a plunge in ice water; this is a shock treatment to keep your green vegetables green and crisp.

Only briefly cooked, blanched vegetables are ready for freezing or to be finished as part of a dish.

If they are left to cook fully, they are then known as boiled vegetables.

COUSCOUS

A brief history

More than just historical, couscous is the stuff of legend, with so many origins attributed to it and coming in so many variations. Legend has it that after King Solomon fell in love with the Queen of Sheba, he was so besotted with her that he could no longer eat or sleep. The court physician hastened to prepare a dish of semolina fragrant with herbs, which restored his strength and delighted him.

The word "couscous" can be confusing, as it refers to both the pasta pellets themselves and the dishes made with them. Couscous (the pasta) may be more or less fine-grained in size. It is typically made from semolina wheat, but couscous dishes are also made from barley in Morocco, green wheat in Algeria, cassava in the Ivory Coast, millet in Senegal and Sudan, and even rice in Niger.

As for the garnishes, they depend on the season and vary according to region. The best known couscous dish is lamb couscous, but anything goes: Sicilian *cusucù* gives prominence to fish; couscous with wild figs from the Atlas Mountains is vegetarian; while couscous made with tripe, dried meat, and green vegetables, among other items, can't be overlooked.

Couscous is traditionally prepared for a large number of guests and special occasions. There is not one kind of couscous, but what they all have in common is warmth and being shareable..

Spices

- **Saffron:** From the Arabic *az-za'faran*, this yellow spice is the most highly prized and costly in the world. As many as 150,000 *Crocus sativus* flowers are needed to make a single kilogram or just over two pounds of saffron. Whether in threads or powdered, it adds an unforgettable flavor to fish and chicken couscous, and it combines wonderfully with ginger.
- **Turmeric:** From the ginger family, turmeric has a musky and earthy flavor that makes it a perfect match for lamb.
- **Ginger:** Whether fresh or powdered, ginger adds heat and acidity. Historically, it was used in place of pepper, which was much more expensive.
- **Ras-el-hanout:** This Moroccan blend contains 27 ingredients: spices (including cinnamon, turmeric, clove, ginger, long pepper), flowers (rose, lavender), and even, surprisingly, belladonna berries and cantharides (the beetle known as Spanish fly, long rumored to be an aphrodisiac).
- **Chili:** Spicy chili is traditionally served separately in the form of Tunisian harissa, which has to be diluted.
- **Paprika:** With its sweet flavor, paprika adds a touch of color and fragrance to beef and fish couscous dishes.

Flavor, color

Be inventive and have fun with spices to create broths to color the couscous: paprika and turmeric for red and orange; but also fresh herbs for green. Try edible flowers (jasmine, lavender) for added sweetness.

Caution, chili

Chile burns and stains. Always use gloves or wash your hands thoroughly after preparing it. Avoid using a cutting board, or it will become permanently stained and flavored.

Couscous

Serves 4
Preparation time: 6 minutes
Cooking time: 10 minutes
Resting time: 20 minutes

INGREDIENTS

- 400 g – 14 ounces (2 1/3 cups) fine- or medium-grain couscous
- 4 g – 0.14 ounce (heaping 1/2 teaspoon) salt
- 60 ml – 1/4 cup fruity olive oil
- 500 ml – 2 cups broth or stock (pair the type of stock with the finished dish)

FOR COLORED COUSCOUS

- Paprika, saffron, fresh herbs, dried flowers (of your choice)

Couscous was traditionally rubbed using *smen*, clarified sheep's milk butter. You can add 50 g – 1.75 ounces (3 1/2 tablespoons) of softened unsalted butter while rubbing the grains, provided the amount of olive oil is reduced to 20 ml – 1 tablespoon plus 1 teaspoon.

1

Put the couscous into a bowl and add a generous amount of cold water. Rinse by shaking the bowl from side to side.

2

Drain through a fine strainer (sieve).

Return the moist couscous to the bowl. Season with salt, then add the olive oil. Let stand for 10 minutes.

3

Rub the couscous between your outspread palms for 3 minutes to coat the grains with the oil; the grains should be glossy.

4

If you are adding spices to your broth, choose the ones you want to use: chili powder, saffron, turmeric, cumin, or something else. Dissolve the spices in the cold broth and gradually bring to a boil.

Add any herbs or flowers to the cold broth and bring to a boil. Next, cover and let infuse for 10 minutes off the heat, then strain.

5

Pour the hot broth in a thin stream over the couscous. Cover with plastic wrap (cling film) and let the grains swell for 10 minutes.

6

Place the top pot of the couscoussier on a plate and throw the couscous against the sides (to prevent the grains from falling through the holes).

Put the broth and garnish into the bottom pot of the couscoussier, or use 1 liter – 4 1/4 cups water if you are preparing the couscous in advance, and bring to a boil. If the liquid doesn't boil, the couscous will stick to the bottom of the pot.

7

Place the top pot over the bottom pot at a boil, cover, and cook for 10 minutes, counting from the moment the steam begins to pass through the couscous.

8

Transfer the couscous to a bowl and loosen the grains with a fork. Serve, or set aside in a warm place covered with plastic wrap.

HARISSA

Preparation time: 20 minutes
For 1 small bowl

INGREDIENTS
- 40 g – 1.4 ounces fresh red chilies
- 2 cloves garlic
- 1 teaspoon salt
- 1/2 teaspoon caraway or cumin seeds
- 1/2 teaspoon coriander seeds
- 40 ml – 2 tablespoons plus 1 1/2 teaspoons olive oil

This Tunisian sauce is made from chilies and garlic pounded to a paste and is served as an accompaniment to lamb or beef couscous. Its intensity varies depending on the chili peppers used, which can have a higher or lower capsaicin content.

To store your homemade harissa, pour it into a jar and cover it with a thin layer of grapeseed oil. This way it should keep for 15 days in the refrigerator.

Resist the urge to taste the harissa with a spoon. Always dilute it with a little broth, or you will be breathing fire.

Another red but much sweeter sauce is tomato harissa. Pound 2 garlic cloves in a mortar together with coriander seeds, salt, and a pinch of sugar. Add 1 red bell pepper, peeled, seeded, and cut into small dice, and 4 dried tomatoes (no seeds) that have been rehydrated.

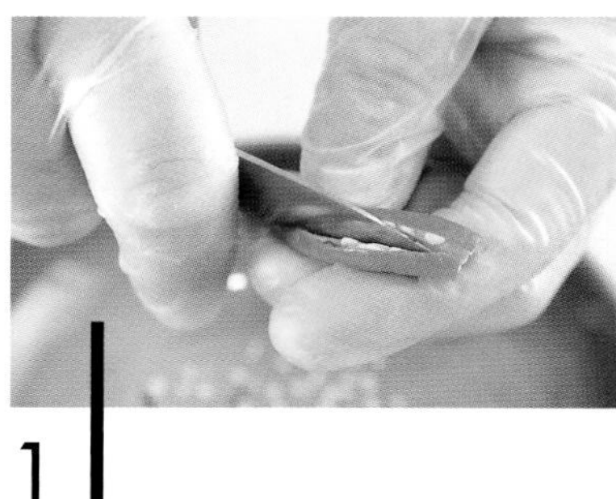

1

After putting on gloves to protect your hands, wash and dry the chilies, remove their stems (stalks), and cut in half lengthwise. Use a knife tip to remove the seeds and white pith.

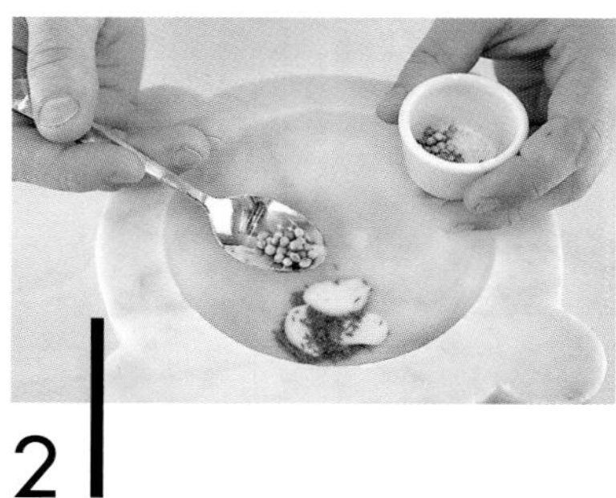

2

Cut the garlic cloves in half and remove the green cores. Peel and put into a mortar. Add the salt. Add the caraway and coriander seeds.

3

Pound to a paste.

4

Add the chilies and crush them coarsely with the pestle. Turn the mortar 90 degrees after each crushing action.

Add 20 ml – 1 tablespoon plus 3/4 teaspoon of olive oil and pound for 10 minutes until you have a paste. Make an emulsion with the remaining oil, as if making mayonnaise.

MARINADES

There is nothing like a well-balanced marinade to give any product a unique flavor. In addition to flavoring, marinades have the special ability to "cook" fish and white meats without heat.

Dry marinade

This is made from dry ingredients (lemon or lime zest, freshly grated ginger, fleur de sel, and freshly ground pepper, for instance), without liquid added. A dry marinade will flavor thin slices of fish in a very short time.

Liquid marinade

The simplest marinade can be made using just lemon juice and olive oil. It can be enhanced with scallions (spring onions) or any other herb.

Gravlax

The process for making gravlax (gravadlax) starts with a dry marinade comprising salt, sugar, pepper, and sometimes fresh dill. As marinating takes a long time (at least 48 hours), a brine is formed from the liquid released by the fish, turning the dry marinade into a liquid marinade. This specialty originated in Sweden, where it is considered a great delicacy.

Interestingly, in the eighteenth century, lightly salted salmon was buried in large holes lined with birch bark, which allowed it to be preserved for a long time. The name of this *gravad lax*, literally "buried salmon," became shortened to gravlax in most European countries.

MASHED POTATOES

Preparation: 20 minutes
Cooking time: 20 minutes

INGREDIENTS

- 700 g – 1 pound 8 ounces Pompadour potatoes
- Kosher (coarse) salt

1

Wash, brush, and peel the potatoes. Cut into pieces.

Pour water into a sauté pan or deep skillet or frying pan, measuring the amount of water you add, and then add 12 g – 0.42 ounce (1 tablespoon) of kosher (coarse) salt for every 1 liter – 4 1/2 cups of water. Add the potatoes and place over medium heat.

Skim while cooking to remove all the froth from the surface. Cook for 20 minutes.

Check that the potatoes are cooked through, using a knife tip, which should pierce a potato easily.

2

Transfer to a colander. Drain until the potato pieces are extremely dry.

3

Put potato pieces in a food mill (fitted with the disk with small holes). Turn the handle to mash the potatoes.

Collect the mash in a bowl. Return the potatoes and pass them through the food mill without adding any water.

Most recipes containing mashed potatoes require them to be very dry. Do not add any liquid while using the food mill. If necessary, dry out the mashed potatoes in a pan over low heat (as if making choux paste).

PARMESAN TUILES

Parmesan tuiles are very easy to make. The trick to making perfect tuiles is to use a round cookie cutter when sprinkling the Parmesan into the pan. These tuiles also make a delicious appetizer for guaranteed impact.

Sprinkle a little finely grated Parmesan cheese into a very hot skillet or frying pan. It will melt, forming bubbles that stick to each other. Push the melted cheese into shape with a spatula.

Take the tuile out of the pan when it is dry and no longer has any white spots.

Drape over a rolling pin and let firm up for 1 minute. Repeat the process to make more tuiles.

RISOTTO: BASICS

Risotto should be cooked slowly.

The secret of a successful risotto is to make the rice "pearly" before incorporating a liquid. This is done by lightly sautéing it for a few minutes in a fat or oil until the grains become shiny and translucent. This process enables the rice grains to open and release their starch while cooking, which gives the dish its creaminess.

A small amount of warm cooking liquid is added regularly to the rice. The choice of liquid will depend on the accompaniment: chicken broth (stock) for a plain or chicken risotto; vegetable broth (stock) for a vegetable risotto; fumet for a rice with seafood; and so forth. This is known as "moistening" the rice.

Moistening is done in three steps, which are repeated several times throughout the cooking process.

First moisten the rice to just cover it with liquid (the equivalent of about a ladle and a half).

Let cook while stirring constantly until the liquid has evaporated, but not completely. The rice should always be moist. To check whether the rice is cooked, cut a grain in half. It should have a small white filament.

The rice must be stirred constantly as it is cooked so that it can release its starch. Don't slack.

Repeat this process until the rice is cooked.

It should take 18 to 20 minutes from when the rice is first moistened.

Here's a tip that lets you enhance the creaminess of this dish. After cooking the risotto, incorporate some butter (or olive oil), Parmesan cheese (except for fish and seafood risottos), and half-whipped cream.

Once you master the technique for risotto, there's no limit to the combinations you can put together. Almost any green vegetable is a good choice for risotto. There are also sweet risottos and risottos made with shellfish or fish.

SOCCA NISSARDA

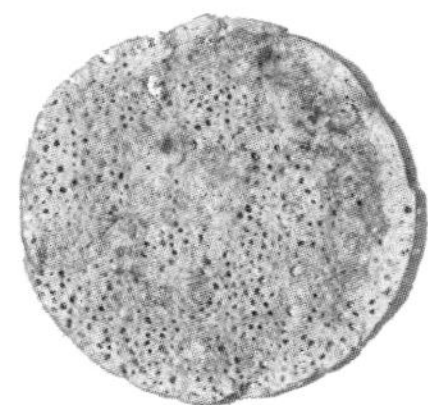

This baked chickpea flour crepe is a part of the culinary tradition of the Mediterranean districts of France, more specifically of the Nice region. The chickpea is a legume (pulse) that held an important place in Provence in the late Middle Ages. Today, its cultivation is limited to the Provence-Alpes-Côte d'Azur region, the southern Drôme region, and Languedoc. The chickpea is also known as the garbanzo bean.

In the Provençal language, it is called *cese* or *pese pounchud*.

Whatever the season, socca can be found in the markets of Nice, often on the large copper trays used to cook them, presenting a golden face to entice customers. This relatively thick crepe (about 1 cm – 1/2 inch) owes its success not only to the quality of the flour used, but also to the proportions of the ingredients used to make it: chickpea flour (also known as besan or gram flour), salt, olive oil, and water.

A little thicker, a little runnier? The results are up to you.

Preparation time: 5 minutes
Resting time: 5 hours
Cooking time: 5 minutes

INGREDIENTS

- 70 g – 2.47 ounces (3/4 cup) chickpea (besan or gram) flour
- 15 ml – 1 tablespoon plus 2 teaspoons olive oil, divided
- Fine salt
- Freshly ground pepper

Put the flour into a bowl. Add 200 ml – 3/4 cup plus 1 tablespoon water while stirring with a whisk. Add 15 ml – 1 tablespoon of olive oil, 2 large pinches of salt, and 5 twists of the peppermill.

Cover with plastic wrap (cling film) and refrigerate for 5 hours.

Blend the socca batter with a hand blender. Heat 1 teaspoon of olive oil in a skillet or frying pan.

Pour in a ladle (about 1/2 cup) of batter. Spread out evenly. When the edges have set, transfer the pan to the oven and cook for 3 minutes.

Lift the socca out with a wide spatula and turn it over onto the work surface.

Sprinkle with freshly ground pepper. Repeat the process to make a second socca.

SOUP COOLING

Empty one or two trays of ice cubes into a large bowl (larger than the bowl or other container that will hold the soup) and add very cold water.

Place the bowl or other container that will hold the soup inside the bowl of ice water.

SUSHI

A brief history

Originally from Japan, a land of innovation and culinary tradition, sushi, principally a combination of vinegared rice and fresh fish in delicious bite-size portions, has crossed borders to appear in the world's best restaurants. While sushi is known to have existed since the eighth century, it was not then as we know it today, given that white rice was a luxury product reserved for the elite. A coarser form of rice was used to wrap fish packed in boxes for transport; the fish was eaten fermented (*narezushi*), while the rice was thrown away. The combination of rice and seafood has far-reaching roots.

However, it was not until the Edo period (1603–1867), a time of stability in Japan, that Hanaya Yohei invented the most famous form of sushi, *nigiri-zushi* (hand-squeezed sushi). Actually, he was not the only cook to offer this new food, but he became particularly famous for turning it into a restaurant-quality dish and for transforming what was a cold snack, sold in the street to be eaten quickly, into the specialty of his establishment. He was actually arrested and tried for selling a cheap meal at a high price, in violation of Japanese sumptuary laws, and for teaching other cooks to do the same. But his name has gone down in history. These differences still endure today. You can find very fast and economical sushi prepared in small inexpensive restaurants, and sushi of extraordinary freshness and refinement in high-quality restaurants.

Buying

Never compromise the freshness of your fish. It should be of excellent quality; check it yourself at a reputable fish merchant.

Preparation

Only use cold water to clean the fish and other ingredients to avoid producing the slightest alteration when cooking. Your hands should also stay cool.

Plating

The choice of dish is also essential. The first precept of Japanese cuisine is that "the plate defines the aesthetics of the flavor." The visual sensation of a dish is as important as the quality of the technique used to make it.

Cutting fish for sushi

The shape, and therefore the art of cutting, is what gives sushi its flavor. Cut the fish quickly and with precision.

Choose a knife with a thin blade (a fillet knife, for example) that has been extremely well sharpened. Slide the blade at a diagonal along a fillet of tuna to obtain even slices about 5 mm – 1/4 inch in thickness.

Preparing wasabi

Preparation time: 10 minutes

INGREDIENTS

- 10 g – 0.35 ounce (2 teaspoons) "Western wasabi" (horseradish) powder

True wasabi is a fragile root plant that is highly sought after and now quite rare. Consequently, the Japanese import stronger-tasting horseradish, which they have christened "Western wasabi." This is why horseradish is used here. Wasabi can also be found in a tube, but it contains other ingredients.

Adjust the amount of wasabi, depending on the recipe and the number of pieces of sushi you are making. Make sure to follow the ratio of wasabi powder and water.

Use a small spoon, preferably made of bamboo, to measure out the wasabi powder.

Add 20 ml – 1 tablespoon plus 1 teaspoon water (you can use bottled water).

Mix with chopsticks. Avoid proximity with your eyes.

Preparing sushi vinegar

Preparation time: 35 minutes
Cooking time: 3 minutes

INGREDIENTS

- 500 ml – 2 cups raspberry vinegar
- 100 g – 3.5 ounces (1/3 cup) salt
- 100 g – 3.5 ounces (1/2 cup) sugar

This version uses raspberry vinegar, but you can use any type of vinegar you prefer and adjust the amount of sugar and salt to your taste.

This preparation will keep for 3 to 4 months in a bottle in the refrigerator. It can be reused.

Prepare all the ingredients and cover the stove top with aluminum foil to protect against splashing.

Pour the vinegar into a saucepan. Add the salt. Then add the sugar and dissolve with a spatula. Bring to a boil, then turn off the heat. Remove from heat. Check that the salt and sugar have dissolved completely. Set aside.

Cooking and preparing the rice (gohan)

Preparation time: 15 minutes
Cooking time: 45 minutes
Resting time: 2 hours

INGREDIENTS
- 600 g – 1 pound 5 ounces (3 cups) Japanese (Japonica) short-grain rice
- 100 ml – 1/3 cup plus 1 tablespoon plus 1 teaspoon vinegar (see opposite)

EQUIPMENT
- 1 electric rice cooker
- 1 flat-bottomed wooden tub (*oke*)

Mix the rice very gently, being careful not to smash it. During the last mixing process, do not spread the vinegar out too evenly. This way the sushi will not be monotonous and will have an interesting flavor.

Tradition dictates that the rice should be fanned. This isn't essential; air flow will suffice. Open a window to prevent hot, moist steam from falling back on the rice.

1

Put the rice into the cooking bowl of the rice cooker and check the quality of the grains. Remove any small stones you find.

Fill the bowl halfway with running water to wash the rice. Stir gently with your hand.

2

Drain the rice in a strainer (sieve). Discard the water. Repeat this process two or three times.

Return the rice to the rice cooker with an equal quantity of water and let soak for at least 2 hours.

3

Cook for 45 minutes. When the rice is cooked, protect your hands as you remove the hot bowl from the rice cooker.

4

Put the rice into the ***oke*** and spread the grains over the bottom with a wooden spatula.

Use a ladle to sprinkle the vinegar over the rice here and there.

5

Turn the rice over in small clumps to mix with the vinegar, but not too much. Set the rice aside until it cools to room temperature.

Making rice balls for nigiri-zushi

This basic technique can be used to make the rice balls for all nigiri-zushi.

Leaving a small air pocket in the rice is the sushi master's secret; the trick is to make the sushi as light as possible by adding air to the rice, making it easier to digest

1

Prepare a bowl of water, a small napkin, and a 20-g – 0.75-ounce rice ball on your work surface.

2

Wet the fingers of one hand.

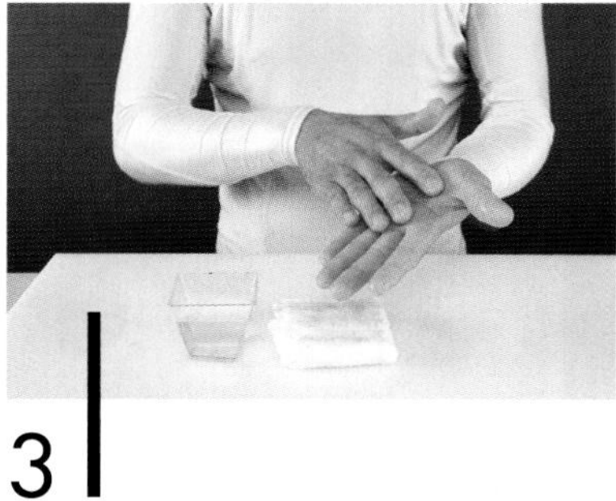

3

Spread the water over the palm of the other hand.

4

Shape the rice into an even ball.

5

Make a hole in the rice ball by pressing with your finger.

6

Pick up the rice ball between your thumb and index finger.

7

Turn it over gently.

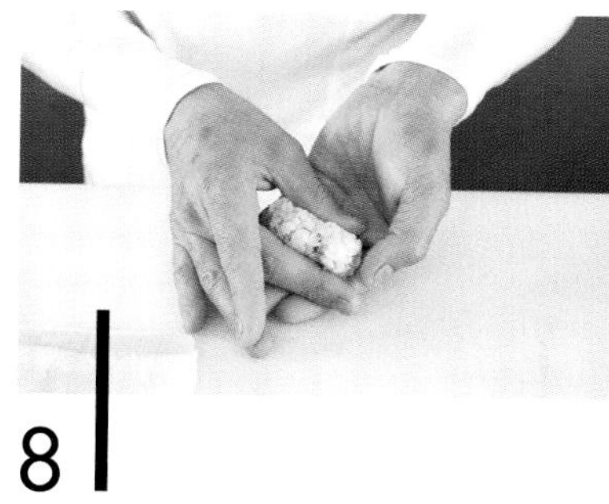

8

Use your thumb and middle finger to elongate it a little.

9

Dry your hand before handling the topping.

Making a japanese omelet (tamagoyaki)

Preparation time: 10 minutes
Cooking time: 10 minutes

INGREDIENTS

- 1/2 teaspoon cornstarch (cornflour)
- 2 tablespoons mirin (sweet cooking rice wine)
- 1/2 teaspoon soy sauce
- 7 eggs
- A little oil

EQUIPMENT

- 1 set bamboo chopsticks
- 1 square skillet or frying pan (18-cm – 7-inch sides)
- 1 bamboo rolling mat

1

Add the cornstarch to a bowl containing the mirin. Mix with the chopsticks.

Add the soy sauce. Mix gently.

Break the eggs into a large bowl. Beat the eggs lightly with the chopsticks.

2

Add the soy sauce mixture. Beat well to mix thoroughly.

Oil the pan with a brush (or use a sheet of paper towel dipped in oil) and heat well.

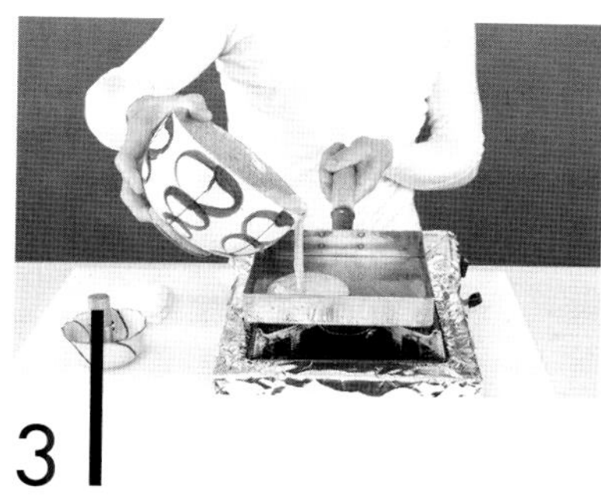

3

Pour a little egg mixture over the bottom of the pan, as if making a crepe Stir the mixture to spread it over the pan, bursting any bubbles with the chopsticks.

4

You now have to roll the omelet four times, starting by folding a quarter. Fold again at halfway. Fold to three-quarters.

5

Fold the last quarter, being careful not to trap any air so that the omelet remains compact.

Lightly oil the empty part of the pan. Push the omelet to the far side of the pan. Oil lightly.

6

Pour in more omelet mixture for a second layer.

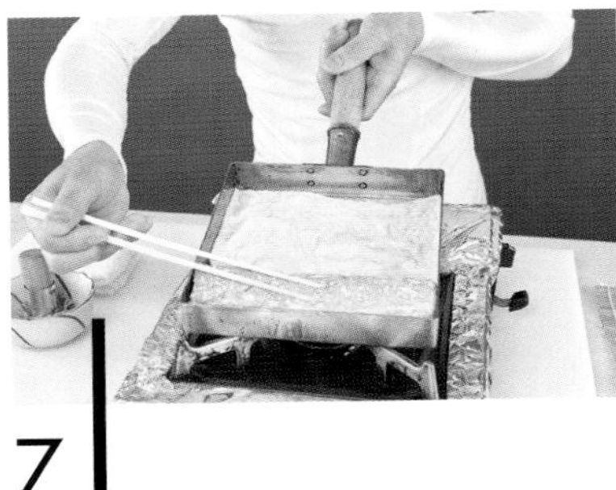

7

Lift up the cooked egg roll so that the mixture can spread around the whole pan. Position the cooked egg over the new, barely set layer.

8

Roll again.

9

Repeat the process until all of the mixture has been used. Turn off the heat. Cover the pan with the bamboo mat.

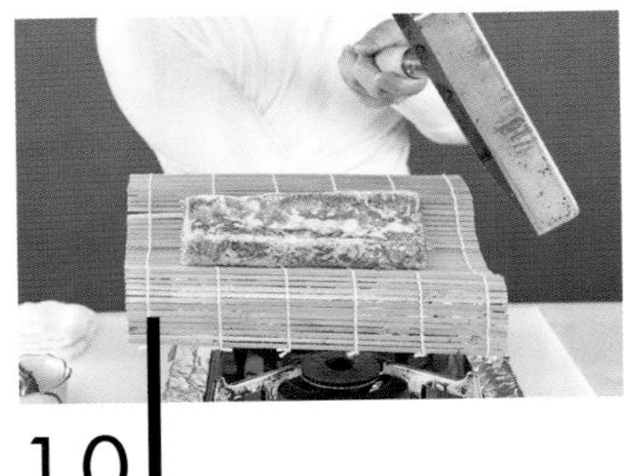

10

Place your hand on the mat. Turn the pan over, moving the omelet to the mat.

11

Fold the two ends of the mat over the top. Press with your fingers and let cool to achieve the final shape.

TOMATO BONBONS

Makes 12 bonbons

INGREDIENTS

- 6 (3-cm- – 1-inch–diameter) tomatoes
- Fine salt
- 250-g – 9-ounce block mozzarella cheese
- Fleur de sel
- Freshly ground pepper

Bring water to a boil. Cut a cross in the bottom of each tomato. Immerse in the boiling water for 10 seconds.

Drain, then immerse in ice water for a few minutes. Peel the tomatoes and remove the stems (stalks). Reserve the skins.

Halve the tomatoes. Use a small spoon to hollow them out. Sprinkle with salt. Let stand for 30 minutes to release any residual water.

Use a melon baller to make 12 mozzarella balls.

Spread plastic wrap (cling film) over the work surface. Cut the plastic into twelve 15-cm – 6-inch squares.

Place one tomato half in the middle of each square. Season with a little fleur de sel and pepper. Fill each tomato half with a mozzarella ball.

Bring the sides of a square together and tightly twist closed. Repeat the process with the remaining tomato halves.

Once the tomatoes have been filled and seasoned with salt and pepper, bring the sides of each square together and tightly twist in a clockwise direction until there is no air left inside.

To eat, put a bonbon into your mouth, holding one end of the plastic, and pull on the plastic to remove.

BASIC SWEET RECIPES AND TECHNIQUES

APPLE JELLY

Save the syrup left over from making apple compote and heat.

After it comes to a gentle boil, reduce over low heat.

Once the syrup thickens enough to coat a spoon, turn off the heat.

The syrup will set naturally as it cooks because of the natural pectin found in apples.

Store in a sealed jar in the refrigerator.

BASIC SYRUP

INGREDIENTS

– 250 g – 9 ounces (1 1/4 cups) sugar

This syrup is mainly used to soak ladyfingers (boudoir biscuits) to make charlottes. It should be warm; if cold, the ladyfingers will soak it up very slowly, and if hot, they may fall apart.

1

2

3

4

5

Pour 600 ml – 2 1/2 cups water into a saucepan.

Add the sugar. Heat over medium heat.

Turn off the heat when the syrup comes to a boil.

Transfer to a container large enough to soak the ladyfingers.

To store, cover with plastic wrap (cling film) or pour into an airtight container to prevent a skin from forming.

BEATING EGG WHITES

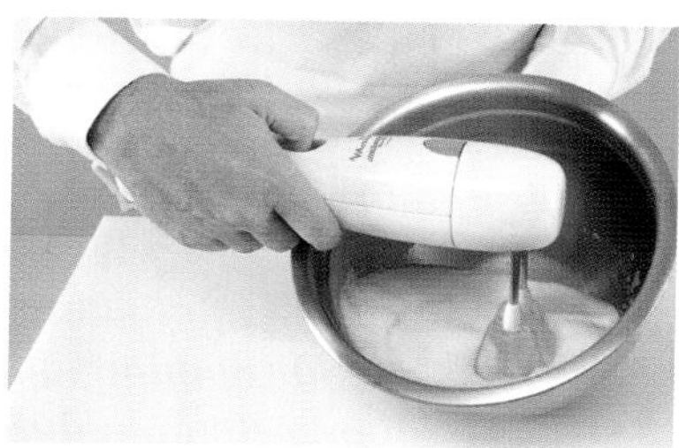

You can beat your egg whites like a pro, using a balloon wire whisk, or if you're feeling lazy (or impatient), use an electric mixer (whisk).

Egg whites beat better in a metal bowl.

BRETON SHORTBREAD COOKIES (BISCUITS)

INGREDIENTS

- 125 g – 4.4 ounces (1 stick plus 1 tablespoon) butter, softened
- 250 g – 9 ounces (2 cups) all-purpose (plain) flour
- 10 g – 0.35 ounce (2 teaspoons) baking powder
- 100 g – 3.5 ounces (1/2 cup) sugar
- 3 g – 0.1 ounce (1/2 teaspoon) salt
- 3 egg yolks
- 1 vanilla bean (pod), halved lengthwise and seeds scraped

Mix the softened butter with the flour, baking powder, sugar, and salt in a bowl.

Add the egg yolks mixed with the seeds scraped from the vanilla bean.

Roll the dough into a cylinder and refrigerate for 30 minutes.

Preheat the oven to 180°C – 350°F (gas mark 4). Cut the cylinder into 5-mm – 1/4-inch slices. Lay them on a baking sheet (tray).

Bake until golden and crisp, about 15 minutes.

BUTTERCREAM

Makes 250 g – 9 ounces (1 3/4 cups)
Preparation time: 25 minutes
Cooking time: 10 minutes
Refrigeration time: 1 hour

INGREDIENTS

- 125 g – 4.4 ounces (1 stick plus 1 tablespoon) butter, softened
- 1 egg + 2 egg yolks
- 88 g – 3.1 ounces (3/4 cup) confectioners' (icing) sugar

EQUIPMENT

- Stand mixer
- 1 cooking or candy thermometer

In this book, buttercream is used for filling coconut, vanilla, hazelnut, and pistachio macarons.

The minimum amount of buttercream that can be prepared is 250 g – 9 ounces; otherwise there will not be enough egg white to beat. Save unused cream to fill other desserts, such as tarts, choux puffs, and millefeuille.

Softened butter is essential for making the buttercream soft. If your butter isn't soft enough, give it a few seconds in the microwave.

If you don't have a thermometer, check the sugar syrup by holding a spoon under cold water, then sticking it very quickly into the sugar. Immediately put it back under the cold water. You should be able to make a small ball with the syrup between your fingers; this is known as the "soft ball" stage.

Weigh out all the ingredients individually.

Whisk the butter until it is very soft and creamy.

Put the egg and the 2 yolks into the bowl of the mixer. Set aside.

Combine the sugar with 25 ml – 1 tablespoon plus 2 teaspoons water in a saucepan and heat to 121°C – 250°F over medium heat.

When the temperature of the syrup reaches 110°C – 230°F, beat the eggs on the highest speed, then once the syrup reaches the appropriate temperature, add the boiling syrup to the eggs while beating.

Continue to beat until the mixture has cooled (about 5 minutes). Add the butter.

Beat for 5 minutes on low speed to obtain a smooth cream.

Cover the buttercream with plastic wrap (cling film) and refrigerate.

CARAMEL

When making a dry caramel, you have to move the pan constantly, because it is less homogeneous than a syrup made with sugar and water. On the other hand, it burns less quickly.

If you want to succeed at making dry caramel, you must not use any utensils to stir it. Hold the handle firmly to control the pan and tilt it in every direction.

1

2

3

4

Add sugar to a skillet or frying pan, a little at a time. This will help it to melt well. If you put all the sugar in at once, you may end up with a lumpy caramel.

Hold the handle and move the pan with a rocking motion to spread the caramel around and mix it.

Continue tilting the pan in every direction. When the caramel is golden, remove from heat.

If the caramel is grainy or the sugar clumps, it means your utensils weren't perfectly clean. It may be helpful to clean the sides of the pan with a wet pastry brush while cooking.

CARAMELIZING A TART SHELL

By applying butter and sugar to a tart shell (base), you caramelize the underside. Whether hot or cold, your tart will have a guaranteed crunch. Be sure to watch it carefully when baking, because the caramel can burn quickly.

On a sheet of parchment (baking) paper, roll out the dough to a thickness of 3 mm – 1/8 inch. Brush with clarified butter. Sprinkle with sugar.

Slide the dough onto a rack and place a baking sheet (tray) upside down on top.

Turn everything over and remove the rack and parchment. Preheat the oven to 210°C – 400°F (gas mark 6-7).

CHANTILLY CREAM

The first rule is to always use a light (single) cream that has not had its fat content reduced.

It has to be very cold; before whipping the cream, put it in the freezer in its packaging for 10 minutes to chill thoroughly. It will whip more easily and quickly.

Another trick is to chill the bowl you'll be using.

A word of caution: Don't overwhip cream, because its fat will turn into butter.

CHOCOLATE CARAMEL

1

2

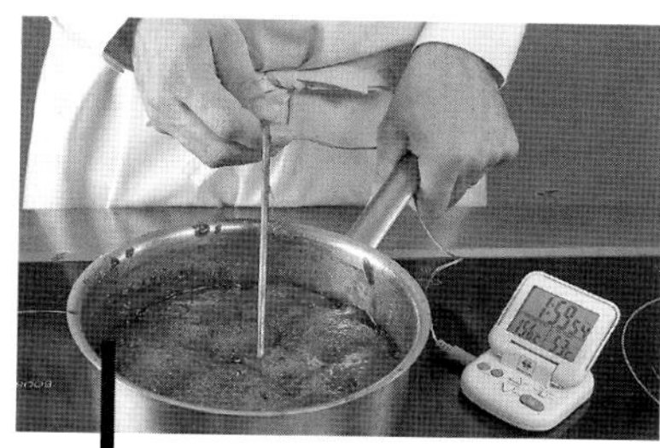

3

4

INGREDIENTS

- 350 g – 12.3 ounces (1 3/4 cups) sugar
- 50 g – 1.75 ounces (3 tablespoons) glucose syrup (page 543)
- 20 g – 0.75 ounce dark chocolate (99% cocoa)
- 8 drops red food coloring
- 10 g – 0.35 ounce (2/3 tablespoon) butter, in cubes

Put the sugar into a saucepan. Add 250 ml – 1 cup of water. Add the glucose syrup and mix. Heat over high heat until it boils. Meanwhile, cut up the chocolate into small pieces with a knife.

As soon as the syrup reaches a low boil, whisk in the chocolate. Mix well. Let boil.

If the mixture isn't perfectly smooth, blend with a hand blender. Check the temperature with a thermometer. Let it reach 156°C – 313°F.

When it reaches this temperature, add the red food coloring. Mix well and remove from heat.

Add the butter. Stir well.

CHOCOLATE COATING

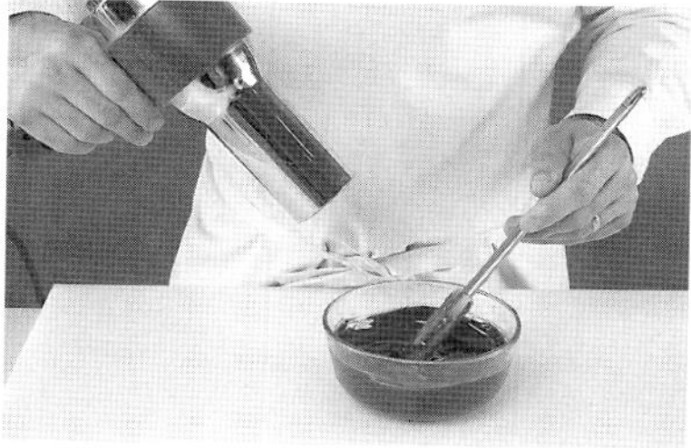

INGREDIENTS

- 100 g – 3.5 ounces dark chocolate (56% cocoa)

Break the chocolate into pieces and place in a heatproof bowl.

Place it over a saucepan with water (bain-marie) and heat over medium heat. Use a thermometer to monitor the temperature, which should reach 55°C – 130°F.

In the meantime, put cold water and ice cubes into a container a little larger than the bowl used for the chocolate.

Stir the chocolate. When it reaches 55°C – 130°F, remove from heat.

Remove the bowl from the bain-marie and put it in the ice bath. Check the thermometer to be sure the temperature falls to 27°C – 81°F.

While stirring constantly, use a hair dryer to increase the temperature to 30°C – 86°F. Use immediately.

LADYFINGERS (BOUDOIR BISCUITS)

Preparation time: 10 minutes
Cooking time: 8 minutes (plain) or 5 minutes (chocolate)
Makes 60 cookies

INGREDIENTS

- 4 eggs (for 125 g – 4.4 ounces egg white and 80 g – 2.82 ounces egg yolk)
- 50 g – 1.75 ounces (1/3 cup plus 1 tablespoon plus 1 teaspoon) flour
- 50 g – 1.75 ounces (1/3 cup plus 1 tablespoon plus 1 teaspoon) cornstarch (cornflour)
- 100 g – 3.5 ounces (1/2 cup) sugar
- 50 g – 1.75 ounces (1/3 cup plus 1 tablespoon plus 1 teaspoon) confectioners' (icing) sugar for dusting

For chocolate ladyfingers, add

- 30 g – 1.06 ounces (1/4 cup) unsweetened cocoa powder
- 50 g – 1.75 ounces (1/3 cup plus 1 tablespoon plus 1 teaspoon) confectioners' (icing) sugar for dusting
- 20 g – 0.75 ounce (2 tablespoons plus 2 1/4 teaspoons) confectioners' (icing) sugar for dusting

EQUIPMENT

- 1 pastry (piping) bag
- 1 plain pastry tip (nozzle) 14 mm – 1/2 inch in diameter

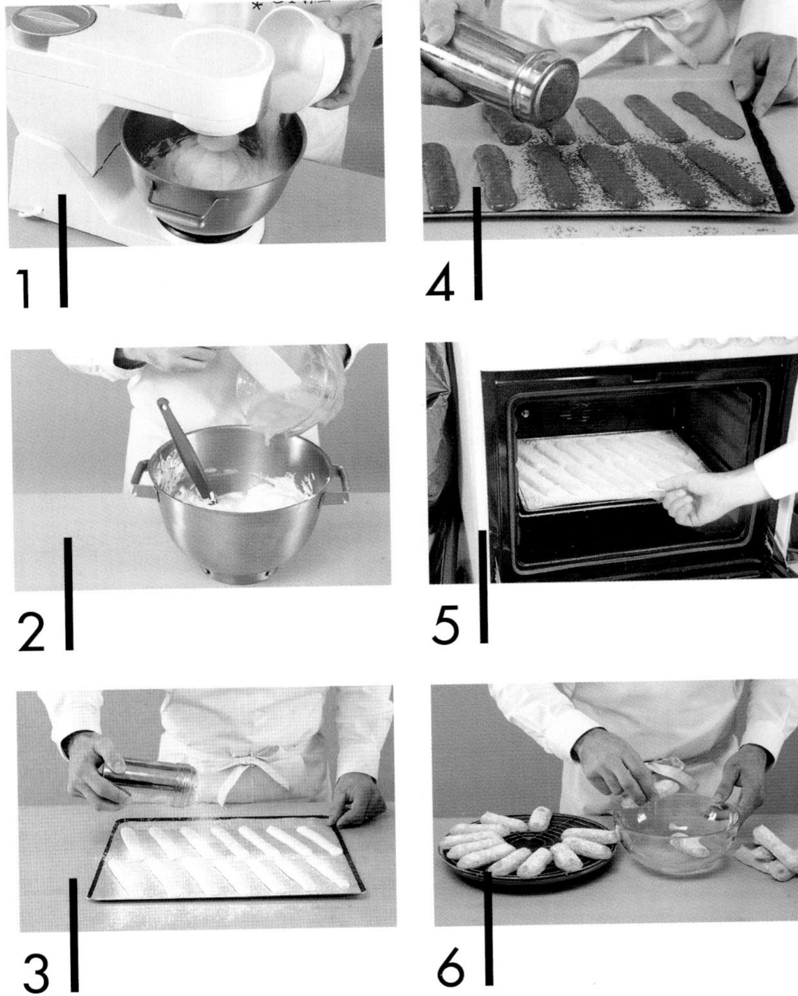

Preheat the oven to 190°C – 375°F (gas mark 5, convection or fan assist, if possible). Break the eggs and separate the whites from the yolks. Weigh out the required amounts.

Sift the flour and cornstarch (and cocoa for the chocolate ladyfingers) through a fine strainer (sieve). Mix these dry ingredients.

Put the egg whites into the bowl of a mixer. Beat to soft peaks on medium speed.

Add the sugar while beating. Increase the speed and beat to firm peaks.

Remove the bowl from the mixer. Fold in the egg yolks.

Add the sifted ingredients. Fold gently to prevent the egg whites from collapsing.

Fill a pastry bag with the batter. Pipe lines of batter 8–10 cm – 3–4 inches in length on a baking sheet (tray) lined with parchment (baking) paper, leaving plenty of space between them.

Dust with confectioners' sugar for plain ladyfingers or with cocoa for chocolate ladyfingers.

Dust again with confectioners' sugar (for both types) to form a crust.

Bake for 8 minutes (plain) or 5 minutes (chocolate). Transfer to a cooling rack.

SOAKING THE LADYFINGERS IN SYRUP

Ladyfingers "drink" very quickly, even more so if they are very dry.

Don't soak them in advance. Soak them, one at a time, when they are ready for placing in the mold.

Put them on a rack and let them drain so that they don't turn too soft. However, if syrup runs out through the bottom of your charlotte, mop it up with paper towel and don't soak the ladyfingers you place at the bottom; they'll gorge themselves on the excess.

MERINGUES

The secrets to making a successful meringue: perfectly clean and dry utensils; eggs brought to room temperature in advance; sugar added very gradually to give it time to dissolve; and as little handling as possible so that it doesn't collapse.

INGREDIENTS

- 80 g – 2.82 ounces egg whites (about 4 large/UK medium eggs)
- 80 g – 2.82 ounces (1/3 cup plus 1 tablespoon) sugar
- 80 g – 2.82 ounces (2/3 cup) confectioners' (icing) sugar, plus more for dusting

EQUIPMENT

- 1 stand mixer
- Pastry (piping) bag + plain tip (nozzle) 10-mm – 3/8-inch diameter

Preheat the oven to 90°C – 194°F (gas mark 1/4). Put the egg whites in the bowl of the mixer. Beat on high speed.

When the egg whites form soft peaks, gradually add the sugar while beating on medium speed (for about 10 minutes).

When the whites are very stiff, smooth, and shiny and they stick to the spatula, stop the mixer.

Gradually add the 80 g – 2.82 ounces confectioners' sugar. Gently fold in.

Fit the pastry bag with the tip and fill with the meringue.

Pipe long lines of meringue onto a baking sheet (tray) lined with parchment (baking) paper. Dust with additional confectioners' sugar.

Bake at 110–130°C – 225–250°F (gas mark 1/4–1/2) until dry and hard, 1 hour to 1 hour 30 minutes. Set aside.

1

2

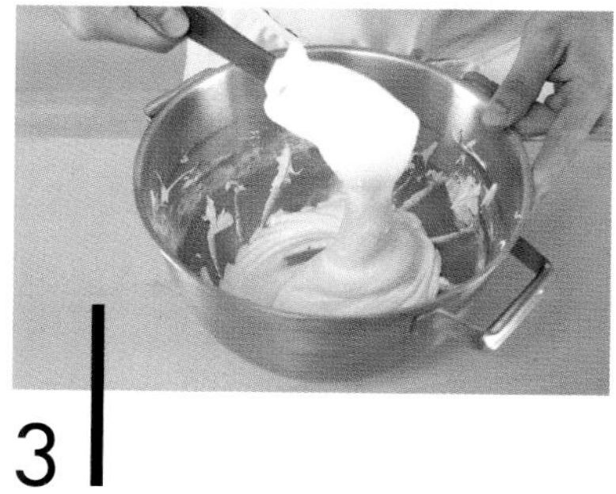

3

4

MOUSSELINE CREAM

Preparation time: 30 minutes
Cooking time: 5 minutes

INGREDIENTS
- 100 g – 3.5 ounces (7 tablespoons) butter, in cubes
- 300 g – 10.5 ounces vanilla pastry cream (opposite)

EQUIPMENT
- 1 stand mixer

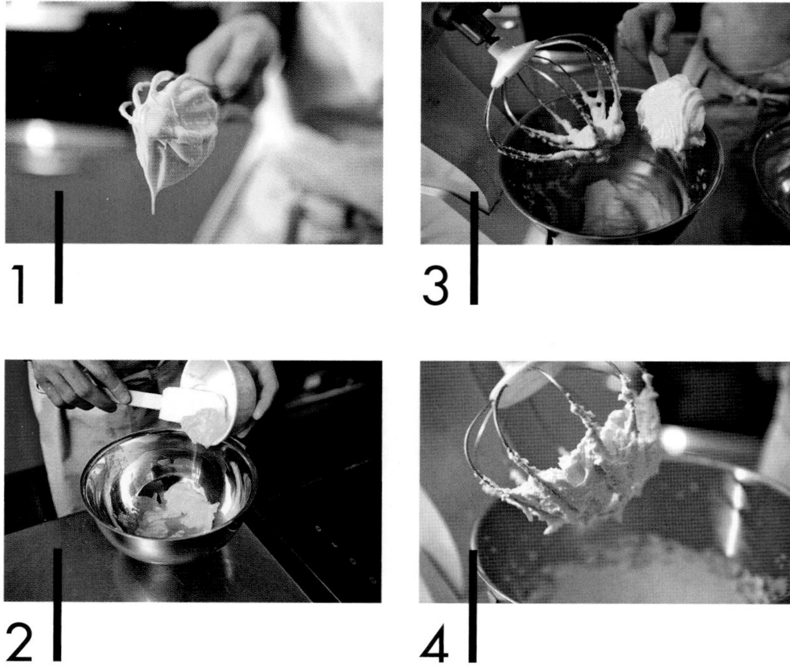

Soften the butter for 40 seconds in a microwave (600 W) until it has the same consistency as the pastry cream.

Combine the butter and the pastry cream and beat on high speed in the mixer until smooth.

Scrape any butter from the bottom or edges of the bowl with a silicone spatula.

Beat again, then refrigerate until use.

VANILLA PASTRY CREAM

Makes 400 g – 14 ounces (about 1 2/3 cups)
Cooking time: 15 minutes
Refrigeration time: 1 hour

INGREDIENTS

- 1 vanilla bean (pod)
- 250 g – 9 ounces (1 cup) milk
- 3 egg yolks
- 50 g – 1.75 ounces (1/4 cup) sugar
- 20 g – 0.75 ounce (2 tablespoons plus 1 1/2 teaspoons) flour
- 20 g – 0.75 ounce (2 tablespoons plus 1 1/2 teaspoons) cornstarch (cornflour)

Use extra-large (UK medium) eggs (60 g – 2.11 ounces: 1 white weighs 30 g – 1.06 ounces; 1 yolk weighs 20 g – 0.75 ounce; and count 10 g – 0.35 ounce for the shell).

Do not let any sugar remain on the egg yolks without stirring; the sugar will "cook" the yolks. Whisk the mixture immediately until thick and pale, a sign that the sugar has dissolved.

Immediately after transferring the pastry cream to a dish, cover it to prevent the formation of a skin.

1

2

3

4

5

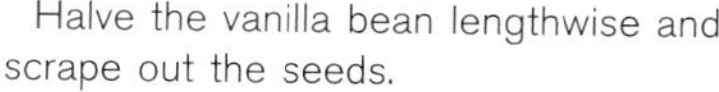

Halve the vanilla bean lengthwise and scrape out the seeds.

Pour the milk into a saucepan. Add the vanilla bean and seeds and stir to distribute the seeds evenly throughout the milk.

Slowly bring to a boil, stirring from time to time.

Remove the vanilla bean just before the milk comes to a boil.

Put the egg yolks into a bowl with the sugar and whisk.

Add the flour and mix; then add the cornstarch and whisk again.

Add two small portions of hot milk (about 3/4 cup) to the bowl and mix.

Pour the contents of the bowl into the saucepan over the heat and cook, stirring vigorously, until the cream thickens.

Remove from heat. Add the rest of the mixture, scraping the bowl well with a silicone spatula.

If the cream sticks to the whisk, it is not cooked. Return to heat and whisk for another minute to cook completely.

Line a dish with plastic wrap (cling film), pour the cream into it, and cover the top with more plastic wrap. Let cool, then refrigerate.

INDEX BY LEVEL OF DIFFICULTY

EASY

Aïoli 8
All-chocolate muffins 100
Anchoïade 9
Apple, artichoke, and beet carpaccio 18
Apple compote 82
Apple crisp 92
Apple shortbread barquettes and granita 122
Apple sorbet 120
Apple tart 88–89, 90
Apple tiramisu 70
Apples in syrup 64
Apricot and lavender macarons 106
Baked apples 86
Boulangère potatoes 52
Brownies 94
Celeriac and apple rémoulade 16
Chicken and Granny Smith apple salad with tangy cream 22
Chilled tomato soup 28
Chocolate îles flottantes 80
Chocolate macalongs 118
Chocolate macarons 114–115, 116
Chocolate truffles 132
Cold couscous salad with crunchy vegetables 20
Confiture de lait (caramel) 68
Cookies 102
Cream of squash soup 34
Dauphine potatoes 49
Desert roses in three chocolates 130
Duchess potatoes 46
Eggplant caviar 10
Eggs en cocotte with salmon and spinach 58
Exotic apple salad 84
Foie gras butter 12
Gratin dauphinois 50
Leek and potato soup 32
Lyonnaise salad 24
Marinated cod appetizers with fragrant rice 62
Mediterranean tian of zucchini, tomatoes, and mozzarella 56
Mint pastilles 124
Niçoise salad 14
Orange-lavender scones 104
Panna cotta with peaches and caramelized almonds 72
Potato croquettes 48
Potato pie 54
Pralines and caramelized hazelnuts 134
Raspberry macarons 110
Raspberry muffins 98
Ratatouille 42
Salmon tartare 60
Soupe au pistou (Provençal vegetable soup with pistou) 38
Stewed apples 66
Tapenade 11
Three-chocolate crème brûlée 78
Three-chocolate panna cotta 74
Three-chocolate pots de crème 76
Tiramisu-style charlotte 96
Vanilla marshmallows 126
Warm Ratte and Vitellote potato salad 26
Zucchini flower fritters 41

INTERMEDIATE

Apple and vanilla charlotte 346
Apple turnovers 376
Artichoke tians 186
Avocado mousse with crayfish 192
Barigoule artichokes 158
Beef carpaccio pearls 148
Bouillabaisse 246
Broiled lamb skewers, red bell pepper coulis, and pan-fried sucrine lettuce 290
Candied orange and orangettes 388
Caramelized veal spareribs with mashed potatoes 274
Cheese puffs 138
Chicken couscous with almonds, raisins, and saffron 278
Chocolat liégeois 326
Chocolate and banana charlotte 362
Chocolate caramel lollipops 400
Chocolate chouquettes 372
Chocolate mousse 336
Choux sticks with hazelnut and chocolate cream 324
Citrus charlotte 358
Coconut macarons 382
Cod confit with cranberry bean puree 222
Cod sticks with red bell pepper sauce 206
Cod tian with spinach and potato 204
Coffee éclairs 332
Couscous with paprika and spiced meatballs 280
Crispy salad with flash-seared tuna 152
Darphin potatoes 160
Daube de boeuf à l'orange (braised beef with orange) 312
Deconstructed rice with mussels and saffron sauce 194
Duck breast with bigarade sauce 270
Duck roulade with apple chutney 144
Duck tian with oranges and turnips 266
Eggs florentine 316
Fish stew with saffron couscous 200
Foie gras en papillote with figs and porcini 264
Foie gras on toast with apples 252
Foie gras terrine with pears 254

Fruits déguisés (dried fruit with marzipan) 390
Gravlax-style cod with mango sauce 216
Grilled salmon 230
Hazelnut macarons 384
Lamb curry with coconut rice 286
Lamb tagine with couscous and nuts 284
Lemon candies 396
Mont Blanc–style charlotte 366
Montélimar nougat 394
Navarin of lamb with spring vegetables 304
One-sided salmon 226
Pan-fried cod with spinach and almonds 212
Pan-fried cod with spring vegetables 210
Pan-fried crusted salmon with black rice 228
Pan-fried salmon with nuts 232
Paris-style salmon 234
Passion fruit and mango with a crumb topping 318
Pets-de-nonne ("nun's farts") 374
Pissaladière 156
Pistachio macarons 380
Plain chouquettes 370
Plain risotto 168
Poached cod brandade 220
Poached salmon with green beans and button mushrooms 236
Potato and tapenade fritters 140
Potato gnocchi with poivrade artichokes 164
Potato rolls 142
Potatoes Anna 162
Potatoes Maxim's 163
Potted rabbit 250
Profiteroles 328
Provençal-style grilled lamb chops with vegetable millefeuille 294
Raspberry and chocolate-raspberry pâte de fruit (fruit jellies) 386
Raspberry charlotte 354–355, 356
Rice pudding and pan-fried fruit 338
Risotto with crispy vegetables 170–171, 172
Roasted leg of lamb and garlic bonbons 296
Roasted shoulder of lamb 300
Roseval potatoes, smoked salmon, and lemon cream 141
Salmon en papillote with mango chutney 242
Salmon nigiri sushi 188
Salmon pies with endives and oranges 244
Salted butter caramels 398
Sardine tian with mint pesto 198
Scallop and fennel tian 202
Seven-hour leg of lamb served with a spoon 308
Shallow-braised salmon with potatoes and sorrel sauce 238
Shortbread cookies in three chocolates 368
Shortbread cookies with chocolate Chantilly cream 322
Shrimp nigiri sushi 190
Squash risotto with crispy bacon 178
Steamed foie gras with green lentils 260–261, 262
Steamed salmon with shiitake mushrooms and sea beans 240
Strawberry charlotte 350
Strawberry éclairs 334
Strawberry tian 342
Summer tian 154
Tarte tatin with apples 344
Tomato risotto 174
Traditional foie gras terrine 256–257, 258
Tropical fruit vacherin 320
Vanilla macarons 378
Vegetarian couscous 182

DIFFICULT

Avocado maki rolls 412
California roll 414
Cheesecake 470
Chocolate and coconut puffs 466
Chocolate caramel chestnuts 498
Crisp and tender chicken with herbs 446
Crispy chocolate tart 488
Doughnuts 492
Foie gras poached in broth 456
Fondant cake in three chocolates 484
Futomaki rolls 416
Gravlax cannelloni 430
Lobster and fava beans with cold soup 442
Macafraise 474
Paris-Brest with hazelnuts 480
Poached cod in a millefeuille 438
Potato ravioli 408
Praline bonbons 496
Rabbit and potato tian 450
Rack of lamb with herb crust 460
Risotto al salto 454
Risotto with red mullet and saffron 420
Roasted loin of lamb stuffed with spinach and almonds 462
Saint Honoré cake 476
Steamed cod with socca and citrus 434
Steamed shrimp, spiced broth, and applesauce 426
Stuffed sardines 422
Stuffed vegetables 404–405, 406
Whole braised foie gras 458

ALPHABETICAL INDEX OF RECIPES

Aïoli 8

All-chocolate muffins 100

Anchoïade 9

Apple and vanilla charlotte 346

Apple compote 82

Apple crisp 92

Apple shortbread barquettes and granita 122

Apple sorbet 120

Apple tart 88–89, 90

Apple tiramisu 70

Apple turnovers 376

Apple, artichoke, and beet carpaccio 18

Apples in syrup 64

Apricot and lavender macarons 106

Artichoke tians 186

Avocado maki rolls 412

Avocado mousse with crayfish 192

Baked apples 86

Barigoule artichokes 158

Beef carpaccio pearls 148

Bouillabaisse 246

Boulangère potatoes 52

Broiled lamb skewers, red bell pepper coulis, and pan-fried sucrine lettuce 290

Brownies 94

California roll 414

Candied orange and orangettes 388

Caramelized veal spareribs with mashed potatoes 274

Celeriac and apple rémoulade 16

Cheese puffs 138

Cheesecake 470

Chicken and Granny Smith apple salad with tangy cream 22

Chicken couscous with almonds, raisins, and saffron 278

Chilled tomato soup 28

Chocolat liégeois 326

Chocolate and banana charlotte 362

Chocolate and coconut puffs 466

Chocolate caramel chestnuts 498

Chocolate caramel lollipops 400

Chocolate chouquettes 372

Chocolate îles flottantes 80

Chocolate macalongs 118

Chocolate macarons 114–115, 116

Chocolate mousse 336

Chocolate truffles 132

Choux sticks with hazelnut and chocolate cream 324

Citrus charlotte 358

Coconut macarons 382

Cod confit with cranberry bean puree 222

Cod sticks with red bell pepper sauce 206

Cod tian with spinach and potato 204

Coffee éclairs 332

Cold couscous salad with crunchy vegetables 20

Confiture de lait (caramel) 68

Cookies 102

Couscous with paprika and spiced meatballs 280

Cream of squash soup 34

Crisp and tender chicken with herbs 446

Crispy chocolate tart 488

Crispy salad with flash-seared tuna 152

Darphin potatoes 160

Daube de boeuf à l'orange (braised beef with orange) 312

Dauphine potatoes 49

Deconstructed rice with mussels and saffron sauce 194

Desert roses in three chocolates 130

Doughnuts 492

Duchess potatoes 46

Duck breast with bigarade sauce 270

Duck roulade with apple chutney 144

Duck tian with oranges and turnips 266

Eggplant caviar 10

Eggs en cocotte with salmon and spinach 58

Eggs florentine 316

Exotic apple salad 84

Fish stew with saffron couscous **200**

Foie gras butter **12**

Foie gras en papillote with figs and porcini **264**

Foie gras on toast with apples **252**

Foie gras poached in broth **456**

Foie gras terrine with pears **254**

Fondant cake in three chocolates **484**

Fruits déguisés (dried fruit with marzipan) **390**

Futomaki rolls **416**

Gratin dauphinois **50**

Gravlax cannelloni **430**

Gravlax-style cod with mango sauce **216**

Grilled salmon **230**

Hazelnut macarons **384**

Lamb curry with coconut rice **286**

Lamb tagine with couscous and nuts **284**

Leek and potato soup **32**

Lemon candies **396**

Lobster and fava beans with cold soup **442**

Lyonnaise salad **24**

Macafraise **474**

Marinated cod appetizers with fragrant rice **62**

Mediterranean tian of zucchini, tomatoes, and mozzarella **56**

Mint pastilles **124**

Mont Blanc–style charlotte **366**

Montélimar nougat **394**

Navarin of lamb with spring vegetables **304**

Niçoise salad **14**

One-sided salmon **226**

Orange-lavender scones **104**

Pan-fried cod with spinach and almonds **212**

Pan-fried cod with spring vegetables **210**

Pan-fried crusted salmon with black rice **228**

Pan-fried salmon with nuts **232**

Panna cotta with peaches and caramelized almonds **72**

Paris-Brest with hazelnuts **480**

Paris-style salmon **234**

Passion fruit and mango with a crumb topping **318**

Pets-de-nonne ("nun's farts") **374**

Pissaladière **156**

Pistachio macarons **380**

Plain chouquettes **370**

Plain risotto **168**

Poached cod brandade **220**

Poached cod in a millefeuille **438**

Poached salmon with green beans and button mushrooms **236**

Potato and tapenade fritters **140**

Potato croquettes **48**

Potato gnocchi with poivrade artichokes **164**

Potato pie **54**

Potato ravioli **408**

Potato rolls **142**

Potatoes Anna **162**

Potatoes Maxim's **163**

Potted rabbit **250**

Praline bonbons **496**

Pralines and caramelized hazelnuts **134**

Profiteroles 328

Provençal-style grilled lamb chops with vegetable millefeuille 294

Rabbit and potato tian 450

Rack of lamb with herb crust 460

Raspberry and chocolate-raspberry pâte de fruit (fruit jellies) 386

Raspberry charlotte 354–355, 356

Raspberry macarons 110

Raspberry muffins 98

Ratatouille 42

Rice pudding and pan-fried fruit 338

Risotto al salto 454

Risotto with crispy vegetables 170–171, 172

Risotto with red mullet and saffron 420

Roasted leg of lamb and garlic bonbons 296

Roasted loin of lamb stuffed with spinach and almonds 462

Roasted shoulder of lamb 300

Roseval potatoes, smoked salmon, and lemon cream 141

Saint Honoré cake 476

Salmon en papillote with mango chutney 242

Salmon nigiri sushi 188

Salmon pies with endives and oranges 244

Salmon tartare 60

Salted butter caramels 398

Sardine tian with mint pesto 198

Scallop and fennel tian 202

Seven-hour leg of lamb served with a spoon 308

Shallow-braised salmon with potatoes and sorrel sauce 238

Shortbread cookies in three chocolates 368

Shortbread cookies with chocolate Chantilly cream 322

Shrimp nigiri sushi 190

Soupe au pistou (Provençal vegetable soup with pistou) 38

Squash risotto with crispy bacon 178

Steamed cod with socca and citrus 434

Steamed foie gras with green lentils 260–261, 262

Steamed salmon with shiitake mushrooms and sea beans 240

Steamed shrimp, spiced broth, and applesauce 426

Stewed apples 66

Strawberry charlotte 350

Strawberry éclairs 334

Strawberry tian 342

Stuffed sardines 422

Stuffed vegetables 404–405, 406

Summer tian 154

Tapenade 11

Tarte tatin with apples 344

Three-chocolate crème brûlée 78

Three-chocolate panna cotta 74

Three-chocolate pots de crème 76

Tiramisu-style charlotte 96

Tomato risotto 174

Traditional foie gras terrine 256–257, 258

Tropical fruit vacherin 320

Vanilla macarons 378

Vanilla marshmallows 126

Vegetarian couscous 182

Warm Ratte and Vitellote potato salad 26

Whole braised foie gras 458

Zucchini flower fritters 41

INDEX BY TYPES OF DISHES

BITES

Cheese puffs 138
Duck roulade with apple chutney 144
Potato and tapenade fritters 140
Potato rolls 142
Roseval potatoes, smoked salmon, and lemon cream 141

CONDIMENTS AND BASICS

Aïoli 8
Anchoïade 9
Eggplant caviar 10
Foie gras butter 12
Plain risotto 168
Tapenade 11

CONFECTIONERY

Candied orange and orangettes 388
Chocolate caramel chestnuts 498
Chocolate caramel lollipops 400
Chocolate truffles 132
Desert roses in three chocolates 130
Fruits déguisés (dried fruit with marzipan) 390
Lemon candies 396
Mint pastilles 124
Montélimar nougat 394
Praline bonbons 496
Pralines and caramelized hazelnuts 134
Salted butter caramels 398
Vanilla marshmallows 126

DESSERTS AND PASTRIES

All-chocolate muffins 100
Apple turnovers 376
Apricot and lavender macarons 106
Chocolate chouquettes 372
Chocolate macalongs 118
Chocolate macarons 114–115, 116
Coconut macarons 382
Cookies 102
Doughnuts 492
Hazelnut macarons 384
Orange-lavender scones 104
Pets-de-nonne ("nun's farts") 374
Pistachio macarons 380
Plain chouquettes 370
Raspberry and chocolate-raspberry pâte de fruit (fruit jellies) 386
Raspberry macarons 110
Raspberry muffins 98
Shortbread cookies in three chocolates 368
Vanilla macarons 378

DESSERTS, PLATED

Apple tiramisu 70
Chocolat liégeois 326
Chocolate and coconut puffs 466
Chocolate îles flottantes 80
Chocolate mousse 336
Choux sticks with hazelnut and chocolate cream 324
Coffee éclairs 332
Panna cotta with peaches and caramelized almonds 72
Passion fruit and mango with a crumb topping 318
Profiteroles 328
Rice pudding and pan-fried fruit 338
Shortbread cookies with chocolate chantilly cream 322
Strawberry charlotte 350
Three-chocolate crème brûlée 78
Three-chocolate panna cotta 74
Three-chocolate pots de crème 76
Tropical fruit vacherin 320

DESSERTS, SHARED

Apple and vanilla charlotte 346
Apple compote 82
Apple crisp 92
Apple tart 88–89, 90
Baked apples 86
Brownies 94
Cheesecake 470
Chocolate and banana charlotte 362
Citrus charlotte 358
Crispy chocolate tart 488
Exotic apple salad 84
Fondant cake in three chocolates 484
Macafraise 474
Mont Blanc–style charlotte 366
Paris-Brest with hazelnuts 480
Raspberry charlotte 354–355, 356

Saint Honoré cake 476

Strawberry éclairs 334

Strawberry tian 342

Tarte tatin with apples 344

Tiramisu-style charlotte 96

EGGS

Eggs en cocotte with salmon and spinach 58

Eggs florentine 316

FISH, SEAFOOD, AND SHELLFISH

Fish

Marinated cod appetizers with fragrant rice 62

Salmon nigiri sushi 188

Salmon tartare 60

Seafood

Bouillabaisse 246

California roll 414

Cod confit with cranberry bean puree 222

Cod sticks with red bell pepper sauce 206

Cod tian with spinach and potato 204

Deconstructed rice with mussels and saffron sauce 194

Fish stew with saffron couscous 200

Futomaki rolls 416

Gravlax cannelloni 430

Gravlax-style cod with mango sauce 216

Grilled salmon 230

Lobster and fava beans with cold soup 442

One-sided salmon 226

Pan-fried cod with spinach and almonds 212

Pan-fried cod with spring vegetables 210

Pan-fried crusted salmon with black rice 228

Pan-fried salmon with nuts 232

Paris-style salmon 234

Poached cod brandade 220

Poached cod in a millefeuille 438

Poached salmon with green beans and button mushrooms 236

Risotto with red mullet and saffron 420

Salmon en papillote with mango chutney 242

Salmon pies with endives and oranges 244

Sardine tian with mint pesto 198

Scallop and fennel tian 202

Shallow-braised salmon with potatoes and sorrel sauce 238

Steamed cod with socca and citrus 434

Steamed salmon with shiitake mushrooms and sea beans 240

Steamed shrimp, spiced broth, and applesauce 426

Stuffed sardines 422

Shellfish

Avocado mousse with crayfish 192

Shrimp nigiri sushi 190

ICE CREAM AND SORBET

Apple shortbread barquettes and granita 122

Apple sorbet 120

MEAT AND POULTRY

Beef

Couscous with paprika and spiced meatballs 280

Daube de boeuf à l'orange (braised beef with orange) 312

Chicken

Chicken couscous with almonds, raisins, and saffron 278

Crisp and tender chicken with herbs 446

Duck

Duck breast with bigarade sauce 270

Duck tian with oranges and turnips 266

Foie gras

Foie gras en papillote with figs and porcini 264

Foie gras on toast with apples 252

Foie gras poached in broth 456

Foie gras terrine with pears 254

Steamed foie gras with green lentils 260–261, 262

Traditional foie gras terrine 256–257, 258

Whole braised foie gras 458

Lamb

Broiled lamb skewers, red bell pepper coulis, and pan-fried sucrine lettuce 290

Lamb curry with coconut rice 286

Lamb tagine with couscous and nuts 284

Navarin of lamb with spring vegetables 304

Provençal-style grilled lamb chops with vegetable millefeuille 294

Rack of lamb with herb crust 460

Roasted leg of lamb and garlic bonbons 296

Roasted loin of lamb stuffed with spinach and almonds 462

Roasted shoulder of lamb 300

Seven-hour leg of lamb served with a spoon 308

Poultry

Risotto al salto 454

Rabbit

Potted rabbit 250

Rabbit and potato tian 450

Veal

Caramelized veal spareribs with mashed potatoes 274

ONE-DISH MEALS

Potato pie 54

SALADS

Apple, artichoke, and beet carpaccio 18

Beef carpaccio pearls 148

Celeriac and apple rémoulade 16

Chicken and Granny Smith apple salad with tangy cream 22

Cold couscous salad with crunchy vegetables 20

Crispy salad with flash-seared tuna 152

Lyonnaise salad 24

Niçoise salad 14

Summer tian 154

Warm Ratte and Vitellote potato salad 26

SOUPS

Chilled tomato soup 28

Cream of squash soup 34

Leek and potato soup 32

Soupe au pistou (Provençal vegetable soup with pistou) 38

SWEET CONDIMENTS AND BASICS

Apples in syrup 64

Confiture de lait (caramel) 68

Stewed apples 66

VEGETABLES

Barigoule artichokes 158

Boulangère potatoes 52

Darphin potatoes 160

Dauphine potatoes 49

Duchess potatoes 46

Gratin dauphinois 50

Pissaladière 156

Potato croquettes 48

Potato gnocchi with poivrade artichokes 164

Potatoes Anna 162

Potatoes Maxim's 163

Ratatouille 42

Risotto with crispy vegetables 170–171, 172

Squash risotto with crispy bacon 178

Stuffed vegetables 404–405, 406

Tomato risotto 174

Vegetarian couscous 182

Zucchini flower fritters 41

VEGETARIAN PLATES

Artichoke tians 186

Avocado maki rolls 412

Mediterranean tian of zucchini, tomatoes, and mozzarella 56

Potato ravioli 408

INDEX BY INGREDIENT

Almond 18, 72, 212, 232, 278, 284, 334, 394, 462, 480

Almond meal (ground almonds) 86, 92, 100, 106, 110, 114, 118, 202, 206, 228, 318, 368, 378, 380, 382, 390, 470

Anchovy 9, 11, 14, 156, 460

Apple 16, 18, 22, 64, 66, 70, 82, 84, 86, 88, 92, 120, 122, 144, 252, 338, 344, 346, 376, 426

Apricot 106

Artichoke 18, 148

Asparagus 270

Avocado 154, 192, 412, 414

Bacon 24, 34, 158, 178, 186, 308, 312

Banana 338, 362

Basil 11, 14, 38, 42, 60, 152, 158, 210, 226, 404, 420, 446, 450, 462

Bass 200

Beef 148, 280, 312

Beet (beetroot) 18

Bell pepper 14, 20, 42, 182, 192, 198, 206, 210, 242, 280, 290

Brousse cheese 158, 430

Butternut squash 34

Candied (glacéd) cherry 390

Carrot 34, 158, 172, 182, 186, 222, 226, 242, 262, 286

Celeriac 16

Celery 14, 22, 158, 182, 226, 242, 286, 312, 442

Chestnut 366, 458, 498

Chicken 22, 278, 446, 454

Chickpea 182, 200

Chocolate 74, 76, 78, 80, 94, 100, 102, 114, 118, 130, 132, 322, 324, 326, 328, 336, 362, 368, 372, 386, 388, 400, 466, 484, 488, 496, 498

Cider, hard 64, 346

Coconut 286, 382, 466

Cod 62, 204, 206, 210, 212, 216, 220, 222, 434, 438

Coffee 96, 332

Conger 246

Cornflakes 130, 362, 496

Couscous 20, 182, 200, 280, 284

Cucumber 14, 20, 28, 416

Cured ham 408

Date 390

Dried apricots 284

Dried navy (haricot) beans 38, 222

Dried tomato 152, 422

Duck 144, 266, 270

Eggplant 10, 42, 198, 294

Eggs 46, 48, 58, 60, 70, 76, 78, 80, 86, 94, 98, 100, 102, 104, 106, 110, 116, 126, 138, 140, 154, 164, 204, 232, 234, 242, 244, 246, 264, 280, 308, 321, 326, 328, 332, 338, 346, 350, 362, 366, 368, 370, 372, 376, 380, 382, 384, 390, 394, 408, 470, 492

Emmental 22

Endive 244

Fava (broad) bean 182, 442

Fennel 14, 170, 182, 194, 202, 210, 246, 420, 426, 442

Figs 264, 338, 456

Foie gras 12, 252, 254, 256, 260, 264, 456, 458

Ginger 62, 200, 242, 374, 442

Grapefruit 154, 434

Grapes 458

Green beans 38, 182, 236

Hazelnuts 98, 102, 134, 324, 384, 480, 496

Honey 102, 104, 266, 394, 446

Kiwi fruit 338

Ladyfingers 96, 346, 354, 358, 362, 366

Lamb 284, 286, 290, 294, 296, 300, 304, 308, 460, 462

Leek 32, 52, 222, 226, 242, 262, 312, 434

Lemon 8, 10, 16, 20, 22, 60, 64, 106, 124, 130, 141, 148, 152, 154, 182, 198, 202, 212, 216, 228, 270, 274, 286, 346, 350, 358, 386, 390, 396, 426, 438, 442, 446

Lentils 260

Lettuce 152, 222, 290, 446

Lime 62

Lobster 442

Mango 216, 242, 318, 320

Mascarpone 70, 96, 184

Mint 20, 84, 124, 198, 406

Monkfish 200, 246

Mozzarella 56

Mushrooms 182, 236, 240, 264, 270, 294, 316

Nuts 232

Olive 9, 11, 140, 152, 156, 290, 294, 450

Onion 22, 24, 25, 26, 34, 38, 42, 54, 56, 70, 144, 154, 156, 168, 172, 174, 178, 186, 198, 200, 202, 206, 210, 216, 222, 226, 232, 242, 246, 250, 262, 266, 270, 278, 280, 284, 286, 290, 294, 300, 304, 308, 312, 406, 420, 422, 430, 442, 446, 450, 454

Orange 104, 244, 266, 270, 276, 312, 358, 388, 394, 434

Paprika 216, 280

Parmesan cheese 18, 38, 138, 148, 168, 170, 174, 178, 184, 406, 422, 450, 454

Parsley 20, 26, 52, 172, 212, 220, 222, 226, 230, 234, 240, 262, 280, 294, 312, 446, 460

Passion fruit 84, 318

Peach 72

Pear 254, 338

Pecans 94

Petits pois 182

Pine nuts 38, 192, 284

Pineapple 320, 338

Pistachio 130, 380, 394

Poivrade artichoke 14, 148, 158, 164, 170, 186

Potato 8, 26, 32, 34, 38, 46, 48, 49, 50, 52, 54, 60, 140, 141, 142, 160, 162, 163, 164, 204, 220, 238, 246, 276, 304, 408, 438, 450

Prune 390

Quail eggs 14, 24

Rabbit 250, 450

Raisin 284

Raspberry 98, 110, 334, 354, 386, 474

Red currant 318

Red mullet 420

Rice 62, 168, 170, 174, 178, 188, 190, 194, 228, 286, 338, 412, 414, 416, 420, 454

Saffron 194, 200, 244, 246, 278, 284, 420

Salmon 58, 60, 141, 188, 226, 228, 230, 232, 234, 236, 238, 240, 242, 244, 414, 430

Salmon roe 60

Salted side bacon 54

Sardine 198, 422

Scallion 10, 14, 18, 20, 62, 148, 152, 164, 182, 192, 234

Scallops 202

Scorpion fish 200

Shrimp (prawns) 154, 190, 192, 228, 416, 426

Sorrel 238

Spinach 58, 164, 204, 212, 232, 316, 408, 422, 430, 462

Strawberry 320, 334, 342, 350, 474

Sultana 278

Tomato 14, 20, 28, 38, 42, 56, 152, 172, 174, 182, 200, 204, 206, 216, 230, 246, 278, 289, 294, 406, 426, 442, 446

Tuna 14, 152

Turnip 182, 226, 266, 304

Vanilla 34, 68, 72, 76, 82, 86, 98, 106, 126, 134, 202, 318, 338, 342, 344, 346, 366, 378, 390, 398, 470, 474

Veal 276

Walnut 144

Winter squash 178

Zucchini 38, 42, 56, 170, 182, 200, 210, 290, 404

Zucchini flower 40, 404

INDEX BY COOKING UTENSILS

BROILER

Duck tian with oranges and turnips 266

Grilled salmon 230

Provençal-style grilled lamb chops with vegetable millefeuille 294

Risotto al salto 454

COUSCOUSSIER

Chicken couscous with almonds, raisins, and saffron 278

Couscous with paprika and spiced meatballs 280

Fish stew with saffron couscous 200

Lamb tagine with couscous and nuts 284

Vegetarian couscous 182

DEEP (FAT) FRYER

Dauphine potatoes 49

Doughnuts 492

Potato and tapenade fritters 140

Potato croquettes 48

Zucchini flower fritters 41

DUTCH OVEN OR CASSEROLE DISH

Navarin of lamb with spring vegetables 304

Scallop and fennel tian 202

Seven-hour leg of lamb served with a spoon 308

Whole braised foie gras 458

MICROWAVE

Cheesecake 470

Chocolate îles flottantes 80

OVEN

All-chocolate muffins 100

Apple crisp 92

Apple shortbread barquettes and granita 122

Apple tart 88

Apple turnovers 376

Apricot and lavender macarons 106

Artichoke tians 186

Avocado mousse with crayfish 192

Baked apples 86

Beef carpaccio pearls 148

Boulangère potatoes 52

Broiled lamb skewers, red bell pepper coulis, and pan-fried sucrine lettuce 290

Brownies 94

Candied orange and orangettes 388

Caramelized veal spareribs with mashed potatoes 274

Cheese puffs 138

Cheesecake 470

Chocolate and coconut puffs 466

Chocolate chouquettes 372

Chocolate macalongs 118

Chocolate macarons 114–115, 116

Choux sticks with hazelnut and chocolate cream 324

Coconut macarons 382

Cod sticks with red bell pepper sauce 206

Cod tian with spinach and potato 204

Coffee éclairs 332

Cookies 102

Crispy chocolate tart 488

Duchess potatoes 46

Duck tian with oranges and turnips 266

Duck roulade with apple chutney 144

Eggplant caviar 10

Foie gras en papillote with figs and porcini 264

Fondant cake in three chocolates 484

Gratin dauphinois 50

Hazelnut macarons 384

Lyonnaise salad 24

Macafraise 474

Mediterranean tian of zucchini, tomatoes, and mozzarella 56

Mont Blanc–style charlotte 366

Montélimar nougat 394

Orange-lavender scones 104

Pan-fried cod with spring vegetables 210

Panna cotta with peaches and caramelized almonds 72

Paris-Brest with hazelnuts 480

Passion fruit and mango with a crumb topping 318

Pissaladière 156

Pistachio macarons 380

Plain chouquettes 370

Poached cod brandade 220

Poached cod in a millefeuille 438

Potato gnocchi with poivrade artichokes 164

Potato pie 54

Potato rolls 142

Potatoes Anna 162

Potatoes Maxim's 163

Potted rabbit 250

Profiteroles 328

Rabbit and potato tian 450

Rack of lamb with herb crust 460

Raspberry charlotte 354–355, 356

Raspberry muffins 98

Roasted leg of lamb and garlic bonbons 296

Roasted loin of lamb stuffed with spinach and almonds 462

Roasted shoulder of lamb 300

Saint Honoré cake 476

Salmon en papillote with mango chutney 242

Salmon pies with endives and oranges 244

Sardine tian with mint pesto 198

Scallop and fennel tian 202

Shortbread cookies in three chocolates 368

Shortbread cookies with chocolate chantilly cream 322

Squash risotto with crispy bacon 178

Steamed cod with socca and citrus 434

Strawberry éclairs 334

Strawberry tian 342

Stuffed sardines 422

Stuffed vegetables 404

Summer tian 154

Tarte tatin with apples 344

Three-chocolate crème brûlée 78

Traditional foie gras terrine 256–257, 258

Vanilla macarons 378

PRESSURE COOKER

Caramelized veal spareribs with mashed potatoes 274

Confiture de lait (caramel) 68

Cream of squash soup 34

Eggs en cocotte with salmon and spinach 58

Steamed shrimp, spiced broth, and applesauce 426

RICE COOKER

Avocado maki rolls 412

California roll 414

Futomaki rolls 416

Salmon nigiri sushi 188

Shrimp nigiri sushi 190

SAUCEPAN

Apple and vanilla charlotte 346

Apple compote 82

Apple shortbread barquettes and granita 122

Apple tart 88–89, 90

Apple turnovers 376

Apricot and lavender macarons 106

Broiled lamb skewers, red bell pepper coulis, and pan-fried sucrine lettuce 290

Brownies 94

Candied orange and orangettes 388

Caramelized veal spareribs with mashed potatoes 274

Cheese puffs 138

Cheesecake 470

Chilled tomato soup 28

Chocolat liégeois 326

Chocolate and banana charlotte 362

Chocolate and coconut puffs 466

Chocolate caramel chestnuts 498

Chocolate caramel lollipops 400

Chocolate chouquettes 372

Chocolate îles flottantes 80

Chocolate macalongs 118

Chocolate macarons 114–115, 116

Chocolate mousse 336

Chocolate truffles 132

Citrus charlotte 358

Cod confit with cranberry bean puree 222

Cod sticks with red bell pepper sauce 206

Coffee éclairs 332

Cookies 102

Crispy chocolate tart 488

Daube de boeuf à l'orange (braised beef with orange) 312

Deconstructed rice with mussels and saffron sauce 194

Desert roses in three chocolates 130

Duck breast with bigarade sauce 270

Duck roulade with apple chutney 144

Exotic apple salad 84

Foie gras on toast with apples 252

Fondant cake in three chocolates 484

Fruits déguisés (dried fruit with marzipan) 390

Gratin dauphinois 50

Gravlax-style cod with mango sauce 216

Grilled salmon 230
Leek and potato soup 32
Lemon candies 396
Lobster and fava beans with cold soup 442
Lyonnaise salad 24
Marinated cod appetizers with fragrant rice 62
Mint pastilles 124
Montélimar nougat 394
Niçoise salad 14
One-sided salmon 226
Orange-lavender scones 104
Pan-fried cod with spring vegetables 210
Pan-fried crusted salmon with black rice 228
Pan-fried salmon with nuts 232
Panna cotta with peaches and caramelized almonds 72
Paris-Brest with hazelnuts 480
Pets-de-nonne ("nun's farts") 374
Poached cod brandade 220
Poached cod in a millefeuille 438
Poached salmon with green beans and button mushrooms 236
Pralines and caramelized hazelnuts 134
Profiteroles 328
Raspberry and chocolate-raspberry pâte de fruit (fruit jellies) 386
Raspberry charlotte 354–355, 356
Raspberry macarons 110
Ratatouille 42
Rice pudding and pan-fried fruit 338
Risotto with crispy vegetables 170–171, 172
Roasted shoulder of lamb 300
Roseval potatoes, smoked salmon, and lemon cream 141
Saint Honoré cake 476
Salmon en papillote with mango chutney 242
Salmon tartare 60
Salted butter caramels 398
Shallow-braised salmon with potatoes and sorrel sauce 238
Shortbread cookies with chocolate Chantilly cream 322
Shrimp nigiri sushi 190
Steamed foie gras with green lentils 260–261, 262
Steamed salmon with shiitake mushrooms and sea beans 240
Stewed apples 66
Strawberry éclairs 334
Stuffed sardines 422
Stuffed vegetables 404
Three-chocolate crème brûlée 78
Three-chocolate panna cotta 74
Three-chocolate pots de crème 76
Tomato risotto 174
Tropical fruit vacherin 320
Vanilla marshmallows 126
Warm Ratte and Vitellote potato salad 26

SKILLET OR PAN

Apple and vanilla charlotte 346
Apples in syrup 64
Artichoke tians 186
Barigoule artichokes 158
Beef carpaccio pearls 148
Broiled lamb skewers, red bell pepper coulis, and pan-fried sucrine lettuce 290
Chicken couscous with almonds, raisins, and saffron 278
Chocolate and banana charlotte 362
Cod confit with cranberry bean puree 222
Cod tian with spinach and potato 204
Cream of squash soup 34
Crisp and tender chicken with herbs 446
Crispy salad with flash-seared tuna 152
Darphin potatoes 160
Duck breast with bigarade sauce 270
Duck roulade with apple chutney 144
Duck tian with oranges and turnips 266
Foie gras on toast with apples 252
Foie gras terrine with pears 254
Lamb curry with coconut rice 286
One-sided salmon 226
Pan-fried cod with spinach and almonds 212
Pan-fried crusted salmon with black rice 228
Pan-fried salmon with nuts 232
Paris-style salmon 234
Passion fruit and mango with a crumb topping 318
Pissaladière 156
Plain risotto 168
Potato gnocchi with poivrade artichokes 164
Potato ravioli 408
Potted rabbit 250
Rabbit and potato tian 450
Rack of lamb with herb crust 460
Ratatouille 42
Rice pudding and pan-fried fruit 338
Risotto al salto 454

Risotto with crispy vegetables 170

Risotto with red mullet and saffron 420

Roasted loin of lamb stuffed with spinach and almonds 462

Roasted shoulder of lamb 300

Salmon pies with endives and oranges 244

Salmon tartare 60

Shallow-braised salmon with potatoes and sorrel sauce 238

Squash risotto with crispy bacon 178

Steamed salmon with shiitake mushrooms and sea beans 240

Strawberry charlotte 350

Strawberry tian 342

Stuffed vegetables 404

Summer tian 154

Tarte tatin with apples 344

Tomato risotto 174

STEAM

Steamed cod with socca and citrus 434

Steamed foie gras with green lentils 260

Steamed salmon with shiitake mushrooms and sea beans 240

STOCKPOT

Bouillabaisse 246

Chicken couscous with almonds, raisins, and saffron 278

Couscous with paprika and spiced meatballs 280

Crisp and tender chicken with herbs 446

Daube de boeuf à l'orange (braised beef with orange) 312

Deconstructed rice with mussels and saffron sauce 194

Duck breast with bigarade sauce 270

Eggs florentine 316

Fish stew with saffron couscous 200

Foie gras poached in broth 456

Lobster and fava beans with cold soup 442

Potato ravioli 408

Potato rolls 142

Roasted loin of lamb stuffed with spinach and almonds 462

Sardine tian with mint pesto 198

Soupe au pistou (Provençal vegetable soup with pistou) 38

Vegetarian couscous 182

TAGINE POT

Lamb tagine with couscous and nuts 284

WOK

Pan-fried cod with spinach and almonds 212

INDEX BY COOKING TIME

UNDER 15 MINUTES

Aïoli 8

Avocado maki rolls 412

Crispy salad with flash-seared tuna 152

Potato and tapenade fritters 140

UNDER 30 MINUTES

Apple, artichoke, and beet carpaccio 18

California roll 414

Celeriac and apple rémoulade 16

Chicken and Granny Smith apple salad with tangy cream 22

Darphin potatoes 160

Eggs en cocotte with salmon and spinach 58

Niçoise salad 14

Pan-fried cod with spring vegetables 210

Pan-fried salmon with nuts 232

Paris-style salmon 234

Potatoes Maxim's 163

Provençal-style grilled lamb chops with vegetable millefeuille 294

Rack of lamb with herb crust 460

Roseval potatoes, smoked salmon, and lemon cream 141

Salmon nigiri sushi 188

Salmon tartare 60

Shortbread cookies in three chocolates 368

Stewed apples 66

Tapenade 11

Warm Ratte and Vitellote potato salad 26

UNDER 45 MINUTES

All-chocolate muffins 100

Apple compote 82

Apple turnovers 376

Artichoke tians 186

Avocado mousse with crayfish 192

Chocolate caramel lollipops 400

Cream of squash soup 34

Duchess potatoes 46

Eggs florentine 316

Exotic apple salad 84

Foie gras butter 12

Foie gras en papillote with figs and porcini 264

Foie gras on toast with apples 252

Futomaki rolls 416

Leek and potato soup 32

Passion fruit and mango with a crumb topping 318

Pets-de-nonne ("nun's farts") 374

Plain risotto 168

Poached salmon with green beans and button mushrooms 236

Pralines and caramelized hazelnuts 134

Raspberry muffins 98

Rice pudding and pan-fried fruit 338

Risotto with crispy vegetables 170–171, 172

Risotto with red mullet and saffron 420

Shrimp nigiri sushi 190

Whole braised foie gras 458

UNDER 1 HOUR

Apple crisp 92

Apple sorbet 120

Apple tart 88–89, 90

Apples in syrup 64

Barigoule artichokes 158

Beef carpaccio pearls 148

Brownies 94

Chocolate chouquettes 372

Dauphine potatoes 49

Duck roulade with apple chutney 144

Fruits déguisés (dried fruit with marzipan) 390

Grilled salmon 230

Mediterranean tian of zucchini, tomatoes, and mozzarella 56

Pan-fried crusted salmon with black rice 228

Paris-Brest with hazelnuts 480

Plain chouquettes 370

Potatoes Anna 162

Roasted loin of lamb stuffed with spinach and almonds 462

Roasted shoulder of lamb 300

Scallop and fennel tian 202

Steamed salmon with shiitake mushrooms and sea beans 240

Steamed shrimp, spiced broth, and applesauce 426

Summer tian 154

UNDER 2 HOURS

Baked apples 86

Broiled lamb skewers, red bell pepper coulis, and pan-fried sucrine lettuce 290

Cheese puffs 138

Chocolate caramel chestnuts 498

Choux sticks with hazelnut and chocolate cream 324

Coconut macarons 382

Cod sticks with red bell pepper sauce 206

Confiture de lait (caramel) 68

Deconstructed rice with mussels and saffron sauce 194

Desert roses in three chocolates 130

Duck tian with oranges and turnips 266

Fish stew with saffron couscous 200

Gratin dauphinois 50

Lemon candies 396

Lyonnaise salad 24

Macafraise 474

Marinated cod appetizers with fragrant rice 62

One-sided salmon 226

Pan-fried cod with spinach and almonds 212

Panna cotta with peaches and caramelized almonds 72

Pistachio macarons 380

Poached cod brandade 220

Poached cod in a millefeuille 438

Potato croquettes 48

Potato gnocchi with poivrade artichokes 164

Potato pie 54

Potato rolls 142

Praline bonbons 496

Profiteroles 328

Rabbit and potato tian 450

Ratatouille 42

Salmon en papillote with mango chutney 242

Salmon pies with endives and oranges 244

Shallow-braised salmon with potatoes and sorrel sauce 238

Squash risotto with crispy bacon 178

Strawberry tian 342

Stuffed sardines 422

Stuffed vegetables 404

Tarte tatin with apples 344

Tomato risotto 174

Tropical fruit vacherin 320

Vanilla macarons 378

Vegetarian couscous 182

Zucchini flower fritters 41

UNDER 4 HOURS

Anchoïade 9

Apple tiramisu 70

Apricot and lavender macarons 106

Bouillabaisse 246

Boulangère potatoes 52

Chocolate îles flottantes 80

Chocolate macarons 114–115, 116

Cod tian with spinach and potato 204

Coffee éclairs 332

Cold couscous salad with crunchy vegetables 20

Cookies 102

Couscous with paprika and spiced meatballs 280

Crisp and tender chicken with herbs 446

Duck breast with bigarade sauce 270

Eggplant caviar 10

Hazelnut macarons 384

Lobster and fava beans with cold soup 442

Navarin of lamb with spring vegetables 304

Pissaladière 156

Potato ravioli 408

Potted rabbit 250

Raspberry and chocolate-raspberry pâte de fruit (fruit jellies) 386

Raspberry macarons 110

Roasted leg of lamb and garlic bonbons 296

Saint Honoré cake 476

Salted butter caramels 398

Sardine tian with mint pesto 198

Shortbread cookies with chocolate chantilly cream 322

Steamed foie gras with green lentils 260–261, 262

Strawberry éclairs 334

Three-chocolate crème brûlée 78

Three-chocolate pots de crème 76

Vanilla marshmallows 126

UNDER 12 HOURS

Apple shortbread barquettes and granita 122

Chocolate and coconut puffs 466

Chocolate mousse 336

Crispy chocolate tart 488

Daube de boeuf à l'orange (braised beef with orange) 312

Doughnuts 492

Lamb tagine with couscous and nuts 284

Mint pastilles 124

Montélimar nougat 394

Orange-lavender scones 104

Seven-hour leg of lamb served with a spoon 308

Steamed cod with socca and citrus 434

SEVERAL DAYS

Apple and vanilla charlotte 346

Candied orange and orangettes 388

Caramelized veal spareribs with mashed potatoes 274

Cheesecake 470

Chicken couscous with almonds, raisins, and saffron 278

Chilled tomato soup 28

Chocolat liégeois 326

Chocolate and banana charlotte 362

Chocolate macalongs 118

Chocolate macarons 114–115, 116

Chocolate truffles 132

Citrus charlotte 358

Cod confit with cranberry bean puree 222

Foie gras poached in broth 456

Foie gras terrine with pears 254

Fondant cake in three chocolates 484

Gravlax cannelloni 430

Gravlax-style cod with mango sauce 216

Lamb curry with coconut rice 286

Mont Blanc–style charlotte 366

Raspberry charlotte 354

Risotto al salto 454

Soupe au pistou (Provençal vegetable soup with pistou) 38

Strawberry charlotte 350

Three-chocolate panna cotta 74

Tiramisu-style charlotte 96

Traditional foie gras terrine 256–257, 258

THE CHEFS

BENOÎT WITZ –
With more than twenty years' experience as a chef, Benoît Witz joined Alain Ducasse's Le Louis XV restaurant in Monaco in 1987. In 1996, he became the chef of La Bastide de Moustiers, then of the l'Hostellerie de l'Abbaye de la Celle.

SÉBASTIEN SERVEAU –
Sébastien Serveau started his career in cooking, then devoted himself completely to pastry making in 1994. He worked in the hotel, retail, and restaurant businesses before joining the staff at the Alain Ducasse Institute. He is now the executive pastry chef at the Ritz, Paris.

ROMAIN CORBIÈRE –
Romain Corbière is a thirty-three-year-old chef. After he trained at Le Louis XV restaurant in Monaco, Alain Ducasse placed him at the helm of the Le Relais du Parc restaurant in Paris, where he earned his first Michelin star. He spent more than ten years developing his skill with the Ducasse mindset and flavors. He has been the executive chef of the Alain Ducasse Institute since 2009.

HISAYUKI TAKEUCHI –
The son of farmers on the Japanese island of Shikoku, Hisayuki Takeuchi came to France to work in the field of artistic creativity after training as a chef specializing in French cuisine in Tokyo. In Paris, he has been a force behind Japanese nouvelle cuisine, a culinary style involving aesthetics, flavor, and health-consciousness. His restaurant (and laboratory), Kaiseki, has been sharing its creations with customers from all over the world since 1999.

First published in English in 2016
by Rizzoli International Publications, Inc.
300 Park Avenue South
New York, NY 10010
www.rizzoliusa.com

Originally published in France in 2011
by Alain Ducasse Édition
2 rue Paul Vaillant Couturier
92530 Levallois Perret
www.alain-ducasse.com

English translation by Cillero & De Motta
English edition cover designed by Kayleigh Jankowski

2016 2017 2018 / 10 9 8 7 6 5 4 3 2 1

Distributed to the U.S. trade by
Random House, New York

Printed in China

ISBN-13: 978-0-7893-3259-2
Library of Congress Control Number: 2016940466

COLLECTION DIRECTOR
Alain Ducasse
MANAGING DIRECTOR
Aurore Charoy
EDITORIAL MANAGER
Alice Gouget
EDITOR
Émilie Morin
GRAPHIC DESIGN
Soins graphiques
Our thanks to Sophie
MARKETING AND COMMUNICATIONS
Camille Gonnet
camille.gonnet@alain-ducasse.com

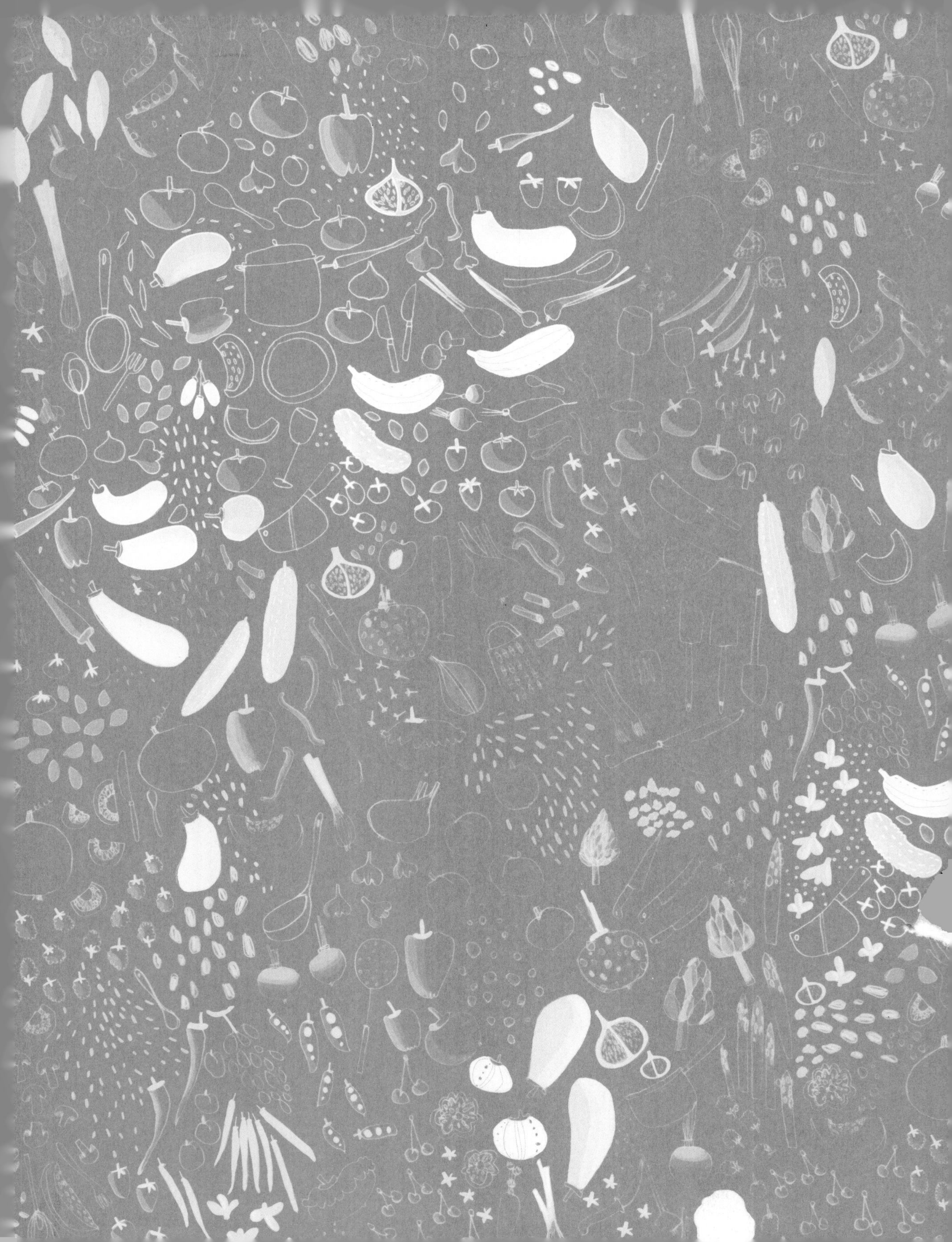